More iPhone 3 Development:

Tackling iPhone SDK 3

Dave Mark

Jeff LaMarche

Apress®

More iPhone 3 Development: Tackling iPhone SDK 3

ISBN-13 (pbk): 978-1-4302-2505-8

ISBN-13 (electronic): 978-1-4302-2743-4

Printed and bound in the United States of America 9 8 7 6 5 4 3 2 1

Trademarked names may appear in this book. Rather than use a trademark symbol with every occurrence of a trademarked name, we use the names only in an editorial fashion and to the benefit of the trademark owner, with no intention of infringement of the trademark.

President and Publisher: Paul Manning
Lead Editor: Clay Andres
Developmental Editor: Douglas Pundick
Technical Reviewer: Mark Dalrymple
Editorial Board: Clay Andres, Steve Anglin, Mark Beckner, Ewan Buckingham, Gary Cornell, Jonathan Gennick, Jonathan Hassell, Michelle Lowman, Matthew Moodie, Duncan Parkes, Jeffrey Pepper, Frank Pohlmann, Douglas Pundick, Ben Renow-Clarke, Dominic Shakeshaft, Matt Wade, Tom Welsh
Coordinating Editor: Kelly Moritz
Copy Editor: Marilyn Smith and Ralph Moore
Compositor: MacPS, LLC
Indexers: John Collin and Julie Grady
Artist: April Milne
Cover Designer: Anna Ishchenko

Distributed to the book trade worldwide by Springer-Verlag New York, Inc., 233 Spring Street, 6th Floor, New York, NY 10013. Phone 1-800-SPRINGER, fax 201-348-4505, e-mail orders-ny@springer-sbm.com, or visit http://www.springeronline.com.

For information on translations, please e-mail info@apress.com, or visit http://www.apress.com.

Apress and friends of ED books may be purchased in bulk for academic, corporate, or promotional use. eBook versions and licenses are also available for most titles. For more information, reference our Special Bulk Sales–eBook Licensing web page at http://www.apress.com/info/bulksales.

The information in this book is distributed on an "as is" basis, without warranty. Although every precaution has been taken in the preparation of this work, neither the author(s) nor Apress shall have any liability to any person or entity with respect to any loss or damage caused or alleged to be caused directly or indirectly by the information contained in this work.

The source code for this book is available to readers at http://www.apress.com. You will need to answer questions pertaining to this book in order to successfully download the code.

To Deneen, Daniel, Kelley, and Ryan, LFU4FRNMWWA. . .

—Dave

To the most important people in my life, my wife and kids.

—Jeff

Contents at a Glance

Contents at a Glance iv

Contents v

About the Authors xii

About the Technical Reviewer xiii

Acknowlegments xiv

Preface xv

Chapter 1: Here We Go Round Again 1

Part I: Core Data 7

Chapter 2: The Anatomy of Core Data 9

Chapter 3: A Super Start: Adding, Displaying, and Deleting Data 41

Chapter 4: The Devil in the Detail View 83

Chapter 5: Preparing for Change: Migrations and Versioning 127

Chapter 6: Custom Managed Objects 137

Chapter 7: Relationships, Fetched Properties, and Expressions 169

Part II: Further Explorations 223

Chapter 8: Peer-to-Peer Over Bluetooth Using GameKit 225

Chapter 9: Online Play: Bonjour and Network Streams 271

Chapter 10: Working with Data from the Web 329

Chapter 11: MapKit 359

Chapter 12: Sending Mail 391

Chapter 13: iPod Library Access 405

Chapter 14: Keeping Your Interface Responsive 451

Chapter 15: Debugging 495

Chapter 16: The Road Goes Ever On… 527

Index 531

Contents

Contents at a Glance iv

Contents v

About the Authors xii

About the Technical Reviewer xiii

Acknowledgments xiv

Preface xv

Chapter 1: Here We Go Round Again 1

What This Book Is 1

What You Need to Know 1

What You Need Before You Can Begin 2

What's In this Book 4

Are You Ready? 6

Part I: Core Data 7

Chapter 2: The Anatomy of Core Data 9

A Brief History of Core Data 10

Creating a Core Data Template Application 10

Core Data Concepts and Terminology 12

The Data Model and Persistent Store 13

The Data Model Class: NSManagedObjectModel 14

The Persistent Store and the Persistent Store Coordinator 16

Reviewing the Data Model 18

Entities and the Data Model Editor 18

Entities 18

Properties 19

Managed Objects 21

Key-Value Coding 21

Managed Object Context 22

Saves on Terminate 23

Loading Data from the Persistent Store 24

The Fetched Results Controller 26

Creating a Fetched Results Controller 26

The Fetched Results Controller Delegate Methods.. 29

Retrieving a Managed Object from the Fetched Results Controller................................ 36

Creating and Inserting a New Managed Object 36

Deleting Managed Objects.. 38

Putting Everything in Context 39

■ Chapter 3: A Super Start: Adding, Displaying, and Deleting Data 41

Setting up the Xcode Project 42

Application Architecture 43

Modifying the Application Delegate Interface.. 44

Adding to the Application Delegate Implementation 45

Creating the Table View Controller 46

Setting up MainWindow.xib 47

Connecting the Outlets 50

Designing the Data Model 50

Adding an Entity 51

Editing the New Entity 52

Adding Attributes to the New Entity 54

Adding the Name Attribute 54

Editing the Attribute... 55

Creating HeroListViewController... 60

Declaring the Fetched Results Controller 60

Drag Two Icons to Your Project 63

Designing the HeroListViewController Interface 64

Implementing the Hero View Controller 66

Let 'Er Rip 79

Done, but Not Done 81

■ Chapter 4: The Devil in the Detail View 83

Table-Based vs. Nib-Based Detail Views.. 84

Detail Editing View Challenges 85

Controlling Table Structure with Arrays 87

Paired Arrays 87

Nested Arrays 88

Paired Nested Arrays 89

Representing Our Table Structure with Arrays... 89

Nested Arrays, Categorically Speaking 90

Updating the SuperDB Project 90

Formatting of Attributes 92

Creating the Detail View Controller 94

Declaring Instance Variables and Properties... 96

Implementing the Viewing Functionality 97

Using the New Controller.. 103

Trying Out the View Functionality... 106

Adding Editing Subcontrollers 107

Creating the Superclass 108

Creating the String Attribute Editor 112

Creating the Date Attribute Editor... 115

Using the Attribute Editors.. 118

Implementing a Selection List 120
    Creating the Generic Selection List Controller 120
Devil's End 125

■Chapter 5: Preparing for Change: Migrations and Versioning 127
About Data Models 128
    Data Models Are Compiled 128
    Data Models Can Have Multiple Versions 129
    Data Model Version Identifiers 131
    Using the Versioned Data Model 132
Migrations 133
    Lightweight vs. Standard 134
    Standard Migrations 134
    Setting up Your App to Use Lightweight Migrations 134
Time to Migrate On 136

■Chapter 6: Custom Managed Objects 137
Updating the Data Model 140
    Adding the Age Attribute 141
    Adding the Favorite Color Attribute 141
    Adding a Minimum Length to the Name Attribute 142
Creating the Hero Class 143
Tweaking the Hero Header 145
Defaulting 146
Validation 147
    Single-Attribute Validations 148
    Multiple-Attribute Validations 150
Virtual Accessors 151
Adding Validation Feedback 152
    Updating the ManagedObjectAttributeEditor Header File 152
    Updating the ManagedObjectAttributeEditor Implementation File 153
    Updating the Subclasses to Use Validation 154
Creating the Value Transformer 155
Creating the Color Attribute Editor 158
Displaying the New Attributes in Hero Edit Controller 161
The Display Problem 163
Adding View-Only Support to Hero Edit Controller 165
    Hiding the Disclosure Indicator 165
    Handling Taps on Read-Only Attributes 166
Color Us Gone 167

■Chapter 7: Relationships, Fetched Properties, and Expressions 169
Expanding Our Application: Superpowers and Reports 170
Relationships 172
    To-One Relationships 173
    To-Many Relationships 174
    Inverse Relationships 176
    Delete Rules 177
Fetched Properties 178
Creating Relationships and Fetched Properties in the Data Model Editor 179
    Adding the Power Entity 179
    Creating the Powers Relationship 180

Creating the Inverse Relationship..181

Creating the *olderHeroes* Fetched Property 181

Creating the *youngerHeroes* Fetched Property...185

Creating the *sameSexHeroes* Fetched Property..186

Creating the *oppositeSexHeroes* Fetched Property..187

Adding Relationships and Fetched Properties to the Hero Class......................................189

The Big Refactor...190

Renaming the Class..191

Refactoring the hero Instance Variable 193

Removing the Arrays 193

Supporting Save and Cancel Buttons 193

Adding Support for To-Many Relationships...197

Using the New Generic Controller..211

Adding Factory Methods for Hero and Power 211

Deleting the Nib Instance 215

Updating HeroListController 215

Creating the Fetched Property Attribute Controller 216

Cleaning Up Deleted Objects 218

Wonderful to the Core...221

Part II: Further Explorations..223

■ Chapter 8: Peer-to-Peer Over Bluetooth Using GameKit 225

This Chapter's Application 226

Network Communication Models 229

Client-Server Model..229

Peer-to-Peer Model 230

Hybrid Client-Server/Peer-to-Peer 231

The GameKit Session 232

Creating the Session 232

Finding and Connecting to Other Sessions..233

Listening for Other Sessions...234

Sending Data to a Peer...234

Packaging Up Information to Send 235

Receiving Data from a Peer 236

Closing Connections 237

The Peer Picker 237

Creating the Peer Picker...237

Handling a Peer Connection 238

Creating the Session 238

Creating the Project..239

Turning Off the Idle Timer...239

Importing the GameKit Framework 240

Designing the Interface 241

Trying It Out 268

Game On!...269

■ Chapter 9: Online Play: Bonjour and Network Streams 271

This Chapter's Application 271

Overview of the Process..273

Setting Up a Listener 273

Callback Functions and Run Loop Integration 274

Configuring a Socket 275
Specifying a Port for Listening 277
Registering the Socket with the Run Loop 280
Implementing the Socket Callback Function 280
Stopping the Listener 281
Bonjour 281
Creating a Service for Publication 282
Searching for Published Bonjour Services 285
Browser Delegate Methods 286
Resolving a Discovered Service 287
Streams 288
Opening a Stream 289
The Stream and Its Delegate 289
Receiving Data from a Stream 290
Sending Data Through the Stream 291
Putting It All Together 292
Updating Tic-Tac-Toe for Online Play 292
Adding the Packet Categories 293
Implementing the Online Session Object 295
Creating the Listener Object 306
Creating the Peer Browser 311
Updating TicTacToeViewController to Support Online Play 318
Time to Play 328

■Chapter 10: Working with Data from the Web 329
Setting Up the Application Skeleton 331
Declaring Actions and Outlets 331
Designing the Interface 333
Implementing the Stubs 335
Retrieving Data Using Foundation Objects 336
Retrieving Data Synchronously 339
The URL Request 339
Retrieving Data Asynchronously 344
NSURLConnection Delegate Methods 345
Adding Asynchronous Retrieval to WebWorks 346
Request Types and Form Parameters 350
Specifying the HTTP Request Types 350
Form Parameters 351
Building the RequestTypes Application 353
404 Conclusion Not Found 358

■Chapter 11: MapKit 359
This Chapter's Application 360
Overview and Terminology 361
The Map View 362
Map Types 362
User Location 364
Coordinate Regions 364
Setting the Region to Display 367
The Map View Delegate 367
Annotations 369
The Annotation Object 370

The Annotation View 370

Adding and Removing Annotations 371

Selecting Annotations 372

Providing the Map View with Annotation Views 372

Reverse Geocoding 373

Building the MapMe Application 375

Declaring Outlets and Actions 375

Building the Interface 376

Writing the Annotation Object Class 378

Implementing MapMeViewController 381

Linking the Map Kit and Core Location Frameworks 389

Go East, Young Programmer 390

■ Chapter 12: Sending Mail 391

This Chapter's Application 391

The MessageUI Framework 394

Creating the Mail Compose View Controller 394

Prepopulating the Subject Line 394

Prepopulating Recipients 394

Setting the Message Body 395

Adding Attachments 395

Presenting the Mail Compose View 395

The Mail Compose View Controller Delegate Method 395

Building the MailPic Application 396

Declaring Outlets and Actions 397

Building the User Interface 397

Implementing the View Controller 398

Linking the MessageUI Framework 403

Mailing It In… 403

■ Chapter 13: iPod Library Access 405

This Chapter's Application 405

Working with the iPod Library 407

Media Items 408

Media Item Collections 413

Media Queries and Media Property Predicates 414

The Media Picker Controller 417

The Music Player Controller 418

Building the Simple Player Application 424

Adding Media Item Collection Functionality 424

Declaring Outlets and Actions 428

Building the User Interface 430

Implementing the Simple Player View Controller 434

Taking Simple Player for a Spin 448

Avast! Rough Waters Ahead! 448

■ Chapter 14: Keeping Your Interface Responsive 451

Exploring the Concurrency Problem 453

Creating the Stalled Application 454

Declaring Actions and Outlets 454

Designing the Interface 454

Implementing the Stalled View Controller 455

Timers 458

Creating a Timer 458

Stopping a Timer 459

Limitations of Timers 459

Fixing Stalled with a Timer 460

Creating the Batch Object 460

Updating the Controller Header 462

Updating the Nib 463

Updating the View Controller Implementation 463

Operation Queues & Concurrency 468

Threads 469

Operations 475

Operation Queues 478

Fixing Stalled with an Operation Queue 479

Creating SquareRootApplication 480

Changes to StalledViewController.h 485

Adjusting the User Interface 486

Updating StalledViewController.m 487

Queue 'em Up 493

■Chapter 15: Debugging 495

The Debugger 496

Breakpoints 497

The GDB Console 513

Static Analysis 516

Specific Bugs 517

Overreleasing Memory 517

Infinite Recursion 523

Missed Outlet and Action Connections 525

GDB: Stopped at Concluding Paragraph 525

■Chapter 16: The Road Goes Ever On… 527

Getting Unstuck 527

Apple's Documentation 528

Mailing Lists 528

Discussion Forums 528

Web Sites 529

Blogs 529

And If All Else Fails… 530

Farewell 530

■Index 531

About the Authors

Dave Mark is a longtime Mac developer and author, who has written a number of books on Mac development, including *Beginning iPhone 3 Development* (Apress, 2009), *Learn C on the Mac* (Apress, 2008), *The Macintosh Programming Primer* series (Addison-Wesley, 1992), and *Ultimate Mac Programming* (Wiley, 1995). Dave loves the water and spends as much time as possible on it, in it, or near it. He lives with his wife and three children in Virginia.

Jeff LaMarche is a Mac and iPhone developer with more than 20 years of programming experience. This is his second book on iPhone development. He has also written about Cocoa and Objective-C for *MacTech Magazine*, as well as articles for Apple's Developer Technical Services web site. He has experience working in enterprise software as a developer for PeopleSoft, starting in the late 1990s, and later as an independent consultant. He now focuses exclusively on programming for the Mac and iPhone.

About the Technical Reviewer

 **Mark Dalrymple** is a longtime Mac and Unix programmer, working on cross-platform toolkits, Internet publishing tools, high-performance web servers, and end-user desktop applications. He is also the principal author of *Advanced Mac OS X Programming* (Big Nerd Ranch, 2005) and *Learn Objective-C on the Mac* (Apress, 2009). In his spare time, Mark plays trombone and bassoon, and makes balloon animals.

Acknowledgments

This book could not have been written without our mighty, kind, and clever families, friends, and cohorts. First and foremost, eternal thanks to Terry and Deneen for putting up with us, and for keeping the rest of the universe at bay while we toiled away on this book. This project saw us tucked away in our writers' cubby for many long hours, and somehow, you didn't complain once. We are lucky men.

This book could not have been written without the fine folks at Apress. Clay Andres brought us to Apress in the first place and carried this book on his back. Dominic Shakeshaft was the gracious mastermind who dealt with all of our complaints with a smile on his face, and somehow found solutions that made sense and made this book better. Kelly Moritz, our wonderful and gracious coordinating editor, was the irresistible force to our slowly movable object. Douglas Pundick, our developmental editor, helped us with some terrific feedback along the way. They kept the book on the right track and always pointed in the right direction. Marilyn Smith and Ralph Moore, copy editors extraordinaire, you were both such a pleasure to work with! Jeffrey Pepper, Frank McGuckin, Angie MacAllister, and the Apress production team took all these pieces and somehow made them whole. Leo Cuellar and Jeff Stonefield assembled the marketing message and got it out to the world. To all the folks at Apress, thank you, thank you, thank you!

A very special shout out to our incredibly talented technical reviewer, Mark Dalrymple. In addition to providing insightful feedback, Mark tested all the code in this book, and helped keep us on the straight and narrow. Thanks, Mark!

Finally, thanks to our children for their patience while their dads were working so hard. This book is for you, Maddie, Gwynnie, Ian, Kai, Daniel, Kelley, and Ryan.

Preface

The preface to our previous book, *Beginning iPhone 3 Development*, started with the phrase, "What an amazing journey!" Well, it's true. We're having a blast, making a lot of new friends and, above all, learning, learning, learning. The iPhone SDK continues to evolve, and with each new release, it brings new concepts to explore and new design patterns to master.

As its name implies, *More iPhone 3 Development* assumes you've read *Beginning iPhone 3 Development* or one of the other terrific titles out there, or have tackled the iPhone dev learning curve on your own. If you are a beginner, not to worry, our approach is the same. We talk you through the concepts, and then build a new project and walk you through the source code, with a sprinkling of tips and cautions along the way.

The book starts off with a series of chapters that cover Core Data, Apple's official iPhone persistence framework. If the concept of persistence is new to you, don't be intimidated by the name. When you want your data to stick around from one run of your app to the next, that's persistence. *Beginning iPhone 3 Development* touched on the topic with a brief introduction to Core Data, but *More iPhone 3 Development* starts from scratch and gives you a complete tour through Core Data, with a lot of reusable code. By the time you are finished with the Core Data chapters, you should have everything you need to add Core Data to your own iPhone apps.

Next up, we offer a series of chapters on GameKit and networking. The GameKit framework makes it easy to add Bluetooth connectivity to your apps. We bring GameKit to life by building a simple, two-person game. We then follow that up by taking iPhone networking to the next level, showing you how to expand your networking skill set to include game play over a local area network. Once you've mastered those techniques, it's just a short step to adding Internet play. Our final networking chapter explores techniques for pulling data from the Internet and interacting with web servers.

Those chapters cover the most widely requested topics by our readers. We hope you'll find them worth the price of admission. But wait, there's more! We also cover MapKit, in-application e-mail, and adding iPod functionality to your applications via the MediaPlayer framework. Finally, we wrap up things with chapters on concurrency and debugging techniques.

Before we leave you to your reading, we just want to say how much we appreciate your support. You've truly made this a gratifying experience for us both. As always, be sure to check out http://iphonedevbook.com/forum, and drop us a line to let us know about your amazing new apps. We look forward to seeing you on the forum. Happy coding!

Dave and Jeff

Chapter 1

Here We Go Round Again

So, you're still creating iPhone applications, huh? Great! The iPhone and the App Store have been a tremendous success, fundamentally changing the way mobile applications are delivered and completely changing what people expect from their mobile phones. Since the first release of the iPhone Software Development Kit (SDK) way back in March 2008, Apple has been busily adding new functionality and improving what was already there. It's no less exciting of a platform than it was back when it was first introduced. In fact, in many ways, it's more exciting, because Apple keeps expanding the amount of functionality available to third-party developers like us.

What This Book Is

This book is a guide to help you continue down the path to creating better iPhone applications. In *Beginning iPhone 3 Development* (Apress, 2009), our goal was to get you past the initial learning curve, and to help you get your arms around the fundamentals of building your first iPhone applications. In this book, we're assuming you already know the basics. So, in addition to showing you how to use several of the new APIs introduced with iPhone SDK 3.0, we're also going to weave in some more advanced techniques that you'll need as your iPhone development efforts grow in size and complexity.

In *Beginning iPhone 3 Development*, every chapter was self-contained, each presenting its own unique project or set of projects. We'll be using a similar approach in the second half of this book, but in Chapters 2 through 7, we'll focus on a single, evolving Core Data application. Each chapter will cover a specific area of Core Data functionality as we expand the application. We'll also be strongly emphasizing techniques that will keep your application from becoming unwieldy and hard to manage as it gets larger.

What You Need to Know

This book assumes that you already have some programming knowledge and that you have a basic understanding of the iPhone SDK, either because you've worked through *Beginning iPhone 3 Development* or because you've gained a similar foundation from other sources. We assume that you've experimented a little with the SDK, perhaps written a small program or two on your own, and have a general feel for how Xcode and Interface Builder work.

COMPLETELY NEW TO THE IPHONE?

If you are completely new to iPhone development, there are other books you probably should read before this one. If you don't already understand the basics of programming and syntax of the C language, you should check out *Learn C on the Mac* by Dave Mark (Apress, 2008), which is a comprehensive introduction to the C language for Macintosh programmers:

`http://www.apress.com/book/view/1430218096`

If you already understand C, but don't have any experience programming with objects, check out *Learn Objective-C on the Mac* (Apress, 2009), an excellent and approachable introduction to Objective-C by Mac programming experts Mark Dalrymple and Scott Knaster:

`http://www.apress.com/book/view/1430218150`

Next, navigate over to the Apple iPhone Development Center and download a copy of *The Objective-C 2.0 Programming Language*, a very detailed and extensive description of the language and a great reference guide:

`http://developer.apple.com/iphone/library/documentation/Cocoa/Conceptual/ObjectiveC/`

Note that you'll need to log in (we'll get to registration in the next section) before you are taken to the start of this document.

Once you have a firm handle on Objective-C, you need to master the fundamentals of the iPhone SDK. For that, you should check out the prequel to this book, *Beginning iPhone 3 Development* (Apress 2008):

`http://www.apress.com/book/view/1430216263`

What You Need Before You Can Begin

Before you can write software for iPhone, you need a few things. For starters, you'll need an Intel-based Macintosh running Snow Leopard (Mac OS X 10.6.2 or later). Any Macintosh computer—laptop or desktop—that has been released since 2006 should work just fine, but make sure your machine is Intel-based and is capable of running Snow Leopard.

> **NOTE:** You actually can develop for the iPhone using Leopard (Mac OS X 10.5 or later), but there are many great new features in Xcode that are available only on Snow Leopard. Therefore, we highly recommend upgrading to Snow Leopard if you are using an earlier release.

This may seem obvious, but you'll also need an iPhone or iPod touch. While much of your code can be tested using the iPhone simulator, not all programs will run in the simulator. And you'll want to thoroughly test any application you create on an actual device before you ever consider releasing it to the public.

Finally, you'll need to sign up to become a Registered iPhone Developer. Apple requires this step before it will allow you to download the iPhone SDK. If you're already a Registered iPhone Developer, go ahead and download the latest and greatest iPhone development tools, and skip ahead to the next section.

If you're new to Apple's Registered iPhone Developer programs, navigate to `http://developer.apple.com/iphone/`, which will bring you to a page similar to that shown in Figure 1-1. Just below the iPhone Dev Center banner, on the right side of the page, you'll find links labeled *Log in* and *Register.* Click the *Register* link. On the page that appears, click the *Continue* button. Follow the sequence of instructions to use your existing Apple ID or create a new one.

Figure 1-1. *Apple's iPhone Dev Center web site*

At some point, as you register, you'll be given a choice of several paths, all of which will lead you to the SDK download page. The three choices are free, commercial, and enterprise. All three options give you access to the iPhone SDK and Xcode, Apple's integrated development environment (IDE). Xcode includes tools for creating and debugging source code, compiling applications, and performance-tuning the applications you've written.

The free option is, as its name implies, free. It lets you develop iPhone apps that run on a software-only iPhone simulator, but does not allow you to download those apps to your iPhone or iPod touch, nor sell your apps on Apple's App Store. In addition, some programs in this book will run only on your device, not in the simulator, which means you will not be able to run them if you choose the free solution. That said, the free solution is a fine place to start if you don't mind learning without doing for those programs that won't run in the simulator.

The other two options are to sign up for an iPhone Developer Program: either the Standard (commercial) Program or the Enterprise Program. The Standard Program costs $99. It provides a host of development tools and resources, technical support, distribution of your application via Apple's App Store, and, most important, the ability to test and debug your code on an iPhone rather than just in the simulator. The Enterprise Program, which costs $299, is designed for companies developing proprietary, in-house applications for the iPhone and iPod touch. For more details on these two programs, check out `http://developer.apple.com/iphone/program/`.

> **NOTE:** If you are going to sign up for the Standard or Enterprise Program, you should go do it right now. It can take a while to get approved, and you'll need that approval to be able to run applications on your iPhone. Don't worry, though—the projects in the early chapters of this book will run just fine on the iPhone simulator.

Because iPhone is an always-connected mobile device that uses another company's wireless infrastructure, Apple has placed far more restrictions on iPhone developers than it ever has on Macintosh developers, who are able to write and distribute programs with absolutely no oversight or approval from Apple. Apple is not doing this to be mean, but rather to minimize the chances of people distributing malicious or poorly written programs that could degrade performance on the shared network. It may seem like a lot of hoops to jump through, but Apple has gone through quite an effort to make the process as painless as possible.

What's In this Book

As we said earlier, Chapters 2 through 7 of this book focus on Core Data, Apple's primary persistence framework. The rest of the chapters cover specific areas of functionality that are either new with iPhone SDK 3.0 or were simply too advanced to include in *Beginning iPhone 3 Development*.

Here is a very brief overview of the chapters that follow:

- *Chapter 2, The Anatomy of Core Data*: In this chapter, we'll introduce you to Core Data. You'll learn why Core Data is a vital part of your iPhone development arsenal. We'll dissect a simple Core Data application and show you how all the individual parts of a Core Data-backed application fit together.

- *Chapter 3, A Super Start: Adding, Displaying and Deleting Data*: Once you have a firm grasp on Core Data's terminology and architecture, you'll learn how to do some basic tasks, including inserting, searching for, and retrieving data.

- *Chapter 4, The Devil in the Detail View*: In this chapter, you'll learn how to let your users edit and change the data stored by Core Data. We'll explore techniques for building generic, reusable views so you can leverage the same code to present different types of data.

- *Chapter 5, Preparing for Change: Migrations and Versioning*: Here, we'll look at Apple tools that you can use to change your application's data model, while still allowing your users to continue using their data from previous versions of your application.

- *Chapter 6, Custom Managed Objects*: To really unlock the power of Core Data, you can subclass the class used to represent specific instances of data. In this chapter, we'll show you how to use custom managed objects, as well as demonstrate some of the benefits of doing so.

- *Chapter 7, Relationships, Fetched Properties, and Expressions*: In this final chapter on Core Data, we'll cover some mechanisms that allow you to expand your applications in powerful ways. We'll also refactor the application we've built in the previous chapters, so that we don't need to add new classes as we expand our data model.

- *Chapter 8, Peer-to-Peer Over Bluetooth Using GameKit*: One of the coolest new features of SDK 3.0 is the GameKit framework. This framework makes it easy to create programs that communicate over Bluetooth, such as multiplayer games for the iPhone and iPod touch. We'll explore GameKit by building a simple two-player game.

- *Chapter 9, Online Play: Bonjour and Network Streams*: GameKit doesn't provide the ability to make multiplayer games that work over Wi-Fi or the Internet. In this chapter, we'll expand our simple two-player game so it can also be played over non-Bluetooth networks.

- *Chapter 10, Working with Data from the Web*: The iPhone is an always-connected device, so learning how to pull data from the Web or other places on the Internet can be very valuable. In this chapter, we'll look at several different techniques for interacting with web servers.

- *Chapter 11, MapKit*: This chapter explores another great new piece of functionality added to the iPhone SDK with the 3.0 release, MapKit. This framework allows you to leverage Google Maps directly from your application.

- *Chapter 12, Sending Mail*: In the original iPhone SDK, if your application wanted to send e-mail, it needed to launch the Mail application to do so. Now, thanks to the 3.0 version, we have the ability to send e-mail directly from our applications. We'll show you how to implement that functionality in this chapter.

- *Chapter 13, iPod Library Access*: It's now possible to programmatically get access to your users' complete library of audio tracks stored on their iPhone or iPod touch. In this chapter, we'll look at the various techniques used to find, retrieve, and play music and other audio tracks.

- *Chapter 14, Keeping Your Interface Responsive*: Long-running programming tasks can easily bog down the iPhone's user interface. In this chapter, we'll take a look at implementing different forms of concurrency so that your application remains responsive.

- *Chapter 15, Debugging*: No program is ever perfect. Bugs and defects are a natural part of the programming process. In this chapter, we'll cover various techniques for finding and fixing bugs in iPhone SDK programs.

- *Chapter 16, The Road Goes Ever On…*: Sadly, every journey must come to an end. We'll wrap up this book with fond farewells and some resources we hope you'll find useful.

Are You Ready?

As we said in *Beginning iPhone 3 Development*, iPhone is an incredible computing platform, an ever-expanding frontier for your development pleasure. In this book, we're going to take you further down the iPhone development road, digging deeper into the SDK, touching on new and, in some cases, more advanced topics.

Read the book, and be sure to build the projects yourself—don't just copy them from the archive and run them once or twice. You'll learn most by doing. Make sure you understand what you did, and why, before moving on to the next project. Don't be afraid to make changes to the code. Experiment, tweak the code, observe the results. Rinse and repeat.

Got your iPhone SDK installed? Turn the page, put on some tunes, and let's go. Your continuing journey awaits.

Part I

Core Data

Core Data is Apple's framework for persisting data to the file system. Using Core Data, you deal with your program's data as objects, and let the framework deal with the gnarly specifics of how to save, find, and retrieve those objects. Over the next several chapters, you'll see how to use Core Data so that you can develop your apps more quickly and get better performance than with traditional persistence mechanisms.

Chapter 2

The Anatomy of Core Data

Core Data is a framework and set of tools that allow you to persist your application's data to the iPhone's file system automatically. Core Data is a form of something called **object-relational mapping**, or **ORM**, which is just a fancy way of saying that Core Data takes the data stored in your Objective-C objects and translates (or **maps**) that data into another form so that it can be easily stored in a database, such as SQLite, or into a flat file.

Core Data can seem like magic when you first start using it. Objects are simply dealt with as objects, and they seem to know how to save themselves into the database or file system. You won't create SQL strings or make file management calls—ever. Core Data insulates you from some complex and difficult programming tasks, which is great for you. By using Core Data, you can develop applications with complex data models much, much faster than you could using straight SQLite, object archiving, or flat files.

Technologies that hide complexity the way Core Data does can encourage "voodoo programming"—that most dangerous of programming practices where you include code in your application that you don't necessarily understand. Sometimes, that mystery code arrives in the form of a project template. Or, perhaps, you downloaded a utilities library that did a task for you that you just don't have the time or expertise to do for yourself. That voodoo code does what you need it to do, and you don't have the time or inclination to step through it and figure it out, so it just sits there, working its magic … until it breaks. Though this is not always the case, as a general rule, if you find yourself with code in your own application that you don't fully understand, it's a sign you should go do a little research, or at least find a more experienced peer to help you get a handle on your mystery code.

The point is that Core Data is one of those complex technologies that can easily turn into a source of mystery code that will make its way into many of your projects. Although you don't need to know exactly how Core Data accomplishes everything it does, you should invest some time and effort into understanding the overall Core Data architecture.

In this chapter, we'll start with a brief history of Core Data, and then dive into the Core Data template itself. By dissecting Xcode's default Core Data template, you'll find it much easier to understand the more complex Core Data projects we get into in the following chapters.

A Brief History of Core Data

Core Data has been around for quite some time, but it just became available on the iPhone with the release of iPhone SDK 3.0. Core Data was originally introduced with Mac OS X 10.4 (Tiger), but some of the DNA in Core Data actually goes back about 15 years, to a NeXT framework called Enterprise Objects Framework (EOF), part of NeXT's WebObjects web development tool set.

EOF was designed to work with remote databases, and it was a pretty revolutionary tool when it first came out. Although there are now many good ORM tools for almost every language, when WebObjects was in its infancy, most web applications were written to use handcrafted SQL or file system calls to persist their data. Back then, writing web applications was incredibly time- and labor-intensive. WebObjects, in part because of EOF, cut the development time needed to create complex web applications by an order of magnitude.

In addition to being part of WebObjects, EOF was also used by NeXTSTEP, which was the predecessor to Cocoa. When Apple bought NeXT, the Apple developers used many of the concepts from EOF to develop a new persistence tool called Core Data. Core Data does for desktop applications what EOF had previously done for web applications: It dramatically increases developer productivity by removing the need to write file system code or interact with an embedded database.

Let's take a look at a Core Data Xcode template.

Creating a Core Data Template Application

Fire up Xcode and select **New Project…** from the **File** menu, or press ⇧⌘N. When the new project assistant comes up, select *Application* under the *iPhone OS* heading in the left column, and then select *Navigation-based Application* from the upper-right pane. In the lower-right pane, make sure the box labeled *Use Core Data for storage* is checked, as in Figure 2–1. That check box is how we tell Xcode to give us all the code and extra stuff we need to start using Core Data. Not all Xcode project templates have this option, but it's available for both the Navigation-based Application and Window-based Application templates.

Figure 2–1. *Creating a project in Xcode that uses Core Data*

Call your project *CoreData*. Now build and run the application. It will work fine in either the simulator or on a physical device. It should look something like Figure 2–2.

Figure 2–2. *The application created by compiling the Core Data Navigation-based Application project*

If you press the plus icon in the upper-right corner, it will insert a new row into the table that shows the exact date and time the plus button was pressed. You can also use the *Edit* button to delete rows. Exciting, huh?

> **CAUTION:** Early versions of the Core Data Navigation-based Application template had a small bug. If you deleted the last row, the application would crash. This was fixed in SDK 3.1.

Under the hood of this simple application, a lot is happening. Think about it—without adding a single class, or any code to persist data to a file or interact with a database, pressing the plus button created an object, populated it with data, and saved it to a SQLite database created for us automatically. There's plenty of free functionality here.

Now that you've seen an application in action, let's take a look at what's going on behind the scenes.

Core Data Concepts and Terminology

Like most complex technologies, Core Data has its own terminology that can be a bit intimidating to newcomers. Let's break down the mystery and get our arms around Core Data's nomenclature.

Figure 2–3 shows a simplified, high-level diagram of the Core Data architecture. Don't expect it all to make sense now, but as we look at different pieces, you might want to refer back to the diagram to cement your understanding of how they fit together.

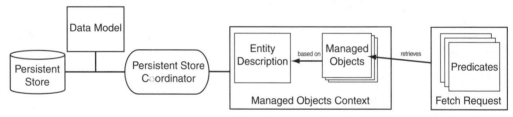

Figure 2–3. *A high-level view of the Core Data architectures. We'll be looking at each of these pieces in this chapter.*

There are five key concepts to focus on here. As you proceed through this chapter, make sure you understand each of the following:

- Persistent store

- Data model

- Persistent store coordinator

- Managed object and managed object context

- Fetch request

Once again, don't let the names throw you. Follow along, and you'll see how all these pieces fit together.

The Data Model and Persistent Store

The **persistent store**, which is sometimes referred to as a **backing store**, is where Core Data stores its data. By default on the iPhone, Core Data will use a SQLite database contained in your application's documents folder as its persistent store. But this can be changed without impacting any of the other code you write by tweaking a single line of code. We'll show you the actual line of code to change in a few moments.

> **CAUTION:** Do not change the type of persistent store once you have posted your application to the App Store. If you must change it for any reason, you will need to write code to migrate data from the old persistent store to the new one, or else your users will lose all of their data—something that will likely make them quite unhappy.

Every persistent store is associated with a single data model, which defines the types of data that the persistent store can store. If you expand the *Resources* folder in the *Groups & Files* pane in Xcode, you'll see a file called *CoreData.xcdatamodel*. That file is the default **data model** for your project. The project template we chose gave us a single persistent store and an associated data model. Single-click *CoreData.xcdatamodel* now to bring up Xcode's **data model editor**. Your editing pane in Xcode should now look like Figure 2–4. As you design your own applications, this is where you'll build your application's data model.

In this chapter, we'll explore the data model that comes with the template. In Chapter 3, we'll actually use the editor to create a custom data model.

Take a look at the data model editor. Notice the single rounded rectangle in the middle of the editing window. That rectangle is known as an **entity**. In effect, an entity is like a class definition, wrapping your various data elements under a single umbrella. This particular entity has the name *Event*, and it features sections for *Attributes* and *Relationships*. There's a single attribute, named *timeStamp*, and no relationships.

Click off the entity rectangle. The title bar should turn a light pink. Click back on the entity, and it will turn blue, indicating the entity is selected.

The entity was created as part of this template. If you use this template to create your own Core Data application, you get the Event entity for free. As you design your own data models, you'll most likely delete the Event entity and create your own entities from scratch.

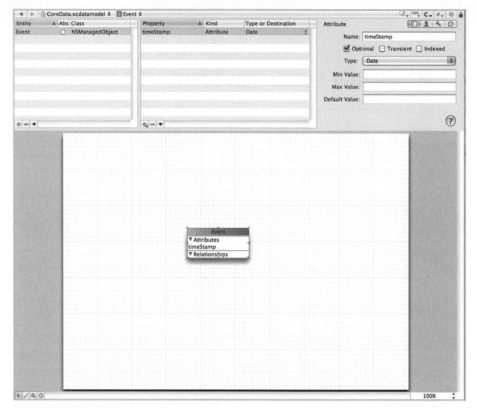

Figure 2–4. *The editing pane for a data model class allows you to design your data model visually.*

A moment ago, you ran your Core Data sample application in the simulator. When you pressed the plus icon, a new instance of an Event was created. Entities, which we'll look at more closely in a few pages, replace the Objective-C data model class you would otherwise use to hold your data.

We'll get back to the data model editor in just a minute to see how it works. For now, just remember that the persistent store is where Core Data stores its data, and the data model defines the form of that data. Also remember that every persistent store has one, and only one, data model.

The Data Model Class: NSManagedObjectModel

Although you won't typically access your application's data model directly, you should be aware of the fact that there is an Objective-C class that represents the data model in memory. This class is called NSManagedObjectModel, and the template automatically creates an instance of NSManagedObjectModel based on the data model file in your project. Let's take a look at the code that creates it now.

In your project window's *Groups & Files* pane, open the *Classes* group and single-click *CoreDataAppDelegate.m*. At the top of the editor pane, click the function menu to bring up a list of the methods in this class (see Figure 2–5). Select *-managedObjectModel*, which will take you to the method that creates the object model based on the *CoreData.xcdatamodel* file.

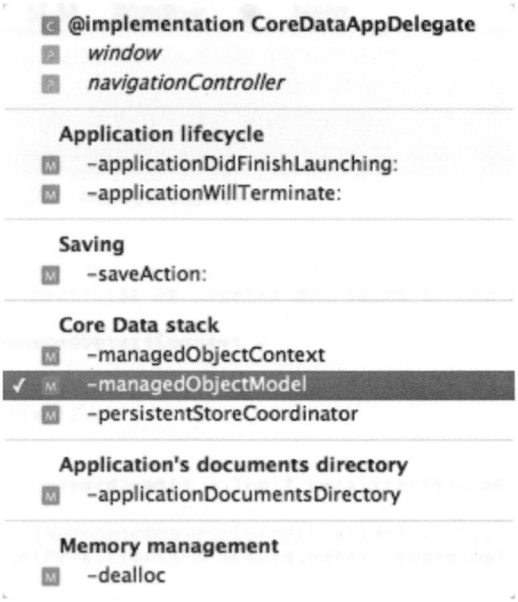

© **@implementation CoreDataAppDelegate**
▣ *window*
▣ *navigationController*

Application lifecycle
Ⓜ   –applicationDidFinishLaunching:
Ⓜ   –applicationWillTerminate:

Saving
Ⓜ   –saveAction:

Core Data stack
Ⓜ   –managedObjectContext
✓ **Ⓜ**   –managedObjectModel
Ⓜ   –persistentStoreCoordinator

Application's documents directory
Ⓜ   –applicationDocumentsDirectory

Memory management
Ⓜ   –dealloc

Figure 2–5. *The editor pane's pop-up menu*

The method should look like this:

```
/**
 Returns the managed object model for the application.
 If the model doesn't already exist, it is created by merging all of the models
 found in the application bundle.
 */
- (NSManagedObjectModel *)managedObjectModel {
    if (managedObjectModel != nil) {
        return managedObjectModel;
    }
    managedObjectModel = [[NSManagedObjectModel mergedModelFromBundles:nil] retain];
    return managedObjectModel;
}
```

The first thing it does is check the instance variable managedObjectModel to see if it's nil. This accessor method uses a form of lazy loading. The underlying instance variable doesn't actually get instantiated until the first time the accessor method is called. For this reason, you should never, ever access managedObjectModel directly (except within the accessor method itself, of course). Always make sure to use the accessor methods. Otherwise, you could end up trying to make calls on an object that hasn't been created yet.

> **TIP:** The data model class is called NSManagedObjectModel because, as you'll see a little later in the chapter, instances of data in Core Data are called **managed objects**.

If managedObjectModel is nil, we'll go get our data models. Remember how we said that a persistent store was associated with a single data model? Well, that's true, but it doesn't tell the whole story. You can combine multiple *.xcdatamodel* files into a single instance of NSManagedObjectModel, creating a single data model that combines all the entities from multiple files. This line of code takes any *.xcdatamodel* files that might be in your Xcode project and combines them together into a single instance of NSManagedObjectModel:

```
managedObjectModel = [[NSManagedObjectModel mergedModelFromBundles:nil] retain];
```

So, for example, if you were to create a second data model file and add it to your project, that new file would be combined with *CoreData.xcdatamodel* into a single managed object model that contained the contents of both files. This allows you to split up your application's data model into multiple smaller and more manageable files.

The vast majority of iPhone applications that use Core Data have a single persistent store and a single data model, so the default template code will work beautifully most of the time, and will let you spread your data model out over multiple files. That said, Core Data does support the use of multiple persistent stores. You could, for example, design your application to store some of its data in a SQLite persistent store and some of it in a binary flat file. If you find that you need to use multiple data models, remember to change the template code here to load the managed object models individually, using initWithContentsOfURL:.

The Persistent Store and the Persistent Store Coordinator

The persistent store isn't actually represented by an Objective-C class. Instead, a class called NSPersistentStoreCoordinator controls access to the persistent store. In essence, it takes all the calls coming from different classes that trigger reads or writes to the persistent store and serializes them so that multiple calls against the same file are not being made at the same time, which could result in problems due to file or database locking.

As is the case with the managed object model, the template provides us with a method in the application delegate that creates and returns an instance of a persistent store coordinator. Other than creating the store and associating it with a data model and a location on disk (which is done for you in the template), you will rarely need to interact with the persistent store coordinator directly. You'll use high-level Core Data calls, and Core Data will interact with the persistent store coordinator to retrieve or save the data.

Let's take a look at the method that returns the persistent store coordinator. In *CoreDataAppDelegate.m*, select *-persistentStoreCoordinator* from the function pop-up menu. Here's the method:

```
/**
 Returns the persistent store coordinator for the application.
 If the coordinator doesn't already exist, it is created and the application's store
 added to it.
 */
- (NSPersistentStoreCoordinator *)persistentStoreCoordinator {

    if (persistentStoreCoordinator != nil) {
        return persistentStoreCoordinator;
    }

    NSURL *storeUrl = [NSURL fileURLWithPath: [[self applicationDocumentsDirectory]
        stringByAppendingPathComponent: @"CoreData.sqlite"]];

    NSError *error;
    persistentStoreCoordinator = [[NSPersistentStoreCoordinator alloc]
        initWithManagedObjectModel: [self managedObjectModel]];
    if (![persistentStoreCoordinator addPersistentStoreWithType:NSSQLiteStoreType
        configuration:nil URL:storeUrl options:nil error:&error]) {
        // Handle error
    }

    return persistentStoreCoordinator;
}
```

As with the managed object model, this persistentStoreCoordinator accessor method uses lazy loading and doesn't instantiate the persistent store coordinator until the first time it is accessed. Then it creates a path to a file called *CoreData.sqlite* in the documents directory in your application's sandbox. The template will always create a filename based on your project's name. If you want to use a different name, you can change it here, though it generally doesn't matter what you call the file, since the user will never see it.

CAUTION: If you do decide to change the filename, make sure you don't change it after you've posted your application to the App Store, or else future updates will cause your users to lose all of their data.

Take a look at this line of code:

```
if (![persistentStoreCoordinator addPersistentStoreWithType:NSSQLiteStoreType
        configuration:nil URL:storeUrl options:nil error:&error]) {
```

The first parameter to this method, NSSQLiteStoreType, determines the type of the persistent store. NSSQLiteStoreType is a constant that tells Core Data to use a SQLite database for its persistent store. If you want your application to use a single, binary flat file instead of a SQLite database, you could specify the constant NSBinaryStoreType instead of NSSQLiteStoreType. The vast majority of the time, the default setting is the best choice, so unless you have a compelling reason to change it, leave it alone.

> **NOTE:** A third type of persistent store supported by Core Data on the iPhone is called **in-memory store**. The primary use of this option is to create a caching mechanism, storing the data in memory instead of in a database or binary file. To use an in-memory store, specify a store type of `NSInMemoryStoreType`.

Reviewing the Data Model

Before we move on to other parts of Core Data, let's quickly review how the pieces we've looked at so far fit together. You might want to refer back to Figure 2–3.

The persistent store (or backing store) is a file on the iPhone's file system that can be either a SQLite database or a binary flat file. A data model file, contained in one or more files with an extension of *.xcdatamodel*, describes the structure of your application's data. This file can be edited in Xcode. The data model tells the persistent store coordinator the format of all data stored in that persistent store. The persistent store coordinator is used by other Core Data classes that need to save, retrieve, or search for data. Easy enough, right? Let's move on.

Entities and the Data Model Editor

Let's go back to the data model editor and take a closer look at the simple data model that was provided as part of the template. Single-click *CoreData.xcdatamodel* again. Your editor pane (the large pane at the bottom of the window) should look similar to the one shown earlier in Figure 2–4.

Entities

As we said before, the rounded rectangle in the center is an entity. In effect, an entity is like an Objective-C class declaration. Each data model class you would create if you didn't use Core Data translates to an entity when you do use Core Data.

Each entity has a name—in this case, *Event*—which must begin with a capital letter. In the template application you ran earlier, each time you pressed the plus button, a new instance of *Event* was created and stored in the application's persistent store.

In the data model editor, you can tell if an entity is selected by its color. A selected entity will have a blue title bar and be surrounded by eight resize handles. An unselected entity will have a reddish-gray title bar, and it will not have any resize handles. Single-click the *Event* entity title bar to select it.

As you select the *Event* entity, take a look at the top-left pane, known as the **entity pane**. The entity pane is a list of all the entities that have been defined in this data model. The template we used for this project creates a single entity, *Event*. Selecting *Event* in the entity pane is the same as selecting the rounded rectangle in the bottom pane. Try it: Click outside the entity in the bottom pane to deselect it, and then click the *Event* line in the entity pane. The entity in the bottom pane will also be selected. The upper-left and bottom panes show two different views of the same entity list.

Properties

While the entity pane lists all the data model's entities, the upper-middle pane, known as the **property pane**, lists the **properties** that belong to the selected entity.

The entity itself has no mechanism for storing data. Instead, entities are made up of one or more properties that define it. When you select an entity in the entity pane, its properties are displayed in the property pane.

An entity can be made up of any number of properties. There are four different types of properties: **attributes**, **relationships**, **fetched properties**, and **fetch requests**.

Attributes

The property that you'll use the most when creating entities is the attribute, which serves the same function in a Core Data entity as an instance variable does in an Objective-C class—they both hold data. If you look at your data model editor (or at Figure 2–4), you'll see that the *Event* entity has one property: an attribute named *timeStamp*. The *timeStamp* attribute holds the date and time when a given *Event* instance was created. In our sample application, when you click the plus sign, a new row is added to the table displaying a single *Event*'s *timeStamp*.

Just like an instance variable, each attribute has a **type**, which is set using a pop-up menu in the third column of the attribute pane. Let's take a look at that pop-up menu. Make sure *Event* is selected in the entity pane, and then select *timeStamp* in the attribute pane. Note the word *Date* in the third column of the *timeStamp* attribute. That's a pop-up menu (see Figure 2–6). Select it, but don't change its value (leave it as *Date*). You can see the range of options for attribute type. We'll look at the different attribute types in the next few chapters when we begin building our own data models.

A date attribute, such as *timeStamp*, corresponds to an instance of NSDate. If you want to set a new value for a date attribute, you need to provide an instance of NSDate to do so. A string attribute corresponds to an instance of NSString, and most of the numeric types correspond to an instance of NSNumber.

> **TIP:** Don't worry too much about all the other buttons, text fields, and check boxes in the data model editor. As you make your way through the next few chapters, you'll get a sense of what each does.

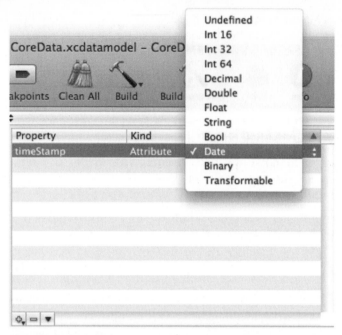

Figure 2–6. *The attribute type pop-up menu appears when you click an attribute in the Type or Destination column.*

Relationships

As the name implies, a relationship defines the associations between two different entities. In the template application, no relationships are defined for the *Event* entity. We'll begin discussing relationships in Chapter 7, but here's an example just to give you a sense of how they work.

Suppose we created an *Employee* entity and wanted to reflect each *Employee*'s employer in the data structure. We could just include an *employer* attribute, perhaps an NSString, in the *Employee* entity, but that would be pretty limiting. A more flexible approach would be to create an *Employer* entity, and then create a relationship between the *Employee* and *Employer* entities.

Relationships can be **to one** or **to many**, and they are designed to link specific objects. The relationship from *Employee* to *Employer* might be a to-one relationship, if we assume that your *Employee*s do not moonlight and have only a single job. On the other hand, the relationship from *Employer* to *Employee* is to many, since an *Employer* might employ many *Employee*s.

To put this in Objective-C terms, a to-one relationship is like using an instance variable to hold a pointer to an instance of another Objective-C class. A to-many relationship is more like using a pointer to a collection class like NSMutableArray or NSSet, which can contain multiple objects.

Fetched Properties

A fetched property is like a query that originates with a single managed object. For example, suppose we added a *birthdate* attribute to *Employee*. We might add a fetched property, called *sameBirthdate*, to find all *Employee*s with the same *birthdate* as the current *Employee*.

Unlike relationships, fetched properties are not loaded along with the object. For example, if *Employee* has a relationship to *Employer*, when an *Employee* instance is loaded, the corresponding *Employer* instance will be loaded, too. But when an *Employee* is loaded, *sameBirthdate* is not evaluated. This is a form of lazy loading. You'll learn more about fetched properties in Chapter 7.

Fetch Requests

While a fetched property is like a query that originates with a single managed object, a fetch request is more like a class method that implements a canned query. For example, we might build a fetch request named *canChangeLightBulb* that returns a list of *Employee*s who are taller than 80 inches (about 2 meters). We can run the fetch request any time we need a light bulb changed. When we run it, Core Data searches the persistent store to find the current list of potential light-bulb-changing *Employee*s.

We will create many fetch requests programmatically in the next few chapters, and we'll be looking at a simple one a little later in this chapter, in the "Creating a Fetched Results Controller" section.

Managed Objects

Entities define the structure of your data, but they do not actually hold any data themselves. The instances of data are called **managed objects**. Every instance of an entity that you work with in Core Data will be an instance of the class NSManagedObject or a subclass of NSManagedObject.

Key-Value Coding

The NSDictionary class allows you to store objects in a data structure and retrieve an object using a unique key. Like the NSDictionary class, NSManagedObject supports the key-value methods valueForKey: and setValue:forKey: for setting and retrieving attribute values. It also has additional methods for working with relationships. You can, for example, retrieve an instance of NSMutableSet representing a specific relationship. Adding managed objects to this mutable set, or removing them will add or remove objects from the relationship it represents.

If the NSDictionary class is new to you, take a few minutes to fire up Xcode and read about NSDictionary in the documentation viewer. The important concept to get your head around is **key-value coding**, or **KVC**. Core Data uses KVC to store and retrieve data from its managed objects.

In our template application, consider an instance of NSManagedObject that represents a single *Event*. We could retrieve the value stored in its *timeStamp* attribute by calling valueForKey:, like so:

```
NSDate *timeStamp = [managedObject valueForKey:@"timeStamp"];
```

Since *timeStamp* is an attribute of type date, we know the object returned by valueForKey: will be an instance of NSDate. Similarly, we could set the value using setValue:ForKey:. The following code would set the *timeStamp* attribute of managedObject to the current date and time:

```
[managedObject setValue:[NSDate date] forKey:@"timeStamp"];
```

KVC also includes the concept of a **keypath**. Keypaths allow you iterate through object hierarchies using a single string. So, for example, if we had a relationship on our *Employee* entity called *whereIWork*, which pointed to an entity named *Employer*, and the *Employer* entity had an attribute called *name*, then we could get to the value stored in *name* from an instance of *Employee* using a keypath like so:

```
NSString *employerName = [managedObject valueForKeyPath:@"whereIWork.name"];
```

Notice that we use valueForKeyPath: instead of valueForKey:, and we provide a dot-separated value for the keypath. KVC parses that string using the dots, so in this case, it would parse it into two separate values: *whereIWork*, and *name*. It uses the first one (*whereIWork*) on itself, and retrieves the object that corresponds to that key. It then takes the next value in the keypath (name) and retrieves the object stored under that key from the object returned by the previous call. Since *Employer* is a to-one relationship, the first part of the keypath would return a managed object instance that represented the *Employee*'s employer. The second part of the keypath would then be used to retrieve the *name* from the managed object that represents the *Employer*.

> **NOTE:** If you've used bindings in Cocoa, you're probably already familiar with KVC and keypaths. If not, don't worry—they will become second nature to you before long. Keypaths are really quite intuitive.

Managed Object Context

Core Data maintains an object that acts as a gateway between your entities and the rest of Core Data. That gateway is called a **managed object context** (often just referred to as a **context**). The context maintains state for all the managed objects that you've loaded or created. The context keeps track of changes that have been made since the last time a managed object was saved or loaded. When you want to load or search for objects, for example, you do it against a context. When you want to commit your changes to the persistent store, you save the context. If you want to undo changes to a managed object, you just ask the managed object context to undo. (Yes, it even handles all the work needed to implement undo and redo for your data model.)

When building iPhone applications, the vast majority of the time, you will have only a single context. However, you can have more than one context. For example, if your application supports threading or some other form of concurrency, such as NSOperationQueue, you'll need more than one context, since contexts are not thread-safe and cannot be shared across threads. This means that the same managed object can exist in two different places with different values if you're not careful.

Because every application needs at least one managed object context to function, the template has very kindly provided us with one. Click *CoreDataAppDelegate.m* again, and select *-managedObjectContext* from the function menu. You will see a method that looks like this:

```
/**
 Returns the managed object context for the application.
 If the context doesn't already exist, it is created and bound to the persistent
 store coordinator for the application.
*/
- (NSManagedObjectContext *) managedObjectContext {

    if (managedObjectContext != nil) {
        return managedObjectContext;
    }

    NSPersistentStoreCoordinator *coordinator = [self persistentStoreCoordinator];
    if (coordinator != nil) {
        managedObjectContext = [[NSManagedObjectContext alloc] init];
        [managedObjectContext setPersistentStoreCoordinator: coordinator];
    }
    return managedObjectContext;
}
```

This method is actually pretty straightforward. Using lazy loading, managedObjectContext is checked for nil. If it is not nil, its value is returned. If managedObjectContext is nil, we check to see if our NSPersistentStoreCoordinator exists. If so, we create a new managedObjectContext, then use setPersistentStoreCoordinator: to tie the current coordinator to our managedObjectContext. When we're finished, we return managedObjectContext.

Note that managed object contexts do not work directly against a persistent store; they go through a persistent store coordinator. As a result, every managed object context needs to be provided with a pointer to a persistent store coordinator in order to function. Multiple managed object contexts can work against the same persistent store coordinator, however.

Saves on Terminate

While we're in the application delegate, let's scroll up to another method called applicationWillTerminate:, which saves changes to the context if any have been made. The changes are saved to the persistent store. As its name implies, this method is called just before the application exits.

```
/**
 applicationWillTerminate: saves changes in the application's managed object context
before the application terminates.
 */
- (void)applicationWillTerminate:(UIApplication *)application {

    NSError *error;
    if (managedObjectContext != nil) {
        if ([managedObjectContext hasChanges] && ![managedObjectContext
            save:&error]) {
            // Handle error.
            NSLog(@"Unresolved error %@, %@", error, [error userInfo]);
            exit(-1);   // Fail
        }
    }
}
```

This is a nice bit of functionality, but there may be times when you don't want the data to be saved. For example, what if the user quits after creating a new entity, but before entering any data for that entity? In that case, do you really want to save that empty managed object into the persistent store? Possibly not. We'll look at dealing with situations like that in the next few chapters.

Loading Data from the Persistent Store

Run the Core Data application we built earlier and press the plus button a few times (see Figure 2–7). Quit the simulator, and then run the application again. Note that the timestamps from our previous runs were saved into the persistent store and loaded back in for this run.

Click *RootViewController.m* so you can see how this happens. As you can probably guess from the filename, RootViewController is the view controller class that acts as our application's, well, root view controller. This is the view controller for the view you can see in Figure 2–7 and which is, in fact, the only view in the template application.

Once you've clicked the filename, you can use the function menu to find the viewDidLoad: method, although it will probably be on your screen already, since it's the first method in the class. The default implementation of the method looks like this:

```
- (void)viewDidLoad {
    [super viewDidLoad];

    // Set up the edit and add buttons.
    self.navigationItem.leftBarButtonItem = self.editButtonItem;

    UIBarButtonItem *addButton = [[UIBarButtonItem alloc]
        initWithBarButtonSystemItem:UIBarButtonSystemItemAdd target:self
        action:@selector(insertNewObject)];
    self.navigationItem.rightBarButtonItem = addButton;
    [addButton release];

    NSError *error = nil;
    if (![[self fetchedResultsController] performFetch:&error]) {
        // Update to handle the error appropriately.
```

```
        NSLog(@"Unresolved error %@, %@", error, [error userInfo]);
        exit(-1);  // Fail
    }
}
```

Figure 2–7. *The template application saves your application data when you quit. When you launch it again, it loads all the existing data from the persistent store.*

The first thing the method does is call super. Next, it sets up the *Edit* and *Add* buttons. Note that RootViewController inherits from UIViewController. UIViewController provides a property named editButtonItem, which returns an *Edit* button. Using dot notation, we retrieve editButtonItem and pass it to the mutator for leftBarButtonItem. Now the *Edit* button is the left button in the navigation bar.

Let's do the *Add* button. Since UIViewController does not provide an *Add* button, we'll use alloc to create one from scratch and add it as the right button in the navigation bar. The next chunk of code may seem a bit strange:

```
NSError *error;
if (![[self fetchedResultsController] performFetch:&error]) {
```

This code calls performFetch: on an object returned by the method fetchedResultsController. The method fetchedResultsController returns an instance of NSFetchedResultsController, which is a new generic controller class added with version 3.0 of the SDK. Let's take a look at how the fetched results controller works.

The Fetched Results Controller

Conceptually speaking, the fetched results controller isn't quite like the other generic controllers you've seen in the iPhone SDK. If you've used Cocoa bindings and the generic controller classes available on the Mac, such as NSArrayController, then you're already familiar with the basic idea. If you're not familiar with those generic controller classes, a little explanation is probably in order.

Most of the generic controller classes in the iPhone SDK—such as UINavigationController, UITableViewController, and UIViewController—are designed to act as the controller for a specific type of view. View controllers, however, are not the only types of controller classes that Cocoa Touch provides, although they are the most common. NSFetchedResultsController is an example of a controller class that is not a view controller.

NSFetchedResultsController is designed to handle one very specific job, which is to manage the objects returned from a Core Data fetch request. NSFetchedResultsController makes displaying data from Core Data easier than it would otherwise be, because it handles a bunch of tasks for you. It will, for example, purge any unneeded objects from memory when it receives a low-memory warning and reload them when it needs them again. If you specify a delegate for the fetched results controller, your delegate will be notified when certain changes are made to its underlying data.

Creating a Fetched Results Controller

You start by creating a fetch request, and then use that fetch request to create a fetched results controller. In our template, this is done in *RootViewController.m*, in the fetchedResultsController method. fetchedResultsController starts by creating a new fetch request. A fetch request is basically a specification that lays out the details of the data to be fetched. You'll need to tell the fetch request which entity to fetch. In addition, you'll want to add a **sort descriptor** to the fetch request. The sort descriptor determines the order in which the data is organized.

Once the fetch request is complete, the fetched results controller is created. The fetched results controller is an instance of the class NSFetchedResultsController. Remember that the fetched results controller's job is to use the fetch request to keep its associated data as fresh as possible.

Once the fetched results controller is created, you'll do your initial fetch. We do this in *RootViewController.m* at the end of ViewDidLoad, by sending our fetched results controller the PerformFetch message.

Now that you have your data, you're ready to be a data source and a delegate to your table view. When your table view wants the number of sections for its table, it will call numberOfSectionsInTableView:. In our version, we get the section information by passing the appropriate message to fetchResultsController. Here's the version from *RootViewController.m*:

```
- (NSInteger)numberOfSectionsInTableView:(UITableView *)tableView {
```

```
    return [[fetchedResultsController sections] count];
}
```

The same strategy applies in tableView:numberOfRowsInSection:

```
- (NSInteger)tableView:(UITableView *)tableView
        numberOfRowsInSection:(NSInteger)section {
    id <NSFetchedResultsSectionInfo> sectionInfo =
        [[fetchedResultsController sections] objectAtIndex:section];
    return [sectionInfo numberOfObjects];
}
```

You get the idea. You used to need to do all this work yourself. Now you can ask your fetched results controller to do all the data management for you. It's an amazing time-saver!

Let's take a closer look at the creation of the fetched results controller. In *RootViewController.m*, use the function menu to go to the method -fetchedResultsController. It should look like this:

```
- (NSFetchedResultsController *)fetchedResultsController {
    if (fetchedResultsController != nil) {
        return fetchedResultsController;
    }

    /*
     Set up the fetched results controller.
    */
    // Create the fetch request for the entity.
    NSFetchRequest *fetchRequest = [[NSFetchRequest alloc] init];
    // Edit the entity name as appropriate.
    NSEntityDescription *entity = [NSEntityDescription entityForName:@"Event"
        inManagedObjectContext:managedObjectContext];
    [fetchRequest setEntity:entity];

    // Set the batch size to a suitable number.
    [fetchRequest setFetchBatchSize:20];

    // Edit the sort key as appropriate.
    NSSortDescriptor *sortDescriptor = [[NSSortDescriptor alloc]
        initWithKey:@"timeStamp" ascending:NO];
    NSArray *sortDescriptors = [[NSArray alloc] initWithObjects:sortDescriptor,
        nil];

    [fetchRequest setSortDescriptors:sortDescriptors];

    // Edit the section name key path and cache name if appropriate.
    // nil for section name key path means "no sections".
    NSFetchedResultsController *aFetchedResultsController =
        [[NSFetchedResultsController alloc] initWithFetchRequest:fetchRequest
        managedObjectContext:managedObjectContext sectionNameKeyPath:nil
        cacheName:@"Root"];
    aFetchedResultsController.delegate = self;
    self.fetchedResultsController = aFetchedResultsController;
```

```
   [aFetchedResultsController release];
    [fetchRequest release];
    [sortDescriptor release];
    [sortDescriptors release];

   return fetchedResultsController;
}
```

This method uses lazy loading. The first thing it does is check fetchedResultsController for nil. If fetchedResultsController already exists, it is returned; otherwise, the process of creating a new fetchedResultsController is started.

As the first step, we'll need to create an NSFetchRequest and NSEntityDescription, and then attach the NSEntityDescription to the NSFetchRequest:

```
NSFetchRequest *fetchRequest = [[NSFetchRequest alloc] init];
// Edit the entity name as appropriate.
NSEntityDescription *entity = [NSEntityDescription entityForName:@"Event"
    inManagedObjectContext:managedObjectContext];
[fetchRequest setEntity:entity];
```

Remember, we're building a fetched results controller, and the fetch request is part of that. Next, we set the batch size to 20. This tells Core Data that this fetch request should retrieve its results 20 at a time. This is sort of like a file system's block size.

```
// Set the batch size to a suitable number.
[fetchRequest setFetchBatchSize:20];
```

Next, we build an NSSortDescriptor and specify that it use timeStamp as a key, sorting the timestamps in ascending order (earlier dates first).

```
// Edit the sort key as appropriate.
NSSortDescriptor *sortDescriptor = [[NSSortDescriptor alloc]
    initWithKey:@"timeStamp" ascending:YES];
```

Now we create an array of sort descriptors. Since we'll be using only one, we pass in sortDescriptor and follow it with nil to let initWithObjects know we'll just have a single element in the array. (Note that the template could have used initWithObject instead.)

```
NSArray *sortDescriptors = [[NSArray alloc] initWithObjects:sortDescriptor,
    nil];

[fetchRequest setSortDescriptors:sortDescriptors];
```

Try this experiment: Change ascending:YES to ascending:NO and run the application again. What do you think will happen? Don't forget to change it back when you are finished.

> **TIP:** If you need to restrict a fetch request to a subset of the managed objects stored in the persistent store, you use a **predicate**. There's an entire chapter dedicated to predicates in *Learn Objective-C on the Mac* by Mark Dalrymple and Scott Knaster (Apress, 2009). The default template does not use predicates, but we'll be working with them in the next several chapters.

Now we create an NSFetchedResultsController using our fetch request and context. We'll cover the third and fourth parameters, sectionNameKeyPath and cacheName, in Chapter 3.

```
// Edit the section name key path and cache name if appropriate.
// nil for section name key path means "no sections".
NSFetchedResultsController *aFetchedResultsController =
    [[NSFetchedResultsController alloc] initWithFetchRequest:fetchRequest
    managedObjectContext:managedObjectContext sectionNameKeyPath:nil
    cacheName:@"Root"];
```

Next, we set self as the delegate, and set fetchedResultsController to the fetched results controller we just created.

```
aFetchedResultsController.delegate = self;
self.fetchedResultsController = aFetchedResultsController;
```

Finally, we release our locals and return our newly created fetchedResultsController:

```
[aFetchedResultsController release];
[fetchRequest release];
[sortDescriptor release];
[sortDescriptors release];

    return fetchedResultsController;
}
```

Don't worry too much about the details here. Try to get your head around the big picture. As you make your way through the next few chapters, the details will come into focus.

The Fetched Results Controller Delegate Methods

The fetched results controller must have a delegate, and that delegate must provide four methods, which we will describe in the pages that follow. These four methods are defined in the protocol NSFetchedResultsControllerDelegate. The fetched results controller monitors its managed object context and calls its delegates as changes are made to its context.

Will Change Content Delegate Method

When the fetched results controller observes a change that affects it—such as an object it manages being deleted or changed, or when a new object is inserted that meets the criteria of the fetched results controller's fetch request—the fetched results controller will notify its delegate before it makes any changes, using the method controllerWillChangeContent:.

The vast majority of the time, a fetched results controller will be used along with a table view, and all you need to do in that delegate method is to inform the table view that updates about to be made might impact what it is displaying. Here is how you do that:

```
- (void)controllerWillChangeContent:(NSFetchedResultsController *)controller {
    [self.tableView beginUpdates];
}
```

As of this writing, the Xcode project templates do not handle most of the fetched results controller delegate task for you, so you will usually need to add the methods in this section to your controller classes. If there is an existing `controllerWillChangeContent:` method, replace it with this one.

> **NOTE:** The `NSFetchedResultsController` was a brand-new object with SDK 3.0. The Core Data Navigation-based Application project template, which uses it, has changed several times since the initial release. The earliest version did not implement any of the fetched results controller delegate methods. Later versions implemented the `controllerWillChangeContent:` delegate method, but just triggered a table reload. The implementations we're providing in this section are generic and robust. You should be able to just copy them into your template and go.

Did Change Content Delegate Method

After the fetched results controller makes its changes, it will then notify its delegate using the method `controllerDidChangeContent:`. At that time, if you're using a table view (and you almost certainly will be), you need to tell the table view that the updates you told it were coming in `controllerWillChangeContent:` are now complete. You do that like so:

```
- (void)controllerDidChangeContent:(NSFetchedResultsController *)controller {
    [self.tableView endUpdates];
}
```

Did Change Object Delegate Method

When the fetched results controller notices a change to a specific object, it will notify its delegate using the method `controller:didChangeObject:forChangeType:newIndexPath:`. This method is where you need to handle updating, inserting, deleting, or moving rows in your table view to reflect whatever change was made to the objects managed by the fetched results controller. Here is a standard implementation of the delegate method that will take care of updating the table view for you:

```
- (void)controller:(NSFetchedResultsController *)controller
    didChangeObject:(id)anObject
       atIndexPath:(NSIndexPath *)indexPath
     forChangeType:(NSFetchedResultsChangeType)type
      newIndexPath:(NSIndexPath *)newIndexPath {
    switch(type) {
        case NSFetchedResultsChangeInsert:
            [self.tableView insertRowsAtIndexPaths:[NSArray
                arrayWithObject:newIndexPath]
                withRowAnimation:UITableViewRowAnimationFade];
            break;
        case NSFetchedResultsChangeDelete:
            [self.tableView deleteRowsAtIndexPaths:[NSArray
```

```objc
            arrayWithObject:indexPath]
            withRowAnimation:UITableViewRowAnimationFade];
        break;
    case NSFetchedResultsChangeUpdate: {
        NSString *sectionKeyPath = [controller sectionNameKeyPath];
        if (sectionKeyPath == nil)
            break;
        NSManagedObject *changedObject = [controller
            objectAtIndexPath:indexPath];
        NSArray *keyParts = [sectionKeyPath componentsSeparatedByString:@"."];
        id currentKeyValue = [changedObject valueForKeyPath:sectionKeyPath];
        for (int i = 0; i < [keyParts count] - 1; i++) {
            NSString *onePart = [keyParts objectAtIndex:i];
            changedObject = [changedObject valueForKey:onePart];
        }
        sectionKeyPath = [keyParts lastObject];
        NSDictionary *committedValues = [changedObject
            committedValuesForKeys:nil];

        if ([[committedValues valueForKeyPath:sectionKeyPath]
            isEqual:currentKeyValue])
            break;

        NSUInteger tableSectionCount = [self.tableView numberOfSections];
        NSUInteger frcSectionCount = [[controller sections] count];
        if (tableSectionCount != frcSectionCount) {
            // Need to insert a section
            NSArray *sections = controller.sections;
            NSInteger newSectionLocation = -1;
            for (id oneSection in sections) {
                NSString *sectionName = [oneSection name];
                if ([currentKeyValue isEqual:sectionName]) {
                    newSectionLocation = [sections indexOfObject:oneSection];
                    break;
                }
            }
            if (newSectionLocation == -1)
                return; // uh oh
            if (!((newSectionLocation == 0) && (tableSectionCount == 1)
                    && ([self.tableView numberOfRowsInSection:0] == 0)))
                [self.tableView insertSections:[NSIndexSet
                    indexSetWithIndex:newSectionLocation]
                    withRowAnimation:UITableViewRowAnimationFade];
            NSUInteger indices[2] = {newSectionLocation, 0};
            newIndexPath = [[[NSIndexPath alloc] initWithIndexes:indices
                length:2] autorelease];
        }
    }
    case NSFetchedResultsChangeMove:
        if (newIndexPath != nil) {
            [self.tableView deleteRowsAtIndexPaths:[NSArray
                arrayWithObject:indexPath]
                withRowAnimation:UITableViewRowAnimationFade];
            [self.tableView insertRowsAtIndexPaths: [NSArray
                arrayWithObject:newIndexPath]
                withRowAnimation: UITableViewRowAnimationRight];
        }
```

```
            else {
                [self.tableView reloadSections:[NSIndexSet
                    indexSetWithIndex:[indexPath section]]
                    withRowAnimation:UITableViewRowAnimationFade];
            }
            break;
        default:
            break;
    }
}
```

Most of this code is fairly straightforward. If a row has been inserted, we receive a type of NSFetchedResultsChangeInsert, and we insert a new row into the table. If a row was deleted, we receive a type of NSFetchedResultsChangeDelete, and we delete the corresponding row in the table. If a type of NSFetchedResultsChangeMove was received, we know that a row was moved, so we delete it from the old location and insert it at the location specified by newIndexPath.

The one section that's not so straightforward is NSFetchedResultsChangeUpdate, which is received when one of the objects the fetched results controller manages changes. Most of the time, you don't need to do anything when that happens. That's a lot of code for doing nothing, isn't it?

The problem is that an update might impact the table view. If you change the field that is used to order the rows or to divide the rows into sections, then you need to take further actions. As of this writing, for example, when changing an object causes it to move to a new section, you are not notified of a move or a section insert—just of the change. The gnarly code under NSFetchedResultsChangeUpdate handles this problem. Don't worry if you don't fully understand that code. It has been written generically, so you should be able to just use it as is. It is advanced code, and understanding it involves understanding things that will be explained in the next chapters.

HANDLING FETCHED RESULTS CONTROLLER OBJECT UPDATES

You don't need to understand how the logic to handle object updates works. This is advanced juju, and it's fine to just use this code without understanding it. But if you're truly curious, we'll step through the process of handling object change scenarios in the delegate method. We do recommend working through the rest of the chapters on Core Data before going through these details, though.

The first thing we do is retrieve the sectionKeyPath our fetched results controller is using. This is the key value used to divide the table's data into sections. If it's nil, then we have nothing more to do, and we break out of the switch statement. Otherwise, we also grab a reference to the object whose change triggered this method call.

```
        case NSFetchedResultsChangeUpdate: {
            NSString *sectionKeyPath = [controller sectionNameKeyPath];
            if (sectionKeyPath == nil)
                break;
            NSManagedObject *changedObject = [controller
                objectAtIndexPath:indexPath];
```

The next thing we do is split up the section name keypath into components. Although most of the time, section name keypaths will just be single property name, like @"foo", they can contain multiple components, each separated by a period, like @"foo.bar". We'll talk more about why a keypath would have multiple components in Chapter 7, when we talk about Core Data relationships.

```
NSArray *keyParts = [sectionKeyPath
    componentsSeparatedByString:@"."];
```

We need to iterate through the keypath to find the object referred to by this keypath. Usually, it will be the object that was changed, but if the keypath has multiple period-separated values, then we know it's actually another, nested object, and we must retrieve that object. We exclude the last string from the keypath, because that part of a keypath refers to the actual property, not the object.

```
id currentKeyValue = [changedObject valueForKeyPath:sectionKeyPath];
for (int i = 0; i < [keyParts count] - 1; i++) {
    NSString *onePart = [keyParts objectAtIndex:i];
    changedObject = [changedObject valueForKey:onePart];
}
```

At this point, changedObject now refers to the object where the section key resides, and we truncate the keypath so that it includes only the last period-separated component. Now we know both the object and the specific property that are being used to divide the rows into sections. Next, we need to determine the prior value for that property and see if that value has changed. All we know now is that this object changed. We don't know if it changed in a way that would require moving the object to a new section. If the value hasn't changed, we break, which ends the method and bypasses the rest of the code in this section.

```
sectionKeyPath = [keyParts lastObject];
NSDictionary *committedValues = [changedObject
    committedValuesForKeys:nil];

if ([[committedValues valueForKeyPath:sectionKeyPath]
    isEqual:currentKeyValue])
    break;
```

If we didn't break and we get to the code below, we know we're dealing with a change to a value that affects the way the objects are divided up into sections, so we need to compare the number of sections in the fetched results controller with the table to see if they are different. Just because an object moved to a new section doesn't necessarily mean that a new section needs to be inserted. It could result in a move to a section that already exists.

```
NSUInteger tableSectionCount = [self.tableView numberOfSections];
NSUInteger frcSectionCount = [[controller sections] count];
if (tableSectionCount != frcSectionCount) {
```

If the fetched results controller and table don't have the same number of sections, we need to loop through the fetched results controller's sections to figure out where the new section needs to get inserted. We loop through and compare the section name with the section key value from the changed object. When we find it, we set newSectionLocation to the index of the found section and break, which stops the loop.

```
// Need to insert a section
NSArray *sections = controller.sections;
NSInteger newSectionLocation = -1;
for (id oneSection in sections) {
    NSString *sectionName = [oneSection name];
    if ([currentKeyValue isEqual:sectionName]) {
        newSectionLocation = [sections
        indexOfObject:oneSection];
```

```
                break;
        }
    }
```

Next, just to make sure, we check `newSectionLocation` to make sure it's not -1. In theory, this shouldn't happen, but we don't want to pass a -1 when we insert a new section, because that would generate an exception at runtime.

```
        if (newSectionLocation == -1)
            return; // uh oh
```

Finally, we insert the new section if needed. Remember that table views must have at least one section. An empty table already has one section, so we don't insert a section if we're inserting the first section into an empty table. It would be rare to be inserting a first row when we get an object-changed notification, since the object must have already existed; however, the object might not have previously matched the criteria in the predicate used by the fetch request underlying the fetched results controller. The change might have moved the object into our fetched results controller's result set as the first object.

```
        if (!((newSectionLocation == 0) && (tableSectionCount == 1)
                && ([self.tableView numberOfRowsInSection:0] == 0)))
            [self.tableView insertSections:[NSIndexSet
                indexSetWithIndex:newSectionLocation]
                withRowAnimation:UITableViewRowAnimationFade];
```

We also create a new `NSIndexPath` instance and assign it to `newIndexPath`. The variable `newIndexPath` points to the location in the table where a row should be moved when we are notified of an object moving. For a change update, as we have here, this value will always be `nil`. We need to create a new index path that points to the first row in the newly created section, since that's where we want the new row to go.

```
        NSUInteger indices[2] = {newSectionLocation, 0};
        newIndexPath = [[[NSIndexPath alloc] initWithIndexes:indices
            length:2] autorelease];
    }
}
```

Notice that we don't have a `break` statement before the next `case` statement. Everything is set up so we fall through to the move logic and leverage that. The next `case` statement will delete the existing row and insert a new row in the newly added section, and all will be right with the world.

```
    case NSFetchedResultsChangeMove:
...
```

Don't worry if this all seemed a bit overwhelming. You'll rarely be called upon to write code like this. As we've said, you don't need to understand how or why it works to be able to use a fetched results controller.

Did Change Section Delegate Method

Lastly, if a change to an object affects the number of sections in the table, the fetched results controller will call the delegate method controller:didChangeSection:atIndex:forChangeType:. If you specify a sectionNameKeyPath when you create your fetched results controller, you need to implement this delegate method to take care of adding and deleting sections from the table as needed. If you don't, you will get runtime errors when the number of sections in the table doesn't match the number of sections in the fetched results controller. Here is a fairly standard implementation of that delegate method that should work for most situations:

```
- (void)controller:(NSFetchedResultsController *)controller
  didChangeSection:(id <NSFetchedResultsSectionInfo>)sectionInfo
          atIndex:(NSUInteger)sectionIndex
     forChangeType:(NSFetchedResultsChangeType)type {

    switch(type) {
        case NSFetchedResultsChangeInsert:
            if (!((sectionIndex == 0) && ([self.tableView numberOfSections] == 1)
                    && ([self.tableView numberOfRowsInSection:0] == 0)))
                [self.tableView insertSections:[NSIndexSet
                    indexSetWithIndex:sectionIndex]
                    withRowAnimation:UITableViewRowAnimationFade];
            break;
        case NSFetchedResultsChangeDelete:
            if (!((sectionIndex == 0) && ([self.tableView numberOfSections] == 1)
                    && ([self.tableView numberOfRowsInSection:0] == 0)))
                [self.tableView deleteSections:[NSIndexSet
                    indexSetWithIndex:sectionIndex]
                    withRowAnimation:UITableViewRowAnimationFade];
            break;
        case NSFetchedResultsChangeMove:
        case NSFetchedResultsChangeUpdate:
        default:
            break;
    }
}
```

Once you've implemented these four delegate methods, if you add a new managed object, the fetched results controller will detect that, and your table will be updated automatically. If you delete or change an object, the controller will detect that, too. Any change that affects the fetched results controller will automatically trigger an appropriate update to the table view, including properly animating the process. This means that you don't need to litter your code with calls to reloadData every time you make a change that might impact your dataset.

Retrieving a Managed Object from the Fetched Results Controller

Our table view delegate methods became much shorter and more straightforward, since our fetched results controller does much of the work that we previously did in those methods. For example, to retrieve the object that corresponds to a particular cell, which we often need to do in `tableView:cellForRowAtIndexPath:` and `tableView:didSelectRowAtIndexPath:`, we can just call `objectAtIndexPath:` on the fetched results controller and pass in the `indexPath` parameter, and it will return the correct object:

```
NSManagedObject *managedObject = [fetchedResultsController
    objectAtIndexPath:indexPath];
```

Creating and Inserting a New Managed Object

From the function menu in the editor pane, select *insertNewObject*, which is the method that is called when the plus button is pressed in the sample application. It's a nice, simple example of how to create a new managed object, insert it into a managed object context, and then save it to the persistent store.

```
- (void)insertNewObject {

    // Create a new instance of the entity managed by the fetched results
    // controller.
    NSManagedObjectContext *context =
        [fetchedResultsController managedObjectContext];
    NSEntityDescription *entity = [[fetchedResultsController fetchRequest] entity];
    NSManagedObject *newManagedObject = [NSEntityDescription
        insertNewObjectForEntityForName:[entity name]
        inManagedObjectContext:context];

    // If appropriate, configure the new managed object.
    [newManagedObject setValue:[NSDate date] forKey:@"timeStamp"];

    // Save the context.
    NSError *error;
    if (![context save:&error]) {
        // Handle the error...
    }
}
```

Notice that the first thing the code does is to retrieve a managed object context from the fetched results controller. In this simple example, where there's only one context, we could also have retrieved the same context from the application delegate. There are a few reasons why the default code uses the context from the fetched results controller. First of all, we already have an instance variable that points to the fetched results controller, so we can get to the context in just one line of code:

```
NSManagedObjectContext *context =
        [fetchedResultsController managedObjectContext];
```

More important, though, a fetched results controller always knows which context its managed objects are contained by, so even if you decide to create an application with multiple contexts, you'll be sure that you're using the correct context if you pull it from the fetched results controller.

Just as we did when we created a fetch request, when inserting a new object, we need to create an entity description to tell Core Data which kind of entity we want to create an instance of. The fetched results controller also knows what entity the objects it manages are, so we can just ask it for that information:

```
NSEntityDescription *entity = [[fetchedResultsController fetchRequest] entity];
```

Then it's simply a matter of using a class method on NSEntityDescription to create the new object and insert it into a context:

```
NSManagedObject *newManagedObject = [NSEntityDescription
    insertNewObjectForEntityForName:[entity name]
    inManagedObjectContext:context];
```

It does seem a little odd that we use a class method on NSEntityDescription, rather than an instance method on the context we want to insert the new object into, but that's the way it's done.

Though this managed object has now been inserted into the context, it still exists in the persistent store. In order to insert it from the persistent store, we must save the context, which is what happens next in this method:

```
NSError *error;
if (![context save:&error]) {
    // Handle the error...
}
```

Notice that we don't call reloadData on our table view. The fetched results controller will realize that we've inserted a new object that meets its criteria and call the delegate method, which will automatically reload the table.

INSERTING NEW ENTITIES USING NSMANAGEDOBJECTCONTEXT

If it really bothers you that you use a method on NSEntityDescription to insert a new object into an NSManagedObjectContext, rather than an instance method on NSManagedObjectContext, you can add an instance method to NSManagedObjectContext using a category. To do that, create two new text files: one called *NSManagedObject-Insert.h* and one called *NSManagedObject-Insert.m*.

In *NSManagedObject-Insert.h*, place the following code:

```
#import <Cocoa/Cocoa.h>
@interface NSManagedObjectContext(insert)
-(NSManagedObject *) insertNewEntityWithName:(NSString *)name;
@end
```

In *NSManagedObject-Insert.m*, place this code:

```
#import "NSManagedObjectContext-insert.h"
```

```
@implementation NSManagedObjectContext(insert)
-(NSManagedObject *) insertNewEntityWithName:(NSString *)name
{
    return [NSEntityDescription insertNewObjectForEntityForName:name
        inManagedObjectContext:self];
}
@end
```

Save both files.

You can add these two files to your Xcode project and import *NSManagedObject-Insert.m* anywhere you wish to use this new method. Then replace the insert calls against NSEntityDescription, like this one:

```
NSManagedObject *newManagedObject = [NSEntityDescription
    insertNewObjectForEntityForName:[entity name]
    inManagedObjectContext:context];
```

with the shorter and more intuitive one:

```
[context insertNewEntityWityName:[entity name]];
```

Ain't categories grand?

Deleting Managed Objects

Deleting managed objects is pretty easy when using a fetched results controller. Use the function menu to navigate to the method called tableView:commitEditingStyle:forRowAtIndexPath:. That method should look like this:

```
// Override to support editing the table view.
- (void)tableView:(UITableView *)tableView
    commitEditingStyle:(UITableViewCellEditingStyle)editingStyle
    forRowAtIndexPath:(NSIndexPath *)indexPath {

    if (editingStyle == UITableViewCellEditingStyleDelete) {
        // Delete the managed object for the given index path
        NSManagedObjectContext *context =
            [fetchedResultsController managedObjectContext];
        [context deleteObject:[fetchedResultsController
            objectAtIndexPath:indexPath]];

      // Save the context.
        NSError *error;
        if (![context save:&error]) {
            // Update to handle the error appropriately.
            NSLog(@"Unresolved error %@, %@", error, [error userInfo]);
            exit(-1);  // Fail
        }
    }
}
```

The method first makes sure that we're in a delete transaction (remember that this same method is used for deletes and inserts):

```
    if (editingStyle == UITableViewCellEditingStyleDelete) {
```

Next, we retrieve the context:

```
NSManagedObjectContext *context =
    [fetchedResultsController managedObjectContext];
```

Then the context is asked to delete that object:

```
[context deleteObject:[fetchedResultsController
    objectAtIndexPath:indexPath]];
```

Next, the managed object context's save: method is called to cause that change to be committed to the persistent store:

```
NSError *error;
if (![context save:&error]) {
    // Update to handle the error appropriately.
    NSLog(@"Unresolved error %@, %@", error, [error userInfo]);
    exit(-1);  // Fail
}
```

And that's all there is to deleting managed objects.

Putting Everything in Context

At this point, you should have a pretty good handle on the basics of using Core Data. You've learned about the architecture of a Core Data application and the process of using entities and properties. You've seen how the persistent store, managed object model, and managed object context are created by your application delegate. You learned how to use the data model editor to build entities that can be used in your program to create managed objects. You also learned how to retrieve, insert, and delete data from the persistent store.

So, enough with the theory. Let's move on and build us some Core Data applications, shall we?

Chapter 3

A Super Start: Adding, Displaying, and Deleting Data

Well, if that last chapter didn't scare you off, then you're ready to dive in and move beyond the basic template we explored in Chapter 2.

In this chapter, we're going to create an application designed to track some superhero data. Our application will be based on the *Window-based Application* template. We'll use the data model editor to design our superhero entity. And then we'll create a new controller class, derived from `UIViewController`, that will allow us to add, display, and delete superheroes. In Chapter 4, we'll extend our application further and add code to allow the user to edit their superhero data.

Take a look at Figure 3-1 to get a sense of what our app will look like when it runs. Looks a lot like the template app. The major differences lie in the entity at the heart of the application and in the addition of a tab bar at the bottom of the screen. Let's get to work.

Figure 3-1. *The SuperDB application as it will look once we've finished this chapter*

Setting up the Xcode Project

Time to get our hands dirty. Launch Xcode if it's not open, and type ⇧⌘N to bring up our old friend, the new project assistant (Figure 3-2).

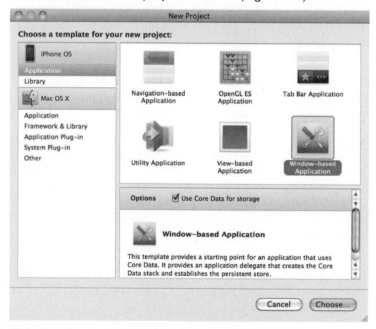

Figure 3-2. *Our dear old friend, Xcode's new project assistant*

In the last chapter, we started with the *Navigation-based Application* template. When you create your own navigation applications, that's a good template to use, as it gives you a lot of the code you're likely to need in your application. However, to make it easier to explain where to add or modify code and also to reinforce your understanding of how applications are constructed, we're going to build the *SuperDB* application from scratch, just as we did throughout most of *Beginning iPhone 3 Development* (Apress, 2009).

Select *Window-based Application*, and make sure that the *Use Core Data for storage* check box is checked. When prompted for a project name, type in *SuperDB*.

When the project window appears, expand both the *Classes* and the *Resources* groups to make it easier to get to the main files with which we'll be working.

Application Architecture

As you can see from Figure 3-1, we're going to create an application with both a tab bar and a navigation controller. Before we start writing code, we need to put a little thought into our application's structure. We need to know, for example, whether our application's root view controller will be a navigation controller, tab bar controller, or something else entirely.

There's not a single right architecture for every application. One obvious approach would be to make the application's root view controller a UITabBarController, and then add a separate navigation controller for each tab. In a situation where each tab corresponds to a completely different view showing different types of data, that approach would make perfect sense. In *Beginning iPhone 3 Development*, in Chapter 7, we used that exact approach because every single tab corresponded to a different view controller with different outlets and different actions.

In our case, however, we're going to implement two tabs (with more to be added in later chapters), but each tab will show exactly the same data, just ordered differently. When one tab is selected, the table will be ordered by the superhero's name. If the other tab is selected, the same data will be shown, ordered by the superhero's secret identity.

Regardless of which tab is selected, tapping a row on the table will do the same thing: drill down to a new view where you can edit the information about the superhero you selected (which we will add in the next chapter). Regardless of which tab is selected, tapping the add button will add a new instance of the same entity. When you drill down to another view to view or edit a hero, the tabs are no longer relevant.

For our application, the tab bar is just modifying the way the data in a single table is presented. There's no need for it to actually swap in and out other view controllers. Why have multiple navigation controller instances all managing identical sets of data and responding the same way to touches? Why not just use one table controller, and have it change the way it presents the data based on which tab is selected? That's the approach we're going to take in this application. As a result, we won't be using UITabBarController at all.

Our root view controller will be a navigation controller, and we'll use a tab bar purely to receive input from the user. The end result that is shown to the user will be identical to what they'd see if we created separate navigation controllers and table view controllers for each tab, but behind the scenes, we'll be using less memory and won't have to worry about keeping the different navigation controllers in sync with each other.

Our application's root view controller will be an instance of UINavigationController. We'll create our own custom view controller class, HeroListViewController, to act as the root view controller for this UINavigationController. HeroListViewController will display the list of superheroes along with the tabs that control how the heroes are displayed and ordered.

Here's how the app will work. When the application starts, the UINavigationController instance is created from the nib file and the navigation controller's view is added as a subview to the application's window so it can be seen. The rest of the window will be taken up by a content pane for its subcontroller views. Next, the instance of HeroListViewController will be loaded from the nib, and the view from its associated nib file will be added as a subview to the navigation controller's content pane. This view (the one associated with HeroListViewController) contains our tab bar and our superhero table view.

In Chapter 4, we'll add a table view controller into the mix that implements a detail superhero view. When the user taps on a superhero in the superhero list, this detail controller will be pushed onto the navigation stack and its view will temporarily replace the HeroListViewController's view in the UINavigationController's content view. No need to worry about the detail view now, we just wanted you to see what's coming.

Modifying the Application Delegate Interface

Given our approach, we need to declare an outlet to our application's root view controller on our application delegate. Single-click on *SuperDBAppDelegate.h* and add the code in bold:

```
@interface SuperDBAppDelegate : NSObject <UIApplicationDelegate> {
    NSManagedObjectModel *managedObjectModel;
    NSManagedObjectContext *managedObjectContext;
    NSPersistentStoreCoordinator *persistentStoreCoordinator;

    UIWindow *window;

    UINavigationController  *navController;
}

@property (nonatomic, retain, readonly) NSManagedObjectModel *managedObjectModel;
@property (nonatomic, retain, readonly) NSManagedObjectContext
    *managedObjectContext;
@property (nonatomic, retain, readonly) NSPersistentStoreCoordinator
    *persistentStoreCoordinator;

@property (nonatomic, retain) IBOutlet UIWindow *window;
```

```
@property (nonatomic, retain) IBOutlet UINavigationController *navController;

- (NSString *)applicationDocumentsDirectory;
@end
```

As you probably realized, the `navController` outlet will point to an instance of `UINavigationController` that will act as our application's root view controller. Other view controllers will be pushed onto the navigation stack when they need to be displayed, and will be popped off of the stack when they are done.

Adding to the Application Delegate Implementation

Before we head over to Interface Builder, let's quickly finish up with our Application delegate by adding the following code at the beginning of *SuperDBAppDelegate.m*:

```
#import "SuperDBAppDelegate.h"

@implementation SuperDBAppDelegate

@synthesize window;
@synthesize navController;

#pragma mark -
#pragma mark Application lifecycle

- (void)applicationDidFinishLaunching:(UIApplication *)application {

    // Override point for customization after app launch
    [window insertSubview:navController.view atIndex:0];
    [window makeKeyAndVisible];
}

...
```

There shouldn't be too much there that's unfamiliar to you. We synthesize our new property, just as we always do. In our `applicationDidFinishLaunching:` method, we add the `view` property from `navController`, our application's root view controller, as a subview of `contentView` so that it will be displayed to the user.

Now, scroll down to the bottom of *SuperDBAppDelegate.m*. We need to add a few lines to the `dealloc` method to make sure we're being good memory citizens. Make the following additions at the bottom of the file:

```
...

- (void)dealloc {
    [managedObjectContext release];
    [managedObjectModel release];
    [persistentStoreCoordinator release];

    [window release];

    [navController release];

    [super dealloc];
```

```
}
@end
```

Make sure you save both *SuperDBAppDelegate.h* and *SuperDBAppDelegate.m* before continuing.

Creating the Table View Controller

Our application's root view controller is going to be a stock `UINavigationController`, so we don't need to define a class for the app's root view controller, but we do need to create a controller class to display the list of heroes and act as the root of the navigation controllers' stack. Even though we will be using a table to display the list of heroes, we're not going to subclass `UITableViewController`. Because we also need to add a tab bar to our interface, we're going to create a subclass of `UIViewController` and create our interface in Interface Builder. The table that will display the list of heroes will be a subview of our view controller's content pane.

Single-click the *Classes* folder in the *Groups & Files* pane, then type ⌘N to bring up the new file assistant or select **New File...** from the **File** menu.

When the new file assistant pops up (Figure 3-3), select *Cocoa Touch Class* from under the iPhone OS heading in the upper-left pane, then select *UIViewController subclass* from the upper-right pane. Now make sure the *UITableViewController subclass* check box is *not* checked, but the check box labeled *With XIB for user interface* check box is checked since, unlike with most table-based views, we *will* need a nib file. With that done, click the *Next* button.

Figure 3-3. *Selecting the Objective-C subclass template in the new file assistant*

When prompted for a filename, type in *HeroListViewController.m* and make sure the check box labeled *Also create "HeroListViewController.h"* is checked. Press return to add the files to your project. After the files are created, click and drag *HeroListViewController.xib* from the *Classes* folder, where Xcode created it, to the *Resources* folder where it belongs.

For now, that's all we need in this controller class. In order to create an instance of the class in Interface Builder, we first needed the class definition to exist in Xcode.

Setting up MainWindow.xib

Interface Builder should now be open and should look something like Figure 3-4. You're probably well-acquainted with Interface Builder by now, but let's just quickly review the names of the various windows so that we're all on the same page. The top-left window, the one with *MainWindow.xib* in the title bar, is the nib file's main window. Below that, the window with the imaginative name of *Window* represents our application's one and only instance of UIWindow. Double-clicking the *Window* icon in the nib file's main window will reopen this if it gets closed.

The window with the small title bar to the right of the nib's main window is the context-sensitive *Inspector* where you can change the attributes of whatever item is currently selected in the active window. And finally, the right-most window is the *Library*, which contains pre-configured items that you can add to a nib.

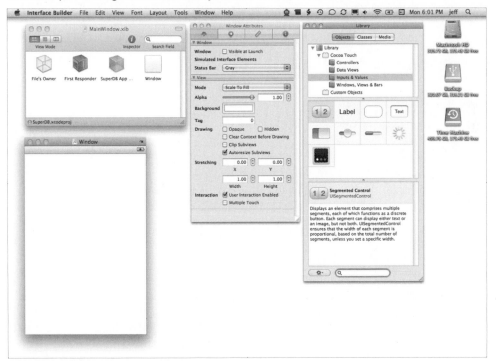

Figure 3-4. *MainWindow.xib in Interface Builder*

In the library, select the *Controllers* folder in the top-most pane (inside *Library*, then inside *Cocoa Touch*). With *Controllers* selected in the top pane, look in the middle pane for the *Navigation Controller* icon (Figure 3-5). Drag one of these to your nib file's main window. Once you do that, your nib's main window will gain an additional icon called *Navigation Controller* (or *Navigation Co...* if you're in icon view mode, which truncates longer names), and a new window should have just popped up (Figure 3-6).

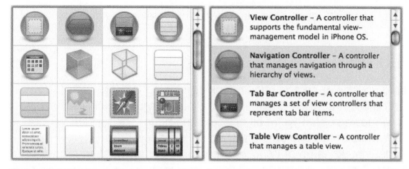

Figure 3-5. *The Navigation Controller icon. Depending on the version of Interface Builder you are using, the Library may default to displaying items in one of two ways. You might see just the icon (left), or the icon and a short description (right). You can change how the library items are displayed by right-clicking on the middle pane.*

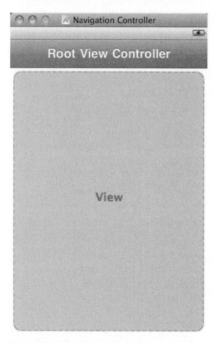

Figure 3-6. *Adding a Navigation Controller to your nib causes a new window to pop up*

The new window has a grey rounded rectangle with a dashed outline labeled *View* and a title of *Root View Controller*. This is Interface Builder's way of reminding us that a navigation controller needs at least one child view controller in order to function. We can set the root view controller right here in Interface Builder. The easiest way to do this is to put our nib's main window in list mode by clicking the middle of the three *View Mode* icons (Figure 3-7).

Figure 3-7. *The nib's main window in list view mode*

With your nib in list view mode, you should notice that *Navigation Controller* has a disclosure triangle next to it. That means it has sub-items of some form. Different items can contain different types of sub-items. Instances of view classes, for example, can contain subviews. View controller classes generally have either the views they control or the subordinate view controllers they're responsible for managing (or both). Expand *Navigation Controller* by single-clicking its disclosure triangle. Underneath it, you'll find a navigation bar instance, and a view controller with the rather long and unwieldy name of *View Controller (Root View Controller).* The view controller represents the navigation controller's root view controller. As we said earlier, HeroListViewController was designed to act as the navigation controller's root view controller. We need to change the class of the root view controller to *HeroListViewController*.

Single-click *View Controller (Root View Controller)* and press ⌘4 to bring up the identity inspector (Figure 3-8). Change the underlying class in the identity inspector from *UIViewController* to *HeroListViewController*. This will cause a single instance of HeroListViewController to get created when our application launches.

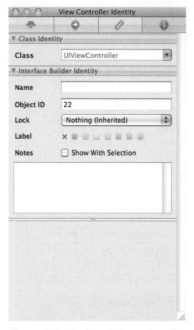

Figure 3-8. *The identity inspector allows us to change the underlying class for the navigation controller's root view controller to our custom controller class.*

Now we've got a navigation controller and an instance of our custom controller class in our nib.

Connecting the Outlets

Earlier we created an outlet in our application delegate for the navigation controller. We've added an instance of `UINavigationController` to our nib, so let's connect the outlet. Control-drag from *SuperDB App Delegate* in the nib's main window to the *Navigation Controller* also in the nib's main window. When the black menu pops up, select the outlet called *navController* to connect that outlet.

And with that, we have received final clearance to land our nib. Save and head on back to Xcode to pick up your luggage.

Designing the Data Model

As we discussed in Chapter 2, Xcode's data model editor is where you design your application's data model. In your project window's *Resources* group, single-click on *SuperDB.xcdatamodel*. This should bring up the data model editor (Figure 3-9).

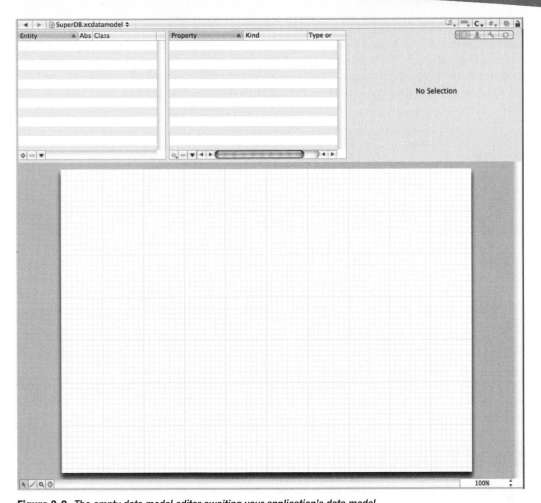

Figure 3-9. *The empty data model editor awaiting your application's data model.*

Unlike the template we used in Chapter 2, this template provides us with a completely empty data model, so we can just dive right in and start building without deleting anything. The first thing we need to add to our data model is an entity. Remember, entities are like class definitions. Although they don't store any data themselves, without at least one entity in your data model, your application won't be able to store any data.

Adding an Entity

Since the purpose of our application is to track information about superheroes, it seems logical that we're going to need an entity to represent a hero. We're going to start off simple in this chapter and track only a few pieces of data about each hero: their name, secret identity, date of birth, and sex. We'll add more data elements in future chapters, but this will give us a basic foundation upon which to build.

In the entity pane, which is the upper-left pane of the data model editor, you should notice buttons with a plus and a minus icon in the lower-left corner (Figure 3-10). As you might have guessed, the button with the plus icon adds a new entity to the data model, and the button with the minus icon removes the currently selected one. Since there's no entity to delete, the minus button is disabled. Click the plus button now to add a new entity.

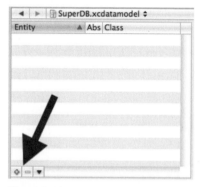

Figure 3-10. *The plus and minus buttons in the entity pane allow you to add and remove entities from the data model*

As soon as you click the plus button, a new entity, named *Entity*, should appear in the entity pane. This entity should be selected for you automatically, which means that the detail pane in the upper-right corner of the data model editor lists details about this new entity and the entity will be selected in the editing pane at the bottom of the data model editor (Figure 3-11).

Editing the New Entity

Now that you've now added an entity to your data model, you'll need to change its name. The easiest way to do that is to change it in the detail pane. Conveniently enough, the *Name* text field in the detail pane is highlighted and has the focus, so you can just start typing the new name to change the entity's name. Type *Hero*.

Below the *Name* field in the detail pane is a text field called *Class*. Leave this at the default value of *NSManagedObject*. In Chapter 6, you'll see how to use this field to create custom subclasses of NSManagedObject to add functionality.

Below that is a pop-up menu labeled *Parent*. Within a data model, you have the ability to specify a parent entity, which is very similar to subclassing in Objective-C. When you specify another entity as your parent, the new entity receives all the properties of *Parent* along with any additional ones that you specify.

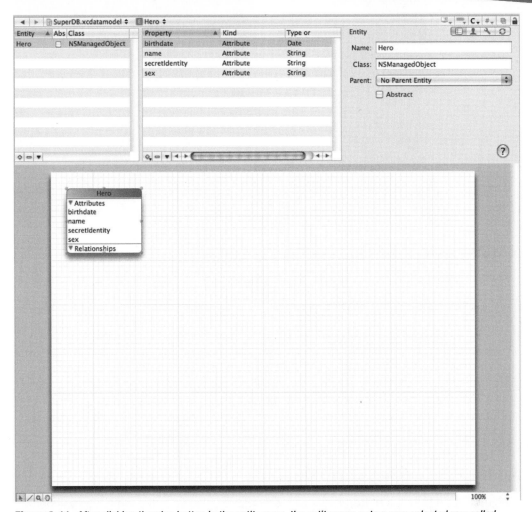

Figure 3-11. *After clicking the plus button in the entity pane, the entity pane gets a new selected row called* Entity, *the diagram view shows the new entity as a rounded rectangle, and the detail pane shows information about the selected entity*

Below the *Parent* pop-up menu is a check box called *Abstract*. This check box allows you to create an entity that cannot be used to create managed objects at runtime. The reason you might create an abstract entity is if you have several properties that are common to multiple entities. In that case, you might create an abstract entity to hold the common fields and then make every entity that uses those common fields a child of that abstract entity. Doing that would mean that if you needed to change those common fields, you'd only need to do it in one place.

Leave the parenting pop-up set to *No Parent Entity* and leave the *Abstract* check box unchecked.

> **NOTE:** You may be wondering about the button bar in the upper-left of the detail pane. These buttons give you access to more advanced configuration parameters that are only rarely used. We won't be changing any of the configuration options except those visible when the *General* button is selected (the default button, the one we're on now).
>
> If you're interested in finding out more about these advanced options, you can read more about them in the Core Data Programming Guide at http://developer.apple.com/ documentation/Cocoa/Conceptual/CoreData/ and the Core Data Model Versioning and Data Migration Guide at http://devworld.apple.com/documentation/ Cocoa/Conceptual/CoreDataVersioning/index.html

Adding Attributes to the New Entity

Now that we have an entity, we have to give it attributes in order for managed objects based on this entity to be able to store any data. For this chapter, we need four attributes: name, secret identity, birth date, and sex.

In the data model editor, to the right of the entity pane is the property pane. This is where you can add properties, including attributes, to the currently selected entity. In the lower-left of the property pane, you should see buttons similar to the ones in the lower-left of the entity pane. Because there is more than one type of property, the button with the plus on it also has a little triangle on it as well. This indicates that when you click the button, you will get a pop-up menu asking you to select exactly which type of property you want to add. Let's add our four attributes now.

Adding the Name Attribute

Single-click on the plus button in the property pane. Once you click on it, you will be presented with a drop-down menu that looks like Figure 3-12. Since we want to add an attribute, select **Add Attribute** from the menu.

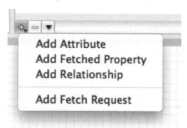

Figure 3-12. *Clicking the plus button in the property pane gives you a menu from which you can select the type of property you wish to add*

Editing the Attribute

The *Hero* entity should now have an attribute called *newAttribute*. Just as when you created a new entity, the newly added attribute has been automatically selected for you, which also causes its information to be displayed in the detail pane. Also just like before, the *Name* field should have focus, so you can just type the new name for the attribute. Type *name* now so that your detail pane looks like Figure 3-13.

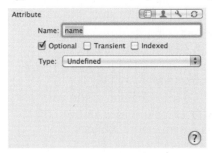

Figure 3-13. *The detail pane after typing the new attribute's name*

> **TIP:** It's not an accident that we chose to start our entity *Hero* with a capital H, but our attribute *name* with a lowercase n. This is the accepted naming convention for entities and properties. Entities begin with a capital letter, properties begin with a lowercase letter. In both cases, if the name of the entity or property consists of more than one word, the first letter of each new word is capitalized.

Below the *Name* field are three check boxes: *Optional*, *Transient*, and *Indexed*. If *Optional* is checked, then this entity can be saved even if this attribute has no value assigned to it. If we uncheck it, then any attempt to save a managed object based on this entity when the *name* attribute is nil will result in a validation error that will prevent the save. In this particular case, *name* is the main attribute that we will use to identify a given hero, so we probably want to require this attribute. Single-click the *Optional* check box to uncheck it, making this field required.

The second check box, *Transient*, allows you to create attributes that are not saved in the persistent store. They can also be used to create custom attributes that store non-standard data. For now, don't worry too much about *Transient*. Just leave it unchecked and we'll revisit this check box in Chapter 6.

The final check box, *Indexed*, tells the underlying data store to add an index on this attribute. Not all persistent stores support indices, but the default store (SQLite) does. The database uses an index to improve search speeds when searching or ordering based on that field. We will be ordering our superheroes by name, so let's check the *Indexed* check box to tell SQLite to create an index on the column that will be used to store this attribute's data.

CAUTION: Properly used, indices can greatly improve performance in a SQLite persistent store. Adding indices where they are not needed, however, can actually degrade performance. If you don't have a reason for selecting *Indexed*, leave it unchecked.

Attribute Types

Every attribute has a type, which identifies the kind of data that the attribute is capable of storing. If you single-click the *Type* drop-down (which should currently be set to *Undefined*), you can see the various datatypes that Core Data supports out of the box (Figure 3-14). These are all the types of data that you can store without having to implement a custom attribute, like we're going to do in Chapter 6. Each of the datatypes correspond to an Objective-C class that is used to set or retrieve values and you must make sure to use the correct object when setting values on managed objects.

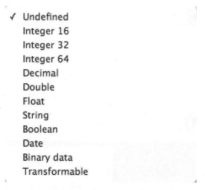

Figure 3-14. *The datatypes supported by Core Data*

The Integer Datatypes

Integer 16, *Integer 32*, and *Integer 64* all hold signed integers (whole numbers). The only difference between these three number types is the minimum and maximum size of the values they are capable of storing. In general, you should pick the smallest-size integer that you are certain will work for your purposes. For example, if you know your attribute will never hold a number larger than a thousand, make sure to select *Integer 16* rather than *Integer 32* or *Integer 64*. The minimum and maximum values that these three datatypes are capable of storing is as follows:

Datatype	Minimum	Maximum
Integer 16	−32,768	32, 767
Integer 32	−2,147,483,648	2,147,483,647
Integer 64	−9,223,372,036,854,775,808	9,223,372,036,854,775,807

At runtime, you set integer attributes of a managed object using instances of NSNumber created using a factory method such as numberWithInt:, or numberWithLong:.

The Decimal, Double, and Float Datatypes

The *Decimal*, *Double*, and *Float* datatypes all hold decimal numbers. *Double* and *Float* hold floating-point representations of decimal numbers similar to the C datatypes of double and float, respectively. Floating-point representations of decimal numbers are always an approximation due to the fact that they use a fixed number of bytes to represent data. The larger the number to the left of the decimal point, the less bytes there are available to hold the fractional part of the number. The *Double* datatype uses 64 bits to store a single number while the *Float* datatype uses 32 bits of data to store a single number. For many purposes, these two datatypes will work just fine. However, when you have data, such as currency, where small rounding errors would be a problem, Core Data provides the *Decimal* datatype, which is not subject to rounding errors. The *Decimal* type can hold numbers with up to 38 significant digits stored internally using fixed-point numbers so that the stored value is not subject to the rounding errors that can happen with floating-point numbers.

At runtime, you set *Double* and *Float* attributes using instances of NSNumber created using the NSNumber factory method numberWithFloat: or numberWithDouble:. Decimal attributes, on the other hand, must be set using an instance of the class NSDecimalNumber.

The String Datatype

The *String* datatype is one of the most common attribute types you will use. *String* attributes are capable of holding text in nearly any language or script since they are stored internally using Unicode. *String* attributes are set at runtime using instances of NSString.

The Boolean Datatype

Boolean values (YES or NO) can be stored using the *Boolean* datatype. Boolean attributes are set at runtime using instances of NSNumber created using numberWithBOOL:.

The Date Datatype

Dates and timestamps can be stored in Core Data using the *Date* datatype. At runtime, Date attributes are set using instances of NSDate.

The Binary Datatype

The *Binary* datatype is used to store any kind of binary data. Binary attributes are set at runtime using NSData instances. Anything that can be put into an NSData instance can be stored in a Binary attribute. However, you generally can't search or sort on binary datatypes.

The Transformable Datatype

The `Transformable` datatype is a special datatype that works along with something called a **value transformer** to let you create attributes based on any Objective-C class, even those for which there is no corresponding Core Data datatype. You would use `Transformable` datatypes to store a `UIImage` instance, for example, or to store a `UIColor` instance. You'll see how `Transformable` attributes work in Chapter 6.

Setting the Name Attributes's Type

A name, obviously, is text, so the obvious type for this attribute is *String*. Select *String* from the *Type* drop-down. After selecting it, a few new fields will appear in the detail pane (Figure 3-15). Just like Interface Builder's inspector, the detail pane in the data model editor is context-sensitive. Some attribute types, such as the *String* type, have additional configuration options.

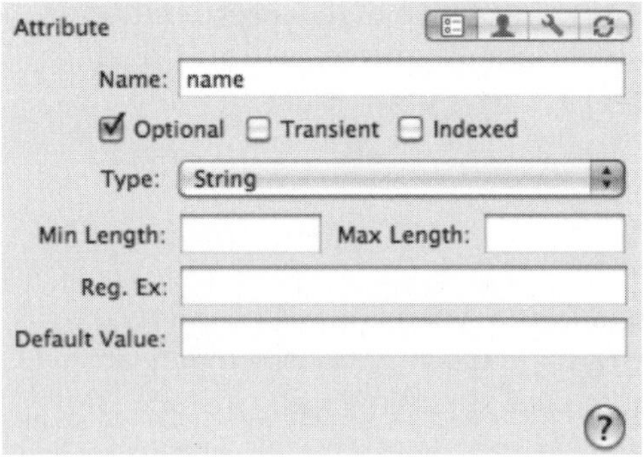

Figure 3-15. *The detail pane after selecting the String type*

The *Min Length:* and *Max Length:* fields allow you to set a minimum and maximum number of characters for this field. If you enter a number into either field, any attempt to save a managed object that has less characters than the *Min Length:* or more characters than *Max Length:* stored in this attribute will result in a validation error at save time.

Note that this enforcement happens in the data model, not in the user interface. Unless you specifically enforce limitations through your user interface, these validations won't happen until you actually save the data model. In most instances, if you enforce a minimum or maximum length, you should also take some steps to enforce that in your user interface. Otherwise, the user won't be informed of the error until they go to save, which could be quite a while after they've entered data into this field. You'll see an example of enforcing this in Chapter 6.

The next field is labeled *Reg. Ex.:* and that stands for **regular expression**. This field allows you to do further validation on the entered text using regular expressions, which are special text strings that you can use to express patterns. You could, for example, use an attribute to store an IP address in text and then ensure that only valid numerical IP addresses are entered by entering the regular expression \b\d{1,3}\.\d{1,3}\.\d{1,3}\.\d{1,3}\b. We're not going to use regular expressions for this attribute, so leave the *Reg. Ex.* field blank.

> **NOTE:** Regular expressions are a very complex topic on which many full books have been written. Teaching regular expressions is way beyond the scope of this book, but if you're interested in using regular expressions to do data model-level validation, a good starting point is the Wikipedia page on regular expressions at `http://en.wikipedia.org/wiki/Regular_expression`, which covers the basic syntax and contains links to many regular expression-related resources.

Finally, you can use the field labeled *Default Value:* to, well, set a default value for this property. If you type a value into this field, any managed object based on this entity will automatically have its corresponding property set to whatever value you type in here. So, in this case, if you were to type *Untitled Hero* into this field, any time you created a new Hero managed object, the *name* property would automatically get set to *Untitled Hero*. Heck, that sounds like a good idea, so type *Untitled Hero* into this field. Then, for good measure, save.

Adding the Rest of the Attributes

Our *Hero* entity needs three more attributes, so let's add them now. Click the plus button in the properties pane again and select **Add Attribute** once more. Give this one a name of *secretIdentity* and a type of *String*. Since, according to Mr. Incredible, every superhero has a secret identity, we'd better uncheck the *Optional* check box. We will be sorting and searching on secret identity, so check the *Indexed* box. For *Default Value:*, type in *Unknown*. Because we've made the field mandatory by unchecking the *Optional* check box, it's a good idea to provide a default value. Leave the rest of the fields as is.

> **CAUTION:** Be sure you enter default values for the name and `secretIdentity` attributes. If you don't, the program will behave badly. If your program crashes, check to make sure you've saved your source code files and your nib files.

Click the plus button a third time to add yet another attribute, giving it a name of *birthdate* and a type of *Date*. Leave the rest of the fields at their default values for this attribute. We may not know the birthdate for all of our superheroes, so we want to leave this attribute as optional. As far as we know now, we won't be doing a lot of searching or ordering on birthdate, so there's no need to make this attribute indexed. We could do some additional validation here by setting a minimum, maximum, or default date, but there really isn't much need. There's no default value that would make sense, and setting a minimum or maximum date would preclude the possibility of an immortal superhero or a time-traveling one, which we certainly don't want to do!

That leaves us with one more attribute for this first iteration of our application: sex. There are a number of ways that we could choose to store this particular piece of information. For simplicity's sake (and because it will help us show you a few helpful techniques in Chapter 6), we're just going to store a character string of either *Male* or *Female*. Add another attribute and select a *Type* of *String*. Let's leave this as an optional setting— there might just be an androgynous masked avenger or two out there. We could use the regular expression field to limit inputs to either *Male* or *Female* but, instead, we're going to enforce that in the user interface by presenting a selection list rather than enforcing it here in the data model.

Guess what? You've now completed the data model for the first iteration of the *SuperDB* application. Save it and let's go create our controller.

Creating HeroListViewController

If you look back at Figure 3-1, you can see that our application displays a list of heroes, and it can sort that list by either name or secret identity. As we discussed earlier in the chapter, we're using a single controller to handle both of the sort options rather than using separate controllers for each one. In order to retrieve the results from our persistent store, we're going to use a fetched results controller just as the template code we looked at in the last chapter did. However, we are not using a table view controller, so we have to design our user interface in our nib. Before we do that, though, we should declare the outlets that we're going to need.

Declaring the Fetched Results Controller

Single-click on *HeroListViewController.h* to bring up the header file for our class. We need to declare our property and instance variable for the fetched results controller, so make the following changes to your file:

```
#import <UIKit/UIKit.h>

#define kSelectedTabDefaultsKey @"Selected Tab"

enum {
    kByName,
    kBySecretIdentity,
};

@interface HeroListViewController : UIViewController
    <UITableViewDelegate, UITableViewDataSource, UITabBarDelegate,
    UIAlertViewDelegate, NSFetchedResultsControllerDelegate>
{
    UITableView *tableView;
    UITabBar    *tabBar;

@private
```

```
    NSFetchedResultsController *_fetchedResultsController;
}

@property (nonatomic, retain) IBOutlet UITableView *tableView;
@property (nonatomic, retain) IBOutlet UITabBar *tabBar;
@property (nonatomic, readonly) NSFetchedResultsController
    *fetchedResultsController;

- (void)addHero;
- (IBAction)toggleEdit;

@end
```

This looks just a little different than what we've done before, so let's discuss what's going on here. First, we define a constant that will be used as a key to store and retrieve a preference value in the user defaults. When our program launches, we want to take the user back to the same tab they were on when they last used the program. This constant will be used to store that information in our application's preferences.

After that, we define an enumeration that gives us constants for the individual tabs used in the tab bar, just to make our code a bit more readable. The number 0 can mean lots of different things in the context of our code, but the constant kByName makes it obvious that this time, it's referring to the tab called *By Name*.

Next, we conform our class to a whole bunch of protocols. Because we're not subclassing UITableViewController, we have to manually conform to UITableViewDelegate and UITableViewDataSource. We also conform to UITabBarDelegate because we're also going to act as the tab bar delegate. Doing so will cause us to be notified whenever the user selects a new tab without having to utilize action methods.

If we encounter a fatal error, we're going to show the user an alert before quitting, so we have to become the alert's delegate in order to be notified when the alert is dismissed. That's why we also need to conform to UIAlertViewDelegate. The template code just logs errors to the console and quits, but we're going to be a little more user-friendly than that and let the user know when something has gone wrong.

Finally, we conform to NSFetchedResultsControllerDelegate because we're going to be using a fetched results controller and will need to be notified when its data changes.

After that, we create instance variables to serve as outlets for the tab bar and table view. Then, we specify the @private keyword, which indicates that all instance variables that follow have a private scope and cannot be accessed directly by other classes. We then create a private instance variable in which to store our fetched results controller. Notice that we've called the instance variable _fetchedResultsController, yet if you look down a few lines later, the property is actually named fetchedResultsController, without the underscore.

By default, properties expect their underlying instance variable to have the same name as the property. However, that is just the default behavior and is not required. When you synthesize your property in the implementation file using the @synthesize keyword, you can specify the name of the underlying instance variable to be used to store the property's data. The specified name can be anything at all. It doesn't need to be related to or similar to the property name at all.

When we synthesize this property, we'll use this line of code:

```
@synthesize fetchedResultsController=_fetchedResultsController;
```

The property name goes immediately after the @synthesize keyword, just as always, but it is then followed by an equal sign and then the name of the instance variable to be used. This particular convention of using the same name as the property but prefixed with an underscore is one you see a lot, even in Apple's sample code. Some programmers use this naming convention for all of their properties. We tend to use it only when there's a specific reason to not want other objects mucking with an instance variable.

This naming convention should prevent us from accidentally confusing the property and instance variable in our code. By using different names for each, we are far less likely to access the instance variable directly when we intend to use the property.

You might remember from the last chapter that our fetchedResultsController was lazily loaded. As a result, it is critical that references to the fetchedResultsController be done through the accessor, since the accessor will make sure that our fetchedResultsController was properly loaded. We're going to be doing the same thing in this chapter. This naming convention and the use of the @private keyword will help prevent unintentional direct access to the instance variable that could cause problems if the fetched results controller hasn't been loaded by an earlier use of the accessor.

> **NOTE:** You may hear developers claim that using the underscore prefix is reserved by Apple and that you shouldn't use it. This is a misconception. Apple does, indeed, reserve the underscore prefix for the names of methods. It does not make any similar reservation when it comes to the names of instance variables. You can read Apple's naming convention for instance variables, which makes no restriction on the use of the underscore, here: http://developer.apple.com/documentation/Cocoa/Conceptual/CodingGuidelin es/Articles/NamingIvarsAndTypes.html

Notice that the fetchedResultsController property is declared with the readonly keyword. We will be lazily loading the fetched results controller in the accessor method. We do not want other classes to be able to set fetchedResultsController, so we declare it readonly to prevent that from happening.

SYNTHESIZED INSTANCE VARIABLES

There's a new feature of the Objective-C 2.0 runtime that hasn't been talked about much and that we haven't had you use at all. It's called **synthesized instance variables**. The Objective-C 2.0 runtime will actually create instance variables for you if you declare a property and don't give it an underlying instance variable. So, for example, this is a perfectly valid class interface:

```
#import <Cocoa/Cocoa.h>

@interface TestController : NSObject {
}
@property (retain) NSString *testString;
@end
```

Notice that there's no instance variable declaration for testString; it's not needed. Well, that is, it's not needed if you're compiling 64-bit Cocoa applications or iPhone applications.

Unfortunately, though, the iPhone simulator is a 32-bit Mac application, and 32-bit Mac applications cannot take advantage of instance variable synthesis. That means iPhone programs running in the simulator cannot take advantage of this feature either. In other words, the following class is a perfectly valid class when compiled for the device, but will fail with errors when compiled against the simulator:

```
#import <UIKit/UIKit.h>

@interface MyViewController : UITableViewController {
}
@property (nonatomic, retain) NSManagedObject *myObject;
@end
```

You could utilize this feature on the iPhone and still create programs that can compile on the simulator by using platform macros, like this:

```
#import <UIKit/UIKit.h>

@interface MyViewController : UITableViewController {
#if  TARGET_IPHONE_SIMULATOR
    NSManagedObject *myObject;
#endif
}
@property (nonatomic, retain) NSManagedObject *myObject;
@end
```

But, there's a catch. Synthesized instance variables cannot be accessed directly, even from within your class. You have to use the accessor and mutator methods everywhere.

So, what's the advantage of not declaring the underlying instance variable? On the iPhone, it doesn't save you any typing unless you never, ever run your program in the simulator. That means that for most iPhone developers, there really is no advantage to using this feature right now. In the future, it is possible, and maybe even likely, that there will be compiler optimizations behind the scenes that your program will take advantage of if you've let the runtime create your instance variables for you. As of right now, however, there's no real advantage to using this feature unless you plan to always test on an iPhone, in which case, it can save you a little typing.

Drag Two Icons to Your Project

Before writing our implementation of HeroListViewController, we need to head over to Interface Builder to design the interface and connect our outlets. Before we do that, however, you need to copy two image files into your Xcode project so that they'll be available to you in Interface Builder. If you look in the project archive that accompanies this book, in the *03 - SuperDB* folder, you'll find files called *name_icon.png* and *secret_icon.png*. These are the images that you will use on the two tabs. Add them both to your project in the *Resources* group. Once you've done that, you can double-click *HeroListViewController.xib* to open up Interface Builder.

Designing the HeroListViewController Interface

When the nib file opens, the *View* window should show up. If it doesn't, double-click the *View* icon in the nib's main window to open it. We need to add a tab bar and a table view to our nib, and then make the connections.

Let's add the tab bar first. Look in the Library for a tab bar (Figure 3-16). Make sure you're grabbing a tab bar and not a tab bar controller. We only want the user interface item.

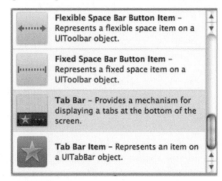

Figure 3-16. *The tab bar in the Library*

Drag a tab bar from the library to the window called View, and place it snugly in the bottom of the window, as we've done in Figure 3-17.

Figure 3-17. *The tab bar placed snugly against the bottom of the screen*

The default tab bar has two tabs, which is exactly the number we want. Let's change the icon and label for each. With the tab bar still selected, click on the star above Favorites and then press ⌘1 to bring up the attribute inspector.

If you've correctly selected the tab bar item, the inspector window should have the title *Tab Bar Item Attributes* and the *Identifier* pop-up should say *Favorites*. In the attribute inspector, give this tab a *Title* of *By Name*, and an *Image* of *name_icon.png* (Figure 3-18). Now click on the three dots above the word *More* on the tab bar to select the right tab. Using the inspector, give this tab a *Title* of *By Secret Identity* and an *Image* of *secret_icon.png*.

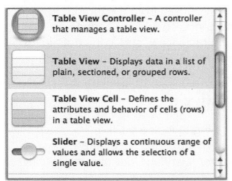

Figure 3-18. *Setting the attributes of the left tab*

Back in the library, look for a *Table View* (Figure 3-19). Again, make sure you're getting the user interface element, not a *Table View Controller*. Drag this to the space above the tab bar. It should resize automatically to fit the space available. After you drop it, it should look like Figure 3-20.

Figure 3-19. *The Table View in the library*

Figure 3-20. *The HeroListViewController interface after dropping the table on it*

With the table in place, the HeroListViewController interface is complete, we just need to make the outlet, delegate, and datasource connections. Control-drag from *File's Owner* to the table view and select the *tableView* outlet, then control-drag again from *File's Owner* to the tab bar and select the *tabBar* outlet. That takes care of the outlet connections. Let's move on to the delegate and datasource connections.

Control-drag twice from the table view to *File's Owner*, selecting the *dataSource* outlet one time, and the *delegate* outlet the other. Then control-drag from the tab bar to *File's Owner* and select the *delegate* outlet. Now our controller's outlets are connected, and our controller is the delegate for both the tab bar and table view, and is the data source for the table view as well. Our job here is done. Save the nib and go back to Xcode.

Implementing the Hero View Controller

The implementation of HeroListViewController is going to look a bit like RootViewController from the previous chapter, even though they have different superclasses. Replace the current contents of your *HeroListViewController.m* file with the following code. Once you've done that, we'll talk about the new stuff it contains.

```
#import "HeroListViewController.h"
#import "SuperDBAppDelegate.h"

@implementation HeroListViewController
```

```objc
#pragma mark Properties
@synthesize tableView;
@synthesize tabBar;
@synthesize fetchedResultsController = _fetchedResultsController;

#pragma mark -
- (void)addHero {
    NSManagedObjectContext *context =
        [self.fetchedResultsController managedObjectContext];
    NSEntityDescription *entity =
        [[self.fetchedResultsController fetchRequest] entity];
    NSManagedObject *newManagedObject = [NSEntityDescription
        insertNewObjectForEntityForName:[entity name]
        inManagedObjectContext:context];

    NSError *error;
    if (![context save:&error])
        NSLog(@"Error saving entity: %@", [error localizedDescription]);

    // TODO: Instantiate detail editing controller and push onto stack
}

- (IBAction)toggleEdit {
    BOOL editing = !self.tableView.editing;
    self.navigationItem.rightBarButtonItem.enabled = !editing;
    self.navigationItem.leftBarButtonItem.title = (editing) ?
        NSLocalizedString(@"Done", @"Done") : NSLocalizedString(@"Edit", @"Edit");
    [self.tableView setEditing:editing animated:YES];
}

- (void)viewDidLoad {
    [super viewDidLoad];
    NSError *error = nil;
    if (![[self fetchedResultsController] performFetch:&error]) {
        UIAlertView *alert = [[UIAlertView alloc]
            initWithTitle:NSLocalizedString(@"Error loading data",
                @"Error loading data")
            message:[NSString stringWithFormat:NSLocalizedString(
                @"Error was: %@, quitting.", @"Error was: %@, quitting."),
                [error localizedDescription]]
            delegate:self
            cancelButtonTitle:NSLocalizedString(@"Aw, Nuts", @"Aw, Nuts")
            otherButtonTitles:nil];
        [alert show];

    }

    NSUserDefaults *defaults = [NSUserDefaults standardUserDefaults];
    NSInteger selectedTab = [defaults integerForKey:kSelectedTabDefaultsKey];
    UITabBarItem *item = [tabBar.items objectAtIndex:selectedTab];
    [tabBar setSelectedItem:item];
}

- (void)viewDidAppear:(BOOL)animated {
    UIBarButtonItem *editButton = self.editButtonItem;
    [editButton setTarget:self];
    [editButton setAction:@selector(toggleEdit)];
```

```objc
        self.navigationItem.leftBarButtonItem = editButton;

        UIBarButtonItem *addButton = [[UIBarButtonItem alloc]
            initWithBarButtonSystemItem:UIBarButtonSystemItemAdd
            target:self
            action:@selector(addHero)];
        self.navigationItem.rightBarButtonItem = addButton;
        [addButton release];
}

- (void)viewDidUnload {
    self.tableView = nil;
    self.tabBar = nil;
}

- (void)dealloc {
    [tableView release];
    [tabBar release];
    [_fetchedResultsController release];
    [super dealloc];
}

#pragma mark -
#pragma mark Table View Methods
- (NSInteger)numberOfSectionsInTableView:(UITableView *)theTableView {
    NSUInteger count = [[self.fetchedResultsController sections] count];
    if (count == 0) {
        count = 1;
    }
    return count;
}

- (NSInteger)tableView:(UITableView *)tableView
    numberOfRowsInSection:(NSInteger)section {
    NSArray *sections = [self.fetchedResultsController sections];
    NSUInteger count = 0;
    if ([sections count]) {
        id <NSFetchedResultsSectionInfo> sectionInfo =
            [sections objectAtIndex:section];
        count = [sectionInfo numberOfObjects];
    }
    return count;
}

- (UITableViewCell *)tableView:(UITableView *)theTableView
cellForRowAtIndexPath:(NSIndexPath *)indexPath {

    static NSString *HeroTableViewCell = @"HeroTableViewCell";

    UITableViewCell *cell = [tableView
        dequeueReusableCellWithIdentifier:HeroTableViewCell];
    if (cell == nil) {
        cell = [[[UITableViewCell alloc] initWithStyle:UITableViewCellStyleSubtitle
            reuseIdentifier:HeroTableViewCell] autorelease];
    }
    NSManagedObject *oneHero = [self.fetchedResultsController
        objectAtIndexPath:indexPath];
```

```objc
        NSInteger tab = [tabBar.items indexOfObject:tabBar.selectedItem];
        switch (tab) {
            case kByName:
                cell.textLabel.text = [oneHero valueForKey:@"name"];
                cell.detailTextLabel.text = [oneHero valueForKey:@"secretIdentity"];
                break;
            case kBySecretIdentity:
                cell.detailTextLabel.text = [oneHero valueForKey:@"name"];
                cell.textLabel.text = [oneHero valueForKey:@"secretIdentity"];
            default:
                break;
        }
        return cell;
}

- (void)tableView:(UITableView *)theTableView
    didSelectRowAtIndexPath:(NSIndexPath *)indexPath {
    // TODO: Instantiate detail editing view controller and push onto stack
}

- (void)tableView:(UITableView *)tableView
commitEditingStyle:(UITableViewCellEditingStyle)editingStyle
forRowAtIndexPath:(NSIndexPath *)indexPath {

    if (editingStyle == UITableViewCellEditingStyleDelete) {
        NSManagedObjectContext *context = [self.fetchedResultsController
            managedObjectContext];
        [context deleteObject:[self.fetchedResultsController
            objectAtIndexPath:indexPath]];

        NSError *error;
        if (![context save:&error]) {
            NSLog(@"Unresolved error %@, %@", error, [error userInfo]);
            UIAlertView *alert = [[UIAlertView alloc] initWithTitle:
                NSLocalizedString(@"Error saving after delete",
                @"Error saving after delete.")
              message:[NSString stringWithFormat:NSLocalizedString(
                  @"Error was: %@, quitting.",@"Error was: %@, quitting."),
                  [error localizedDescription]]
              delegate:self
              cancelButtonTitle:NSLocalizedString(@"Aw, Nuts", @"Aw, Nuts")
                                              otherButtonTitles:nil];
            [alert show];
        }
    }
}

#pragma mark -
#pragma mark Fetched results controller
- (NSFetchedResultsController *)fetchedResultsController {

    if (_fetchedResultsController != nil) {
        return _fetchedResultsController;
    }

    NSFetchRequest *fetchRequest = [[NSFetchRequest alloc] init];
```

```objc
    SuperDBAppDelegate *appDelegate = UIApplication
        sharedApplication] delegate];
    NSManagedObjectContext *managedObjectContext = appDelegate.managedObjectContext;

    NSEntityDescription *entity = [NSEntityDescription entityForName:@"Hero"
        inManagedObjectContext:managedObjectContext];

    NSUInteger tab = [tabBar.items indexOfObject:tabBar.selectedItem];
    if (tab == NSNotFound) {
        NSUserDefaults *defaults = [NSUserDefaults standardUserDefaults];
        tab = [defaults integerForKey:kSelectedTabDefaultsKey];
    }

    NSString *sectionKey = nil;
    switch (tab) {
        case kByName: {
            NSSortDescriptor *sortDescriptor1 = [[NSSortDescriptor alloc]
                initWithKey:@"name" ascending:YES];
            NSSortDescriptor *sortDescriptor2 = [[NSSortDescriptor alloc]
                initWithKey:@"secretIdentity" ascending:YES];
            NSArray *sortDescriptors = [[NSArray alloc]
                initWithObjects:sortDescriptor1, sortDescriptor2, nil];
            [fetchRequest setSortDescriptors:sortDescriptors];
            [sortDescriptor1 release];
            [sortDescriptor2 release];
            [sortDescriptors release];
            sectionKey = @"name";
            break;
        }
        case kBySecretIdentity:{
            NSSortDescriptor *sortDescriptor1 = [[NSSortDescriptor alloc]
                initWithKey:@"secretIdentity" ascending:YES];
            NSSortDescriptor *sortDescriptor2 = [[NSSortDescriptor alloc]
                initWithKey:@"name" ascending:YES];
            NSArray *sortDescriptors = [[NSArray alloc]
                initWithObjects:sortDescriptor1, sortDescriptor2, nil];
            [fetchRequest setSortDescriptors:sortDescriptors];
            [sortDescriptor1 release];
            [sortDescriptor2 release];
            [sortDescriptors release];
            sectionKey = @"secretIdentity";
            break;
        }
        default:
            break;

    }
    [fetchRequest setEntity:entity];
    [fetchRequest setFetchBatchSize:20];

    NSFetchedResultsController *frc = [[NSFetchedResultsController alloc]
        initWithFetchRequest:fetchRequest
        managedObjectContext:managedObjectContext
        sectionNameKeyPath:sectionKey
        cacheName:@"Hero"];
    frc.delegate = self;
    _fetchedResultsController = frc;
```

```objc
        [fetchRequest release];

    return _fetchedResultsController;
}

- (void)controllerWillChangeContent:(NSFetchedResultsController *)controller {
    [self.tableView beginUpdates];
}

- (void)controllerDidChangeContent:(NSFetchedResultsController *)controller {
    [self.tableView endUpdates];
}

- (void)controller:(NSFetchedResultsController *)controller
    didChangeObject:(id)anObject atIndexPath:(NSIndexPath *)indexPath
      forChangeType:(NSFetchedResultsChangeType)type
       newIndexPath:(NSIndexPath *)newIndexPath {
    switch(type) {
        case NSFetchedResultsChangeInsert:
            [self.tableView insertRowsAtIndexPaths:[NSArray
                arrayWithObject:newIndexPath]
                withRowAnimation:UITableViewRowAnimationFade];
            break;
        case NSFetchedResultsChangeDelete:
            [self.tableView deleteRowsAtIndexPaths:[NSArray
            arrayWithObject:indexPath]
            withRowAnimation:UITableViewRowAnimationFade];
            break;
        case NSFetchedResultsChangeUpdate: {
            NSString *sectionKeyPath = [controller sectionNameKeyPath];
            if (sectionKeyPath == nil)
                break;
            NSManagedObject *changedObject = [controller
                objectAtIndexPath:indexPath];
            NSArray *keyParts = [sectionKeyPath componentsSeparatedByString:@"."];
            id currentKeyValue = [changedObject valueForKeyPath:sectionKeyPath];
            for (int i = 0; i < [keyParts count] - 1; i++) {
                NSString *onePart = [keyParts objectAtIndex:i];
                changedObject = [changedObject valueForKey:onePart];
            }
            sectionKeyPath = [keyParts lastObject];
            NSDictionary *committedValues = [changedObject
                committedValuesForKeys:nil];

            if ([[committedValues valueForKeyPath:sectionKeyPath]
                isEqual:currentKeyValue])
                break;

            NSUInteger tableSectionCount = [self.tableView numberOfSections];
            NSUInteger frcSectionCount = [[controller sections] count];
            if (tableSectionCount != frcSectionCount) {
                // Need to insert a section
                NSArray *sections = controller.sections;
                NSInteger newSectionLocation = -1;
                for (id oneSection in sections) {
                    NSString *sectionName = [oneSection name];
```

```
                    if ([currentKeyValue isEqual:sectionName]) {
                        newSectionLocation = [sections indexOfObject:oneSection];
                        break;
                    }
                }
                if (newSectionLocation == -1)
                    return; // uh oh

                if (!(newSectionLocation == 0 && tableSectionCount == 1) &&
                    [self.tableView numberOfRowsInSection:0] == 0)
                    [self.tableView insertSections:[NSIndexSet
                        indexSetWithIndex:newSectionLocation]
                        withRowAnimation:UITableViewRowAnimationFade];
                NSUInteger indices[2] = {newSectionLocation, 0};
                newIndexPath = [[[NSIndexPath alloc] initWithIndexes:indices
                    length:2] autorelease];
            }
        }
        case NSFetchedResultsChangeMove:
            if (newIndexPath != nil) {
                [self.tableView deleteRowsAtIndexPaths:[NSArray
                    arrayWithObject:indexPath]
                    withRowAnimation:UITableViewRowAnimationFade];
                [self.tableView insertRowsAtIndexPaths: [NSArray
                    arrayWithObject:newIndexPath]
                    withRowAnimation: UITableViewRowAnimationRight];

            }
            else {
                [self.tableView reloadSections:[NSIndexSet
                    indexSetWithIndex:[indexPath section]]
                    withRowAnimation:UITableViewRowAnimationFade];
            }
            break;
        default:
            break;
    }
}

- (void)controller:(NSFetchedResultsController *)controller
  didChangeSection:(id <NSFetchedResultsSectionInfo>)sectionInfo
        atIndex:(NSUInteger)sectionIndex
    forChangeType:(NSFetchedResultsChangeType)type {
    switch(type) {
        case NSFetchedResultsChangeInsert:
            if (!(sectionIndex == 0 && [self.tableView numberOfSections] == 1) &&
                [self.tableView numberOfRowsInSection:0] == 0)
                [self.tableView insertSections:[NSIndexSet
                    indexSetWithIndex:sectionIndex]
                    withRowAnimation:UITableViewRowAnimationFade];
            break;
        case NSFetchedResultsChangeDelete:
            if (!(sectionIndex == 0 && [self.tableView numberOfSections] == 1) &&
                [self.tableView numberOfRowsInSection:0] == 0)
                [self.tableView deleteSections:[NSIndexSet
                    indexSetWithIndex:sectionIndex]
                    withRowAnimation:UITableViewRowAnimationFade];
```

```
                break;
          case NSFetchedResultsChangeMove:
                break;
          case NSFetchedResultsChangeUpdate:
                break;
          default:
                break;
      }
}

#pragma mark -
#pragma mark UIAlertView Delegate
- (void)alertView:(UIAlertView *)alertView
    didDismissWithButtonIndex:(NSInteger)buttonIndex {
    exit(-1);
}

#pragma mark -
#pragma mark Tab Bar Delegate
- (void)tabBar:(UITabBar *)theTabBar didSelectItem:(UITabBarItem *)item {
    NSUserDefaults *defaults = [NSUserDefaults standardUserDefaults];
    NSUInteger tabIndex = [tabBar.items indexOfObject:item];
    [defaults setInteger:tabIndex forKey:kSelectedTabDefaultsKey];

    _fetchedResultsController.delegate = nil;
    [_fetchedResultsController release];
    _fetchedResultsController = nil;

    NSError *error;
    if (![self.fetchedResultsController performFetch:&error])
        NSLog(@"Error performing fetch: %@", [error localizedDescription]);
    [self.tableView reloadData];
}

@end
```

Okay, that was a lot of code. As you were typing it, a lot of it probably looked familiar. Let's start at the top and work our way down until we've covered all the new stuff.

The first few lines are pretty straightforward. We import our header file, and also import the header file from our application delegate because we'll be using our application delegate in a few methods.

```
#import "HeroListViewController.h"
#import "SuperDBAppDelegate.h"

@implementation HeroListViewController
```

Then we synthesize our properties, making sure to identify the instance variable that backs the fetchedResultsController since its underlying instance variable has a different name:

```
#pragma mark Properties
@synthesize tableView;
@synthesize tabBar;
@synthesize fetchedResultsController = _fetchedResultsController;
```

After that, we first have our method for adding new heroes. This method is nearly identical to the `insertNewObjects:` method from last chapter. If `save:` encounters an error, it will return `NO` and we'll send an error to the console.

```
- (void)addHero {
    NSManagedObjectContext *context =
        [self.fetchedResultsController managedObjectContext];
    NSEntityDescription *entity =
        [[self.fetchedResultsController fetchRequest] entity];
    NSManagedObject *newManagedObject = [NSEntityDescription
        insertNewObjectForEntityForName:[entity name]
        inManagedObjectContext:context];

    NSError *error;
    if (![context save:&error])
        NSLog(@"Error saving entity: %@", [error localizedDescription]);

    // TODO: Instantiate detail editing controller and push onto stack
}
```

> **NOTE:** You will get a warning about the unused variable `newManagedObject` when you compile this code. We actually need this line of code because it creates a new managed object and inserts that object into the context. We don't use the pointer returned by this call, and that's why we get the warning. Normally, we just wouldn't save the returned value, but we will be using this pointer in Chapter 4 when we expand our application. So live with the warning for now and know that we will be making use of `newManagedObject` in the next chapter.

Notice that comment at the end of the method? Some comments that begin with certain strings have special meaning in Xcode, and this is one of those strings. A comment that begins with `// TODO:` will be included in the function pop-up menu (Figure 3-21). These comments are designed to work as a reminder to ourselves to come back later and finish this incomplete piece of functionality. In this case, it's a reminder to instantiate the detail editing pane that will allow the user to edit the newly added hero and push it onto the navigation stack, which we'll do in the next chapter.

> **TIP:** There are other special comments that will show up in the function pop-up menu in addition to `// TODO:`. If you want to indicate a problem that needs to be fixed, you can insert a comment that begins with `// FIXME:`. Comments beginning with either `// ???:` or `// !!!:` will also show up in the function pop-up, the former typically being used to indicate a question or something puzzling in the code, and the latter typically being used to mark something urgent or surprising in the code. You can also just put an entry in the function menu using comments that begin with `// MARK:`, which will cause anything on the line after the colon to show up in the function menu the way using `#pragma mark` does.

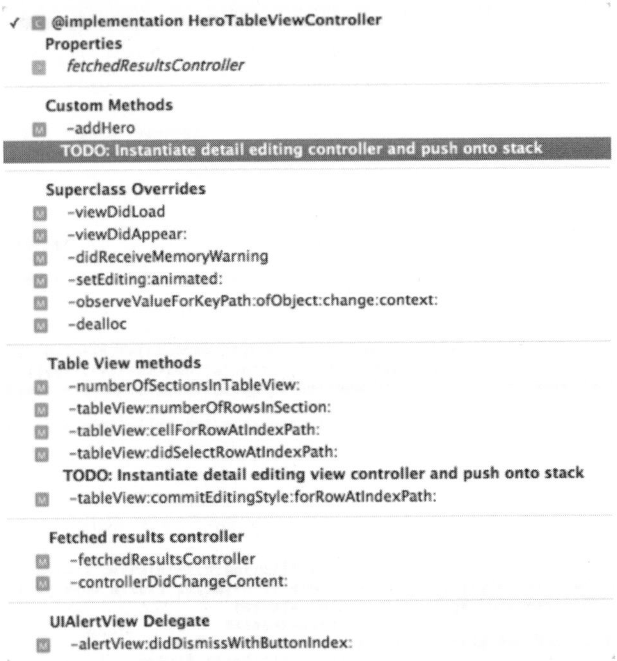

✓ ☐ @implementation HeroTableViewController
    Properties
    ☐ *fetchedResultsController*

    Custom Methods
    Ⓜ –addHero
    TODO: Instantiate detail editing controller and push onto stack

    Superclass Overrides
    Ⓜ –viewDidLoad
    Ⓜ –viewDidAppear:
    Ⓜ –didReceiveMemoryWarning
    Ⓜ –setEditing:animated:
    Ⓜ –observeValueForKeyPath:ofObject:change:context:
    Ⓜ –dealloc

    Table View methods
    Ⓜ –numberOfSectionsInTableView:
    Ⓜ –tableView:numberOfRowsInSection:
    Ⓜ –tableView:cellForRowAtIndexPath:
    Ⓜ –tableView:didSelectRowAtIndexPath:
    TODO: Instantiate detail editing view controller and push onto stack
    Ⓜ –tableView:commitEditingStyle:forRowAtIndexPath:

    Fetched results controller
    Ⓜ –fetchedResultsController
    Ⓜ –controllerDidChangeContent:

    UIAlertView Delegate
    Ⓜ –alertView:didDismissWithButtonIndex:

Figure 3-21. *Certain comments will show up in the function pop-up menu, such as this TODO comment we added to our code*

Next comes `toggleEdit`, our action method for turning on and off our table view's edit mode. In addition to simply toggling the table view's edit mode, we also have a bit of housekeeping to attend to, to make sure the user interface works as the user expects it to. Because we've subclassed `UIViewController` instead of `UITableViewController`, we have to maintain the *Edit* button's label ourselves. We change the title of the edit button to either *Edit* or *Done* based on whether the table is in editing mode or not. We also hide the right nav bar button, which is used to add new rows, based on whether editing mode is being turned on or off. We don't want the user to be able to add new rows while we're in edit mode.

```
- (IBAction)toggleEdit {
    BOOL editing = !self.tableView.editing;
    self.navigationItem.rightBarButtonItem.enabled = !editing;
    self.navigationItem.leftBarButtonItem.title = (editing) ?
        NSLocalizedString(@"Done", @"Done") : NSLocalizedString(@"Edit", @"Edit");
    [self.tableView setEditing:editing animated:YES];
}
```

At first glance, viewDidLoad looks like the version from the template. We start by calling the same method on super, and then we get the fetched results controller and call performFetch:.

```
- (void)viewDidLoad {
    [super viewDidLoad];
    NSError *error = nil;
    if (![[self fetchedResultsController] performFetch:&error]) {
```

If an error is encountered, however, we no longer just log and quit. Instead, we show an alert informing the user of the error. We still log more detailed information to the console, and we still quit, but at least we tell the user that we're quitting and why before we do it. The actual command to quit is actually in the alert view delegate method alertView:didDismissButtonWithIndex:, which will cause the program to quit after the user dismisses the alert.

```
        UIAlertView *alert = [[UIAlertView alloc]
                initWithTitle:NSLocalizedString(@"Error loading data",
                    @"Error loading data")
                message:[NSString stringWithFormat:@"Error was: %@, quitting.",
                    [error localizedDescription]]
                delegate:self
                cancelButtonTitle:NSLocalizedString(@"Aw, Nuts", @"Aw, Nuts")
                otherButtonTitles:nil];
        [alert show];
    }
}
```

The viewDidAppear: method is nearly identical to the one from the previous chapter. It makes sure that the edit and add buttons are in the navigation bar.

```
- (void)viewDidAppear:(BOOL)animated {
    self.navigationItem.leftBarButtonItem = self.editButtonItem;
    UIBarButtonItem *addButton = [[UIBarButtonItem alloc]
        initWithBarButtonSystemItem:UIBarButtonSystemItemAdd
        target:self
        action:@selector(addHero)];
    self.navigationItem.rightBarButtonItem = addButton;
    [addButton release];
}
```

After that, we override setEditing:animated:, which is the method that gets called when the *edit* button is tapped, or when the user swipes a row.

```
- (void)setEditing:(BOOL)editing animated:(BOOL)animated {
    self.navigationItem.rightBarButtonItem.enabled = !editing;
    self.navigationItem.leftBarButtonItem.title = (editing) ?
        NSLocalizedString(@"Done", @"Done") :
        NSLocalizedString(@"Edit", @"Edit");
    [self.tableView setEditing:editing animated:animated];
}
```

The table view delegate and datasource methods are pretty straightforward, so let's skip down to fetchedResultsController. Everything there starts out pretty much the same as the version in the last chapter:

```
- (NSFetchedResultsController *)fetchedResultsController {
    if (_fetchedResultsController != nil) {
        return _fetchedResultsController;
    }

    NSFetchRequest *fetchRequest = [[NSFetchRequest alloc] init];

    SuperDBAppDelegate *appDelegate = (SuperDBAppDelegate *)[[UIApplication
        sharedApplication] delegate];
    NSManagedObjectContext *managedObjectContext = appDelegate.managedObjectContext;
```

```
NSEntityDescription *entity = [NSEntityDescription entityForName:@"Hero"
    inManagedObjectContext:managedObjectContext];
```

Because our sort descriptors are going to depend on the currently selected tab, we need to find out which tab is currently selected. If no tab is selected, as might be the case if this method is called before the nib has loaded, we'll grab the last used value from preferences.

```
NSUInteger tab = [tabBar.items indexOfObject:tabBar.selectedItem];
if (tab == NSNotFound) {
    NSUserDefaults *defaults = [NSUserDefaults standardUserDefaults];
    tab = [defaults integerForKey:kSelectedTabDefaultsKey];
}
```

Next, we create sort descriptors and a fetch request much as the template did in the last chapter, only we use different sort descriptors based on the currently selected tab. We're also going to use another feature of the fetched results controller that wasn't used in the template. If we specify a **section name keypath** when we create our fetched results controller, our fetched results controller will automatically divide the result set into sections. The most common scenario is to simply pass the same key used in the first sort descriptor. So, if you're sorting by name, and pass in @"name" as the section name keypath and sections will automatically be created based on the first letter of the hero's name. We won't be able to see this functionality in action until the next chapter when we add the ability to edit heroes.

Here, we set the sort descriptor and section name keypath based on the currently selected tab:

```
NSString *sectionKey = nil;
switch (tab) {
    case kByName: {
        NSSortDescriptor *sortDescriptor1 = [[NSSortDescriptor alloc]
            initWithKey:@"name" ascending:YES];
        NSSortDescriptor *sortDescriptor2 = [[NSSortDescriptor alloc]
            initWithKey:@"secretIdentity" ascending:YES];
        NSArray *sortDescriptors = [[NSArray alloc]
            initWithObjects:sortDescriptor1, sortDescriptor2, nil];
        [fetchRequest setSortDescriptors:sortDescriptors];
        [sortDescriptor1 release];
        [sortDescriptor2 release];
        [sortDescriptors release];
        sectionKey = @"name";
        break;
    }
    case kBySecretIdentity:{
        NSSortDescriptor *sortDescriptor1 = [[NSSortDescriptor alloc]
            initWithKey:@"secretIdentity" ascending:YES];
        NSSortDescriptor *sortDescriptor2 = [[NSSortDescriptor alloc]
            initWithKey:@"name" ascending:YES];
        NSArray *sortDescriptors = [[NSArray alloc]
            initWithObjects:sortDescriptor1, sortDescriptor2, nil];
        [fetchRequest setSortDescriptors:sortDescriptors];
        [sortDescriptor1 release];
        [sortDescriptor2 release];
```

```
            [sortDescriptors release];
            sectionKey = @"secretIdentity";
            break;
        }
    default:
        break;
    }
fetchRequest setEntity:entity];
[fetchRequest setFetchBatchSize:20];

NSFetchedResultsController *frc = [[NSFetchedResultsController alloc]
    initWithFetchRequest:fetchRequest managedObjectContext:managedObjectContext
    sectionNameKeyPath:sectionKey
    cacheName:@"Hero"];
```

After that, we just make `self` the delegate of the fetched results controller so that we get notified of changes, assign the new fetched results controller to our private instance variable, and then return that instance variable. Notice that we don't release `frc`. This is intentional. Since we're assigning the controller directly to the instance variable, it does not get retained automatically. That means that `_fetchedResultsController` already has a retain count of 1, which is what we want.

```
    frc.delegate = self;
    _fetchedResultsController = frc;

    return _fetchedResultsController;
}
```

Next are the four fetched results controller delegate methods. Our implementation here is exactly the same as we discussed last chapter, so if you're unclear as to what these four methods are doing, go back to Chapter 2 and re-read the section called *Working With a Fetched Results Controller*.

The alert view delegate method, which gets called when the user dismisses an alert view, does nothing more than quit the application. In this controller, the only reason that we've used alert view is to inform the user of a fatal error.

```
#pragma mark -
#pragma mark UIAlertView Delegate
- (void)alertView:(UIAlertView *)alertView
    didDismissWithButtonIndex:(NSInteger)buttonIndex {
    exit(-1);
}
```

Finally, we have the tab bar delegate method `tabBar:didSelectItem:`, which gets called whenever the user changes the selected tab in our tab bar. In this method, we start by storing the index of the tab the user selected into user defaults. Although tab bar controllers use tab indices to identify which tab is selected, tab bars themselves don't use indices. Instead, we're actually passed the tab bar item that was selected, and we have to determine the index of the tab. It's easy enough to do. `UITabBar` maintains an array of its items called `items`. The index of the tab bar item in that array is the tab index, so we can use NSArray's `indexOfObject:` method to determine it:

```
#pragma mark -
#pragma mark Tab Bar Delegate
```

```
- (void)tabBar:(UITabBar *)theTabBar didSelectItem:(UITabBarItem *)item {
    NSUserDefaults *defaults = [NSUserDefaults standardUserDefaults];
    NSUInteger tabIndex = [tabBar.items indexOfObject:item];
    [defaults setInteger:tabIndex forKey:kSelectedTabDefaultsKey];
```

The next thing we do is set the fetched results controller to nil. By doing this, the next time the fetchedResultsController accessor method is called, it will reload the result set from the persistent store using the criteria based on the new tab selection. Before we set it to nil, however, we set its delegate property to nil. We were the fetched results controller's delegate, but once we set it to nil, we don't want to be its delegate any more.

> **NOTE:** Setting the delegate property to nil when you're done is good form, but if you fail to do it, it usually won't cause any major problems. Although there are a few exceptions in the system, generally speaking, objects do not retain their delegates, so failing to set a delegate to nil won't prevent an object's retain count from reaching zero when it is another object's delegate.

```
    _fetchedResultsController.delegate = nil;
    [_fetchedResultsController release];
    _fetchedResultsController = nil;
```

After we set the fetched results controller to nil, we then call performFetch:, just like we did in viewDidLoad so that the data gets reloaded immediately based on the new criteria. This is the one situation when it's important to call reloadData when using a fetched results controller. Since we release the old fetched results controller and create a new one, we can't rely on the fetched results controller delegate methods to update the table for us.

```
    NSError *error;
    if (![self.fetchedResultsController performFetch:&error])
        NSLog(@"Error performing fetch: %@", [error localizedDescription]);
    [self.tableView reloadData];
}
```

And that's pretty much everything.

Let 'Er Rip

Well, what are you waiting for? That was a lot of work; you deserve to try it out. Make sure everything is saved, then select **Build and Run** from the **Build** menu in Xcode to try things out.

If everything went okay, when the application first launches, you should be presented with an empty table with a navigation bar at the top and a tab bar at the bottom (Figure 3-22). Pressing the right button in the navigation bar will add a new unnamed superhero to the database. Pressing the *Edit* button will allow you to delete heroes.

NOTE: If your app crashed when you ran it, there's a couple of things to look for. First, make sure you saved all your source code and nib files before you ran your project. Also, make sure that you have defaults specified for your hero's name and secretIdentity in your data model editor. If you did that and your app still crashes, try resetting your simulator. Here's how you do that. Bring up the simulator. From the iPhone Simulator menu, select **Reset Contents and Settings...**. That should do it. In Chapter 5, we'll show you how to ensure that changes to your data model don't cause such problems.

Figure 3-22. *The SuperDB application at launch time*

Make sure you try out the two tabs and make sure that the display changes when you select a new tab. When you select the *By Name* tab, it should look like Figure 3-1, but when you select the *By Secret Identity* tab, it should look like Figure 3-23.

Figure 3-23. *Pressing the Secret Identity tab doesn't change the order of the rows yet, but it does change which value is displayed first*

Done, but Not Done

In this chapter, you did a lot of work. You saw how to set up a navigation-based application that uses a tab bar, and learned how to design a basic Core Data data model by creating an entity and giving it several attributes.

This application isn't done, but you've now laid a solid foundation on which to move forward. When you're ready, turn the page, and we'll create a detail editing page to allow the user to edit their superheroes.

Chapter 4

The Devil in the Detail View

In Chapter 3, we built our application's main table view controller. We set it up to display heroes ordered by their name or their secret identity, and we put in place the infrastructure needed to save, delete, and add new heroes. What we didn't do was give the user a way to edit the information about a particular hero, which means we're limited to creating and deleting superheroes named *Untitled Hero*. I guess we can't ship our application yet, huh?

That's okay. Application development is an iterative process, and the first several iterations of any application likely won't have enough functionality to stand on its own. In this chapter, we're going to create an **editable detail view** to let the user edit the data for a specific superhero.

The controller we're going to write will be a subclass of `UITableViewController`, and we're going to use an approach that is somewhat conceptually complex, but that will be easy to maintain and expand. This is important, because we're going to be adding new attributes to the *Hero* managed object, as well as expanding it in other ways and we'll need to keep changing the user interface to accommodate those changes.

Instead of hard-coding the table's structure in our code, we're going to use `NSArray` instances to represent the structure of our tables. By changing the contents of those arrays, we will be able to change the number, order, and content of the sections and rows in our table, meaning that the code we write in our table view data source and delegate methods will not have to change when we make changes to our table's structure. This will make our application easier to expand in future chapters.

After we've written our detail view controller, we will then write additional controller classes, each of which will be designed to let the user edit a single type of data. This will give us the abilty to use the same class for multiple attributes, yet the flexibility to handle special cases when the need arises.

Table-Based vs. Nib-Based Detail Views

In Chapters 3 and 4 of *Beginning iPhone 3 Development* (Apress, 2009), we showed how to build a user interface using Interface Builder. Building your editable detail views in Interface Builder is definitely one way to go. But another common approach is to implement your detail view as a grouped table. Take a look at your iPhone's Contacts application or the Contacts tab of the Phone application (Figure 4–1). The detail editing view in Apple's navigation applications are often implemented using a grouped table rather than using an interface designed in Interface Builder.

The *Human Interface Guidelines* do not give any real guidance as to when you should use a table-based detail view as opposed to a detail view designed in Interface Builder, so it comes down to a question of which feels right. Here's our take: If you're building a navigation-based application, and the data can reasonably and efficiently be presented in a grouped table, it probably should be. Since our superhero data is structured much like the data displayed in the Contacts application, a table-based detail view seems the obvious choice.

Figure 4–2 shows what this chapter's detail view will look like by the end of this chapter.

Figure 4–1. *The Contacts tab of the Phone application uses a table-based detail editing view*

Figure 4–2. *The detail editing view that we'll be building in this application is modeled very closely on Apple's approach in the Phone application*

The table view shown in Figure 4–2 displays data from a single hero, which means that everything in that table comes from a single managed object. Each row corresponds to a different attribute of the managed object. The first section's only row displays the hero's name, for example. The disclosure indicator on that row tells the user that tapping that row will take them to a new view where they can change this hero's name.

The organization of the sections and the order in which attributes are displayed are not determined by the managed object. Instead, they are the results of design decisions we, as the developers, have to make by trying to anticipate what will make sense to our users. We could, for example, put the attributes in alphabetical order, which would put birthdate first. That wouldn't have been very intuitive because birthdate is not the most important or defining attribute of a hero. In our minds, the hero's name and secret identity are the most important attributes and are the first two elements presented in our table view.

Detail Editing View Challenges

The table view architecture was designed to efficiently present data stored in collections. For example, you might use a table view to display data in an NSAarray or in a fetched results controller. When you're creating a detail editing view, however, you're typically presenting data from a single object, in this case an instance of NSManagedObject that represents a single superhero. A managed object uses key-value coding but has no mechanism to present its attributes in a meaningful order. For example, NSManagedObject has no idea that the name attribute is the most important one or that it should be in its own section the way it is in Figure 4–2.

Coming up with a good, maintainable way to specify the sections and rows in a detail editing view is a non-trivial task. The most obvious solution, and one you'll frequently see in online sample code, uses an enum to list the table sections, followed by additional enums for each section, containing constants and a count of rows for each section, like so:

```
enum HeroEditControllerSections {
    HeroEditControllerSectionName = 0,
    HeroEditControllerSectionGeneral,
    HeroEditControllerSectionCount
};

enum HeroEditControllerNameSection {
    HeroEditControllerNameRow = 0,
    HeroEditControllerNameSectionCount
};

enum HeroEditControllerGeneralSection {
    HeroEditControllerGeneralSectionSecretIdentityRow,
    HeroEditControllerGeneralSectionBirthdateRow,
    HeroEditControllerGeneralSectionSexRow,
    HeroEditControllerGeneralSectionCount
};
```

Then, in every method where you are provided with an index path, you can take the appropriate action based on the row and section represented by the index path, using switch statements, like this:

```
- (void)tableView:(UITableView *)tableView
didSelectRowAtIndexPath:(NSIndexPath *)indexPath {
    NSUInteger section = [indexPath section];
    NSUInteger row = [indexPath row];

    switch (section) {
        case HeroEditControllerSectionName:
            switch (row)
            {
                case HeroEditControllerNameRow :
                    // Create a controller to edit name
                    // and push it on the stack
                    ...
                    break;
                default:
                    break;
            }
            break;
        case HeroEditControllerSectionGeneral:
            switch (row) {
                case HeroEditControllerGeneralSectionSecretIdentityRow:
                    // Create a controller to edit secret identity
                    // and push it on the stack
                    ...
```

```
                    break;
            case HeroEditControllerGeneralSectionBirthdateRow:
                // Create a controller to edit birthdate and
                // push it on the stack
                ...
                break;
            case HeroEditControllerGeneralSectionSexRow:
                // Create a controller to edit sex and push it
                // on the stack
                ...
                break;
            default:
                break;
        }
        break;
    default:
        break;
    }
}
```

The problem with this approach is that it doesn't scale very well at all. A nested set of switch statements like this will need to appear in almost every table view delegate or datasource method that takes an index path, which means that adding or deleting rows or sections involves updating your code in multiple places.

Additionally, the code under each of the case statements is going to be relatively similar. In this particular case, we will have to create a new instance of a controller or use a pointer to an existing controller, set some properties to indicate which values need to get edited, then push the controller onto the navigation stack. If we discover a problem in our logic anywhere in these switch statements, chances are we're going to have to change that logic in several places, possibly even dozens.

Controlling Table Structure with Arrays

As you can see here, the most obvious solution isn't always the best one. We don't want to have very similar chunks of code scattered throughout our controller class, and we don't want to have to maintain multiple copies of a complex decision tree. There's a better way to do this.

We can use arrays to mirror the structure of our table. As the user descends into our table, we can use the data stored in an array to construct the appropriate table. The key to this approach is a combination of paired arrays and nested arrays.

Paired Arrays

As the name implies, paired arrays are a pair of arrays whose contents are kept in sync. Paired arrays always have the same number of rows, and the object at a given index in one of the arrays corresponds to the object at the same index in the other paired array. Let's look at a simple example. Figure 4–3 represents a list of peoples' first and last names using paired arrays.

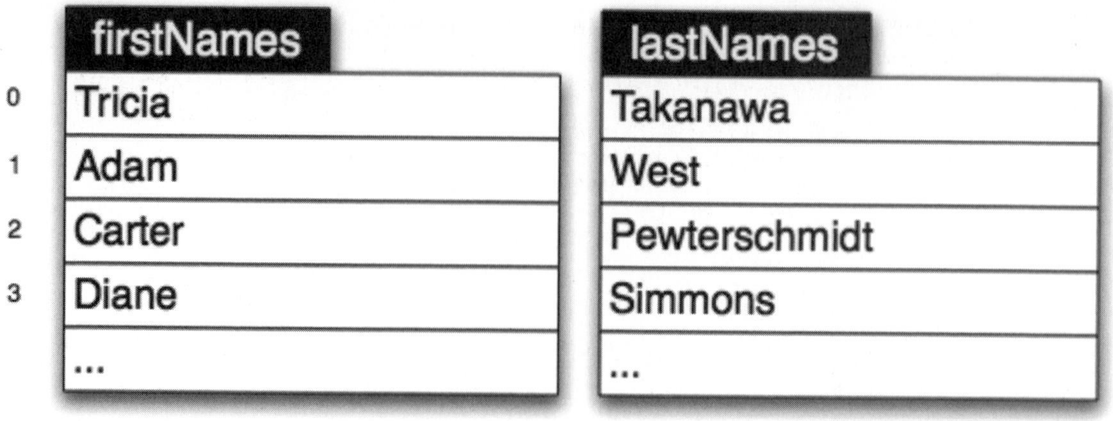

	firstNames		lastNames
0	Tricia		Takanawa
1	Adam		West
2	Carter		Pewterschmidt
3	Diane		Simmons
	...		...

Figure 4–3. *A simple visualization of a paired array*

If you look at Figure 4–3 and look at the first row (index zero), you'll notice that the firstNames array has a value of *Tricia* and the lastNames array has a value of *Takanawa*. That means that index zero in this array pair represents *Tricia Takanawa*. Pretty easy, right? It's not a difficult concept, but it can be a powerful one, as you'll see in a few minutes.

Nested Arrays

Nested arrays are nearly as simple as paired arrays. A nested array is nothing more than an array—in our case, it will be an instance of NSArray—that contains other arrays. A nested array can be used to represent the sections and rows in a table view. You can see a visual representation of this in Figure 4–4. The main array, or **outer array**, contains a series of **subarrays**, each of which represents a section in our table. Each subarray is another instance of NSArray and contains a series of NSString instances, each of which represents a single row in its section.

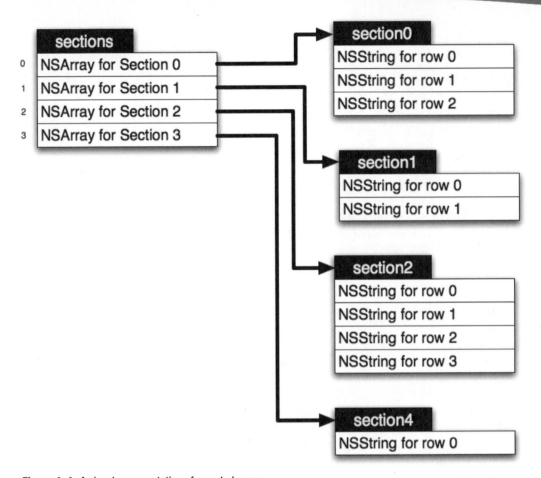

Figure 4–4. *A visual representation of a nested array*

Paired Nested Arrays

We can take these two concepts and combine them. Paired nested arrays are simply nested arrays with the same number of subarrays and where the same index in each subarray corresponds to different information about the same item. Read on to see how we do this.

Representing Our Table Structure with Arrays

Let's use these concepts to represent the structure of our detail view table. The first thing we need is a simple NSArray instance that defines the sections in our table. Each object in this array, which we'll call sectionNames, will be an instance of NSString that represents the section's name, which will be displayed above the section in the table. For sections with no name, we'll use an instance of the class NSNull instead of an NSString to indicate that a section exists, but doesn't have a title.

> **NOTE:** Collection classes like NSArray and NSDictionary cannot contain nil values. NSNull was created specifically as a placeholder for nil. It is an object that can go into collections, but it doesn't really do anything other than take up space. NSNull is implemented as a singleton, which means that there's ever only a single instance of NSNull, but it can be used in as many places as you need.

Next, we need a nested array to hold the name of the attribute that will be displayed in a particular row. We'll call this array rowKeys. Now, we could derive the label to be displayed on each row from the row key. So, for example, if the row key was *name*, we could capitalize it to create a label of *Name*. We're not going to do that, however. To give ourselves more flexibility and the ability to localize our application into other languages, we'll create a second nested array called rowLabels that will hold the label to be displayed on each row next to the attribute value (the words to the left of each field in Figure 4–2).

Finally, we need one last nested array that will contain the name of the controller class that will be used to edit this row's attribute. We'll use Objective-C's dynamic nature to let us create instances at runtime based on the name of a class.

That should be all the data structures we need to represent the table's structure for now. Fortunately, if we discover that we need additional information for each row, we can always add an additional nested array later without impacting our existing design.

Nested Arrays, Categorically Speaking

In order to make our life easier when it comes time to retrieve data from our nested arrays, let's write a category on NSArray that will add two new methods specifically designed for those situations. The first of these methods will take an NSIndexPath and return the corresponding object from the nested subarray. This will allow us, in one line, to retrieve the object we need from any nested array.

In the table view datasource method tableView:cellForRowAtIndexPath:, we'll use this method to turn an NSIndexPath into its corresponding row key and row label. We'll also write a method that returns the count of a specific subarray, which we will later use in tableView:numberOfRowsInSection: to return the correct number of rows for a particular section.

Updating the SuperDB Project

Find your *SuperDB* project folder from Chapter 3 and make a copy of it. That way, if things go south when we add our new code for this chapter, you won't have to start at the very beginning. Open this new copy of your project in Xcode.

Single-click your project's root node (the top row in the *Groups & Files* pane) and select **New Group** from the **Project** menu. This will create a new folder in your *Groups & Files* pane. Rename this new group *Categories*.

Single-click the new *Categories* folder and select **New File…** from the **File** menu. Select *Cocoa Touch Class* from under the *iPhone OS* heading in the left pane, then select the Objective-C Class icon from the upper-right and make sure that the *Subclass of* pop-up menu reads *NSObject*. If you don't see these options, look instead for an icon called *NSObject subclass*. We're not actually going to create a subclass of NSObject, we're going to create a category. Xcode currently has no template for creating a category. We could choose to create two empty files, but since this template will give us both header and implementation files that are already correctly named, we'll choose it and then just delete the code that the template gives us.

Name the new "class" *NSArray-NestedArrays.m* and make sure that *Also create "NSArray-NestedArrays.h"* is checked.

Once the files are created, single-click *NSArray-NestedArrays.h* and replace any existing content with the following category header:

```
#import <Foundation/Foundation.h>

@interface NSArray(NestedArrays)
/**
 This method will return an object contained with an array
 contained within this array. It is intended to allow
 single-step retrieval of objects in the nested array
 using an index path
 */
- (id)nestedObjectAtIndexPath:(NSIndexPath *)indexPath;

/**
 This method will return the count from a subarray.
 */
- (NSInteger)countOfNestedArray:(NSUInteger)section;
@end
```

TIP: Did you notice the format of the comments above each of the methods? This is called **javadoc notation**. There are several tools you can use to automatically create API documentation from your Objective-C code based on class structure and the comments you place in your code using this format, or alternatively, a format called **headerdoc notation**. Apple maintains an open source program called HeaderDoc that will create the documentation for you; there's a third-party tool called Doxygen that can also create API documentation for most popular programming languages, including Objective-C.

Headerdoc can be found here: `http://developer.apple.com/opensource/tools/headerdoc.html`

Doxygen is located here: `http://www.doxygen.org/`

Now, single-click on *NSArray-NestedArrays.m* and replace the contents with the following code:

```
#import "NSArray-NestedArrays.h"

@implementation NSArray(NestedArrays)

- (id)nestedObjectAtIndexPath:(NSIndexPath *)indexPath {
        NSUInteger row = [indexPath row];
        NSUInteger section = [indexPath section];
        NSArray *subArray = [self objectAtIndex:section];

        if (![subArray isKindOfClass:[NSArray class]])
                return nil;

        if (row >= [subArray count])
                return nil;

        return [subArray objectAtIndex:row];
}

- (NSInteger)countOfNestedArray:(NSUInteger)section {
        NSArray *subArray = [self objectAtIndex:section];
        return [subArray count];
}

@end
```

Now, thanks to the chewy goodness of categories, NSArray now has two new methods, nestedObjectAtIndexPath: and countOfNestedArray:.

Formatting of Attributes

One issue with our table-based approach is that we have attributes of different types to display to the user. Although string attributes can just be displayed as is, most other attributes will have to be converted to a string to be displayed in a table.

There are several approaches we can take to format our attributes. We could create a subclass of NSFormatter for each attribute. NSFormatter is a class specifically designed for converting data for display. However, NSFormatter is overkill for our situation. We can find something simpler.

Another approach is to use the description method, which is declared in NSObject. This is the method that gets sent to an object when you use a format string and the %@ token, like this:

```
        NSLog(@"My object value: %@", theObject);
```

In this line of code, which is likely similar to code you've written before, NSLog() sends theObject a description message and replaces the %@ token in the string with the string returned by description.

This method is a good starting point, and it would work for most attribute types. NSNumber, for example, returns the number it represents as a string and NSString simply returns itself. NSDate, however, returns the date it represents like this:

```
2009-09-02 20:28:19 -0400
```

There are two problems with this display. First, it's not all that user-friendly. Most people aren't used to seeing dates displayed like this. The second problem is that this format is too long to fit in the space available using the default table view font.

Instead, we're going to send the attribute objects a custom message called heroValueDisplay. We'll create categories on each of the classes that are used to represent attributes and add a category method that, as needed, formats that attribute's data as a string, formatted exactly the way we want it to be.

Single-click the *Categories* folder in the *Groups & Files* pane and select **New File…** from the **File** menu again.

Select *Cocoa Touch Class* from under the *iPhone OS* heading in the left pane, then select the *Objective-C Class* icon from the upper-right and make sure that the *Subclass of* pop-up menu reads *NSObject*. As with last time, if you don't see these options, look instead for an icon called *NSObject subclass* and select that. When prompted for a name, type *HeroValueDisplay.m* and make sure that *Also create "HeroValueDisplay.h"* is checked.

We're going to put multiple categories into a single file. This is perfectly okay. Although the majority of the time, each class and category is placed into its own header and implementation file pair, there's absolutely no reason why you can't put multiple categories or classes in the same file pair if it make sense and helps organize your project. These categories are all very small and all serve the same purpose, so putting them into a single file pair seems to make sense.

In that file, we're also going to create a protocol that defines the heroValueDisplay method. This will afford us some type safety later when we send the heroValueDisplay message to objects retrieved using objectForKey:.

Single-click *HeroValueDisplay.h* and replace the contents of the file with the following:

```objc
#import <Foundation/Foundation.h>

@protocol HeroValueDisplay
- (NSString *)heroValueDisplay;
@end

@interface NSString (HeroValueDisplay) <HeroValueDisplay>
- (NSString *)heroValueDisplay;
@end

@interface NSDate (HeroValueDisplay) <HeroValueDisplay>
- (NSString *)heroValueDisplay;
@end

@interface NSNumber (HeroValueDisplay) <HeroValueDisplay>
- (NSString *)heroValueDisplay;
```

```
@end

@interface NSDecimalNumber (HeroValueDisplay) <HeroValueDisplay>
- (NSString *)heroValueDisplay;
@end
```

Notice that each of our categories conforms their class to the HeroValueDisplay protocol. Our code that sends the heroValueDisplay message won't know what type of object it's dealing with since the same exact code will handle every row, regardless of the attribute's type. By creating a protocol and conforming all of these objects to that protocol, we'll be able to send this message without getting compiler warnings, as you'll see a little later.

Single-click *HeroValueDisplay.m* and replace the contents with this code:

```
#import "HeroValueDisplay.h"

@implementation NSString (HeroValueDisplay)
- (NSString *)heroValueDisplay {
        return self;
}
@end

@implementation NSDate (HeroValueDisplay)

- (NSString *)heroValueDisplay {
        NSDateFormatter *formatter = [[NSDateFormatter alloc] init];
        [formatter setDateStyle:NSDateFormatterMediumStyle];
        NSString *ret = [formatter stringFromDate:self];
        [formatter release];
        return ret;
}
@end

@implementation NSNumber (HeroValueDisplay)
- (NSString *)heroValueDisplay {
    return [self descriptionWithLocale:[NSLocale currentLocale]];
}
@end

@implementation NSDecimalNumber (HeroValueDisplay)
- (NSString *)heroValueDisplay {
    return [self descriptionWithLocale:[NSLocale currentLocale]];
}
@end
```

With these categories defined, we can send any of our attributes the heroValueDisplay message and show the returned string in the table.

Creating the Detail View Controller

The next file we need to create is the detail view controller itself. Remember that we're creating a table-based editing view, so we want to subclass UITableViewController.

Single-click the *Classes* folder in Xcode's *Groups & Files* pane and type ⌘N to create a new file, which should bring up the new file assistant (Figure 4–5).

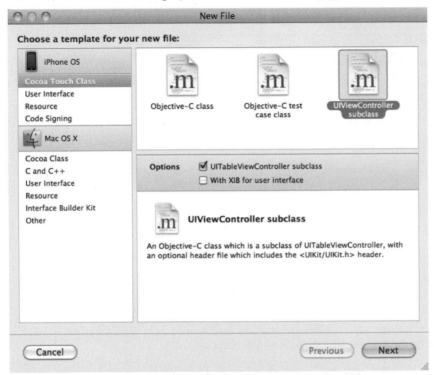

Figure 4–5. *Using the new file assistant to create a new table view controller subclass*

CAUTION: The arrangement of the new file assistant has changed a little in each of the last several releases of the iPhone SDK. As a result, the step-by-step instructions on this page may not exactly match what you need to do if you are on an older release (pre 3.1). You need to create a table view controller subclass. If you don't see those options under *UIViewController*, check under *Objective-C class*. If you are given the opportunity to create an *XIB for user interface* as in the screenshot in Figure 4–5, do not select that option because table view controllers generally don't need a nib file.

Select *Cocoa Touch Class* from under the *iPhone OS* heading in the left pane, then select the *UIViewController subclass*. Make sure the check box labeled *UITableViewController subclass* is checked, but that the *With XIB for user interface* checkbox is not. If you don't see these options, check the previous tech block for more information.

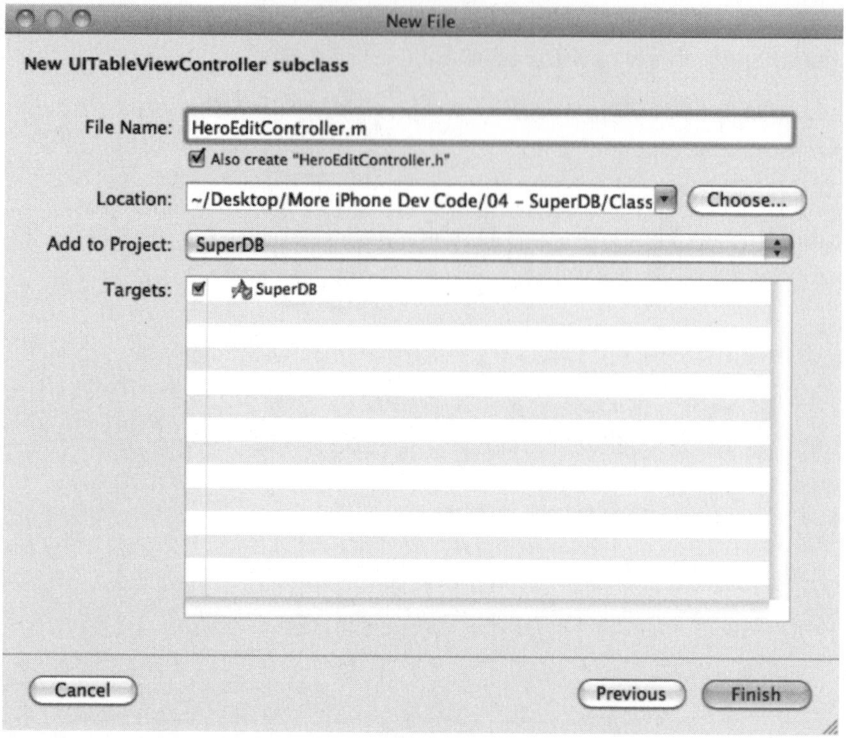

Figure 4–6. *Entering the name for the detail editing view controller class*

When prompted for a filename (Figure 4–6), type in *HeroEditController.m* and make sure that *Also create "HeroEditController.h"* is checked. Once the two new files are created, single-click on *HeroEditController.h* so you can add the necessary instance variables and properties.

Declaring Instance Variables and Properties

Since this editing view will display and allow the editing of a single hero, it needs an NSManagedObject instance variable to hold the hero to be displayed or edited. We also need instance variables to hold the various paired arrays we discussed earlier that define the layout of the table. Make the following changes to *HeroEditController.h*:

```
#import <UIKit/UIKit.h>

@interface HeroEditController : UITableViewController {
    NSManagedObject *hero;

@private
    NSArray          *sectionNames;
    NSArray          *rowLabels;
    NSArray          *rowKeys;
    NSArray          *rowControllers;
}
```

```
@property (nonatomic, retain) NSManagedObject *hero;
@end
```

Notice that we've created five instance variables but only one property. While properties are useful for making memory management easier, they are not always appropriate. In this case, we don't want other objects to be able to change our table structure and there's no real reason why they would ever access these arrays. Therefore, we make them @private and do not declare properties for them, which restricts their use to our class.

You might be wondering why we didn't choose to also make hero a private instance variable. There's nothing particularly sensitive or unusual about this particular instance variable that makes it dangerous and there are valid reasons why a subclass might need to access this directly. The default visibility for instance variables in Objective-C 2.0 is @protected, not @public, so there's really no danger in having hero above the @private. @protected instance variables can be freely accessed by subclasses, but not by other classes, which seems like appropriate behavior.

> **CAUTION:** While the scope limiters @private and @protected are enforced on the iPhone, they are not enforced in the iPhone Simulator. As of this writing, the iPhone Simulator is still a 32-bit Mac application that can't take advantage of all the features of the Objective-C 2.0 runtime. On the simulator, accessing another class's @private or @protected instance variables will result in a compiler warning, but the code will work. On the device, it will not work, and will generate a compiler error instead of a warning. This should serve as just another reason to do something you were going to do anyway (right?), which is to make sure you test your applications thoroughly on a physical device before shipping.

Implementing the Viewing Functionality

We're going to approach the implementation of our controller in two stages. First, we're going to make sure the controller displays its information correctly, then we're going to implement editing.

Single-click on *HeroEditController.m*. The template we chose gave us a lot of stubs and commented-out code. Rather than try to give you instructions on how to make changes to the existing file, just delete the code that the template provided and replace it with this:

```
#import "HeroEditController.h"
#import "NSArray-NestedArrays.h"
#import "HeroValueDisplay.h"

@implementation HeroEditController
@synthesize hero;
```

```objc
- (void)viewDidLoad {
    sectionNames = [[NSArray alloc] initWithObjects:
        [NSNull null],
        NSLocalizedString(@"General", @"General"),
        nil];
    rowLabels = [[NSArray alloc] initWithObjects:

        // Section 1
        [NSArray arrayWithObjects:NSLocalizedString(@"Name", @"Name"), nil],

        // Section 2
        [NSArray arrayWithObjects:NSLocalizedString(@"Identity", @"Identity"),
        NSLocalizedString(@"Birthdate", @"Birthdate"),
        NSLocalizedString(@"Sex", @"Sex"),
        nil],

        // Sentinel
        nil];

    rowKeys = [[NSArray alloc] initWithObjects:

        // Section 1
        [NSArray arrayWithObjects:@"name", nil],

        // Section 2
        [NSArray arrayWithObjects:@"secretIdentity", @"birthdate", @"sex", nil],

      // Sentinel
        nil];

    // TODO: Populate the rowControllers array

    [super viewDidLoad];
}

- (void)dealloc {
    [hero release];
    [sectionNames release];
    [rowLabels release];
    [rowKeys release];
    [rowControllers release];
    [super dealloc];
}

#pragma mark -
#pragma mark Table View Methods
- (NSInteger)numberOfSectionsInTableView:(UITableView *)theTableView {
    return [sectionNames count];
}

- (NSString *)tableView:(UITableView *)theTableView
titleForHeaderInSection:(NSInteger)section {
    id theTitle = [sectionNames objectAtIndex:section];
    if ([theTitle isKindOfClass:[NSNull class]])
        return nil;

    return theTitle;
```

```
}

- (NSInteger)tableView:(UITableView *)theTableView
numberOfRowsInSection:(NSInteger)section {
    return [rowLabels countOfNestedArray:section];
}

- (UITableViewCell *)tableView:(UITableView *)theTableView
cellForRowAtIndexPath:(NSIndexPath *)indexPath {

    static NSString *CellIdentifier = @"Hero Edit Cell Identifier";

    UITableViewCell *cell = [theTableView
        dequeueReusableCellWithIdentifier:CellIdentifier];
    if (cell == nil) {
        cell = [[[UITableViewCell alloc] initWithStyle:UITableViewCellStyleValue2
            reuseIdentifier:CellIdentifier] autorelease];
    }

    NSString *rowKey = [rowKeys nestedObjectAtIndexPath:indexPath];
    NSString *rowLabel = [rowLabels nestedObjectAtIndexPath:indexPath];

    id <HeroValueDisplay, NSObject> rowValue = [hero valueForKey:rowKey];

    cell.detailTextLabel.text = [rowValue heroValueDisplay];
    cell.textLabel.text = rowLabel;
    cell.accessoryType = UITableViewCellAccessoryDisclosureIndicator;
    return cell;
}

- (void)tableView:(UITableView *)theTableView
didSelectRowAtIndexPath:(NSIndexPath *)indexPath {
    // TODO: Push editing controller onto the stack.
}

@end
```

Let's take a look at the code we just wrote. Notice first that we import both of the categories we created earlier. If we don't import the category headers, the compiler doesn't know that those methods exist and will give us compile warnings. We also synthesize our only property:

```
#import "HeroEditController.h"
#import "NSArray-NestedArrays.h"
#import "HeroValueDisplay.h"
@implementation HeroEditController
@synthesize hero;
```

Next comes viewDidLoad. In this method, we create and populate those various arrays we discussed earlier that will define the structure of our tables. For now, we're just going to create the arrays here in code. If our table gets more complex, we might want to consider putting the contents of the arrays into property lists or text files and creating the arrays from those files rather than hardcoding them as we've done here. That would reduce the size and complexity of our controller class. At this point, there doesn't seem to be much benefit to doing that. One of the nice things about this approach is that since the arrays' contents drive the table structure and the rest of the code in this controller class is relatively generic, we can change how we create our arrays without impacting the functionality of the rest of the code in this controller.

The first array we populate is the sectionNames array. Notice that because we are not using a property, we don't have an accessor. Since we're not using an accessor that will retain the instance for us, we don't release it. After this line of code, sectionNames has a retain count of 1, which is exactly what it would be if we assigned it to a property specified with the retain keyword, and then released it after making the assignment.

```
- (void)viewDidLoad {
    sectionNames = [[NSArray alloc] initWithObjects:
        [NSNull null],
        NSLocalizedString(@"General", @"General"),
        nil];
```

> **TIP:** Notice that we pass a nil as the last parameter to initWithObjects:. This is important. initWithObjects: is a **variadic** method, which is just a fancy way of saying it takes a variable number of arguments. We can pass in any number of objects to this method, and they will all get added to this array. The terminating nil is how we tell the initWithObjects: method that we've got not more objects for it. This terminating nil is called a **sentinel**. Starting with Snow Leopard, Xcode will warn you if you forget the sentinel, but on Leopard, a missing sentinel can be a very hard-to-debug problem.

After this line of code fires, sectionNames has two elements. The first one is that special placeholder, NSNull, we talked about. If you look at Figure 4–2, you can see that the first section has no header. This is how we're going to indicate that there's a section, but that it doesn't have a header. The second object in the array is a localized string that contains the word "General." By creating a localized string, we have the ability to translate this header into whatever languages we wish. If you need a refresher on localizing your apps, the topic is covered in Chapter 17 of *Beginning iPhone 3 Development*.

Next, we populate the rowLabels array. This is the array that defines the blue labels displayed on each row that you can see in Figure 4–2. Notice again, that we've used localized strings so that if we want to later translate our labels into other languages, we have the ability to do so without having to change our code. Because we've got nested object creation here, we've added comments so that when we revisit this somewhat complex code, we'll remember what each bit of code is used for.

```
    rowLabels = [[NSArray alloc] initWithObjects:

        // Section 1
        [NSArray arrayWithObjects:NSLocalizedString(@"Name", @"Name"), nil],

        // Section 2
        [NSArray arrayWithObjects:NSLocalizedString(@"Identity", @"Identity"),
        NSLocalizedString(@"Birthdate", @"Birthdate"),
        NSLocalizedString(@"Sex", @"Sex"),
        nil],
```

```
    // Sentinel
    nil];
```

The code that populates the rowKeys array is very similar, except we don't localize the strings. These are key values that are used to indicate which attribute gets shown in which row, and localizing them would break the functionality. The key is the same regardless of the language our user understands.

```
rowKeys = [[NSArray alloc] initWithObjects:

    // Section 1
    [NSArray arrayWithObjects:@"name", nil],

    // Section 2
    [NSArray arrayWithObjects:@"secretIdentity",
        @"birthdate",
        @"sex",
        nil],

    // Sentinel
    nil];
```

We have one more array, but we're not populating it yet. The last array defines which controller classes are used to edit which rows. We haven't written any such controller classes yet, so we've got nothing to put in that array. We're also not yet accessing this array anywhere, so it's okay to just put in a reminder to do it later. As you've already seen, when developing more complex applications, you will often have to implement some functionality in an incomplete manner and then come back later to finish it.

```
    // TODO: Populate the rowControllers array

    [super viewDidLoad];
}
```

The next method we implemented was dealloc, and there shouldn't be anything too surprising here. We release all of the objects that we've retained, both those that are associated with properties, and those that aren't. Remember, in viewDidLoad, we left our various structure arrays at a retain count of 1, so we have to release them here to avoid leaking memory.

```
- (void)dealloc {
    [hero release];
    [sectionNames release];
    [rowLabels release];
    [rowKeys release];
    [rowControllers release];
    [super dealloc];
}
```

Even though we haven't yet created or populated rowControllers, it's perfectly okay to release it here. Sending a release message to nil is just fine and dandy in Objective-C.

Next up are the table view datasource methods. The first one we implement tells our table view how many sections we have. We return the count from sectionNames here. By doing that, if we change the number of objects in the sectionNames array, we automatically change the number of sections in the table and don't have to touch this method.

```
#pragma mark -
#pragma mark Table View Methods

- (NSInteger)numberOfSectionsInTableView:(UITableView *)theTableView {
    return [sectionNames count];
}
```

Since sections have an optional header displayed, we also implement `tableView:titleForHeaderInSection:`. For this, we just need to return the value from `sectionNames`. If the value NSNull is stored as a section name, we need to convert it to nil, since that's what UITableView expects for a section with no header.

```
- (NSString *)tableView:(UITableView *)theTableView
titleForHeaderInSection:(NSInteger)section {
    id theTitle = [sectionNames objectAtIndex:section];
    if ([theTitle isKindOfClass:[NSNull class]])
        return nil;

    return theTitle;
}
```

In addition to telling our table view the number of sections, we need to tell it the number of rows in each section. Thanks to that category on `NSArray` we wrote earlier, this can be handled with one line of code. It doesn't matter which of the paired arrays we use, since they should all have the same number of rows in every subarray. We obviously can't use `rowControllers`, since we haven't populated it yet. We chose `rowLabels`, but `rowKeys` would have worked exactly the same.

```
- (NSInteger)tableView:(UITableView *)theTableView
numberOfRowsInSection:(NSInteger)section {
    return [rowLabels countOfNestedArray:section];
}
```

The `tableView:cellForRowAtIndexPath:` method is where we actually create the cell to be displayed. We start out almost exactly in the same way as every other table view controller, by looking for a dequeued cell and using it, or creating a new cell if there aren't any dequeued cells.

```
- (UITableViewCell *)tableView:(UITableView *)theTableView
cellForRowAtIndexPath:(NSIndexPath *)indexPath {

    static NSString *CellIdentifier = @"Hero Edit Cell Identifier";

    UITableViewCell *cell = [theTableView
        dequeueReusableCellWithIdentifier:CellIdentifier];
    if (cell == nil) {
        cell = [[[UITableViewCell alloc] initWithStyle:UITableViewCellStyleValue2
            reuseIdentifier:CellIdentifier] autorelease];
    }
```

Next, we retrieve the attribute name and the label for this row, again using that category method we added to `NSArray` to retrieve the correct object based on index path.

```
    NSString *rowKey = [rowKeys nestedObjectAtIndexPath:indexPath];
```

```
    NSString *rowLabel = [rowLabels nestedObjectAtIndexPath:indexPath];
```

Once we know the attribute name, we can retrieve the object that's used to represent this attribute using valueForKey:. Notice that we declare our rowValue object as id. We do this because the returned object could be instances of any number of different classes. We put HeroValueDisplay between angle brackets to indicate that we know the returned object will be an object that conforms to that HeroValueDisplay protocol we created earlier. This gives us the ability to call the heroValueDisplay method on whatever was returned without having to figure out what type of object it was.

```
    id <HeroValueDisplay, NSObject> rowValue = [hero valueForKey:rowKey];
```

Finally, we assign the label and value to the cell's labels, and then return the cell.

```
    cell.detailTextLabel.text = [rowValue heroValueDisplay];
    cell.textLabel.text = rowLabel;
    cell.accessoryType = UITableViewCellAccessoryDisclosureIndicator;
    return cell;
}
```

The final method in our controller class is just a stub with a reminder to add this functionality later.

```
- (void)tableView:(UITableView *)theTableView
didSelectRowAtIndexPath:(NSIndexPath *)indexPath {
    // TODO: Push editing controller onto the stack.
}
```

```
@end
```

Using the New Controller

Now that we have our new controller class, we have to create instances of it somewhere and push those onto the stack. To do that, we have to revisit HeroListViewController. We could create a new instance of HeroEditController every time a row is tapped. Only one copy of HeroEditController will ever need to be on the navigation stack at a time. As a result, we can reuse a single instance over and over. We can also save ourselves several lines of code by adding an instance of HeroEditController to *MainWindow.xib* and adding an outlet to that instance to HeroListViewController. Remember, when you add an icon to a nib, an instance of that object gets created when the nib loads.

Declaring the Outlet

Single-click *HeroListViewController.h*, and add the following code to add an outlet for the instance of *HeroEditController* we're going to add to *MainWindow.xib*:

```
#import <UIKit/UIKit.h>

#define kSelectedTabDefaultsKey @"Selected Tab"
enum {
    kByName = 0,
```

```
        kBySecretIdentity,
};

@class HeroEditController;
@interface HeroListViewController : UIViewController  <UITableViewDelegate,
UITableViewDataSource, UITabBarDelegate, UIAlertViewDelegate,
NSFetchedResultsControllerDelegate>{

    UITableView *tableView;
    UITabBar    *tabBar;
    HeroEditController *detailController;

@private
    NSFetchedResultsController *_fetchedResultsController;
}

@property (nonatomic, retain) IBOutlet UITableView *tableView;
@property (nonatomic, retain) IBOutlet UITabBar *tabBar;
@property (nonatomic, retain) IBOutlet HeroEditController *detailController;
@property (nonatomic, readonly) NSFetchedResultsController
    *fetchedResultsController;
- (void)addHero;
- (IBAction)toggleEdit;

@end
```

Now that we've got it declared, save *HeroListViewController.h*, and we'll go add the instance to *MainWindow.xib*.

Adding the Instance to MainWindow.xib

Double-click on *MainWindow.xib* to open the nib file in Interface Builder. Look in the library for a *Table View Controller*, and drag one of those over to the nib's main window. The newly added controller should be selected, so press ⌘4 to bring up the identity inspector and change the underlying class from *UITableViewController* to *HeroEditController*.

Next, in the main nib window, click on the *Hero Edit Controller* disclosure triangle and double-click on the *Table View* that appears. Alternatively, you can just click in the Hero Edit Controller window so the Table View shown in that window is selected. Now, press ⌘1 to bring up the attribute inspector. You'll know you've got the right item selected when the inspector window's title changes from *Hero Edit Controller Attributes* to *Table View Attributes*. Change the table's *Style* from *Plain* to *Grouped*.

Back in the main nib window, open the disclosure triangle to the left of *Navigation Controller* to reveal an item named *Hero List View Controller (Root View Controller)*. Control-drag from that item to the *Hero Edit Controller* icon and select the *detailController* outlet.

> **NOTE:** Note that your *Hero List View Controller (Root View Controller)* might instead have the name *Hero List View Controller (SuperDB)*. No worries, it should work just fine.

Save and close this nib and go back to Xcode.

Pushing the New Instance onto the Stack

Single-click *HeroListViewController.m*. There are two methods that we need to implement. When a user taps a row, we want to use the detail controller to show them information about the hero on which they tapped. When they add a new hero, we also want to take them down to the newly added hero so they can edit it. We haven't implemented the editing functionality yet, but we can still configure and push detailController onto the stack now, so let's do that.

First, we need to import *HeroEditController.h* and synthesize the detailController outlet:

```
#import "HeroListViewController.h"
#import "SuperDBAppDelegate.h"
#import "HeroEditController.h"

@implementation HeroListViewController
@synthesize tableView;
@synthesize tabBar;
@synthesize detailController;
@synthesize fetchedResultsController = _fetchedResultsController;
...
```

Now, find the addHero method, and add the following new code to it. You can also delete the old TODO comment.

```
- (void)addHero {
    NSManagedObjectContext *context = [self.fetchedResultsController
        managedObjectContext];
    NSEntityDescription *entity = [[self.fetchedResultsController fetchRequest]
        entity];
    NSManagedObject *newManagedObject = [NSEntityDescription
        insertNewObjectForEntityForName:[entity name] inManagedObjectContext:context];

    NSError *error;
    if (![context save:&error])
        NSLog(@"Error saving entity: %@", [error localizedDescription]);

    // TODO: Instantiate detail editing controller and push onto stack
    detailController.hero = newManagedObject;
    [self.navigationController pushViewController:detailController animated:YES];
}
```

We assign the new managed object to detailController's hero property, which is how we tell that controller that this is the hero to be viewed and/or edited. Then, we push it onto the stack. Easy enough?

Now, find tableView:didSelectRowAtIndexPath:. It should just be a stub with a TODO comment. Replace it with this new version:

```
- (void)tableView:(UITableView *)theTableView
didSelectRowAtIndexPath:(NSIndexPath *)indexPath {
    detailController.hero = [self.fetchedResultsController
        objectAtIndexPath:indexPath];
    [self.navigationController pushViewController:detailController animated:YES];
    [theTableView deselectRowAtIndexPath:indexPath animated:YES];
}
```

That should look pretty familiar. We're doing almost the same thing, except instead of pushing a new managed object onto the stack, we're retrieving the object that corresponds to the row on which the user tapped.

Trying Out the View Functionality

Save *HeroListViewController.m* and then build and run your application. Try adding new rows, or tapping on an existing row. You still don't have the ability to edit them, but when you add a new row, you should get a new screen of data that looks like Figure 4–7.

Figure 4–7. *Adding a new hero now takes you to the new controller class*

All that's missing is the ability to edit the individual fields, so let's add that now.

Adding Editing Subcontrollers

Our next step is to create a series of new controllers, each of which can be used to edit an individual value on a hero. For now, we need one that can edit string attributes (Figure 4–8) and one that can edit date attributes (Figure 4–9). We'll be adding other controllers later. All of these controllers have common functionality. They'll all take a managed object and the name of the attribute on that managed object to be edited. They'll all need a *Save* button and a *Cancel* button.

Figure 4–8. *The subcontroller that will allow the user to edit string attributes. Here, it's being used to edit the* name *attribute.*

Figure 4–9. *The subcontroller that allows editing date attributes. Here, it's being used to edit the birthdate attribute.*

Creating the Superclass

Whenever you are about to implement multiple objects that have some common functionality, you should put some thought into whether that common functionality can be put into a single class that the other controllers can then subclass. In this case, there is enough common functionality that a common superclass is appropriate. Let's create that common superclass now.

Single-click the *Classes* folder in the *Groups & Files* pane and select **New File…** from the **File** menu. Create another UITableViewController subclass, as you did earlier when you created the HeroEditController class. Call this new class *ManagedObjectAttributeEditor* and make sure you create both the implementation and header file but do *not* create a nib file.

Single-click *ManagedObjectAttributeEditor.h*, and replace the contents with this code:

```
#import <UIKit/UIKit.h>
#define kNonEditableTextColor    [UIColor colorWithRed:.318 green:0.4 blue:.569 ↵
alpha:1.0]

@interface ManagedObjectAttributeEditor : UITableViewController {
    NSManagedObject        *managedObject;
    NSString               *keypath;
    NSString               *labelString;
}
```

```
@property (nonatomic, retain) NSManagedObject *managedObject;
@property (nonatomic, retain) NSString *keypath;
@property (nonatomic, retain) NSString *labelString;
-(IBAction)cancel;
-(IBAction)save;

@end
```

> **TIP:** Wondering about that funky looking arrow (◄─) at the end of the #define in the previous chunk of code? That's a continuation character. Don't type it! It just means that the current line and the following line should be joined together as a single line.

The constant kNonEditableTextColor is defined to match the color used in the table view cell style UITableViewCellStyleValue2. We can't use the default cell styles and let the user edit values using a text field, but we want to match the appearance as closely as we can (Figure 4–8).

We could have called the managedObject attribute hero instead, but by using more generic terms, it'll be easier to reuse this code in future projects. Having a property called hero wouldn't make much sense if we were writing an application to keep track of recipes, for example.

Instead of attribute name, we've defined a property called keypath. This will be the attribute name, but by using keypath instead of key, we'll have the ability to edit attributes on other objects, not just on the one we're editing. Don't worry if that doesn't make much sense now; you'll see why we chose keypath instead of attribute or key in Chapter 7 when we start talking about relationships and fetched properties. We've also provided a property for a label. Not all subclasses will need this, but many will, so we'll provide the instance variable and property definition here in our superclass.

We also define two methods, cancel and save, that will be called when the user presses either of the buttons that will be presented. Switch over to *ManagedObjectAttributeEditor.m* and replace the existing contents with the following code:

```
#import "ManagedObjectAttributeEditor.h"

@implementation ManagedObjectAttributeEditor
@synthesize managedObject;
@synthesize keypath;
@synthesize labelString;

- (void)viewWillAppear:(BOOL)animated  {
    UIBarButtonItem *cancelButton = [[UIBarButtonItem alloc]
        initWithTitle:NSLocalizedString(@"Cancel",
            @"Cancel - for button to cancel changes")
        style:UIBarButtonSystemItemCancel
        target:self
        action:@selector(cancel)];
    self.navigationItem.leftBarButtonItem = cancelButton;
    [cancelButton release];
    UIBarButtonItem *saveButton = [[UIBarButtonItem alloc]
        initWithTitle:NSLocalizedString(@"Save",
```

```
                @"Save - for button to save changes")
            style:UIBarButtonItemStyleDone
            target:self
            action:@selector(save)];
        self.navigationItem.rightBarButtonItem = saveButton;
        [saveButton release];
        [super viewWillAppear:animated];
    }

    -(IBAction)cancel {
        [self.navigationController popViewControllerAnimated:YES];
    }

    -(IBAction)save {
        // Objective-C has no support for abstract methods, so we're going
        // to take matters into our own hands.
        NSException *ex = [NSException exceptionWithName:
                @"Abstract Method Not Overridden"
            reason:NSLocalizedString(@"You MUST override the save method",
                @"You MUST override the save method")
            userInfo:nil];
        [ex raise];
    }

    -(void)dealloc {
        [managedObject release];
        [keypath release];
        [labelString release];
        [super dealloc];
    }

    @end
```

Much of this should make sense to you, but there are a few things that warrant explanation. In the viewWillAppear: method, we are creating two bar button items to go in the navigation bar. You can see these two buttons, labeled *Cancel* and *Save*, in Figure 4–8.

Bar button items are similar to standard controls like UIButtons, but they are a special case, designed to be used on navigation bars and toolbars only. One key difference between a bar button item and a regular UIButton is that bar button items only have one target and action. They don't recognize the concept of control events. Bar button items send their message on the equivalent of *touch up inside* only. Here's where we create the *Cancel* button. The code that creates the *Save* button is nearly identical:

```
    UIBarButtonItem *cancelButton = [[UIBarButtonItem alloc]
        initWithTitle:NSLocalizedString(@"Cancel",
            @"Cancel - for button to cancel changes")
        style:UIBarButtonSystemItemCancel
        target:self
        action:@selector(cancel)];
    self.navigationItem.leftBarButtonItem = cancelButton;
    [cancelButton release];
```

When we create the button, notice that we're once again using the NSLocalizedString macro to make sure that any text to be displayed to the user can be translated. There are several bar button styles, including one intended for *Cancel* buttons called UIBarButtonSystemItemCancel, which we've used here.

We also have to provide a target and action for the bar button item. The target is self, because we want it to call a method on the instance of this controller that is active. The action is a selector to one of those action methods we declared in the header file. Setting a target and action like this is exactly equivalent to control-dragging from a button to a controller class and selecting an action method, we're just doing it in code this time because we don't have a nib.

The cancel method does nothing more than pop the subcontroller off the navigation stack, which returns the user to the previous screen. In this case, it will return them to the detail view for the hero. Since we don't take any steps to capture the input from the user, the managed object stays the same as it was before.

> **NOTE:** Strictly speaking, the save and cancel methods do not need to be declared with the IBAction keyword, since we're not triggering those methods from a nib. They are, however, action methods, and it is conceivable that at some point in the future, we could convert this controller to using a nib file, so we declare both of the action methods with the IBAction keyword just to be safe and to advertise that these are, indeed, methods that will be triggered by user interface controls.

The save method is a little unusual here. We will never actually create an instance of this class. We're creating this class only to contain common functionality that we expect to exist among classes we're going to write. In most languages, we would define this as an abstract class. But Objective-C doesn't have abstract classes, and it doesn't have a mechanism to force a subclass to implement a given method. Therefore, just to be safe, we throw an exception in our save method. That way, if we ever forget to implement save in a subclass we create, we'll know about it instantly. Instead of unpredictable behavior, we'll get slammed with a runtime exception. While that may be a little unpleasant when it happens, it will be very easy to debug because our exception will tell us exactly what we did wrong.

```
NSException *ex = [NSException exceptionWithName:
        @"Abstract Method Not Overridden"
    reason:NSLocalizedString(@"You MUST override the save method",
        @"You MUST override the save method")
    userInfo:nil];
[ex raise];
```

> **CAUTION:** Objective-C does have exceptions, as you can see here. Objective-C does not use exceptions the way many other languages, such as Java and C++, do. In Objective-C, exceptions are used only for truly exceptional situations and are usually an indication of a problem within your code. They should never be used just to report a run-of-the-mill error condition. Exceptions are used with much less frequency in Objective-C then they are in many other languages.

Creating the String Attribute Editor

Now it's time to create a generic controller class to handle the editing of string attributes. Single-click on *Classes* and create a new implementation and header file pair. Just as you did before, create a subclass of `UITableViewController` and do *not* create a nib file. Name the class *ManagedObjectStringEditor*. Single-click *ManagedObjectStringEditor.h*, and replace the contents with the following code:

```
#import <UIKit/UIKit.h>
#import "ManagedObjectAttributeEditor.h"

#define kLabelTag        1
#define kTextFieldTag    2

@interface ManagedObjectStringEditor : ManagedObjectAttributeEditor {
}

@end
```

As you can see, we're not adding any additional properties or instance variables. We do change the subclass to `ManagedObjectAttributeEditor` so that we inherit the functionality we implemented there, and we also define two constants that will be used in a moment to let us retrieve subviews from the table view cell. The default table view cell styles don't allow in-place editing, so we have to customize the contents of our cell. Since we don't have a nib, we don't have a way to connect outlets, so instead of using outlets, we'll assign tags to each of the subviews we add to the table view cell, and then we'll use that tag later to retrieve them.

Save *ManagedObjectStringEditor.h* and switch over to *ManagedObjectStringEditor.m*. Replace the contents of that file with this code:

```
#import "ManagedObjectStringEditor.h"

@implementation ManagedObjectStringEditor

#pragma mark -
#pragma mark Table View methods
- (NSInteger)tableView:(UITableView *)tableView
        numberOfRowsInSection:(NSInteger)section {
    return 1;
}

- (UITableViewCell *)tableView:(UITableView *)tableView
        cellForRowAtIndexPath:(NSIndexPath *)indexPath {
    static NSString *ManagedObjectStringEditorCell =
    @"ManagedObjectStringEditorCell";

    UITableViewCell *cell = [tableView dequeueReusableCellWithIdentifier:
        ManagedObjectStringEditorCell];
    if (cell == nil) {
        cell = [[[UITableViewCell alloc] initWithStyle:UITableViewCellStyleDefault
            reuseIdentifier:ManagedObjectStringEditorCell] autorelease];

        UILabel *label = [[UILabel alloc] initWithFrame:CGRectMake(10, 10, 80, 25)];
        label.textAlignment = UITextAlignmentRight;
```

```objc
        label.tag = kLabelTag;
        UIFont *font = [UIFont boldSystemFontOfSize:14.0];
        label.textColor = kNonEditableTextColor;
        label.font = font;
        [cell.contentView addSubview:label];
        [label release];

        UITextField *theTextField = [[UITextField alloc]
                                initWithFrame:CGRectMake(100, 10, 190, 25)];

        [cell.contentView addSubview:theTextField];
        theTextField.tag = kTextFieldTag;
        [theTextField release];
    }
    UILabel *label = (UILabel *)[cell.contentView viewWithTag:kLabelTag];

    label.text = labelString;
    UITextField *textField = (UITextField *)[cell.contentView
                                        viewWithTag:kTextFieldTag];
    NSString *currentValue = [self.managedObject valueForKeyPath:self.keypath];

    NSEntityDescription *ed = [self.managedObject entity];
    NSDictionary *properties = [ed propertiesByName];
    NSAttributeDescription *ad = [properties objectForKey:self.keypath];
    NSString *defaultValue = nil;
    if (ad != nil)
        defaultValue = [ad defaultValue];
    if (![currentValue isEqualToString:defaultValue])
        textField.text =  currentValue;

    [textField becomeFirstResponder];
    return cell;
}

- (void)tableView:(UITableView *)tableView didSelectRowAtIndexPath:
        (NSIndexPath *)indexPath {
    [tableView deselectRowAtIndexPath:indexPath animated:YES];
}

-(IBAction)save {
    NSUInteger onlyRow[] = {0, 0};
    NSIndexPath *onlyRowPath = [NSIndexPath indexPathWithIndexes:onlyRow length:2];
    UITableViewCell *cell = [self.tableView cellForRowAtIndexPath:onlyRowPath];
    UITextField *textField = (UITextField *)[cell.contentView
                                        viewWithTag:kTextFieldTag];
    [self.managedObject setValue:textField.text forKey:self.keypath];

    NSError *error;
    if (![managedObject.managedObjectContext save:&error])
        NSLog(@"Error saving: %@", [error localizedDescription]);

    [self.navigationController popViewControllerAnimated:YES];
}

@end
```

Almost everything we do in this class is covered in Chapters 8 and 9 of *Beginning iPhone 3 Development*, but there's some code in `tableView:cellForRowAtIndexPath:` that is worth taking a look at. We've set default values for two of our attributes because they were required fields. When the user taps one of those rows, they aren't going to want to have to delete the default value before typing in the new value. So, we've added some code to check to see if the current value is the same as the default value and, if it is, we tell the text field to clear on editing.

Here's the code from `tableView:cellForRowAtIndexPath:` that does that. First, we grab the current value held by the attribute.

```
NSString *currentValue = [self.managedObject valueForKeyPath:self.keypath];
```

Next, we grab the managed object's entity. Information about an entity is returned in an NSEntityDescription instance:

```
NSEntityDescription *ed = [self.managedObject entity];
```

We can retrieve a dictionary with the properties, which includes attributes, by calling propertiesByName on the entity description.

```
NSDictionary *properties = [ed propertiesByName];
```

We can retrieve the NSAttributeDescription that stores information about the attribute we're editing from that dictionary using key-value coding:

```
NSAttributeDescription *ad = [properties objectForKey:self.keypath];
```

One piece of information that the attribute description holds is its default value, if any, so we retrieve the default value.

```
NSString *defaultValue = nil;
if (ad != nil)
    defaultValue = [ad defaultValue];
```

Once we have the default value, we compare it to the current value. If they're not the same, then we set the text field's value. If they are the same, then we won't bother populating the text field with the current value because we know they're going to change it.

```
if (![currentValue isEqualToString:defaultValue])
    textField.text =  currentValue;
```

> **NOTE:** Little details like not making your users spend time deleting default values can make the difference between a good application and a great one. Don't expect to anticipate every possible detail in advance, however. These are the kind of things that often don't become obvious until you start testing and actually using the application, but when they become apparent, make sure you deal with them. Annoying customers is not a good strategy.

You should also notice that we implement the save method, overriding the one in our superclass, which throws an exception. Looking at that save method, you might also be wondering if we made a mistake in this controller. In *Beginning iPhone 3 Development*, we warned against relying on controls on table view cells to maintain state for you, since cells can get dequeued and reused to represent a different row. Yet we are doing just that here. We are relying on a text field on a table view cell to keep track of the changes the user has made to the attribute until they tap *Save*, at which point, we copy the value from the text field back into the attribute. In this particular case, we know that there will always be exactly one row in this table. Since a table view is always capable of displaying one row, this cell can never get dequeued. That makes this scenario an exception to the general rule that you shouldn't rely on table view cells to maintain state for you.

Creating the Date Attribute Editor

Create yet another table view subclass, this time calling the class *ManagedObjectDateEditor*. Once you've created the file, single-click on *ManagedObjectDateEditor.h* and replace the contents with the following code:

```
#import <Foundation/Foundation.h>
#import "ManagedObjectAttributeEditor.h"

@interface ManagedObjectDateEditor : ManagedObjectAttributeEditor {
    UIDatePicker    *datePicker;
    UITableView     *dateTableView;
}

@property (nonatomic, retain) UIDatePicker *datePicker;
@property (nonatomic, retain) UITableView *dateTableView;

- (IBAction)dateChanged;

@end
```

The controller for editing dates is slightly more complex than the one for editing a string. If you look at Figure 4–9, you'll see that there is a text field that displays the current value, and there is also a date picker that can be used to change the date.

Save *ManagedObjectDateEditor.h* then single-click *ManagedObjectDateEditor.m* and replace its contents with the following code:

```
#import "ManagedObjectDateEditor.h"

@implementation ManagedObjectDateEditor
@synthesize datePicker;
@synthesize dateTableView;

- (IBAction)dateChanged {
    [self.dateTableView reloadData];
}

#pragma mark -
#pragma mark Superclass Overrides
-(IBAction)save {
    [self.managedObject setValue:self.datePicker.date forKey:self.keypath];
```

```objc
        NSError *error;
        if (![managedObject.managedObjectContext save:&error])
            NSLog(@"Error saving: %@", [error localizedDescription]);

        [self.navigationController popViewControllerAnimated:YES];
    }

- (void)loadView {
    [super loadView];

    UIView *theView = [[UIView alloc] initWithFrame:[[UIScreen mainScreen] bounds]];
    self.view = theView;
    [theView release];

    UITableView *theTableView = [[UITableView alloc] initWithFrame:
        CGRectMake(0.0, 67.0, 320.0, 480.0) style:UITableViewStyleGrouped];
    theTableView.delegate = self;
    theTableView.dataSource = self;
    [self.view addSubview:theTableView];
    self.dateTableView = theTableView;
    [theTableView release];

    UIDatePicker *theDatePicker = [[UIDatePicker alloc]
        initWithFrame:CGRectMake(0.0, 200.0, 320.0, 216.0)];
    theDatePicker.datePickerMode = UIDatePickerModeDate;
    self.datePicker = theDatePicker;
    [theDatePicker release];
    [datePicker addTarget:self action:@selector(dateChanged)
        forControlEvents:UIControlEventValueChanged];
    [self.view addSubview:datePicker];
    self.view.backgroundColor = [UIColor groupTableViewBackgroundColor];
}

- (void)viewWillAppear:(BOOL)animated {
    if ([managedObject valueForKeyPath:self.keypath] != nil)
        [self.datePicker setDate:[managedObject
            valueForKeyPath:keypath] animated:YES];
    else
        [self.datePicker setDate:[NSDate date] animated:YES];
    [self.tableView reloadData];

    [super viewWillAppear:animated];
}

-(void)dealloc {
    [datePicker release];
    [dateTableView release];
    [super dealloc];
}

#pragma mark -
#pragma mark Table View Methods
- (NSInteger)tableView:(UITableView *)tableView numberOfRowsInSection:(NSInteger)section
{
        return 1;
}
```

```
- (UITableViewCell *)tableView:(UITableView *)tableView
        cellForRowAtIndexPath:(NSIndexPath *)indexPath {
    static NSString *GenericManagedObjectDateEditorCell =
    @"GenericManagedObjectDateEditorCell";

    UITableViewCell *cell = [tableView dequeueReusableCellWithIdentifier:
        GenericManagedObjectDateEditorCell];
    if (cell == nil)
    {
        cell = [[[UITableViewCell alloc] initWithStyle:UITableViewCellStyleDefault
            reuseIdentifier:GenericManagedObjectDateEditorCell] autorelease];
        cell.textLabel.font = [UIFont systemFontOfSize:17.0];
        cell.textLabel.textColor = [UIColor colorWithRed:0.243 green:0.306
                                                    blue:0.435 alpha:1.0];
    }
    NSDateFormatter *formatter = [[NSDateFormatter alloc] init];
    [formatter setDateStyle:NSDateFormatterMediumStyle];
    cell.textLabel.text = [formatter stringFromDate:[self.datePicker date]];
    [formatter release];

    return cell;
}
@end
```

Most of what's going on in this class should be familiar to you. The one thing that's somewhat strange with this is how we've implemented the date picker view. If we had just created a UIDatePicker and added it as a subview of our table view, then the picker would have scrolled with the table and been unusable. Instead, we use loadView, which is used to create a user interface programmatically, and we create both a UIDatePicker and a second UITableView. We make both of these new objects subviews of our view property. This controller is actually modeled after the way that Apple's Contacts application accepts date inputs (Figure 4–10).

Figure 4–10. *When you add a date field to a person's record in the Contacts application, this is the screen. Our date editing view controller recreates, pixel-for-pixel, this view.*

Using the Attribute Editors

There's just one last task that we need to handle before we can try out our new iteration of the SuperDB application. We have to add code to use these new attribute editors. Single-click *HeroEditController.m*. First, add the following declaration to the top of the file:

```
#import "ManagedObjectAttributeEditor.h"
```

Next, in the viewDidLoad method, get rid of the TODO comment, and replace it with the code that follows. This will define which controller class gets used for each row in each section.

```
rowControllers = [[NSArray alloc] initWithObjects:
    // Section 1
    [NSArray arrayWithObject:@"ManagedObjectStringEditor"],

    // Section 2
    [NSArray arrayWithObjects:@"ManagedObjectStringEditor",
        @"ManagedObjectDateEditor",
        @"ManagedObjectStringEditor", nil],

    // Sentinel
    nil];
```

Now, replace the `tableView:didSelectRowAtIndexPath:` method with the following:

```
- (void)tableView:(UITableView *)tableView
        didSelectRowAtIndexPath:(NSIndexPath *)indexPath {
    NSString *controllerClassName = [rowControllers
        nestedObjectAtIndexPath:indexPath];
    NSString *rowLabel = [rowLabels nestedObjectAtIndexPath:indexPath];
    NSString *rowKey = [rowKeys nestedObjectAtIndexPath:indexPath];
    Class controllerClass = NSClassFromString(controllerClassName);
    ManagedObjectAttributeEditor *controller =
        [controllerClass alloc];
    controller = [controller initWithStyle:UITableViewStyleGrouped];
    controller.keypath = rowKey;
    controller.managedObject = hero;
    controller.labelString = rowLabel;
    controller.title = rowLabel;
    [self.navigationController pushViewController:controller animated:YES];
    [controller release];
}
```

This may be new to you, so let's review it. The first thing we do is retrieve the name of the controller class that should be used to edit this particular row.

```
NSString *controllerClassName = [rowControllers
    nestedObjectAtIndexPath:indexPath];
```

We also retrieve the attribute name and label for the selected row.

```
NSString *rowLabel = [rowLabels nestedObjectAtIndexPath:indexPath];
NSString *rowKey = [rowKeys nestedObjectAtIndexPath:indexPath];
```

Next, we use a special function called `NSClassFromString()` that creates an instance of a class based on its name stored in an `NSString` instance.

```
Class controllerClass = NSClassFromString(controllerClassName);
```

After this line of code, controllerClass will be the class object for the class whose name we put in the `rowController` array. You can use a Class object just like you can the name of the class when you `alloc` a new object. So, if `controllerClassName` was Foo, then doing

```
id theObject = [controllerClass alloc];
```

would be exactly the same as calling

```
id theObject = [foo alloc];
```

So, in the next line of code, we do this:

```
ManagedObjectAttributeEditor *controller =
    [controllerClass alloc];
```

Here, we're actually creating an instance of the class that will be used to edit this particular attribute. That's probably a little confusing and, if so, don't worry too much. It can take some time to get used to Objective-C's dynamic nature. We've already allocated the controller. Now, we just need to initialize it, set its properties, then push it onto the navigation stack, like so:

```
controller = [controller initWithStyle:UITableViewStyleGrouped];
controller.keypath = rowKey;
controller.managedObject = hero;
controller.labelString = rowLabel;
controller.title = rowLabel;
[self.navigationController pushViewController:controller animated:YES];
[controller release];
```

Save *HeroEditController.m* and build and run your application. You should be able to edit all the attributes by tapping a row.

Implementing a Selection List

There's one last loose end to take care of. This version of our application uses the string attribute editor to solicit the sex (sorry, we couldn't resist!) of the superhero. This means that there is no validation on the input other than that it's a valid string. A user could type *M*, *Male*, *MALE*, or *Yes, Please*, and they would all be happily accepted by the string attribute editor. That means, later on, if we want to let the user sort or search their heroes by gender, we could have problems, because the data won't be structured in a consistent manner.

As you saw earlier, we could have enforced a specific sex spelling by using a regular expression, putting up an alert if the user typed something besides *Male* or *Female*. This would have prevented values other than the ones we want from getting entered, but this approach is not all that user friendly. We don't want to annoy our user. Why make them type anything at all? There are only two possible choices here. Why not present a selection list and let the user just tap the one they want? Hey, that sounds like a great idea! We're glad you thought of it. Let's implement it now, shall we?

We could, of course, write a special controller to present a two-item list, but that wouldn't be the best use of our time. Such a controller would only be useful when we were soliciting sex (gee, did we do that again?). Wouldn't it be more useful to create a controller that can be used for any selection list? Of course it would, so let's do that.

Creating the Generic Selection List Controller

Create a new table view controller as you did previously, calling this class *ManagedObjectSingleSelectionListEditor*. After you create the files, single-click on *ManagedObjectSingleSelectionListEditor.h* and replace its contents with the following code:

```
#import <UIKit/UIKit.h>
#import "ManagedObjectAttributeEditor.h"

@interface ManagedObjectSingleSelectionListEditor :
    ManagedObjectAttributeEditor {
    NSArray          *list;
```

```
@private
    NSIndexPath         *lastIndexPath;
}
@property (nonatomic, retain) NSArray *list;
@end
```

The structure here might seem somewhat familiar. It's almost identical to one of the controllers from the *Nav* application in Chapter 9 of *Beginning iPhone 3 Development*. The list property will contain the array of values from which the user can select, and lastIndexPath will be used to keep track of the selection.

Save *ManagedObjectSingleSelectionListEditor.h* and single-click on *ManagedObjectSingleSelectionListEditor.m*. Replace the contents of that file with the following code:

```
#import "ManagedObjectSingleSelectionListEditor.h"

@implementation ManagedObjectSingleSelectionListEditor
@synthesize list;
-(IBAction)save {
    UITableViewCell *selectedCell = [self.tableView
        cellForRowAtIndexPath:lastIndexPath];
    NSString *newValue = selectedCell.textLabel.text;
    [self.managedObject setValue:newValue forKey:self.keypath];
    NSError *error;
    if (![self.managedObject.managedObjectContext save:&error])
        NSLog(@"Error saving: %@", [error localizedDescription]);

    [self.navigationController popViewControllerAnimated:YES];
}

- (void)viewWillAppear:(BOOL)animated
{
    NSString *currentValue = [self.managedObject valueForKey:self.keypath];
    for (NSString *oneItem in list) {
        if ([oneItem isEqualToString:currentValue]) {
            NSUInteger newIndex[] = {0, [list indexOfObject:oneItem]};
            NSIndexPath *newPath = [[NSIndexPath alloc] initWithIndexes:
                newIndex length:2];
            [lastIndexPath release];
            lastIndexPath = newPath;
            break;
        }
    }
    [super viewWillAppear:animated];
}

- (void)dealloc {
    [list release];
    [lastIndexPath release];
    [super dealloc];
}

#pragma mark -
#pragma mark Table View Methods
```

```objc
- (NSInteger)tableView:(UITableView *)tableView numberOfRowsInSection:(NSInteger)section
{
    return [list count];
}

- (void)tableView:(UITableView *)tableView
        didSelectRowAtIndexPath:(NSIndexPath *)indexPath {
    int newRow = [indexPath row];
    int oldRow = [lastIndexPath row];

    if (newRow != oldRow || newRow == 0) {
        UITableViewCell *newCell = [tableView cellForRowAtIndexPath:indexPath];
        newCell.accessoryType = UITableViewCellAccessoryCheckmark;

        UITableViewCell *oldCell = [tableView cellForRowAtIndexPath:lastIndexPath];
        oldCell.accessoryType = UITableViewCellAccessoryNone;

        [lastIndexPath release];
        lastIndexPath = indexPath;
    }
    [tableView deselectRowAtIndexPath:indexPath animated:YES];
}

- (UITableViewCell *)tableView:(UITableView *)tableView
        cellForRowAtIndexPath:(NSIndexPath *)indexPath {
    static NSString *GenericManagedObjectListSelectorCell =
        @"GenericManagedObjectListSelectorCell";

    UITableViewCell *cell = [tableView
        dequeueReusableCellWithIdentifier:GenericManagedObjectListSelectorCell];
    if (cell == nil) {
        cell = [[[UITableViewCell alloc] initWithStyle:UITableViewCellStyleDefault
        reuseIdentifier:GenericManagedObjectListSelectorCell] autorelease];
    }
    NSUInteger row = [indexPath row];
    NSUInteger oldRow = [lastIndexPath row];
    cell.textLabel.text = [list objectAtIndex:row];
    cell.accessoryType = (row == oldRow && lastIndexPath != nil) ?
        UITableViewCellAccessoryCheckmark : UITableViewCellAccessoryNone;
    return cell;
}

@end
```

There's really nothing new here. The logic we're using is exactly the same that we used in the *Nav* application. If you aren't sure what's going on here, go back and take a look through Chapter 9 of *Beginning iPhone 3 Development*. The only difference here is that we're using the keypath and managedObject to determine the initial selection and then pushing the final selection back into managedObject when the user presses the *Save* button.

Now, the question is, how do we provide the values (*Male* and *Female*) to this subcontroller? Remember: we want to avoid creating special cases. We want to keep our code as generic as possible. We don't want to, for example, hard code a check for this new controller's class, and then set the list property. That would work, but we want to find a solution that's flexible, reusable, and easy to maintain as our application grows.

What we're going to do is create another paired nested array to hold additional arguments to be passed on to the subordinate controller. Anything we put into this dictionary for a given row will be passed along to the subordinate controller using key-value coding. This gives us the flexibility to pass on any information to any controller we create.

The first step toward implementing this is to add an instance variable for the new nested array. Single-click *HeroEditController.h* and add the following line of code:

```
#import <UIKit/UIKit.h>

@interface HeroEditController : UITableViewController {
    NSManagedObject *hero;

@private
    NSArray         *sectionNames;
    NSArray         *rowLabels;
    NSArray         *rowKeys;
    NSArray         *rowControllers;
    NSArray         *rowArguments;
}

@property (nonatomic, retain) NSManagedObject *hero;

@end
```

Save *HeroEditController.h* and flip over to *HeroEditController.m*. We need to make two changes here. First, we need to create and populate the new `rowArguments` array. And second, we need to write code to pass the key/value pairs from that array on to the subordinate controller.

First, look for the `viewDidLoad` method. Find where we create and populate `rowControllers`, and replace that code with the following version, which changes the controller used for the row that represents the hero's sex.

```
    rowControllers = [[NSArray alloc] initWithObjects:
        // Section 1
        [NSArray arrayWithObject:@"ManagedObjectStringEditor"],

        // Section 2
        [NSArray arrayWithObjects:@"ManagedObjectStringEditor",
            @"ManagedObjectDateEditor",
            @"ManagedObjectSingleSelectionListEditor", nil],

        // Sentinel
        nil];

    rowArguments = [[NSArray alloc] initWithObjects:

        // Section 1
        [NSArray arrayWithObject:[NSNull null]],

        // Section 2,
        [NSArray arrayWithObjects:[NSNull null],
```

```
            [NSNull null],
            [NSDictionary dictionaryWithObject:[NSArray
                arrayWithObjects:@"Male", @"Female", nil]
                forKey:@"list"],
            nil],

        // Sentinel
        nil];
```

Pretty straightforward, right? Most of the rows don't need any arguments, so we use our friend NSNull again as placeholders for those rows in the rowArguments array. We could have also created empty instances of NSArray to represent rows that need no arguments passed on, but it seemed silly to create new instances when we have a singleton object instance already around and ready made just for this kind of work.

Now, find tableView:didSelectRowAtIndexPath: and insert the following code, which retrieves the arguments for this row and, if the object retrieved is a dictionary, it loops through the keys contained in that dictionary and passes the key and value on to the controller.

```
- (void)tableView:(UITableView *)tableView
        didSelectRowAtIndexPath:(NSIndexPath *)indexPath {
    NSString *controllerClassName = [rowControllers
        nestedObjectAtIndexPath:indexPath];
    NSString *rowLabel = [rowLabels nestedObjectAtIndexPath:indexPath];
    NSString *rowKey = [rowKeys nestedObjectAtIndexPath:indexPath];
    Class controllerClass = NSClassFromString(controllerClassName);
    AbstractManagedObjectAttributeEditor *controller =
        [controllerClass alloc];
    controller = [controller initWithStyle:UITableViewStyleGrouped];
    controller.keypath = rowKey;
    controller.managedObject = hero;
    controller.labelString = rowLabel;
    controller.title = rowLabel;

    NSDictionary *args = [rowArguments nestedObjectAtIndexPath:indexPath];
    if ([args isKindOfClass:[NSDictionary class]]) {
        if (args != nil) {
            for (NSString *oneKey in args) {
                id oneArg = [args objectForKey:oneKey];
                [controller setValue:oneArg forKey:oneKey];
            }
        }
    }

    [self.navigationController pushViewController:controller animated:YES];
    [controller release];
}
```

> **TIP:** The isKindOfClass: method that we used in this new chunk of code is a method that will return YES when called on an instance of a specific class or an instance of any class that descends from that class. In this case, since we pass the NSArray class object in as an argument, the method will return YES if args was an instance of NSDictionary or if it was an instance of NSMutableDictionary, but would return NO if args is the singleton NSNull.

Save *HeroEditController.m* and build and run the application. This time, when you tap on the row labeled *Sex*, you should get a nice, user-friendly list like in Figure 4–11.

Figure 4–11. *The selection list controller being used to present two options for the sex attribute*

Devil's End

Well, we're at the end of a long and conceptually difficult chapter. You should congratulate yourself on making it all the way through with us. Table-based detail editing view controllers are some of the hardest controller classes to write well, but now you have a handful of tools in your toolbox to help you create them. You've seen how to use nested and paired arrays to define your table view's structure, you've seen how to create generic classes that can be used to edit multiple types of data, and you've also seen how to use Objective-C's dynamic nature to create instances of classes based on the name of the class stored in an NSString instance.

Ready to move on? Turn the page. Let's get going!

Chapter 5

Preparing for Change: Migrations and Versioning

By the time you reached the end of Chapter 4, you mastered a great deal of the Core Data architecture and functionality. Together, we built a fully functioning, albeit somewhat simple, Core Data application. You've now got enough Core Data chops to build a solid app, send it to your testers, and then on to the App Store.

But what happens if you change your data model and send a new version of your application out to testers who already have the previous version? Consider our *SuperDB* app. Let's say we decide to add a new attribute to the Hero entity, make one of the existing, currently optional attributes required, and then add a new entity. Can we just send the program out to our users, or is this going to cause problems with their data?

As things stand right now, if you make changes to your data model, the existing data sitting in the user's persistent store on their iPhone will be unusable in the new version of your application. Your application will crash on launch. If you launch the new version from Xcode, you will see a big, scary error message like the following:

```
2009-09-08 14:37:26.392 SuperDB[4138:207] Unresolved error Error
Domain=NSCocoaErrorDomain Code=134100 UserInfo=0x14049d0 "Operation could not be
completed. (Cocoa error 134100.)", {
    metadata =     {
        NSPersistenceFrameworkVersion = 241;
        NSStoreModelVersionHashes =         {
            Hero = <209a8e07 84180c10 08c4a2fe a68af2a1 e0d620b1 f592e6b0 66ea6663
ef6bc252>;
        };
        NSStoreModelVersionHashesVersion = 3;
        NSStoreModelVersionIdentifiers =         (
        );
        NSStoreType = SQLite;
        NSStoreUUID = "663F93E0-BD32-4F80-87F2-D72011101610";
    };
    reason = "The model used to open the store is incompatible with the one used to
create the store";
}
```

If this happens in development, it's not usually a big deal. If nobody else has a copy of your app and you don't have any irreplaceable data stored in it, you can just select **Reset Content and Settings…** from the **iPhone Simulator** menu in the simulator or uninstall the application from your iPhone using Xcode's Organizer window, and Core Data will create a new persistent store based on the revised data model next time you install and run your application.

If, however, you have given the application to others, they will be stuck with an unusable application on their iPhone unless they uninstall and re-install the application, thereby losing all of their existing data.

As you probably imagine, this is not something that makes for particularly happy customers. In this chapter, we're going to show you how to **version** your data model, then we'll talk a little bit about Apple's mechanism for converting data between different data model versions, which are called **migrations**. We'll talk a little about the difference between the two types of migrations: **lightweight migrations** and **standard migrations**. Then we will set up our *SuperDB* Xcode project to use lightweight migrations so that the changes we make in the next few chapters won't cause problems for our (admittedly non-existent) users.

At the end of this chapter, our *SuperDB* application will be all set up and ready for new development, including changes to our data model, without having to worry about our users losing their data when we ship our new verion.

About Data Models

When you create a new Xcode project using a template that supports Core Data, you are provided with a single data model in the form of an *.xcdatamodel* file in your project's *Resources* folder. In Chapter 2, we saw how this file was loaded into an instance of NSManagedObjectModel at runtime in the application delegate's managedObjectModel method. In order to understand versioning and migrations, it's important to look a little deeper under the hood to see what's going on.

Data Models Are Compiled

The *.xcdatamodel* class in your project does not get copied into your application's bundle the way other resources do. The data model file contains a lot of information that your application doesn't need. For example, it contains information about the layout of the objects in Xcode's data model editor's diagram view (Figure 5–1) that is only there to make your life easier. Your application doesn't care about how those rounded rectangles are laid out, so there's no reason to include that information inside your application bundle.

Instead, your *.xcdatamodel* files get compiled into a new type of file with an extension of *.mom*, which stands for managed object model (sorry, Mom). This is a much more compact binary file that contains just the information that your application needs. This *.mom* file is what is actually loaded to create instances of NSManagedObjectModel.

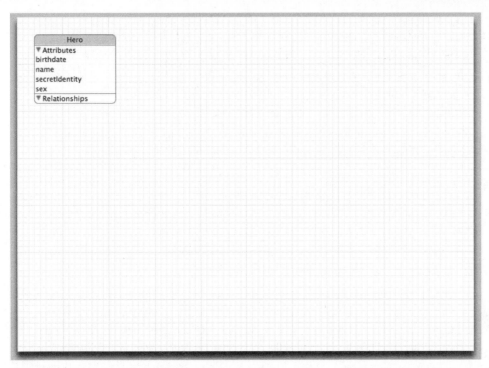

Figure 5–1. *The fact that the rounded rectangle representing our* Hero *entity is in the upper-left corner and the disclosure triangle next to* Attributes *and* Relationships *are expanded is stored in the* .xcdatamodel *file but not in the* .mom *file*

Data Models Can Have Multiple Versions

You most likely understand what versioning means, in a general sense. When a company releases a new version of a piece of software with new features, it typically has a new number or designation. For example, you are working on a specific version of Xcode (for us, it's 3.2.1), and a specific version of Mac OS X (for us it's 10.6.2, also known as Snow Leopard).

These are what are called **marketing version identifiers** or numbers, as they are primarily intended to let customers tell the difference between different released versions of the software. Marketing versions are incremented when a new version of the program is released to customers.

There are other, finer-grained forms of versioning used by developers, however. If you've ever used a concurrent versioning system such as cvs, svn, or git, you're probably aware of how this all works. Versioning software keeps track of the changes over time to all of the individual source code and resource files that make up your project (among other things).

NOTE: We're not going to be discussing regular version control, but it's a good thing to know about if you're a developer. Fortunately, there are a lot of resources on the Web for learning to use and install different version-control software packages. A good place to start is the Wikipedia page on version control at: http://en.wikipedia.org/wiki/Revision_control.

Xcode integrates with several version-control software packages, but it also has some built-in version-control mechanisms, including one that's intended for use with Core Data data models. Creating new versions of your data models is the key to keeping your users happy. Every time you release a version of your application to the public, you should create a new version of your data model. This will create a new copy so that the old version can be kept around to help the system figure out how to update the data from a persistent store made with one version to a newer version.

Creating a New Data Model Version

Single-click *SuperDB.xcdatamodel* in Xcode. Now click the **Design** menu, select the **Data Model** sub-menu and, finally, select **Add Model Version**. You just added a new version of your data model. Once you select that, the *SuperDB.xcdatamodel* file will disappear from your *Resources* group and be replaced by a new resource with the extension *.xcdatamodeld* with a disclosure triangle next to it. This is your indication that you have a versioned data model (Figure 5–2).

Figure 5–2. *The .xcdatamodeld extension indicates a versioned data model*

If you expand the disclosure triangle next to *SuperDB.xcdatamodeld*, you can see all the different versions of your data model. The icon for one of the versions will have a green checkmark on it (Figure 5–3). This indicates the current version, which is the one that your application will use. By default, when you create a new version, the current version continues to be the one with the original name, and the copy is created with the same name but an incrementally larger number affixed to the end. In our case, the one we just created, *SuperDB 2.xcdatamodel*, is the original data model that represents what our data model looked like at the time we created the new version. It should be left untouched.

The fact that the higher number is the older file might seem a little weird but, as more versions accumulate, the numbering will make more sense. The next time we create a new version, the old version will be named *SuperDB 3.xcdatamodel*, and so on. The numbering makes sense for all the non-current versions, since each version will have a number one higher than the previous one. By keeping the name of the current model the same, it's easy to tell which one you should be making changes to.

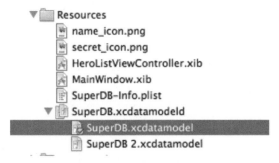

Figure 5–3. *A versioned data model contains the current version, marked with a green checkmark on its icon, along with every previous version*

The Current Data Model Version

In Figure 5–3, *SuperDB.xcdatamodel* is the current version of the data model, and *SuperDB 2.xcdatamodel* is the previous version. You can now safely make changes to the current version, knowing that a copy of the previous version exists, frozen in time, which will give us the ability to migrate our users' data from the old version to the next version when we release it.

You can change which version is the current version. To do this, select the data model you want to make current, then select **Set Current Version** from the **Design** menu, **Data Model** submenu. You won't do this often, but you might do it if you needed to revert to an older version of the application for some reason. You can use migrations to go back to an older version as well as move to a new version.

Data Model Version Identifiers

Although you can assign version identifiers like *1.1* or *Version A* to data models by selecting the data model in the *Groups & Files* pane and pressing ⌘I to bring up the Info window (Figure 5–4), this identifier is purely for your own use and is completely ignored by Core Data.

Instead, Core Data performs a mathematical calculation called a **hash** on each entity in your data model file. The hash values are stored in your persistent store. When Core Data opens your persistent store, Core Data uses these hash values to ensure that the version of your data stored in the store are compatible with the current data model.

Since Core Data does its version validation using the stored hash values, you don't need to worry about incrementing version numbers for versioning to work. Core Data will just know which version a persistent store was created for by looking at the stored hash value and comparing it to the hash calculated on the current version of the data model.

Figure 5–4. *The Info window for a data model will allow you to set a version identifier.*

Using the Versioned Data Model

Back in Chapter 2, when we walked through the Core Data template, we looked at this accessor method:

```
- (NSManagedObjectModel *)managedObjectModel {

    if (managedObjectModel != nil) {
        return managedObjectModel;
    }
    managedObjectModel = [[NSManagedObjectModel mergedModelFromBundles:nil] retain];
    return managedObjectModel;
}
```

During our discussion, we said that mergedModelFromBundles: iterated through all the resources in your application's bundle and loaded any data models it found. Well, that's perfectly true, but this can cause a problem when you're using versioned data models.

When versioned data models are compiled, they get compiled to a *.momd,* which is a versioned managed object model containing the current data model and all previous versions of it. Before we versioned our data model, it was getting compiled to a *.mom* file. The NSManagedObjectModel class is capable of working with either a *.mom* or a

.momd file, but just to be safe, we're going to point it to the *.momd* file now that we've versioned our data model to make sure it's loading the correct one.

Strictly speaking, this isn't necessary; however, unless you do a clean build after versioning your data model, the existing *.mom* file will still be part of your application. When `mergedModelFromBundles:` is used in this scenario, it attempts to load both the versioned and non-versioned data model into a single instance of `NSManagedObjectModel`. Since a managed object model can only have one copy of any entity and these two data models will contain at least some of the same entities, this call will fail.

If you experience this problem, selecting **Clean…** from the **Build** menu will delete the old data model file, fixing the problem. We like to take the uncertainty out of the situation by tweaking the way our `NSManagedObjectModel` instance is created so that it always loads the correct file no matter what our application bundle contains. This is an optional step; however, it will avoid some potentially hard-to-debug scenarios.

In Xcode, single-click on the *SuperDBAppDelegate.m* file and scroll down to the method called `managedObjectModel`. Replace the existing version with this new version:

```
- (NSManagedObjectModel *)managedObjectModel {
    if (managedObjectModel != nil) {
        return managedObjectModel;
    }

    NSString *path = [[NSBundle mainBundle] pathForResource:@"SuperDB"
        ofType:@"momd"];
    NSURL *momURL = [NSURL fileURLWithPath:path];
    managedObjectModel = [[NSManagedObjectModel alloc]
        initWithContentsOfURL:momURL];

    return managedObjectModel;
}
```

This is pretty straightforward. Instead of using the factory method `mergedModelFromBundles:`, we're allocating an instance of `NSManagedObjectModel` from a single managed object model, but notice the type of the resource we're requesting. We're not specifying a regular managed object model (*.mom*), we're specifying the versioned object model (*.momd*). By specifying the *.momd* file, we're telling Core Data to only use the versioned data model. Core Data is savvy enough to only load the current version, and will use the other ones only if a migration is necessary.

Which is a nice segue into…

Migrations

As you saw at the beginning of the chapter, when Core Data detects that the persistent store in use is incompatible with the current data model, it throws an exception. The solution is to provide a migration to tell Core Data how to move data from the old persistent store to a new one that matches the current data model.

Lightweight vs. Standard

There are two different types of migrations supported by Core Data. The first, called a **lightweight migration**, is only available in the case of relatively straightforward modifications to your data model. If you add or remove an attribute from an entity or add or delete an entity from the data model, for example, Core Data is perfectly capable of figuring out how to migrate the existing data into the new model. In the case of a new attribute, it simply creates storage for that attribute, but doesn't populate it with data for the existing managed objects. In a lightweight migration, Core Data actually analyzes the two data models and creates the migration for you.

If you make a change that's not straightforward and thus can't be resolved by the lightweight migration mechanism, then you have to use a **standard migration**. A standard migration involves creating a **mapping model** and possibly writing some code to tell Core Data how to move the data from the old persistent store to the new one.

Standard Migrations

The changes we will be making to the *SuperDB* application in this book are all pretty straightforward, and an in-depth discussion of standard migrations is beyond the scope of this book. Apple has documented the process fairly thoroughly in the developer documentation, though, so you can read more about standard migrations at `http://developer.apple.com/mac/library/documentation/Cocoa/Conceptual/CoreDataV ersioning/index.html`.

Setting up Your App to Use Lightweight Migrations

On the other hand, we will be using lightweight migrations a lot through the rest of the book. In every remaining Core Data chapter, we will create a new version of our data model and let lightweight migrations handle moving the data. However, lightweight migrations are not turned on by default, so we need to make some more changes to our application delegate to enable them.

Back in Xcode, *SuperDBAppDelegate.m* should still be showing in the editing pane. If it's not, single-click *SuperDBAppDelegate.m*. Use the function pop-up menu to navigate to the existing `persistentStoreCoordinator` method. It should look basically like this:

```
- (NSPersistentStoreCoordinator *)persistentStoreCoordinator {

    if (persistentStoreCoordinator != nil) {
        return persistentStoreCoordinator;
    }

    NSURL *storeUrl = [NSURL fileURLWithPath: [[self applicationDocumentsDirectory]
        stringByAppendingPathComponent: @"SuperDB.sqlite"]];


    NSError *error = nil;
    persistentStoreCoordinator = [[NSPersistentStoreCoordinator alloc]
```

```
        initWithManagedObjectModel:[self managedObjectModel]];
    if (![persistentStoreCoordinator addPersistentStoreWithType:NSSQLiteStoreType
        configuration:nil URL:storeUrl options:nil error:&error]) {

        // error handling code goes here
    }
    return persistentStoreCoordinator;
}
```

The way that we turn on lightweight migrations is to pass a dictionary in to the `options` argument when we call the `addPersistentStoreWithType:configuration:URL:options:error:` method to add our newly created persistent store to the persistent store coordinator. In that dictionary, we use two system-defined constants, `NSMigratePersistentStoresAutomaticallyOption` and `NSInferMappingModelAutomaticallyOption`, as keys in the dictionary, and store an `NSNumber` under both of those keys that holds an Objective-C `YES` value. By passing a dictionary with these two values in when we add the persistent store to the persistent store coordinator, we indicate to Core Data that we want it to attempt to automatically create migrations if it detects a change in the data model version, and if it's able to create the migrations, to automatically use those migrations to migrate the data to a new persistent store based on the current data model.

Replace the existing version with this new one.

```
- (NSPersistentStoreCoordinator *)persistentStoreCoordinator {

    if (persistentStoreCoordinator != nil) {
        return persistentStoreCoordinator;
    }

    NSURL *storeUrl = [NSURL fileURLWithPath: [[self applicationDocumentsDirectory]
        stringByAppendingPathComponent: @"SuperDB.sqlite"]];

    NSDictionary *options = [NSDictionary dictionaryWithObjectsAndKeys:
        [NSNumber numberWithBool:YES], NSMigratePersistentStoresAutomaticallyOption,
        [NSNumber numberWithBool:YES], NSInferMappingModelAutomaticallyOption, nil];

    NSError *error = nil;
    persistentStoreCoordinator = [[NSPersistentStoreCoordinator alloc]
        initWithManagedObjectModel:[self managedObjectModel]];
    if (![persistentStoreCoordinator addPersistentStoreWithType:NSSQLiteStoreType
        configuration:nil URL:storeUrl options:options error:&error]) {

        NSLog(@"Unresolved error %@, %@", error, [error userInfo]);
        abort();
    }

    return persistentStoreCoordinator;
}
```

And that's it. With these changes made to our project, we are ready to start making changes to our data model without fear. Well, maybe not completely without fear. By using lightweight migrations, we limit the complexity of the changes we're able to make. For example, we won't be able to split an entity up into two different entities or move attributes from one entity to another, but the majority of changes you'll need to make outside of major refactoring can be handled by lightweight migrations, and once you set your project up the way we've done in this chapter, that functionality is basically free.

Time to Migrate On

After a couple of long, conceptually difficult chapters, taking a break to set up our project to use migrations gave us a nice breather, but don't underestimate the importance of migrations. The people who use your applications are trusting you to take a certain amount of care with their data. Putting some effort into making sure that your changes don't cause major problems for your users is important.

Any time you put out a new release of your application with a new data model version, make sure you test the migration thoroughly. This is true regardless of whether you're using the lightweight migrations we set up in this chapter or the heavier-duty standard migrations.

Migrations, especially lightweight migrations, are relatively easy to use, but they hold the potential for causing your users significant inconvenience, so don't get lulled into a false sense of security by how easy they are to use. Test every migration thoroughly with as much realistic data as you can.

And with that warning out of the way, let's continue adding functionality to our *SuperDB* application. Up next? Custom managed objects for fun and profit.

Chapter 6

Custom Managed Objects

At the moment, our *Hero* entity is represented by instances of the class NSManagedObject. Thanks to key value coding, we have the ability to create entire data models without ever having to create a class specifically designed just to hold our application's data.

There are some drawbacks to this approach, however. For one thing, when using key value coding with managed objects, we use NSString constants to represent our attributes in code, but these constants are not checked in any way by the compiler. If we mistype the name of an attribute, the compiler won't catch it. It can also be a little tedious, having to use valueForKey: and setValue:forKey: all over the place instead of just using properties and dot notation.

Although you can set default values for some types of data model attributes, you can't, for example, set conditional defaults such as defaulting a date attribute to today's date. For some types of attributes, there's no way at all to set a default in the data model. Validation is similarly limited. Although you can control certain elements of some attributes, like the length of a string, or max value of a number, there's no way to do complex or conditional validation, or to do validation that depends on the values in multiple attributes.

Fortunately, NSManagedObject can be subclassed, just like other Objective-C classes, and that's the key to doing more advanced defaulting and validation. It also opens the door to adding additional functionality to your entity by adding methods. You can, for example, create a method to return a value calculated from one or more of the entity's attributes.

In this chapter, we're going to create a custom subclass of NSManagedObject for our *Hero* entity, then we're going to use that subclass to add some additional functionality. We're also going to add two new attributes to *Hero*. One is the hero's age. Instead of storing the age, we're going to calculate it based on their birthdate. As a result, we won't need Core Data to create space in the persistent store for the hero's age, so we're going to use the *Transient* attribute type and then write an accessor method to calculate and return the hero's age. The *Transient* attribute type tells Core Data not to create storage for that attribute. In our case, we'll calculate the hero's age as needed at run time.

The second attribute we're going to add is the hero's favorite color. Now, there is no attribute type for colors, so we're going to implement something called a **transformable attribute**. Transformable attributes use a special object called a **value transformer** to convert custom objects to instances of NSData so they can be stored in the persistent store. We'll write a value transformer that will let us save UIColor instances this way. In Figure 6–1, you can see what the detail editing view will look like at the end of the chapter with the two new attributes in place. Notice that the row for *Age* doesn't have a disclosure indicator next to it. That's our users' clue that it's not an editable field.

Figure 6–1. *The hero detail editing view as it will look at the end of the chapter*

Of course, we don't have an attribute editor for colors, so we'll have to write one of those to let the user select the hero's favorite color. We're just going to create a simple, slider-based color chooser (Figure 6–2).

Because there's no way to set a default color in the data model, we're going to write code to default the favorite color attribute to white. If we don't do that, then the color will be nil when the user goes to edit it the first time, which will cause problems.

Finally, we'll add validation to the date field to prevent the user from selecting a birthdate that occurs in the future and we're also going to tweak our attribute editors so that they notifiy the user when an entered attribute has failed validation. We'll give the user the option to go back and fix the attribute, or to just cancel the changes they made (Figure 6–3).

Figure 6–2. *The color attribute editor that we will be building in this chapter*

Figure 6–3. *When attempting to save an attribute that fails validation, the user will have the option of fixing the problem, or cancelling their changes*

Although we're only going to be adding validation to the *Birthdate* field, the reporting mechanism we're going to write will be generic and reusable if you add validation to another field. You can see an example of our generic error alert in Figure 6–4.

Figure 6–4. *Since our goal is generally to write reusable code, our validation mechanism will also enforce validations done on the data model, such as minimum length.*

There's a fair amount of work to do, so let's get started. We're going to continue working with the same *SuperDB* application from last chapter. Make sure that you created a new version of your data model and that you turned on lightweight migrations as shown in the last chapter.

Updating the Data Model

The first order of business is to add our two new attributes to the data model. Make sure that the disclosure triangle next to *SuperDB.xcdatamodeld* in the *Resources* folder is expanded, and single-click on the current version of the data model, the one with the green check mark icon on it.

Once the data model editor comes up, select the *Hero* entity by clicking either on the rounded rectangle in the diagram view or on the row labeled *Hero* in the entity pane (Figure 6–5).

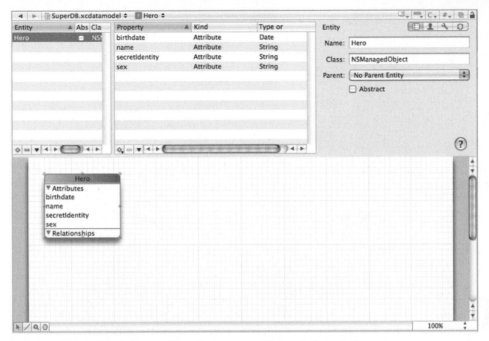

Figure 6–5. *Selecting the* Hero *entity so that we can add new attributes to it*

Adding the Age Attribute

Click the plus icon in the lower left of the property pane and select **Add Attribute** to add a new attribute. Change the new attribute's name to *age*, then check the *Transient* check box. That will tell Core Data that we don't need to store a value for this attribute. In our case, since we're using SQLite for our persistent store, this will tell Core Data not to add a column for *age* to the database table used to store hero data. Change the type to *Integer 16*; we're going to calculate age as a whole number. That's all we have to do for now for the *age* attribute. Of course, as things stand, we can't do anything meaningful with this particular attribute, because it can't store anything, and we don't yet have any way to tell it how to calculate the age. That will change in a few minutes, when we create a custom subclass of NSManagedObject.

Adding the Favorite Color Attribute

Click the plus icon in the property pane again and select **Add Attribute** one more time. This time, call the new attribute *favoriteColor* and set the *Type* to *Transformable*. Once you've changed the *Type* pop-up to *Transformable*, you should notice a new field called *Value Transformer Name:* (Figure 6–6).

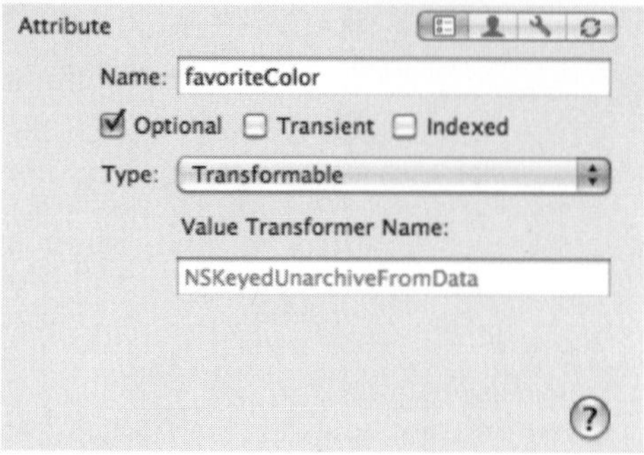

Figure 6–6. *Making the* favoriteColor *attribute a transformable attribute*

The *Value Transformer Name:* field is the key to using transformable attributes. We'll discuss value transformers in more depth in just a few minutes, but we'll populate this field now to save ourselves a trip back to the data model editor later. This field is where we need to put the name of the **value transformer** class that will be used to convert whatever object represents this attribute into an NSData instance for saving in the persistent store, and vice versa. The default value, *NSKeyedUnarchiveFromData*, will work with a great many objects by using NSKeyedArchiver and NSKeyedUnarchiver to convert any object that conforms to the NSCoding protocol into an instance of NSData. For most types of objects, this default transformer will work just fine, and our work would be basically done. Unfortunately, UIColor does not conform to NSCoding, which means that this value won't work for our situation. Instead, we need to write a custom value transformer class and provide its name here.

Because we have a crystal ball (well, OK, because we wrote the code), we know that we're going to call our value transformer *UIColorRGBValueTransformer*, so type that into the *Value Transformer Name:* field now.

> **CAUTION:** The data model editor does not validate the *Value Transformer Name:* field to make sure it is a valid class. We're utilizing that fact right now to let us put in the name of a non-existent class that we'll write later. It's a double-edged sword, however, since mistyping the name of the value transformer won't show up as a problem until runtime and can be hard to debug, so make sure you are very careful about typing the correct name in this field.

Adding a Minimum Length to the Name Attribute

Next, let's add some validation to ensure that our *name* attribute is at least one character long. Single-click the *name* attribute to select it. In the *Min. Length* field, enter *1* to specify that the value entered into this field has to be at least one character long. This may seem like a redundant validation, since we already unchecked *Optional* in a previous chapter for this attribute, but the two do not do exactly the same thing. Because the *Optional* check box is unchecked, the user will be prevented from saving if *name* is nil. However, our application takes pains to ensure that *name* is never nil. For example, we give *name* a default value. If the user deletes that value, the text field will still return an empty string instead of `nil`. Therefore, to ensure that an actual name is entered, we're going to add this validation.

Save the data model.

Creating the Hero Class

It's now time to create our custom subclass of `NSManagedObject`. This will give us the flexibility to add custom validation and defaulting as well as the ability to use properties instead of key value coding, which will make our code easier to read and give us additional checks at compile time.

Single-click the *Classes* folder in the *Groups & Files* pane of Xcode. The data model editor should still be showing in the editing pane. If it's not, single-click the current version of the data model again, and then select the *Classes* folder. Now, single-click anywhere in the diagram pane. As you'll see in a moment, in order for our next step to work, the data model editor must be in the editing pane and the editing pane must be the active pane.

Now, select **New File…** from the **File** menu or press ⌘N. When the new file assistant pops up, select *Cocoa Touch Class* from under the iPhone OS heading in the left pane, then look for an icon in the upper-right pane that you've probably never seen before: *Managed Object Class*. This template is only available when the editing pane is currently showing a Core Data data model and is the active pane. Select it, and click the *Next* button.

Figure 6–7. *Selecting the* Managed Object Class *template*

Instead of prompting you for a file name, it's going to present you with a slightly different dialog than the one you usually see (Figure 6–8). This new dialog asks you only where it should put the generated file or files, but not what they should be called. It will name the subclasses automatically based on their entity name. Click the *Next* button again.

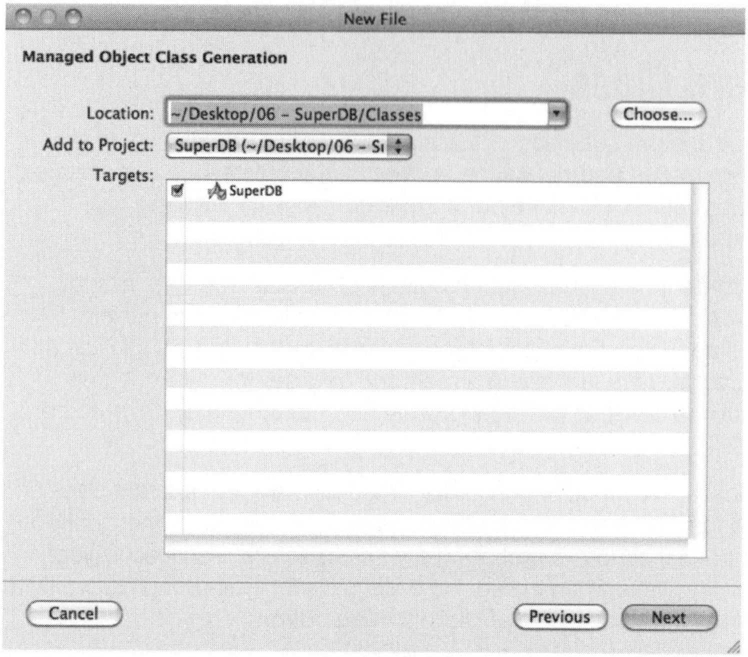

Figure 6–8. *With the* Managed Object Class *template, you are not prompted for a name*

After clicking *Next*, you'll get a new dialog that lists all the entities in the active data model. In our case, we only have a single entity, so it's a pretty short list (Figure 6–9).

Make sure that the *Hero* entity is checked and that both *Generate accessors* and *Generate Obj-C 2.0 Properties* are checked. That will cause Xcode to create properties in the new class automatically for all the attributes. Leave the *Generate validation methods* check box unchecked. That option will generate method stubs for validating our attributes. Since we're going to write code to validate only one attribute, we'll write the methods by hand. If we were to select this, it would give us method stubs for validating every property in our entity. Once your screen looks like Figure 6–9, click the *Finish* button.

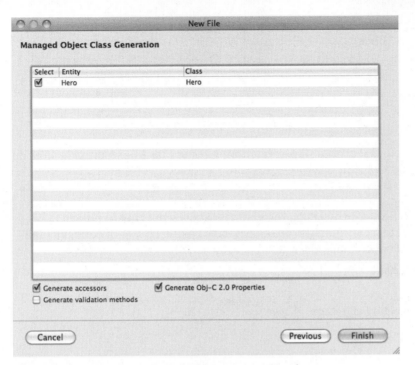

Figure 6–9. *Selecting the entities for which to create custom classes*

Tweaking the Hero Header

You should now have a pair of files called *Hero.h* and *Hero.m* in your *Classes* folder. Xcode also tweaked your data model so that the *Hero* entity uses this class rather than NSManagedObject at runtime. Single-click on the new *Hero.h* file now. It should look something look like this, though the exact order of your property declarations may not be exactly the same as ours:

```
#import <CoreData/CoreData.h>

@interface Hero :  NSManagedObject
{
}

@property (nonatomic, retain) NSNumber * age;
@property (nonatomic, retain) NSString * secretIdentity;
@property (nonatomic, retain) NSString * sex;
@property (nonatomic, retain) NSString * name;
@property (nonatomic, retain) NSDate * birthdate;
@property (nonatomic, retain) id favoriteColor;

@end
```

> **CAUTION:** If your *Hero.h* file does not include declarations of age and `favoriteColor`, chances are you did not save properly somewhere along the way. If so, select *Hero.h* and *Hero.m* in your project file and press Delete, being sure the files are moved to the trash. Then go back, make sure your attributes were properly created in your data model, make sure the data model was saved, then recreate *Hero.h* and *Hero.m*.

We need to make two quick changes here. First, we want to make age read-only. We're not going to allow people to set a hero's age, we're just going to calculate it based on the birthdate. We also want to change `favoriteColor` from the generic `id` to `UIColor` to indicate that our `favoriteColor` attribute is, in fact, an instance of `UIColor`. This will give us some additional type safety by letting the compiler know what type of object represents the `favoriteColor` attribute. We also need to add a couple of constants that will be used in our validation methods. Make the following changes to *Hero.h*:

```
#import <CoreData/CoreData.h>

#define kHeroValidationDomain          @"com.Apress.SuperDB.HeroValidationDomain"
#define kHeroValidationBirthdateCode   1000

@interface Hero :  NSManagedObject
{
}

@property (nonatomic, retain) id favoriteColor;
@property (nonatomic, retain) UIColor * favoriteColor;
@property (nonatomic, retain) NSNumber * age;
@property (nonatomic, readonly) NSNumber * age;
@property (nonatomic, retain) NSString * secretIdentity;
@property (nonatomic, retain) NSString * sex;
@property (nonatomic, retain) NSString * name;
@property (nonatomic, retain) NSDate * birthdate;

@end
```

Don't worry too much about the two constants. We'll explain error domains and error codes in a few moments. Switch over to *Hero.m*. We've got a bit more work to do in the implementation file. Before we do that, let's talk about what we're going to do.

Defaulting

One of the most common Core Data tasks that requires you to subclass `NSManagedObject` is setting conditional default values for attributes, or setting the default value for attribute types that can't be set in the data model, such as default values for transformable attributes.

`NSManagedObject` has a method called `awakeFromInsert` that is specifically designed to be overridden by subclasses for the purpose of setting default values. It gets called immediately after a new instance of an object is inserted into a managed object context and before any code has a chance to make changes to or use the object.

In our case, we have a transformable attribute called `favoriteColor` that we want to default to white. To accomplish that, add the following method before the @end declaration in *Hero.m*:

```
- (void) awakeFromInsert {
    self.favoriteColor = [UIColor colorWithRed:1.0 green:1.0 blue:1.0 alpha:1.0];
    [super awakeFromInsert];
}
```

Notice the use of the @dynamic keyword in *Hero.m*. This tells the compiler not to generate accessors and mutators for the property that follows. The idea here is that the accessors and mutators will be provided by the superclass at runtime. Don't worry too much about the specifics here, just know that this bit of complexity is required in order for Core Data to work properly.

> **TIP:** Notice that we didn't use `[UIColor whiteColor]` for the default. The reason we used the `colorWithRed:green:blue:alpha:` factory method is because it always creates an RGBA color. `UIColor` supports several different color models. Later, we're going to be breaking the `UIColor` down into its separate components (one each for red, green, blue, and alpha) in order to save it in the persistent store. We're also going to be letting the user select a new color by manipulating sliders for each of these components. The `whiteColor` method, however, doesn't create a color using the RGBA color space. Instead, it creates a color using the grayscale color model, which represents colors with only two components, gray and alpha.

Simple enough. We just create a new instance of `UIColor` and assign it to `favoriteColor`. Another common usage of `awakeFromInsert` is for defaulting date attributes to the current date. We could, for example, default the `birthdate` attribute to the current date by adding the following line of code to `awakeFromInsert`:

```
self.birthdate = [NSDate date];
```

Validation

Core Data offers two mechanisms for doing attribute validation in code, one that's intended to be used for single-attribute validations, and one that's intended to be used when a validation depends on the value of more than one attribute. Single attribute validations are relatively straightforward. You might want to make sure that a date is valid, a field is not `nil`, or that a number attribute is not negative. Multi-field validations are a little more complex. Let's say that you had a *Person* entity, and it had a string attribute called *legalGuardian* where you keep track of the person who is legally responsible and able to make decisions for a person if they are a minor. You might want to make sure this attribute is populated, but you'd only want to do that for minors, not for adults. Multi-attribute validation would let you make the attribute required, if the person's *age* attribute is less than 18, but not otherwise.

Single-Attribute Validations

NSManagedObject provides a method for validating single attributes, called validateValue:forKey:error:. This method takes a value, key, and an NSError handle.

You could override this method and perform validation by returning YES or NO, based on whether the value is valid. If it doesn't pass, you would also be able to create an NSError instance to hold specific information about what is not valid and why.

You could do that. But don't. You never actually need to override this method because the default implementation uses a very cool mechanism to dynamically dispatch error handling to special validation methods that aren't defined in the class.

For example, let's say you have a field called, oh, say, birthdate. NSManagedObject will, during validation, automatically look for a method on our subclass called validateBirthdate:error:. It will do this for every attribute, so if you want to validate a single attribute, all you have to do is declare a method that follows the naming convention validateXxx:error: (where xxx is the name of the attribute to be validated), returning a BOOL that indicates whether the new value passed validation.

Let's use this mechanism to prevent the user from entering birthdates that occur in the future. Above the @end declaration in *Hero.m*, add the following method:

```
-(BOOL)validateBirthdate:(id *)ioValue error:(NSError **)outError{
    NSDate *date = *ioValue;
    if ([date compare:[NSDate date]] == NSOrderedDescending) {
        if (outError != NULL) {
            NSString *errorStr = NSLocalizedString(
                @"Birthdate cannot be in the future",
                @"Birthdate cannot be in the future");
            NSDictionary *userInfoDict = [NSDictionary dictionaryWithObject:errorStr
                forKey:NSLocalizedDescriptionKey];
            NSError *error = [[[NSError alloc] initWithDomain:kHeroValidationDomain
                code:kHeroValidationBirthdateCode
                userInfo:userInfoDict] autorelease];
            *outError = error;
        }
        return NO;
    }
    return YES;
}
```

> **TIP:** Are you wondering why we're passed a pointer to a pointer to an NSError rather than just a pointer? Pointers to pointers allow a pointer to be passed by reference. In Objective-C methods, arguments, including object pointers, are passed by value, which means that the called method gets its own copy of the pointer that was passed in. So if the called method wants to change the pointer, as opposed to the data the pointer points to, we need another level of indirection. Thus, the pointer to the pointer.

As you can see from the preceding method, we return NO if the date is in the future, and YES if the date is in the past. If we return NO, we also take some additional steps. We create a dictionary, and store an error string under the key NSLocalizedDescriptionKey, which is a system constant that exists for this purpose. We then create a new instance of NSError and pass that newly created dictionary as the NSError's userInfo dictionary. This is the standard way to pass back information in validation methods and pretty much every other method that takes a handle to an NSError as an argument.

Notice that when we create the NSError instance, we use the two constants we defined earlier, kHeroValidationDomain and kHeroValidationBirthdateCode:

```
NSError *error = [[[NSError alloc] initWithDomain:kHeroValidationDomain
        code:kHeroValidationBirthdateCode
        userInfo:userInfoDict] autorelease];
```

> **TIP** Notice that we don't call super in the single-attribute validation methods. It's not that these methods are defined as abstract, it's that they simply don't exist. These methods are created dynamically at runtime, so not only is there no point in calling super, there's actually no method on super to call.

Every NSError requires an error domain and an error code. Error codes are integers that uniquely identify a specific type of error. An error domain defines the application or framework that generated the error. For example, there's an error domain called NSCocoaErrorDomain that identifies errors created by code in Apple's Cocoa frameworks. We defined our own error domain for our application using a reverse DNS-style string and assigned that to the constant kHeroValidationDomain. We'll use that domain for any error created as a result of validating the Hero object. We could also have chosen to create a single domain for the entire *SuperDB* application, but by being more specific, our application will be easier to debug.

By creating our own error domains, we can be as specific as we want to be. We also avoid the problem of searching through long lists of system-defined constants, looking for just the right code that covers a specific error. kHeroValidationBirthdateCode is the first code we've created in our domain, and we just picked the value 1000 for it arbitrarily. It would have been perfectly valid to choose 0, 1, 10000, or 34848 for this error code. It's our domain, we can do what we want.

NIL VS. NULL

In our validation methods, you may have noticed that we're comparing `outError` to NULL to see if we've been provided a valid pointer, rather than comparing to `nil` as we typically do. Both `nil` and NULL serve the same purpose (to represent empty pointers) and, in fact, they are defined to the same thing: the number zero. In terms of your code functioning, `nil` and NULL are 100% interchangeable.

That being said, you should endeavor to use the right one at the right time. Which one you use will be a clue to your future self, as well as any other developers who work with your code, as to what you are doing.

When you are checking an Objective-C object pointer, compare to `nil`. With any other C pointers, use NULL. In this case, we're dealing with a pointer to a pointer, so we use NULL. If a pointer doesn't directly reference an Objective-C object, NULL is the appropriate comparison value, even if the pointer it references points to an object.

Multiple-Attribute Validations

When you need to validate a managed object based on the values of multiple fields, the approach is a little different. After all the single-field validation methods have fired, another method will be called to let you do more complex validations. There are actually two such methods, one that is called when an object is first inserted into the context, and another when you save changes to an existing managed object.

When inserting a new managed object into a context, the multiple-attribute method you use is called `validateForInsert:`. When updating an existing object, the validation method you implement is called `validateForUpdate:`. In both cases, you return YES if the object passes validation, and NO if there's a problem. As with single-field validation, if you return NO, you should also create an NSError instance that identifies the specifics of the problem encountered.

In many instances, the validation you want to do at insert and at update are identical. In those cases, do not copy the code from one and paste it into the other. Instead, create a new validation method and have both `validateForInsert:` and `validateForUpdate:` call that new validation method.

In our application, we don't yet really have a need for any multiple-attribute validations, but let's say, hypothetically, that instead of making both name and `secretIdentity` required, we only wanted to require one of the two. We could accomplish that by making both name and `secretIdentity` optional in the data model, then using the multiple-attribute validation methods to enforce it. To do that, we would add the following three methods to our Hero class:

```
- (BOOL)validateNameOrSecretIdentity:(NSError **)outError {
    if (([self.name length] == 0) &&
        ([self.secretIdentity length] == 0)) {
        if (outError != NULL) {
            NSString *errorStr = NSLocalizedString(
                @"Must provide name or secret identity.",
                @"Must provide name or secret identity.");
```

```
        NSDictionary *userInfoDict = [NSDictionary dictionaryWithObject:errorStr
            forKey:NSLocalizedDescriptionKey];
        NSError *error = [[[NSError alloc] initWithDomain:kHeroValidationDomain
            code:kHeroValidationNameOrSecretIdentityCode
            userInfo:userInfoDict] autorelease];
        *outError = error;
        }
    }
    return YES;
}

- (BOOL)validateForInsert:(NSError **)outError {
    return [self validateNameOrSecretIdentity:outError];
}

- (BOOL)validateForUpdate:(NSError **)outError {
    return [self validateNameOrSecretIdentity:outError];
}
```

Virtual Accessors

At the beginning of the chapter, we added a new attribute, called age, to our data model. We don't need to store the hero's age, however, because we can calculate it based on the hero's birthdate. Calculated attributes like this are often referred to as **virtual accessors**. They look like accessors, and as far as other objects are concerned, they can be treated just like the other attributes. The fact that we're calculating the value at runtime rather than retrieving it from the persistent store is simply an implementation detail.

As our Hero object stands right now, the age accessor will always return nil because we've told our data model not to create storage space for it in the persistent store and have made it read only. In order to make it behave correctly, we have to implement the logic to calculate age in a method that looks like an accessor (hence, the name "virtual accessor"). To do that, add the following method to *Hero.m*, just before @end:

```
- (NSNumber *)age {
    NSCalendar *gregorian = [[NSCalendar alloc]
        initWithCalendarIdentifier:NSGregorianCalendar];

    NSDateComponents *components = [gregorian
        components:NSYearCalendarUnit
        fromDate:self.birthdate
        toDate:[NSDate date]
        options:0];
    NSInteger years = [components year];

    [gregorian release];

    return [NSNumber numberWithInteger:years];
}
```

Now, any code that uses the age property accessor will be returned an NSNumber instance with the calculated age of the superhero.

Adding Validation Feedback

In Chapter 4, we created an abstract class named ManagedObjectAttributeEditor that encapsulates the common functionality shared by the various attribute editors. The ManagedObjectAttributeEditor class does not include code designed to save its managed object. We push that job to the subclasses, because we know that the actual mechanism for retrieving values from the user interface and putting them into an attribute is going to vary from subclass to subclass. But now, we want to add validation feedback when the edited attribute fails validation, and we don't want to duplicate the same functionality in each subclass's save method.

If you look at the subclasses of ManagedObjectAttributeEditor, you'll notice that they all share a bit of logic at the end of their save methods:

```
NSError *error;
if (![managedObject.managedObjectContext save:&error])
    NSLog(@"Error saving: %@", [error localizedDescription]);

[self.navigationController popViewControllerAnimated:YES];
```

Every attribute editor has to save the managed object after updating it with the newly edited value. At this point in the save method, we'll find out about any validation error, so this is where we need to add the code to notify the user of those errors. Let's refactor this shared functionality into ManagedObjectAttributeEditor.

Now, we could put this code in the save method of ManagedObjectAttributeEditor and have each of the subclasses call super after copying the data from their user interface to the managed object. However, it's still important to make sure that subclasses do actually implement save. If we have the subclasses call super, then we've got no place to place an exception. Instead, we'll leave the exception in ManagedObjectAttributeEditor's save method. If a subclass does not implement save, ManagedObjectAttributeEditor's save will be called and this exception will be thrown.

To complement this strategy, we'll create a new method on ManagedObjectAttributeEditor called validateAndPop that will attempt to save the managed object. If the object passes validation, it will pop the controller off the navigation stack, returning the user to the previous level in the nagivation hierarchy. If validation fails, however, we will present an alert telling the user what went wrong. We'll present them with the option of fixing it, or canceling their changes and reverting to the previous value.

Updating the ManagedObjectAttributeEditor Header File

Single-click on *ManagedObjectAttributeEditor.h*. We need to make two changes to this file. First, we need to conform the class to UIAlertViewDelegate. We're going to be using an alert view to notify the user if validation failed, and we need to conform to this protocol to find out whether the user chose to fix the problem or to cancel the change. We also need to add a declaration for the new validateAndPop: method. Here are the necessary changes:

```
#import <UIKit/UIKit.h>
#define kNonEditableTextColor     [UIColor colorWithRed:.318 green:0.4 blue:.569
alpha:1.0]

@interface ManagedObjectAttributeEditor : UITableViewController
    <UIAlertViewDelegate> {
    NSManagedObject        *managedObject;
    NSString               *keypath;
    NSString               *labelString;

}

@property (nonatomic, retain) NSManagedObject *managedObject;
@property (nonatomic, retain) NSString *keypath;
@property (nonatomic, retain) NSString *labelString;

-(IBAction)cancel;
-(IBAction)save;
-(IBAction)validateAndPop;

@end
```

Save *ManagedObjectAttributeEditor.h* and switch to *ManagedObjectAttributeEditor.m*.

Updating the ManagedObjectAttributeEditor Implementation File

Add the following method to the ManagedObjectAttributeEditor implementation, somewhere between the @implementation and @end tags. We put it right after the save method, but feel free to put it anywhere that makes sense to you as long as it's within the class implementation. It's your code, after all, and you're the one who may need to find this method again.

```
-(IBAction)validateAndPop {
    NSError *error;
    if (![managedObject.managedObjectContext save:&error]) {

        NSString *message = nil;
        if ([[error domain] isEqualToString:@"NSCocoaErrorDomain"]) {
            NSDictionary *userInfo = [error userInfo];
            message = [NSString stringWithFormat:NSLocalizedString(
                @"Validation error on %@\rFailed condition: %@",
                @"Validation error on %@, (failed condition: %@)"),
                [userInfo valueForKey:@"NSValidationErrorKey"],
                [userInfo valueForKey:@"NSValidationErrorPredicate"]];
        }
        else
            message = [error localizedDescription];

        UIAlertView *alert = [[UIAlertView alloc] initWithTitle:
            NSLocalizedString(@"Validation Error", @"Validation Error")
            message:message
            delegate:self
            cancelButtonTitle:NSLocalizedString(@"Cancel", @"Cancel")
```

```
                    otherButtonTitles:NSLocalizedString(@"Fix", @"Fix"), nil];
            [alert show];
            [alert release];
        }
        else
            [self.navigationController popViewControllerAnimated:YES];
    }
```

There's nothing really new here. We attempt to save and, if the attempt fails, we pull the information out of the returned NSError object. The only unusual thing here is that we retrieve the information a little bit differently if the error came from our application than if was the result of a validation error generated by the data model. Either way, we present an alert with two buttons, one to cancel the changes, and the other to stay in the editor and make changes to fix the problem.

Next, we need to add our alert view delegate method, which will get called when the user presses one of the two buttons on the alert view. Add the following code to your class implementation also. We like to put the delegate methods at the end of the file, right before the @end statement.

```
#pragma mark -
#pragma mark Alert View Delegate
- (void)alertView:(UIAlertView *)alertView clickedButtonAtIndex:(NSInteger)buttonIndex {
    if (buttonIndex == [alertView cancelButtonIndex]) {
        [self.managedObject.managedObjectContext rollback];
        [self.navigationController popViewControllerAnimated:YES];
    }
}
```

If the user pressed the *Cancel* button, we roll back the managed object context, which returns the context back to the state it was in when it was last saved. If we didn't do this, then the change the user made would still be in memory, it just wouldn't have been saved to the persistent store, and that would cause problems with any future saves. It would also simply be wrong, because the user would see the unsaved, changed value in the user interface, even though they just did a cancel.

After restoring the hero in memory to its last saved state, our controller then pops itself off the stack, which returns the user to the previous view. In our case, the previous view is the hero editing view.

Updating the Subclasses to Use Validation

We currently have three subclasses of ManagedObjectAttributeEditor, and all three of them currently handle saving and popping themselves off the stack themselves. We need to modify the save method of all three classes to use the new functionality in their superclass instead.

Updating ManagedObjectStringEditor

Single-click *ManagedObjectStringEditor.m* and look for the save method. Remove the existing code to save and pop the controller off the navigation stack and replace it with a call to the superclass's `validateAndPop` method. When you're done, the save method should look like this:

```
-(IBAction)save {
    NSUInteger onlyRow[] = {0, 0};
    NSIndexPath *onlyRowPath = [NSIndexPath indexPathWithIndexes:onlyRow length:2];
    UITableViewCell *cell = [self.tableView cellForRowAtIndexPath:onlyRowPath];
    UITextField *textField = (UITextField *)[cell.contentView
                                             viewWithTag:kTextFieldTag];
    [self.managedObject setValue:textField.text forKey:self.keypath];

    [self validateAndPop];
}
```

Save *ManagedObjectStringEditor.m*.

Updating ManagedObjectDateEditor

Next, single-click *ManagedObjectDateEditor.m* and do the same thing. When you're done, it should look like this:

```
-(IBAction)save {
    [self.managedObject setValue:self.datePicker.date forKey:self.keypath];
    [self validateAndPop];
}
```

Save *ManagedObjectDateEditor.m*.

Updating ManagedObjectSingleSelectionListEditor

Finally, single-click *ManagedObjectSingleSelectionListEditor.m* and repeat the process one more time. When you're done, the save method should look like this:

```
-(IBAction)save {
    UITableViewCell *selectedCell = [self.tableView
        cellForRowAtIndexPath:lastIndexPath];
    NSString *newValue = selectedCell.textLabel.text;
    [self.managedObject setValue:newValue forKey:self.keypath];
    [self validateAndPop];
}
```

Save *ManagedObjectSingleSelectionListEditor.m*.

Creating the Value Transformer

Earlier in the chapter, we added an attribute called *favoriteColor*, and set its type to *Transformable*. As we stated then, often you'll be able to leave the transformable attribute's transformer class at *NSKeyedUnarchiveFromData* and be completely done with the process, since that provided class will use an NSKeyedArchiver to convert an object instance into an NSData object that can be stored in the persistent store, and an NSKeyedUnarchiver to take the NSData object from the persistent store and reconstitute it back into an object instance.

In the case of UIColor, we can't do that, because UIColor doesn't conform to NSCoding and can't be archived using an NSKeyedArchiver. As a result, we have to manually write a value transformer to handle the transformation.

Writing a value transformer is actually quite easy. We start by subclassing the NSValueTransformer class. We then override transformedValueClass, which is a method that returns the class of objects that this transformer can convert. Our value transformer will return an instance of the class UIColor because that's the type of attribute we want to store. Transformable Core Data attributes have to be able to both convert from an instance of UIColor to an instance of NSData and back from an instance of NSData to an instance of UIColor. Otherwise, we wouldn't be able to both save and retrieve values from the persistent store. As a result, we also need to override a method called allowsReverseTransformation, returning YES to indicate that our converter supports two-way conversions.

After that, we override two methods. One, transformedValue:, takes an instance of the class we want to convert and returns the converted object. For transformable Core Data attributes, this method will take an instance of the attribute's underlying class and will return an instance of NSData. The other method we have to implement, reverseTransformedValue:, takes a converted object instance and reconstitutes the original object. For a Core Data transformable attribute, that means taking an instance of NSData and returning an object that represents this attribute. Let's do it.

Single-click the *Classes* folder in the *Groups & Files* pane and create a new file. Xcode doesn't provide a file template for value transformers, so select the *Objective-C class* template and create a subclass of NSObject and name it *UIColorRGBValueTransformer.m*.

> **TIP** Some of the class names we're creating may seem unnecessarily long, but it's important that class names be descriptive. UIColor supports many color models but, for our needs, we only need to convert RGBA colors, because we're only going to allow the user to create RGBA colors. It's important to indicate this limitation in the class name because at some point in the future we may need a UIColor value transformer that supports all color models. When we revisit this code in the future, we'll have a built-in reminder that this class only handles one of the possible color models that UIColor supports.

Single-click *UIColorRGBValueTransformer.h* and change the superclass from NSObject to NSValueTransformer.

In addition, since UIColor is part of UIKit, not Foundation, change the line that currently reads:

```
#import <Foundation/Foundation.h>
```

to read:

```
#import <UIKit/UIKit.h>
```

Once you've made those two changes, save the file and switch over to *UIColorRGBValueTransformer.m*.

Now, we have to implement the four methods that will allow our value transformer class to convert instances of UIColor to NSData and vice versa. Add the following four methods to your class:

```
#import "UIColorRGBValueTransformer.h"


@implementation UIColorRGBValueTransformer
+ (Class)transformedValueClass {
    return [NSData class];
}

+ (BOOL)allowsReverseTransformation {
    return YES;
}

// Takes a UIColor, returns an NSData
- (id)transformedValue:(id)value {
    UIColor *color = value;
    const CGFloat *components = CGColorGetComponents(color.CGColor);
    NSString *colorAsString = [NSString stringWithFormat:@"%f,%f,%f,%f",
        components[0], components[1], components[2], components[3]];
    return [colorAsString dataUsingEncoding:NSUTF8StringEncoding];
}

// Takes an NSData, returns a UIColor
- (id)reverseTransformedValue:(id)value {
    NSString *colorAsString = [[[NSString alloc] initWithData:value
        encoding:NSUTF8StringEncoding] autorelease];
    NSArray *components = [colorAsString componentsSeparatedByString:@","];
    CGFloat r = [[components objectAtIndex:0] floatValue];
    CGFloat g = [[components objectAtIndex:1] floatValue];
    CGFloat b = [[components objectAtIndex:2] floatValue];
    CGFloat a = [[components objectAtIndex:3] floatValue];
    return [UIColor colorWithRed:r green:g blue:b alpha:a];
}

@end
```

There are many approaches we could have used to convert a UIColor instance into an NSData instance. We opted for a relatively simple one here. We store the color's four component values in a string with commas between the values. Since we're only dealing with RGBA colors, we know we will always and only have four components, so we're able to simplify the transformation greatly. Now we have a way to store colors in Core Data, so let's create a way for the user to enter a color.

Creating the Color Attribute Editor

Single-click the *Classes* folder in Xcode's *Groups & Files* pane and select **New File…** from the **File** menu. When prompted, select *Objective-C Class* from the *Cocoa Touch Class* category and make sure the *Subclass of* pop-up is set to *NSObject*. When prompted for a name, type *ManagedObjectColorEditor.m* and make sure that *Also create "ManagedObjectColorEditor.h"* is checked. Once the files are created, single-click *ManagedObjectColorEditor.h* and replace the existing contents with the following:

```
#import <UIKit/UIKit.h>
#import "ManagedObjectAttributeEditor.h"

#define kNumberOfSections          2
#define kNumberOfRowsInSection0    1
#define kSliderTag                 5000
#define kColorViewTag              5001

enum colorSliders {
    kRedRow = 0,
    kGreenRow,
    kBlueRow,
    kAlphaRow,
    kNumberOfColorRows
};

@interface ManagedObjectColorEditor : ManagedObjectAttributeEditor {
    UIColor *color;
}

@property (nonatomic, retain) UIColor *color;
- (IBAction)sliderChanged;
@end
```

If you look back at Figure 6–2, you can see that our color editor is going to consist of a table with two sections. The first section will have a single row that will display the currently selected color. The second section will have four rows with sliders, one for each of the four components of an RGBA color. The first two constants and the enum will be used to make our code more legible when referring to section and rows. kSliderTag and kColorViewTag will be used as tags on the slider and color views to make them easier to retrieve from the cell they're on, just as we did in Chapter 8 of *Beginning iPhone 3 Development* (Apress, 2009).

We've subclassed ManagedObjectAttributeEditor once again, so we inherit the keypath, labelString, and managedObject properties, but we do need to add a property to hold the color as it's being edited. We also create an action method that the four sliders can call when they've changed so that we can update the interface and show the new colors indicated by the sliders. Save *ManagedObjectColorEditor.h* and switch over to the implementation file. Replace the existing contents of that file with the following code to implement the color attribute editor:

```
#import "ManagedObjectColorEditor.h"

@implementation ManagedObjectColorEditor
```

```
@synthesize color;
- (void)viewWillAppear:(BOOL)animated {
    [super viewWillAppear:animated];
    self.color = [self.managedObject valueForKey:self.keypath];
}

- (IBAction)sliderChanged {

    CGFloat components[4];
    for (int i = 0; i < kNumberOfColorRows; i++) {
        NSUInteger indices[] = {1, i};
        NSIndexPath *indexPath = [NSIndexPath indexPathWithIndexes:indices
            length:2];
        UITableViewCell *cell = [self.tableView cellForRowAtIndexPath:indexPath];
        UISlider *slider = (UISlider *)[cell viewWithTag:kSliderTag];
        components[i] = slider.value;
    }
    self.color = [UIColor colorWithRed:components[0] green:components[1]
        blue:components[2] alpha:components[3]];

    NSUInteger indices[] = {0,0};
    NSIndexPath *indexPath = [NSIndexPath indexPathWithIndexes:indices length:2];
    UITableViewCell *colorCell = [self.tableView cellForRowAtIndexPath:indexPath];
    UIView *colorView = [colorCell viewWithTag:kColorViewTag];
    colorView.backgroundColor = self.color;
}

-(IBAction)save {
    [self.managedObject setValue:self.color forKey:self.keypath];
    [self validateAndPop];
}

- (void)dealloc {
    [color release];
    [super dealloc];
}

#pragma mark -
#pragma mark Table View Methods
- (NSInteger)numberOfSectionsInTableView:(UITableView *)tableView {
    return kNumberOfSections;
}

- (NSInteger)tableView:(UITableView *)tableView numberOfRowsInSection:(NSInteger)section
{
    if (section == 0)
        return kNumberOfRowsInSection0;
    else
        return kNumberOfColorRows;
}

- (UITableViewCell *)tableView:(UITableView *)tableView
cellForRowAtIndexPath:(NSIndexPath *)indexPath  {

    static NSString *GenericManagedObjectColorEditorColorCell =
        @"GenericManagedObjectColorEditorColorCell";
    static NSString *GenericManagedObjectColorEditorSliderCell =
```

```
        @"GenericManagedObjectColorEditorSliderCell";

    NSString *cellIdentifier = nil;

    NSUInteger row = [indexPath row];
    NSUInteger section = [indexPath section];
    if (section == 0)
        cellIdentifier = GenericManagedObjectColorEditorColorCell;
    else
        cellIdentifier = GenericManagedObjectColorEditorSliderCell;


    UITableViewCell *cell = [tableView
        dequeueReusableCellWithIdentifier:cellIdentifier];
    if (cell == nil) {
        cell = [[[UITableViewCell alloc]
            initWithStyle:UITableViewCellStyleDefault
            reuseIdentifier:cellIdentifier] autorelease];

        UIView *contentView = cell.contentView;

        if (section == 0){
            UIView *colorView = [[UIView alloc] initWithFrame:
                CGRectMake(5.0, 5.0, 290.0, 33.0)];
            colorView.backgroundColor = self.color;
            colorView.tag = kColorViewTag;
            [contentView addSubview:colorView];
        }
        else {

            if (color == nil)
            self.color = [UIColor colorWithRed:1.0 green:1.0 blue:1.0
                alpha:1.0];

            components = CGColorGetComponents(color.CGColor);

          UISlider * slider = [[UISlider alloc] initWithFrame:
              CGRectMake(70.0, 10.0, 210.0, 20.0)];
            slider.tag = kSliderTag;
            slider.maximumValue = 1.0;
            slider.minimumValue = 0.0;
            slider.value = components[row];
            [slider addTarget:self action:@selector(sliderChanged)
                forControlEvents:UIControlEventValueChanged];
            UILabel *label = [[UILabel alloc] initWithFrame:
                CGRectMake(20.0, 10.0, 50.0, 20.0)];
            switch (row) {
                case kRedRow:
                    label.text = NSLocalizedString(@"R",
                        @"R (short for red)");
                    label.textColor = [UIColor redColor];
                    break;
                case kGreenRow:
                    label.text = NSLocalizedString(@"G",
                        @"G (short for green)");
                    label.textColor = [UIColor greenColor];
                    break;
```

```
            case kBlueRow:
                label.text = NSLocalizedString(@"B",
                    @"B (short for blue)");
                label.textColor = [UIColor blueColor];
                break;
            case kAlphaRow:
                label.text = NSLocalizedString(@"A",
                    @"A (short for alpha)");
                label.textColor = [UIColor colorWithRed:0.0
                    green:0.0 blue:0.0 alpha:0.5];
                break;
            default:
                break;
        }
        [contentView addSubview:slider];
        [contentView addSubview:label];

        [slider release];
        [label release];
    }

    }
    return cell;
}

- (NSIndexPath *)tableView:(UITableView *)tableView
willSelectRowAtIndexPath:(NSIndexPath *)indexPath {
    return nil;
}

@end
```

There's nothing really new there. Look over the code and make sure you know what it's doing, but there's nothing there that should really need explanation.

Displaying the New Attributes in Hero Edit Controller

We've added two new attributes to our data model, but we haven't added them to our user interface yet. Remember from Chapter 4 that the attributes displayed by HeroEditController are controlled by those paired, nested arrays we create in viewDidLoad. Until we add rows to those arrays to represent the new attributes, they won't show up or be editable. Single-click *HeroEditController.m* and replace viewDidLoad: with this new version that adds rows to each of the paired, nested arrays for the calculated attribute age and the transformable attribute favoriteColor.

```
- (void)viewDidLoad {
    sectionNames = [[NSArray alloc] initWithObjects:
        [NSNull null],
        NSLocalizedString(@"General", @"General"),
        nil];

    rowLabels = [[NSArray alloc] initWithObjects:

        // Section 1
```

```
            [NSArray arrayWithObject:NSLocalizedString(@"Name", @"Name")],

            // Section 2
            [NSArray arrayWithObjects:
                NSLocalizedString(@"Identity", @"Identity"),
                NSLocalizedString(@"Birthdate", @"Birthdate"),
                NSLocalizedString(@"Age", @"Age"),
                NSLocalizedString(@"Sex", @"Sex"),
                NSLocalizedString(@"Fav. Color", @"Favorite Color"),
                nil],

             // Sentinel
             nil];

    rowKeys = [[NSArray alloc] initWithObjects:

            // Section 1
            [NSArray arrayWithObjects:@"name", nil],

            // Section 2
            [NSArray arrayWithObjects:@"secretIdentity", @"birthdate",
                @"age", @"sex", @"favoriteColor", nil],

            // Sentinel
            nil];

    rowControllers = [[NSArray alloc] initWithObjects:

            // Section 1
            [NSArray arrayWithObject:@"ManagedObjectStringEditor"],

            // Section 2
            [NSArray arrayWithObjects:@"ManagedObjectStringEditor",
                @"ManagedObjectDateEditor",
                [NSNull null],
                @"ManagedObjectSingleSelectionListEditor",
                @"ManagedObjectColorEditor",
                nil],

            // Sentinel
            nil];

    rowArguments = [[NSArray alloc] initWithObjects:

            // Section 1
            [NSArray arrayWithObject:[NSNull null]],

            // Section 2,
            [NSArray arrayWithObjects:[NSNull null],
                [NSNull null],
                [NSNull null],
                [NSDictionary dictionaryWithObject:[NSArray
                    arrayWithObjects:@"Male", @"Female", nil]
                    forKey:@"list"],
                [NSNull null],
                [NSNull null],
                nil],
```

```
    // Sentinel
      nil];

    [super viewDidLoad];
}
```

Notice that in `rowControllers`, for the age row, we've used our good old friend `NSNull`. We're using that to indicate that there is no controller class for that row. The user can't drill down to edit this value. In other words, it's read only.

The Display Problem

If you build and run your application, you'll run into a subtle problem. Here's a hint. It has something to do with the display of `UIColor`. Can you guess what it is?

The problem is that `UIColor` doesn't respond to the `heroValueDisplay` method. We could create a category to add that method to `UIColor`, but the real problem is this: how do we meaningfully represent a color using an instance of `NSString`, the type returned by `heroValueDisplay`? We could create a string that displays the four components of the color, but to most end users, those numbers are meaningless. Our users are going to expect to see the actual color when they're viewing the hero, and we don't have any mechanism right now for showing colors on a row.

The question at this point is, do we go back and re-architect our application so that it can support the display of a UIColor on a table view row? We could resolve this issue, for example, by changing the `heroValueDisplay` protocol and methods that currently return an `NSString` instance and have them return a `UIView` instance, where the `UIView` contains everything that we want to display in a particular row. That's a good idea, but it will require some relatively extensive changes in many different places in our application's code.

Bottom line, we need to figure out if it makes sense to do major renovations to our code to accommodate this need. Is this a one time thing, or do we need do some fairly intrusive refactoring to create a more general solution? We don't want to over-engineer. We don't want to have to do complex changes to multiple classes to support functionality that we'll never need outside of this single instance.

There isn't really One Right Answer™ here. For the sake of argument, we're going to say that we don't foresee needing the ability to display a color anywhere else in our application. Then the question becomes whether there is a less intrusive way of handling this that's not going to make our code significantly harder to maintain. In this situation, there is, and we're going to use it. We can implement the functionality we need by conforming `UIColor` to the `HeroValueDisplay` protocol and then adding just two lines of code to `HeroEditController`.

Single-click *HeroValueDisplay.h* (it's in the *Categories* group) and add the following category declaration at the bottom of the file:

```
@interface UIColor (HeroValueDisplay) <HeroValueDisplay>
- (NSString *)heroValueDisplay;
```

@end

Save *HeroValueDisplay.h* and switch over to *HeroValueDisplay.m* to write the implementation of the heroValueDisplay method for UIColor. Add the following at the end of the file:

```
@implementation UIColor (HeroValueDisplay)
- (NSString *)heroValueDisplay {
    return [NSString stringWithFormat:@"%C%C%C%C%C%C%C%C%C%C",0x2588, 0x2588,
        0x2588, 0x2588, 0x2588, 0x2588, 0x2588, 0x2588, 0x2588, 0x2588];
}
@end
```

This is probably non-obvious, so we'll explain. What we're doing here is creating an NSString instance that contains a sequence of Unicode characters. The 0x2588 character is the Unicode full block character, which is a solid rectangle that takes up the full space of the glyph. If you place several full blocks together in a string, they appear as a rectangle like the one you see in the bottom row of Figure 6–1. Now, we just need to make that rectangle display in color.

Single-click *HeroEditController.m* and add the following two lines of code to tableView:cellForRowAtIndexPath:.

```
- (UITableViewCell *)tableView:(UITableView *)tableView
  cellForRowAtIndexPath:(NSIndexPath *)indexPath {

    static NSString *CellIdentifier = @"Hero Edit Cell Identifier";

    UITableViewCell *cell = [tableView
                        dequeueReusableCellWithIdentifier:CellIdentifier];
    if (cell == nil) {
        cell = [[[UITableViewCell alloc] initWithStyle:UITableViewCellStyleValue2
                                reuseIdentifier:CellIdentifier] autorelease];
    }

    NSString *rowKey = [rowKeys nestedObjectAtIndexPath:indexPath];
    NSString *rowLabel = [rowLabels nestedObjectAtIndexPath:indexPath];

    id <HeroValueDisplay, NSObject> rowValue = [hero valueForKey:rowKey];

    cell.detailTextLabel.text = [rowValue heroValueDisplay];
    cell.textLabel.text = rowLabel;
    cell.accessoryType = UITableViewCellAccessoryDisclosureIndicator;

    if ([rowValue isKindOfClass:[UIColor class]])
        cell.detailTextLabel.textColor = (UIColor *)rowValue;

    return cell;
}
```

The two lines of code we just added look at the underlying class of the attribute we're displaying, and if it's UIColor, or a subclass of UIColor, then we set the text label's textColor property to the value stored in the hero's favoriteColor attribute. This will cause that string of Unicode full blocks to be drawn in that color. Compile and run the application, and the two new attributes should be there (Figure 6–10).

Figure 6–10. *Almost there. The new values are being displayed and the favorite color attribute can be edited.*

This is almost done. There's just one little detail we need to take care of. Look at the *Age* row. Something's not right there. Age is calculated and can't be edited by the user. Yet there's a disclosure indicator on the row, which tells us as a user that we can tap it to edit it. Go ahead and tap it if you want. We'll wait. After it crashes, come on back and we can chat about how to fix it.

Adding View-Only Support to Hero Edit Controller

We need to do two things here. First, we need to get rid of the disclosure indicator so the user doesn't think they can drill down into that attribute to edit it. Then, we need to change the code so that even if a user does tap that row, nothing bad happens. You know, this is actually a pretty good task for you to try on your own if you want. Give it a try. We'll wait right here.

Hiding the Disclosure Indicator

In *HeroEditController.m*, find the method `tableView:cellForRowAtIndexPath:` and replace this line of code:

```
cell.accessoryType = UITableViewCellAccessoryDisclosureIndicator;
```

with these lines of code:

```
id rowController = [rowControllers
```

```
        nestedObjectAtIndexPath:indexPath];
    cell.accessoryType = UITableViewCellAccessoryDisclosureIndicator;
    cell.accessoryType = (rowController == [NSNull null]) ?
        UITableViewCellAccessoryNone :
        UITableViewCellAccessoryDisclosureIndicator;
    if ([rowValue isKindOfClass:[UIColor class]])
        cell.detailTextLabel.textColor = (UIColor *)rowValue;
```

Previously, we were just setting every row to use the disclosure indicator. Now, instead, we retrieve that singleton instance of NSNull and the name of the class that is responsible for editing this type of attribute. If that controller class is NSNull, it means there is no controller class to drill down into. If there's no controller class, then we set the accessory type to UITableViewCellAccessoryNone, which means there will be nothing in the accessory view of this row. If there is a controller class to drill down into, we set the accessory view to show the disclosure indicator, just like we were previously doing. Simple enough, right? Let's take care of the other half of the equation.

Handling Taps on Read-Only Attributes

As you may remember from *Beginning iPhone 3 Development*, table view delegates have a way of disallowing a tap on a specific row. If we implement the method tableView:willSelectRowAtIndexPath: and return nil, the row won't get selected. Add the following method to *HeroEditController.m*, down in the table view portion of the code:

```
- (NSIndexPath *)tableView:(UITableView *)tableView
        willSelectRowAtIndexPath:(NSIndexPath *)indexPath {
    id controllerClassName = [rowControllers nestedObjectAtIndexPath:indexPath];
    return (controllerClassName == (id)[NSNull null]) ? nil : indexPath;
}
```

In this method, we retrieve the controller class for the tapped row. If we get an instance of NSNull back, we return nil to indicate that the user cannot select this row. If we retrieve any other value, we return indexPath, which allows the selection to continue.

By disallowing the selection when the row has no controller, the code in tableView:didSelectRowAtIndexPath: will never get called when a read-only row is tapped. As a result, we don't have to make any changes to that method, so we're ready to go. Build and run your project and play around with *SuperDB* some more. The editing view should now look like Figure 6–1. If you tap the *Fav. Color* row, it should drill down to something that looks like Figure 6–2. If you tap on the *Age* row, it should do nothing. If you try to enter an invalid value into any attribute, you should get an alert and be given the opportunity to fix or cancel the changes you made. And all is right with the world. Well, at least with our app. For now.

Color Us Gone

By now, you should have a good grasp on just how much power you gain from subclassing NSManagedObject. You've seen how to use it to do conditional defaulting and both single-field and multi-field validation. You also saw how to use custom managed objects to create virtual accessors.

You saw how to politely inform your user when they've entered an invalid attribute that causes a managed object to fail validation, and you saw how to use transformable attributes and value transformers to store custom objects in Core Data.

This was a dense chapter, but you should really be starting to get a feel for just how flexible and powerful Core Data can be. We've got one more chapter on Core Data before we move on to other parts of the iPhone 3 SDK. When you're ready, turn the page to learn about relationships and fetched properties.

Chapter 7

Relationships, Fetched Properties, and Expressions

Welcome to the final chapter on Core Data. So far, our application includes only a single entity: *Hero*. In this chapter, we're going to show you how managed objects can incorporate and reference other managed objects through the use of **relationships** and **fetched properties**. This will give you the ability to make applications of much greater complexity than our current SuperDB application. That's not the only thing we're going to do in this chapter, however.

Throughout the book, we've endeavored to write our code in a generic fashion. We created our `HeroEditController`, for example, so that the structure and content were completely controlled by a handful of arrays, and we implemented error validation in our managed object attribute editors by adding generic code to their common superclass. In this chapter, we're going to reap the benefits of writing our code that way. We'll introduce a new entity, yet we won't need to write a new controller class to display that entity and let the user edit it. Our code is generic enough that we're simply going to refactor our existing `HeroEditController` into a generic class that can display and edit any managed object just by changing the data stored in those paired, nested arrays. This will greatly reduce the number of controller classes we need in our application as the complexity of the data model increases. Instead of having dozens of individual controller classes for each entity that needs to be edited by or displayed to the user, we'll have a single, generic controller class capable of displaying and editing the contents of any managed object.

We have a lot to do in this chapter, so no dallying. Let's get started.

Expanding Our Application: Superpowers and Reports

Before we talk about the nitty-gritty, let's quickly look at the changes we're going to make to the SuperDB application in this chapter. On the surface, the changes look relatively simple. We'll add the ability to specify any number of superpowers for each hero, and also add a number of reports that show other superheroes that meet certain criteria, including heroes who are either younger or older than this hero, or who are the same sex or the opposite sex (Figure 7–1).

Figure 7–1. *At the end of our chapter, we'll have added the ability to specify any number of superpowers for each hero, as well as provided a number of reports that let us find other heroes based on how they relate to this hero.*

Heroes' powers will be represented by a new entity that we'll create and imaginatively call *Power*. When users add or edit a power, they will be presented with a new view (Figure 7–2), but in reality, under the hood, it will be a new instance of the same object used to edit and display heroes.

Figure 7–2. *The new view for editing powers is actually an instance of the same object used to edit heroes.*

When users drill down into one of the reports, they will get a list of the other heroes that meet the selected criteria (Figure 7–3).

Figure 7–3. *The Reports section on our hero will let us find other heroes who meet certain criteria in relation to the hero we're currently editing. Here, for example, we're seeing all the heroes who were born after Ultra Guy.*

Tapping any of the rows will take you to another view where you can edit that hero, using another instance of the same generic controller class. Our users will be able to drill down an infinite number of times (limited only by memory), all courtesy of a single class.

Before we start implementing these changes, we need to talk about a few concepts, and then make some changes to our data model.

Relationships

We introduced the concept of Core Data relationships back in Chapter 2. Now we will go into more detail, and see how these can be used in applications. The **relationship** is one of the most important concepts in Core Data. Without relationships, entities would be isolated. There would be no way to have one entity contain another entity or reference another entity. Let's look at a hypothetical header file for a simple example of an old-fashioned data model class to give us a familiar point of reference:

```
#import <UIKit/UIKit.>

@class Address;

@interface Person : NSObject {

    NSString        *firstName;
    NSString        *lastName;
    NSDate          *birthdate;
    UIImage         *image;

    Address         *address;

    Person          *mother;
    Person          *father;

    NSMutableArray  *children;
}

@property (nonatomic, retain) NSString *firstName;
@property (nonatomic, retain) NSString *lastName;
@property (nonatomic, retain) NSDate *birthdate;
@property (nonatomic, retain) UIImage *image;
@property (nonatomic, retain) Address *address;
@property (nonatomic, retain) Person *mother;
@property (nonatomic, retain) Person *father;
@property (nonatomic, retain) NSMutableArray *children;

@end
```

Here, we have a class that represents a single person. We have instance variables to store a variety of information about that person and properties to expose that information to other objects. There's nothing earth-shattering here. Now, let's think about how we could re-create this object in Core Data.

The first four instance variables—firstName, lastName, birthDate, and image—can all be handled by built-in Core Data attribute types, so we could use attributes to store that information on the entity. The two NSString instances would become *String* attributes, the NSDate instance would become a *Date* attribute, and the UIImage instance would become a *Transformable* attribute, handled in the same way as UIColor in the previous chapter.

After that, we have an instance of an Address object. This object probably stores information like street address, city, state or province, and postal code. That's followed by two Person instance variables and a mutable array designed to hold pointers to this person's children. Most likely, these arrays are intended to hold pointers to more Person objects.

In object-oriented programming, including a pointer to another object as an instance variable is called **composition**. Composition is an incredibly handy device, because it lets us create much smaller classes and reuse objects, rather then have data duplicated.

In Core Data, we don't have composition per se, but we do have relationships, which essentially serve the same purpose. Relationships allow managed objects to include references to other managed objects of a specific entity, known as **destination entities**, or sometimes just **destinations**. Relationships are Core Data properties, just as attributes are. As such, they have an assigned name, which serves as the key value used to set and retrieve the object or objects represented by the relationship. Relationships are added to entities in Xcode's data model editor in the same way attributes are added. You'll see how to do that in a few minutes. There are two basic types of relationships: **to-one relationships** and **to-many relationships**.

To-One Relationships

When you create a to-one relationship, you are saying that one object can contain a pointer to a single managed object of a specific entity. In our example, the *Person* entity has a single to-one relationship to the *Address* entity.

Once you've added a to-one relationship to an object, you can assign a managed object to the relationship using key-value coding (**KVC**). For example, you might set the *Address* entity of a *Person* managed object like so:

```
NSManagedObject *address = [NSEntityDescription insertNewObjectForEntityForName:
    @"Address" inManagedObjectContext:thePerson.managedObjectContext];
[thePerson setValue:address forKey:@"address"];
```

Retrieving the object can also be accomplished using KVC, just with attributes:

```
NSManagedObject *address = [thePerson valueForKey:@"address"];
```

When you create a custom subclass of NSManagedObject, as we did in the previous chapter, you can use Objective-C properties and dot notation to get and set those properties. The property that represents a to-one relationship is an instance of NSManagedObject or a subclass of NSManagedObject, so setting the address looks just like setting attributes:

```
NSManagedObject *address = [NSEntityDescription insertNewObjectForEntityForName:
    @"Address" inManagedObjectContext:thePerson.managedObjectContext];
thePerson.address = address;
```

And retrieving a to-one relationship becomes as follows:

```
NSManagedObject *address = thePerson.address;
```

In almost every respect, the way you deal with a to-one relationship in code is identical to the way we've been dealing with Core Data attributes. We use KVC to get and set the values using Objective-C objects. Instead of using Foundation classes that correspond to different attribute types, we use NSManagedObject or a subclass of NSManagedObject that represents the entity.

To-Many Relationships

To-many relationships allow you to use a relationship to associate multiple managed objects to a particular managed object. This is equivalent to using composition with a collection class such as NSMutableArray or NSMutableSet in Objective-C, as with the children instance variable in the Person class we looked at earlier. In that example, we used an NSMutableArray, which is an editable, ordered collection of objects. That array allows us to add and remove objects at will. If we want to indicate that the person represented by an instance of Person has children, we just add the instance of Person that represents that person's children to the children array.

In Core Data, it works a little differently. To-many relationships are unordered. They are represented by instances of NSSet, which is an unordered, immutable collection that you can't change, or by NSMutableSet, an unordered collection that you can change. Here's how getting a to-many relationship and iterating over its contents might look with an NSSet:

```
NSSet *children = [person valueForKey:@"children"];
for (NSManagedObject *oneChild in children) {
    // do something
}
```

> **NOTE:** Do you spot a potential problem from the fact that to-many relationships are returned as an unordered NSSet? When displaying them in a table view, it's important that the objects in the relationship are ordered consistently. If the collection is unordered, you have no guarantee that the row you tap will bring up the object you expect. You'll see how to deal with that a little later in the chapter.

On the other hand, if you wish to add or remove managed objects from a to-many relationship, you must ask Core Data to give you an instance of NSMutableSet, by calling mutableSetValueForKey: instead of valueForKey:, like so:

```
NSManagedObject *child = [NSEntityDescription insertNewObjectForEntityForName:
    @"Person" inManagedObjectContext:thePerson.managedObjectContext];
NSMutableSet *children = [person mutableSetValueForKey:@"children"];
```

```
[children addObject:child];
[children removeObject:childToBeRemoved];
```

If you don't need to change which objects a particular relationship contains, use valueForKey:, just as with to-one arrays. Don't call mutableSetValueForKey: if you don't need to change which objects make up the relationship, as it incurs slightly more overhead than just calling valueForKey:.

In addition to using valueForKey: and mutableSetValueForKey:, Core Data also provides special methods, created dynamically at runtime, that let you add and delete managed objects from a to-many relationship. There are four of these methods per relationship. Each method name incorporates the name of the relationship. The first allows you to add a single object to a relationship:

```
- (void)addXxxObject:(NSManagedObject *)value;
```

where Xxx is the capitalized name of the relationship, and value is either an NSManagedObject or a specific subclass of NSManagedObject. In the Person example we've been working with, the method to add a child to the children relationship looks like this:

```
- (void)addChildrenObject:(Person *)value;
```

The method for deleting a single object follows a similar form:

```
- (void)removeXxxObject:(NSManagedObject *)value;
```

The dynamically generated method for adding multiple objects to a relationship takes the following form:

```
- (void)addXxx:(NSSet *)values;
```

The method takes an instance of NSSet containing the managed objects to be added. So, the dynamically created method for adding multiple children to our Person managed object is as follows:

```
- (void)addChildren:(NSSet *)values;
```

Finally, here's the method used to remove multiple managed objects from a relationship:

```
- (void)removeXxx:(NSSet *)values;
```

Remember that these methods are generated for you when you declare a custom NSManagedObject subclass. When Xcode encounters your NSManagedObject subclass declaration, it creates a category on the subclass that declares the four dynamic methods using the relationship name to construct the method names. Since the methods are generated at runtime, you won't find any source code in your project that implements the methods. If you never call the methods, you'll never see the methods. As long as you've already created the to-many relationship in your data model editor, you don't need to do anything extra to access these methods. They are created for you and ready to be called.

> **NOTE:** There's one tricky point associated with the methods generated for to-many relationships. Xcode declares the four dynamic methods when you first generate the NSManagedObject subclass files from the template. If you have an existing data model with a to-many relationship and a subclass of NSManagedObject, what happens if you decide to add a new to-many relationship to that data model? If you add the to-many relationship to an existing NSManagedObject subclass, you'll need to add the category containing the dynamic methods yourself, which is what we'll do a little later in the chapter.

There is absolutely no difference between using these four methods and using mutableSetValueForKey:. The dynamic methods are just a little more convenient and make your code easier to read.

Inverse Relationships

In Core Data, every relationship can have an **inverse relationship**. A relationship and its inverse are two sides of the same coin. In our Person object example, the inverse relationship for the children relationship might be a relationship called parent. A relationship does not need to be the same kind as its inverse. A to-one relationship, for example, can have an inverse relationship that is to-many. In fact, this is pretty common. If you think about it in real-world terms, a person can have many children. The inverse is that a child can have only one biological mother and one biological father, but the child can have multiple parents and guardians. So, depending on your needs and the way you modeled the relationship, you might choose to use either a to-one or a to-many relationship for the inverse.

If you add an object to a relationship, Core Data will automatically take care of adding the correct object to the inverse relationship. So, if you had a Person named steve and added a child to steve, Core Data would automatically make the child's parent steve.

Although relationships are not required to have an inverse, Apple generally recommends that you always create and specify the inverse, even if you won't need to use the inverse relationship in your application. In fact, the compiler will actually warn you if you fail to provide an inverse. There are some exceptions to this general rule, specifically when the inverse relationship will contain an extremely large number of objects, since removing the object from a relationship triggers its removal from the inverse relationship. Removing the inverse will require iterating over the set that represents the inverse, and if that's a very large set, there could be performance implications. But unless you have a specific reason not to do so, you should model the inverse, as it helps Core Data ensure data integrity. If you have performance issues as a result, it's relatively easy to remove the inverse relationship later.

NOTE: You can read more about how the absence of inverse relationships can cause integrity problems here:
`http://developer.apple.com/mac/library/documentation/Cocoa/Concept`
`ual/CoreData/Articles/cdRelationships.html#//apple_ref/doc/uid/TP4`
`0001857-SW6`

Delete Rules

Every relationship, regardless of its type, has something called a **delete rule**, which specifies what happens when one object in the relationship is deleted. There are four possible delete rules:

- *Nullify*: This is the default delete rule. With this delete rule, when one object is deleted, the inverse relationship is just updated so that it doesn't point to anything. If the inverse relationship is a to-one relationship, it is set to `nil`. If the inverse relationship is a to-many relationship, the deleted object will be removed from the inverse relationship. This option ensures that there are no references to the object being deleted, but does nothing more.

- *No Action*: If you specify a delete rule of *No Action*, when you delete one object from a relationship, nothing happens to the other object. Instances where you would use this particular rule are extremely rare, and are generally limited to one-way relationships with no inverse. This action is rarely used because the other object's inverse relationship would end up pointing to an object that no longer exists.

- *Cascade*: If you set the delete rule to *Cascade*, when you delete a managed object, all the objects in the relationship are also removed. This is a more dangerous option than *Nullify*, in that deleting one object can result in the deletion of other objects. You would typically want to choose *Cascade* when a relationship's inverse relationship is to-one and the related object is not used in any other relationships. If the object or objects in the relationship are used only for this relationship and not for any other reason, then you probably do want a cascade rule, so that you don't leave orphaned objects sitting in the persistent store taking up space.

- *Deny*: This delete rule option will actually prevent an object from being deleted if there are any objects in this association, making it the safest option in terms of data integrity. The *Deny* option is not used frequently, but if you have situations where an object shouldn't be deleted as long as it has any objects in a specific relationship, this is the one you would choose.

Fetched Properties

Relationships allow you to associate managed objects with specific other managed objects. In a way, relationships are sort of like iTunes playlists, where you can put specific songs into a list and then play them later. If you're an iTunes user, you know that there are things called Smart Playlists, which allow you to create playlists based on criteria rather than a list of specific songs. You can create a Smart Playlist, for example, that includes all the songs by a specific artist. Later on, when you buy new songs from that artist, they are added to that Smart Playlist automatically, because the playlist is based on criteria and the new songs meet those criteria.

Core Data has something similar. There's another type of attribute you can add to an entity that will associate a managed object with other managed objects based on criteria, rather than associating specific objects. Instead of adding and removing objects, fetched properties work by creating a predicate that defines which objects should be returned. Predicates, as you may recall, are objects that represent selection criteria. They are primarily used to sort collections and fetch results.

> **TIP:** If you're rusty on predicates, *Learn Objective-C on the Mac* by Scott Knaster and Mark Dalrymple (Apress, 2009) devotes an entire chapter to the little beasties.

Fetched properties are always immutable. You can't change their contents at runtime. The criteria are usually specified in the data model (a process that we'll look at shortly), and then you access the objects that meet that criteria using properties or KVC.

Unlike to-many relationships, fetched properties are ordered collections and can have a specified sort order. Oddly enough, the data model editor doesn't allow you to specify how fetched properties are sorted. If you care about the order of the objects in a fetched property, you must actually write code to do that, which we'll look at later in this chapter.

Once you've created a fetched property, working with it is pretty straightforward. You just use `valueForKey:` to retrieve the objects that meet the fetched property's criteria in an instance of `NSArray`:

```
NSArray *olderPeople = [person valueForKey:@"olderPeople"];
```

If you use a custom `NSManagedObject` subclass and define a property for the fetched property, you can also use dot notation to retrieve objects that meet the fetched property's criteria in an `NSArray` instance, like so:

```
NSArray *olderPeople = person.olderPeople;
```

Creating Relationships and Fetched Properties in the Data Model Editor

The first step in using relationships or fetched properties is to add them to your data model. Let's add the relationship and fetched properties we'll need in our SuperDB application now. If you look back at Figure 7–1, you can probably guess that we're going to need a new entity to represent the heroes' powers, as well as a relationship from our existing *Hero* entity to the new *Power* entity we're going to create. We'll also need four fetched properties to represent the four different reports.

Before we start making changes, create a new version of your data model by single-clicking the current version in the *Groups & Files* pane (the one with the green check mark), and then selecting **Add Model Version** from the **Data Model** submenu of the **Design** menu. This ensures that the data we collected using the previous data models migrate properly to the new version we'll be creating in this chapter.

Adding the Power Entity

Click the current data model to bring up the data model editor. Using the plus icon in the lower-left corner of the data model editor's entity pane, add a new entity and call it *Power*. You can leave all the other fields at their default values (Figure 7–4).

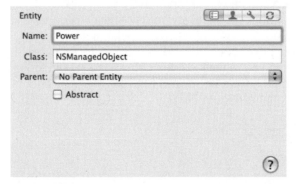

Figure 7–4. *Rename the new entity* Power *and leave the other fields at their default values.*

If you look back at Figure 7–2, you can see that our *Power* object has two fields: one for the name of the power and another that identifies the source of this particular power. In the interest of keeping things simple, the two attributes will just hold string values.

With *Power* still selected in the property pane, add two attributes using the property pane. Call one of them *name*, uncheck the *Optional* check box, set its *Type* to *String*, and give it a *Default* value of *New Power*. Give the second one a name of *source*, and set its *Type* to *String* as well. Leave *Optional* checked. There is no need for a default value. Once you're finished, you should have two rounded rectangles in the data model editor's diagram view (Figure 7–5).

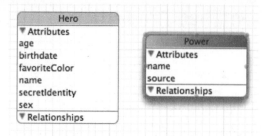

Figure 7–5. *We now have two entities, but they are not related in any way.*

Creating the Powers Relationship

Right now, the *Power* entity is selected. Single-click the rounded rectangle that represents the *Hero* entity, or select *Hero* in the entity pane to select it. Now, in the properties pane, click the plus button and select *Add Relationship*. In the data model editor's detail pane, change the name of the new relationship to *powers* and the *Destination* to *Power*. The *Destination* field specifies which entity's managed objects can be added to this relationship, so by selecting *Power*, we are indicating that this relationship stores powers.

We can't specify the inverse relationship yet, but we do want to check the *To-Many Relationship* box to indicate that each hero can have more than one power. Also, change the *Delete Rule* to *Cascade*. In our application, every hero will have his or her own set of powers—we won't be sharing powers between heroes. When a hero is deleted, we want to make sure that hero's powers are deleted as well, so we don't leave orphaned data in the persistent store. Once you're finished, the detail pane should look like Figure 7–6, and the diagram view should have a line drawn between the *Hero* and *Power* entities to represent the new relationship (Figure 7–7).

Relationship	
Name:	powers
	☑ Optional ☐ Transient
Destination:	Power
Inverse:	No Inverse Relationship
	☑ To-Many Relationship
Min Count:	none Max Count: none
Delete Rule:	Cascade

Figure 7–6. *The detail pane view of the powers relationship*

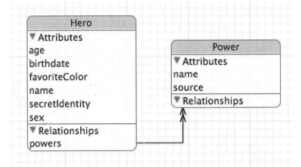

Figure 7–7. *Relationships are represented in the diagram view by lines drawn between rounded rectangles. A single arrowhead represents a to-one relationship, and a double arrowhead (as shown here) represents a to-many relationship.*

Creating the Inverse Relationship

We won't actually need the inverse relationship in our application, but we're going to follow Apple's recommendation and specify one. Since the inverse relationship will be to-one, it doesn't present any performance implications. Select the *Power* entity again, and add a relationship to it using the property pane. Name this new relationship *hero*, and select a *Destination* entity of *Hero*. If you look at your diagram view now, you should see two lines representing the two different relationships we've created.

Next, click the *Inverse* pop-up menu and select *powers*. This indicates that the relationship is the inverse of the one we created earlier. Once you've selected it, the two relationship lines in the diagram view will merge together into a single line with arrowheads on both sides (Figure 7–8).

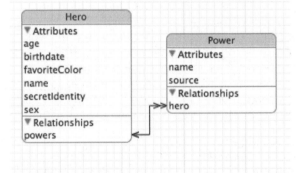

Figure 7–8. *Inverse relationships are represented as a single line with arrowheads on both sides, rather than two separate lines.*

Creating the *olderHeroes* Fetched Property

Select the *Hero* entity again so that you can add some fetched properties to it. In the property pane, select the plus button and choose *Add Fetched Property*. Call the new fetched property *olderHeroes*, and select a *Destination* of *Hero*. Notice that there is only one other field that can be set on the detail pane: a big white box called *Predicate* (Figure 7–9).

TIP: Both relationships and fetched properties can use their own entity as the *Destination*.

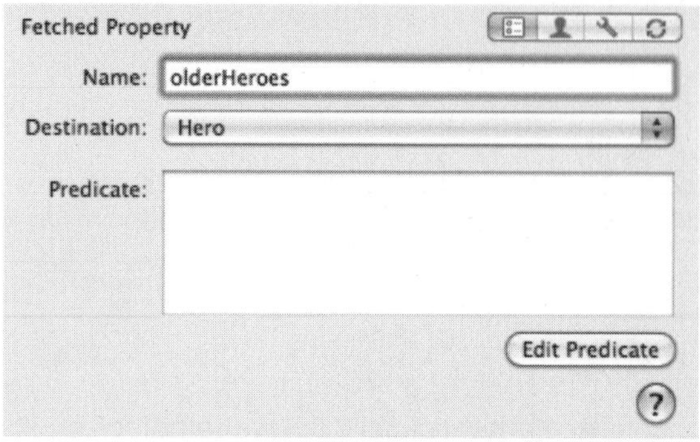

Figure 7–9. *The detail pane showing a fetched property*

Although the *Predicate* field is a text field, it's not directly editable. Once you've created a predicate, it will show a string representation of that predicate, but you can't actually type into the field. Instead, to set the predicate for this fetched property, you click the *Edit Predicate* button to enter Xcode's **predicate builder**. Let's do that now. Go ahead. It's perfectly safe. No, seriously—click the darn button already.

The predicate builder is a visual tool for building criteria (Figure 7–10), and it can be used to specify some relatively sophisticated logic. We're going to start with a fairly simple predicate, and then we'll build a little more complex one later.

When the predicate builder opens, it contains a single row that represents the first criterion. Without at least one criterion, a predicate serves no purpose, so Xcode gives you the first one automatically. The pop-up menu on the left side allows you to select among the properties on the destination entity, as well as some other options that we'll look at later. The predicate we're building now needs to be based on *birthdate*, so single-click the pop-up menu and select *birthdate*, and then change the second pop-up menu (the one currently set to =) to <. For another hero to be older than this hero, that hero's birth date must be earlier.

When you change the leftmost pop-up menu to *birthdate*, the text field on the row changes into a date-picker control. If we wanted the comparison to be against a date constant, we would enter that date value there. That's not what we want, however. The way to change this is not obvious. Control-click in the space between the date field and the minus button. That brings up a contextual menu, and one of the things you can do with this contextual menu is change the operator type.

Figure 7–10. *The predicate builder when first opened*

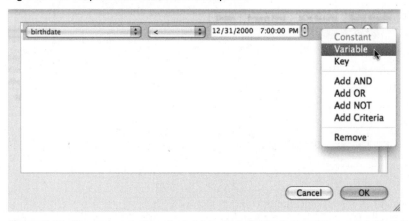

Figure 7–11. *The super-secret predicate trick: right-clicking in the white space to the left of the minus button lets you change the type of operand.*

Three types of operands are available in the predicate builder, and both the left and right operand can be changed to any of these three types:

- *Constant*: A constant is a specified value you enter into a field. Constants never change value.

- *Key*: A key is a value on the object to be retrieved that is specified using KVC. The left operand always defaults to a key, so when we selected *birthdate* a moment ago, we were setting a key operand.

- *Variable*: A variable is a special value that is entered into a text field and evaluated at runtime. The primary usage of variable operands is to allow you to compare attributes on the entities being evaluated with the attributes on the source object where the fetched property is being called.

Your first instinct might be to specify *Key* for the right operand, since we want to compare to the *birthdate* attribute on this object. However, it doesn't work that way. Key operators always and only refer to keys on the managed objects being retrieved—no matter on which side of the equation they appear. So, if we were to select *Key* here, we would be comparing each hero's birth date to his or her own birth date. Instead, we want to choose *Variable*. Do that now, and the date field should turn back into a text field, where you can type.

The *Variable* option allows you to use special predicate builder variables that are evaluated at runtime. These variables also can be combined with keypaths to get to specific attributes of that object. The variable that's used to refer to the object where the fetched property is being executed is called *$FETCH_SOURCE*. To specify the birth date value on the source object, type *FETCH_SOURCE.birthdate* in the text field (without the dollar sign), which tells Core Data that we want to compare to the *birthdate* value on the object where the fetched property is being executed.

> **CAUTION:** The dollar sign is, in fact, part of the variable name. However, the predicate builder automatically prefixes whatever you type in the variable field with a dollar sign, so it's important that you don't type it in, as that would result in two dollar signs being used.

Now click the *OK* button, because this predicate is done. The detail pane for your new fetched property should look like Figure 7–12.

> **NOTE:** The variable text field is not big enough to show the entire value you just typed. Just type carefully, and everything will be okay.

Fetched Property	
Name:	olderHeroes
Destination:	Hero
Predicate:	birthdate < $FETCH_SOURCE.birthdate
	Edit Predicate

Figure 7–12. *The finished fetched property. Notice that the predicate in the box includes a dollar sign before FETCH_SOURCE, even though you didn't type one.*

Here are a few points of caution:

- When you add or change a predicate, always take a look at the result before you run the application.

- Make sure variables start with a dollar sign and are not surrounded by quotes.

- Make sure you did not choose *Constant* instead of *Variable* (a common mistake).

If you've checked these things and still run into problems, try doing a clean build. Sometimes that helps.

> **NOTE:** In addition to $FETCH_SOURCE, Core Data also offers the variable $FETCHED_PROPERTY, which points to the description of a fetched property. You might use this is you want to compare an object attribute with the name of the fetched property being run. We won't use $FETCHED_PROPERTY in this book, but you can find out more about it by reading the *Core Data Programming Guide*:
>
> ```
> http://developer.apple.com/mac/library/documentation/Cocoa/Concept
> ual/CoreData/Articles/cdRelationships.html
> ```

Creating the *youngerHeroes* Fetched Property

Add another fetched property named *youngerHeroes*. The *Destination* will be *Hero* again, and the predicate should be the same as the previous one, except the operator will be > instead of <. However, we're not going to build this one in quite the same way we did the previous one. Instead, we're going to show you another way of entering criteria in the predicate builder.

In addition to specifying criteria using the pop-up menus as we just did, Xcode's predicate builder also allows us to use something called an **expression**. In the context of a predicate, an expression is just a string that represents one or more criteria. (For those who have worked with SQL, a predicate's expression is similar to a SQL statement's WHERE clause, although the syntax is different.)

Click the *Edit Predicate* button again to open the predicate builder for this new fetched property. From the pop-up menu on the left, instead of selecting *birthdate*, select *Expression*, which should be the topmost item in the menu. A large text field appears to the right of the pop-up button. In that text field, type the following expression string:

```
birthdate > $FETCH_SOURCE.birthdate
```

Once you're finished typing this expression, your predicate builder sheet should look like Figure 7–13.

> **NOTE:** The syntax for expressions is documented in the *Predicates Programming Guide*:
>
> ```
> http://developer.apple.com/mac/library/DOCUMENTATION/Cocoa/Concept
> ual/Predicates/predicates.html
> ```

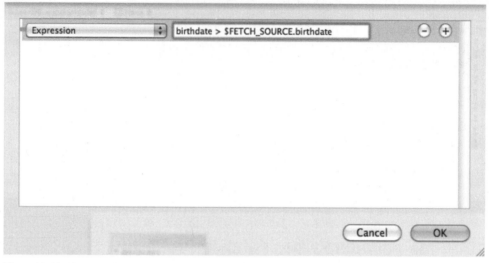

Figure 7–13. *You can also enter criteria as expressions.*

Hit the *OK* button, and this predicate is done.

One thing to be aware of is that a fetched property retrieves all matching objects, potentially including the object on which the fetch is being performed. This means it is possible to create a **result set** that, when executed on Ultra Guy, returns Ultra Guy.

Both the *youngerHeroes* and *olderHeroes* fetched properties automatically exclude the hero being evaluated. Heroes cannot be older or younger than themselves; their birth date will always exactly equal their own birth date, and so no hero will ever meet the two criteria we just created.

Let's now add a fetched property that has slightly more complex criteria.

Creating the *sameSexHeroes* Fetched Property

The next fetched property we're going to create is called *sameSexHeroes*, and it returns all heroes who are the same sex as this hero. We can't just specify to return all heroes of the same sex, however, because we don't want this hero to be included in the fetched property. Ultra Guy is the same sex as Ultra Guy, but users will not expect to see Ultra Guy when they look at a list of the heroes who are the same sex as Ultra Guy.

Create another fetched property, naming it *sameSexHeroes*. Assign the new fetched property a *Destination* of *Hero*, and then open the predicate builder. In the pop-up menu on the left, select *sex*. Right-click in the blank area to the left of the plus and minus buttons, change the right operand to *Variable*, and type in *FETCH_SOURCE.sex*. The operator should have defaulted to =, but if not, change it to =. Now our predicate specifies all heroes who are the same sex as this hero, but we need another criterion to exclude the hero for whom this fetched property is being executed.

Right-click in the space to the left of the plus and minus buttons again. Notice that there are some other options below the operand types. Select *Add AND* to add another

criterion to this predicate. You could also have accomplished this by clicking the +
button, but we wanted you to see this other way. After you add the second criteria, your
predicate should look like Figure 7–14.

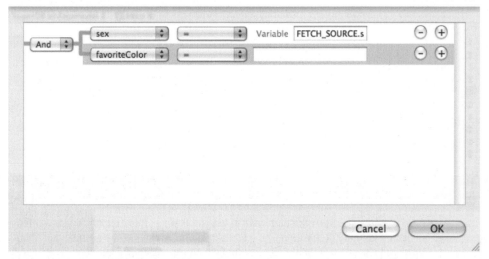

Figure 7–14. *The predicate builder allows you to build complex criteria using Boolean logic. Here, we have two criteria being joined by an* AND *operator.*

Because we selected *AND*, this fetched property will return only heroes that meet both
criteria. So, what should the second criterion be?

We could just compare names and exclude heroes with the same name as ours. That
might work, except for the fact that two heroes might have the same name. Maybe using
name isn't the best idea. But what value is there that uniquely identifies a single hero?
There isn't one, really.

Fortunately, predicate builder expressions recognize a special value called *SELF*, which
returns the object being compared. The *$FETCH_SOURCE* variable represent the object
where the fetch request is happening. Therefore, to exclude the object where the fetch
request is firing, we just need to require it to return only objects where *SELF !=*
$FETCH_SOURCE. To prevent this predicate from including the object where the
selection is happening, click the left pop-up menu on the second row and select
Expression. In the text field that appears, type the following:

```
SELF != $FETCH_SOURCE
```

Creating the *oppositeSexHeroes* Fetched Property

Create a new fetched property called *oppositeSexHeroes* and give it a *Destination* of
Hero. Use the predicate editor to retrieve all heroes of the opposite sex. We're not going
to give you the exact steps for this one, but your completed fetched property should
look like Figure 7–15. Make sure you save your data model before continuing.

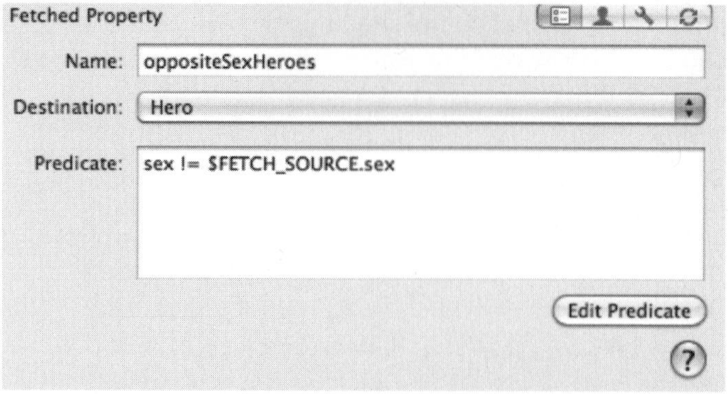

Figure 7–15. *This is how the final fetched property should look when you're finished.*

EXPRESSIONS AND AGGREGATES

Another use of expressions is to aggregate attributes without loading them all into memory. If you wanted to get the average, median, minimum, or maximum for a specific attribute, such as the average age of our heroes or count of female heroes, you can do that (and more) with an expression. In fact, that's how you should do it. To understand why, you need to know a little about the way Core Data works under the hood.

The fetched results controller we're using in `HeroListController` contains objects for all of the heroes in our database, but it doesn't have all of them fully loaded into memory as managed objects. Core Data has a concept of a **fault**. A fault is sort of like a stand-in for a managed object. A fault object knows a bit about the managed object it's standing in for, such as its unique ID and perhaps the value of one attribute being displayed, but it's not a full managed object.

A fault turns into a full-fledged managed object when something **triggers** the fault. Triggering a fault usually happens when you access an attribute or key that the fault doesn't know about. Core Data is smart enough to turn a fault into a managed object when necessary, so your code usually doesn't need to worry about whether it's dealing with a fault or a managed object. However, it's important to know about this behavior, so you don't unintentionally cause performance problems by triggering faults unnecessarily.

Most likely, the faults in our fetched results controller don't know anything about the `sex` attribute of `Hero`. So, if we were to loop through the heroes in our fetched results controller to get a count of the female heroes, we would be triggering every fault to become a managed object. That's inefficient, because it uses a lot more memory and processing power than necessary. Instead, we can use expressions to retrieve aggregate values from Core Data without triggering faults.

Here's an example of how we would use an expression to retrieve the average birth date calculated for all female heroes in our application (we can't use `age` in a fetch request because it's a transient attribute that isn't stored).

```
NSExpression *ex = [NSExpression expressionForFunction:@"average:"
    arguments:[NSArray arrayWithObject:[NSExpression
    expressionForKeyPath:@"birthdate"]]];
NSPredicate *pred = [NSPredicate predicateWithFormat:@"sex == 'Female'"];

NSExpressionDescription *ed = [[NSExpressionDescription alloc] init];
[ed setName:@"averageBirthdate"];
[ed setExpression:ex];
[ed setExpressionResultType:NSDateAttributeType];
```

```
    NSArray *properties = [NSArray arrayWithObject:ed];

    NSFetchRequest *request = [[NSFetchRequest alloc] init];
    [request setPredicate:pred];
    [request setPropertiesToFetch:properties];
    [request setResultType:NSDictionaryResultType];

    NSEntityDescription *entity = [NSEntityDescription entityForName:@"Hero"
        inManagedObjectContext:context];
    [request setEntity:entity];

    NSArray *results = [context executeFetchRequest:request error:nil];
    NSDate *date = [results objectAtIndex:0];
    NSLog(@"Average birthdate for female heroes: %@", date);
```

Aggregate expressions are relatively new to Core Data. As of this writing, the process of using expressions to obtain aggregates is not thoroughly documented, but the preceding code sample, along with the API documentation for NSExpression and NSExpressionDescription, should get you pointed in the right direction for working with aggregates.

Adding Relationships and Fetched Properties to the Hero Class

Since we created a custom subclass of NSManagedObject, we need to update that class to include the new relationship and fetched properties. If we had not made any changes to the Hero class, we could just regenerate the class definition from our data model, and the newly generated version would include properties and methods for the relationships and fetched properties we just added to our data model. Since we have added validation code, we'll need to update it manually. Single-click *Hero.h* and add the following code:

```
#import <CoreData/CoreData.h>

#define kHeroValidationDomain            @"com.Apress.SuperDB.HeroValidationDomain"
#define kHeroValidationBirthdateCode     1000
#define kHeroValidationNameOrSecretIdentityCode 1001

@class Power;

@interface Hero :  NSManagedObject
{
}

@property (nonatomic, readonly) NSNumber * age;
@property (nonatomic, retain) NSString * secretIdentity;
@property (nonatomic, retain) NSString * sex;
@property (nonatomic, retain) NSString * name;
@property (nonatomic, retain) NSDate * birthdate;
@property (nonatomic, retain) UIColor * favoriteColor;

@property (nonatomic, retain) NSSet* powers;
```

```
@property (nonatomic, readonly) NSArray *olderHeroes;
@property (nonatomic, readonly) NSArray *youngerHeroes;
@property (nonatomic, readonly) NSArray *sameSexHeroes;
@property (nonatomic, readonly) NSArray *oppositeSexHeroes;
@end

@interface Hero (PowerAccessors)
- (void)addPowersObject:(Power *)value;
- (void)removePowersObject:(Power *)value;
- (void)addPowers:(NSSet *)value;
- (void)removePowers:(NSSet *)value;
@end
```

Save the file.

Switch over to *Hero.m*, and make the following changes:

```
#import "Hero.h"

@implementation Hero

@dynamic age;
@dynamic secretIdentity;
@dynamic sex;
@dynamic name;
@dynamic birthdate;
@dynamic favoriteColor;
@dynamic powers;
@dynamic olderHeroes, youngerHeroes, sameSexHeroes, oppositeSexHeroes;

- (void) awakeFromInsert
{
...
```

The Big Refactor

Our data model is now complete. Next, we need to make changes to our user interface to let the user see the fetched properties and to view and edit powers. In order to let our users view the fetched properties, we'll create a new generic attribute controller, such as the one found in *ManagedObjectStringEditor.m*, that will be used to display all four fetched properties. We'll also be able to use this controller in the future to display any other fetched properties we add. How should we implement a controller for editing powers?

Throughout the book, we've been harping on writing code generically. We've talked about and demonstrated some of the benefits of doing that. We're now able to add and remove attributes from our user interface without needing to write any substantive code. This means it will be easy to extend and maintain HeroEditController as our application grows. There's also another benefit.

Powers and heroes are both represented by managed objects. Since we've written HeroEditController so generically, we could just copy the contents of

HeroEditController into a new controller class called PowerEditController. Then all we would need to do is change the array that is created in viewDidLoad:, and everything should pretty much work, right?

Yes, but …

Any time you find yourself copying and pasting large amounts of code, you need to take a step back and ask yourself if there isn't some way to avoid duplicating logic. What happens if you discover a bug in the controller logic? If you copy that logic over to a new controller class, you'll need to fix it in two places. In this case, we want to look for a way to leverage the same code to display both the Hero and Power managed object, and also to handle any additional entities that we might create in the future.

By writing our code generically, we have done almost all the work needed to display and edit any Core Data managed object. We have a class, HeroEditController, that with a little restructuring can be used to display any managed object. Having a generic managed object editor will make our life much easier as we expand our application in the future, so let's refactor now.

We're going to start by renaming HeroEditController to ManagedObjectEditor. We'll remove all of the hero-specific code from that the renamed class and move it to a category on ManagedObjectEditor that will contain all of our project-specific code. This will allow us to reuse the class in other projects, without needing to copy code that's specific to another project. After that, we'll make a handful of changes so that the class is more generic and to handle the display of relationships.

Renaming the Class

The name HeroEditController was very descriptive up to now, because that was exactly the job this controller was performing. By the end of this chapter, however, it will be used to display and edit two completely different entities, and will be capable of displaying others. Therefore, a new name seems to be in order. HeroAndPowerAndOtherManagedObjectsEditController is one candidate, but that's a little long, even in the iPhone development world. Let's go with ManagedObjectEditor.

In the *Groups & Files* pane, single-click *HeroEditController.h*. Find the following line:

```
@interface HeroEditController : UITableViewController {
```

In this line, double-click the word HeroEditController to select it. Now, from the **Edit** menu, select **Refactor…**, or press ⌘⇧J, to bring up the refactor window (Figure 7–16). This window will allow you to change the name of a class or an instance variable. It will go through your project and change any references to the old name to the new name. In the text field, type *ManagedObjectEditor*, and then click the *Preview* button.

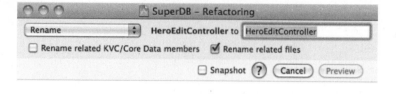

Figure 7–16. *The refactor window allows you to rename classes and instance variables.*

The preview will show you all the changes that Xcode will make for you if you decide to apply the change. If you select any of the listed filenames, it will show you all the changes that will be made to that file. The existing file will be displayed on the left, and the refactored view will appear on the right (Figure 7–17).

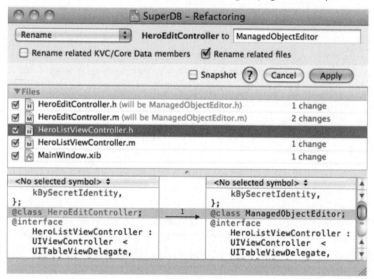

Figure 7–17. *Xcode's refactoring allows you to preview the changes that will be made.*

Click the *Apply* button to commit the changes, and then press ⌘⌥S to save all the affected files.

Refactoring the hero Instance Variable

In our ManagedObjectEditor class, we have an instance variable called hero. That variable name is no longer representative of what that variable holds, so let's refactor that as well. Single-click *ManagedObjectEditor.h*, and then double-click the hero instance variable to select it. Press ⌘⇧J to bring up the refactor window again, and change its name to *managedObject*. Don't forget to save all the affected files after you apply the changes.

Removing the Arrays

Currently, our one instance of ManagedObjectEditor (formerly HeroEditController) is contained in *MainWindow.xib*, and the arrays that define the table structure are created in viewDidLoad:. Since viewDidLoad: will be called no matter which entity is being displayed, we need to move the arrays somewhere else. For now, this object-specific code doesn't belong in a generic class, so we'll delete it. We'll re-create the code a little later in a new location outside the main class definition.

Single-click *ManagedObjectEditor.m* and delete all of the code from the viewDidLoad: method except the call to super. Here's the new version of viewDidLoad::

```
- (void)viewDidLoad {
    [super viewDidLoad];
}
```

Don't worry—we'll write code elsewhere to populate the arrays. Before we do that, though, we have a few other changes to make.

Supporting Save and Cancel Buttons

One difference between HeroEditController and ManagedObjectEditor is that HeroEditController always existed at the same spot in the navigation hierarchy. You could drill down to it from one, and only one, place: the navigation controller's root view controller. When we use the class to let users edit and display powers, however, we're giving them the ability to add a new object by tapping a row on another object. As was the case with our generic attribute editors, our users are going to expect to be able to save or cancel when they are in the process of adding a new power. In addition, since this same code will be used to display a selected hero, we need to handle the case where save and cancel are not needed. Our new generic controller handles both cases.

Single-click *ManagedObjectEditor.h* and make the following changes:

```
#import <UIKit/UIKit.h>

#define kToManyRelationship     @"ManagedObjectToManyRelationship"
#define kSelectorKey            @"selector"

@interface ManagedObjectEditor : UITableViewController {
    NSManagedObject *managedObject;
    BOOL            showSaveCancelButtons;
```

```
@private
    NSArray          *sectionNames;
    NSArray          *rowLabels;
    NSArray          *rowKeys;
    NSArray          *rowControllers;
    NSArray          *rowArguments;

}
@property (nonatomic, retain) NSManagedObject *managedObject;
@property BOOL showSaveCancelButtons;
- (IBAction)save;
- (IBAction)cancel;

@end
```

We first define a couple of constants that we'll need later. Don't worry about them for now. We'll explain what they're used for later when we use them in code. Next, we need an instance variable to keep track of whether we should show the *Save* and *Cancel* buttons, so we declare showSaveCancelButtons. We also declare a corresponding property of the same name to expose this variable to other objects. We then add two action methods to handle the result of pressing either of the two buttons. Don't forget to save this file.

Flip over to *ManagedObjectEditor.m*. Synthesize the showSaveCancelButtons property and add the implementation of the save and cancel methods, as follows:

```
#import "ManagedObjectEditor.h"
#import "NSArray-NestedArrays.h"
#import "HeroValueDisplay.h"
#import "ManagedObjectAttributeEditor.h"
@implementation ManagedObjectEditor
@synthesize managedObject;
@synthesize showSaveCancelButtons;

- (IBAction)save {
    NSError *error;
    if (![self.managedObject.managedObjectContext save:&error])
        NSLog(@"Error saving: %@", [error localizedDescription]);

    [self.navigationController popViewControllerAnimated:YES];
}

- (IBAction)cancel {
    if ([self.managedObject isNew])
        [self.managedObject.managedObjectContext deleteObject:self.managedObject];
    [self.navigationController popViewControllerAnimated:YES];
}

- (void)viewWillAppear:(BOOL)animated {
...
```

Notice that we're only logging errors in save, and not reporting them to the user. This is because we validate and save every time an individual attribute is edited. Doing it here would be redundant; we just log the error to help us with debugging. In theory, once our application has been tested, the code here should never actually encounter an error in the wild.

The cancel method might look a little odd. Remember that this same class is used to create and edit powers. If it's a new object, then *Cancel* means the new object that was created needs to be deleted before we go back to the previous level in the navigation hierarchy. If we're just editing an existing object, we don't want to delete it—we just move back up to the previous view in the hierarchy.

Adding the isNew Method to NSManagedObject

In the cancel method, we used a method on NSManagedObject called isNew that returns YES if this object has not been saved to the database. This is a handy method. Unfortunately, it doesn't exist on NSManagedObject, so we need to add it using a category. Single-click the *Categories* folder in the *Groups & Files* pane, and then select **New File...** from the **File** menu and select *Objective-C class* from under the *Cocoa Touch Class* heading. Make the file a subclass of *NSObject*. Name the new file *NSManagedObject-IsNew.m*, and make sure you check the box to have it create the header file.

Single-click *NSManagedObject-IsNew.h* and replace its contents with the following:

```
#import <Foundation/Foundation.h>

@interface NSManagedObject(IsNew)
/**
    Returns YES if this managed object is new and has not yet been saved in the
persistent store.
*/
-(BOOL)isNew;
@end
```

Switch over to *NSManagedObject-IsNew.m* and replace its contents with this:

```
#import "NSManagedObject-IsNew.h"

@implementation NSManagedObject(IsNew)
-(BOOL)isNew
{
    NSDictionary *vals = [self committedValuesForKeys:nil];
    return [vals count] == 0;
}
@end
```

This method relies on the fact that managed objects maintain a dictionary of **committed values**, which are the values of attributes that have already been saved in the persistent store. This is the way it tells if values have been changed since the last save. If there aren't any attributes in the dictionary returned by committedValuesForKeys:, then the object must be new, because that indicates that there are no values saved in the persistent store.

Make sure both of these files are saved. Then go back to *ManagedObjectEditor.m* and add this `import` statement to the top to prevent compiler warnings about the `isNew` method not existing:

```
#import "ManagedObjectEditor.h"
#import "NSArray-NestedArrays.h"
#import "HeroValueDisplay.h"
#import "ManagedObjectAttributeEditor.h"
#import "NSManagedObject-IsNew.h"

@implementation ManagedObjectEditor
@synthesize managedObject;
@synthesize showSaveCancelButtons;

- (IBAction)save {
...
```

Adding the Save and Cancel Buttons

The property `showSaveCancelButtons` tracks whether we should show the *Save* and *Cancel* buttons. Now we need to add code to `viewWillAppear:` to actually add those buttons to the navigation bar. Since it's possible that an instance of `ManagedObjectEditor` will be reused for different managed objects, we also need to make sure that we're not showing buttons from a previous use when `showSaveCancelButtons` is NO. Still in *ManagedObjectEditor.m*, add the following code to `viewWillAppear:`.

```
- (void)viewWillAppear:(BOOL)animated {
    [self.tableView reloadData];
    if (showSaveCancelButtons) {
        UIBarButtonItem *cancelButton = [[UIBarButtonItem alloc]
            initWithTitle:NSLocalizedString(@"Cancel",
            @"Cancel - for button to cancel changes")
            style:UIBarButtonSystemItemCancel
            target:self
            action:@selector(cancel)];
        self.navigationItem.leftBarButtonItem = cancelButton;
        [cancelButton release];
        UIBarButtonItem *saveButton = [[UIBarButtonItem alloc]
            initWithTitle:NSLocalizedString(@"Save",
            @"Save - for button to save changes")
            style:UIBarButtonItemStyleDone
            target:self
            action:@selector(save)];
        self.navigationItem.rightBarButtonItem = saveButton;
        [saveButton release];
    }
    else {
        self.navigationItem.leftBarButtonItem = nil;
        self.navigationItem.rightBarButtonItem = nil;
    }
    [super viewWillAppear:animated];
}
```

Adding Support for To-Many Relationships

If you look back at Figure 7–1, you'll see that we display a row for every power in the powers relationship and also use our table view's editing mode buttons to let the user delete powers or insert powers. We're going to use functionality built into UITableView to handle the deletes and inserts for to-many relationships. This is the presentation that the users will expect based on their experiences with built-in iPhone applications like Contacts and Calendar. It also allows us to leverage built-in code, rather than writing our own.

Turning on Edit Mode

In order to leverage the table's built-in editing functionality, we need to turn on edit mode for our table view. Unlike in previous examples, we're going to leave edit mode on all the time. This is a controller intended specifically for editing, so we're not going to make the users take an extra step to turn on edit mode before they're allowed to add or delete objects from a relationship. Let's turn on edit mode in viewDidLoad: by adding the following two lines of code:

```
- (void)viewDidLoad {
    self.tableView.editing = YES;
    self.tableView.allowsSelectionDuringEditing = YES;

    [super viewDidLoad];
}
```

The first line of code turns on the table view's edit mode. The second line allows rows to be selected when edit mode is on. Ordinarily, there would be no need to select a row while in edit mode, because you would be in edit mode only for the time it takes to delete or move a row, and being able to accidentally select a row could get in the way of that functionality. As a result, by default, you can't select a row when edit mode is turned off. We need it turned back on so that the user can interact with our rows and drill down to edit attributes.

Setting Row Indentation

By default, any row that can be edited gets indented so that there's room for the delete or insert button to the left of the cell. In our design, rows in sections that represent to-many relationships will always be indented. All the rows in the *Powers* section will be indented to make room for the delete or insert button. Note that all to-many sections will always have at least one row labeled *Add New...*, and that section will always feature an insert button, as shown in Figure 7–1.

Our goal here is to build a generic managed object editor that we can use for the *Powers* section, as well as for any other to-many sections we might add to our application in the future.

We use the rowControllers subarray to represent a table section. We'll embed the constant kToManyRelationship we defined earlier inside any subarray pointed to by rowControllers when that subarray represents a to-many section.

Let's add a method to ManagedObjectEditor now that takes a section index and returns a BOOL that identifies whether the section is a regular section or a to-many relationship section. Later in the chapter, we'll add the code that embeds the kToManyRelationship constant in the section array if the section does represent a to-many relationship.

Insert the code shown in bold into *ManagedObjectEditor.m*:

```
#import "ManagedObjectEditor.h"
#import "NSArray-NestedArrays.h"
#import "HeroValueDisplay.h"
#import "ManagedObjectAttributeEditor.h"
#import "NSArray-Set.h"
#import "NSManagedObject-IsNew.h"

@interface ManagedObjectEditor()
- (BOOL)isToManyRelationshipSection:(NSInteger)section;
@end

@implementation ManagedObjectEditor
@synthesize managedObject
@synthesize showSaveCancelButtons;

- (BOOL)isToManyRelationshipSection:(NSInteger)section
{
    NSArray *controllersForSection = [rowControllers objectAtIndex:section];

    if ([controllersForSection count] == 0)
        return NO;

    NSString *controllerForRow0 = [controllersForSection objectAtIndex:0];
    NSArray *sectionKeys = [rowKeys objectAtIndex:section];

    return [sectionKeys count] == 1 && [controllerForRow0
        isEqualToString:kToManyRelationship];
}

- (IBAction)save {
...
```

Since this method is not one that would ever be used outside our class, we're not going to declare it in our header. If we declared it there, we would advertise it to other classes. Instead, we'll use an **Objective-C extension** to declare it. Doing this lets the compiler know about the existence of our method without advertising it outside our class.

> **NOTE:** Extensions are new to Objective-C 2.0. They exist specifically to let you declare a method without exposing it in your header file.

The isToManyRelationshipSection: method grabs the controller for the specified section. Unlike other sections, to-many sections will have only a single value in the rowControllers subarray. If the specified section array does not contain a row (is empty), then we know it's not a to-many section, and we return NO because there's no point in doing any further work. Otherwise, we look at the controller class, and if there's only one row and that row contains the constant kToManyRelationship, then we return YES. For any other values, we return NO.

Now that we have the ability to determine if a section is a to-many section, we can implement the delegate method that identifies which rows should be indented. Add the following method just about the @end declaration in *ManagedObjectEditor.m*:

```
- (BOOL)tableView:(UITableView *)tableView
  shouldIndentWhileEditingRowAtIndexPath:(NSIndexPath *)indexPath {
    return [self isToManyRelationshipSection:[indexPath section]];
}
```

Now, any row that represents a to-many section will get indented and leave room for the insert or delete button. Any other row will appear unindented, as in the previous iterations of the application.

Setting the Correct Number of Rows for To-Many Sections

That's not all there is to supporting to-many relationships. We also need to change the tableView:numberOfRowsInSection: method so that it returns a value based on the number of objects in a to-many relationship when a section is a to-many section. Replace the existing method in *ManagedObjectEditor.m* with this new version:

```
- (NSInteger)tableView:(UITableView *)tableView
      numberOfRowsInSection:(NSInteger)section {
    if ([self isToManyRelationshipSection:section]) {
        NSArray *sectionKeys = [rowKeys objectAtIndex:section];
        NSString *row0Key = [sectionKeys objectAtIndex:0];
        return [[managedObject valueForKey:row0Key] count] + 1;
    }
    return [rowLabels countOfNestedArray:section];
}
```

Notice that we actually return a number that is one higher than the number of objects in the to-many relationship. If you look at Figure 7–1, you'll see that we need an additional row to allow the user to insert a new power. You cannot have an insert and a delete button on the same row, so we need an additional row to let the user insert new values.

> **NOTE:** Yes, the Contacts application on the iPhone has both a plus button and a minus button on some rows. That ability has not been exposed through public APIs, however, so we can't easily provide that same functionality without violating the iPhone SDK agreement that prohibits the use of private APIs.

The Set Problem

We mentioned earlier that to-many relationships are represented as an unordered collection using NSSet. What's critical is that the list of to-many objects be consistently represented in the same order.

Before we modify our delegate and data source methods to handle to-many relationships, let's create a category on NSArray that will allow us to create an array from a set by specifying a key that should be used for ordering the objects. If we pass an NSSet into this method, it will always spit out an array with the same objects that are in the NSSet, only in a specific order.

In your *Groups & Files* pane, select the *Categories* folder. Then select ⌘N from the **File** menu and choose *Objective-C class*, with a subclass of *NSObject*. Call the file *NSArray-Set.m*, and make sure to have it create the header file as well.

Single-click *NSArray-Set.h* and replace the contents with the following:

```
#import <Foundation/Foundation.h>

@interface NSArray(Set)
+ (id)arrayByOrderingSet:(NSSet *)set byKey:(NSString *)key ascending:(BOOL)ascending;

@end
```

Save your changes.

Now switch over to *NSArray-Set.m* and replace its contents with the following:

```
#import "NSArray-Set.h"

@implementation NSArray(Set)
+ (id)arrayByOrderingSet:(NSSet *)set byKey:(NSString *)key ascending:(BOOL)ascending {
    NSMutableArray *ret = [NSMutableArray arrayWithCapacity:[set count]];
    for (id oneObject in set)
        [ret addObject:oneObject];

    NSSortDescriptor *descriptor = [[NSSortDescriptor alloc] initWithKey:key
        ascending:ascending];
    [ret sortUsingDescriptors:[NSArray arrayWithObject:descriptor]];
    [descriptor release];
    return ret;
}
@end
```

Now, we have the ability to quickly and easily create ordered arrays from unordered sets. We can create order from chaos. We are now truly masters of the universe.

Okay, that might be overstating the case just a touch, but it's still pretty cool. Since we're going to be using this category in several methods in the ManagedObjectEditor class, insert the following import statement near the top of *ManagedObjectEditor.m*:

```
#import "ManagedObjectEditor.h"
#import "NSArray-NestedArrays.h"
#import "HeroValueDisplay.h"
#import "ManagedObjectAttributeEditor.h"
#import "NSManagedObject-IsNew.h"
#import "NSArray-Set.h"

@interface ManagedObjectEditor()
...
```

Specifying the Editing Style for the Rows

The default editing style for all rows in a table is the delete style. Since our table view will always be in edit mode, if we stay with the delete style, a delete button will always appear next to each of our table rows. That's not what we want. Instead, we want insert and delete buttons only in to-many sections. To do that, add the following method just above the @end declaration in *ManagedObjectEditor.m*:

```
- (UITableViewCellEditingStyle)tableView:(UITableView *)tableView
editingStyleForRowAtIndexPath:(NSIndexPath *)indexPath {

    if ([self isToManyRelationshipSection:[indexPath section]]) {
        NSUInteger newPath[] = {[indexPath section], 0};
        NSIndexPath *row0IndexPath = [NSIndexPath indexPathWithIndexes:
            newPath length:2];

        NSString *rowKey = [rowKeys nestedObjectAtIndexPath:row0IndexPath];
        NSString *rowLabel = [rowLabels nestedObjectAtIndexPath:row0IndexPath];
        NSMutableSet *rowSet = [managedObject mutableSetValueForKey:rowKey];
        NSArray *rowArray = [NSArray arrayByOrderingSet:rowSet byKey:rowLabel
            ascending:YES];

        if ([indexPath row] >= [rowArray count])
            return UITableViewCellEditingStyleInsert;

        return UITableViewCellEditingStyleDelete;
    }
    return UITableViewCellEditingStyleNone;
}
```

For sections that hold to-many relationships, we return UITableViewCellEditingStyleDelete, which shows the delete button, unless it's that last additional row in the section—the one that allows the user to *Add New....* In that case, we return UITableViewCellEditingStyleInsert, which shows an insert button. For all other rows, we return UITableViewCellEditingStyleNone, which tells the table view to show neither button.

Displaying To-Many Sections

We need to update tableView:cellForRowAtIndexPath: so that it knows about to-many sections. This requires some substantial changes, because we must add a new cell identifier with a different cell style for the to-many sections. For the existing rows, we'll continue to use UITableViewCellStyleValue2, which has two fields: a blue text label and a larger black text label. We don't want to use that style for to-many sections. We want to use the default style with just a single black text label.

Because the changes to this method are so extensive, we'll just replace the existing tableView:cellForRowAtIndexPath: in *ManagedObjectEditor.m* with the following new version:

```
- (UITableViewCell *)tableView:(UITableView *)tableView
        cellForRowAtIndexPath:(NSIndexPath *)indexPath {
    static NSString *defaultIdentifier = @"Managed Object Cell Identifier";
```

```objc
static NSString *relationshipIdentifier =
    @"Managed Object Relationship Cell Identifier";

id rowController = [rowControllers nestedObjectAtIndexPath:indexPath];
NSString *rowKey = [rowKeys nestedObjectAtIndexPath:indexPath];
NSString *rowLabel = [rowLabels nestedObjectAtIndexPath:indexPath];

if (rowController == nil) {
    NSUInteger newPath[] = {[indexPath section], 0};
    NSIndexPath *row0IndexPath = [NSIndexPath indexPathWithIndexes:newPath
        length:2];
    rowController = [rowControllers nestedObjectAtIndexPath:row0IndexPath];
    rowKey = [rowKeys nestedObjectAtIndexPath:row0IndexPath];
    rowLabel = [rowLabels nestedObjectAtIndexPath:row0IndexPath];
}

NSString *cellIdentifier = nil;
UITableViewCellStyle cellStyle;
if ([rowController isEqual:kToManyRelationship]) {
    cellIdentifier = relationshipIdentifier;
    cellStyle = UITableViewCellStyleDefault;
}
else {
    cellIdentifier = defaultIdentifier;
    cellStyle = UITableViewCellStyleValue2;
}

UITableViewCell *cell = [tableView
                         dequeueReusableCellWithIdentifier:cellIdentifier];
if (cell == nil) {
    cell = [[[UITableViewCell alloc] initWithStyle:cellStyle
                                   reuseIdentifier:cellIdentifier] autorelease];
}

if ([rowController isEqual:kToManyRelationship]) {
    NSSet *rowSet = [managedObject valueForKey:rowKey];
    if ([rowSet count] == 0 || [indexPath row] >= [rowSet count]) {
        cell.textLabel.text = NSLocalizedString(@"Add New…", @"Add New…");
        cell.editingAccessoryType = UITableViewCellAccessoryDisclosureIndicator;
    }
    else {
        NSArray *rowArray = [NSArray arrayByOrderingSet:rowSet byKey:rowLabel
            ascending:YES];
        NSUInteger row = [indexPath row];
        NSManagedObject *relatedObject = [rowArray objectAtIndex:row];
        NSString *rowValue = [[relatedObject valueForKey:rowLabel]
            heroValueDisplay];
        cell.textLabel.text = rowValue;
        cell.editingAccessoryType = UITableViewCellAccessoryDisclosureIndicator;
    }
} else if ([rowController isEqual:@"ManagedObjectFetchedPropertyDisplayer"]) {
    cell.detailTextLabel.text = rowLabel;
    cell.editingAccessoryType = UITableViewCellAccessoryDisclosureIndicator;
    cell.textLabel.text = @"";
} else {
    id <HeroValueDisplay, NSObject> rowValue = [managedObject
        valueForKey:rowKey];
```

```
            cell.detailTextLabel.text = [rowValue heroValueDisplay];
            cell.textLabel.text = rowLabel;
            cell.editingAccessoryType = (rowController == [NSNull null]) ?
                UITableViewCellAccessoryNone :
                UITableViewCellAccessoryDisclosureIndicator;

            if ([rowValue isKindOfClass:[UIColor class]])
                cell.detailTextLabel.textColor = (UIColor *)rowValue;
            else
                cell.detailTextLabel.textColor = [UIColor blackColor];
        }
        return cell;
}
```

This is a little more complex than the old version, so let's step through what we're doing.

First, we define two cell identifiers, one for each of the types of cells that we want to use in our table:

```
static NSString *defaultIdentifier = @"Managed Object Cell Identifier";
static NSString *relationshipIdentifier =
    @"Managed Object Relationship Cell Identifier";
```

Basically, a **managed object relationship cell** is a row in our table that appears in a to-many section. All other rows are **managed object cells**.

Next, we retrieve the controller, key, and label from our nested arrays using indexPath, which identifies the current section and row, just as we did previously.

```
id rowController = [rowControllers nestedObjectAtIndexPath:indexPath];
NSString *rowKey = [rowKeys nestedObjectAtIndexPath:indexPath];
NSString *rowLabel = [rowLabels nestedObjectAtIndexPath:indexPath];
```

Next, we check to see if rowController is nil. This will happen only if the current section is a to-many section and we are in the second row or greater. Why? Because in managed object sections (which are not to-many sections), every row will have an associated row controller. In addition, in a to-many section, the first item will have a value in the row controller field of kToManyRelationship. So if rowController is nil, we know we're in row 2+ of a to-many section, and we go back and get the values from the first row in the section, which we do by creating a new index path:

```
if (rowController == nil) {
    NSUInteger newPath[] = {[indexPath section], 0};
    NSIndexPath *row0IndexPath = [NSIndexPath indexPathWithIndexes:newPath
        length:2];
    rowController = [rowControllers nestedObjectAtIndexPath:row0IndexPath];
    rowKey = [rowKeys nestedObjectAtIndexPath:row0IndexPath];
    rowLabel = [rowLabels nestedObjectAtIndexPath:row0IndexPath];
}
```

After that, we declare local variables to represent the cell identifier and style, and then set them based on whether indexPath points to a row in a to-many section or a regular section:

```
NSString *cellIdentifier = nil;
UITableViewCellStyle cellStyle;
if ([rowController isEqual:kToManyRelationship]) {
```

```
        cellIdentifier = relationshipIdentifier;
        cellStyle = UITableViewCellStyleDefault;
}
else {
        cellIdentifier = defaultIdentifier;
        cellStyle = UITableViewCellStyleValue2;
}
```

Once we have the style and identifier, we dequeue or create a new cell as normal:

```
UITableViewCell *cell = [tableView
                        dequeueReusableCellWithIdentifier:cellIdentifier];
if (cell == nil) {
    cell = [[[UITableViewCell alloc] initWithStyle:cellStyle
                                reuseIdentifier:cellIdentifier] autorelease];
}
```

Now things get a little hairy. We check to see if we have a to-many relationship:

```
if ([rowController isEqual:kToManyRelationship]) {
```

Then we grab the set that represents the to-many relationship and check to see if the row that this cell represents is greater than or equal to the number of objects in the relationship. If it is, then this row is that special insert row that doesn't actually represent any object in the relationship, so we set the cell label to the string constant @"Add New...":

```
        NSSet *rowSet = [managedObject valueForKey:rowKey];
        if ([rowSet count] == 0 || [indexPath row] >= [rowSet count]) {
            cell.textLabel.text = NSLocalizedString(@"Add New…", @"Add New…");
            cell.editingAccessoryType = UITableViewCellAccessoryDisclosureIndicator;
        }
```

If it's not the last row, we need to order the set into an array. Since we don't need to display a label on each row for to-many arrays, we're repurposing that subarray for to-many sections to hold a key value that identifies which value on the other managed object should be displayed in the text label for the row. That key value will also be used to order the rows in the relationship, so they are always in the same order. Later, when we re-create the table structure arrays, we'll specify @"name" in that subarray for the powers to-many section to indicate that it should order the powers by the name attribute and display the name attribute in the table view cell.

> **NOTE:** Yes, this is a little confusing. Bear with us. It probably would have been clearer to declare another array to hold the key value for to-many sections. However, since we already have a nested array that isn't needed by to-many sections, and we would need another nested array that is used only for to-many sections, we're trading off a little complexity for improved efficiency. We'll just need to make sure we document the fact that the rowLabels subarrays serve a slightly different purpose for to-many sections.

```
        else {
            NSArray *rowArray = [NSArray arrayByOrderingSet:rowSet byKey:rowLabel
                ascending:YES];
```

```
        NSUInteger row = [indexPath row];
        NSManagedObject *relatedObject = [rowArray objectAtIndex:row];
        NSString *rowValue = [[relatedObject valueForKey:rowLabel]
            heroValueDisplay];
        cell.textLabel.text = rowValue;
        cell.editingAccessoryType = UITableViewCellAccessoryDisclosureIndicator;
    }
```

A little later in the chapter, we're going to write a controller class to display fetched properties. You can see what the end result of that controller class will look like in Figure 7–3. To avoid going back and forth later on, we're going to write the code for those rows now, since they require slightly different logic than other attributes. If you look at Figure 7–1, you'll see that we use only one of the two labels for the fetched properties, so the next chunk of code handles the display of fetched properties by setting the unused text label to display an empty string:

```
    } else if ([rowController isEqual:@"ManagedObjectFetchedPropertyDisplayer"]) {
        cell.detailTextLabel.text = rowLabel;
        cell.editingAccessoryType = UITableViewCellAccessoryDisclosureIndicator;
        cell.textLabel.text = @"";
    }
```

Otherwise, we have the same basic logic we used before:

```
    else {
        id <HeroValueDisplay, NSObject> rowValue = [managedObject
            valueForKey:rowKey];
        cell.detailTextLabel.text = [rowValue heroValueDisplay];
        cell.textLabel.text = rowLabel;
        cell.editingAccessoryType = (rowController == [NSNull null]) ?
            UITableViewCellAccessoryNone :
            UITableViewCellAccessoryDisclosureIndicator;

        if ([rowValue isKindOfClass:[UIColor class]])
            cell.detailTextLabel.textColor = (UIColor *)rowValue;
        else
            cell.detailTextLabel.textColor = [UIColor blackColor];
    }
```

Of course, once we're finished, we return the cell:

```
    return cell;
}
```

Updating Row Selection for To-Many Relationships

Just as we did in the previous section, what we do when a user taps on a row depends on whether it's a row in a to-many section or just a regular section. Replace your existing tableView:didSelectRowAtIndexPath: method with this new version:

```
- (void)tableView:(UITableView *)tableView
didSelectRowAtIndexPath:(NSIndexPath *)indexPath {

    if ([self isToManyRelationshipSection:[indexPath section]]) {

        NSUInteger newPath[] = {[indexPath section], 0};
```

```
        NSIndexPath *row0IndexPath = [NSIndexPath indexPathWithIndexes:newPath
            length:2];

        NSString *rowKey = [rowKeys nestedObjectAtIndexPath:row0IndexPath];
        NSString *rowLabel = [rowLabels nestedObjectAtIndexPath:row0IndexPath];
        NSSet *rowSet = [managedObject valueForKey:rowKey];
        NSDictionary *args = [rowArguments nestedObjectAtIndexPath:row0IndexPath];
        NSString *selectorString = [args objectForKey:kSelectorKey];

        NSEntityDescription *ed = [managedObject entity];
        NSRelationshipDescription *rd = [[ed relationshipsByName]
            valueForKey:rowKey];
        NSEntityDescription *dest = [rd destinationEntity];
        NSString *entityName = [dest name];

        ManagedObjectEditor *controller = [ManagedObjectEditor
            performSelector:NSSelectorFromString(selectorString)];

        NSMutableSet *relationshipSet = [self.managedObject
            mutableSetValueForKey:rowKey];
        if ([rowSet count] == 0 || [indexPath row] >= [rowSet count]) {
            NSManagedObject *object = [NSEntityDescription
                insertNewObjectForEntityForName:entityName
                inManagedObjectContext:[self.managedObject managedObjectContext]];
                controller.managedObject = object;
            [relationshipSet addObject:object];
            controller.title = [NSString stringWithFormat:@"New %@", entityName];
        }
        else {
            NSArray *relationshipArray = [NSArray arrayByOrderingSet:relationshipSet
                byKey:rowLabel ascending:YES];
            NSManagedObject *selectedObject = [relationshipArray
                objectAtIndex:[indexPath row]];
            controller.managedObject = selectedObject;
            controller.title = entityName;
        }
        controller.showSaveCancelButtons = YES;
        [self.navigationController pushViewController:controller animated:YES];
    }
    else {
        NSString *controllerClassName = [rowControllers
                                    nestedObjectAtIndexPath:indexPath];
        NSString *rowLabel = [rowLabels nestedObjectAtIndexPath:indexPath];
        NSString *rowKey = [rowKeys nestedObjectAtIndexPath:indexPath];
        Class controllerClass = NSClassFromString(controllerClassName);
        ManagedObjectAttributeEditor *controller =
        [controllerClass alloc];
        controller = [controller initWithStyle:UITableViewStyleGrouped];
        controller.keypath = rowKey;
        controller.managedObject = managedObject;
        controller.labelString = rowLabel;
        controller.title = rowLabel;

        NSDictionary *args = [rowArguments nestedObjectAtIndexPath:indexPath];
        if ([args isKindOfClass:[NSDictionary class]]) {
            if (args != nil) {
                for (NSString *oneKey in args) {
```

```
                    id oneArg = [args objectForKey:oneKey];
                    [controller setValue:oneArg forKey:oneKey];
                }
            }
        }
        [self.navigationController pushViewController:controller animated:YES];
        [controller release];
    }
}
```

This code may look a little scary, but it's not really that bad. Let's break it down.

First, we check to see if we're dealing with a to-many relationship:

```
    if ([self isToManyRelationshipSection:[indexPath section]]) {
```

If we are, then we create an NSIndexPath instance that points to the first row in the nested arrays, because that's where the information for a to-many relationship is stored:

```
        NSUInteger newPath[] = {[indexPath section], 0};
        NSIndexPath *row0IndexPath = [NSIndexPath indexPathWithIndexes:newPath
            length:2];
```

Then we use that index path to get the various values we need from our nested arrays:

```
        NSString *rowKey = [rowKeys nestedObjectAtIndexPath:row0IndexPath];
        NSString *rowLabel = [rowLabels nestedObjectAtIndexPath:row0IndexPath];
        NSSet *rowSet = [managedObject valueForKey:rowKey];
        NSDictionary *args = [rowArguments nestedObjectAtIndexPath:row0IndexPath];
```

Earlier in the chapter, we defined the two constants kToManyRelationship and kSelectorKey. We used one of them to identify when a section was a to-many section. Now, we're going to use the other one, which will be used as a key in the rowArguments dictionary. Later, when we re-create our table structure arrays, we'll store the name of an Objective-C method, under the kSelectorKey key, into the rowArguments subarray for the heroes section. That method name will be a class method that can be called on ManagedObjectEditor. That class method will return an instance of ManagedObjectEditor with the nested arrays all populated for the display of the *Power* entity. Later, we'll use categories to add factory methods to ManagedObjectEditor for each entity that we let the user edit. Here, we retrieve the value stored under that key:

```
        NSString *selectorString = [args objectForKey:kSelectorKey];
```

We also need to know the name of the destination entity used in this relationship. We can get that information from the data model, although it takes a couple of calls to get to the information we need:

```
        NSEntityDescription *ed = [managedObject entity];
        NSRelationshipDescription *rd = [[ed relationshipsByName]
            valueForKey:rowKey];
        NSEntityDescription *dest = [rd destinationEntity];
        NSString *entityName = [dest name];
```

Next, we create a new instance of ManagedObjectEditor that will be used to display and edit the object on which the user tapped. So, if the user tapped on a power in Figure 7–1, here, we would be creating a new instance of ManagedObjectEditor configured to allow editing of *Power* managed objects.

This code takes advantage of Objective-C's dynamic nature. We take the name of the factory method that we just retrieved from the `rowArguments` nested array and use `NSSelectorFromString()` to turn it into a selector. We then perform that selector on `ManagedObjectEditor`, which is how you call class methods dynamically:

```
ManagedObjectEditor *controller = [ManagedObjectEditor
    performSelector:NSSelectorFromString(selectorString)];
```

If the user tapped on the last row in the section, we need to create a new object, since this is the *Add New...* row. The next chunk of code checks if the user tapped the last row, and then it creates a new entity if necessary:

```
NSMutableSet *relationshipSet = [self.managedObject
    mutableSetValueForKey:rowKey];
if ([rowSet count] == 0 || [indexPath row] >= [rowSet count]) {

    NSManagedObject *object = [NSEntityDescription
        insertNewObjectForEntityForName:entityName
        inManagedObjectContext:[self.managedObject managedObjectContext]];
    controller.managedObject = object;
    [relationshipSet addObject:object];
    controller.title = [NSString stringWithFormat:@"New %@", entityName];
}
```

If the user tapped on any other row besides the last one in the section, then we retrieve the object that corresponds to the row tapped. We need to create an ordered array from the set so we know which object was tapped:

```
else {
    NSArray *relationshipArray = [NSArray arrayByOrderingSet:relationshipSet
        byKey:rowLabel ascending:YES];
    NSManagedObject *selectedObject = [relationshipArray
        objectAtIndex:[indexPath row]];
    controller.managedObject = selectedObject;
    controller.title = entityName;
}
```

Once we have the controller, and have either retrieved the object to be edited or created a new object, we set `showSaveCancelButtons` to tell the new instance of `ManagedObjectEditor` to show the *Save* and *Cancel* buttons, and then we push it onto the navigation stack so the user sees it:

```
    controller.showSaveCancelButtons = YES;
    [self.navigationController pushViewController:controller animated:YES];
}
```

If the row isn't a to-many section, then we use the previous logic that grabs the information from the nested arrays and pushes the appropriate attribute editor onto the stack for the attribute that corresponds to the row that was tapped:

```
else {
    NSString *controllerClassName = [rowControllers
                            nestedObjectAtIndexPath:indexPath];
    NSString *rowLabel = [rowLabels nestedObjectAtIndexPath:indexPath];
    NSString *rowKey = [rowKeys nestedObjectAtIndexPath:indexPath];
    Class controllerClass = NSClassFromString(controllerClassName);
    ManagedObjectAttributeEditor *controller =
```

```
        [controllerClass alloc];
        controller = [controller initWithStyle:UITableViewStyleGrouped];
        controller.keypath = rowKey;
        controller.managedObject = managedObject;
        controller.labelString = rowLabel;
        controller.title = rowLabel;

        NSDictionary *args = [rowArguments nestedObjectAtIndexPath:indexPath];
        if ([args isKindOfClass:[NSDictionary class]]) {
            if (args != nil) {
                for (NSString *oneKey in args) {
                    id oneArg = [args objectForKey:oneKey];
                    [controller setValue:oneArg forKey:oneKey];
                }
            }
        }
        [self.navigationController pushViewController:controller animated:YES];
        [controller release];
    }
}
```

Handling To-Many Inserts and Deletes

When the user taps on a delete or insert icon, our delegate method
tableView:commitEditingStyle:forRowAtIndexPath: is called. In that method, if the
delete button was tapped, we need to handle deleting the selected object and removing
it from the relationship. If the insert button was tapped, we need to handle that as well.
Add the following method to *ManagedObjectEditor.m*, just before the @end declaration:

```
- (void)tableView:(UITableView *)tableView
      commitEditingStyle:(UITableViewCellEditingStyle)editingStyle
      forRowAtIndexPath:(NSIndexPath *)indexPath {
    if (editingStyle == UITableViewCellEditingStyleInsert) {
        [self tableView:tableView didSelectRowAtIndexPath:indexPath];
    }

    else if (editingStyle == UITableViewCellEditingStyleDelete) {
        NSUInteger newPath[] = {[indexPath section], 0};
        NSIndexPath *row0IndexPath = [NSIndexPath indexPathWithIndexes:newPath
            length:2];

        NSString *rowKey = [rowKeys nestedObjectAtIndexPath:row0IndexPath];
        NSString *rowLabel = [rowLabels nestedObjectAtIndexPath:row0IndexPath];

        NSMutableSet *rowSet = [self.managedObject mutableSetValueForKey:rowKey];

        NSArray *rowArray = [NSArray arrayByOrderingSet:rowSet byKey:rowLabel
            ascending:YES];
        NSManagedObject *objectToRemove = [rowArray objectAtIndex:[indexPath row]];
        [rowSet removeObject:objectToRemove];
        [self.tableView deleteRowsAtIndexPaths:[NSArray arrayWithObject:indexPath]
            withRowAnimation:UITableViewRowAnimationFade];
        [[objectToRemove managedObjectContext] deleteObject:objectToRemove];
        NSError *error;
        if (![self.managedObject.managedObjectContext save:&error])
            NSLog(@"Error saving: %@", [error localizedDescription]);
```

```
    }
}
```

This method is considerably shorter and less complex than the last few, but it's still important to understand.

The first thing we do here is check the editing style, which will tell us which button was tapped. In the case of an insert, we call the `tableView:cellForRowAtIndexPath:` method. If you recall, we already wrote functionality in that method so that a tap on the last row in a to-many section will add a new managed object. There's no point in doing it again, so we just call that method:

```
if (editingStyle == UITableViewCellEditingStyleInsert) {
    [self tableView:tableView didSelectRowAtIndexPath:indexPath];
}
```

Otherwise, we're dealing with a delete. We use an `else` if just to be safe. Although currently this method will be called only with either `UITableViewCellEditingStyleDelete` or `UITableViewCellEditingStyleInsert`, we want to code defensively so our application doesn't break if Apple someday adds another editing style into the mix.

```
else if (editingStyle == UITableViewCellEditingStyleDelete) {
```

If it's a delete, we know that we're dealing with a to-many relationship, so we create an index path pointing to the first object in the nested subarrays, and use it to retrieve the row key and label:

```
NSUInteger newPath[] = {[indexPath section], 0};
NSIndexPath *row0IndexPath = [NSIndexPath indexPathWithIndexes:newPath
    length:2];

NSString *rowKey = [rowKeys nestedObjectAtIndexPath:row0IndexPath];
NSString *rowLabel = [rowLabels nestedObjectAtIndexPath:row0IndexPath];
```

Next, we get the set that represents the relationship. We use `mutableSetValueForKey:` instead of `valueForKey:`, so that we can remove objects from the relationship:

```
NSMutableSet *rowSet = [self.managedObject mutableSetValueForKey:rowKey];
```

We need to order the set into an array so we know which object the user tapped:

```
NSArray *rowArray = [NSArray arrayByOrderingSet:rowSet byKey:rowLabel
    ascending:YES];
```

Then we can get the actual object that needs to be deleted and removed from the relationship. Once we have it, we remove it from the mutable set, which removes it from the relationship. We then delete the row from the table, delete the object from the persistent store, and save.

```
NSManagedObject *objectToRemove = [rowArray objectAtIndex:[indexPath row]];
[rowSet removeObject:objectToRemove];
[self.tableView deleteRowsAtIndexPaths:[NSArray arrayWithObject:indexPath]
    withRowAnimation:UITableViewRowAnimationFade];
[[objectToRemove managedObject] deleteObject:objectToRemove];
NSError *error;
if (![self.managedObject.managedObjectContext save:&error])
    NSLog(@"Error saving: %@", [error localizedDescription]);
}
```

> **CAUTION:** In our application, each hero has his or her own powers. Powers are not shared, so we just delete them with impunity. Not all relationships in all applications you write will be this way. Often, the inverse relationship will be to-many also, and objects will be shared. In those instances, you will need to be sure to delete the object only if there are no other objects in the inverse relationship. If other objects exist, you shouldn't delete the selected object, but just remove it from the relationship.

Well, congratulations. You now have a generic controller class for editing data stored in Core Data. But before you get too excited, we still have work to do. For one thing, we completely broke our application when we took the code to create the nested arrays out of `viewDidLoad:` earlier. If you run the application now, it will not work. Let's fix things.

Using the New Generic Controller

Refactoring can be hard, confusing work. The payoff is going to be substantial and have lasting effects, so stick with us. The next thing we need to do is fix the application so that it uses this new class to edit heroes and their powers. To accomplish that, we need to add factory methods to `ManagedObjectEditor` to return a fully initialized controller for each entity we want to use.

Adding Factory Methods for Hero and Power

Because we have created a generic controller, we don't want it to have code that ties it to our specific data model. So, we'll create a project-specific category on `ManagedObjectEditor` that will contain the code to create the arrays. This will maximize reusability of our code, because what's contained in *ManagedObjectEditor.m* will be completely generic and can be copied to other projects.

In the *Groups & Files* pane in Xcode, select the *Categories* folder and select ⌘N from the File menu to create a new file. Select the Objective-C Class template, subclass of *NSObject*, and name the file *ManagedObjectEditor-SuperDB.m*. Make sure you also have it create the corresponding header file. Once the file has been created, single-click *ManagedObjectEditor-SuperDB.h* and replace the contents with the following:

```
#import "ManagedObjectEditor.h"

@interface ManagedObjectEditor(HeroEditor)
+ (id)controllerForHero;
- (id)initHeroEditor;
@end

@interface ManagedObjectEditor(PowerEditor)
+ (id)controllerForPower;
- (id)initPowerEditor;
@end
```

Save the file.

We're actually creating two categories in this one file pair. We could have just as easily added these four methods in a single category, but to make things more organized, we're separating the methods by the entity that they are used to edit.

Switch over to *ManagedObjectEditor-SuperDB.m* and replace its contents with the following:

```objc
#import "ManagedObjectEditor-SuperDB.h"

@implementation ManagedObjectEditor (HeroEditor)

+ (id)controllerForHero {
    id ret = [[[self class] alloc] initHeroEditor];
    return [ret autorelease];
}

- (id)initHeroEditor {
    if (self = [super initWithStyle:UITableViewStyleGrouped])
    {
        sectionNames = [[NSArray alloc] initWithObjects:
            [NSNull null],
            NSLocalizedString(@"General", @"General"),
            NSLocalizedString(@"Powers", @"Powers"),
            NSLocalizedString(@"Reports", @"Reports"),
            nil];

        rowLabels = [[NSArray alloc] initWithObjects:

            // Section 1
            [NSArray arrayWithObjects:NSLocalizedString(@"Name", @"Name"), nil],

            // Section 2
            [NSArray arrayWithObjects:NSLocalizedString(@"Identity", @"Identity"),
                NSLocalizedString(@"Birthdate", @"Birthdate"),
                NSLocalizedString(@"Age", @"Age"),
                NSLocalizedString(@"Sex", @"Sex"),
                NSLocalizedString(@"Fav. Color", @"Favorite Color"),
                nil],

            // Section 3
            [NSArray arrayWithObject:@"name"], // label here is the key on the
                                               // other object to use as the label

            // Section 4
            [NSArray arrayWithObjects:
                NSLocalizedString(@"All Older Heroes", @"All Older Heroes"]),
                NSLocalizedString(@"All Younger Heroes", @"All Younger Heroes"),
                NSLocalizedString(@"Same Sex Heroes", @"Same Sex Heroes"),
                NSLocalizedString(@"Opposite Sex Heroes", @" Opposite Sex Heroes"),
                nil],

            // Sentinel
            nil];

        rowKeys = [[NSArray alloc] initWithObjects:
```

```
    // Section 1
    [NSArray arrayWithObjects:@"name", nil],

    // Section 2
    [NSArray arrayWithObjects:@"secretIdentity", @"birthdate", @"age",
    @"sex", @"favoriteColor", nil],

    // Section 3
    [NSArray arrayWithObject:@"powers"],

    // Section 4
    [NSArray arrayWithObjects:@"olderHeroes", @"youngerHeroes",
        @"sameSexHeroes", @"oppositeSexHeroes", nil],

    // Sentinel
    nil];

rowControllers = [[NSArray alloc] initWithObjects:

    // Section 1
    [NSArray arrayWithObject:@"ManagedObjectStringEditor"],

    // Section 2
    [NSArray arrayWithObjects:@"ManagedObjectStringEditor",
        @"ManagedObjectDateEditor",
        [NSNull null],
        @"ManagedObjectSingleSelectionListEditor",
        @"ManagedObjectColorEditor",
        nil],

    // Section 3
    [NSArray arrayWithObject:kToManyRelationship],

    // Section 4
    [NSArray arrayWithObjects:
        @"ManagedObjectFetchedPropertyDisplayer",
        @"ManagedObjectFetchedPropertyDisplayer",
        @"ManagedObjectFetchedPropertyDisplayer",
        @"ManagedObjectFetchedPropertyDisplayer",
        nil],

    // Sentinel
    nil];
rowArguments = [[NSArray alloc] initWithObjects:

    // Section 1
    [NSArray arrayWithObject:[NSNull null]],

    // Section 2
    [NSArray arrayWithObjects:[NSNull null],
        [NSNull null],
        [NSNull null],
        [NSDictionary dictionaryWithObject:
            [NSArray arrayWithObjects:@"Male", @"Female", nil]
            forKey:@"list"],
        [NSNull null],
```

```objc
                            [NSNull null],
                        nil],

                // Section 3
                [NSArray arrayWithObject:[NSDictionary dictionaryWithObjectsAndKeys:
                    @"controllerForPower", kSelectorKey, nil]],

                //Section 4
                [NSArray arrayWithObjects:
                    [NSDictionary dictionaryWithObjectsAndKeys:
                        @"name", @"displayKey", @"controllerForHero",
                        @"controllerFactoryMethod", nil],
                    [NSDictionary dictionaryWithObjectsAndKeys:
                        @"name", @"displayKey", @"controllerForHero",
                        @"controllerFactoryMethod", nil],
                    [NSDictionary dictionaryWithObjectsAndKeys:
                        @"name", @"displayKey", @"controllerForHero",
                        @"controllerFactoryMethod", nil],
                    [NSDictionary dictionaryWithObjectsAndKeys:
                        @"name", @"displayKey", @"controllerForHero",
                        @"controllerFactoryMethod", nil],
                    nil],

                // Sentinel
                nil];
    }
    return self;
}
@end

@implementation ManagedObjectEditor (PowerEditor)

+ (id)controllerForPower {
    id ret = [[[self class] alloc] initPowerEditor];
    return [ret autorelease];
}

- (id)initPowerEditor {
    if (self = [[[self class] alloc] initWithStyle:UITableViewStyleGrouped]) {
        sectionNames = [[NSArray alloc] initWithObjects:[NSNull null],
            [NSNull null], nil];
        rowLabels = [[NSArray alloc] initWithObjects:
            [NSArray arrayWithObject:NSLocalizedString(@"Name", @"Name")],
            [NSArray arrayWithObject:NSLocalizedString(@"Source", @"Source")],
            nil];

        rowKeys = [[NSArray alloc] initWithObjects:
            [NSArray arrayWithObject:@"name"],
            [NSArray arrayWithObject:@"source"],
            nil];

        rowControllers = [[NSArray alloc] initWithObjects:
            [NSArray arrayWithObject:@"ManagedObjectStringEditor"],
            [NSArray arrayWithObject:@"ManagedObjectStringEditor"],
            nil];

        rowArguments = [[NSArray alloc] initWithObjects:
```

```
                    [NSArray arrayWithObject:[NSNull null]],
                    [NSArray arrayWithObject:[NSNull null]],
                    nil];
        }
        return self;
    }
}

@end
```

The two init methods should look familiar to you. They set up the structure arrays, just as in `viewDidLoad`. The contents of the `Hero` arrays have gotten a little more complex, since we've added a to-many relationship and four fetched properties, but the basic concept is unchanged from before.

You should look these over to make sure you understand what they're doing. We've been working with the nested arrays long enough now that we're not going to step through them line by line.

Deleting the Nib Instance

We need to delete the instance of `ManagedObjectEditor` in *MainWindow.xib*. If you remember from the earlier chapters, there is an instance of `HeroEditController` in the nib, and that instance is used to edit all heroes. When we refactored `HeroEditController`, the instance of the nib became an instance of `ManagedObjectEditor`.

We can no longer instantiate our controller class from the nib file because the nested arrays won't be set up properly if we leave it like this. We used to create the arrays in `viewDidLoad`, but that is no longer the case, so we need to create the controller instance in code to make sure that those arrays are created.

Double-click *MainWindow.xib* in the *Groups & Files* pane to open Interface Builder. Look in the nib's main window for an icon labeled *Managed Object Editor*. Single-click it to select it, and then press the Delete key on your keyboard to delete it. Note that if you are in list mode, *Managed Object Editor* will also have a child *Table View*. No worries—that child view will disappear when you delete the parent. Save the nib and go back to Xcode.

Updating HeroListController

Now that we're not creating an instance of `ManagedObjectEditor` in *MainWindow.xib*, we need to take care of that task in code. We will do this in `HeroListViewController`, which is the navigation controller's root view controller. Single-click *HeroListViewController.m* and add the following `import` statements at the top of the file:

```
#import "HeroListViewController.h"
#import "SuperDBAppDelegate.h"
#import "ManagedObjectEditor.h"
#import "Hero.h"
#import "ManagedObjectEditor-SuperDB.h"
```

```
@implementation HeroListViewController
...
```

Next, we need to create the controller class in `viewDidLoad`. Insert the following line of code into `viewDidLoad` to accomplish that:

```
- (void)viewDidLoad {
    [super viewDidLoad];
    self.detailController = [ManagedObjectEditor controllerForHero];
    NSError *error = nil;
    ...
```

Because we're using the factory method `controllerForHero`, the controller class that is created will have all the arrays populated so that it works correctly and allows the user to edit the *Hero* entity.

Creating the Fetched Property Attribute Controller

At this point, the application should run and work mostly okay, with the exception of the fetched properties. We haven't written the controller to display them yet. Let's do that now. You've written enough of these attribute editing classes, so we won't walk through this one step by step.

Create a new file by single-clicking the *Classes* folder and selecting ⌘N from the **File** menu. Use the Objective-C class template, subclass *NSObject*, and name the new file *ManagedObjectFetchedPropertyDisplayer.m*, making sure to create the header file as well. Once the file is created, single-click *ManagedObjectFetchedPropertyDisplayer.h* and replace the contents with the following:

```
#import <Foundation/Foundation.h>
#import "ManagedObjectAttributeEditor.h"

@interface ManagedObjectFetchedPropertyDisplayer : ManagedObjectAttributeEditor {
    NSString    *displayKey;
    NSString    *controllerFactoryMethod;
}
@property (nonatomic, retain) NSString *displayKey;
@end
```

Save the file.

Switch over to *ManagedObjectFetchedPropertyDisplayer.m* and replace its contents with the following:

```
#import "ManagedObjectFetchedPropertyDisplayer.h"
#import "NSArray-Set.h"
#import "ManagedObjectEditor.h"

@implementation ManagedObjectFetchedPropertyDisplayer

@synthesize displayKey;

- (void)viewWillAppear:(BOOL)animated {
    [super viewWillAppear:animated];
```

```objectivec
        self.navigationItem.leftBarButtonItem = nil;
        self.navigationItem.rightBarButtonItem = nil;
}

- (void)dealloc {
    [displayKey release];
    [super dealloc];
}

#pragma mark -
#pragma mark Table View Methods
- (NSInteger)tableView:(UITableView *)theTableView
numberOfRowsInSection:(NSInteger)section {
    NSArray *array = [self.managedObject valueForKey:keypath];
    return [array count];
}

- (UITableViewCell *)tableView:(UITableView *)theTableView
        cellForRowAtIndexPath:(NSIndexPath *)indexPath {
    static NSString *CellIdentifier = @"Fetched Property Display Cell";

    UITableViewCell *cell = [theTableView
        dequeueReusableCellWithIdentifier:CellIdentifier];
    if (cell == nil) {
        cell = [[[UITableViewCell alloc] initWithStyle:UITableViewCellStyleDefault
            reuseIdentifier:CellIdentifier] autorelease];
    }
    NSArray *array = [self.managedObject valueForKey:keypath];

    NSManagedObject *oneObject = [array objectAtIndex:[indexPath row]];
    cell.textLabel.text = [oneObject valueForKey:displayKey];
    cell.accessoryType = UITableViewCellAccessoryDisclosureIndicator;
    return cell;
}

- (void)tableView:(UITableView *)tableView
        didSelectRowAtIndexPath:(NSIndexPath *)indexPath {
    NSArray *array = [self.managedObject valueForKey:keypath];
    NSManagedObject *oneObject = [array objectAtIndex:[indexPath row]];
    SEL factorySelector = NSSelectorFromString(controllerFactoryMethod);
    ManagedObjectEditor *controller = [ManagedObjectEditor
        performSelector:factorySelector];
    controller.managedObject = oneObject;
    [self.navigationController pushViewController:controller animated:YES];
}

@end
```

This attribute editor uses Objective-C's dynamic dispatching to let the calling object specify a factory method that can be used to edit any of the objects in the fetched relationship. Selecting a hero in one of the lists drills down and lets you edit that hero in a new instance of ManagedObjectEditor. In fact, you can drill down endlessly, even in our simple application—at least until you run out of memory.

Build and run the application, and then test it. Try out the four fetched properties, and make sure you see the heroes you expect to see in each one. Try drilling down to edit the heroes from the fetched property.

It's pretty good, and you can extend this application quite a bit without writing any code except new factory methods to populate those arrays.

Cleaning Up Deleted Objects

There is still one minor problem to address. Select a hero or create a new one, and then hit the plus button to add a new power to the hero. Once the new view comes up, immediately hit the *Cancel* button. When you get back to the original hero, you'll see two insert rows, as shown in Figure 7–18.

Figure 7–18. *Oops! That's not good.*

Here's what's happening. When we added the new power, the power instance was added to the managed object context in memory. When we pressed the *Cancel* button, we deleted the object from the context. But instead, the delete rule should have come into play, and the object should have been deleted from the data structure that Core Data uses to represent the relationship in memory. This is a bug—at least as of this writing. We could have ignored this, hoping that the bug was fixed before the book was released, but we didn't want to leave you hanging. There are a number of ways that we could handle this.

We could, for example, give the `ManagedObjectEditor` class a property that points to its parent controller—the one that created it and pushed it onto the navigation stack. With that information, we could then remove the offending object from the relationship when we delete it. That creates a dependency, however. It operates under the assumption that the parent view controller is the same class, and we know that that's not always true, because `HeroListController` is the parent view controller for one instance of this class.

How can we fix the problem, then?

What we can do is loop through the properties of the managed object looking for instances of `NSSet`, which we know will represent to-many relationships. When we find one, we can loop through the objects in the relationship, and if we find a deleted one, we can remove it.

In order to get access to information about an object's properties, we need to use the Objective-C runtime, which is a library of C functions that are responsible for Objective-C's dynamic nature.

Single-click *ManagedObjectEditor.m*. In order to call any of the Objective-C runtime's functions, we need to import two header files. Insert the following two lines of code near the top of the file:

```objc
#import "ManagedObjectEditor.h"
#import "NSArray-NestedArrays.h"
#import "HeroValueDisplay.h"
#import "ManagedObjectAttributeEditor.h"
#import "NSManagedObject-IsNew.h"
#import "NSArray-Set.h"

#import <objc/runtime.h>
#import <objc/message.h>
...
```

Now, look for the `viewWillAppear:` method. At the very beginning of that method, insert the following code:

```objc
- (void)viewWillAppear:(BOOL)animated {

    unsigned int outCount;
    objc_property_t *propList =
        class_copyPropertyList([self.managedObject class], &outCount);

    for (int i = 0; i < outCount; i++) {
        objc_property_t oneProp = propList[i];
        NSString *propName = [NSString
            stringWithUTF8String:property_getName(oneProp)];
        NSString *attrs = [NSString stringWithUTF8String:
            property_getAttributes(oneProp)];

        if ([attrs rangeOfString:@"NSSet"].location != NSNotFound) {

            NSMutableSet *objects = [self.managedObject
```

```
                valueForKey:propName];
        NSMutableArray *toDelete = [NSMutableArray array];
        for (NSManagedObject *oneObject in objects) {
            if ([oneObject isDeleted])
                [toDelete addObject:oneObject];
        }
        for (NSManagedObject *oneObject in toDelete) {
            [objects removeObject:oneObject];
            NSError *error;
            if (![self.managedObject.managedObjectContext save:&error])
                NSLog(@"Error saving: %@", [error localizedDescription]);
        }
    }
}
free(propList);

[self.tableView reloadData];
...
```

> **NOTE:** The Objective-C runtime is fairly advanced juju, so if you don't 100% understand this right now, don't worry about it. You can read up on the Objective-C runtime in Apple's documentation:
>
> http://developer.apple.com/mac/library/documentation/Cocoa/Referen ce/ObjCRuntimeRef/Reference/reference.html

This is the first time we've worked with the Objective-C runtime directly. Although for most programming jobs there's no need to dive down into the runtime, having access to the same functions that are used to implement Objective-C gives us an incredible amount of power. Let's quickly run through what we're doing here, but don't feel like you have to grok this one the first time through.

First, we declare an int, which will hold the number of properties that managedObject has. Then we declare a pointer to an objc_property_t, which is a datatype that represents Objective-C 2.0 properties, and use a runtime function called class_copyPropertyList() to retrieve the list of pointers to the managedObject properties. This function also populates outCount with the number of properties.

```
unsigned int outCount;
objc_property_t *propList =
    class_copyPropertyList([self.managedObject class], &outCount);
```

Next, we use a for loop to iterate over the properties:

```
for (int i=0; i < outCount; i++) {
```

We grab a reference to the structure that points to one property in the list, and then get the property's name as an NSString instance. We also get the property's attributes, which are contained in a string. The format for the attribute string is documented in

Apple's Objective-C runtime documentation, but for our purposes, all we need to know is that it contains (among other things) the class of the property.

```
objc_property_t oneProp = propList[i];
NSString *propName = [NSString
    stringWithUTF8String:property_getName(oneProp)];
NSString *attrs = [NSString stringWithUTF8String:
    property_getAttributes(oneProp)];
```

We check to see if the attribute string contains @"NSSet":

```
if ([attrs rangeOfString:@"NSSet"].location != NSNotFound) {
```

If it does, we then retrieve the set and create an instance of NSMutableArray to keep track of the objects that need to be deleted. It is not safe to delete objects from a collection while we are iterating over it, so we'll stick them in an array. Then, when we're finished iterating, we'll iterate through the array of objects that need to be deleted and remove them.

```
NSMutableSet *objects = [self.managedObject
    valueForKey:propName];
NSMutableArray *toDelete = [NSMutableArray array];
for (NSManagedObject *oneObject in objects) {
    if ([oneObject isDeleted])
        [toDelete addObject:oneObject];
}
for (NSManagedObject *oneObject in toDelete) {
    [objects removeObject:oneObject];
    NSError *error;
    if (![self.managedObject.managedObjectContext save:&error])
        NSLog(@"Error saving: %@", [error localizedDescription]);
}
}
}
```

And, believe it or not, the application is done. Build and run it, and try it out. See how many times you can drill down. Try creating new powers, deleting existing powers, and canceling when editing both new and existing powers.

Now, if you really want to challenge yourself, try adding more entities and relationships and using ManagedObjectEditor instances and its nested arrays to allow editing of those new entities. In short, play. Get used to this application. Expand it. Change it. Break it. And then fix it. That's the best way to cement your understanding of everything we did in this chapter.

Wonderful to the Core

This chapter and the previous chapters have given you a solid foundation in the use of Core Data. Along the way, we've also tried to give you some information about how to design complex iPhone applications so that they can be maintained and expanded without writing unnecessary code or repeating the same logic in multiple places. We've demonstrated just how much benefit you can get from taking the time to write code generically. We've showed you how to look for opportunities to refactor your code to make it smaller, more efficient, easier to maintain, and just generally more pleasant to be around.

We could go on for several more chapters about Core Data and not exhaust the topic. But Core Data is not the only new framework introduced in iPhone SDK 3. At this point, you should have a solid enough understanding of Core Data to be able to, armed with Apple's documentation, take your explorations even further.

Now it's time to leave our friend Core Data behind and explore some of the other aspects of iPhone SDK 3.

Part II

Further Explorations

We've devoted six chapters to the biggest of the new APIs, but Core Data is not all that iPhone SDK 3 brings to the table for iPhone developers. A whole slew of new functionality has been made available, including peer-to-peer connectivity, mapping, push services, in-application e-mail, copy and paste, and undo—to name just a few. In the next chapters, we're going to show you how to use several of these exciting new APIs in your own applications, as well as dive into a few more advanced topics such as networking and concurrency.

Chapter 8

Peer-to-Peer Over Bluetooth Using GameKit

One of the coolest new frameworks added to the iPhone 3 SDK is called GameKit. GameKit makes it easy to wirelessly connect multiple iPhones or iPod touches using Bluetooth. Bluetooth is a wireless networking option built into all but the first-generation iPhone and iPod touch. GameKit allows any supported devices to communicate with any other supported devices that are within roughly 30 feet (about 10 meters) of each other. Though the name implies differently, GameKit is useful for nongaming apps, too. For example, you might build a social networking app that allows people to easily transfer contact information over Bluetooth.

CAUTION: The code in this chapter will not run in the simulator because the simulator does not support Bluetooth. The only way to build and debug apps on a device attached to your machine is by joining the paid iPhone Developer Program. So you'll need to do that if you want to fully experience this chapter's chewy goodness.

In addition, the game we're building in this chapter requires the use of two second-generation devices (iPhone 3G or 3Gs, or second-generation iPod touch) to run and test. As of this writing, you cannot play GameKit games between a device and the simulator. If you have only one device, you will not be able to try out the game in this chapter. We will be adding online play in the next chapter, so you might want to follow along, even if you can't test your application yet.

As of this writing, GameKit has three basic components:

- The **session** allows iPhone OS devices running the same application to easily send information back and forth over Bluetooth without writing any networking code.

- The **peer picker** provides an easy way to find other devices without writing any networking or discovery (Bonjour) code.

■ The **in-game voice** functionality allows users to send voice communications using GameKit sessions or over the Internet.

> **NOTE:** We won't use in-game voice in this chapter's example, but it's actually pretty straightforward. If you want to learn more about it, here's a link to the official Apple doc:
>
> http://developer.apple.com/iPhone/library/documentation/Networking
> Internet/Conceptual/GameKit_Guide/InGameVoice/InGameVoice.html

Under the hood, GameKit sessions leverage **Bonjour**, Apple's technology for zero-configuration network device discovery. As a result, devices using GameKit are capable of finding each other on the network without the user needing to enter an IP address or domain name.

This Chapter's Application

In this chapter, we're going to explore GameKit by writing a simple networked game. We'll write a two-player version of tic-tac-toe (Figure 8–1) that will use GameKit to let people on two different iPhones or iPod touches play against each other over Bluetooth. We won't be implementing online play over the Internet or local area network in this chapter. However, we will discuss online communications in the next chapter.

Figure 8–1. *We'll use a simple game of tic-tac-toe to show you the basics of GameKit.*

When users launch our application, they will be presented with an empty tic-tac-toe board and a single button labeled *New Game*. (For the sake of simplicity, we're not going to implement a single-device mode to let two players play on the same device.) When the user presses the *New Game* button, the application will start looking for Bluetooth peers using the peer picker (Figure 8–2).

Figure 8–2. *When the user presses the* New Game *button, it will launch the peer picker to look for other devices running the tic-tac-toe game.*

If another device within range runs the TicTacToe application, and the user also presses the *New Game* button, then the two devices will find each other, and the peer picker will present a dialog to the users, letting them choose among the available peers (Figure 8–3).

Figure 8–3. *When another device within range starts a game, the two devices will show up in each other's peer picker dialog.*

After one player selects a peer, the other person will be asked to accept or refuse the connection. If the connection is accepted, the two applications will negotiate to see who goes first. Each side will randomly select a number, the numbers will be compared, and the highest number will go first. Once that decision is made, play will commence (Figure 8–4) until someone wins (Figure 8–5).

Figure 8–4. *The user whose turn it is can tap any available space. That space will get an X or an O on both users' devices.*

Figure 8–5. *Play continues until one player wins or there is a tie.*

Network Communication Models

Before we look at how GameKit and the peer picker work, let's talk generally about communication models used in networked programs, so that we're all on the same page in terms of terminology.

Client-Server Model

You're probably familiar with the client-server model, as it is the model used by the World Wide Web. Machines called **servers** listen for connections from other machines, referred to as **clients**. The server then takes actions based on the requests received from the clients. In the context of the Web, the client is usually a web browser, and there can be any number of clients attaching to a single server. The clients never communicate with each other directly, but direct all communications through the server. Most massively multiplayer online role-playing games (MMORPGs) like World of Warcraft also use this model. Figure 8–6 represents a client-server scenario.

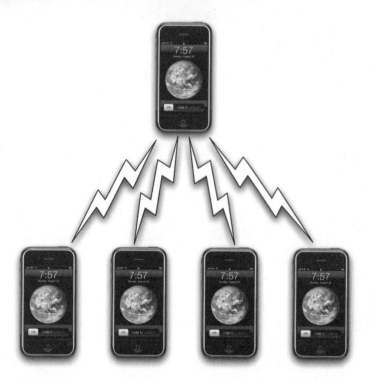

Figure 8–6. *The client-server model features one machine acting as a server with all communications—even communications between clients—going through the server.*

In the context of an iPhone application, a client-server setup is where one phone acts as a server and listens for other iPhones running the same program. The other phones can then connect to that server. If you've ever played a game where one machine "hosts" a game and others then join the game, that game is almost certainly using a client-server model.

A drawback with the client-server model is that everything depends on the server, which means that the game cannot continue if anything happens to the server. If the user whose phone is acting as the server quits, crashes, or moves out of range, the entire game is ended. Since all the other machines communicate through the central server, they lose the ability to communicate if the server is unavailable. This is generally not an issue with client-server games where the client is a hefty server farm connected to the Internet by redundant high-speed lines, but it certainly can be an issue with mobile games.

Peer-to-Peer Model

In the peer-to-peer model, all the individual devices (called **peers**) can communicate with each other directly. A central server may be used to initiate the connection or to facilitate certain operations, but the main distinguishing feature of the peer-to-peer model is that peers can talk to each other directly, and can continue to do so even in the absence of a server (Figure 8–7).

The peer-to-peer model was popularized by file-sharing services like BitTorrent. A centralized sever is used to find other peers that have the file you are looking for, but once the connection is made to those other peers, they can continue, even if the server goes offline.

Figure 8–7. *In the peer-to-peer model, peers can talk to each other directly, and can continue to do so even in the absence of a server.*

The simplest and probably the most common implementation of the peer-to-peer model on the iPhone is when you have two devices connected to each other. This is the model you use in head-to-head games, for example. GameKit makes this kind of peer-to-peer network exceedingly simple to set up and configure, as you'll see in this chapter.

Hybrid Client-Server/Peer-to-Peer

The client-server and peer-to-peer models of network communication are not mutually exclusive, and it is possible to create programs that utilize a hybrid of both. For example, a client-server game might allow certain communications to go directly from client to client, without going through the server. In a game that had a chat window, it might allow messages intended for only one recipient to go directly from the machine of the sender to the machine of the intended recipient, while any other kind of chat would go to the server to be distributed to all clients.

You should keep these different networking models in mind as we discuss the mechanics of making connections and transferring data between application nodes. **Node** is a generic term that refers to any computer connected to an application's network. A client, server, or peer is a node. The game we will be writing in this chapter will use a simple, two-machine, peer-to-peer model.

The GameKit Session

The key to GameKit is the session, represented by the class GKSession. The session represents our end of a network connection with one or more other iPhones. Regardless of whether you are acting as a client, a server, or a peer, an instance of GKSession will represent the connections you have with other phones. You will use GKSession whether you employ the peer picker or write your own code to find machines to connect to and let the user select from them.

> **NOTE:** As you make your way through the next few pages, don't worry too much about where each of these elements is implemented. This will all come together in the project you create in this chapter.

You will also use GKSession to send data to connected peers. You will implement session delegate methods to get notified of changes to the session, such as when another node connects or disconnects, as well as to receive data sent by other nodes.

Creating the Session

To use a session, you must first create allocate and initialize a GKSession object, like so:

```
GKSession *theSession = [[GKSession alloc] initWithSessionID:@"com.apress.Foo"
displayName:nil sessionMode:GKSessionModePeer];
```

There are three arguments you pass in when initializing a session:

■ The first argument is a **session identifier**, which is a string that is unique to your application. This is used to prevent your application's sessions from accidentally connecting to sessions from another program. Since the session identifier is a string, it can be anything, though the convention is to use a reverse DNS-style name, such as *com.apress.Foo*. By assigning session identifiers in this manner, rather than by just randomly picking a word or phrase, you are less likely to accidentally choose a session identifier that is used by another application on the App Store.

- The second argument is the **display name**. This is a name that will be provided to the other nodes to uniquely identify your phone. If you pass in nil, the display name will default to the device's name as set in iTunes. If multiple devices are connected, this will allow the other users to see which devices are available and connect to the correct one. In Figure 8–3, you can see an example of where the unique identifier is used. In that example, one other device is advertising itself with the same session identifier as us, using a display name of *iPhone*.

- The last argument is the **session mode**. Session modes determine how the session will behave once it's all set up and ready to make connections. There are three options:

  - If you specify GKSessionModeServer, your session will advertise itself on the network so that other devices can see it and connect to it, but it won't look for other sessions being advertised.

  - If you specify GKSessionModeClient, the session will not advertise itself on the network, but will look for other sessions that are advertising themselves.

  - If you specify GKSessionModePeer, your session will both advertise its availability on the network and also look for other sessions.

NOTE: Although you will generally use GKSessionModePeer when establishing a peer-to-peer network, and GKSessionModeServer and GKSessionModeClient when setting up a client-server network, these constants dictate only whether an individual session will advertise its availability on the network using Bonjour, or look for other available nodes. They are not necessarily indicative of which of the network models is being used by the application.

Regardless of the type of session you create, it won't actually start advertising its availability or looking for other available nodes until you tell it to do so. You do that by setting the session property available to YES. Alternatively, you can have the node stop advertising its availability and/or stop looking for other available nodes by setting available to NO.

Finding and Connecting to Other Sessions

When a session that was created using GKSessionModeClient or GKSessionModePeer finds another node advertising its availability, it will call the method session:peer:didChangeState: and pass in a state of GKPeerStateAvailable. This same method will be called every time a peer becomes available or unavailable, as well as when a peer connects or disconnects. The second argument will tell you which peer's state changed, and the last argument will tell you its new state.

If you find one or more other sessions that are available, you can choose to connect the session to one of the available sessions by calling connectToPeer:withTimeout:. Here's an example of session:peer:didChangeState: that connects to the first available peer it finds:

```
- (void)session:(GKSession *)session peer:(NSString *)peerID
      didChangeState:(GKPeerConnectionState)inState {
    if (inState == GKPeerStateAvailable) {
        [session connectToPeer:peerID withTimeout:60];
        session.available = NO;
    }
}
```

This isn't a very realistic example, as you would normally allow the user to choose the node to which they connect. It's a good example though, because it shows both of the basic functions of a client node. In this example, we've set available to NO after we connect. This will cause our session to stop looking for additional sessions. Since a session can connect to multiple peers, you won't always want to do this. If your application supports multiple connections, then you will want to leave it at YES.

Listening for Other Sessions

When a session is specified with a session mode of GKSessionModeServer or GKSessionModePeer, it will be notified when another node attempts to connect. When this happens, the session will call the method session:didReceiveConnectionRequestFromPeer:. You can choose to accept the connection by calling acceptConnectionFromPeer:error:, or you can reject it by calling denyConnectionFromPeer:. The following is an example that assumes the presence of a Boolean instance variable called amAcceptingConnections. If it's set to YES, it accepts the connection, and if it's set to NO, it rejects the connection.

```
- (void)session:(GKSession *)session
didReceiveConnectionRequestFromPeer:(NSString *)peerID {
    if (amAcceptingConnections) {
        NSError *error;
        if (![session acceptConnectionFromPeer:peerID error:&error])
            // Handle error
    } else {
        [session denyConnectionFromPeer:peerID];
    }
}
```

Sending Data to a Peer

Once you have a session that is connected to another node, it's very easy to send data to that node. All you need to do is call one of two methods. Which method you call depends on whether you want to send the information to all connected sessions or to just specific ones. To send data to just specified peers, you use the method sendData:toPeers:withDataMode:error:, and to send data to every connected peer, you use the method sendDataToAllPeers:withDataMode:error:.

In both cases, you need to specify a **data mode** for the connection. The data mode tells the session how it should try to send the data. There are two options:

- GKSendDataReliable: This option ensures that the information will arrive at the other session. It will send the data in chunks if it's over a certain size, and wait for an acknowledgment from the other peer for every chunk.

- GKSendDataUnreliable: This mode sends the data immediately and does not wait for acknowledgment. It's much faster than GKSendDataReliable, but there is a small chance of the complete message not arriving at the other node.

Usually, the GKSendDataReliable data mode is the one you'll want to use, though if you have a program where speed of transmission matters more than accuracy, then you'll want to consider GKSendDataUnreliable.

Here is what it looks like when you send data to a single peer:

```
NSError *error = nil;
If (![session sendData:theData toPeers:[NSArray arrayWithObject:thePeerID]
    withDataMode:GKSendDataReliable error:&error]) {
    // Do error handling
}
```

And here's what it looks like to send data to all connected peers:

```
NSError *error = nil;
if (![session sendDataToAllPeers:data withDataMode:GKSendDataReliable
    error:&error]) {
    // Do error handling
}
```

Packaging Up Information to Send

Any information that you can get into an instance of NSData can be sent to other peers. There are two basic approaches to doing this for use in GameKit. The first is to use archiving and unarchiving, just as we did in the archiving section of Chapter 11 of *Beginning iPhone 3 Development* (Apress, 2009).

With the archiving/unarchiving method, you define a class to hold a single packet of data to be sent. That class will contain instance variables to hold whatever types of data you might need to send. When it's time to send a packet, you create and initialize an instance of the packet object, and then you use NSKeyedArchiver to archive the instance of that object into an instance of NSData, which can be passed to sendData:toPeers:withDataMode:error: or to sendDataToAllPeers:withDataMode:error:. We'll use this approach in this chapter's example. However, this approach incurs a small amount of overhead, since it requires the creation of objects to be passed, along with archiving and unarchiving those objects.

Although archiving objects is the best approach in many cases, because it is easy to implement and it fits well with the design of Cocoa Touch, there may be some cases where applications need to constantly send a lot of data to their peers, and this overhead might be unacceptable. In those situations, a faster option is to just use a static array (a regular old C array, not an NSArray) as a local variable in the method that sends the data.

You can copy any data you need to send to the peer into this static array, and then create an NSData instance from that static array. There's still some object creation involved in creating the NSData instance, but it's one object instead of two, and you don't have the overhead of archiving. Here's a simple example of sending data using this faster technique:

```
NSUInteger packetData[2];
packet[0] = foo;
packet[1] = bar;
NSData *packet = [NSData dataWithBytes:packetData
    length:2 * sizeof(packetData)];
NSError *error = nil;
if (![session sendDataToAllPeers:packet withDataMode:GKSendDataReliable
    error:&error]) {
    // Handle error
}
```

Receiving Data from a Peer

When a session receives data from a peer, the session passes the data to a method on an object known as a **data receive handler**. The method is receiveData:fromPeer:inSession:context:. By default, the data receive handler is the session's delegate, but it doesn't have to be. You can specify another object to handle the task by calling setDataReceiveHandler:withContext: on the session and passing in the object you want to receive data from the session.

Whichever object is specified as the data receive handler must implement receiveData:fromPeer:inSession:context:, and that method will be called any time new data comes in from a peer. There's no need to acknowledge receipt of the data or worry about waiting for the entire packet. You can just use the provided data as is appropriate for your program. All the gnarly aspects of network data transmission are handled for you. Every call to sendDataToAllPeers:withDataMode:error: made by other peers, and every call to sendData:toPeers:withDataMode:error: made by other peers who specify your peer identifier, will result in one call of the data receive handler.

Here's an example of a data receive handler method that would be the counterpart to our earlier send example:

```
- (void) receiveData:(NSData *)data fromPeer:(NSString *)peer
inSession: (GKSession *)theSession context:(void *)context {
    NSUInteger *packet = [data bytes];
    NSUInteger foo = packet[0];
    NSUInteger bar = packet[0];
    // Do something with foo and bar
}
```

We'll look at receiving archived objects when we build this chapter's example.

Closing Connections

When you're finished with a session, before you release the session object, it's important to do a little cleanup. Before releasing the session object, you must make the session unavailable, disconnect it from all of its peers, set the data receive handler to nil, and set the session delegate to nil. Here's what the code in your dealloc method (or any other time your need to close the connections) might look like:

```
session.available = NO;
[session disconnectFromAllPeers];

[session setDataReceiveHandler: nil withContext: nil];
session.delegate = nil;
[session release];
```

If, instead, you just want to disconnect from one specific peer, you can call disconnectPeerFromAllPeers:, which will disconnect the remote peer from all the peers to which it was connected. Use this method with caution, as it will cause the peer on which it was called to disconnect from all remote peers, not just your application. Here's what using it might look like:

```
[session disconnectPeerFromAllPeers:thePeer];
```

The Peer Picker

Although GameKit does not need to be used only for games, network games are clearly the primary motivator behind the technology—at least if the name Apple chose is any clue. The most common type of network model for mobile games is the head-to-head or simple peer-to-peer model, where one player plays a game against one other player. Because this scenario is so common, Apple has provided a mechanism called the **peer picker** for easily setting up this simple type of peer-to-peer network.

Creating the Peer Picker

The peer picker was designed specifically to connect one device to a single other device using Bluetooth. Though limited in this way, the peer picker is incredibly simple to use, and a great choice if it meets your needs. To create and show the peer picker, you just create an instance of GKPeerPickerController, set its delegate, and then call its show method, like so:

```
GKPeerPickerController *picker;
picker = [[GKPeerPickerController alloc] init];
picker.delegate = self;
[picker show];
```

One important thing to note here is that it looks like we're leaking the picker here (we've used alloc with no corresponding release), but that's not the case. This is one of those unusual exceptions to the general rule. The reason it's okay to leak the memory is that the delegate (which is the object where the preceding code appears, since it's set to self) will be called again when the user is finished interacting with the peer picker. The delegate method will be passed back a reference to the same peer picker controller instance that was leaked here. At that point, the delegate can release the peer picker, and no memory will have been leaked during the filming of this application.

Handling a Peer Connection

When the user has selected a peer and the sessions have been connected to each other, the delegate method peerPickerController:didConnectToPeer:toSession: will be called. In your implementation of that method, you need to do a few things. First, you might want to store the **peer identifier**, which is a string that identifies the device to which you're connected. The peer identifier defaults to the iPhone's device name, though you can specify other values. You also need to save a reference to the session so you can use it to send data and to disconnect the session later. Additionally, it's important to dismiss the peer picker and make sure that its memory is not leaked. Remember that you didn't retain it when you created it, so you are responsible for releasing it here.

We use autorelease, instead of release, to give the calling object (which is, in fact, picker) the ability to finish the method that's currently executing—the one that called this delegate method. If we were to use release, the object could (and probably would) be released immediately, which would mean the calling method would never finish, and the connection might not finish being established. By putting picker into the autorelease pool, we ensure that it won't be deallocated until the end of the current run loop, so it will have the opportunity to finish any work it's in the process of doing, yet we'll still avoid leaking memory. It is still true that you should avoid unnecessary use of the autorelease pool, but here it isn't unnecessary.

```
- (void)peerPickerController:(GKPeerPickerController *)picker
didConnectPeer:(NSString *)thePeerID
toSession:(GKSession *)theSession {
    self.peerID = thePeerID;

    self.session = theSession;
    self.session.delegate = self;
    [self.session setDataReceiveHandler:self withContext:NULL];

    [picker dismiss];
    picker.delegate = nil;
    [picker autorelease];
}
```

Creating the Session

There's one last delegate task that you must handle when using the peer picker, which is to create the session when the picker asks for a session. You don't need to worry about most of the other tasks related to finding and connecting to other peers when using the peer picker, but you are responsible for creating the session for the picker to use. Here's what that method typically looks like:

```
- (GKSession *)peerPickerController:(GKPeerPickerController *)picker
sessionForConnectionType:(GKPeerPickerConnectionType)type{
    GKSession *theSession = [[GKSession alloc] initWithSessionID:@"a session id"
        displayName:nil sessionMode:GKSessionModePeer];
    return [theSession autorelease];
}
```

We've already talked about the session, so there shouldn't be anything in this method that's confusing.

> **NOTE:** There's actually another peer picker delegate method that you need to implement if you want to support online play over the Internet with the peer picker:
> `peerPickerController:didSelectConnectionType:`. We'll look at that method in the next chapter.

Well, that's enough discussion. Let's start building our application.

Creating the Project

Okay, you know the drill. Fire up Xcode if it's not already open and create a new project. Use the *View-based Application* template and call the project *TicTacToe*. Once the project is open, look in the project archives that accompany this book, in the folder *08 – TicTacToe*. Find the image files called *wood_button.png*, *board.png*, *O.png*, and *X.png*, and copy them into the *Resources* folder of your project. There's also an icon file called *icon.png*, which you can copy into your project if you want to use it.

Turning Off the Idle Timer

The first thing we want to do is to turn off the **idle timer**. The idle timer is what tells your iPhone to go to sleep if the user has not interacted with it in a while. Because the user won't be tapping the screen during the opponent's turn, we need to turn this off to prevent the phone from going to sleep if the other user takes a while to make a move. Generally speaking, you don't want networked applications to go to sleep, because sleeping breaks the network connection. Most of the time, with networked iPhone games, disabling the idle timer is the best approach.

Expand the *Classes* folder in the *Groups & Files* pane in Xcode and single-click *TicTacToeAppDelegate.m*. Add the following line of code to applicationDidFinishLaunching: to disable the idle timer.

```
- (void)applicationDidFinishLaunching:(UIApplication *)application {
    // Override point for customization after app launch
    [window addSubview:viewController.view];
    [window makeKeyAndVisible];

    [[UIApplication sharedApplication] setIdleTimerDisabled:YES];
}
```

NOTE: There may be rare times when you want to leave the idle timer functioning and just close your sessions when the app goes to sleep, but closing sessions on sleep is not quite as straightforward as it would seem. The application delegate method `applicationWillResignActive:` is called before the phone goes to sleep, but unfortunately, it's also called at other times. In fact, it's called any time that your application loses the ability to respond to touch events. That makes it close to impossible to differentiate between when the user has been presented a system alert, such as from a push notification or a low-battery warning (which won't result in broken connections), and when the phone is actually going to sleep. So, until Apple provides a way to differentiate between these scenarios, your best bet is to simply disallow sleep while a networked program is running.

Importing the GameKit Framework

GameKit is not one of the frameworks that is automatically linked by the Xcode project template, so we need to manually link it ourselves in order to access the session and peer picker methods. Select the *Frameworks* folder in the *Groups & Files* pane. Now, right-click the *Frameworks* folder and select **Add** from the context menu, and then choose **Existing Frameworks...**.

If you're using Xcode 3.2 or higher (which requires Snow Leopard), you'll notice that there's a new, easier way to select frameworks (Figure 8–8). You can just select *GameKit.framework* from a provided list of frameworks and then hit the *Add* button. If you're still running Leopard or an earlier version of Xcode, you'll need to link the old-fashioned way: by navigating through the file system to the *Frameworks* folder for the version of the iPhone SDK that you're using, and then selecting *GameKit.framework*. The *Frameworks* folder is at the following location:

```
/Developer/Platforms/iPhoneOS.platform/Developer/SDKs/iPhoneOSx.y.z.sdk/System/Library/Frameworks
```

In this path, *x*, *y*, and *z* denote the release number. For iPhone SDK 3.1.2, for example (the current version as of this writing), *x* is 3, *y* is 1, and *z* is 2. In that case, you would need to navigate to this location:

```
/Developer/Platforms/iPhoneOS.platform/Developer/SDKs/iPhoneOS3.1.2.sdk/System/Library/Frameworks
```

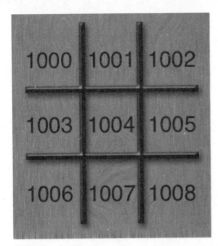

Figure 8–8. *The new Snow Leopardy way of linking frameworks.*

Designing the Interface

Now, we're going to design our game's user interface. Since tic-tac-toe is a relatively simple game, we'll design our user interface in Interface Builder, rather than by using OpenGL ES.

Each of the spaces on the board will be a button. When the user taps a button that hasn't already been selected (which we'll determine by seeing if the button has an image assigned), we'll set the image to either *X.png* or *O.png* (which you added to your project a few minutes ago). We'll then send that information to the other device. We're also going to use the button's tag value to differentiate the buttons and make it easier to determine when someone has won. We'll assign each of the buttons that represents a space on the board with a sequential tag, starting in the upper-left corner. You can see which space will have which tag value by looking at Figure 8–9.

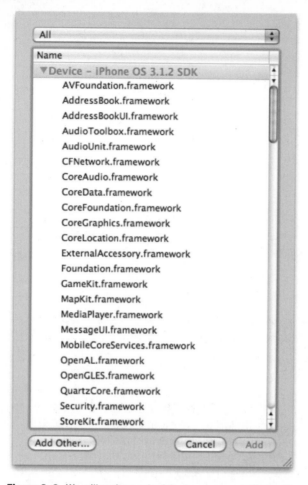

Figure 8–9. *We will assign each of the game space buttons a tag value. This way, we can identify which button was pressed without needing to have separate action methods for each button.*

Setting Up the View Controller Header

Before we head over to Interface Builder to actually create our user interface, we want to declare the actions and outlets that we'll need to connect once we get there. While we're in the header file, we'll also declare the rest of the methods we'll be using, as well as some constants and enumerations to make our code easier to read.

Single-click *TicTacToeViewController.h* and make the following changes:

```
#import <UIKit/UIKit.h>
#import <GameKit/GameKit.h>

#define kTicTacToeSessionID      @"com.apress.TicTacToe.session"
#define kTicTacToeArchiveKey     @"com.apress.TicTacToe"

typedef enum GameStates {
```

```
        kGameStateBeginning,
        kGameStateRollingDice,
        kGameStateMyTurn,
        kGameStateOpponentTurn,
        kGameStateInterrupted,
        kGameStateDone
} GameState;

typedef enum BoardSpaces {
    kUpperLeft = 1000, kUpperMiddle, kUpperRight,
    kMiddleLeft, kMiddleMiddle, kMiddleRight,
    kLowerLeft, kLowerMiddle, kLowerRight
} BoardSpace;

typedef enum PlayerPieces {
    kPlayerPieceUndecided,
    kPlayerPieceO,
    kPlayerPieceX
} PlayerPiece;

@class TicTacToePacket;
@interface TicTacToeViewController : UIViewController
@interface TicTacToeViewController : UIViewController <GKPeerPickerControllerDelegate,
GKSessionDelegate, UIAlertViewDelegate> {
    UIButton    *newGameButton;
    UILabel     *feedbackLabel;

    GKSession   *session;
    NSString    *peerID;

    GameState   state;

    NSInteger   myDieRoll;
    NSInteger   opponentDieRoll;

    PlayerPiece piece;
    UIImage     *xPieceImage;
    UIImage     *oPieceImage;

    BOOL        dieRollReceived;
    BOOL        dieRollAcknowledged;

}
@property(nonatomic, retain) IBOutlet UIButton *newGameButton;
@property(nonatomic, retain) IBOutlet UILabel *feedbackLabel;

@property(nonatomic, retain) GKSession   *session;
@property(nonatomic, copy)   NSString    *peerID;

@property(nonatomic, retain) UIImage *xPieceImage;
@property(nonatomic, retain) UIImage *oPieceImage;

- (IBAction)newGameButtonPressed;
- (IBAction)gameSpacePressed:(id)sender;
```

```
- (void)resetBoard;
- (void)startNewGame;
- (void)resetDieState;
- (void)sendPacket:(TicTacToePacket *)packet;
- (void)sendDieRoll;
- (void)checkForGameEnd;
@end
```

The first thing we need to do is import the GameKit headers so that the compiler knows about the objects and methods from GameKit:

```
#import <GameKit/GameKit.h>
```

Next, we define two constants. One will be our session identifier, which GameKit will use to make sure we connect only to devices running the same program. The other is an archiving key that we will use when packaging data to send to the other node.

```
#define kTicTacToeSessionID     @"com.apress.TicTacToe.session"
#define kTicTacToeArchiveKey    @"com.apress.TicTacToe"
```

Adding networking to even a simple application creates a fair bit of complexity, because network communications are asynchronous. You can't make any assumptions about the order that data will be received. To help us keep track of where we are, we define an enum with a bunch of different game states that identify what's going on right now in our game:

```
typedef enum GameStates {
    kGameStateBeginning,
    kGameStateRollingDice,
    kGameStateMyTurn,
    kGameStateOpponentTurn,
    kGameStateInterrupted,
    kGameStateDone
} GameState;
```

When a game has not yet begun, the state will be kGameStateBeginning. After the devices connect, or when a new game is started, the two nodes will negotiate who goes first by each generating a random number, which is equivalent to flipping a coin or rolling a die in real life. When who goes first is being negotiated, the state is kGameStateRollingDice. When it's our turn to make a move, the state will be kGameStateMyTurn, and when it's the opponent's turn, the state will be kGameStateOpponentTurn. If the connection is interrupted for any reason, we'll set the state to kGameStateInterrupted. Finally, if there are no more possible moves or a player gets three in a row, the state will move to kGameStateDone.

Next, we define another enumeration to refer to each of the spaces on the board by their tag:

```
typedef enum BoardSpaces {
    kUpperLeft = 1000, kUpperMiddle, kUpperRight,
    kMiddleLeft, kMiddleMiddle, kMiddleRight,
    kLowerLeft, kLowerMiddle, kLowerRight
} BoardSpace;
```

In tic-tac-toe, the player who goes first is O, and the other player is X. To identify who is X and who is O, we have one more enumeration:

```
typedef enum PlayerPieces {
    kPlayerPieceUndecided,
    kPlayerPieceO,
    kPlayerPieceX
} PlayerPiece;
```

After that, we tell the compiler that there is a class called `TicTacToePacket`. This class doesn't exist yet, but we'll write it shortly. A `@class` declaration doesn't cause the compiler to look for the class' header file—it's just a promise that a class really exists, so it's okay to declare it this way before actually creating or writing the class.

```
@class TicTacToePacket;
```

Our controller class needs to conform to a few protocols. Our controller will be the delegate of the peer picker, the session. We'll also be using alert views to inform the user when there's a problem, so we conform our class to the three protocols used to define the delegate methods for each of these jobs.

```
@interface TicTacToeViewController : UIViewController <GKPeerPickerControllerDelegate,
GKSessionDelegate, UIAlertViewDelegate> {
```

If you look at the interface in Figures 8–1 and 8–4, you can see that there's a button for starting a game, as well as a label that's used to tell users if it's their turn, or if they've won or lost. We need instance variables for outlets to both of those:

```
    UIButton    *newGameButton;
    UILabel     *feedbackLabel;
```

We also need instance variables for the GameKit session and to hold the peer identifier of the one connected node.

```
    GKSession   *session;
    NSString    *peerID;
```

A moment ago, we defined an enumeration with the various game states, but we need an instance variable to keep track of the current state:

```
    GameState   state;
```

Because we don't know whether we will roll the die or receive our opponent's die roll first, we need variables to hold them both. Once we have both, we can compare them and start the game:

```
    NSInteger   myDieRoll;
    NSInteger   opponentDieRoll;
```

Once we know who goes first, we can store whether we're O or X in this instance variable:

```
    PlayerPiece piece;
```

We'll also load both of the images representing the two game pieces when our view is loaded, and keep a reference to them in these pointers:

```
    UIImage     *xPieceImage;
```

```
    UIImage      *oPieceImage;
```

Finally, we have two more Booleans to keep track of whether we've received the opponent's die roll and whether our opponent has acknowledged receipt of ours. We don't want to begin the game until we have both die rolls and we know our opponent has both as well. When both of these are YES, we'll know it's time to start the actual game play:

```
    BOOL         dieRollReceived;
    BOOL         dieRollAcknowledged;
}
```

Next, we define properties for our outlets, as well as some of our instance variables:

```
@property(nonatomic, retain) IBOutlet UIButton *newGameButton;
@property(nonatomic, retain) IBOutlet UILabel *feedbackLabel;

@property(nonatomic, retain) GKSession *session;
@property(nonatomic, copy)   NSString  *peerID;

@property(nonatomic, retain) UIImage *xPieceImage;
@property(nonatomic, retain) UIImage *oPieceImage;
```

And, finally, we declare our action methods and a bunch of other methods that we'll need in our game. We'll discuss the specific methods in more detail when we implement our controller later, after we design our user interface.

```
- (IBAction)newGameButtonPressed;
- (IBAction)gameSpacePressed:(id)sender;
- (void)resetBoard;
- (void)startNewGame;
- (void)resetDieState;
- (void)sendPacket:(TicTacToePacket *)packet;
- (void)sendDieRoll;
- (void)checkForGameEnd;
@end
```

Save this file.

Now, expand the *Resources* folder in the *Groups & Files* pane, if it's not already expanded, and double-click *TicTacToeViewController.xib* to open Interface Builder.

Designing the Game Board

Once Interface Builder is open, look in the library for an *Image View* and drag that to the window labeled *View*. Because it's the first object you're adding to the view, it should resize to take up the full view. Place it so that it fills the entire view, and then press ⌘1 to bring up the attribute inspector. At the top of the attribute inspector, set the *Image* field to *board.png*, which is one of the images you added to your project earlier.

Next, drag a *Round Rect Button* from the library over to the top of the view. The exact placement doesn't matter yet. After it's placed, use the attribute inspector to change the button type from *Rounded Rect* to *Custom*. In the *Image* field of the attribute inspector, select *wood_button.png*, and then press ⌘= to change the button's size to match the image we assigned to it. Now use the blue guidelines to center the button in the view and place it against the top blue margin so it looks like Figure 8–10.

Figure 8–10. *Your interface after sizing and placing the button*

Control-drag from *File's Owner* to the button and select the *newGameButton* outlet. Then Control-drag from the button back to *File's Owner*, and select the *newGameButtonPressed* action.

Look again in the library for a *Label*, and drag it to the view. Place the label in the top of the view so it runs from the left blue margin to the right blue margin horizontally, and from the top blue margin down to just above the tic-tac-toe board. It will overlap the button we just added, and that's okay, because the label will display text only when the button isn't visible. Use the attribute inspector to center the text, and the font palette (⌘T) to increase the size of the font to 60 points. Feel free to also set the text to a nice bright color if you want. Once you have the label the way you want it, double-click it to edit the starting text, and press the Delete key to delete it, so that it doesn't display anything at application start.

Control-drag from *File's Owner* to the new label and select the *feedbackLabel* outlet.

Now, we need to add a button for each of the nine game spaces and assign them each a tag value so that our code will have a way to identify which space on the board each button represents. Drag nine *Round Rect Buttons* to the view, and use the attribute inspector to change their type to *Custom*. Use the size inspector to place them in the locations specified in Table 8–1, and use the attribute inspector to assign them the listed tag value. Here's one shortcut to consider: Create one, set its size and attributes, and then start making copies.

Table 8-1. *Game Space Locations, Sizes, and Tags*

Game Space	X	Y	Width	Height	Tag
Upper Left	24	122	86	98	1000
Upper Middle	120	122	86	98	1001
Upper Right	217	122	86	98	1002
Middle Left	24	230	86	98	1003
Middle	120	230	86	98	1004
Middle Right	217	230	86	98	1005
Lower Left	24	336	86	98	1006
Lower Middle	120	336	86	98	1007
Lower Right	217	336	86	98	1008

Once you have the buttons in place, Control-drag from each of the nine buttons to *File's Owner* and select the *gameSpacePressed:* action.

Finally, save the nib, and then quit Interface Builder.

Creating the TicTacToePacket Object

Once you're back in Xcode, single-click the *Classes* folder in the *Groups & Files* pane, and select **New File...** from the **File** menu. Select the *Objective-C class* template, with *NSObject* selected for the *Subclass of* pop-up menu. We're going to create the class that will be used to send information back and forth between the two nodes, so name this file *TicTacToePacket.m* and make sure the *Also create "TicTacToePacket.h"* check box is checked.

Once the files are created, single-click *TicTacToePacket.h* and replace its contents with the following:

```
#import <Foundation/Foundation.h>
#import "TicTacToeViewController.h"

#define dieRoll() (arc4random() % 1000000)
#define kDiceNotRolled  INT_MAX

typedef enum PacketTypes {
    kPacketTypeDieRoll,     // used to determine who goes first
    kPacketTypeAck,         // used to acknowledge die roll packet receipt
    kPacketTypeMove,        // used to send information about a player's move
    kPacketTypeReset,       // used to inform the peer that we're starting over
} PacketType;
```

```objc
@interface TicTacToePacket : NSObject <NSCoding> {
    PacketType  type;
    NSUInteger  dieRoll;
    BoardSpace  space;
}
@property PacketType type;
@property NSUInteger dieRoll;
@property BoardSpace space;
- (id)initWithType:(PacketType)inType
    dieRoll:(NSUInteger)inDieRoll
    space:(BoardSpace)inSpace;
- (id)initDieRollPacket;
- (id)initDieRollPacketWithRoll:(NSUInteger)inDieRoll;
- (id)initMovePacketWithSpace:(BoardSpace)inSpace;
- (id)initAckPacketWithDieRoll:(NSUInteger)inDieRoll;
- (id)initResetPacket;
@end
```

Much of this code should be fairly intuitive. We define a macro for generating a random number to resolve who goes first. It generates a number between 0 and 999,999. We're using a large number here so that the chance of both devices rolling the same value (which would require a reroll) will be extremely low. We also define a constant that will identify when the die has not yet been rolled. Remember that we're storing both our die roll and our opponent's die roll in NSInteger instance variables. On the iPhone, NSInteger is the same as an int. We use the value INT_MAX to identify when those values have not yet been determined. INT_MAX is the largest value that an int can hold on the platform. Since the largest number our dieRoll() macro will generate is 999,999, we can safely use INT_MAX to identify when a die hasn't been rolled, because INT_MAX equals 2,147,483,647 on current iPhones. If INT_MAX ever changes, it will likely get bigger, not smaller.

```objc
#define dieRoll() (arc4random() % 1000000)
#define kDiceNotRolled  INT_MAX
```

We define an enum with each of the different types of packets we'll need to send to the other node:

```objc
typedef enum PacketTypes {
    kPacketTypeDieRoll,     // used to determine who goes first
    kPacketTypeAck,         // used to acknowledge die roll packet receipt
    kPacketTypeMove,        // used to send information about a player's move
    kPacketTypeReset,       // used to inform the peer that we're starting over
} PacketType;
```

In our class definition, we have only three instance variables: one to identify the type of packet and two others to hold information that might need to be sent as part of that packet. The only other pieces of information we ever need to send are the results of a die roll and which space on the game board a player placed an X or O. We also conform our class to the NSCoding protocol so that we can archive it into an NSData instance to send through the GameKit session:

```objc
@interface TicTacToePacket : NSObject <NSCoding> {
    PacketType  type;
    NSUInteger  dieRoll;
```

```
        BoardSpace  space;
}
```

We expose all three instance variables using properties:

```
@property PacketType type;
@property NSUInteger dieRoll;
@property BoardSpace space;
```

And we declare a handful of init methods for creating the different types of packets we will send:

```
- (id)initWithType:(PacketType)inType
    dieRoll:(NSUInteger)inDieRoll
    space:(BoardSpace)inSpace;
- (id)initDieRollPacket;
- (id)initDieRollPacketWithRoll:(NSUInteger)inDieRoll;
- (id)initMovePacketWithSpace:(BoardSpace)inSpace;
- (id)initAckPacketWithDieRoll:(NSUInteger)inDieRoll;
- (id)initResetPacket;
@end
```

Save *TicTacToePacket.h*.

Next, switch over to *TicTacToePacket.m* and replace the contents of the file with this new version:

```
#import "TicTacToePacket.h"

@implementation TicTacToePacket
@synthesize type;
@synthesize dieRoll;
@synthesize space;

#pragma mark -
- (id)initWithType:(PacketType)inType dieRoll:(NSUInteger)inDieRoll
space:(BoardSpace)inSpace {
    if (self = [super init]) {
        type = inType;
        dieRoll = inDieRoll;
        space = inSpace;
    }
      return self;
}

- (id)initDieRollPacket {
    int roll = dieRoll();
    return [self initWithType:kPacketTypeDieRoll dieRoll:roll space:0];
}

- (id)initDieRollPacketWithRoll:(NSUInteger)inDieRoll {
    return [self initWithType:kPacketTypeDieRoll dieRoll:inDieRoll space:0];
}

- (id)initMovePacketWithSpace:(BoardSpace)inSpace{
    return [self initWithType:kPacketTypeMove dieRoll:0 space:inSpace];
}

- (id)initAckPacketWithDieRoll:(NSUInteger)inDieRoll {
```

```
    return [self initWithType:kPacketTypeAck dieRoll:inDieRoll space:0];
}

- (id)initResetPacket {
    return [self initWithType:kPacketTypeReset dieRoll:0 space:0];
}

#pragma mark -
- (NSString *)description {
    NSString *typeString = nil;
    switch (type) {
        case kPacketTypeDieRoll:
            typeString = @"Die Roll";
            break;
        case kPacketTypeMove:
            typeString = @"Move";
            break;
        case kPacketTypeAck:
            typeString = @"Ack";
            break;
        case kPacketTypeReset:
            typeString = @"Reset";
        default:
            break;
    }
    return [NSString stringWithFormat:@"%@ (dieRoll: %d / space: %d)", typeString,
        dieRoll, space];
}

#pragma mark -
#pragma mark NSCoder (Archiving)
- (void)encodeWithCoder:(NSCoder *)coder {
    [coder encodeInt:[self type] forKey:@"type"];
    [coder encodeInteger:[self dieRoll] forKey:@"dieRoll"];
    [coder encodeInt:[self space] forKey:@"space"];
}

- (id)initWithCoder:(NSCoder *)coder  {
    if (self = [super init]) {
        [self setType:[coder decodeIntForKey:@"type"]];
        [self setDieRoll:[coder decodeIntegerForKey:@"dieRoll"]];
        [self setSpace:[coder decodeIntForKey:@"space"]];
    }
    return self;
}

@end
```

TicTacToePacket is a fairly straightforward class. There shouldn't be anything in its implementation that you haven't seen before. Save *TicTacToePacket.m*. Next, we'll write our view controller and finish up our application.

Implementing the Tic-Tac-Toe View Controller

Single-click *TicTacToeViewController.m*. There's a lot of code to write in this controller class, so let's just replace this file with the following version:

```
#import "TicTacToeViewController.h"
#import "TicTacToePacket.h"

@implementation TicTacToeViewController

#pragma mark -
#pragma mark Synthesized Properties
@synthesize newGameButton;
@synthesize feedbackLabel;
@synthesize session;
@synthesize peerID;
@synthesize xPieceImage;
@synthesize oPieceImage;
#pragma mark -
#pragma mark Game-Specific Methods

- (IBAction)newGameButtonPressed {
    dieRollReceived = NO;
    dieRollAcknowledged = NO;

    newGameButton.hidden = YES;
    GKPeerPickerController *picker = [[GKPeerPickerController alloc] init];

    picker.delegate = self;

    [picker show];
}

- (IBAction)gameSpacePressed:(id)sender {
    UIButton *buttonPressed = (UIButton *)sender;
    if (state == kGameStateMyTurn &&
        [buttonPressed imageForState:UIControlStateNormal] == nil) {
        [buttonPressed setImage:(piece == kPlayerPieceO) ? oPieceImage : xPieceImage
            forState:UIControlStateNormal];
        feedbackLabel.text = NSLocalizedString(@"Opponent's Turn",
            @"Opponent's Turn");
        state = kGameStateOpponentTurn;

        TicTacToePacket *packet = [[TicTacToePacket alloc]
            initMovePacketWithSpace:buttonPressed.tag];
        [self sendPacket:packet];
        [packet release];

        [self checkForGameEnd];
    }
}

- (void)startNewGame {
    [self resetBoard];
    [self sendDieRoll];
}
```

```objc
- (void)resetBoard {
    for (int i = kUpperLeft; i <= kLowerRight; i++) {
        UIButton *oneButton = (UIButton *)[self.view viewWithTag:i];
        [oneButton setImage:nil forState:UIControlStateNormal];
    }

    feedbackLabel.text = @"";

    TicTacToePacket *resetPacket = [[TicTacToePacket alloc] initResetPacket];
    [self sendPacket:resetPacket];
    [resetPacket release];

    piece = kPlayerPieceUndecided;
}

- (void)resetDieState {
    dieRollReceived = NO;
    dieRollAcknowledged = NO;
    myDieRoll = kDiceNotRolled;
    opponentDieRoll = kDiceNotRolled;
}

- (void)startGame {
    if (myDieRoll == opponentDieRoll) {
        myDieRoll = kDiceNotRolled;
        opponentDieRoll = kDiceNotRolled;
        [self sendDieRoll];
        piece = kPlayerPieceUndecided;
    }
    else if (myDieRoll < opponentDieRoll) {
        state = kGameStateOpponentTurn;
        piece = kPlayerPieceX;
        feedbackLabel.text = NSLocalizedString(@"Opponent's Turn",
            @"Opponent's Turn");

    }
    else {
        state = kGameStateMyTurn;
        piece = kPlayerPieceO;
        feedbackLabel.text = NSLocalizedString(@"Your Turn", @"Your Turn");
    }
    [self resetDieState];
}

- (void)checkForGameEnd {
    NSInteger moves = 0;

    UIImage     *currentButtonImages[9];
    UIImage     *winningImage = nil;

    for (int i = kUpperLeft; i <= kLowerRight; i++) {
        UIButton *oneButton = (UIButton *)[self.view viewWithTag:i];
        if ([oneButton imageForState:UIControlStateNormal])
            moves++;
        currentButtonImages[i - kUpperLeft] = [oneButton
            imageForState:UIControlStateNormal];
```

```
        }

        // Top Row
        if (currentButtonImages[0] == currentButtonImages[1] &&
            currentButtonImages[0] == currentButtonImages[2] &&
            currentButtonImages[0] != nil)
            winningImage = currentButtonImages[0];

    // Middle Row
        else if (currentButtonImages[3] == currentButtonImages[4] &&
                 currentButtonImages[3] == currentButtonImages[5] &&
                 currentButtonImages[3] != nil)
            winningImage = currentButtonImages[3];

        // Bottom Row
        else if (currentButtonImages[6] == currentButtonImages[7] &&
                 currentButtonImages[6] == currentButtonImages[8] &&
                 currentButtonImages[6] != nil)
            winningImage = currentButtonImages[6];

        // Left Column
        else if (currentButtonImages[0] == currentButtonImages[3] &&
                 currentButtonImages[0] == currentButtonImages[6] &&
                 currentButtonImages[0] != nil)
            winningImage = currentButtonImages[0];

        // Middle Column
        else if (currentButtonImages[1] == currentButtonImages[4] &&
                 currentButtonImages[1] == currentButtonImages[7] &&
                 currentButtonImages[1] != nil)
            winningImage = currentButtonImages[1];

        // Right Column
        else if (currentButtonImages[2] == currentButtonImages[5] &&
                 currentButtonImages[2] == currentButtonImages[8] &&
                 currentButtonImages[2] != nil)
            winningImage = currentButtonImages[2];
        // Diagonal starting top left
        else if (currentButtonImages[0] == currentButtonImages[4] &&
                 currentButtonImages[0] == currentButtonImages[8] &&
                 currentButtonImages[0] != nil)
            winningImage = currentButtonImages[0];

    // Diagonal starting top right
        else if (currentButtonImages[2] == currentButtonImages[4] &&
                 currentButtonImages[2] == currentButtonImages[6] &&
                 currentButtonImages[2] != nil)
            winningImage = currentButtonImages[2];


        if (winningImage == xPieceImage) {
            if (piece == kPlayerPieceX) {
                feedbackLabel.text = NSLocalizedString(@"You Won!", @"You Won!");
                state = kGameStateDone;
            }
            else {
                feedbackLabel.text = NSLocalizedString(@"Opponent Won!",
```

```
                @"Opponent Won!");
            state = kGameStateDone;
        }
    }
    else if (winningImage == oPieceImage) {
        if (piece == kPlayerPieceO){
            feedbackLabel.text = NSLocalizedString(@"You Won!", @"You Won!");
            state = kGameStateDone;
        }
        else {
            feedbackLabel.text = NSLocalizedString(@"Opponent Won!",
                @"Opponent Won!");
            state = kGameStateDone;
        }

    }
    else {
        if (moves >= 9) {
            feedbackLabel.text = NSLocalizedString(@"Cat Wins!", @"Cat Wins!");
            state = kGameStateDone;
        }
    }

    if (state == kGameStateDone)
        [self performSelector:@selector(startNewGame) withObject:nil
            afterDelay:3.0];
}

#pragma mark -
#pragma mark Superclass Overrides
- (void)viewDidLoad {
    [super viewDidLoad];
    myDieRoll = kDiceNotRolled;
    self.oPieceImage = [UIImage imageNamed:@"O.png"];
    self.xPieceImage = [UIImage imageNamed:@"X.png"];
}

- (void)viewDidUnload {
    [super viewDidUnload];
    self.newGameButton = nil;
    self.xPieceImage = nil;
    self.oPieceImage = nil;
}

- (void)dealloc {
    [newGameButton release];
    [feedbackLabel release];
    [xPieceImage release];
    [oPieceImage release];

    session.available = NO;
    [session disconnectFromAllPeers];
    [session setDataReceiveHandler: nil withContext: nil];
    session.delegate = nil;
    [session release];
    [peerID release];
    [super dealloc];
```

```objc
}

#pragma mark -
#pragma mark GameKit Peer Picker Delegate Methods
- (GKSession *)peerPickerController:(GKPeerPickerController *)picker
sessionForConnectionType:(GKPeerPickerConnectionType)type{
    GKSession *theSession = [[GKSession alloc]
        initWithSessionID:kTicTacToeSessionID displayName:nil
        sessionMode:GKSessionModePeer];
    return [theSession autorelease];
}

- (void)peerPickerController:(GKPeerPickerController *)picker
didConnectPeer:(NSString *)thePeerID toSession:(GKSession *)theSession {
    self.peerID = thePeerID;

    self.session = theSession;
    self.session.delegate = self;
    [self.session setDataReceiveHandler:self withContext:NULL];

    [picker dismiss];
    picker.delegate = nil;
    [picker release];

    [self startNewGame];
}

- (void)peerPickerControllerDidCancel:(GKPeerPickerController *)picker {
    newGameButton.hidden = NO;
}

#pragma mark -
#pragma mark GameKit Session Delegate Methods
- (void)session:(GKSession *)theSession didFailWithError:(NSError *)error {
    UIAlertView *alert = [[UIAlertView alloc] initWithTitle:
        NSLocalizedString(@"Error Connecting!", @"Error Connecting!")
        message:NSLocalizedString(@"Unable to establish the connection.",
            @"Unable to establish the connection.")
        delegate:self
        cancelButtonTitle:NSLocalizedString(@"Bummer", @"Bummer")
        otherButtonTitles:nil];
    [alert show];
    [alert release];
    theSession.available = NO;
    [theSession disconnectFromAllPeers];
    theSession.delegate = nil;
    [theSession setDataReceiveHandler:nil withContext:nil];
    self.session = nil;
}

- (void)session:(GKSession *)theSession peer:(NSString *)peerID
didChangeState:(GKPeerConnectionState)inState {
    if (inState == GKPeerStateDisconnected) {
        state = kGameStateInterrupted;
        UIAlertView *alert = [[UIAlertView alloc] initWithTitle:
            NSLocalizedString(@"Peer Disconnected!", @"Peer Disconnected!")
            message:NSLocalizedString(@"Your opponent has disconnected, or ↵
```

```
                            the connection has been lost",
                        @"Your opponent has disconnected, or the connection has been lost")
                delegate:self
                cancelButtonTitle:NSLocalizedString(@"Bummer", @"Bummer")
                otherButtonTitles:nil];
            [alert show];
            [alert release];
            theSession.available = NO;
            [theSession disconnectFromAllPeers];
            theSession.delegate = nil;
            [theSession setDataReceiveHandler:nil withContext:nil];
            self.session = nil;
        }
}

#pragma mark -
#pragma mark GameKit Send & Receive Methods
- (void)sendDieRoll {
    state = kGameStateRollingDice;
    TicTacToePacket *rollPacket;
    if (myDieRoll == kDiceNotRolled) {
        rollPacket = [[TicTacToePacket alloc] initDieRollPacket];
        myDieRoll = rollPacket.dieRoll;
    }
    else
        rollPacket = [[TicTacToePacket alloc] initDieRollPacketWithRoll:myDieRoll];
    [self sendPacket:rollPacket];
    [rollPacket release];

}

- (void) receiveData:(NSData *)data fromPeer:(NSString *)peer
inSession:(GKSession *)theSession context:(void *)context
{
    NSKeyedUnarchiver *unarchiver = [[NSKeyedUnarchiver alloc]
        initForReadingWithData:data];
    TicTacToePacket *packet = [unarchiver decodeObjectForKey:kTicTacToeArchiveKey];

    switch (packet.type) {
        case kPacketTypeDieRoll:
            opponentDieRoll = packet.dieRoll;
            TicTacToePacket *ack = [[TicTacToePacket alloc]
                initAckPacketWithDieRoll:opponentDieRoll];
            [self sendPacket:ack];
            [ack release];
            dieRollReceived = YES;
            break;
        case kPacketTypeAck:
            if (packet.dieRoll != myDieRoll) {
                NSLog(@"Ack packet doesn't match opponentDieRoll (mine: %d, ↩
send: %d", packet.dieRoll, myDieRoll);
            }
            dieRollAcknowledged = YES;
            break;
        case kPacketTypeMove:{
            UIButton *theButton = (UIButton *)[self.view viewWithTag:packet.space];
            [theButton setImage:(piece == kPlayerPieceO) ? xPieceImage : oPieceImage
```

```
                forState:UIControlStateNormal];
            state = kGameStateMyTurn;
            feedbackLabel.text = NSLocalizedString(@"Your Turn", @"Your Turn");
            [self checkForGameEnd];
        }
            break;
        case kPacketTypeReset:
            if (state == kGameStateDone)
                [self resetDieState];
            break;
        default:
            break;
    }

    if (dieRollReceived == YES && dieRollAcknowledged == YES)
        [self startGame];

    [unarchiver release];
}

- (void) sendPacket:(TicTacToePacket *)packet {
    NSMutableData *data = [[NSMutableData alloc] init];
    NSKeyedArchiver *archiver = [[NSKeyedArchiver alloc]
        initForWritingWithMutableData:data];
    [archiver encodeObject:packet forKey:kTicTacToeArchiveKey];
    [archiver finishEncoding];

    NSError *error = nil;

    if (![session sendDataToAllPeers:data withDataMode:GKSendDataReliable
        error:&error]) {
        // You will do real error handling
        NSLog(@"Error sending data: %@", [error localizedDescription]);
    }
    [archiver release];
    [data release];
}

#pragma mark -
#pragma mark Alert View Delegate Methods
- (void)alertView:(UIAlertView *)alertView
willDismissWithButtonIndex:(NSInteger)buttonIndex {
    [self resetBoard];
    newGameButton.hidden = NO;
}

@end
```

Whoa. Deep breath now. That was a lot of code, huh? Let's break it down.

The first method we wrote is the action method that is called when the *New Game*
button is pressed. When that happens, we set dieRollReceived and
dieRollAcknowledged to NO, because we know neither of these things has happened yet
for the new game.

```
- (IBAction)newGameButtonPressed {
    dieRollReceived = NO;
```

```
        dieRollAcknowledged = NO;
```

Next, we hide the button, because we don't want our player to request a new game while we're looking for peers or playing the game. Then we create an instance of GKPeerPickerController, set self as the delegate, and show the peer picker controller.

```
    newGameButton.hidden = YES;
    GKPeerPickerController *picker = [[GKPeerPickerController alloc] init];

    picker.delegate = self;

    [picker show];
}
```

That's all we need to do to kick off the process of letting the user select another device to play against. The peer picker will handle everything, and then call delegate methods when we need to take some action.

We also wrote an action method that is called when the user taps one of the nine game spaces. The first thing we do is cast sender to a UIButton. We know sender will always be an instance of UIButton, and doing this will prevent us from needing to cast sender every time we use it.

```
- (IBAction)gameSpacePressed:(id)sender {
    UIButton *buttonPressed = (UIButton *)sender;
```

Next, we check the game state. We don't want to let the user select a space if it's not that player's turn. We also check to make sure that the button pressed has no image already assigned. If it has an image assigned to it, then there's already either an X or an O in the space this button represents, and the user is not allowed to select it.

```
    if (state == kGameStateMyTurn &&
        [buttonPressed imageForState:UIControlStateNormal] == nil) {
```

If the space has no image assigned and it is our turn, we set the image to whichever image is appropriate for our player, based on whether we went first or second. The piece variable will get set later when we compare die rolls. We also set the feedback label to inform the users that it's no longer their turn, and change the state to reflect that as well.

```
        [buttonPressed setImage:(piece == kPlayerPieceO) ? oPieceImage : xPieceImage
            forState:UIControlStateNormal];
        feedbackLabel.text = NSLocalizedString(@"Opponent's Turn",
            @"Opponent's Turn");
        state = kGameStateOpponentTurn;
```

We must inform the other device that we've made our move, so we create an instance of TicTacToePacket, passing the tag value from the button that was pressed to identify which space our player selected. We use a method called sendPacket:, which we'll look at in a moment, to send the instance of TicTacToePacket to the other node, and then we release packet:

```
        TicTacToePacket *packet = [[TicTacToePacket alloc]
            initMovePacketWithSpace:buttonPressed.tag];
        [self sendPacket:packet];
        [packet release];
```

Finally, we check to see if the game is over. The method checkForGameEnd determines if either player won or if there are no spaces on the board, which would mean it's a tie.

```
        [self checkForGameEnd];
    }
}
```

The method startNewGame is very simple. It just calls a method to reset the board, and then calls another method to roll the die and send the result to the other node. Both of these actions can happen at times other than game start. For example, we reset the board if the connection is lost, and we send the die roll if both nodes roll the same number.

```
- (void)startNewGame {
    [self resetBoard];
    [self sendDieRoll];
}
```

Resetting the board involves removing the images from all of the buttons that represent spaces on the game board. Rather than declare nine outlets—one to point at each button—we just loop through the nine tag values and retrieve the buttons from our content view using viewWithTag:.

```
- (void)resetBoard {
    for (int i = kUpperLeft; i <= kLowerRight; i++) {
        UIButton *oneButton = (UIButton *)[self.view viewWithTag:i];
        [oneButton setImage:nil forState:UIControlStateNormal];
    }
```

We also blank out the feedback label.

```
    feedbackLabel.text = @"";
```

And we send a packet to the other node telling it that we're resetting. This is done just to make sure that if we follow up with another die roll, the other machine knows not to overwrite it. The fact that network communication happens asynchronously means we can't rely on things always happening in a specific order, as we can with a program running on only one device. It's possible that we'll send the die roll before the other device has finished determining who won. By sending a reset packet, we tell the other node that there may be another die roll coming for a new game, so make sure it's in the right state to accept that new roll. If we didn't do something like this, it might store our die roll, and then overwrite the rolled value when it resets its own board, which would cause a hang because the other device would then be waiting for a die roll that would never arrive.

```
    TicTacToePacket *resetPacket = [[TicTacToePacket alloc] initResetPacket];
    [self sendPacket:resetPacket];
    [resetPacket release];
```

We also need to reset the player's game piece. Because the game is over, we don't know if the player will be X or O for the next game.

```
    piece = kPlayerPieceUndecided;
}
```

Resetting the die state is nothing more than setting `dieRollReceived` and `dieRollAcknowledged` to NO, and setting both our die roll and the opponent's die roll to `kDiceNotRolled`:

```
- (void)resetDieState {
    dieRollReceived = NO;
    dieRollAcknowledged = NO;
    myDieRoll = kDiceNotRolled;
    opponentDieRoll = kDiceNotRolled;
}
```

The next method is called once we have received our opponent's die roll and have also gotten an acknowledgment that it has received ours. First, we make sure that we don't have a tie. If we do have a tie, we kick off the die-rolling process again.

```
- (void)startGame {
    if (myDieRoll == opponentDieRoll) {
        myDieRoll = kDiceNotRolled;
        opponentDieRoll = kDiceNotRolled;
        [self sendDieRoll];
        piece = kPlayerPieceUndecided;
    }
```

Otherwise, we set `state`, `piece`, and the `feedbackLabel`'s text based on whether it's our turn or the opponent's turn to go first.

```
    else if (myDieRoll < opponentDieRoll) {
        state = kGameStateOpponentTurn;
        piece = kPlayerPieceX;
        feedbackLabel.text = NSLocalizedString(@"Opponent's Turn",
            @"Opponent's Turn");
    }
    else {
        state = kGameStateMyTurn;
        piece = kPlayerPieceO;
        feedbackLabel.text = NSLocalizedString(@"Your Turn", @"Your Turn");
    }
```

Then we reset the die state. It may seem odd to do it here, but at this point, we're finished with the die rolling for this game, and because we may receive our opponent's die roll before our code has realized the game is over, we reset now to ensure that the die rolls are not accidentally reused in the next game.

```
    [self resetDieState];
}
```

The `checkForGameEnd` method just checks all nine spaces to see whether they have X or O in them, and then looks for three in a row. It does this by first declaring a variable called `moves` to keep track of how many moves have happened. This is how it will tell if there's a tie. If there have been nine moves, and no one has won, then there are no available spaces left on the board, so it's a tie.

```
- (void)checkForGameEnd {
    NSInteger moves = 0;
```

Next, we declare an array of nine `UIImage` pointers. We're going to pull the images out of the nine buttons representing spaces on the board and put them in this array to make it easier to check if a player won.

```
UIImage     *currentButtonImages[9];
```

If we find three in a row, we'll store one of the three images in this variable so we know which player won the game.

```
UIImage     *winningImage = nil;
```

Next, we loop through the buttons by `tag`, as we did in the `resetBoard` method earlier, storing the images from the buttons in the array we declared earlier.

```
for (int i = kUpperLeft; i <= kLowerRight; i++) {
    UIButton *oneButton = (UIButton *)[self.view viewWithTag:i];
    if ([oneButton imageForState:UIControlStateNormal])
        moves++;
    currentButtonImages[i - kUpperLeft] = [oneButton
        imageForState:UIControlStateNormal];
}
```

The next big chunk of code just checks to see if there are three of the same images in a row anywhere. If it finds three in a row, it stores one of the three images in `winningImage`. When it completes the check, it will know which player, if any, has won.

```
// Top Row
if (currentButtonImages[0] == currentButtonImages[1] &&
    currentButtonImages[0] == currentButtonImages[2] &&
    currentButtonImages[0] != nil)
    winningImage = currentButtonImages[0];

// Middle Row
else if (currentButtonImages[3] == currentButtonImages[4] &&
         currentButtonImages[3] == currentButtonImages[5] &&
         currentButtonImages[3] != nil)
    winningImage = currentButtonImages[3];

// Bottom Row
else if (currentButtonImages[6] == currentButtonImages[7] &&
         currentButtonImages[6] == currentButtonImages[8] &&
         currentButtonImages[6] != nil)
    winningImage = currentButtonImages[6];

// Left Column
else if (currentButtonImages[0] == currentButtonImages[3] &&
         currentButtonImages[0] == currentButtonImages[6] &&
         currentButtonImages[0] != nil)
    winningImage = currentButtonImages[0];

// Middle Column
else if (currentButtonImages[1] == currentButtonImages[4] &&
         currentButtonImages[1] == currentButtonImages[7] &&
         currentButtonImages[1] != nil)
    winningImage = currentButtonImages[1];

// Right Column
else if (currentButtonImages[2] == currentButtonImages[5] &&
```

```
            currentButtonImages[2] == currentButtonImages[8] &&
            currentButtonImages[2] != nil)
        winningImage = currentButtonImages[2];
// Diagonal starting top left
else if (currentButtonImages[0] == currentButtonImages[4] &&
            currentButtonImages[0] == currentButtonImages[8] &&
            currentButtonImages[0] != nil)
        winningImage = currentButtonImages[0];

// Diagonal starting top right
else if (currentButtonImages[2] == currentButtonImages[4] &&
            currentButtonImages[2] == currentButtonImages[6] &&
            currentButtonImages[2] != nil)
        winningImage = currentButtonImages[2];
```

Finally, we check to see if there was a winner, and whether it was our opponent or our
player. If there is a winner, we set the feedback label and state as appropriate.

```
if (winningImage == xPieceImage) {
    if (piece == kPlayerPieceX) {
        feedbackLabel.text = NSLocalizedString(@"You Won!", @"You Won!");
        state = kGameStateDone;
    }
    else {
        feedbackLabel.text = NSLocalizedString(@"Opponent Won!",
            @"Opponent Won!");
        state = kGameStateDone;
    }
}
else if (winningImage == oPieceImage) {
    if (piece == kPlayerPieceO){
        feedbackLabel.text = NSLocalizedString(@"You Won!", @"You Won!");
        state = kGameStateDone;
    }
    else {
        feedbackLabel.text = NSLocalizedString(@"Opponent Won!",
            @"Opponent Won!");
        state = kGameStateDone;
    }
}
```

If there wasn't a winner, then we check to see if any spaces are left on the board by
looking at moves. If no spaces remain, then we know the game is over, and the cat won.

```
else {
    if (moves >= 9) {
        feedbackLabel.text = NSLocalizedString(@"Cat Wins!", @"Cat Wins!");
        state = kGameStateDone;
    }
}
```

NOTE: In tic-tac-toe, a tie is also called a "cat's game." The expression "the cat won" refers to a tie.

If any of the preceding code set the state to kGameStateDone, then we use performSelector:withObject:afterDelay: to start a new game after the user has had time to read who won.

```
if (state == kGameStateDone)
    [self performSelector:@selector(startNewGame) withObject:nil
        afterDelay:3.0];
}
```

In viewDidLoad, we first set myDieRoll to show that we have not yet rolled the die to choose who goes first. Then we load the two images used for the playing pieces and store them in the two properties designed to hold them.

```
- (void)viewDidLoad {
    [super viewDidLoad];
    myDieRoll = kDiceNotRolled;
    self.oPieceImage = [UIImage imageNamed:@"O.png"];
    self.xPieceImage = [UIImage imageNamed:@"X.png"];
}
```

The viewDidUnload method is pretty typical, so it doesn't warrant any discussion.

```
- (void)viewDidUnload {
    [super viewDidUnload];
    self.newGameButton = nil;
    self.xPieceImage = nil;
    self.oPieceImage = nil;
}
```

Most of the dealloc method is pretty standard, too. Just notice that before we release session, we take care of disconnecting from our peers and setting both the delegate and data receive handler to nil, as we discussed earlier in the chapter.

```
- (void)dealloc {
    [newGameButton release];

    [xPieceImage release];
    [oPieceImage release];

    session.available = NO;
    [session disconnectFromAllPeers];
    [session setDataReceiveHandler: nil withContext: nil];
    session.delegate = nil;
    [session release];

    [super dealloc];
}
```

Now, we get into the peer picker delegate methods. This first one is where the picker asks us to provide a session. Because we want all devices to both advertise and look for other devices on the network, we specify GKSessionModePeer for the session mode. Notice that we also use our constant kTicTacToeSessionID, which we defined in the header file to make sure that we connect only to other instances of *TicTacToe*.

```
- (GKSession *)peerPickerController:(GKPeerPickerController *)picker
sessionForConnectionType:(GKPeerPickerConnectionType)type{
    GKSession *theSession = [[GKSession alloc]
```

```
        initWithSessionID:kTicTacToeSessionID displayName:nil
        sessionMode:GKSessionModePeer];
    return [theSession autorelease];
}
```

Because the peer picker is only for simple peer-to-peer games, once we're notified of a connection, we store the session and the peer identifier, and then dismiss the picker. After we've dismissed it, we call startNewGame to get things going.

```
- (void)peerPickerController:(GKPeerPickerController *)picker
didConnectPeer:(NSString *)thePeerID toSession:(GKSession *)theSession {
    self.peerID = thePeerID;

    self.session = theSession;
    self.session.delegate = self;
    [self.session setDataReceiveHandler:self withContext:NULL];

    [picker dismiss];
    picker.delegate = nil;
    [picker release];

    [self startNewGame];
}
```

This method is called if the users select *Cancel* from either the Bluetooth enable or peer picker dialog. It simply makes sure that our *New Game* button is visible if they cancel, so they can still start a new game.

```
- (void)peerPickerControllerDidCancel:(GKPeerPickerController *)picker {
    newGameButton.hidden = NO;
}
```

The next few methods are the session delegate methods. The first one we implement is called if a connection attempt fails. All we do is put up an alert view informing the user that it failed, and then clean up the session. In the alert view delegate method, we reset the board so the users can try again or select a new opponent if they want.

```
- (void)session:(GKSession *)theSession didFailWithError:(NSError *)error {
    UIAlertView *alert = [[UIAlertView alloc] initWithTitle:
        NSLocalizedString(@"Error Connecting!", @"Error Connecting!")
        message:NSLocalizedString(@"Unable to establish the connection.",
            @"Unable to establish the connection.")
        delegate:self
        cancelButtonTitle:NSLocalizedString(@"Bummer", @"Bummer")
        otherButtonTitles:nil];
    [alert show];
    [alert release];
    theSession.available = NO;
    [theSession disconnectFromAllPeers];
    theSession.delegate = nil;
    [theSession setDataReceiveHandler:nil withContext:nil];
    self.session = nil;
}
```

Because we're using the peer picker, we don't need to handle choosing another node or connecting to it. But we must make sure that if the opponent disconnects, we don't keep trying to play that game. The following method is called any time a peer's state changes. If we're notified that another node has disconnected, we again inform the users through an alert view, and when they dismiss it, our alert view delegate method will reset the board.

```
- (void)session:(GKSession *)theSession peer:(NSString *)peerID
        didChangeState:(GKPeerConnectionState)inState {
    if (inState == GKPeerStateDisconnected) {
        state = kGameStateInterrupted;
        UIAlertView *alert = [[UIAlertView alloc] initWithTitle:
            NSLocalizedString(@"Peer Disconnected!", @"Peer Disconnected!")
            message:NSLocalizedString(@"Your opponent has disconnected, or ↵
the connection has been lost",
                @"Your opponent has disconnected, or the connection has been lost")
            delegate:self
            cancelButtonTitle:NSLocalizedString(@"Bummer", @"Bummer")
            otherButtonTitles:nil];
        [alert show];
        [alert release];
        theSession.available = NO;
        [theSession disconnectFromAllPeers];
        theSession.delegate = nil;
        [theSession setDataReceiveHandler:nil withContext:nil];
        self.session = nil;
    }
}
```

This method sends a die roll packet to the other node. The `initDieRollPacket` method automatically generates a packet with a random number.

```
- (void)sendDieRoll {
    state = kGameStateRollingDice;
    TicTacToePacket *rollPacket;
    if (myDieRoll == kDiceNotRolled) {
        rollPacket = [[TicTacToePacket alloc] initDieRollPacket];
        myDieRoll = rollPacket.dieRoll;
    }
    else
        rollPacket = [[TicTacToePacket alloc] initDieRollPacketWithRoll:myDieRoll];
    [self sendPacket:rollPacket];
    [rollPacket release];
}
```

The following is our data receive handler. This method is called whenever we receive a packet from the other node. The first thing we do is unarchive the data into a copy of the original `TicTacToePacket` instance that was sent.

```
- (void) receiveData:(NSData *)data fromPeer:(NSString *)peer
        inSession:(GKSession *)theSession context:(void *)context {
    NSKeyedUnarchiver *unarchiver = [[NSKeyedUnarchiver alloc]
        initForReadingWithData:data];
    TicTacToePacket *packet = [unarchiver decodeObjectForKey:kTicTacToeArchiveKey];
```

Then we use a `switch` statement to take different actions based on the type of packet we received.

```
    switch (packet.type) {
```

If it's a die roll, we store our opponent's value, send back an acknowledgment of the value, and set dieRollReceived to YES.

```
case kPacketTypeDieRoll:
    opponentDieRoll = packet.dieRoll;
    TicTacToePacket *ack = [[TicTacToePacket alloc]
        initAckPacketWithDieRoll:opponentDieRoll];
    [self sendPacket:ack];
    [ack release];
    dieRollReceived = YES;
    break;
```

If we've received an acknowledgment, we make sure the number returned is the same as the one we sent. This is just a consistency check. It shouldn't ever happen that the number is not the same. If it did, it might be an indication of a problem with our code, or it could mean that someone is cheating. Although we doubt that anyone would bother cheating at tic-tac-toe, people have been know to cheat in some networked games, so you might want to consider validating any information exchanged with peers. Here, we're just logging the inconsistency and moving on. In your real-world applications, you might want to take more serious action if you detect a data inconsistency of this nature.

```
case kPacketTypeAck:
    if (packet.dieRoll != myDieRoll) {
        NSLog(@"Ack packet doesn't match opponentDieRoll (mine: %d, ↵
send: %d", packet.dieRoll, myDieRoll);
    }
    dieRollAcknowledged = YES;
    break;
```

If the packet is a move packet, which denotes that the other player chose a space, we update the appropriate space with an X or O image, and change the state and label to reflect the fact that it's now our player's turn. We also check to see if the other player's move resulted in the game being over.

```
case kPacketTypeMove:{
    UIButton *theButton = (UIButton *)[self.view viewWithTag:packet.space];
    [theButton setImage:(piece == kPlayerPiece0) ? xPieceImage : oPieceImage
        forState:UIControlStateNormal];
    state = kGameStateMyTurn;
    feedbackLabel.text = NSLocalizedString(@"Your Turn", @"Your Turn");
    [self checkForGameEnd];
}
    break;
```

When we receive a reset packet, all we do is change the game state to kGameStateDone, so that if a die roll comes in before we've realized the game is over, we don't discard it.

```
case kPacketTypeReset:
    if (state == kGameStateDone)
        [self resetDieState];
default:
    break;
}
```

If we received a packet, and both dieRollReceived and dieRollAcknowledged are now YES, we know it's time to start the game.

```
    if (dieRollReceived == YES && dieRollAcknowledged == YES)
        [self startGame];
```

Of course, before our method is complete, we need to release the unarchiver, since we used `alloc` to create it.

```
    [unarchiver release];
}
```

The next method sends a packet to the other device. It takes an instance of `TicTacToePacket` and archives it into an instance of `NSData`. It then uses the session's `sendDataToAllPeers:withDataMode:error:` method to send it across the wire—well, across the wireless, in this case.

```
- (void) sendPacket:(TicTacToePacket *)packet {
    NSMutableData *data = [[NSMutableData alloc] init];
    NSKeyedArchiver *archiver = [[NSKeyedArchiver alloc]
        initForWritingWithMutableData:data];
    [archiver encodeObject:packet forKey:kTicTacToeArchiveKey];
    [archiver finishEncoding];

    NSError *error = nil;

    if (![session sendDataToAllPeers:data withDataMode:GKSendDataReliable
        error:&error]) {
        // You will do real error handling
        NSLog(@"Error sending data: %@", [error localizedDescription]);
    }
    [archiver release];
    [data release];
}
```

The last method in our controller class is the alert view delegate. This is called any time we show an alert view. The only reason we ever show an alert view in this application is to inform the user that something bad happened. Therefore, if we get here, we know we must reset the board and show the *New Game* button.

```
- (void)alertView:(UIAlertView *)alertView
willDismissWithButtonIndex:(NSInteger)buttonIndex {
    [self resetBoard];
    newGameButton.hidden = NO;
}
@end
```

Trying It Out

Unlike most of the applications we've written together, our `tic-tac-toe` game can't be used in the simulator. It will run there, but the simulator does not support Bluetooth connections. Our app currently relies on Bluetooth connections to work, since we're using GameKit and the peer picker. As a result, you'll need to have two physical devices, and neither of them can be a first-generation device, because the original iPhone and the first-generation iPod touch do not work with GameKit's peer picker.

It also means that you need to have two devices provisioned for development, but note that you do not want to connect both devices to your computer at the same time. This can cause some problems, since there's no way to specify which one to use for debugging. Therefore, you need to build and run on one device, quit, unplug that device, and then plug in the other device and do the same thing. Once you've done that, you will have the application on both devices. You can run it on both devices, or you can launch it from Xcode on one device, so you can debug and read the console feedback.

> **NOTE:** Detailed instructions for installing applications on a device are available at `http://developer.apple.com/iphone` in the developer portal, which is available only to paid iPhone SDK members.

You should be aware that debugging—or even running from Xcode without debugging—will slow down the program running on the connected iPhone, and this can have an affect on network communications. Underneath the hood, all of the data transmissions back and forth between the two devices check for acknowledgments and have a timeout period. If they don't receive a response in a certain amount of time, they will disconnect. So, if you set a breakpoint, chances are that you will break the connection between the two devices when it reaches the breakpoint. This can make figuring out problems in your GameKit application tedious. You often will need to use alternatives to breakpoints, like `NSLog()` or breakpoint actions, so you don't break the network connection between the devices. We'll talk more about debugging in Chapter 15.

Game On!

Another long chapter under your belt, and you should now have a pretty firm understanding of GameKit networking. You've seen how to use the peer picker to let your user select another iPhone or iPod touch to which to connect. You've seen how to send data by archiving objects, and you've gotten a little taste of the complexity that is introduced to your application when you start adding in network multiuser functionality.

In the next chapter, we're going to expand the TicTacToe application to support online play over Wi-Fi using Bonjour. So when you've recovered, skip on over to the next page, and we'll get started.

Chapter 9

Online Play: Bonjour and Network Streams

In the previous chapter, you saw how easy it is to create a networked application using GameKit. GameKit is cool, but currently it only supports online play using Bluetooth. If you want your networked programs to play on first-generation iPhones and iPod touches, or if you want to let people play over their local Wi-Fi connection or the Internet, you need to go beyond GameKit. In this chapter, we're going to do just that.

We'll take our *TicTacToe* project from Chapter 8 and add online play to it. We'll use Bonjour to let you find other players on your local network, and then create objects using **CFNetwork**, Apple's low-level networking framework, and the **Berkeley sockets API** to listen on the network for other devices attempting to connect. We'll then use **network streams** to communicate back and forth with the remote device. By combining these, we can provide the same functionality over the network that GameKit currently provides over Bluetooth.

This Chapter's Application

We're going to continue working with our project from the previous chapter, adding functionality to the existing tic-tac-toe game. At the end of this chapter, when users press the *New Game* button, instead of being presented immediately with a list of peers, they will be presented with the option to select either *Online* or *Nearby* play (Figure 9–1).

Figure 9–1. *When the* New Game *button is pressed, the users will now have the option to select between two different modes of play.* Online *will allow them to play over their Wi-Fi connection with other phones that are also on the Wi-Fi connection.* Nearby *will allow them to play over Bluetooth, as in the original version of the application.*

If users select *Nearby*, they will move to the peer picker and continue just as they did in the original version of the game. If they select *Online*, they will get an application-generated list of devices on the local network that are available to play the game (Figure 9–2).

Figure 9–2. *Our application's equivalent of the GameKit's peer picker*

If either player selects a peer, the game will commence exactly as it did in the previous chapter, but the packets will be sent over the network, rather than over the Bluetooth connection.

Before we start updating our application, we need to look at a few frameworks and objects that we haven't used before, which are required to implement online play. Let's take a few minutes to talk about Bonjour, network streams, and how to listen for connections using CFNetwork, which is the low-level networking API used by all of the Cocoa classes that read from or write to the network.

Overview of the Process

Before we get down into the specific objects and method calls that we need to use to implement online network play, let's look at the process from a very high level.

When the user selects online play, the first thing we're going to do is set up a listener. A **listener** is code that monitors a specific network port for connections. Then we're going to **publish a service** using Bonjour that says, in effect, "Hey world, I'm listening on this port for tic-tac-toe game connections." At the same time, we'll look for other Bonjour services that are also advertising in the same way, and will present a list of any tic-tac-toe games we find to the user.

If the user taps a row, we will stop advertising and listening, and connect to the advertised service on the other machine. Once we have a connection established, either because our user tapped a service name or because our listener detected a connection from another machine, we will use that network connection to transfer data back and forth with our opponent, just as we did over Bluetooth.

Setting Up a Listener

For most of the tasks that we need to do to implement online play, we'll be able to leverage Foundation (Objective-C) objects. There are, for example, high-level objects for publishing and discovering Bonjour services, and for sending and receiving data over a network connection. The way we work with these will be very familiar to you, because they are all Objective-C classes that use delegates to notify your controller class when something relevant has occurred.

> **NOTE:** Remember that Foundation is the name of the framework containing the general-purpose Objective-C classes that are shared between the iPhone and Mac, and includes such classes as NSString and NSArray. Core Foundation is the name given to the collection of C APIs upon which most Foundation objects are built. When you see the prefix *CF*, it is an indication that you are working with a procedural C framework, rather than one written in Objective-C.

Our first step is to set up a listener to detect connection requests from remote machines. This is one task for which we must dive down into CFNetwork, which is the networking library from Apple's Core Foundation, and also a bit into the Berkeley sockets API, which is an even lower-level network programming library atop which CFNetwork sits.

Here, we'll review some basic CFNetwork and socket programming concepts to help you understand what we're doing in this chapter.

> **NOTE:** For the most part, you won't need to do socket programming when working with Objective-C. The vast majority of the networking functionality your applications will need can be handled by higher-level objects like NSURLRequest, as well as the numerous init methods that take NSURL parameters, such as NSString's stringWithContentsOfURL:encoding: error:. Listening for network connections is one of the rare situations in Cocoa Touch where you need to interact with the low-level socket API. If you are really interested in learning more about socket programming, we recommend a good and fairly comprehensive guide to low-level socket programming, *Beej's Guide to Network Programming*, which is available on the Web at http://beej.us/guide/bgnet/.

Callback Functions and Run Loop Integration

Because CFNetwork is a procedural C library, it has no concept of selectors, methods, self, or any of the other dynamic runtime goodies that make Objective-C so much fun. As a result, CFNetwork calls do not use delegates to notify you when something has happened and cannot call methods. CFNetwork doesn't know about objects, so it can't use an objet as a delegate.

CFNetwork integrates with your application's **run loop**. We haven't worked with it directly, but every iPhone program has a main loop that's managed by UIApplication. The main loop keeps running until it receives some kind of input that tells it to quit. In that loop, the application looks for inputs, such as fingers touching the screen or the phone being rotated, and dispatches events through the responder chain based on those inputs. During the run loop, the application also makes any other calls that are necessary, such as calling application delegate methods at the appropriate times.

The application allows you to register certain objects with the run loop. Each time through the run loop, those objects will have a chance to perform tasks and call out to delegates, in the case of Objective-C, or to callback functions, in the case of Core Foundation libraries like CFNetwork. We're not going to delve into the actual process of creating objects that can be registered in the run loop, but it's important to know that CFNetwork and many of the higher-level objective-C networking classes register with the run loop to do their work. This allows them to listen for network connection attempts, for example, or to check if data has been received without needing to create threads or fork child processes.

Because CFNetwork is a procedural library, when you register any CFNetwork functionality with the run loop, it uses good old-fashioned C callbacks when it needs to notify you that something has happened. This means that each of our socket callbacks must take the form of a C function that won't know anything about our application's classes—it's just a chunk of code. We'll look at how to deal with that in a moment.

Configuring a Socket

In order to listen for connections, we need to create a **socket**. A socket represents one end of a network connection, and we can leverage CFNetwork to create it. To do that, first we declare a CFSocketContext, which is a data structure specifically created for configuring a socket.

Declaring a Socket Context

When creating a socket, the CFSocketContext you define to configure it will typically look something like this:

```
CFSocketContext socketCtxt = {0, self, NULL, NULL, NULL};
```

The first value in the struct is a version number that always needs to be set to 0. Presumably, this could change at some point in the future, but at present, you need to set the version to 0, and never any other value.

The second item in the struct is a pointer that will be passed to any callback functions called by the socket we create. This pointer is provided specifically for application use. It allows us to pass any data we might need to the callback functions. We set this pointer to self. Why? Remember that we must implement those callback functions that don't know anything about objects, self, or which object triggered the callback. We include a pointer to self to give the callback function context for which object triggered the callback. If we didn't include a reference to the object that created the socket, our callback function probably wouldn't know what to do, since the rest of our program is implemented as objects, and the function wouldn't have a pointer to any objects.

> **NOTE:** Because Core Foundation can be used outside Objective-C, the callbacks don't take Objective-C objects as arguments, and none of the Core Foundation code uses Objective-C objects. But in your implementation of a Core Foundation callback function, it is perfectly acceptable to use Objective-C objects, as long as your function is contained in a *.m* file rather than a *.c* file. Objective-C is a superset of C, and it's always okay to have any C functionality in your implementation files. Since Objective-C objects are actually just pointers, it's also okay to do what we've done here and pass a pointer to an Objective-C object in any field or argument that is documented as being for application use. C doesn't know about objects, but it does know about pointers and will happily pass the object pointer along to the callback function.

The other three items in this struct are function pointers for optional callback functions supported by CFSocket. The first two are for memory management: one that can be used to retain any objects that need to be retained, and a second that can be used to release objects that were retained in the previous callback. This is important when using CFNetwork from C, because the memory needs to be retained and released, just as with Objective-C objects. We're not going to use these because we do all our memory management in the context of our objects, so we pass NULL for both.

The last function pointer is a callback that can be used to provide a string description of the second element (the one where we specified self). In a complex application, you might use this last element to differentiate the different values that were passed to the callback. We pass NULL for this one also; since we only use the pointer to self, there's no need to differentiate anything.

Creating a Socket

Once we have our CFSocketContext, we call the function CFSocketCreate() to actually create the socket.

```
CFSocketRef socket = CFSocketCreate(kCFAllocatorDefault, PF_INET, SOCK_STREAM,
    IPPROTO_TCP, kCFSocketAcceptCallBack,
    (CFSocketCallBack)&listenerAcceptCallback, &socketCtxt);
```

The first argument is a constant that tells CFNetwork that we don't have any special memory allocation that needs to happen, so it can just use the default memory allocator to create the socket. CFAllocators are special objects used in Core Foundation to handle allocating memory. Because Core Foundation is C-based and not Objective-C–based, it can't do retain counting in quite the same way as in Objective-C, so memory management is handled through a fairly complex set of callbacks that allow you to allocate and release memory.

The second argument, PF_INET, identifies the protocol family to be used. This is a constant defined in the socket libraries that refers to the Internet Protocol (IP). The instances where you would use any other value when specifying a protocol family in a CFNetwork or socket API call are very few and far between, as the world has pretty much standardized on PF_INET at this point.

The third argument, SOCK_STREAM, is another constant from the socket library. There are two primary types of sockets commonly used in network programming: stream sockets and datagram sockets. Stream sockets are typically used with the Transmission Control Protocol (TCP), the most common transmission protocol used with IP. It's so commonly used that the two are often referred to together as TCP/IP. With TCP, a connection is opened, and then data can continuously be sent (or "streamed") to the remote machine (or received from the remote machine) until the connection is closed. Datagram sockets are typically used with an alternative, lesser-used protocol called User Datagram Protocol (UDP). With datagram sockets, the connection is not kept open, and each transmission of data is a separate event. UDP is a lightweight protocol that is less reliable than TCP but faster. It is sometimes used in certain online games where transmission speed is more important than maintaining absolute data integrity. We won't be implementing UDP-based services in this book.

The fourth argument identifies the transmission protocol we want our socket to use. Since we specified SOCK_STREAM for our socket type, we want to specify TCP as our transmission protocol, which is what the constant IPPROTO_TCP does.

For the fifth argument, we pass a CFNetwork constant that tells the socket when to call its callback function. There are a number of different ways you can configure CFSockets. We pass kCFSocketAcceptCallBack to tell it to automatically accept new connections, and then call our callback function only when that happens. In our callback method, we will grab references to the input and output streams that represent that connection, and then we won't need any more callbacks from the socket. We'll talk more about streams a little later in the chapter.

The sixth argument is a pointer to the function we want called when the socket accepts a connection. This is a pointer to a C function that we need to implement. This function must follow a certain format, which can be found in the CFNetwork documentation.

> **NOTE:** Not to worry—we'll show you how to implement these callbacks once we get to our sample code in a bit. In the meantime, you might want to bookmark Apple's CFNetwork documentation, which can be found here:
>
> http://developer.apple.com/mac/library/documentation/Networking/Conceptual/CFNetwork/Introduction/Introduction.html

The last argument is a pointer to the CFSocketContext struct we created. It contains the pointer to self that will be passed to the callback functions.

Once we've created the socket, we need to check socket to make sure it's not NULL. If it is NULL, then the socket couldn't be created. Here's what checking the socket for NULL might look like:

```
if (socket == NULL) {
    if (error) *error = [[NSError alloc]
        initWithDomain:kMyApplicationErrorDomain
        code:kNoSocketsAvailableError
        userInfo:nil];
    return NO;
}
```

Specifying a Port for Listening

Our next task is to specify a **port** for our socket to listen on. A port is a virtual, numbered data connection. Port numbers run from 0 to 65535, with port 0 reserved for system use. Since we'll be advertising our service with Bonjour, we don't want to hard-code a port number and risk a conflict with another running program. Instead, we'll specify port 0, which tells the socket to pick an available port and use it.

MANUALLY ASSIGNING PORTS

If you do decide to listen on a specific, hard-coded port, you should be aware that certain port numbers should not be used.

Ports 0 through 1023 are the **well-known ports**. These are assigned to common protocols such as FTP, HTTP, and SMTP. Generally, you shouldn't use these for your application. In fact, on the iPhone, your application doesn't have permission to do so, so any attempt to listen on a well-known port will fail.

Ports 1024 through 49151 are called **registered ports**. They are used by publicly available online services. There is a registry of these ports maintained by an organization called the Internet Assigned Numbers Authority (IANA). If you plan to use one, you should register the port number you wish to use with the IANA to make sure you don't conflict with an existing service.

Port numbers higher than 49151 are available for application use without any restrictions. So, if you feel you *must* specify a port for your application to listen on, specify one in the range 49152 to 65535

In the following example, we set the listen port to any available port, and then determine which port was used. First, we need to declare a `struct` of the type `sockaddr_in`, which is a data structure from the socket API used for configuring a socket. The socket APIs are very old and are from a time when the names of data structures were kept intentionally terse, so forgive the cryptic nature of this code.

```
struct sockaddr_in addr4;
memset(&addr4, 0, sizeof(addr4));
addr4.sin_len = sizeof(addr4);
addr4.sin_family = AF_INET;
addr4.sin_port = 0;
addr4.sin_addr.s_addr = htonl(INADDR_ANY);
```

NOTE: If you're wondering why the variable ends in 4, it's a clue that we're using IP version 4 (IPv4), currently the most widely used version of the protocol. Because of the widespread popularity of the Internet, at some point in the not-too-distant future, IPv4 will run out of addresses. IP version 6 (IPv6) uses a different addressing scheme with more available addresses. As a result, IPv6 sockets must be created using a different data structure, called `sockaddr_storage` instead of `sockaddr`. Although there's a clear need for additional addresses on the Internet, there's no need to use IPv6 when working on a local area network.

In order to pass this `struct` into a CFNetwork call, we need to turn it into an instance of NSData:

```
NSData *address4 = [NSData dataWithBytes:&addr4 length:sizeof(addr4)];
```

We can then use the Core Foundation function `CFSocketSetAddress` to tell the socket on which port it should listen. If `CFSocketSetAddress` fails, it will return a value other than kCFSocketSuccess, and we do appropriate error handling:

```
if (kCFSocketSuccess != CFSocketSetAddress(socket, (CFDataRef)address4)) {
    if (error) *error = [[NSError alloc]
        initWithDomain:kMyApplicationErrorDomain
```

```
                code:kUnableToSetListenAddressErrorCode
                userInfo:nil];
    if (socket) CFRelease(socket);
    socket = NULL;
    return NO;
}
```

You might have noticed that we actually cast our NSData instance to CFDataRef. Foundation and Core Foundation have a very special relationship. Many of the Objective-C objects that we use from Foundation have counterparts in Core Foundation. Through a special process called **toll-free bridging**, many of those items can be used interchangeably, either as an Objective-C object or as a Core Foundation object. In the preceding code example, we're creating an instance of NSData and passing it into a CFNetwork function called CFSocketSetAddress(), which expects a pointer to a CFData object. When you see a Core Foundation datatype that ends in ref, that means it's a pointer to something. In this case, CFDataRef is a pointer to a CFData. Because CFData and NSData are toll-free bridged, it's okay to simply cast our NSData instance as a CFDataRef.

> **NOTE:** The API documentation for Foundation objects identifies whether an object is toll-free bridged with a Core Foundation counterpart.

Finally, we need to copy the information back from the socket, because the socket will have updated the fields with the correct port and address that were actually used. We need to copy that data back into addr4 so we can determine which port number was used.

```
NSData *addr = [(NSData *)CFSocketCopyAddress(socket) autorelease];
memcpy(&addr4, [addr bytes], [addr length]);
uint16_t port = ntohs(addr4.sin_port);
```

BYTE ORDERING

The functions htonl() and ntohs() are part of a family of functions that convert byte order from your local machine to the network byte order, as follows:

- htonl(), which stands for "host to network long," converts a long from the machine's byte ordering to the network's byte-order.

- ntohs(), which stands for "network to host short," converts a short from the network's byte order to the machine's.

Different machines represent multibyte values differently. For example, the older PowerPC Macs used a byte-ordering called **big-endian**, and current Intel-based Macs use a byte-ordering called **little-endian**. This means that the same int is represented differently in memory on the two machines.

Protocols specify the ordering that they use, and these functions are defined on all platforms to handle any conversion necessary to allow different machines to exchange data over the network, without needing to worry about the byte ordering.

CFNetwork and higher-level networking classes deal with byte ordering for you. However, when working with the socket APIs directly, you need to use these conversion functions any time you specify or pass in a value other than 0 (which is the same regardless of byte ordering) or a defined socket API constant.

You can find out more about byte-ordering at http://en.wikipedia.org/wiki/Endianness.

Registering the Socket with the Run Loop

The last thing we need to do is to register our socket with our run loop. This will allow the socket to poll the specified port for connection attempts, and then call our callback function when a connection is received. Here is how we do that:

```
CFRunLoopRef cfrl = CFRunLoopGetCurrent();
CFRunLoopSourceRef source4 = CFSocketCreateRunLoopSource(kCFAllocatorDefault,
        socket, 0);
CFRunLoopAddSource(cfrl, source4, kCFRunLoopCommonModes);
CFRelease(source4);
```

Implementing the Socket Callback Function

Once our socket is registered with the run loop, any time that we receive a connection from a remote machine, the function we specified when we created the socket will be called. In that function, we need to create a pair of stream objects that represent the connection to the other machine. One of those stream objects will be used to receive data from the other machine, and the other one will be used to send data to the other machine.

Here's how you create the stream pair that represents the connection to the other machine:

```
static void listenerAcceptCallback (CFSocketRef theSocket, CFSocketCallBackType
theType, CFDataRef theAddress, const void *data, void *info) {

    if (theType == kCFSocketAcceptCallBack) {
        CFSocketNativeHandle socketHandle = *(CFSocketNativeHandle *)data;
        uint8_t name[SOCK_MAXADDRLEN];
        socklen_t namelen = sizeof(name);
        NSData *peer = nil;
        if (getpeername(socketHandle, (struct sockaddr *)name, &namelen) == 0) {
            peer = [NSData dataWithBytes:name length:namelen];
        }
        CFReadStreamRef readStream = NULL;
        CFWriteStreamRef writeStream = NULL;
        CFStreamCreatePairWithSocket(kCFAllocatorDefault, socketHandle,
            &readStream, &writeStream);
        if (readStream && writeStream) {
            CFReadStreamSetProperty(readStream,
                kCFStreamPropertyShouldCloseNativeSocket, kCFBooleanTrue);
            CFWriteStreamSetProperty(writeStream,
            kCFStreamPropertyShouldCloseNativeSocket, kCFBooleanTrue);

            self.inStream = readStream;
```

```
            self.outStream = writeStream;
        } else {
            close(socketHandle);
        }
        if (readStream) CFRelease(readStream);
        if (writeStream) CFRelease(writeStream);
    }
}
```

In this particular example, we're just storing a reference to the stream pair. We'll talk about how to use them a little later in the chapter.

Stopping the Listener

To stop listening for new connections, we must invalidate and release the socket. We don't need to remove it from the run loop, because invalidating the socket takes care of that for us. Here's all we need to do when we're finished with our `CFSocket`:

```
if (socket) {
    CFSocketInvalidate(socket);
    CFRelease(socket);
    socket = NULL;
}
```

Bonjour

In the previous chapter, when we were using GameKit's peer picker, each phone was able to find the other phone without the user typing in an IP address or DNS name. That was accomplished using Bonjour (also known as Zeroconf). Bonjour is a protocol specifically designed to let devices find each other on a network. If you buy a new printer and plug it into your AirPort base station, and then tell a Mac on the same network to add a new printer, the new printer will appear automatically. The printer's type will be discovered without the need to type in an IP address or manually search the network. That's Bonjour in action. When you're in the Finder and other Macs on your network show up automatically under the *SHARED* heading (Figure 9–3), that's also Bonjour doing its thing.

If you're young enough not to remember life before Bonjour, consider yourself lucky. Bonjour makes life much easier for computer users. In the "old days" (yes, we walked to school 10 miles through the snow uphill both ways), you needed to know a service or device's IP address to find it on your network. It was often a tedious, frustrating experience. We want life to be easy for our users, don't we? Well, of course we do. So, how do we use Bonjour?

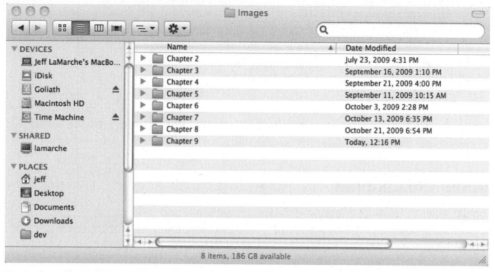

Figure 9–3. *The* SHARED *heading in the Finder's sidebar lists all other Macs on your network that have shared folders. This is just one of the many examples of where Bonjour is used in Mac OS X.*

Creating a Service for Publication

When you advertise a service on the network using Bonjour, it's called **publishing** the service. Published services will be available for other computers to discover and connect to. The process of discovering another published service on the network is called **searching** for services. When you find a service and wish to connect to it, you need to **resolve** the service to get information about the address and port on which the service is running or, alternatively, you can ask the resolved service for a connection in the form of **streams**.

To advertise an available service, you need to create an instance of a class called NSNetService. To do that, you provide four pieces of information:

- *Domain*: The first piece of information is the domain, which is referring to a DNS domain name like www.apple.com. You pretty much always want to specify an empty string for the domain. Although the documentation for NSNetService says to pass @"local." instead of the empty string if you want to support only local connections, *Technote QA1331* (http://developer.apple.com/mac/library/qa/qa2001/qa1331.html) clarifies this point and says that passing @"local." may make your application incompatible with future versions of Mac OS X. It says to always pass an empty string, and NSNetService will "do the right thing."

■ *Service type*: The second piece of information that needs to be passed in is your service type. This is a string that uniquely identifies the protocol or application being run, along with the transmission protocol it uses. This is used to prevent services of different types from trying to connect to each other, much like the session identifier we used in Chapter 8. Unlike GameKit session identifiers, Bonjour identifiers must follow a very specific formula; you can't use just any string. A valid Bonjour type begins with an underscore, followed by a string that identifies the service or protocol being advertised, followed by another period, another underscore, the transmission protocol, and then a terminating period. For Cocoa applications, your transmission type will almost always be TCP, so your Bonjour type will pretty much always end in `._tcp.`.

■ *Name*: The third piece of information you provide is a name that uniquely identifies this particular device on the network. This is the value that is displayed in the list in Figure 9–2. If you pass the empty string, Bonjour will automatically select the device name as set in iTunes, which is usually the owner's first name followed by the type of device (e.g., *Dave's iPhone* or *Jeff's iPod touch*). In most instances, the empty string is the best option for name, although you could solicit a desired name from your users if you wanted to let them specify a different name under which they would appear.

■ *Port number*: Finally, you need to specify the port number that your application is listening on. Each port can be used by only a single application at a time, so it's important that you don't select one that's already in use. In the previous section, we showed how to set up a listener and specify the port, or how to let it pick a port and then find out which one it picked. The number we retrieved from the listener is the number that should be passed here. When you create an instance of `NSNetService`, you are telling the world (or at least your local network) that there is a specific device or service listening on a specific port of this machine. You shouldn't advertise one unless you are actually listening.

Here's what allocating a new net service might look like:

```
NSNetService *svc = [[NSNetService alloc] initWithDomain:@""
    type:@"_myprogram._tcp."
    name:@""
    port:15000];
```

Publishing a Bonjour Service

Once you've created an instance of `NSNetService`, you need to take a few steps before `NSNetService` will start actually advertising your service:

- First, you need to schedule the service in your application's run loop. We introduced run loop integration when we talked about creating a listener earlier in the chapter. Because we're using Foundation rather than Core Foundation, we schedule the service in the run loop using method calls instead of C function calls, but the process is comparable.

- After we schedule the service in the run loop, we need to set a delegate so that the service can notify us when certain things happen, such as when NSNetService is finished publishing or if an error was encountered.

- Finally, we need to actually publish the service, which causes it to start letting other devices on the network know about its existence.

These steps would typically look something like this:

```
[svc scheduleInRunLoop:[NSRunLoop currentRunLoop] forMode:NSRunLoopCommonModes];
[svc setDelegate:self];
[svc publish];
```

Stopping a Bonjour Service

When you stop listening on a port, or simply don't want any new connections, you need to tell the net service to stop advertising using Bonjour, like so:

```
[svc stop];
```

All this does is tell the service not to advertise its existence. You can always start it back up again, by republishing it:

```
[svc publish];
```

Delegate Methods for Publication

Once you've scheduled your service in your application's run loop and have published the service, it will call methods on its delegate when certain things happen. The class that acts as the service's delegate should conform to the NSNetServiceDelegate protocol and should implement any of the methods that correspond to activities it needs to be notified about.

Several of the delegate methods are called during the publication process. For example, when the service has been configured successfully, and just before it begins advertising its existence, it will call the following method on its delegate:

```
-(void)netServiceWillPublish:(NSNetService *)netService;
```

This is a good place to do setup work or configuration that, for some reason, you don't want to occur if the publication isn't going to work. If you're providing feedback to the user about the status of the connection, you can also use this method to let the user know that the server is ready to accept connections.

Similarly, if the service fails to publish for some reason, it will notify its delegate of that as well, using the method netService:didNotPublish:. In that method, you should stop the service. Here is an example implementation of netService:didNotPublish::

```
- (void)netService:(NSNetService *)theNetService
        didNotPublish:(NSDictionary *)errorDict {
    NSNumber *errorDomain = [errorDict valueForKey:NSNetServicesErrorDomain];
    NSNumber *errorCode = [errorDict valueForKey:NSNetServicesErrorCode];
    NSLog(@"Unable to publish Bonjour service (Domain: %@, Error Code: %@)",
        errorDomain, errorCode);
    [theNetService stop];
}
```

The second argument to this delegate method is a dictionary that contains information about the error, including an error domain stored under the key NSNetServicesErrorDomain and an error code stored under the key NSNetServicesErrorCode. These two items will tell you more about why it failed.

> **NOTE:** You can find a list of the error domains and error codes that Bonjour services can generate in the API documentation for NSNetService.

When the service stops, the delegate method netServiceDidStop: will be called, which will give you the opportunity to update the status or to reattempt publication if desired. Often, once a service stops, you are finished with the net service and just want to release the instance of NSNetService that stopped. Here's what the delegate method in that situation might look like:

```
- (void)netServiceDidStop:(NSNetService *)netService {
    netService.delegate = nil;
    self.netService = nil;
}
```

Searching for Published Bonjour Services

The process to discover published services on your local network is fairly similar to that of publishing a service. You first create an instance of NSNetServiceBrowser and set its delegate:

```
NSNetServiceBrowser *theBrowser = [[NSNetServiceBrowser alloc] init];
theBrowser.delegate = self;
```

Then you call searchForServicesOfType:inDomain: to kick off the search. Unlike with NSNetService, you don't need to register a service browser with the run loop, though you do still need to specify a delegate; otherwise, you wouldn't ever find out about the other services. For the first argument, you pass the same Bonjour identifier that we discussed when we talked about publishing the domain. In the second argument, we follow Apple's recommendation and pass the empty string.

```
[theBrowser searchForServicesOfType:@"_myprogram._tcp" inDomain:@""];
```

Browser Delegate Methods

When the browser completes its configuration and is ready to start looking for services, it will call the following method on its delegate:

```
- (void)netServiceBrowserWillSearch:(NSNetServiceBrowser *)browser
```

You do not need to implement this method, as there are no actions you must take at this point for the browser to find other services. It's just notifying you in case you want to update the status or take some action before it starts looking.

If the browser was unable to start a search for some reason, it will call the delegate method netServiceBrowser:didNotSearch: on its delegate. When this happens, you should stop the browser and do whatever error reporting is appropriate for your application. Here is a simple example:

```
- (void)netServiceBrowser:(NSNetServiceBrowser *)browser
          didNotSearch:(NSDictionary *)errorDict {
    NSLog(@"Error browsing for service: %@", [errorDict
        objectForKey:NSNetServicesErrorCode]);
    [self.netServiceBrowser stop];
}
```

You should not release the browser at this point, even if you're finished with it. After you call the stop method here, or at any other time, it will trigger another delegate method call, which is where you should release the browser, like so:

```
- (void)netServiceBrowserDidStopSearch:(NSNetServiceBrowser *)browser {
    browser.delegate = nil;
    self.netServiceBrowser = nil;
}
```

When the browser finds a new service, it will call the delegate method netServiceBrowser:didFindService:moreComing:. The second argument the browser will pass to this method is an instance of NSNetService that can be resolved into an address or port, or turned into a stream pair, which you'll see how to do in a minute.

Typically, when notified about a new service, you add it to an array or other collection, so that you can let your user select from the available services. If the browser knows that there are more services coming, it will indicate this by passing YES for the last argument, which allows you to skip updating the user interface unnecessarily. The following is an example of what an implementation of this method might look like in a table view controller. Notice that we sort the data and reload the table only if there are no more services coming.

```
- (void)netServiceBrowser:(NSNetServiceBrowser *)browser
          didFindService:(NSNetService *)aNetService
             moreComing:(BOOL)moreComing {
    if (![[self.publishedService name] isEqualToString:[aNetService name]])
        [discoveredServices addObject:aNetService];

    if (!moreComing) {
        [self.tableView reloadData];
        NSSortDescriptor *sd = [[NSSortDescriptor alloc] initWithKey:@"name"
            ascending:YES];
```

```
            [discoveredServices sortUsingDescriptors:[NSArray arrayWithObject:sd]];
            [sd release];
        }
}
```

Another thing to notice here is that we're comparing browser's name to the name of another published service. This step is unnecessary if you haven't published a Bonjour service in your app. However, if you're both publishing and browsing, as we're going to do in our application, you typically don't want to display your own service to your users. If you've published one, it will be discovered by your browser, so you must manually exclude it from the list you show to the users.

Finally, if a service becomes unavailable, the browser will call another delegate method, which looks very similar to the last one, to let you know that one of the previously available services can no longer be found. Here's what that method might look like in a table view controller class:

```
- (void)netServiceBrowser:(NSNetServiceBrowser *)browser
         didRemoveService:(NSNetService *)aNetService
               moreComing:(BOOL)moreComing {
    [discoveredServices removeObject:aNetService];

    if(!moreComing)
        [self.tableView reloadData];
}
```

Resolving a Discovered Service

If you want to connect to any of the discovered services, you do it by resolving the instance of NSNetService that was returned by the browser in the netServiceBrowser:didFindService:moreComing: method. To resolve it, all you need to do is call the method resolveWithTimeout:, specifying how long it should attempt to connect, or 0.0 to specify no timeout. If you were storing the discovered services in an array called discoveredServices, here is how you would resolve one of the services in that array:

```
    NSNetService *selectedService = [discoveredServices objectAtIndex:selectedIndex];
    selectedService.delegate = self;
    [selectedService resolveWithTimeout:0.0];
```

Discovered services do not need to be registered with the run loop the way published ones do. Once you call resolveWithTimeout:, the service will then call delegate methods to tell you that the service was resolved, or to tell you that it couldn't be resolved.

If the service could not be resolved, for whatever reason, it will call the delegate method netService:didNotResolve:. At a minimum, you should stop the net service here. You should also do whatever error checking is appropriate to your application. Here's a simple implementation of this delegate method:

```
- (void)netService:(NSNetService *)sender didNotResolve:(NSDictionary *)errorDict {
    [sender stop];
    NSNumber *errorDomain = [errorDict valueForKey:NSNetServicesErrorDomain];
    NSNumber *errorCode = [errorDict valueForKey:NSNetServicesErrorCode];
```

```
    NSLog(@"Unable to resolve Bonjour service (Domain: %@, Error Code: %@)",
        errorDomain, errorCode);
}
```

If the discovered service resolved successfully, then the delegate method `netServiceDidResolveAddress:` will be called. You can call the methods `hostName` and `port` on the service to find out its location and connect to it manually. An easier option is to ask the net service for a pair of streams already configured to connect to the remote service. Here's an example implementation of that delegate method. Note, however, that we don't do anything with the streams yet.

```
- (void)netServiceDidResolveAddress:(NSNetService *)service {

    NSInputStream *tempIn = nil;
    NSOutputStream *tempOut = nil;
    if (![service getInputStream:&tempIn outputStream:&tempOut]){
        NSLog(@"Could not start game with remote device",
            @"Could not start game with remote device") ];
        return;
    }
    // Open and use the streams
}
```

Why didn't we do anything with the streams? Because streams are complex enough to deserve their very own section, so we will now, very smoothly, segue into...

Streams

In the previous sections, we demonstrated how to obtain a pair of **streams**, which represent a connection to another device. In the section on setting up a listener, we showed you how to get a pair of `CFStream` pointers when another computer is connected. When we looked at resolving services with Bonjour, we demonstrated how to get a pair of `NSStreams` (actually an `NSInputStream` and an `NSOutputStream`, but both are subclasses of `NSStream`) to represent the connection to the published services. So, now it's time to talk about how to use streams.

Before we go too far, we should remind you that `CFStream` and `NSStream` are toll-free bridged, so we're not really talking about different objects here. They're all stream objects. If they represent a connection designed to let you send data to another machine, they're an `NSOutputStream` instance; if they're designed to let you read the data sent by another machine, they are instances of `NSInputStream`.

> **NOTE:** In this chapter, we use streams to pass data between different instances of our application over a network. However, streams are also useful in situations that don't involve network connections. For example, streams can be used to read and write files. Any type of data source or destination that sequential bits of data can be sent to or received from can be represented as a stream.

Opening a Stream

The first thing you need to do with any stream object is to open it. You can't use a stream that hasn't been opened.

Opening a stream tells it that you're ready to use it. Until it's open, a stream object really represents a potential rather than an actual stream. After you open a stream, you need to register it with your run loop, so that it can send and receive data without disrupting the flow of your application. And, as you've probably guessed, you need to set a delegate, so that the streams can notify you when things happen.

Here's what opening a pair of streams generally looks like:

```
[inStream scheduleInRunLoop:[NSRunLoop currentRunLoop]
    forMode:NSDefaultRunLoopMode];
[outStream scheduleInRunLoop:[NSRunLoop currentRunLoop]
    forMode:NSDefaultRunLoopMode];

inStream.delegate = self;
outStream.delegate = self;

if ([inStream streamStatus] == NSStreamStatusNotOpen)
    [inStream open];

if ([outStream streamStatus] == NSStreamStatusNotOpen)
    [outStream open];
```

Just to be safe, we actually check the status of the stream and make sure it wasn't already opened elsewhere. With the streams retrieved from Bonjour or from a network listener, the streams won't be open, but we code defensively so we don't get burnt.

The Stream and Its Delegate

Streams have one delegate method—that's it, just one. But they call that one method whenever anything of interest happens on the streams. The delegate method is `stream:handleEvent:`, and it includes an event code that tells you what's going on with the stream. Let's look at the relevant event codes:

- `NSStreamEventOpenCompleted`: When the stream has finished opening and is ready to allow data to be transferred, it will call `stream:handleEvent:` with the event code `NSStreamEventOpenCompleted`. Put another way, once the stream has finished opening, its delegate will receive the `NSStreamEventOpenCompleted` event. Until this event has been received, a stream should not be used. You won't receive any data from an input stream before this event happens, and any attempts to send data to an output stream before its receipt will fail.

- NSStreamEventErrorOccurred: If an error occurs at any time with the stream, it will send its delegate the NSStreamEventErrorOccurred event. When this happens, you can retrieve an instance of NSError with the details of the error by calling streamError on the stream, like so:

```
NSError *theError = [stream streamError];
```

NOTE: An error does not necessarily indicate that the stream can no longer be used. If the stream can no longer be used, you will also receive a separate event informing you of that.

- NSStreamEventEndEncountered: If you encounter a fatal error, or the device at the other end of the stream disconnects, the stream's delegate will receive the NSStreamEventEndEncountered event. When this happens, you should dispose of the streams, because they no longer connect you to anything.

- NSStreamEventHasBytesAvailable: When the device you are connected to sends you data, you will receive one or more NSStreamEventHasBytesAvailable events. One of the tricky things about streams is that you may not receive the data all at once. The data will come across in the same order it was sent, but it's not the case that every discrete send results in one and only one NSStreamEventHasBytesAvailable event. The data from one send could be split into multiple events, or the data from multiple sends could get combined into one event. This can make reading data somewhat complex. We'll look at how to handle that complexity a little later, when we implement online play in our tic-tac-toe game.

- NSStreamEventHasSpaceAvailable: Streams, especially network streams, have a limit to how much data they can accept at a time. When space becomes available on the stream, it will notify its delegate by sending the NSStreamEventHasSpaceAvailable event. At this time, if there is any queued, unsent data, it is safe to send at least some of that data through the stream.

Receiving Data from a Stream

When notified, by receipt of an NSStreamEventHasBytesAvailable event, that there is data available on the stream, you can read the available data, or a portion of it, by calling read:maxLength: on the stream.

The first argument you need to pass is a buffer, or chunk of memory, into which the stream will copy the received data. The second parameter is the maximum number of bytes that your buffer can handle. This method will return the number of bytes actually read, or -1 if there was an error.

Here's an example of reading up to a kibibyte of data (yes, Virginia, there is such a thing as a kibibyte; check out this link to learn more: http://en.wikipedia.org/wiki/Kibibyte) from the stream:

```
uint8_t    buffer[1024];
NSInteger  bytesRead = [inStream read:buffer maxLength:1024];
if (bytesRead == -1) {
    NSError *error = [inStream streamError];
    NSLog(@"Error reading data: %@", [error localizedDescription]);
}
```

> **NOTE:** You'll notice that when we deal with data to be sent over a network connection, we often choose datatypes like `uint8_t` or `int16_t`, rather than more common datatypes like `char` and `int`. These are datatypes that are specified by their byte size, which is important when sending data over a network connection. Conversely, the `int` datatype is based on the register size of the hardware for which it's being compiled. An `int` compiled for one piece of hardware might not be the same size as an `int` compiled for another piece of hardware.
>
> In this case, we want to be able to specify a buffer in bytes, so we use a datatype that's always going to be 8 bits (1 byte) long on all hardware and every platform. The actual datatype of the buffer doesn't matter—what matters is the size of that datatype, because that will affect the size of the buffer we allocate. We know `uint8_t` will always be 1 byte long on all platforms and all hardware, and that fact will be obvious to any programmer looking at our code, since the byte size is part of the datatype name.

Sending Data Through the Stream

To send data to the connected device through the output stream, you call `write:maxLength:`, passing in a pointer to the data to send and the length of that data. Here's how you might send the contents of an `NSData` instance called `dataToSend`:

```
NSUInteger sendLength = [dataToSend length];
NSUInteger written = [outStream write:[dataToSend bytes] maxLength:sendLength];
if (written == -1) {
    NSError *error = [outStream streamError];
    NSLog(@"Error writing data: %@", [error localizedDescription]);
}
```

It's important at this point that you check `written` to make sure it matches `sendLength`. If it doesn't, that means only part of your data went through, and you need to resend the rest when you get another `NSStreamEventHasBytesAvailable` event from the stream.

Putting It All Together

As you can see, adding online play to a program can be complex. If we're not careful, we could end up with messy globs of networking code littered throughout our application, making it hard to maintain and debug. We're still trying to write our code generically, so our goal is to create objects that can be reused, preferably unmodified, in other applications and that encapsulate the new functionality we need.

In this case, fortunately, we already have something we can model our classes on: GameKit. As discussed in the previous chapter, communication in GameKit happens through an object called a GKSession. That object manages both sending data to the remote device and receiving data from it. We call a method and pass in an NSData instance to send data to the other device, and we implement a delegate method to receive data from it. We're going to follow this model to create a similar session object for online play. We'll create two new generic classes, along with a couple of categories to help us convert an array of objects to a stream of bytes and back again. We're also going to need a new view controller.

The category will contain functionality that will assist us in reassembling data sent over a stream. One of the new objects will be called OnlineSession, and it will function similarly to GKSession. Once a stream pair is received from either the listener or from resolving the net service, that stream pair can be used to create a new OnlineSession.

We're also going to create a class called OnlineListener, which will encapsulate all the functionality needed to listen for new connections. Our new view controller class will present a list of available peers, similar to the peer picker in GameKit.

Before we get started writing these new classes, let's consider how we're going to ensure that the NSData objects we send can be reassembled by the other device. Remember that we don't have any control over how many bytes are sent at a time. We might, for example, send a single NSData instance, and the other machine may get that NSData spread over 20 NSStreamEventHasBytesAvailable events. Or we might send a few instances at different times that could be received all together in one NSStreamEventHasBytesAvailable event. To make sure that we can reassemble the stream of bytes into an object, we'll first send the length of the object followed by its bytes. That way, no matter how the stream is divided up, it can always be reassembled. If the other device is told to expect 128 bytes, it knows to keep waiting for data until it gets all 128 bytes before it should reassemble it. The device will also know that if it gets more than 128 bytes, then there's another object.

Let's take all this information and get it into code before our heads explode, shall we?

Updating Tic-Tac-Toe for Online Play

We're going to continue working with the TicTacToe application from the previous chapter. If you don't already have it open, consider making a backup copy before continuing. Because the fundamental game isn't changing, we don't need to touch the existing nibs. Although we will need to make changes to `TicTacToeViewController`, we won't change any of the game logic.

Adding the Packet Categories

We need the ability to convert multiple `NSData` instances into a single stream of bytes containing the length of the data and then the actual bytes. We also need a way to take a stream of bytes and reassemble those back into `NSData` instances. We're going to use categories to add this functionality to existing classes.

Because the stream won't necessarily be able to handle all the data we have to send, we're going to maintain a queue of all the data waiting to be sent in an `NSArray`. One of our categories will be on `NSArray` and will return a single `NSData` instance that holds a buffer of bytes representing everything in the array. We're also going to write a category on `NSData` to take a stream of bytes held in an instance of `NSData` and parse it back into the original objects. These categories will contain a single method each. Since they represent two sides of the same operation, we're going to place both categories in a single pair of files, just to minimize project clutter.

With your *TicTacToe* project open, single-click the *Classes* folder in the *Groups & Files* pane and press ⌘N or select **New File...** from the **File** menu. Under the *Cocoa Touch Class* category, select *Objective-C Class* and select *NSObject* from the *Subclass of* pop-up menu. When prompted for a name, type *PacketCategories.m*, and make sure the check box labeled *Also create "PacketCategories.h"* is selected.

Once the files have been created, single-click *PacketCategories.h* and replace the existing contents with the following:

```
#import <Foundation/Foundation.h>
#define kInvalidObjectException      @"Invalid Object Exception"

@interface NSArray(PacketSend)
-(NSData *)contentsForTransfer;
@end

@interface NSData(PacketSplit)
- (NSArray *)splitTransferredPackets:(NSData **)leftover;
@end
```

The one constant, `kInvalidObjectException`, will be used to throw an exception if our `NSArray` method is called on an array that contains objects other than instances of `NSData`. If we wanted to make this more robust, we might archive other objects into instances of `NSData`, throwing an exception only if the array contains an object that doesn't conform to `NSCoding`. For simplicity's sake and to be consistent with the approach used by `GKSession`, we're going to support just `NSData` instances in our application.

After that, we declare a category on `NSArray` that adds a single method called `contentsForTransfer`, which returns the entire contents of the array, ready to be sent through a stream to the other machine. The second category is on `NSData`. This method will reassemble all of the objects contained in a chunk of received data. In addition to returning an array with those objects, it also takes one argument called `leftover`. This pointer to a pointer will be used to return any incomplete objects. If an object is incomplete, the caller will need to wait for more bytes, append them to `leftover`, and then call this method again.

Switch over to *PacketCategories.m* and replace the existing contents with this:

```objc
#import "PacketCategories.h"

@implementation NSArray(PacketSend)
-(NSData *)contentsForTransfer {
    NSMutableData *ret = [NSMutableData data];
    for (NSData *oneData in self) {
        if (![oneData isKindOfClass:[NSData class]])
            [NSException raise:kInvalidObjectException format:
                @"arrayContentsForTransfer only supports instances of NSData"];

        uint64_t dataSize[1];
        dataSize[0] = [oneData length];
        [ret appendBytes:dataSize length:sizeof(uint64_t)];
        [ret appendBytes:[oneData bytes] length:[oneData length]];
    }
    return ret;
}
@end

@implementation NSData(PacketSplit)
- (NSArray *)splitTransferredPackets:(NSData **)leftover {

    NSMutableArray *ret = [NSMutableArray array];
    const unsigned char *beginning = [self bytes];
    const unsigned char *offset = [self bytes];
    NSInteger bytesEnd = (NSInteger)offset + [self length];

    while ((NSInteger)offset < bytesEnd) {
        uint64_t dataSize[1];
        NSInteger dataSizeStart = offset - beginning;
        NSInteger dataStart = dataSizeStart + sizeof(uint64_t);

        NSRange headerRange = NSMakeRange(dataSizeStart, sizeof(uint64_t));
        [self getBytes:dataSize range:headerRange];

        if ((dataStart + dataSize[0] + (NSInteger)offset) > bytesEnd) {
            NSInteger lengthOfRemainingData = [self length] - dataSizeStart;
            NSRange dataRange = NSMakeRange(dataSizeStart, lengthOfRemainingData);
            *leftover = [self subdataWithRange:dataRange];

            return ret;
        }

        NSRange dataRange = NSMakeRange(dataStart, dataSize[0]);
        NSData *parsedData = [self subdataWithRange:dataRange];

        [ret addObject:parsedData];
        offset = offset + dataSize[0] + sizeof(uint64_t);
```

```
    }
    return ret;
}
@end
```

These two categories might appear a little intimidating because they're dealing with bytes, but they're really quite straightforward. The first just creates an instance of NSMutableData to hold the stream of bytes, and then iterates over the array. For each object, it first adds the length of the object as a 64-byte integer, and then appends the actual data bytes from the object. When it's finished iterating, it returns the mutable data that contains the formatted stream of bytes.

The second method might be a little more intimidating looking, but all it's doing is looping through the bytes of self, which will be an instance of NSData that holds data formatted by the previous method. It first reads a uint64_t, a 64-byte integer that should hold the length of the object that follows, and then reads that number of bytes into a new instance of NSData, which it adds to a mutable array that will be returned. It continues to do this until it reaches the end of the data. If it gets to the end of the data and has an incomplete object, it sends that object's data back to the calling method using that pointer to a pointer argument, leftover.

Implementing the Online Session Object

Now that we have a way to split up and recombine objects from the stream, let's write our OnlineSession object. Create a new file by selecting the *Classes* folder and pressing ⌘N. You can use the same file template you used for creating the category, but call the new class *OnlineSession.m* and make sure it creates *OnlineSession.h* for you.

Single-click *OnlineSession.h* and replace the current contents with this new version:

```
#import <Foundation/Foundation.h>
#define kOnlineSessionErrorDomain    @"Online Session Domain"
#define kFailedToSendDataErrorCode   1000
#define kDataReadErrorCode           1001

#define kBufferSize                  512

@class OnlineSession;
@protocol OnlineSessionDelegate
- (void)onlineSessionReadyForUse:(OnlineSession *)session;
@optional
- (void)onlineSession:(OnlineSession *)session
        receivedData:(NSData *)data;
- (void)onlineSession:(OnlineSession *)session
 encounteredReadError:(NSError *)error;
- (void)onlineSession:(OnlineSession *)session
encounteredWriteError:(NSError *)error;
- (void)onlineSessionDisconnected:(OnlineSession *)session;
@end

@interface OnlineSession : NSObject {
    id                          delegate;
```

```
NSInputStream                    *inStream;
NSOutputStream                   *outStream;

BOOL                             writeReady;
BOOL                             readReady;

NSMutableArray                   *packetQueue;
NSData                           *readLeftover;
NSData                           *writeLeftover;
}
@property (nonatomic, assign) id<OnlineSessionDelegate> delegate;

- (id)initWithInputStream:(NSInputStream *)theInStream
            outputStream:(NSOutputStream *)theOutStream;
- (BOOL)sendData:(NSData *)data error:(NSError **)error;
- (BOOL)isReadyForUse;
@end
```

Let's take a look at what we're doing here. First, we define a few constants for an error domain for our session object, as well as some error codes to represent errors we might encounter:

```
#define kOnlineSessionErrorDomain    @"Online Session Domain"
#define kFailedToSendDataErrorCode   1000
#define kDataReadErrorCode           1001
```

After that, we define another constant that will set the size of our read buffer. Remember that when we read data from a stream, we need to create a buffer of a specific size, and then inform the stream of the maximum number of bytes we can accept in a single read operation. This constant will be used to allocate the memory and also will be passed in to the stream's read method as the maxLength parameter. Depending on the size of the data you need to transfer, you might want to tweak this value, but it's generally a good idea to read from the stream in small chunks. Apple typically recommends either 512 or 1024 per read. Since the data we send in our application is relatively small, we went with the smaller suggested value of 512.

```
#define kBufferSize                  512
```

Our session will have a delegate, and we will inform the delegate when certain things happen. We create a protocol to define the methods that our delegate can and must implement. Because we haven't yet declared our OnlineSession class (which will happen below the protocol), we use the @class keyword to tell the compiler that the class actually exists, even though the compiler hasn't seen it yet. The only required method is the one used to receive data from peers; however, we provide methods to inform the delegate of pretty much any stream event that the application might need to know about.

```
@class OnlineSession;
@protocol OnlineSessionDelegate
- (void)onlineSessionReadyForUse:(OnlineSession *)session;
@optional
- (void)onlineSession:(OnlineSession *)session
          receivedData:(NSData *)data;
- (void)onlineSession:(OnlineSession *)session
 encounteredReadError:(NSError *)error;
```

```
- (void)onlineSession:(OnlineSession *)session
encounteredWriteError:(NSError *)error;
- (void)onlineSessionDisconnected:(OnlineSession *)session;
@end
```

Next, we define the `OnlineSession` class and declare its instance variables:

```
@interface OnlineSession : NSObject {
    id                          delegate;

    NSInputStream               *inStream;
    NSOutputStream              *outStream;

    BOOL                        writeReady;
    BOOL                        readReady;

    NSMutableArray              *packetQueue;
    NSData                      *readLeftover;
    NSData                      *writeLeftover;

}
```

We have a delegate, a stream pair, a pair of `BOOL`s that will be used to keep track of whether the streams are ready to use, and then a mutable array to keep a queue of unsent data. When our write method is called, if the streams aren't ready or if there is no space available on the output stream, we'll queue up the data by adding it to the `packetQueue` array, and then send the queued data when we get a space available event from `outStream`. The last two instance variables are used to keep track of partial packets. Remember that we won't always be able to send an entire object, nor will we always receive objects in a single chunk, so we need a way to keep track of the leftover data.

The only one of our instance variables that ever needs to be changed by another class is `delegate`, so we declare a property for `delegate`. Unlike the underlying instance variable, we declare the property as `id<OnlineSessionDelegate>`, which means that we accept any object, but require it to conform to the `OnlineSessionDelegate` protocol that we defined earlier. If another object tries to assign a delegate that doesn't conform to that protocol, it will generate a compile-time warning, because we've declared the property this way.

```
@property (nonatomic, assign) id<OnlineSessionDelegate> delegate;
```

One really important thing to note here is that we use `assign` rather than `retain` for our delegate. This is a standard convention in Cocoa and Cocoa Touch. Generally speaking, objects should not retain their delegate unless there's a compelling reason to do so. As a result, your delegate properties should always be declared with the `assign` keyword.

Finally, we declare a whopping three instance methods in our header: an init method, a method to send data, and a method to determine if the session is ready for use.

```
- (id)initWithInputStream:(NSInputStream *)theInStream
            outputStream:(NSOutputStream *)theOutStream;
- (BOOL)sendData:(NSData *)data error:(NSError **)error;
- (BOOL)isReadyForUse;
```

Save your file.

Now, switch over to *OnlineSession.m* and replace the contents with the following:

```objc
#import "OnlineSession.h"
#import "PacketCategories.h"

@interface OnlineSession()
- (void)sendQueuedData;
@end

#pragma mark -
@implementation OnlineSession
@synthesize delegate;

#pragma mark -
- (id)initWithInputStream:(NSInputStream *)theInStream
              outputStream:(NSOutputStream *)theOutStream {
    if (self = [super init]) {

        inStream = [theInStream retain];
        outStream = [theOutStream retain];

        [inStream scheduleInRunLoop:[NSRunLoop currentRunLoop]
            forMode:NSDefaultRunLoopMode];
        [outStream scheduleInRunLoop:[NSRunLoop currentRunLoop]
            forMode:NSDefaultRunLoopMode];

        inStream.delegate = self;
        outStream.delegate = self;

        if ([inStream streamStatus] == NSStreamStatusNotOpen)
            [inStream open];

        if ([outStream streamStatus] == NSStreamStatusNotOpen)
            [outStream open];

        packetQueue = [[NSMutableArray alloc] init];
    }
    return self;
}

- (BOOL)sendData:(NSData *)data error:(NSError **)error {

    if (data == nil || [data length] == 0)
        return NO;

    [packetQueue addObject:data];

    if ([outStream hasSpaceAvailable])
        [self sendQueuedData];

    return YES;
}

- (BOOL)isReadyForUse {
    return readReady && writeReady;
}
```

```
- (void)dealloc {
    [inStream close];
    [inStream removeFromRunLoop:[NSRunLoop currentRunLoop]
        forMode:NSDefaultRunLoopMode];
    inStream.delegate = nil;
    [inStream release];

    [outStream close];
    [outStream removeFromRunLoop:[NSRunLoop currentRunLoop]
        forMode:NSDefaultRunLoopMode];
    outStream.delegate = nil;
    [outStream release];

    [packetqueue release];
    [writeLeftover release];
    [readLeftover release];

    [super dealloc];
}

- (void) stream:(NSStream *)stream
    handleEvent:(NSStreamEvent)eventCode {
    switch(eventCode) {
        case NSStreamEventOpenCompleted:
            if (stream == inStream)
                readReady = YES;
            else
                writeReady = YES;
            if ([self isReadyForUse] &&
                [delegate respondsToSelector:@selector(onlineSessionReadyForUse:)])
                [delegate onlineSessionReadyForUse:self];
            break;
        case NSStreamEventHasBytesAvailable:
            if (stream == inStream) {

                if ([inStream hasBytesAvailable]) {

                    NSMutableData *data = [NSMutableData data];

                    if (readLeftover != nil) {
                        [data appendData:readLeftover];
                        [readLeftover release];
                        readLeftover = nil;
                    }

                    NSInteger      bytesRead;
                    static uint8_t buffer[kBufferSize];

                    bytesRead = [inStream read:buffer maxLength:kBufferSize];
                    if (bytesRead == -1 && [delegate respondsToSelector:
                        @selector(onlineSession:encounteredReadError:)]) {
                        NSError *error = [[NSError alloc]
                            initWithDomain:kOnlineSessionErrorDomain
                            code:kDataReadErrorCode userInfo:nil];
                        [delegate onlineSession:self encounteredReadError:error];
                        [error release];
```

```objectivec
                        return;
                    }
                    else if (bytesRead > 0) {
                        [data appendBytes:buffer length:bytesRead];

                        NSArray *dataPackets = [data splitTransferredPackets:
                            &readLeftover];

                        if (readLeftover)
                            [readLeftover retain];

                        for (NSData *onePacketData in dataPackets)
                            [delegate onlineSession:self
                                receivedData:onePacketData];
                    }
                }
            }
            break;
        case NSStreamEventErrorOccurred: {
            NSError *theError = [stream streamError];
            if (stream == inStream)
                if (delegate && [delegate respondsToSelector:
                    @selector(onlineSession:encounteredReadError:)])
                    [delegate onlineSession:self encounteredReadError:theError];
                else{
                    if (delegate && [delegate respondsToSelector:
                        @selector(onlineSession:encounteredWriteError:)])
                        [delegate onlineSession:self
                            encounteredWriteError:theError];
                }

            break;
        }
        case NSStreamEventHasSpaceAvailable:
            if (stream == outStream) {
                [self sendQueuedData];
            }
            break;
        case NSStreamEventEndEncountered:
            if (delegate && [delegate respondsToSelector:
                @selector(onlineSessionDisconnected:)])
                [delegate onlineSessionDisconnected:self];
            readReady = NO;
            writeReady = NO;
            break;
        default:
            break;
    }
}

- (void)sendQueuedData {

    if (writeLeftover == nil && [packetQueue count] == 0)
        return; // Nothing to send!

    NSMutableData *dataToSend = [NSMutableData data];
```

```
    if (writeLeftover != nil) {
        [dataToSend appendData:writeLeftover];
        [writeLeftover release];
        writeLeftover = nil;
    }

    [dataToSend appendData:[packetQueue contentsForTransfer]];
    [packetQueue removeAllObjects];

    NSUInteger sendLength = [dataToSend length];
    NSUInteger written = [outStream write:[dataToSend bytes] maxLength:sendLength];

    if (written == -1) {
        if (delegate && [delegate respondsToSelector:
            @selector(onlineSession:encounteredWriteError:)])
            [delegate onlineSession:self encounteredWriteError:
                [outStream streamError]];
    }
    if (written != sendLength) {
        NSRange leftoverRange = NSMakeRange(written, [dataToSend length] - written);
        writeLeftover = [[dataToSend subdataWithRange:leftoverRange] retain];
    }
}
}

@end
```

This is a little gnarly looking, but we've already covered pretty much everything we do in this class. In the initWithInputStream:outputStream: method, we retain and keep a reference to the two streams, schedule them both with the run loop, and then open the streams if they aren't already open. We also create our mutable array to serve as our packet queue.

```
- (id)initWithInputStream:(NSInputStream *)theInStream
            outputStream:(NSOutputStream *)theOutStream {
    if (self = [super init]) {
        [theInStream retain];
        inStream = theInStream;

        [theOutStream retain];
        outStream = theOutStream;

        [inStream scheduleInRunLoop:[NSRunLoop currentRunLoop]
            forMode:NSDefaultRunLoopMode];
        [outStream scheduleInRunLoop:[NSRunLoop currentRunLoop]
            forMode:NSDefaultRunLoopMode];

        inStream.delegate = self;
        outStream.delegate = self;

        if ([inStream streamStatus] == NSStreamStatusNotOpen)
            [inStream open];

        if ([outStream streamStatus] == NSStreamStatusNotOpen)
            [outStream open];

        packetQueue = [[NSMutableArray alloc] init];
    }
```

```
        return self;
    }
```

In our sendData: method, we add the new object to the queue and, if there's space available, we call the method sendQueuedData, which will attempt to send as much of the queued data as the stream will take. If there is no space available on the stream, we don't do anything other than add the data to the queue. It will be sent when we are notified that there is space available on the stream.

```
- (BOOL)sendData:(NSData *)data error:(NSError **)error {

    if (data == nil || [data length] == 0)
        return NO;

    [packetQueue addObject:data];

    if ([outStream hasSpaceAvailable])
        [self sendQueuedData];

    return YES;
}
```

The isReadyForUse method just does a logical AND operation on the two BOOL instance variables that are used to track whether the two streams are available for use. It returns YES if both streams are ready; otherwise, it returns NO. You'll see where we set these values a little later in the chapter.

```
- (BOOL)isReadyForUse {
    return readReady && writeReady;
}
```

Our dealloc method is pretty standard. The only differences from the regular dealloc methods we're used to writing is that we need to close the streams, remove them from the run loop, and set their delegate to nil.

```
- (void)dealloc {
    [inStream close];
    [inStream removeFromRunLoop:[NSRunLoop currentRunLoop]
        forMode:NSDefaultRunLoopMode];
    inStream.delegate = nil;
    [inStream release];

    [outStream close];
    [outStream removeFromRunLoop:[NSRunLoop currentRunLoop]
        forMode:NSDefaultRunLoopMode];
    outStream.delegate = nil;
    [outStream release];

    [super dealloc];
}
```

The next method is a bit of a doozy. It's that stream delegate method we discussed earlier—the one that is called with different event codes. This is where most of the work happens in our OnlineSession class. Let's look at each of the event codes separately.

If we are notified that a stream has finished opening, we check which stream sent us the event and set the appropriate value to YES. After we do that, we check to see if both are YES and, if they are, we inform our delegate that the session is ready to use if the delegate has implemented that method.

```
case NSStreamEventOpenCompleted:
    if (stream == inStream)
        readReady = YES;
    else
        writeReady = YES;
    if ([self isReadyForUse] &&
        [delegate respondsToSelector:@selector(onlineSessionReadyForUse:)])
        [delegate onlineSessionReadyForUse:self];
    break;
```

If we are notified that there are bytes available on a stream, we first make sure we're getting this event from the input stream. In theory, we should never get this event from an output stream, but we code defensively just in case. We also create an instance of NSMutableData to hold the received data. If there is any leftover data, we combine the new data with the leftover data, which we will be stored in readLeftover, before processing it. This way, every time new data comes in, we have all the unprocessed data in one place.

```
case NSStreamEventHasBytesAvailable:
    if (stream == inStream) {

        if ([inStream hasBytesAvailable]) {

            NSMutableData *data = [NSMutableData data];

            if (readLeftover != nil) {
                [data appendData:readLeftover];
                [readLeftover release];
                readLeftover = nil;
            }
```

Now we read the data into a buffer. We check to make sure we didn't encounter an error and, if we did, we notify our delegate about the error.

```
            NSInteger      bytesRead;
            static uint8_t buffer[kBufferSize];

            bytesRead = [inStream read:buffer maxLength:kBufferSize];
            if (bytesRead == -1 && [delegate respondsToSelector:
                @selector(onlineSession:encounteredReadError:)]) {
                NSError *error = [[NSError alloc]
                    initWithDomain:kOnlineSessionErrorDomain
                    code:kDataReadErrorCode userInfo:nil];
                [delegate onlineSession:self encounteredReadError:error];
                [error release];
                return;
            }
```

If there wasn't an error, we use the category method we created earlier to decode objects from the data we've received. If any objects were decoded, we inform our delegate. If there is any leftover data, we retain it so that it will be here the next time this event is called.

```
else if (bytesRead > 0) {
    [data appendBytes:buffer length:bytesRead];

    NSArray *dataPackets = [data splitTransferredPackets:
        &readLeftover];

    if (readLeftover)
        [readLeftover retain];

    for (NSData *onePacketData in dataPackets)
        [delegate onlineSession:self
            receivedData:onePacketData];
    }
}
}
break;
```

If we get an error event, all we do is pass it on to our delegate method.

```
case NSStreamEventErrorOccurred: {
    NSError *theError = [stream streamError];
    if (stream == inStream)
        if (delegate && [delegate respondsToSelector:
            @selector(onlineSession:encounteredReadError:)])
            [delegate onlineSession:self encounteredReadError:theError];
        else {
            if (delegate && [delegate respondsToSelector:
                @selector(onlineSession:encounteredWriteError:)])
                [delegate onlineSession:self
                    encounteredWriteError:theError];
        }
        break;
}
```

When the output stream tells us that there's space available, we call sendQueuedData to send any unsent data.

```
case NSStreamEventHasSpaceAvailable:
    if (stream == outStream) {
        [self sendQueuedData];
    }
    break;
```

Finally, if we are notified that the stream has been closed for any reason, we inform our delegate of the fact, and mark both streams as no longer ready for use. Because the streams act as a pair, we don't bother to check which one informed us—we just assume that if one is closed, both are closed.

```
case NSStreamEventEndEncountered:
    if (delegate && [delegate respondsToSelector:
        @selector(onlineSessionDisconnected:)])
        [delegate onlineSessionDisconnected:self];
```

```
            readReady = NO;
            writeReady = NO;
        break;
```

We're almost finished with OnlineSession. We just need to look at the sendQueuedData method. First, if there's no leftover data and nothing queued, we return, because there's no reason to do anything else.

```
- (void)sendQueuedData {
    if (writeLeftover == nil && [packetQueue count] == 0)
        return; // Nothing to send!
```

We next create an instance of NSMutableData. We use that instance to combine the queued data with the leftover data into a single chunk, and then clear the queue.

```
    NSMutableData *dataToSend = [NSMutableData data];

    if (writeLeftover!= nil) {
        [dataToSend appendData: writeLeftover];
        [writeLeftover release];
        writeLeftover = nil;
    }

    [dataToSend appendData:[packetQueue contentsForTransfer]];
    [packetQueue removeAllObjects];
```

Now that we have all the data that needs to be sent in a single instance of NSMutableData, we try to send it.

```
    NSUInteger sendLength = [dataToSend length];
    NSUInteger written = [outStream write:[dataToSend bytes] maxLength:sendLength];
```

If we encountered a write error, we notify our delegate.

```
    if (written == -1) {
        if (delegate && [delegate respondsToSelector:
            @selector(onlineSession:encounteredWriteError:)])
            [delegate onlineSession:self encounteredWriteError:
                [outStream streamError]];
    }
```

Then, if the amount sent is not equal to the length of the data we needed to send, we extract the part that didn't get sent and store it in writeLeftover, so we'll have it the next time we try to send queued data.

```
    if (written != sendLength) {
        NSRange leftoverRange = NSMakeRange(written, [dataToSend length] - written);
        writeLeftover = [[dataToSend subdataWithRange:leftoverRange] retain];

    }
}
```

We're finished with *OnlineSession.m*. Make sure you save it.

Creating the Listener Object

As we discussed earlier in the chapter, we need to listen for network connections if we're going to advertise a service using Bonjour. Now, let's create a class to encapsulate listening for a network connection.

Create a new file using the same *Objective-C class* template we've used twice already in this chapter. Name the new file *OnlineListener.m*, and have it create *OnlineListener.h* for you as well.

Once the files are created, single-click *OnlineListener.h* and replace the current contents with the following:

```
#import <Foundation/Foundation.h>
#define kOnlineListenerErrorDomain @"Online Session Listener Session Domain"
#define kOnlineListenerErrorNoSocketsAvailable     1000
#define kOnlineListenerErrorCouldntBindToAddress   1001
#define kOnlineListenerErrorStreamError            1002

@class OnlineListener;
@protocol OnlineListenerDelegate
- (void) acceptedConnectionForListener:(OnlineListener *)theListener
                           inputStream:(NSInputStream *)theInputStream
                          outputStream:(NSOutputStream *)theOutputStream;
@optional
- (void) onlineListener:(OnlineListener *)theListener
        encounteredError:(NSError *)error;
@end

@interface OnlineListener : NSObject {
    id delegate;
    uint16_t port;
    CFSocketRef socket;
}
@property (nonatomic, assign) id<OnlineListenerDelegate> delegate;
@property uint16_t  port;

- (BOOL)startListening:(NSError **)error;
- (void)stopListening;

@end
```

Once again, we have constants for an error domain, a few error codes that we'll need, a formal protocol to define one method that this class's delegate must implement, and a second method that it can define if necessary. The required method will be called when a connection attempt is detected, and it will pass to the delegate the stream pair that was created. The optional method is called when a connection was attempted but failed.

We have three instance variables this time: a delegate, a port number, and a CFSocketRef, which is that CFNetwork socket object we discussed earlier in the chapter. We expose only the delegate and the port number as properties, because there's really no reason why external objects would need direct access to the socket. We're not using a specific port number, which means the object that creates the listener will need to retrieve the port number so it can pass it to Bonjour.

The class itself has only two methods: one to tell it to start listening and one to tell it to stop listening. Nice and simple.

Make sure you save *OnlineListener.h* before continuing.

Single-click *OnlineListener.m* and replace its contents with the following:

```
#import "OnlineListener.h"
#include <sys/socket.h>
#include <netinet/in.h>
#include <unistd.h>
#include <CFNetwork/CFSocketStream.h>

#pragma mark CFNetwork C Callbacks
static void onlineListenerAcceptCallback (CFSocketRef theSocket, CFSocketCallBackType
theType, CFDataRef theAddress, const void *data, void *info) {
    OnlineListener *listener = (OnlineListener *)info;
    id listenerDelegate = listener.delegate;
    if (theType == kCFSocketAcceptCallBack) {
        CFSocketNativeHandle nativeSocket = *(CFSocketNativeHandle *)data;
        uint8_t name[SOCK_MAXADDRLEN];
        socklen_t namelen = sizeof(name);
        NSData *peer = nil;
        if (getpeername(nativeSocket, (struct sockaddr *)name, &namelen) == 0) {
            peer = [NSData dataWithBytes:name length:namelen];
        }
        CFReadStreamRef readStream = NULL;
        CFWriteStreamRef writeStream = NULL;
        CFStreamCreatePairWithSocket(kCFAllocatorDefault, nativeSocket, &readStream,
            &writeStream);
        if (readStream && writeStream) {
            CFReadStreamSetProperty(readStream,
                kCFStreamPropertyShouldCloseNativeSocket, kCFBooleanTrue);
            CFWriteStreamSetProperty(writeStream,
                kCFStreamPropertyShouldCloseNativeSocket, kCFBooleanTrue);
            if (listenerDelegate && [listenerDelegate respondsToSelector:
                @selector(acceptedConnectionForListener:inputStream:outputStream:)]){
                [listenerDelegate acceptedConnectionForListener:listener
                    inputStream:(NSInputStream *)readStream
                    outputStream:(NSOutputStream *)writeStream];
            }
        } else {
            close(nativeSocket);
            if ([listenerDelegate
                respondsToSelector:@selector(onlineListener:encounteredError:)]) {
                NSError *error = [[NSError alloc]
                    initWithDomain:kOnlineListenerErrorDomain
                    code:kOnlineListenerErrorStreamError userInfo:nil];
                [listenerDelegate onlineListener:listener encounteredError:error];
                [error release];
            }
        }
        if (readStream) CFRelease(readStream);
        if (writeStream) CFRelease(writeStream);
    }
}

#pragma mark -
```

```objc
@implementation OnlineListener
@synthesize delegate;
@synthesize port;
#pragma mark -
#pragma mark Listener Methods
- (BOOL)startListening:(NSError **)error {
    CFSocketContext socketCtxt = {0, self, NULL, NULL, NULL};
    socket = CFSocketCreate(kCFAllocatorDefault, PF_INET, SOCK_STREAM, IPPROTO_TCP,
kCFSocketAcceptCallBack, (CFSocketCallBack)&onlineListenerAcceptCallback, &socketCtxt);

    if (socket == NULL) {
        if (error) *error = [[NSError alloc]
            initWithDomain:kOnlineListenerErrorDomain
            code:kOnlineListenerErrorNoSocketsAvailable
            userInfo:nil];
        return NO;
    }

    int ret = 1;
    setsockopt(CFSocketGetNative(socket), SOL_SOCKET, SO_REUSEADDR, (void *)&ret,
        sizeof(ret));

    struct sockaddr_in addr4;
    memset(&addr4, 0, sizeof(addr4));
    addr4.sin_len = sizeof(addr4);
    addr4.sin_family = AF_INET;
    addr4.sin_port = 0;
    addr4.sin_addr.s_addr = htonl(INADDR_ANY);
    NSData *address4 = [NSData dataWithBytes:&addr4 length:sizeof(addr4)];

    if (kCFSocketSuccess != CFSocketSetAddress(socket, (CFDataRef)address4)) {
        if (error) *error = [[NSError alloc]
            initWithDomain:kOnlineListenerErrorDomain
            code:kOnlineListenerErrorCouldntBindToAddress
            userInfo:nil];
        if (socket)
            CFRelease(socket);
        socket = NULL;
        return NO;
    }

    NSData *addr = [(NSData *)CFSocketCopyAddress(socket) autorelease];
    memcpy(&addr4, [addr bytes], [addr length]);
    self.port = ntohs(addr4.sin_port);

    CFRunLoopRef cfrl = CFRunLoopGetCurrent();
    CFRunLoopSourceRef source4 = CFSocketCreateRunLoopSource(kCFAllocatorDefault,
        socket, 0);
    CFRunLoopAddSource(cfrl, source4, kCFRunLoopCommonModes);
    CFRelease(source4);

    return ret;
}

- (void)stopListening {
    if (socket) {
        CFSocketInvalidate(socket);
```

```
        CFRelease(socket);
        socket = NULL;
    }
}

- (void)dealloc {
    [self stopListening];
    [super dealloc];
}

@end
```

We begin by importing some header files you may not have seen before. The first three are part of the old-school socket API. We need to include these because we use some of the constants and functions they contain when we set up our listener. We also import a CFNetwork header file used to retrieve streams from a CFSocket.

```
#include <sys/socket.h>
#include <netinet/in.h>
#include <unistd.h>
#include <CFNetwork/CFSocketStream.h>
```

Next, before our class implementation, we have a C function. This is our socket callback function that will be called whenever a connection attempt is detected.

```
static void onlineListenerAcceptCallback (CFSocketRef theSocket,
    CFSocketCallBackType theType, CFDataRef theAddress,
const void *data, void *info) {
```

Since this is a C function, it does not have access to Objective-C constructs such as self. So how do we access our delegate from within this function? When we created the socket, we created a socket context struct, and embedded a pointer to self in that struct. That embedded pointer is passed to this function as its last parameter, info. We'll cast that pointer to an instance of OnlineListener, which will give us access to the listener's delegate.

```
    OnlineListener *listener = (OnlineListener *)info;
    id listenerDelegate = listener.delegate;
```

Next, we make sure that we got the right type of callback. Although we registered to receive only one type of callback, we still want to code defensively. Remember that CFWriteStreamRef is toll-free bridged to NSOutputStream, and CFReadStreamRef is toll-free bridged to NSInputStream, so once we've created the stream pair, we pass them to the listener's delegate.

```
    if (theType == kCFSocketAcceptCallBack) {
```

Then we retrieve a stream pair that represents the connection that was made:

```
        CFSocketNativeHandle nativeSocket = *(CFSocketNativeHandle *)data;
        uint8_t name[SOCK_MAXADDRLEN];
        socklen_t namelen = sizeof(name);
        NSData *peer = nil;
        if (getpeername(nativeSocket, (struct sockaddr *)name, &namelen) == 0) {
            peer = [NSData dataWithBytes:name length:namelen];
        }
        CFReadStreamRef readStream = NULL;
```

```
            CFWriteStreamRef writeStream = NULL;
            CFStreamCreatePairWithSocket(kCFAllocatorDefault, nativeSocket, &readStream,
                &writeStream);
            if (readStream && writeStream) {
                CFReadStreamSetProperty(readStream,
                    kCFStreamPropertyShouldCloseNativeSocket, kCFBooleanTrue);
                CFWriteStreamSetProperty(writeStream,
                    kCFStreamPropertyShouldCloseNativeSocket, kCFBooleanTrue);
                if (listenerDelegate && [listenerDelegate respondsToSelector:
                    @selector(acceptedConnectionForListener:inputStream:outputStream:)]){
                    [listenerDelegate acceptedConnectionForListener:self
                        inputStream:inStream outputStream:outStream];
            } else {
```

If there was a problem, we close the socket and notify our delegate, assuming it has implemented the onlineListener:encounteredError: method.

```
            close(nativeSocket);
            if ([listenerDelegate
                respondsToSelector:@selector(onlineListener:encounteredError:)]) {
                NSError *error = [[NSError alloc]
                    initWithDomain:kOnlineListenerErrorDomain
                    code:kOnlineListenerErrorStreamError userInfo:nil];
                [listenerDelegate onlineListener:listener encounteredError:error];
                [error release];
            }
        }
```

When we're finished, we release both of the streams. CFRelease acts like release in Objective-C. It doesn't deallocate the object, but just decrements the object's retain count. It will be the delegate's responsibility to retain the streams if it's going to continue using them.

```
        if (readStream) CFRelease(readStream);
        if (writeStream) CFRelease(writeStream);
    }
}
```

The startListening: method goes through the process we described earlier to create and configure a socket, and register it with the run loop. If there's anything here that you're not comfortable with, go back and review the "Setting Up a Listener" section earlier in this chapter.

The next method is stopListening. All it needs to do is invalidate and release the socket.

```
- (void)stopListening {
    if (socket) {
        CFSocketInvalidate(socket);
        CFRelease(socket);
        socket = NULL;
    }
}
```

Creating the Peer Browser

Since we're not using GameKit when the user selects online play, we must implement our own controller class to display the available peers and to let the user select one of them. Our current controller class, `TicTacToeViewController`, will present this new view controller's view modally, which will add just a touch of complexity to our application. The new view controller class will create and be the delegate for an instance of `NSNetServiceBrowser`, but when the user selects a peer, it's actually `TicTacToeViewController` that will need to be the delegate for the resolved service, because the resolution will happen after the modal view has been dismissed.

Creating the Peer Browser Files

Create another new class, and just to shake things up, let's choose a different file template this time. Select *UIViewController subclass*, and make sure the *UITableViewController subclass* check box is not selected, but that the *With XIB for user interface box* is checked (Figure 9–4). Call this new file *OnlinePeerBrowser.m*, and have it create *OnlinePeerBrowser.h* also.

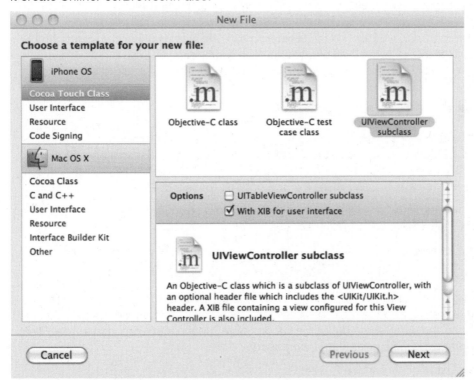

Figure 9–4. *When choosing the file template for creating the peer browser, you should select UIViewController subclass and also check the box labeled* With XIB for user interface.

After it creates the file, you should drag *OnlinePeerBrowser.xib* to the *Resources* folder in the *Groups & Files* pane where it belongs.

Writing the Peer Browser Header

Single-click *OnlinePeerBrowser.h* and replace the contents with the following:

```
#import <UIKit/UIKit.h>

@interface OnlinePeerBrowser : UIViewController
        <UITableViewDelegate, UITableViewDataSource> {

    UITableView          *tableView;
    NSNetServiceBrowser *netServiceBrowser;

    NSMutableArray       *discoveredServices;
}
@property (nonatomic, retain) IBOutlet UITableView *tableView;
@property (nonatomic, retain) NSNetServiceBrowser *netServiceBrowser;
@property (nonatomic, retain) NSMutableArray *discoveredServices;
- (IBAction)cancel;
@end
```

Everything here should be understandable. Because we need a toolbar with a *Cancel* button on it, we're not subclassing UITableViewController, but we will be using a table view, so we conform our class to both UITableViewDelegate and UITableViewDataSource. We have an outlet that will point to the table view, and an action method for the *Cancel* button on the toolbar to call. We also declare an instance of NSNetServiceBrowser, which will be used to search for peers, and a mutable array, called discoveredServices, which will be used to keep track of the found services.

Building the Peer Browser Interface

Double-click *OnlinePeerBrowser.xib* to open Interface Builder. Once it opens, drag a *Toolbar* from the library to the window labeled *View*, and place it snugly against the bottom of the window. Double-click the toolbar's one button to edit the button's title, and change it to say *Cancel*. Press return to commit the title change.

The toolbar button should still be selected. Control-drag from the button to *File's Owner*, and select the *cancel* action to connect the button to that action method.

Next, drag a *Table View* from the library over to the window. As you move it over the *View* window, it should automatically resize itself to the space available above the toolbar. Drop the table onto the view so it takes up the remainder of the space. Press ⌘1 to bring up the attribute inspector and change the table's *Style* to *Grouped*. Then control-drag twice from the table view to *File's Owner*, selecting the *delegate* outlet the first time and the *dataSource* outlet the second time. Now control-drag back from *File's Owner* to the table view and select the *tableView* outlet.

Save the nib and quit Interface Builder.

Implementing the Peer Browser View Controller

Single-click *OnlinePeerBrowser.m*. Replace the current contents of that file with the following:

> **CAUTION:** Do not try to build the project yet. The following code relies on some changes to `TicTacToeViewController` that we haven't made yet.

```objc
#import "OnlinePeerBrowser.h"
#import "TicTacToeViewController.h"

@implementation OnlinePeerBrowser
@synthesize tableView;
@synthesize netServiceBrowser;
@synthesize discoveredServices;

#pragma mark -
#pragma mark Action Methods
- (IBAction)cancel {
    [self.netServiceBrowser stop];
    self.netServiceBrowser.delegate = nil;
    self.netServiceBrowser = nil;

    [(TicTacToeViewController *)self.parentViewController browserCancelled];
}

#pragma mark -
#pragma mark Superclass Overrides
- (void)viewDidLoad {
    NSNetServiceBrowser *theBrowser = [[NSNetServiceBrowser alloc] init];
    theBrowser.delegate = self;

    [theBrowser searchForServicesOfType:kBonjourType inDomain:@""];
    self.netServiceBrowser = theBrowser;
    [theBrowser release];

    self.discoveredServices = [NSMutableArray array];

}

- (void)viewDidUnload {
    self.tableView = nil;
}

- (void)dealloc {
    [tableView release];
    if (netServiceBrowser != nil) {
        [self.netServiceBrowser stop];
        self.netServiceBrowser.delegate = nil;
    }
    [netServiceBrowser release];
    [discoveredServices release];
    [super dealloc];
}
```

```objc
#pragma mark -
#pragma mark Table View Methods
- (NSInteger)tableView:(UITableView *)theTableView
numberOfRowsInSection:(NSInteger)section {
    return [discoveredServices count];
}

- (NSString *)tableView:(UITableView *)theTableView
titleForHeaderInSection:(NSInteger)section {
    return NSLocalizedString(@"Available Peers", @"Available Peers");
}

- (UITableViewCell *)tableView:(UITableView *)theTableView
        cellForRowAtIndexPath:(NSIndexPath *)indexPath {
    static NSString *identifier = @"Browser Cell Identifier";

    UITableViewCell *cell = [tableView
        dequeueReusableCellWithIdentifier:identifier];
    if (cell == nil) {
        cell = [[[UITableViewCell alloc] initWithStyle:UITableViewCellStyleDefault
            reuseIdentifier:identifier] autorelease];
    }
    NSUInteger row = [indexPath row];
    cell.textLabel.text = [[discoveredServices objectAtIndex:row] name];
    return cell;
}

- (void)tableView:(UITableView *)theTableView
        didSelectRowAtIndexPath:(NSIndexPath *)indexPath {
    NSNetService *selectedService = [discoveredServices
        objectAtIndex:[indexPath row]];
    selectedService.delegate = self.parentViewController;
    [selectedService resolveWithTimeout:0.0];

    TicTacToeViewController *parent =
        (TicTacToeViewController *)self.parentViewController;
    parent.netService = selectedService;

    [self.netServiceBrowser stop];

    [self.parentViewController dismissModalViewControllerAnimated:YES];
}

#pragma mark -
#pragma mark Net Service Browser Delegate Methods
- (void)netServiceBrowserDidStopSearch:(NSNetServiceBrowser *)browser {
    self.netServiceBrowser.delegate = nil;
    self.netServiceBrowser = nil;
}

- (void)netServiceBrowser:(NSNetServiceBrowser *)browser
            didNotSearch:(NSDictionary *)errorDict {
    NSLog(@"Error browsing for service: %@", [errorDict
        objectForKey:NSNetServicesErrorCode]);
    [self.netServiceBrowser stop];
}
```

```objc
- (void)netServiceBrowser:(NSNetServiceBrowser *)browser
         didFindService:(NSNetService *)aNetService
             moreComing:(BOOL)moreComing {
    TicTacToeViewController *parent =
        (TicTacToeViewController *)self.parentViewController;
    if (![[parent.netService name] isEqualToString:[aNetService name]]){
        [discoveredServices addObject:aNetService];
        NSSortDescriptor *sd = [[NSSortDescriptor alloc]
            initWithKey:@"name" ascending:YES];
        [discoveredServices sortUsingDescriptors:[NSArray arrayWithObject:sd]];
        [sd release];
    }

    if(!moreComing)
        [self.tableView reloadData];
}

- (void)netServiceBrowser:(NSNetServiceBrowser *)browser
         didRemoveService:(NSNetService *)aNetService
             moreComing:(BOOL)moreComing {
    [discoveredServices removeObject:aNetService];

    if(!moreComing)
        [self.tableView reloadData];
}

@end
```

Most of this is stuff we've talked about before, but it's worth stepping through so you understand how we implemented this controller. The action method, `cancel`, stops the service browser from looking for Bonjour services, and then calls a method that we will write shortly on the parent view controller, which will be an instance of `TicTacToeViewController`. This method will dismiss the modal view controller and will reset the user interface so that the *New Game* button is available. Since no opponent was selected, the user should have the option to begin a new game.

```objc
- (IBAction)cancel {
    [self.netServiceBrowser stop];
    self.netServiceBrowser.delegate = nil;
    self.netServiceBrowser = nil;

    [(TicTacToeViewController *)self.parentViewController browserCancelled];
}
```

In `viewDidLoad`, we create an instance of `NSNetServiceBrowser` and tell it to start searching for services. We specify a constant called `kBonjourType`, which will contain the Bonjour type identifier for our tic-tac-toe game. We also create the mutable array instance that we'll use to keep track of discovered services and that will drive the table.

```objc
- (void)viewDidLoad {
    NSNetServiceBrowser *theBrowser = [[NSNetServiceBrowser alloc] init];
    theBrowser.delegate = self;

    [theBrowser searchForServicesOfType:kBonjourType inDomain:@""];
    self.netServiceBrowser = theBrowser;
```

```
    [theBrowser release];

    self.discoveredServices = [NSMutableArray array];
}
```

The viewDidUnload and dealloc methods are standard and shouldn't require any additional explanation. The first three table view methods are all standard as well. We have a table with a single section, and the row count for that section is dictated by the number of items in the discoveredServices array.

```
- (NSInteger)tableView:(UITableView *)theTableView
numberOfRowsInSection:(NSInteger)section {
    return [discoveredServices count];
}
```

We also return a header for the one section to inform the user what they're viewing.

```
- (NSString *)tableView:(UITableView *)theTableView
titleForHeaderInSection:(NSInteger)section {
    return NSLocalizedString(@"Available Peers", @"Available Peers");
}
```

The tableView:cellForRowAtIndexPath: method is also pretty much the same as many we've written in the past. It just displays the name of one of the discovered services in a cell using the default cell style.

```
- (UITableViewCell *)tableView:(UITableView *)theTableView
        cellForRowAtIndexPath:(NSIndexPath *)indexPath {
    static NSString *identifier = @"Browser Cell Identifier";

    UITableViewCell *cell = [tableView
        dequeueReusableCellWithIdentifier:identifier];
    if (cell == nil) {
        cell = [[[UITableViewCell alloc] initWithStyle:UITableViewCellStyleDefault
            reuseIdentifier:identifier] autorelease];
    }
    NSUInteger row = [indexPath row];
    cell.textLabel.text = [[discoveredServices objectAtIndex:row] name];
    return cell;
}
```

When the user taps a row, tableView:didSelectRowAtIndexPath: is called, and we need to resolve the selected service. When we do that, we don't specify self as the delegate of the net service that was selected. Instead, we specify our parent view controller, which is the view controller that presented our view modally. In our application, that will be TicTacToeViewController, so when the net service resolves, TicTacToeViewController will be notified. This is a good thing, because after that, we stop the browser (we support only one peer in this game) and dismiss the modally presented view controller, meaning this instance won't be around to be notified when the service is resolved.

```
- (void)tableView:(UITableView *)theTableView
didSelectRowAtIndexPath:(NSIndexPath *)indexPath {

    NSNetService *selectedService = [discoveredServices
        objectAtIndex:[indexPath row]];
```

```
    selectedService.delegate = self.parentViewController;
    [selectedService resolveWithTimeout:0.0];

    TicTacToeViewController *parent =
        (TicTacToeViewController *)self.parentViewController;
    parent.netService = selectedService;

    [self.netServiceBrowser stop];

    [self.parentViewController dismissModalViewControllerAnimated:YES];
}
```

Next up are the `NSNetServiceBrowser` delegate methods. When we're notified that a search stopped, we set the browser's delegate to `nil` and release it by assigning `nil` to the `netServiceBrowser` property.

```
- (void)netServiceBrowserDidStopSearch:(NSNetServiceBrowser *)browser {
    self.netServiceBrowser.delegate = nil;
    self.netServiceBrowser = nil;
}
```

If we are notified that the browser wasn't able to search, we log the error and stop the search. In a shipping application, you would probably also want to notify the user of the error. In the interest of not making this chapter any longer than it already is, we opted to just log it here, because this shouldn't be a very common occurrence; if it does happen, the user just won't see any peers, which is hardly catastrophic.

```
- (void)netServiceBrowser:(NSNetServiceBrowser *)browser
           didNotSearch:(NSDictionary *)errorDict {
    NSLog(@"Error browsing for service: %@", [errorDict
        objectForKey:NSNetServicesErrorCode]);
    [self.netServiceBrowser stop];
}
```

When the browser finds a service, it will call the next method. When that happens, we first check to make sure the service that was found wasn't the one that our parent view controller published. If it wasn't, then we add it to the array. If there are no more services coming, we reload the table so the user will see the new services in the view.

```
- (void)netServiceBrowser:(NSNetServiceBrowser *)browser
           didFindService:(NSNetService *)aNetService
              moreComing:(BOOL)moreComing {
    TicTacToeViewController *parent =
        (TicTacToeViewController *)self.parentViewController;
    if (![[parent.netService name] isEqualToString:[aNetService name]]){
        [discoveredServices addObject:aNetService];
        NSSortDescriptor *sd = [[NSSortDescriptor alloc]
            initWithKey:@"name" ascending:YES];
        [discoveredServices sortUsingDescriptors:[NSArray arrayWithObject:sd]];
        [sd release];
    }

    if(!moreComing)
        [self.tableView reloadData];
}
```

When we are notified that a service has become unavailable, we remove it from the array. Again, if there are no more services coming, we reload the table so the user sees the change.

```
- (void)netServiceBrowser:(NSNetServiceBrowser *)browser
        didRemoveService:(NSNetService *)aNetService
              moreComing:(BOOL)moreComing {
    [discoveredServices removeObject:aNetService];

    if(!moreComing)
        [self.tableView reloadData];
}

@end
```

Okay, save *OnlinePeerBrowser.m*.

We have just one last step to get online play working in our game, but it's a somewhat complicated step. We need to update TicTacToeViewController to use these new objects we've created when the user chooses online play.

Updating TicTacToeViewController to Support Online Play

Single-click *TicTacToeViewController.h* so we can make the changes necessary to support online play. Add the bold code shown here to your existing file.

```
#import <UIKit/UIKit.h>
#import <GameKit/GameKit.h>
#import "OnlineSession.h"
#import "OnlineListener.h"

#define kTicTacToeSessionID      @"com.apress.TicTacToe.session"
#define kTicTacToeArchiveKey     @"com.apress.TicTacToe"
#define kBonjourType             @"_tictactoe._tcp."

typedef enum GameStates {
    kGameStateBeginning,
    kGameStateRollingDice,
    kGameStateMyTurn,
    kGameStateOpponentTurn,
    kGameStateInterrupted,
    kGameStateDone
} GameState;

typedef enum BoardSpaces {
    kUpperLeft = 1000, kUpperMiddle, kUpperRight,
    kMiddleLeft, kMiddleMiddle, kMiddleRight,
    kLowerLeft, kLowerMiddle, kLowerRight
} BoardSpace;

typedef enum PlayerPieces {
    kPlayerPieceUndecided,
    kPlayerPieceO,
    kPlayerPieceX
} PlayerPiece;
```

```objc
@class TicTacToePacket;
@interface TicTacToeViewController : UIViewController
    <GKPeerPickerControllerDelegate, GKSessionDelegate, UIAlertViewDelegate
    , OnlineSessionDelegate, OnlineListenerDelegate>
{
    UIButton    *newGameButton;
    UILabel     *feedbackLabel;

    GKSession   *session;
    NSString    *peerID;

    GameState   state;

    NSInteger   myDieRoll;
    NSInteger   opponentDieRoll;

    PlayerPiece piece;
    UIImage     *xPieceImage;
    UIImage     *oPieceImage;

    BOOL        dieRollReceived;
    BOOL        dieRollAcknowledged;

    // Online Play
    NSNetService    *netService;
    OnlineSession   *onlineSession;
    OnlineListener  *onlineSessionListener;

}
@property(nonatomic, retain) IBOutlet UIButton *newGameButton;
@property(nonatomic, retain) IBOutlet UILabel *feedbackLabel;

@property(nonatomic, retain) GKSession      *session;
@property(nonatomic, copy) NSString         *peerID;

@property GameState state;

@property(nonatomic, retain) UIImage *xPieceImage;
@property(nonatomic, retain) UIImage *oPieceImage;

@property (nonatomic, retain) NSNetService      *netService;
@property (nonatomic, retain) OnlineSession     *onlineSession;
@property (nonatomic, retain) OnlineListener    *onlineSessionListener;

- (IBAction)newGameButtonPressed;
- (IBAction)gameSpacePressed:(id)sender;
- (void)resetBoard;
- (void)startNewGame;
- (void)resetDieState;
- (void)sendPacket:(TicTacToePacket *)packet;
- (void)sendDieRoll;
- (void)checkForGameEnd;
- (void)handleReceivedData:(NSData *)data;
- (void)browserCancelled;
@end
```

Most of the new code is self-explanatory. We declared a constant that is a valid Bonjour type identifier for our game. That identifier is used both when we publish our service and when we search for other services. We also conform our class to the two protocols used by `OnlineSession` and `OnlineListener` for their delegates, and we add instance variables to hold an instance of those two classes. The former will be used to communicate with the other peer if we're in online play; the other will be used to listen for connections when we want to start a new game.

We also added two new methods. One is used by the `OnlinePeerBrowser` class and is called when the user presses the *Cancel* button. The other requires a little bit of explanation. In our original version of the app, we had a `switch` statement right in the data receive handler used by GameKit to inform us that there was received data. In order to avoid duplicating the logic that handles those received packets now that we have two potential sources of data, we're going to move the logic to its own method, which will then be called both from GameKit's data receive handler, as well as from the data receive handler for our online session object.

Save *TicTacToeViewController.h*.

Now, switch over to *TicTacToeViewController.m*. At the top of the file, add the bold code shown here.

```objc
#import "TicTacToeViewController.h"
#import "TicTacToePacket.h"
#import "OnlinePeerBrowser.h"

@interface TicTacToeViewController()
- (void)showErrorAlertWithTitle:(NSString *)title message:(NSString *)message;
@end

@implementation TicTacToeViewController
#pragma mark -
#pragma mark Synthesized Properties
@synthesize newGameButton;
@synthesize feedbackLabel;
@synthesize session;
@synthesize peerID;
@synthesize state;
@synthesize xPieceImage;
@synthesize oPieceImage;

@synthesize netService;
@synthesize onlineSession;
@synthesize onlineSessionListener;

#pragma mark -
#pragma mark Private Methods
- (void)showErrorAlertWithTitle:(NSString *)alertTitle message:(NSString *)message {
    UIAlertView *alert = [[UIAlertView alloc] initWithTitle:alertTitle
        message:message delegate:self
        cancelButtonTitle:NSLocalizedString(@"Bummer", @"Bummer")
        otherButtonTitles:nil];
    [alert show];
```

```
    [alert release];
}

#pragma mark -
#pragma mark Game-Specific Methods
- (IBAction)newGameButtonPressed {
...
```

Because we're going to be creating instances of OnlinePeerBrowser, we need to import its header. We also use an Objective-C extension to declare a new private method for showing error alerts. In the previous version of our app, we showed alerts in only a handful of places. We'll add another handful to support errors encountered during online play, and that means we are now going to have that same task, which requires multiple lines of code, in many different places. By creating a method that displays an alert, we can replace several lines of code in multiple places in our class with a one-line call to this method.

Next, look for the existing method called newGameButtonPressed. We're still going to use the peer picker, but we need to tell it that we're also supporting online play. Add the following code to the newGameButtonPressed method to do that:

```
- (IBAction)newGameButtonPressed {

    dieRollReceived = NO;
    dieRollAcknowledged = NO;

    newGameButton.hidden = YES;
    GKPeerPickerController*    picker;

    picker = [[GKPeerPickerController alloc] init];
    picker.delegate = self;

    picker.connectionTypesMask = GKPeerPickerConnectionTypeOnline |
                                 GKPeerPickerConnectionTypeNearby;
    [picker show];
}
```

> **CAUTION:** Currently, GameKit can be used only if you are offering *Nearby* play. Offering *Online* play is optional with the peer picker, but offering *Nearby* is not optional. If you attempt to set the picker's connectionTypesMask without including GKPeerPickerConnectionTypeNearby, you will get an error at runtime.

Scroll down now to just after the checkForGameEnd method but before the viewDidLoad method. We need to add those two new methods we declared in our header, and this is a good place to do it. Add the two new methods in bold after the existing checkForGameEnd method, like so:

```
    if (state == kGameStateDone)
        [self performSelector:@selector(startNewGame) withObject:nil
        afterDelay:3.0];
}
```

```objc
- (void)handleReceivedData:(NSData *)data {

    NSKeyedUnarchiver *unarchiver = [[NSKeyedUnarchiver alloc]
        initForReadingWithData:data];
    TicTacToePacket *packet = [unarchiver decodeObjectForKey:kTicTacToeArchiveKey];

    switch (packet.type) {
        case kPacketTypeDieRoll:
            opponentDieRoll = packet.dieRoll;
            TicTacToePacket *ack = [[TicTacToePacket alloc]
                initAckPacketWithDieRoll:opponentDieRoll];
            [self sendPacket:ack];
            [ack release];
            dieRollReceived = YES;
            break;
        case kPacketTypeAck:
            if (packet.dieRoll != myDieRoll) {
                NSLog(@"Ack packet doesn't match opponentDieRoll (mine: %d, ↩
send: %d", packet.dieRoll, myDieRoll);
            }
            dieRollAcknowledged = YES;
            break;
        case kPacketTypeMove:{
            UIButton *theButton = (UIButton *)[self.view viewWithTag:packet.space];
            [theButton setImage:(piece == kPlayerPieceO) ? xPieceImage : oPieceImage
                forState:UIControlStateNormal];
            state = kGameStateMyTurn;
            feedbackLabel.text = NSLocalizedString(@"Your Turn", @"Your Turn");
            [self checkForGameEnd];
        }
            break;
        case kPacketTypeReset:
            if (state == kGameStateDone)
                [self resetDieState];
        default:
            break;
    }

    if (dieRollReceived == YES && dieRollAcknowledged == YES)
        [self startGame];
}

- (void)browserCancelled {
    [self dismissModalViewControllerAnimated:YES];
    newGameButton.hidden = NO;
    feedbackLabel.text = @"";
}
#pragma mark -
#pragma mark Superclass Overrides

- (void)viewDidLoad {
...
```

Now look for the existing method called sendPacket: and delete it. We're going to replace it with a new version that can send over either a GKSession instance or an OnlineSession instance. Because the new sendPacket: is no longer a GameKit-specific method, we should put this version above viewDidLoad. Insert this new version of sendPacket: above viewDidLoad, directly below the two methods you just added.

> **CAUTION:** It's very important that you delete the old version of the sendPacket: method. You cannot have two copies of the same method in a class. If you fail to delete the old one, you will get a compile error.

```
- (void) sendPacket:(TicTacToePacket *)packet {

    NSMutableData *data = [[NSMutableData alloc] init];
    NSKeyedArchiver *archiver = [[NSKeyedArchiver alloc]
        initForWritingWithMutableData:data];
    [archiver encodeObject:packet forKey:kTicTacToeArchiveKey];
    [archiver finishEncoding];

    NSError *error = nil;

    if (session) {
        if (![session sendDataToAllPeers:data withDataMode:GKSendDataReliable
            error:&error]) {
            // You will do real error handling
            NSLog(@"Error sending data: %@", [error localizedDescription]);
        }
    }else {
        if (![onlineSession sendData:data error:&error]) {
            // Ditto
            NSLog(@"Error sending data: %@", [error localizedDescription]);
        }
    }
    [archiver release];
    [data release];
}
```

The only real difference here is that we check to see if session, which is the GameKit session, is nil. If it's not nil, then we send data using it. If it is nil, we know we're in online play, and we must use onlineSession.

Scroll down some more. If you typed your code exactly the way it appeared in the previous chapter, you should have a #pragma line that identifies when the peer picker delegate methods start. It should look something like this:

```
#pragma mark -
#pragma mark GameKit Peer Picker Delegate Methods
```

Right after that, we need to add another method. If you don't have that #pragma line, then just search for the first method that takes an instance of GKPeerPickercontroller * as an argument, and add the new method before that method.

The peer picker has a delegate method called peerPickerController:didSelect ConnectionType:. We didn't need to implement this method in the previous chapter because we supported only one connection type. If, as we've now done, we tell the peer picker to offer online play, when users make their choice, it will call this delegate method to inform us about which option was selected. If *Online* was selected, we need to dismiss the peer picker and take over manually. If *Nearby* was selected, we don't need to do anything. Add the following new method to handle online play:

```
- (void)peerPickerController:(GKPeerPickerController *)picker
        didSelectConnectionType:(GKPeerPickerConnectionType)type {
    if (type == GKPeerPickerConnectionTypeOnline) {
        picker.delegate = nil;
        [picker dismiss];
        [picker autorelease];

        OnlineListener *theListener = [[OnlineListener alloc] init];
        self.onlineSessionListener = theListener;
        theListener.delegate = self;
        [theListener release];

        NSError *error;
        if (![onlineSessionListener startListening:&error]) {
            [self showErrorAlertWithTitle:NSLocalizedString(
                @"Error starting listener", @"Error starting listener")
                message:NSLocalizedString(
                @"Unable to start online play", @"Unable to start")];
        }

        NSNetService *theService = [[NSNetService alloc] initWithDomain:@""
            type:kBonjourType name:@"" port:onlineSessionListener.port];
        self.netService = theService;
        [theService release];

        [self.netService scheduleInRunLoop:[NSRunLoop currentRunLoop]
            forMode:NSRunLoopCommonModes];
        [self.netService setDelegate:self];
        [self.netService publish];


        OnlinePeerBrowser *controller = [[OnlinePeerBrowser alloc]
            initWithNibName:@"OnlinePeerBrowser" bundle:nil];
        [self presentModalViewController:controller animated:YES];
        [controller release];
    }
}
```

After we dismiss the peer picker, we create and start an instance of `OnlineListener`, which will start listening for connections. We then start advertising our listener using Bonjour. After we do that, we create an instance of `OnlinePeerBrowser` and present it modally so the user can choose who to play against online, if more than one peer is available.

Down a little further in the file, there should be a method called `session:didFailWithError:`. We can shorten that method by a few lines, courtesy of our snazzy new error alert method, like so:

```
- (void)session:(GKSession *)theSession didFailWithError:(NSError *)error {
    UIAlertView *alert = [[UIAlertView alloc] initWithTitle:
        NSLocalizedString(@"Error Connecting!", @"Error Connecting!")
```

```
          message:NSLocalizedString(@"Unable to establish the connection.",
          @"Unable to establish the connection.")
          delegate:self
          cancelButtonTitle:NSLocalizedString(@"Bummer", @"Bummer")
          otherButtonTitles:nil];
    [alert show];
    [alert release];
    [self showErrorAlertWithTitle:NSLocalizedString(@"Peer Disconnected!",
        @"Peer Disconnected!") message:NSLocalizedString(
        @"Your opponent has disconnected, or the connection has been lost",
        @"Your opponent has disconnected, or the connection has been lost")];
    theSession.available = NO;
    [theSession disconnectFromAllPeers];
    theSession.delegate = nil;
    [theSession setDataReceiveHandler:nil withContext:nil];
    self.session = nil;
}
```

There are several other places in the existing code where you can make the same change. We're not going to show you every one, and it won't hurt anything to leave them as they are. But if you want to shorten your code, you can replace any of the existing code that shows an alert with a call to our new alert method.

Next, look for a method called `receiveData:fromPeer:inSession:context:`. It should be in with your other GameKit methods (you can just use the function pop-up to navigate to it). This method currently contains the logic to handle a packet received from the peer. Since we've moved this logic into `handleReceivedData:`, we can trim out the logic and replace it with a single call:

```
- (void)receiveData:(NSData *)data fromPeer:(NSString *)peer
    inSession: (GKSession *)theSession context:(void *)context {
    [self handleReceivedData:data];
}
```

Now, scroll down to the bottom of the file. We need to add a few delegate methods for NSNetService to handle resolving discovered services. We also need to add the delegate methods for `OnlineSession` and `OnlineListener`. We have a bunch of new methods to add. We're going to add a few methods at a time and then explain them, but all of the code from here until the end of the chapter should go at the end of the file, directly above the @end declaration.

First up are the delegate methods that are called when a net service failed to publish or when it is stopped. If the service couldn't publish, we throw up an error alert. When the service stops, we set its delegate to nil and release it.

```
#pragma mark -
#pragma mark Net Service Delegate Methods (Publishing)
- (void)netService:(NSNetService *)theNetService
    didNotPublish:(NSDictionary *)errorDict {
    NSNumber *errorDomain = [errorDict valueForKey:NSNetServicesErrorDomain];
    NSNumber *errorCode = [errorDict valueForKey:NSNetServicesErrorCode];
    [self showErrorAlertWithTitle:NSLocalizedString(@"Unable to connect",
        @"Unable to connect") message:[NSString
        stringWithFormat:NSLocalizedString(
        @"Unable to publish Bonjour service(%@/%@)",
```

```
        @"Unable to publish Bonjour service(%@/%@)"), errorDomain, errorCode] ];

    [theNetService stop];
}

- (void)netServiceDidStop:(NSNetService *)netService {
    self.netService.delegate = nil;
    self.netService = nil;
}
```

Next up is an `NSNetService` delegate that is called whenever an error is encountered. This is called if an error is encountered either with publishing a service or resolving one. All we do is show an alert.

```
#pragma mark -
#pragma mark Net Service Delegate Methods (General)
- (void)handleError:(NSNumber *)error withService:(NSNetService *)service {
    [self showErrorAlertWithTitle:NSLocalizedString(@"A network error occurred.",
        @"A network error occurred.") message:[NSString stringWithFormat:
        NSLocalizedString(
        @"An error occurred with service %@.%@.%@, error code = %@",
        @"An error occurred with service %@.%@.%@, error code = %@"),
        [service name], [service type], [service domain], error]];
}
```

There are two delegate methods related to resolving discovered services: one is called if the service could not be resolved, and one is called if it resolves successfully. If it fails to resolve, we just show an alert and stop trying to resolve the service.

```
#pragma mark -
#pragma mark Net Service Delegate Methods (Resolving)
- (void)netService:(NSNetService *)sender didNotResolve:(NSDictionary *)errorDict {

    NSNumber *errorDomain = [errorDict valueForKey:NSNetServicesErrorDomain];
    NSNumber *errorCode = [errorDict valueForKey:NSNetServicesErrorCode];
    [self showErrorAlertWithTitle:NSLocalizedString(@"Unable to connect",
        @"Unable to connect") message:[NSString stringWithFormat:
        NSLocalizedString(@"Could not start game with remote device (%@/%@)",
        @"Could not start game with remote device (%@/%@)"), errorDomain,
        errorCode] ];
    [sender stop];
}
```

If it resolved successfully, then we stop listening for new connections and get the stream pair for the connection. If we're not able to get the stream pair, we show an error alert; otherwise, we create an `OnlineSession` object with the stream pair.

```
- (void)netServiceDidResolveAddress:(NSNetService *)service {

    [self.onlineSessionListener stopListening];
    self.onlineSessionListener = nil;

    NSInputStream *tempIn = nil;
    NSOutputStream *tempOut = nil;
    if (![service getInputStream:&tempIn outputStream:&tempOut]){
        [self showErrorAlertWithTitle:NSLocalizedString(@"Unable to connect",
            @"Unable to connect") message:NSLocalizedString(
            @"Could not start game with remote device",
```

```
                    @"Could not start game with remote device") ];
            return;
        }

        OnlineSession *theSession = [[OnlineSession alloc]
            initWithInputStream:tempIn outputStream:tempOut];
        theSession.delegate = self;
        self.onlineSession = theSession;
        [theSession release];
}
```

When an `OnlineListener` detects a connection, it notifies its delegate. In that case, we also create an `OnlineSession` object with the stream pair we got from the listener.

```
#pragma mark -
#pragma mark Online Session Listener Delegate Methods
- (void) acceptedConnectionForListener:(OnlineListener *)theListener
                        inputStream:(NSInputStream *)theInputStream
                        outputStream:(NSOutputStream *)theOutputStream {
    OnlineSession *theSession = [[OnlineSession alloc]
        initWithInputStream:theInputStream outputStream:theOutputStream];
    theSession.delegate = self;
    self.onlineSession = theSession;

    [theSession release];
}
```

Our `OnlineSession` object, regardless of whether it was created by resolving a service or by accepting a connection from another machine, will call `onlineSessionReadyForUse:` when both streams are open. In this method, we check to see if we're still presenting a modal view controller, which would be the case if we received a connection from another machine; if so, we dismiss it. Then we start a new game.

```
#pragma mark -
#pragma mark Online Session Delegate Methods
- (void)onlineSessionReadyForUse:(OnlineSession *)session {
    if (self.modalViewController)
        [self dismissModalViewControllerAnimated:YES];

    [self startNewGame];
}
```

When we receive data from the `OnlineSession`, all we need to do is pass that on to the `handleReceivedData:` method.

```
- (void)onlineSession:(OnlineSession *)session receivedData:(NSData *)data {
    [self handleReceivedData:data];
}
```

If any of the three `OnlineSessionDelegate` error methods are called, we throw up an error alert and kill the session.

```
- (void)onlineSession:(OnlineSession *)session
  encounteredReadError:(NSError *)error {
    [self showErrorAlertWithTitle:NSLocalizedString(@"Error reading",
        @"Error Reading") message:NSLocalizedString(@"Could not read sent packet",
        @"Could not read sent packet")];
    self.onlineSession = nil;
```

```
}
- (void)onlineSession:(OnlineSession *)session
    encounteredWriteError:(NSError *)error {
    [self showErrorAlertWithTitle:NSLocalizedString(@"Error Writing",
        @"Error Writing") message:NSLocalizedString(@"Could not send packet",
        @"Could not send packet")];
    self.onlineSession = nil;
}
- (void)onlineSessionDisconnected:(OnlineSession *)session {
    [self showErrorAlertWithTitle:NSLocalizedString(@"Peer Disconnected",
        @"Peer Disconnected") message:NSLocalizedString(
        @"Your opponent disconnected or otherwise could not be reached.",
        @"Your opponent disconnected or otherwise could not be reached")];
    self.onlineSession = nil;
}
@end
```

WHAT ABOUT INTERNET PLAY?

If you want to offer play over the Internet, the process is almost exactly the same. You still need to listen on a port, and you still use streams to exchange data with the remote machine. Generally speaking, you do not use Bonjour to advertise services over the Internet, though. Typically, a dedicated server will be used to find opponents or, more rarely, users will be asked to type in the address and port to which they want to connect.

To find out more about getting a stream connection to a remote machine based on DNS name or IP address and port, you should read Tech Note QA1652, which is available at `http://developer.apple.com/iphone/library/qa/qa2009/qa1652.html`.

Time to Play

And with that marathon of changes, we have now implemented online play in our TicTacToe application. You can select **Build and Run** from the **Build** menu to try it out. About time, huh?

Online play is significantly more complex to implement than GameKit over Bluetooth, but there's good news. The `OnlineSession` and `OnlineListener` objects we just wrote are completely generic. Copy them to a new project, and you can use them unchanged. That means your next application that needs to support network play will be almost as easy to write as it would be to use GameKit.

Before we leave the topic of networking completely, we have one more chapter of network goodness for you. We're going to show you a variety of ways to retrieve information from web servers and RESTful web services.

Chapter 10

Working with Data from the Web

As you saw in the last chapter, writing code to communicate over a network can be complex and, at times, difficult. Fortunately, for many common network-related tasks, Apple has provided higher-level methods and objects that will make your life considerably easier. One fairly common task when you're writing software for a device that's pretty much always connected to the Internet is to retrieve data from web servers. There is a large amount of data available for applications to use on the World Wide Web, and there are countless reasons why an iPhone application might want to pull data from the Web.

> **NOTE:** The applications we're writing in this chapter will work just fine on the simulator. But, as you might expect, since those applications will be retrieving data from the Web, they'll only work if the computer on which the simulator is running has an active connection to the Internet.

There are a number of techniques you can use to grab data from web servers. In this chapter, we're going to show you three of them. We'll first show you how to leverage special methods that exist in several Foundation classes that allow you to retrieve data based on a URL in just a line or two of code. We'll expand on that and show you how to take more control over the process so that you can detect when errors occur. Next, we'll show you how to pull data asynchronously, so your application can do other things while data is being retrieved in the background. And finally, we'll learn how to make different types of HTTP requests and pass form parameters so you can retrieve data from web applications and web services as well as static files.

Since each of these topics stands alone, we'll build our chapter application-iteratively. We'll discuss one type of retrieval, then add it to the application.

We'll start by setting up an application skeleton. Next, we'll add URL-based methods to retrieve both an image and text from the Web. Then we'll talk about doing a more robust form of data retrieval, and then add code to our application to retrieve the same image and text file using that approach. After that, we'll talk about asynchronous data retrieval and then add code to our application to retrieve the text and image in the background. You can look at Figure 10–1 to see what our application will look like when done.

Figure 10–1. *One of the two applications we'll build in this chapter The top row of buttons will retrieve an image file from a web server in one of three different ways. The bottom row of buttons will retrieve a text document in one of three different ways.*

Once we're done with those different ways of retrieving static data, we'll move on to forms and various HTTP request types. Then we will build another small application that uses both kinds of form parameters and two different request types (Figure 10–2).

Figure 10–2. *The second application we're going to build in this chapter shows how to change the request type and how to pass form parameters*

Setting Up the Application Skeleton

We're going to start by creating an application skeleton with **stub methods** for each of the tasks that we're going to implement in the first application. A stub method (sometimes referred to as just a **stub**) is typically an empty method, or one with only one or two lines of code designed to act as a placeholder for a method that you plan to add later. This allows you to set up your user interface before you're ready to write the code behind it. As we discuss the different ways to retrieve data, we will add code to these stubs.

In Xcode, create a new project, select the *View-based Application* template, and call the new project *WebWork*. Once the project is open, find the project archives that accompany this book and look in the *10 – WebWork* folder for the images called *blue_get.png*, *green_get.png*, *lavender_get.png*, *text.png*, and *image.png* and add them all to your project. These are the images you'll need for the buttons as well as the text and image icons that appear to the left of the buttons in Figure 10–1.

Declaring Actions and Outlets

Single-click on *WebWorkViewController.h* so we can add our outlet and action declarations. Replace the existing contents with the following code:

```objc
#import <UIKit/UIKit.h>

#define kImageURL    @"http://iphonedevbook.com/more/10/cover.png"
#define kTextURL     @"http://iphonedevbook.com/more/10/text.txt"

typedef enum RequestTypes {
    kRequestTypeImage,
    kRequestTypeText,
} RequestType;

@interface WebWorkViewController : UIViewController {
    UIActivityIndicatorView *spinner;
    UIImageView             *imageView;
    UITextView              *textView;

    NSMutableData           *receivedData;
    RequestType             requestType;
}

@property (nonatomic, retain) IBOutlet UIActivityIndicatorView *spinner;
@property (nonatomic, retain) IBOutlet UIImageView *imageView;
@property (nonatomic, retain) IBOutlet UITextView *textView;
@property (nonatomic, retain) NSMutableData *receivedData;

- (void)clear;

- (IBAction)getImageUsingNSData;
- (IBAction)getImageSynchronously;
- (IBAction)getImageAsynchronously;

- (IBAction)getTextUsingNSString;
- (IBAction)getTextSynchronously;
- (IBAction)getTextAsynchronously;
@end
```

We start off by defining two constants that point to an image file and a text file that we've hosted on the Internet for your use. This is the data that we'll be pulling into our application. Feel free to use different URLs if you prefer.

```objc
#define kImageURL    @"http://iphonedevbook.com/more/10/cover.png"
#define kTextURL     @"http://iphonedevbook.com/more/10/text.txt"
```

Next, we define a new type along with an enum. In some parts of our code, we will be using delegate methods (surprise!), and we will need a way to know in one of those delegate methods whether the data being we're retrieving holds an image or text. While there are ways to determine that from the web server's response (which we'll see later in the chapter), just keeping track of which we've requested is a lot easier and more efficient.

```objc
typedef enum RequestTypes {
    kRequestTypeImage,
    kRequestTypeText,
} RequestType;
```

We have three views that we'll need outlets to so that we can show the returned data. The UIImageView will be used to show the retrieved image, the UITextView will be used to display the retrieved text, and the `UIActivityIndicatorView` is that white spinning doohickey that tells the user that some action is in progress (you'll know it when you see it). When we retrieve the data asynchronously, we'll show the activity indicator so that the user knows we're in the process of retrieving the data they requested. Once we have the data, we'll hide the activity indicator and show the image or text that was requested.

```
@interface WebWorkViewController : UIViewController {
    UIActivityIndicatorView *spinner;
    UIImageView             *imageView;
    UITextView              *textView;
```

We also declare an instance of `NSMutableData` that will be used to store the data when fetching asynchronously. When we do that, a delegate method that we will implement will be called repeatedly and provided with small chunks of the requested data. We will accumulate those chunks in this instance so that when the process is complete, we'll have the whole image or text file.

```
    NSMutableData           *receivedData;
```

And, here's where we'll keep track of whether an image or text was last requested.

```
    RequestType             requestType;
```

We also declare properties for our instance variables, using the `IBOutlet` keyword for those that will need to be connected to objects in Interface Builder.

```
@property (nonatomic, retain) IBOutlet UIActivityIndicatorView *spinner;
@property (nonatomic, retain) IBOutlet UIImageView *imageView;
@property (nonatomic, retain) IBOutlet UITextView *textView;
@property (nonatomic, retain) NSMutableData *receivedData;
```

And then we have our methods. The first one is just used to clear the requested data so that the application can be used again without restarting.

```
- (void)clear;
```

And we have six action methods, one for each of the buttons you can see in Figure 10–1. Since each button represents a different way to retrieve one kind of data, it makes sense to give each of the buttons its own action method.

```
- (IBAction)getImageUsingNSData;
- (IBAction)getImageSynchronously;
- (IBAction)getImageAsynchronously;

- (IBAction)getTextUsingNSString;
- (IBAction)getTextSynchronously;
- (IBAction)getTextAsynchronously;
```

Designing the Interface

Now that we have our actions and outlets in place, make sure you save first, then double-click *WebWorkViewController.xib* to open up the file in Interface Builder.

Let's start off by dragging an *Image View* from the library over to the window labeled *View*. Interface Builder will resize the image view to take up the whole window, which isn't what we want this time, so press ⌘3 to bring up the size inspector, change the *X* and *Y* value each to 20, set *W* to 280, and set *H* to 255.

Then, control-drag from *File's Owner* to the image view and select the *imageView* outlet. Press ⌘1 and use the attribute inspector to change the *Mode* from *Center* to *Aspect Fit* so that the image will be resized to fit.

Now, drag a *Text View* from the library to the *View* window. Place it in exactly the same location as the image view and make it exactly the same size. Once it's placed, control-drag from *File's Owner* to the text view and select the *textView* outlet. Double-click the text view so that the text it contains is editable, make sure all the text is selected, and hit the delete button. In the attribute inspector, uncheck the box that says *Editable* so that our user can't change the downloaded text.

In the library, look for an *Activity Indicator View* and drag one to the *View* window. Use the blue guidelines to line it up with the horizontal and vertical centers of the text and image views you already added. Then, control-drag from *File's Owner* to the activity indicator and select the *spinner* outlet. Press ⌘1 to bring up the attribute inspector and check *Hide When Stopped* so that when the indicator is not spinning, it won't be visible.

Now, drag another *Image View* to the view. Place it somewhere in the bottom half of the screen; the exact placement doesn't matter for now. Press ⌘1and use the attribute inspector to select the *text.png* for the *Image* field. Press ⌘= to resize the image view to match the image, then place the resized image view in the lower-left of the window, using the blue guidelines to place it against the bottom and left margins.

Bring over another *Image View* and select *image.png* for its image. Use ⌘= to resize the image view and then place it above the image view you placed a moment ago, using Figure 10–1 as a guide.

Next, bring over a *Round Rect Button* from the library, and use the size inspector (⌘3) to change both the height and width of the button to 57 pixels. Place the button to the right of the *image.png* image view. Now, use the attributes inspector to change the button's type from *Rounded Rect* to *Custom* and select *blue_get.png* from the Image pop-up. Option-drag the button to the right to create a second one, then repeat to create a third button. Change the image of the second button to *green_get.png* and change the image of the third button to *lavender_get.png*. Finally, select all three buttons and option-drag them to create three new buttons below the first set of buttons. Use Figure 10–1 as a guide to help you place everything just so.

Now, bring over a *Label* over from the library, and place it above the left-most button, the blue one. Change the font size to 14 points (you can change the font size using the fonts palette ⌘T) and change the text to *Object*. Now option-drag the label to create a second and third copy, placing one above the second and third column of buttons. Change the second label to read *Sync*, and the third label to read *Async*. Again, use Figure 10–1 as a guide.

Now, control-drag from all six of the buttons to *File's Owner* and select the action methods that match the button's position. For the top-left button, for example, you should select *getImageUsingNSData*, and for the bottom-left button you should select *getTextUsingNSString*. Once you have connected all six buttons to the appropriate action method, save the nib and head back to Xcode.

Implementing the Stubs

Now we're going to write our implementation file, but aren't going to write any of the actual code to retrieve the data yet. We're just putting in placeholders so we have a place to add the code later in the chapter. Single-click *WebWorkViewController.m* and replace the current contents with the following:

```objc
#import "WebWorkViewController.h"

@implementation WebWorkViewController
@synthesize spinner;
@synthesize imageView;
@synthesize textView;
@synthesize receivedData;

- (void)clear {
    imageView.hidden = YES;
    textView.hidden = YES;
}

- (IBAction)getImageUsingNSData {
    NSLog(@"Entering %s", __FUNCTION__);
}

- (IBAction)getImageSynchronously {
    NSLog(@"Entering %s", __FUNCTION__);
}

- (IBAction)getImageAsynchronously {
    NSLog(@"Entering %s", __FUNCTION__);
}

- (IBAction)getTextUsingNSString {
    NSLog(@"Entering %s", __FUNCTION__);
}

- (IBAction)getTextSynchronously {
    NSLog(@"Entering %s", __FUNCTION__);
}

- (IBAction)getTextAsynchronously {
    NSLog(@"Entering %s", __FUNCTION__);
}

- (void)viewDidUnload {
    self.spinner = nil;
    self.imageView = nil;
    self.textView = nil;
}

- (void)dealloc {
```

```
    [spinner release];
    [imageView release];
    [textView release];
    [receivedData release];
    [super dealloc];
}

@end
```

The only thing in this file right now that might be new to you are the lines that look like this:

```
    NSLog(@"Entering %s", __FUNCTION__);
```

All this line does is print to the console the name of the method that's being called. __FUNCTION__ is a special macro that compiles into a C-string that holds the name of the function or method currently being executed.

> **NOTE:** It may not be obvious from looking at it on the printed page, but __FUNCTION__ has two underscores at the beginning and another two underscores at the end for a total of four underscore characters.

By doing this, we can quickly check our stubs to make sure they get called when they're supposed to be. Save and then select **Build and Run** from the **Build** menu. You should be able to click all six of the buttons and have the appropriate method for each button print in the console. This is a good way, when building your own applications, to make sure that your nib is set up correctly. A missed nib connection can be surprisingly difficult to debug, so making sure all your connections are made and are made to the correct actions before you start writing application code can be a very good idea (Figure 10–3).

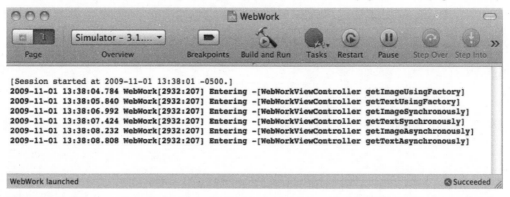

Figure 10–3. *With these stubs in place, you can quickly check out your Interface Builder action connections to make sure every button triggers the right method.*

Retrieving Data Using Foundation Objects

By far, the easiest way to retrieve data from a web server is to use a class that has an init method or factory method whose name contains withContentsOfURL:. These are special methods that take care of all aspects of retrieving a particular kind of data from the Internet. All you have to do is provide these methods with an instance of NSURL, a class that holds a single URL, and it will initialize and return an object containing the data pointed to by the URL.

> **NOTE:** These URL-based methods can also be used to create objects based on data located in a local file or using other Internet protocols like FTP. Basically, any data that can be retrieved using a URL can be used to instantiate these objects.

To initialize an NSData instance from a file on the Web, for example, you could do this:

```
NSString *theUrlString = @"http://domainname.com/filename";
NSURL *url = [NSURL urlWithString:theUrlString];
NSData *imageData = [NSData dataWithContentsOfURL:url];
```

To initialize an NSString instance from a file on the Web, it looks like this:

```
NSString *theUrlString = @"http://domainname.com/filename";
NSURL *url = [NSURL urlWithString:theUrlString];
NSString *string = [NSString stringWithContentsOfURL:url
    encoding:NSUTF8StringEncoding error:nil];
```

These aren't the only two classes that have URL-based init or factory methods, but they are the two that you will most commonly use. Most of the other methods only work if the provided URL points to data of a specific type or that's in a specific format. For NSDictionary and NSArray, for example, the URL has to lead to a property list in the format that those classes need. For AVAudioPlayer, the URL must point to a valid audio file in a format that the iPhone supports natively. How you use all of these objects is identical to the two examples shown in this section, however.

There's no doubt that these methods are convenient. If you compare the three-line process in these examples with the process we went through in the previous chapter to receive data from another device, these methods must seem laughably easy. But they do have some drawbacks. In fact, there are two major drawbacks to this approach that prevent them from being used in a lot of places. First, if anything goes wrong, the only indication you get is that they return nil. You aren't told if the file doesn't exist, or if the network connection is down. You just get a nil, and you should be happy about it. Why, when we were kids, we'd walk 20 miles, barefoot, in a blizzard just for a chance to see a nil. And we liked it!

Okay, a few of these methods will return an NSError object using a pointer to a pointer, as you can see in the last line of the NSString example, so in some instances, you have a little bit more information than just a nil, but with these techniques, you do not get detailed information about how the server responded.

The other drawback is that the process is synchronous, which means that when you call the method, no other code can run (at least on the main thread that controls the user interface) until it has finished downloading the data. If you're pulling down a small text file, that might not be a big deal, but if you're pulling down a high-res image or a video file, it's a very big deal. Your user interface will become unresponsive and your application will be unable to do anything else until the data has all been retrieved.

As a result, you should limit your use of these methods for retrieving data from the network to very small pieces of data, and even then, use them with caution. Users do not appreciate apps that become unresponsive for no apparent reason, and this as a reason will definitely not be apparent to most end users. They also don't like when things don't work and they don't know why. If they are expecting an image, and you give them nothing and no explanation about why they're getting nothing, they're bound to be unhappy about it.

Let's implement the two left-most buttons in our application so you can see this process in action.

Single-click *WebWorkViewController.m* and replace the existing stub implementation of getImageUsingNSData with this new version that retrieves a picture from the Web using NSData:

```
- (IBAction)getImageUsingNSData {
    textView.hidden = YES;
    imageView.hidden = NO;

    NSURL *url = [NSURL URLWithString:kImageURL];
    NSData *imageData = [NSData dataWithContentsOfURL:url];
    imageView.image = [UIImage imageWithData:imageData];
    [self performSelector:@selector(clear) withObject:nil afterDelay:5.0];
}
```

Also replace the existing stub implementation of getTextUsingNSString with this new version:

```
- (IBAction)getTextUsingNSString {
    textView.hidden = NO;
    imageView.hidden = YES;
    NSURL *url = [NSURL URLWithString:kTextURL];
    textView.text = [NSString stringWithContentsOfURL:url
        encoding:NSUTF8StringEncoding error:nil];
    [self performSelector:@selector(clear) withObject:nil afterDelay:5.0];
}
```

In each of these methods, we make sure the appropriate view for the type of data we're using is visible, then create an NSURL instance based on one of the two string constants we declared earlier. Then we retrieve the data from the Web using those special methods and stick the data into the appropriate view. Once we're all done with that, we use performSelector:withObject:afterDelay: to clear the text or image after five seconds so the user can try another button without having to quit.

Now try it out. When you use the top-left button, you should end up with a picture of the cover of this book, like the one shown in Figure 10–1. If you tap the lower-left button, you'll get the first page of the Iliad by Homer (Figure 10–4). Since the image and text being retrieved here are relatively small, you probably won't notice more than a minor hiccup in your application's reponsiveness after you tap the button. If you're on a fast enough connection, you may not even notice that. But, trust us when we say that if you were to do this to retrieve a large data file, the delay would definitely be noticeable.

Figure 10–4. *The bottom row of buttons will retrieve the first page of the Iliad from a web server*

Retrieving Data Synchronously

The code we just added was short and sweet, and it did the job. Mostly. But what if there was a problem? What if the file wasn't found, or the server wasn't responding? What if the user's Internet connection was down for some reason? The URL init or factory methods would return nil, and all we'd know for sure was that something prevented the object from being created. In most cases, we're going to want more information than that. We're going to want to know why our call failed so we can give our users a satisfying answer about what went wrong.

The URL Request

To do that, we have to take a little more control over the situation. Instead of using an init or factory method that takes an NSURL, we have to create an object called an NSURLRequest (or just a "request"), which is used to request data from a remote server using a URL. Here's how we create such a request:

```
NSURLRequest *req = [[NSURLRequest alloc] initWithURL:url];
```

Not too difficult, huh? Okay, so once you have your request, how do you use it to get data? In addition to the request, we also need a connection, which is represented by the class NSURLConnection. To request data synchronously, however, we don't actually have to create a connection, we can just use a class method on `NSURLConnection` to send our request and retrieve the data, like so:

```
NSHTTPURLResponse* response = nil;
NSError* error nil;
NSData *responseData = [NSURLConnection sendSynchronousRequest:req
    returningResponse:&response
    error:&error];
```

As Newton said, every request has an equal and opposite response. Okay, we didn't really pay much attention in Physics class, so that's probably not quite what he said, but it's true in the context of the Web. For every request you send, you get back a response. The `NSHTTPURLResponse` object holds the response from the server if it was able to reach the server, or `nil` if the server could not be reached. On return, the **response object** will contain all the information provided by the server in response to that request except for the actual data from the requested file which, in the this example, is held in `responseData`.

That response object gives us much more information than our previous examples because it tells us exactly what happened. It will contain a **response code**, which tells us if the server was able to fulfill the request, and how. It also contains a `content-type` which tells us what kind of data is contained in `responseData`. We can retrieve the content type and response code like this:

```
NSInteger statusCode = [response statusCode];
NSString *contentType = [[response allHeaderFields]
    objectForKey:@"Content-Type"];
```

> **TIP** You can find a list of the HTTP response codes and response header fields in the HTTP protocol specification at `http://www.w3.org/Protocols/rfc2616/rfc2616-sec6.html`. The IANA (the same organization that keeps the port number registry we talked about in the last chapter) also keep a registry of content-types, which you can find at `http://www.iana.org/assignments/media-types/`.

As we said before, if the server couldn't be reached at all, then `response` will be `nil`. If the server responded, but something went wrong, the response code will give us more information about the problem. If `reponseData` is `nil`, we might find out that the data wasn't found (response code 404) or that it moved to a new location (301) or that we don't have privileges to download it (401). Armed with the list of response codes, we can give our users a much better answer about why we weren't able to get the file for them. We can also ensure that the data we're receiving is the same type that we were expecting. Web servers will often forward requests, so `responseData` might contain, for example, the HTML for a 404 page, or a page full of ads rather than the file we were trying to retrieve.

Let's use this technique to implement the middle two buttons of our application. Single-click *WebWorkViewController.m* if it's not already selected and replace the existing stub implementation of `getImageSynchronously` with the following version:

```objc
- (IBAction)getImageSynchronously {
    textView.hidden = YES;
    imageView.hidden = NO;
    NSURL *url = [[NSURL alloc] initWithString:kImageURL];
    NSURLRequest *req = [[NSURLRequest alloc] initWithURL:url];

    NSHTTPURLResponse* response = nil;
    NSError* error = nil;
    NSData *responseData = [NSURLConnection sendSynchronousRequest:req
                                                returningResponse:&response
                                                            error:&error];

    if (response == nil) {
        UIAlertView *alert = [[UIAlertView alloc] initWithTitle:@"Error!"
            message:@"Unable to contact server."
            delegate:nil
            cancelButtonTitle:@"Bummer"
            otherButtonTitles:nil];
        [alert show];
        [alert release];
    }

    NSInteger statusCode = [response statusCode];
    NSString *contentType = [[response allHeaderFields]
        objectForKey:@"Content-Type"];

    if (statusCode >= 200 && statusCode < 300 && [contentType hasPrefix:@"image"]) {
        imageView.image = [UIImage imageWithData:responseData];
    }
    else {
        UIAlertView *alert = [[UIAlertView alloc] initWithTitle:@"Error!"
            message:[NSString stringWithFormat:
                @"Encountered %d error while loading", statusCode]
            delegate:nil
            cancelButtonTitle:@"Bummer"
            otherButtonTitles:nil];
        [alert show];
        [alert release];
    }

    [url release];
    [req release];
    [self performSelector:@selector(clear) withObject:nil afterDelay:5.0];
}
```

Now, find the getTextSynchronously stub and replace it with this version:

```objc
- (IBAction)getTextSynchronously {
    textView.hidden = NO;
    imageView.hidden = YES;
    NSURL *url = [[NSURL alloc] initWithString:kTextURL];
    NSURLRequest *req = [[NSURLRequest alloc] initWithURL:url];

    NSHTTPURLResponse* response = nil;
    NSError* error = nil;
    NSData *responseData = [NSURLConnection sendSynchronousRequest:req
                                                returningResponse:&response
                                                            error:&error];

    if (response == nil) {
```

```
        UIAlertView *alert = [[UIAlertView alloc] initWithTitle:@"Error!"
            message:@"Unable to contact server."
            delegate:nil
            cancelButtonTitle:@"Bummer"
            otherButtonTitles:nil];
        [alert show];
        [alert release];
        return;
    }

    NSInteger statusCode = [response statusCode];
    NSString *contentType = [[response allHeaderFields]
        objectForKey:@"Content-Type"];

    if (statusCode >= 200 && statusCode < 300 && [contentType hasPrefix:@"text"]) {
        NSString *payloadAsString = [[NSString alloc] initWithData:responseData
            encoding:NSUTF8StringEncoding];
        textView.text = payloadAsString;
        [payloadAsString release];
    }
    else {
        UIAlertView *alert = [[UIAlertView alloc] initWithTitle:@"Error!"
            message:[NSString stringWithFormat:
                @"Encountered %d error while loading", statusCode]
            delegate:nil
            cancelButtonTitle:@"Bummer"
            otherButtonTitles:nil];
        [alert show];
        [alert release];
        return;
    }

    [url release];
    [req release];
    [self performSelector:@selector(clear) withObject:nil afterDelay:5.0];
}
```

In both cases, we create an NSURL and an NSURLRequest, then use NSURLConnection to send the request to the server. If the response is nil, we put up an alert telling our user that the server could not be reached.

If response was not nil, then we check the response code and content type. Generally speaking, the 200 series of response codes (200 through 299) are used to indicate that the server was able to fulfill our request, so if we got a response code in that range, and the content-type matches the type of data we're expecting, we add the text or image it contains to the appropriate view. Otherwise, we show an alert letting the user know that there was a problem. After we're done, we release url and req so that we don't leak memory, and then use performSelector:withObject:afterDelay: to reset the user interface after five seconds.

Try out the new version. If all is right with the world, you should notice no difference between what the middle buttons do and the left buttons do. But, if something does go wrong, we're much better equipped to inform the user. In our simple example here, the user will know if there's something wrong with their Internet connection (Figure 10–5) or if the URL we used was wrong (Figure 10–6). You can test this out if you're using the simulator by turning Airport off or unplugging your Ethernet cable so that the remote server can't be reached. Another way you can test is to change the URL to point to an object that doesn't exist on the server, like so:

```
#define kImageURL   @"http://iphonedevbook.com/more/10/foo.png"
#define kTextURL    @"http://iphonedevbook.com/more/10/foo.txt"
```

Figure 10–5. *If the network connecton isn't working, or the remote server can't be reached, we're able to tell the user that*

That is much better, but we still have that little hiccup when the user presses the button. With synchronous requests, the entire user interface freezes for the length of time it takes to retrieve the data. Not a huge deal here where we're only pulling a few kilobytes of data, but potentially a very big deal in many situations. Let's look at how to fix that by requesting the data asynchronously.

Figure 10–6. *If we are able to reach the server, but the URL doesn't point to what we think it does, we're also able to report that back to our user or take action based on the error code that was received*

Retrieving Data Asynchronously

In the last chapter, we discussed CFNetwork's interaction with an application's run loop and the notifications your application will receive when a variety of events occur, such as receiving data. Well, the URL loading system that we just used to load data synchronously can also leverage the run loop in a similar fashion. This will allow us to request the data pointed to by a URL, and then go about our merry way while the request chugs away in the background. Once the data has been received, we can then take appropriate action, and our user interface will never become unresponsive.

As you've already seen in previous chapters, asynchronous network communication can be hard. It can be. But it doesn't have to be. Apple's URL loading system actually makes it pretty easy to retrieve data asynchronously. We start off in a manner pretty similar to the synchronous request. This time, we will create an instance of NSURL and NSURLRequest, just like before, but we'll also create an instance of NSURLConnection. Last time, we just used a class method on that object to retrieve the data, but this time we're actually going to create an instance. Just by instantiating NSURLConnection, we actually kick off the asynchronous fetch. That's all we have to do. We do have to specify a delegate when we create the connection so NSURLConnection knows what object to notify when something happens. You will usually specify self to make your controller class (or whatever class this code is part of) the delegate. Here's an example that creates a connection object:

```
NSURLRequest *req = [[NSURLRequest alloc] initWithURL:[NSURL
    URLWithString:kTextURL]];
NSURLConnection *con =[[NSURLConnection alloc] initWithRequest:req
    delegate:self];
```

If we were able to create a connection, then we need to make sure we've got a place to store the data as it comes in. The easiest way to do that is to use an instance of NSMutableData, like the one we declared in our header file earlier.

```
if (con) {
    NSMutableData *data = [[NSMutableData alloc] init];
    self.receivedData = data;
    [data release];
}
```

After that, we're done until the delegate calls one of our methods. The only thing we need to do is release the request, because we allocated it:

```
[req release];
```

Notice that we do not release the connection, however. If we released the connection, it would be deallocated because it's not currently retained by anything else. Don't worry, though, we won't leak the memory. When the connection is all finished, it will call one of our delegate methods, and we will have the chance to free up its memory at that time. Let's look at the delegate methods now.

NSURLConnection Delegate Methods

When the connection is established and a response has been received by the NSURLConnection object, the NSURLConnection will call the method connection:didReceiveResponse: on its delegate. At this point, we can check the response code to make sure we've received a valid code, but that's not always necessary. Here's why.

With asynchronous handling, you will be notified multiple times if a request gets forwarded, which isn't an uncommon occurrence when requesting data from web servers. A redirect typically results in a 300 series response code, which is then followed by another response a few moments later with a new code. This often happens, for example, if a resource moves to a new location on the server.

If the connection fails to retrieve the requested data, the connection will call another delegate method to inform you of that, so very often you don't even need to check the response code in this method unless you specifically need to know about things like redirects.

As we stated, if a connection is forwarded, this delegate method may be called multiple times for a single request. One thing you need to do here, as a result, is to reset the mutable data instance's length to 0, which removes any data that it's currently holding. You do not want to include the data from any of the earlier redirect responses in the object. Here's an example implementation of this delegate method:

```
- (void)connection:(NSURLConnection *)connection
didReceiveResponse:(NSURLResponse *)response {
```

```
    // check response code here if necessary
    [receivedData setLength:0];
}
```

After a response is received, if there is data, it will be sent to the delegate using the method `connection:didReceiveData:`. This method typically gets called multiple times, and you must capture all the data sent in the order in which it was sent, to ensure that you have received the complete object. Fortunately, all that usually entails is appending the received data onto the instance of `NSMutableData` being used to accumulate the data, like so:

```
- (void)connection:(NSURLConnection *)connection
    didReceiveData:(NSData *)data {
    [receivedData appendData:data];
}
```

If an error is encountered while trying to retrieve the requested object, the delegate method `connection:didFailWithError:` gets called. Here's a simple implementation of that method that simply logs the error:

```
- (void)connection:(NSURLConnection *)connection
didFailWithError:(NSError *)error {
    [connection release];
    self.receivedData = nil;
    NSLog(@"Error retrieving data for url %@, error was: %@",
        [error localizedDescription], [[error userInfo]
        objectForKey:NSErrorFailingURLStringKey]);
}
```

In real-world applications, you'll typically want to take more significant action when a connection fails, at the very least informing the user of the failure.

When all of the data that makes up the requested object has been retrieved, the connection will call the delegate method `connectionDidFinishLoading:`. When this method is called, the instance of `NSMutableData` in which we've been collecting the received data should have the complete object, and you can do whatever is appropriate with it. You also need to release the connection here so that you don't leak the memory. It's also usually appropriate to release the mutable data instance that was used to accumulate the data, once you've used the data, though that may not always be the case. Here's a simple example that creates an instance of `UIImage` based on the received data and puts it into a `UIImageView`.

```
- (void)connectionDidFinishLoading:(NSURLConnection *)connection {
    imageView.image = [UIImage imageWithData:receivedData];
    [connection release];
    self.receivedData = nil;
}
```

Adding Asynchronous Retrieval to WebWorks

Here we come, rounding third based on our WebWorks application. We're almost done. Find the stub implementation of `getImageAsynchronously` and replace it with this version:

```
- (IBAction)getImageAsynchronously {
```

```
    [spinner startAnimating];

    NSURLRequest *req = [[NSURLRequest alloc] initWithURL:
        [NSURL URLWithString:kImageURL]];
    NSURLConnection *con = [[NSURLConnection alloc] initWithRequest:req
                                                        delegate:self];
    if (con) {
        NSMutableData *data = [[NSMutableData alloc] init];
        self.receivedData = data;
        [data release];
        requestType = kRequestTypeImage;
    }
    else {
        UIAlertView *alert = [[UIAlertView alloc]
            initWithTitle:@"Error"
            message:@"Error connecting to remote server"
            delegate:self
            cancelButtonTitle:@"Bummer"
            otherButtonTitles:nil];
        [alert show];
        [alert release];
    }
    [req release];
}
```

Now find the stub implementation of getTextAsynchronously and replace it with this version:

```
- (IBAction)getTextAsynchronously {
    [spinner startAnimating];

    NSURLRequest *req = [[NSURLRequest alloc] initWithURL:
        [NSURL URLWithString:kTextURL]];
    NSURLConnection *con = [[NSURLConnection alloc] initWithRequest:req
                                                        delegate:self];
    if (con) {
        NSMutableData *data = [[NSMutableData alloc] init];
        self.receivedData = data;
        [data release];
        requestType = kRequestTypeText;
    }
    else {
        UIAlertView *alert = [[UIAlertView alloc]
            initWithTitle:@"Error"
            message:@"Error connecting to remote server"
            delegate:self
            cancelButtonTitle:@"Bummer"
            otherButtonTitles:nil];
        [alert show];
        [alert release];
    }
    [req release];
}
```

In both methods, we follow the same basic logic. First, we create the URL and request, then use those to create an instance of NSURLConnection, specifying self as the delegate. We check to make sure the connection object is not nil, which would indicate that the server could not be reached, and if we have a valid connection, we allocate our NSMutableData instance to hold the data we're about to start receiving.

So now, the right-hand buttons kick off an asynchronous request and shows the activity indicator. Since the retrieval will happen in the background, there shouldn't be a hiccup or any noticeable unresponsiveness in the app. Of course, it also won't ever show the image or text because we haven't implemented our connection delegate methods. Let's do that now. At the end of the file, just above the @end declaration, add the following methods:

```
#pragma mark -
#pragma mark NSURLConnection Callbacks
- (void)connection:(NSURLConnection *)connection
         didReceiveResponse:(NSURLResponse *)response {
    [receivedData setLength:0];
}

- (void)connection:(NSURLConnection *)connection didReceiveData:(NSData *)data {
    [receivedData appendData:data];
}

- (void)connection:(NSURLConnection *)connection
    didFailWithError:(NSError *)error {
    [connection release];
    self.receivedData = nil;

    UIAlertView *alert = [[UIAlertView alloc] initWithTitle:@"Error"
        message:[NSString stringWithFormat:
            @"Connection failed! Error - %@ (URL: %@)",
            [error localizedDescription],[[error userInfo]
            objectForKey:NSErrorFailingURLStringKey]]
        delegate:self
        cancelButtonTitle:@"Bummer"
        otherButtonTitles:nil];
    [alert show];
    [alert release];
    [spinner stopAnimating];
}

- (void)connectionDidFinishLoading:(NSURLConnection *)connection {
    if (requestType == kRequestTypeImage) {
        imageView.hidden = NO;
        textView.hidden = YES;
        imageView.image = [UIImage imageWithData:receivedData];
    }
    else {
        imageView.hidden = YES;
        textView.hidden = NO;
        NSString *payloadAsString = [[NSString alloc] initWithData:receivedData
            encoding:NSUTF8StringEncoding];
        textView.text = payloadAsString;
        [payloadAsString release];
    }

    [connection release];
    self.receivedData = nil;
```

```
    [spinner stopAnimating];
    [self performSelector:@selector(clear) withObject:nil afterDelay:5.0];
}
```

Let's look at what we did. The first connection delegate method we implement gets
called whenever the connection gets a response from the server. Remember, we might
get more than one response if the server forwards our request, so we reset our mutable
data every time this gets called:

```
- (void)connection:(NSURLConnection *)connection
        didReceiveResponse:(NSURLResponse *)response {
    [receivedData setLength:0];
}
```

Every time the connection has a chunk of data for us, it will call the next method we
wrote, so we take the data and append it to our mutable data instance.

```
- (void)connection:(NSURLConnection *)connection
        didReceiveData:(NSData *)data {
    [receivedData appendData:data];
}
```

In the event of an error, the connection will call our delegate method
connection:didFailWithError:. All we do is report the error to the user using an alert,
and release the connection so that we're not leaking memory. We also stop the activity
indicator so that the user doesn't think we're still trying to retrieve the data.

```
- (void)connection:(NSURLConnection *)connection
        didFailWithError:(NSError *)error {
    [connection release];
    self.receivedData = nil;

    UIAlertView *alert = [[UIAlertView alloc] initWithTitle:@"Error"
        message:[NSString stringWithFormat:
        @"Connection failed! Error - %@ (URL: %@)",
        [error localizedDescription],[[error userInfo]
        objectForKey:NSErrorFailingURLStringKey]]
        delegate:self
        cancelButtonTitle:@"Bummer"
        otherButtonTitles:nil];
    [alert show];
    [alert release];
    [spinner stopAnimating];
}
```

Finally, when all the data has been retrieved, our delegate method
connectionDidFinishLoading: gets called. We check the request type that we set
earlier, and use the received data to populate either the text view or the image view. We
also stop the activity indiator, and release the connection so that we don't leak memory.

```
- (void)connectionDidFinishLoading:(NSURLConnection *)connection {
    if (requestType == kRequestTypeImage) {
        imageView.hidden = NO;
        textView.hidden = YES;
        imageView.image = [UIImage imageWithData:receivedData];
    }
    else {
```

```
            imageView.hidden = YES;
            textView.hidden = NO;
            NSString *payloadAsString = [[NSString alloc] initWithData:receivedData
                encoding:NSUTF8StringEncoding];
            textView.text = payloadAsString;
            [payloadAsString release];
        }

        [connection release];
        self.receivedData = nil;
        [spinner stopAnimating];
        [self performSelector:@selector(clear) withObject:nil afterDelay:5.0];
    }
```

Well, that's better. Take it out for a spin. Try changing the two URLs to point to bigger files if you want to really see the difference that asynchronous retrieval can make in your application.

At this point, you should have a pretty good handle on retrieving static data. But there's more to the Web than getting files from static URLs so, before we leave the chapter, let's take a quick look at how to change the request type and pass form parameters so that you can also retrieve information from web applications and web services.

Request Types and Form Parameters

The Web is so much more than a network of static files now. The Internet is chock full of various forms of web applications. If you need to pull data from a web service or other form of web application, then a standard GET request like the ones we've been creating aren't going to cut it for you. Fortunately, the iPhone's URL handling system is capable of creating any type of HTTP request that you might need.

Specifying the HTTP Request Types

The HTTP protocol actually defines multipe types of requests. In addition to the standard GET request that we've been using, there's also something called a POST request, which is used by most web forms. There's also the lesser-used PUT, which is used to add or replace an existing resource with a new one, and DELETE which is used to remove a resource or make it unavailable.

In the early days of the Web, GET was used to retrieve static files and POST was used for pretty much any kind of interactivity. As a result, there are a lot of web applications and services that still use only GET and POST. With the rising popularity of RESTful web services, many newer web applications do require requests to use the proper request type depending on the task they are seeking to perform. We're not going to try and teach you the nuances of when to use each of the different HTTP request types. Our goal is to show you how to specify the type of your request and pass the necessary parameters so that you can retrieve data from web applications regardless of which request type you need to use.

> **NOTE:** If you're interested in finding out more about what the different request types are used for, a good place to start would be the HTTP 1.1 specification available at `http://www.w3.org/Protocols/rfc2616/rfc2616.html`.

The `NSURLRequest` class that we used in the WebWorks application earlier in the chapter is incapable of doing any other type of request besides a GET request. Sorry, nothing we can do about that. Hope you never need to do anything other than a GET.

> **CAUTION:** We'd like to apologize for the attempt at subtle humor you just experienced. Dave and Jeff have been chastised by their editors and promise not to attempt such humor again. It slows down the book and annoys the patrons. Sincerely yours, the management.

Okay, there actually is a way to create other types of requests. There is a mutable subclass of `NSURLRequest` called `NSMutableURLRequest`, and it allows you to specify, among other things, the request type. Here's how you would create one and set the request type to POST:

```
NSMutableURLRequest *req = [[NSMutableURLRequest alloc]
                             initWithURL:url];
[req setHTTPMethod:@"POST"];
```

If you substitute @"PUT" for @"POST", you'll create a PUT request, and if you substitute @"DELETE" instead, you'll create a DELETE request. What could be easier?

MUTABLE URL REQUESTS

Once you create a mutable URL request, you get a lot more control over the request. In addition to specifying the request type, you can also set any HTTP headers. The HTTP header contains the specifics of the request you are making to the server, and includes several pieces of information, including the user-agent, which identifies the browser you're using, and the referrer, which identifies the page that sent you here if you're following a link from another page. So, for example, you could make it look like you were coming to a request from a link on another page by doing this:

```
[req setValue:@"http://domainname.com" forHTTPHeaderField:@"Referer"];
```

Yes, you really do have to spell referrer wrong when you do this. You can use the same method call to set or change the value of any of the HTTP header fields. You can find a list of the HTTP request header fields at `http://en.wikipedia.org/wiki/List_of_HTTP_headers`.

Form Parameters

You can pass parameters to a web server when you make a request. Web applications can read the parameters you pass in and use them to figure out what they should return. If, instead of retrieving a static image, we were retrieving an image from a web application that returns an image of a specific person, we might pass in the person's name or some other kind of identifying value in the parameters so the web application would know what person's image to send back to us.

Parameters come in two flavors, which are named after the two most commonly used request types: GET and POST. As you might have guessed, GET requests usually use GET parameters, and POST requests usually use POST parameters.

GET Parameters

Get parameters are passed in as part of the URL. At the end of the URL, if you add a question mark (?), you are telling the server that everything else after that question mark in the URL is part of the parameters. The parameters are specified as key/value pairs, with each pair separated by an equal sign. If there is more than one pair, the pairs are each separated by ampersand characters (&). A URL that includes get parameters might look like this:

```
http://www.foobar.org/picture?id=1001&size=200x200
```

This particular URL has two parameters, one called *id* which is being set to 1001, and another called *size*, which is being set to 200x200.

When using the URL loading system, the way that you set GET parameters is by appending them to the end of the URL string before creating your instance of NSURL. Nothing fancy, you just do something like this:

```
NSString *url = [NSString stringWithFormat:@"http://www.foo.bar/action?%@=%@",
    paramName, paramValue];
```

POST Parameters

It's not always desirable to have the parameters being passed in as part of the URL. For one thing, the user can see those values in the URL bar of their browser. When submitting web forms, a different kind of parameter, called POST, is used. POST parameters work in pretty much the same way as GET parameters. They are key value pairs with an equal sign between the key and value and with each pair being separated by an ampersand. The difference is that this parameter string isn't passed as part of the URL, it goes as part of the request body, which typically isn't seen by the user and doesn't show up in the URL.

To set the POST parameters for a request, you have to be using an NSMutableURLRequest. Then you just create a string that contains all the parameters you want to pass, convert that string into an instance of NSData, and then set that instance to be the request's body, like so:

```
NSString *paramDataString = [NSString stringWithFormat:@"%@=%@", paramName,
    paramValue];
NSData *paramData = [paramDataString dataUsingEncoding:NSUTF8StringEncoding];
[req setHTTPBody: paramData];
```

Building the RequestTypes Application

In Xcode, create a new project with the *View-based Application* template again, this time calling the project *RequestTypes*. Once the project is open, single-click on *RequestTypesViewController.h* and replace the contents with this version:

```
#import <UIKit/UIKit.h>
#define kFormURL @"http://iphonedevbook.com/more/10/echo.php"

@interface RequestTypesViewController : UIViewController {
    UIWebView        *webView;
    UITextField      *paramName;
    UITextField      *paramValue;

    NSMutableData            *receivedData;
}

@property (nonatomic, retain) IBOutlet UIWebView *webView;
@property (nonatomic, retain) IBOutlet UITextField *paramName;
@property (nonatomic, retain) IBOutlet UITextField *paramValue;

@property (nonatomic, retain) NSMutableData *receivedData;

- (IBAction)doGetRequest;
- (IBAction)doPostRequest;
@end
```

The constant defines a string that holds a URL to a very simple web service that we've set up for you to use. It will echo back to you with the request type used and both the GET and POST parameters you passed in. We're keeping things relatively simple in this application. We have two text fields, one you can use to enter a parameter name, and another you can use to enter a value for that parameter. We also have a web view that we'll use to display the response from the web application. The UIWebView is capable of displaying URLs, or HTML that is contained in a string. We'll be using it for the latter, just so we don't have to do any processing or formatting of the data returned by the web service.

Our class defines two action methods, one to post a GET request using GET parameters, and another button for sending a POST request with POST parameters. Save *RequestTypesViewController.h* and double-click *RequestTypesViewController.xib* to open Interface Builder.

Using Figure 10–7 as a guide, add two *Labels*, two *Text Fields*, two *Round Rect Buttons*, and a *Web View* to the window labeled *View*. Control-drag from *File's Owner* to the two text fields. For the one on the left, select the *paramName* outlet. For the one on the right, select the *paramValue* outlet. Then control-drag again to the web view and select the *webView* outlet. Next, control drag from the left button to *File's Owner* and select the action named *doGetRequest*. Repeat with the button on the right and connect to the *doPostRequest* action. Save the nib and go back to Xcode.

Figure 10–7. *Use this as a guide when building the RequestTypes application interface. The exact placement isn't important.*

Single-click *RequestTypesViewController.m* and replace the contents with this version:

```
#import "RequestTypesViewController.h"

@implementation RequestTypesViewController
@synthesize webView;
@synthesize paramName;
@synthesize paramValue;
@synthesize receivedData;

- (IBAction)doGetRequest {

    NSMutableString *urlWithParameters = [NSMutableString
        stringWithString:kFormURL];

    [urlWithParameters appendFormat:@"?%@=%@", paramName.text, paramValue.text];

    NSURLRequest *req = [[NSURLRequest alloc] initWithURL:[NSURL
        URLWithString:urlWithParameters]];

    NSURLConnection *theConnection=[[NSURLConnection alloc] initWithRequest:req
        delegate:self];
    if (theConnection) {
        NSMutableData *data = [[NSMutableData alloc] init];
        self.receivedData = data;
```

```objc
        [data release];
    }
    else {
        [webView loadHTMLString:@"Unable to make connection!"
            baseURL:[NSURL URLWithString:kFormURL]] ;
    }
    [paramName resignFirstResponder];
    [paramValue resignFirstResponder];
    [req release];
}

- (IBAction)doPostRequest {
        NSURL *url = [[NSURL alloc] initWithString:kFormURL];
        NSMutableURLRequest *req = [[NSMutableURLRequest alloc]
                            initWithURL:url];
        [req setHTTPMethod:@"POST"];


    NSString *paramDataString = [NSString stringWithFormat:@"%@=%@", paramName.text,
        paramValue.text];

    NSData *paramData = [paramDataString dataUsingEncoding:NSUTF8StringEncoding];
    [req setHTTPBody: paramData];

    NSURLConnection *theConnection = [[NSURLConnection alloc]
                                initWithRequest:req
                                delegate:self];
    if (theConnection) {
        NSMutableData *data = [[NSMutableData alloc] init];
        self.receivedData = data;
        [data release];
    }
    else {
        [webView loadHTMLString:@"Unable to make connection!" baseURL:[NSURL
            URLWithString:kFormURL]] ;
    }

    [url release];
    [req release];
    [paramName resignFirstResponder];
    [paramValue resignFirstResponder];
}

- (void)viewDidUnload {
    self.webView = nil;
    self.paramName = nil;
    self.paramValue = nil;
}

- (void)dealloc {
    [webView release];
    [paramName release];
    [paramValue release];
    [receivedData release];
    [super dealloc];
}
```

```
#pragma mark -
#pragma mark NSURLConnection Callbacks
- (void)connection:(NSURLConnection *)connection
didReceiveResponse:(NSURLResponse *)response {
    [receivedData setLength:0];
}

- (void)connection:(NSURLConnection *)connection didReceiveData:(NSData *)data {
    [receivedData appendData:data];
}

- (void)connection:(NSURLConnection *)connection
  didFailWithError:(NSError *)error {
    [connection release];
    self.receivedData = nil;

    UIAlertView *alert = [[UIAlertView alloc] initWithTitle:@"Error"
        message:[NSString stringWithFormat:
            @"Connection failed! Error - %@ (URL: %@)",
            [error localizedDescription], [[error userInfo]
            objectForKey:NSErrorFailingURLStringKey]]
        delegate:self
        cancelButtonTitle:@"Bummer"
        otherButtonTitles:nil];
    [alert show];
    [alert release];
}

- (void)connectionDidFinishLoading:(NSURLConnection *)connection {

    webView.hidden = NO;
    NSString *payloadAsString = [[NSString alloc] initWithData:receivedData
        encoding:NSUTF8StringEncoding];
    [webView loadHTMLString:payloadAsString baseURL:[NSURL URLWithString:kFormURL]];
    [payloadAsString release];

    [connection release];
    self.receivedData = nil;
}

@end
```

Much of this controller class is identical to our earlier asynchronous example. There are a few things you should take notice of. In doGetRequest, we use a mutable string to append parameters onto the URL.

```
NSMutableString *urlWithParameters = [NSMutableString
    stringWithString:kFormURL];

[urlWithParameters appendFormat:@"?%@=%@", paramName.text, paramValue.text];
```

From that point on, everything is the same as our previous examples. Because we're creating a GET request, we don't need a mutable request.

In doPostRequest, things have changed a little more. We start off by allocating a URL and a mutable request and setting the request's type to POST:

```
- (IBAction)doPostRequest {
```

```
NSURL *url = [[NSURL alloc] initWithString:kFormURL];
NSMutableURLRequest *req = [[NSMutableURLRequest alloc]
                            initWithURL:url];
[req setHTTPMethod:@"POST"];
```

We then create a string that holds the parameters entered by our user in the two text fields.

```
NSString *paramDataString = [NSString stringWithFormat:@"%@=%@", paramName.text,
    paramValue.text];
```

We convert that string into an instance of NSData using UTF-8 encoding, which is the default encoding type used by NSMutableURLRequest. Then we set that as the body of the request.

```
NSData *paramData = [paramDataString dataUsingEncoding:NSUTF8StringEncoding];
[req setHTTPBody: paramData];
```

From that point on, everything else is the same. We create the connection just as we did in the asynchronous example and if our connection isn't nil, we allocate an instance of NSMutableData to hold the returned value.

And there you have it. If you type values into the two text fields and hit either button, you'll send different types of requests with different types of parameters. From these two examples, you should be able to craft pretty much any kind of request you need.

As an example, if you press the *Get* button with *foo* in the *Parameter* field and *bar* in the *Value* field, it's as if you sent out this URL:

```
http://iphonedevbook.com/more/10/echo.php?foo=bar
```

If you press the *Post* button, it's as if you had submitted an HTML form with an action of `http://iphonedevbook.com/more/10/echo.php` that contained a text field (or other control) named *foo* and the user entered a value of *bar* into that field before hitting the *Submit* button. These parameters don't actually go in as part of the URL. Instead, they are passed in the body of the request, which typically isn't seen when you're using a browser.

WHAT ABOUT PUT AND DELETE?

The code that you would write for PUT and DELETE requests, which you often have to use to interact with RESTful web services, are almost exactly like GET and POST. In general, PUT requests use POST parameters and DELETE, if it requires any parameters, usually passes them as GET parameters, though you should check with the documentation for the web service you are accessing to find out for sure. There's no reason why a PUT request can't use GET parameters, or a DELETE can't use POST parameters.

There is one small gotcha with PUT requests, which is that you have to manually set the content type of your NSMutableURLRequest instance. For some reason, when you set the request type to POST, it does this automatically, but when you set it to PUT, it does not. Unless you add this line of code, POST parameters will not pass correctly when making a PUT request:

```
[req setValue:@"application/x-www-form-urlencoded"
    forHTTPHeaderField:@"Content-Type"];
```

In every other respect (except the request type, of course), the code for PUT and POST requests is exactly the same. The code for DELETE requests will usually look like our GET example in this application, only with a mutable request whose type has been set to @"DELETE".

404 Conclusion Not Found

So, now, we must bid adieu to our friend the network. We've spent three chapters exploring ways to exchange information with other machines over network connections. In this chapter, you saw how to perform synchronous and asynchronous requests to web servers, saw how to change the request's type, and also saw how to send both kinds of form parameters.

In the next chapter, we're going to look at using MapKit, Apple's framework for displaying locations and directions on a map right in your own application.

Chapter 11

MapKit

iPhones have always had a way to determine where in the world they are. Even though the original iPhone didn't have GPS, it did have a Maps application and was able to represent its approximate location on the map using cell phone triangulation or by looking up its WiFi IP address in a database of known locations. Prior to SDK 3, there was no way to leverage this functionality within your own applications. It was possible to launch the Maps application to show a specific location or route, but it wasn't possible, using only Apple-provided APIs, to show map data without leaving your application.

That changed with the release of the MapKit framework in the 3.0 release of the iPhone SDK. Applications now have the ability to show maps, including the user's current location, and even drop pins and show annotations on those maps. MapKit's functionality isn't limited to just showing maps, either. It includes functionality called reverse geocoding, which allows you to take a set of specific coordinates and turn them into a physical address. Your application can use those coordinates to find out not just where the person is located but, frequently, the actual address associated with that location. You can't always get down to the street address, but you can almost always get the city and state or province no matter where in the world your user is. In this chapter, we're going to look at the basics of adding MapKit functionality to any application.

NOTE: The application we build in this chapter will run just fine in the iPhone Simulator; however, the Simulator won't report your actual location. Instead, it always returns the address of Apple's corporate headquarters at 1 Infinite Loop in Cupertino, California.

TERMS

The MapKit framework uses Google services to provide map data. As a result, if you choose to use MapKit in an application, it binds you to the Google Maps/Google Earth API terms of service. You can find these terms of service at http://code.google.com/apis/maps/iphone/terms.html.

Make sure you've read the terms and are willing to abide by them if you're planning to use MapKit in your applications.

This Chapter's Application

Our chapter's application will start by showing a map of the entire world (Figure 11–1). Other than the map, our interface will be empty except for a single button with the imaginative title of *Go*. When the button is pressed, the application will determine our current location, zoom the map to show that location, and drop a pin to mark the location (Figure 11–2).

Figure 11–1. *Our MapMe application will start out showing a map of the entire world*

Figure 11–2. *After determining the current location, the map will zoom in to give a better view of that location, and then drop a pin to mark the location. We'll then use the reverse geocoder to determine the address that corresponds to the phone's current location and add an annotation view to the map displaying the address.*

We will then use MapKit's reverse geocoder to determine the address of our current location and we'll add an **annotation** to the map to display the specifics of that location.

Despite its simplicity, this application leverages most of the basic MapKit functionality. Before we start building our project, let's explore MapKit, see what makes it tick.

Overview and Terminology

Although MapKit is not particularly complex, it can be a bit confusing. Let's start with a high-level view and nail down the terminology, then we'll dig down into the individual components.

To display map-related data, you add a **map view** to one of your application's views. Map views can have a delegate, and that delegate is usually the controller class responsible for the view in which the map view resides. That's the approach we'll use for this chapter's application. Our application will have a single view and a single view controller. That single view will contain a map view, along with a few other items, and our single view controller will be the map view's delegate.

Map views keep track of locations of interest using a collection of **annotations**. Any time you see an icon on a map, whether it's a pin, a dot, or anything else, it's an annotation. When an annotation is in the part of the map that's being shown, the map view asks its delegate to provide a view for that annotation (called an **annotation view**) that the map view will draw at the specific location on the map.

Annotations are selectable, and a selected annotation will display a **callout**, which is a small view that floats above the map like the *You are Here!* view shown in Figure 11–2. If the user taps an annotation view and that annotation view is selectable, the map view will display the callout associated with that view.

The Map View

The core element of the MapKit framework is the **map view**, represented by the class MKMapView. The map view takes care of drawing the maps and responding to user input. Users can use all the gestures they're accustomed to, including a pinch in or out to do a controlled zoom, a double-tap to zoom in, or a two-finger double tap to zoom out. You can add a map view to your interface and configure it using Interface Builder. Like many iPhone controls, much of the work of managing the map view is done by the map view's delegate.

Map Types

Map views are capable of displaying maps in several different ways. They can display the map as a series of lines and symbols that represent the roadways and other landmarks in the area being shown. This is the default display, and it's known as the **standard map type**. You can also display the map using satellite images by specifying the **satellite map type**, or you can use what's called the **hybrid map type**, where the lines representing roadways and landmarks from the standard type are superimposed on top of the satellite imagery of the satellite type. You can see an example of the default map type in Figure 11–2. Figure 11–3 shows the satellite map type and Figure 11–4 shows the hybrid map type.

Figure 11–3. *The satellite map type shows satellite imagery instead of lines and symbols*

Figure 11–4. *The hybrid type overlays the lines and symbols of the default type on top of the imagery from the satellite type*

You can set the map type in Interface Builder or by setting the map view's `mapType` property to one of the following:

```
mapView.mapType = MKMapTypeStandard;
mapView.mapType = MKMapTypeSatellite;
mapView.mapType = MKMapTypeHybrid;
```

User Location

Map views will, if configured to do so, use Core Location to keep track of the user's location and display it on the map using a blue dot, much like the way the Maps application does. We won't be using that functionality in this chapter's application, but you can turn it on by setting the map view's `showsUserLocation` property to YES, like so:

```
mapView.showsUserLocation = YES;
```

If the map is tracking the user's location, you can determine if their present location is visible in the map view by using the read-only property `userLocationVisible`. If the user's current location is being displayed in the map view, `userLocationVisible` will return YES.

You can get the specific coordinates of the user's present location from the map view by first setting `showsUserLocation` to YES, and then accessing the `userLocation` property. This property returns an instance of `MKUserLocation`. `MKUserLocation` is an object and has a property called `location` which itself is a `CLLocation` object. A `CLLocation` contains a property called `coordinate` that points to a set of coordinates. All this means you can get the actual coordinates from the `MKUserLocation` object, like so:

```
CLLocationCoordinate2D coords = mapView.userLocation.location.coordinate;
```

Coordinate Regions

A map view wouldn't be much good if you couldn't tell it what to display or find out what part of the world it's currently showing. With map views, the key to being able to do those tasks is the `MKCoordinateRegion`, a `struct` that contains two pieces of data that together define the portion of the map to be shown in a map view.

The first member of `MKCoordinateRegion` is called `center`. This is another `struct` of type `CLLocationCoordinate2D`, which you may remember from the chapter on Core Location in *Beginning iPhone 3 Development* (Apress, 2009). A `CLLocationCoordinate2D` contains two floating point values, a `latitude` and `longitude`, and is used to represent a single spot on the globe. In the context of a coordinate region, that spot on the globe is the spot that represents the center of the map view.

The second member of `MKCoordinateRegion` is called `span`, and it's a `struct` of type `MKCoordinateSpan`. The `MKCoordinateSpan` struct has two members called `latitudeDelta` and `longitudeDelta`. These two numbers are used to set the zoom level of the map by identifying how much of the area around `center` should be displayed. These values represent that distance in degrees latitude and longitude. If `latitudeDelta` and `longitudeDelta` are small numbers, the map will be zoomed in very close; if they are large, the map will be zoomed out and show a much larger area.

Figure 11–5 shows the makeup of the `MKCoordinateRegion` struct.

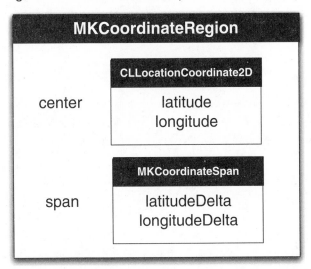

Figure 11–5. *The MKCoordinateRegion represented graphically. It contains two members, both of which are, in turn, structs that own two members.*

If you look back at Figure 11–2, the point of the pin you can see is at the coordinates that were passed in `MKCoordinateRegion.center`. The distance from the top of the map to the bottom of the map was passed in, represented as degrees latitude, using the `MKCoordinateRegion.span.latitudeDelta`. Similarly, the distance from the left side of the map to the right side of the map was passed in, represented as degrees longitude, as the `MKCoordinateRegion.span.longitudeDelta`.

> **TIP:** If you have trouble remembering which lines are latitude and which are longitude, here's a tip from our third grade geography teacher, Mrs. Krabappel (pronounced, kruh-bopple). Latitude sounds like altitude, so latitude tells you how high on the globe you are. The equator is a line of latitude. And the Prime Meridian is a line of longitude. Thanks, Mrs. Krabappel!

There are two challenges that this approach presents to the programmer. First, who thinks in degrees latitude or longitude? Although degrees latitude represent roughly the same distance everywhere in the world, degrees longitude vary greatly in the amount of distance they represent as you move from the pole to the equator, so calculating the degrees longitude isn't as straightforward.

The second challenge is that a map view has a specific width-to-height ratio (called an **aspect ratio**), and the `latitudeDelta` and `longitudeDelta` you specify have to represent an area with that same aspect ratio. Fortunately, Apple provides tools for dealing with both of these issues.

Converting Degrees to Distance

Each degree of latitude represents approximately 69 miles, or about 111 kilometers, no matter where you are. This makes determining the number to pass in as the `latitudeDelta` of an `MKCoordinateSpan` fairly easy to calculate. You can just divide the lateral distance you want to display by 69 if you're using miles, or 111 if you're using kilometers.

> **NOTE:** Since the earth isn't a perfect sphere (technically speaking, it's close to being an oblate spheroid), there actually is some variation between the amount of distance that one degree latitude represents, but it's not enough variation to bother factoring into our calculation, since it's only about a one degree variation from pole to equator. At the equator, one degree of latitude equals 69.046767 miles or 111.12 kilometers and the number gets a little smaller as you move toward the poles. We chose 69 and 111 because they're nice round numbers that are within 1% of the actual distance pretty much everywhere.

The distance represented by one degree longitude, however, is not quite so easy to calculate. To do the same calculation for longitude, you have to take the latitude into account, because the distance represented by one degree longitude depends on where you are in relation to the equator. To calculate the distance represented by degrees longitude, you have to perform some gnarly math. Fortunately, Apple has done the gnarly math for you and provides a method called `MKCoordinateRegionMakeWithDistance()` that you can use to create a region. You provide coordinates to act as the center, along with the distance in meters for the latitudinal and longitudinal span. The function will look at the latitude in the coordinates provided and calculate both delta values for you in degrees. Here is how you might create a region to show one kilometer on each side of a specific location represented by a `CLLocationCoordinate2D` called `center`:

```
MKCoordinateRegion viewRegion = MKCoordinateRegionMakeWithDistance(center,
    2000, 2000);
```

To show a kilometer on each side of center, we have to specify 2000 meters total for each span: 1000 to the left, 1000 to the right, 1000 to the top, and 1000 to the bottom. After this call, `viewRegion` will contain a properly formatted `MKCoordinateRegion` that's almost ready for use. All that's left is taking care of the aspect ratio problem.

THE GNARLY MATH

The math to calculate the distance of one degree longitude really isn't that gnarly, so we thought we'd show those of you who are interested what the man behind the curtain is doing. To calculate the distance for one degree longitude at a given latitude, the calculation is:

$$\frac{\pi}{180°} \times \text{radius of the Earth} \times \cos(\text{lat}°)$$

If Apple didn't provide a function for us, we could create a couple of macros that would accomplish the same thing just by following this formula. The radius of the earth is roughly 3963.1676 miles, or 6378.1 kilometers. So, to calculate the distance for one degree of longitude at a specific latitude contained in the variable `lat`, you would do this:

```
double longitudeMiles = ((M_PI/180.0) × 3963.1676 × cos(latitude));
```

You can do the same calculation to determine the distance of one degree longitude in kilometers, like so:

```
double longitudeKilometers = ((M_PI/180.0) × 6378.1 × cos(latitude));
```

If you're interested, you can find macros in the provided *11 – MapMe* project in the project archive that accompanies this book. Look in the file called *MapMeViewController.h* for macros that implement these calculations. In this chapter, we'll use the function provided by Apple to calculate the span, but we've provided these macros for the curious, or for those who prefer to work in miles or kilometers rather than meters.

Accommodating Aspect Ratio

In the previous section, we showed how to create a span that showed one kilometer on each side of a given location. However, unless the map view is perfectly square, there's no way that the view can show exactly one kilometer on each of the four sides of `center`. If the map view is wider than it is tall, the `longitudeDelta` will need to be larger than the `latitudeDelta`. If the map view is taller than it is wide, the opposite is true.

The `MKMapView` class has an instance method that will adjust a coordinate region to match the map view's aspect ratio. That method is called `regionThatFits:`. To use it, you just pass in the coordinate region you created, and it will return a new coordinate region that is adjusted to the map view's aspect ratio. Here's how you would use it:

```
MKCoordinateRegion adjustedRegion = [mapView regionThatFits:viewRegion];
```

Setting the Region to Display

Once you've created a coordinate region, you can tell a map view to display that region by calling the method `setRegion:animated:`. If you pass YES for the second parameter, the map view will zoom, shift, or otherwise animate the view from its current location to its new location. Here is an example that creates a coordinate region, adjusts it to the map views's aspect ratio, and then tells the map view to display that region:

```
MKCoordinateRegion viewRegion =
    MKCoordinateRegionMakeWithDistance(center, 2000, 2000);
MKCoordinateRegion adjustedRegion = [mapView regionThatFits:viewRegion];
[mapView setRegion:adjustedRegion animated:YES];
```

The Map View Delegate

As we mentioned earlier, map views can have delegates. Map views, unlike table views and pickers, can function without a delegate. On a map view delegate, there are a number of methods you can implement if you need to be notified about certain map-related tasks. They allow you, for example, to get notified when the user changes the part of the map they're looking at, either by dragging to reveal a new section of the map, or by zooming to reveal a smaller or larger area. You can also get notified when the map view loads new map data from the server, or when the map view fails to do so. The map view delegate methods are contained in the `MKMapViewDelegate` protocol, and any class that is used as a map view delegate should conform to that protocol.

Map Loading Delegate Methods

The MapKit framework uses Google Maps to do its job. It doesn't store any map data locally except for temporary caches. Whenever the map view needs to go to Google's servers to retrieve new map data, it will call the delegate method `mapViewWillStartLoadingMap:`, and when it has successfully retrieved the map data it needs, it will call the delegate method `mapViewDidFinishLoadingMap:`. If you have any application-specific processing that needs to happen at either time, you can implement the appropriate method on the map view's delegate.

If MapKit encounters an error loading map data from the server, it will call the method `mapViewDidFailLoadingMap:withError:` on its delegate. At very least, you should implement this delegate method and inform your user of the problem so they aren't sitting there waiting for an update that will never come. Here's a very simple implementation of that method that just shows an alert and lets the user know that something went wrong:

```
- (void)mapViewDidFailLoadingMap:(MKMapView *)mapView
                     withError:(NSError *)error {
    UIAlertView *alert = [[UIAlertView alloc]
        initWithTitle:NSLocalizedString(@"Error loading map",
            @"Error loading map")
        message:[error localizedDescription]
        delegate:nil
        cancelButtonTitle:NSLocalizedString(@"Okay", @"Okay")
        otherButtonTitles:nil];
    [alert show];
    [alert release];
}
```

Region Change Delegate Methods

If your map view is enabled, the user will be able to interact with it using the standard iPhone gestures, like drag, pinch in, pinch out, and double-tap. Doing so will change the region being displayed in the view. There are two delegate methods that will get called whenever this happens, if the map view's delegate implements those methods. As the gesture starts, the delegate method `mapView:regionWillChangeAnimated:` gets called. When the gesture stops, the method `mapView:regionDidChangeAnimated:` gets called. You would implement these if you had functionality that needed to happen while the view region was changing, or after it had finished changing.

DETERMINING IF COORDINATES ARE VISIBLE

One task that you may need to do quite often in the region change delegate methods is to determine if a particular set of coordinates are currently visible on screen. For annotations, and for the user's current location (if it is being tracked), the map view will take care of figuring that out for you. There will still be times, however, when you need to know if a particular set of coordinates is currently within the map view's displayed region.

Here's how you can determine that:

```
CLLocationDegrees leftDegrees = mapView.region.center.longitude -
    (mapView.region.span.longitudeDelta / 2.0);
CLLocationDegrees rightDegrees = mapView.region.center.longitude +
    (mapView.region.span.longitudeDelta / 2.0);
CLLocationDegrees bottomDegrees = mapView.region.center.latitude -
    (mapView.region.span.latitudeDelta / 2.0);
CLLocationDegrees topDegrees = self.region.center.latitude +
    (mapView.region.span.latitudeDelta / 2.0);

if (leftDegrees > rightDegrees) { // Int'l Date Line in View
    leftDegrees = -180.0 - leftDegrees;
    if (coords.longitude > 0) // coords to West of Date Line
        coords.longitude = -180.0 - coords.longitude;
}

If (leftDegrees <= coords.longitude && coords.longitude <= rightDegrees &&
    bottomDegrees <= coords.latitude && coords.latitude <= topDegrees) {
    // Coordinates are being displayed
}
```

In the *11 - MapMe* project in the book's project archive, you can find a category on `MKMapView` that incorporates this logic. The files that implement that category are *MKMapView-CoordsDispay.h* and *MKMapView-CoordsDispay.m*.

Before we move on to the rest of the map view delegate methods, we need to first discuss the topic of annotations.

Annotations

Map views offer the ability to tag a specific location with a set of supplementary information. That information, along with its graphic representation on the map, is called an **annotation**. The pin we drop in the application we're going to write (see Figure 11–2) is a form of annotation. The annotation is composed of two components, the **annotation object**, and an **annotation view**. The map view will keep track of its annotations and will call out to its delegate when it needs to display any of its annotations.

The Annotation Object

Every annotation must have an annotation object, which is almost always going to be a custom class that you write and that conforms to the protocol `MKAnnotation`. An annotation object is typically a fairly standard data model object whose job it is to hold whatever data is relevant to the annotation in question. The annotation object has to respond to two methods and implement a single property. The two methods that an annotation object must implement are called `title` and `subtitle`, and they are the information that will be displayed in the annotation's callout, the little floating view that pops up when the annotation is selected. Back in Figure 11–4, you can see the title and subtitle displayed in the callout. In that instance, the annotation object returned a title of *You are Here!*, and a subtitle of *Infinite Loop • Cupertino, CA*.

An annotation object must also have a property called `coordinate` that returns a `CLLocationCoordinate2D` specifying where in the world (geographically speaking) the annotation should be placed. The map view will use that location to determine where to draw the annotation.

The Annotation View

As we said before, when a map view needs to display any of its annotations, it will call out to its delegate to retrieve an annotation view for that annotation. It does this using the method `mapView:viewForAnnotation:`, which needs to return an `MKAnnotationView` or a subclass of `MKAnnotationView`. The annotation view is the object that gets displayed on the map, not the floating window that gets displayed when the annotation is selected. In Figure 11–4, the annotation view is the pin in the center of the window. It's a pin because we're using a provided subclass of `MKAnnotationView` called `MKPinAnnotationView`, which is designed to draw a red, green, or purple pushpin. It also adds some additional functionality that `MKAnnotationView` doesn't have, such as the pin drop animation.

You can subclass `MKAnnotationView` and implement your own `drawRect:` method if you have advanced drawing needs for your annotation view. Subclassing `MKAnnotationView` is often unnecessary, however, because you can create an instance of `MKAnnotationView` and set its image property to whatever image you want. This opens up a whole world of possibilities without having to ever subclass or add subviews to `MKAnnotationView` (see Figure 11–6).

Figure 11–6. *By setting the image property of an MKAnnotationView, you can display just about anything on the map. In this example, we've replaced the pin with a blood orange, because that's the way we roll.*

Adding and Removing Annotations

The map view keeps track of all of its annotations, so adding an annotation to the map is simply a matter of calling the map view's addAnnotation: method and providing an object that conforms to the MKAnnotation protocol:

```
[mapView addAnnotation:annotation];
```

You can also add multiple annotations by providing an array of annotations, using the method addAnnotations:.

```
[mapView addAnnotations:[NSArray arrayWithObjects:annotation1, annotation2, nil]];
```

You can remove annotations by using either the removeAnnotation: method, and passing in a single annotation to be removed, or by calling removeAnnotations: and passing in an array containing multiple annotations to be removed. All the map view's annotations are accessible using a property called annotations, so if you wanted to remove all annotations from the view, you could to this:

```
[mapView removeAnnotations:mapView.annotations];
```

Selecting Annotations

At any given time, one and only one annotation can be selected. The selected annotation will usually display a **callout**, which is that floating bubble or other view that gives more detailed information about the annotation. The default callout shows the title and subtitle from the annotation. However, you can actually customize the callout, which is just an instance of `UIView`. We won't be providing custom callout views in this chapter's application, but the process is very similar to customizing table view cells the way we did in Chapter 8 of *Beginning iPhone 3 Development*. For more information on customizing a callout, check the documentation for `MKAnnotationView`.

> **NOTE:** Although only a single annotation can currently be selected, `MKMapView` actually uses an instance of `NSMutableArray` to keep track of the selected annotations. This may be an indication that at some point in the future, map views will support selecting multiple annotations at once. Currently, if you provide a `selectedAnnotations` array with more than one annotation, only the first object in that array will be selected.

If the user taps an annotation's image (the push pin in Figure 11–4, or the blood orange in Figure 11–6), it selects that annotation. You can also select an annotation programmatically using the method `selectAnnotation:animated:` and can deselect an annotation programmatically using `deselectAnnotation:animated:`, passing in the annotation you want to select or deselect. If you pass `YES` to the second parameter, it will animate the appearance or disappearance of the callout.

Providing the Map View with Annotation Views

Map views ask their delegate for the annotation view that corresponds to a particular annotation using a delegate method called `mapView:viewForAnnotation:`. This method is called anytime an annotation moves into the map view's displayed region.

Very much like the way table view cells work, annotation views are dequeued, but not deallocated when they scroll off of the screen. Implementations of `mapView:viewForAnnotation:` should ask the map view if there are any dequeued annotation views before allocating a new one. That means that `mapView:viewForAnnotation:` is going to look a fair amount like the many `tableView:cellForRowAtIndexPath:` methods we've written. Here's an example that creates an annotation view, sets its image property to display a custom image, and returns it:

```
- (MKAnnotationView *) mapView:(MKMapView *)theMapView
            viewForAnnotation:(id <MKAnnotation>) annotation {
    static NSString *placemarkIdentifier = @"my annotation identifier";
    if ([annotation isKindOfClass:[MyAnnotation class]]) {
        MKAnnotationView *annotationView = [theMapView
            dequeueReusableAnnotationViewWithIdentifier:placemarkIdentifier];
        if (annotationView == nil)  {
            annotationView = [[MKAnnotationView alloc] initWithAnnotation:annotation
```

```
            reuseIdentifier:placemarkIdentifier];
        annotationView.image = [UIImage imageNamed:@"blood_orange.png"];
    }
    else
        annotationView.annotation = annotation;
    return annotationView;
}
    return nil;
}
```

A few things to notice, here. First, notice that we check the annotation class to make sure it's an annotation we know about. The map view's delegate doesn't only get notified of our custom annotations. Remember, earlier, we talked about the MKUserLocation object that encapsulated the user's location. Well, that's an annotation also, and when you turn on user tracking for a map, your delegate method gets called whenever the user location needs to be displayed. You could provide your own annotation view for that, but if you return nil, the map view will use the default annotation view for it. Generally speaking, for any annotation you don't recognize, your method should return nil and the map view will probably handle it correctly.

Notice we also have an identifier value called placemarkIdentifier. This allows us to make sure we're dequeing the right kind of annotation view. We're not limited to using only one type of annotation view for all of our map's annotations, and the identifier is the way we tell which ones are used for what.

If we did dequeue an annotation view, it's important that we set its annotation property to the annotation that was passed in (annotation in the preceding example). The dequeued annotation view is almost certainly linked to some annotation, and not necessarily the one it should be linked to.

Reverse Geocoding

The map view may be the core of MapKit's functionality, but there's more to explore. Another big feature of MapKit is the ability to do reverse geocoding, which turns a set of coordinates into an address. Reverse geocoding works by comparing a set of coordinates with values stored in a large database (in the case of MapKit, it's Google's database) and returning data about that location. In almost all locations, reverse geocoding will be able to tell you the country and state or province that you're in. The more densely populated the area, the more information you're likely to get. If you're downtown in a large city, you might very well retrieve the street address of the building in which you are located. In most cities and towns, reverse geocoding will, at the very least, get you the name of the street you are on. The tricky thing is, you never know for sure what level of detail you're going to get back.

Reverse geocoding is handled by the MKReverseGeocoder class. It works asynchronously in the background, in much the same way as the networking classes we used in the last three chapters.

To perform reverse geocoding, you start by creating an instance of `MKReverseGeocoder` and initializing it with the coordinates you want to reverse geocode. Then you tell it to start.

```
MKReverseGeocoder *geocoder = [[MKReverseGeocoder alloc]
    initWithCoordinate:coordinates];
geocoder.delegate = self;
[geocoder start];
```

If the instance of `MKReverseGeocoder` is unable to resolve the coordinates, it will call the method `reverseGeocoder:didFailWithError:` on its delegate. Here's a simple implementation of that method that just logs the error. In your real-world applications, you'll probably want to take other actions, such as to inform the user of the problem.

```
- (void)reverseGeocoder:(MKReverseGeocoder *)geocoder
    didFailWithError:(NSError *)error {
NSLog(@"Error resolving coordinates: %@", [error localizedDescription]);
geocoder.delegate = nil;
[geocoder autorelease];
}
```

Assuming the reverse geocoder doesn't hit an error, it will call the method `reverseGeocoder:didFindPlacemark:` to provide its delegate with all the information about the coordinates that it was able to discern. A placemark, represented by the class `MKPlacemark`, contains information about a specific location. It's designed to hold an address for any location in the world. As a result, it doesn't use, perhaps, the terminology you might expect it to use. You won't see street address, city, state, or ZIP. Instead, you'll see properties like `thoroughfare`, `subthoroughfare`, `locality`, and `administrativeArea`.

Here is a handy table to help map `MKPlacemark`'s terminology to the terms with which you might be more familiar:

MKPlacemark Property	Meaning
thoroughfare	Street address. First line if multiple lines.
subthoroughfare	Street address, second line (e.g., apartment or unit number, box number)
locality	City
sublocality	This might contain a neighborhood or landmark name, though it's often nil
administrativeArea	State, province, territory, or other similar unit
subAdministrativeArea	County
postalCode	ZIP code
country	Country
countryCode	Two-digit ISO country code (see: http://en.wikipedia.org/wiki/ISO_3166-1_alpha-2)

Here's an example that pulls information from a placemark in the `reverseGeocoder:didFindPlacemark:` method:

```
- (void)reverseGeocoder:(MKReverseGeocoder *)geocoder
        didFindPlacemark:(MKPlacemark *)placemark {
    NSString *streetAddress = placemark.thoroughfare;
    NSString *city = placemark.locality;
    NSString *state = placemark.administrativeArea;
    NSString *zip = placemark.postalCode;

    // Do something with information

    geocoder.delegate = nil;
    [geocoder autorelease];
}
```

Notice that in both of the reverse geocoder delegate methods, when we're all done, we set the geocoder's delegate to `nil` and release it. Once a geocoder has either found a placemark or failed to do so, there's not much purpose it can serve, so it makes sense to clean it up forthwith.

You know what? That's enough talking about MapKit. Let's start actually using it.

Building the MapMe Application

Let's build an application that shows some of the basic features of the MapKit. Start by creating a new project in Xcode using the *View-based Application* template. Call the new project *MapMe*.

Declaring Outlets and Actions

Before we head over to Interface Builder to design our application's interface, let's declare the outlets and actions we need. We've only got one button, so we only need one action method. We also need an outlet to that button, so we can hide it when it's not available, as well as an outlet to a progress indicator, an outlet to a label, and, of course, an outlet to a map view.

Single-click *MapMeViewController.h*, and replace the contents with the following:

```
#import <UIKit/UIKit.h>
#import <MapKit/MapKit.h>
#import <CoreLocation/CoreLocation.h>

@interface MapMeViewController : UIViewController
    <CLLocationManagerDelegate, MKReverseGeocoderDelegate, MKMapViewDelegate,
    UIAlertViewDelegate> {
    MKMapView          *mapView;
    UIProgressView     *progressBar;
    UILabel            *progressLabel;
    UIButton           *button;
}

@property (nonatomic, retain) IBOutlet MKMapView *mapView;
```

```
@property (nonatomic, retain) IBOutlet UIProgressView *progressBar;
@property (nonatomic, retain) IBOutlet UILabel *progressLabel;
@property (nonatomic, retain) IBOutlet UIButton *button;

- (IBAction)findMe;

@end
```

NOTE: Although map views are capable of tracking the user's current location, we're going to track the user's location manually using Core Location in this application. By doing it manually, we can show you more MapKit features. If you need to track the user's location in your own applications, just let the map view do it for you.

For starters, we import both the MapKit and CoreLocation header files, because we're going to use both Core Location and Map Kit in this application. Then we conform our class to a whole bunch of delegate protocols. We conform to `CLLocationManagerDelegate` so we can get notified by Core Location of the user's current location, `MKReverseGeocoderDelegate` because we're going to use MapKit's reverse geocoder, `MKMapKitDelegate` because we're going to be our map view's delegate and, finally, we conform to the `UIAlertViewDelegate` so we can get notified when the user has dismissed the alert views that we'll use to inform the user if something went wrong.

After that, we have four instance variables for each of the user interface items we're going to add in Interface Builder, and four properties, one for each instance variable, all specified with the `IBOutlet` keyword. We only have one action method, called `findMe`, which will be called when our application's lone button is pressed.

Save *MapMeViewController.h* and double-click *MapMeViewController.xib* to launch Interface Builder.

Building the Interface

Once Interface Builder opens, look in the library for a *Map View* (Figure 11–7). Drag the map view over to the window titled *View*. Interface Builder will resize the view to fit the entire window since it's the first object we're adding. Drop it on the view so it takes up the entire area, then click and drag up on the bottom-middle resize handle to shorten the view and leave some room at the bottom for the other controls like in Figure 11–8. We made the map view 400 pixels tall, though you don't have to match that exactly. Note that you also accomplish this by typing ⌘3 and entering *400* in the *Map View*'s height field.

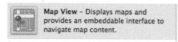

Figure 11–7. *The Map View as it appears in Interface Builder's library*

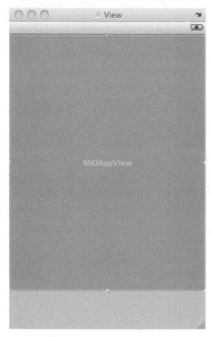

Figure 11–8. *Shortening the map view to leave room for the other controls*

Control-drag from the map view to the *File's Owner* icon in the nib's main window and select *delegate* to make `MapMeViewController` the map view's delegate. Next, control-drag back from *File's Owner* to the map view and select the *mapView* outlet.

Next, drag a *Round Rect Button* from the library over to the window, and place it in the space below the map view, against the right margin. Double-click the newly placed button to edit its title, and type *Go*. Control-drag from the button you just placed to *File's Owner* and select the *findMe* action so that the new button triggers our application's one action method. Then, control-drag back from *File's Owner* to the button and select the *button* outlet.

Drag a *Progress View* from the library, and place it to the left of the button, with the top of the progress view and the top of the button aligned. Resize using the blue guidelines so it extends horizontally from the left margin to the right margin. It will overlap the button, and that's okay. Control-drag from *File's Owner* to the progress view and select the *progressBar* outlet. Press ⌘1 to bring up the attribute inspector. Click in the check box that's labeled *Hidden* so that the progress bar will not be visible until we want to report progress to the user.

Finally, drag a *Label* from the library over to the view and place it below the progress bar. Resize it horizontally so that it takes up the entire width from the left margin guides to the right margin guides. Control-drag from *File's Owner* to the label and select the *progressLabel* outlet. Now, use the attribute inspector to center the label's text then press ⌘T to bring up the text palette and change the font size to 13 so that the text will fit better. Double-click the label and press the delete button to delete the word *Label*.

Save the nib and go back to Xcode.

Writing the Annotation Object Class

We need to create a class to hold our annotation object. We're going to build a simple one that stores some address information, which we'll pull from the reverse geocoder. Single-click the *Classes* folder in the *Groups & Files* pane and then press ⌘N to create a new file. Select the *Objective-C class* template and make sure the *Subclass of* pop-up menu is set to *NSObject*. Name the new file *MapLocation.m* and have Xcode create *MapLocation.h* for you as well.

Once the new files have been created, single-click *MapLocation.h*. Replace the existing file with the following class header:

```
#import <Foundation/Foundation.h>
#import <MapKit/MapKit.h>

@interface MapLocation : NSObject <MKAnnotation, NSCoding> {
    NSString *streetAddress;
    NSString *city;
    NSString *state;
    NSString *zip;

    CLLocationCoordinate2D coordinate;
}

@property (nonatomic, copy) NSString *streetAddress;
@property (nonatomic, copy) NSString *city;
@property (nonatomic, copy) NSString *state;
@property (nonatomic, copy) NSString *zip;
@property (nonatomic, readwrite) CLLocationCoordinate2D coordinate;

@end
```

We did say that annotations were pretty standard data model classes, didn't we? We conformed this to MKAnnotation, and also to NSCoding. We're not actually going to use the archiving functionality, but it's just good habit to conform data model classes to NSCoding. We have four NSString instance variables and corresponding properties that we'll use to store address data, along with a CLLocationCoordinate2D, which will be used to track this annotation's location on the map.

Notice that we've specifically declared the coordinate property to be readwrite. The MKAnnotation protocol declares this property as readonly. We could have declared it that way as well, and then just set the coordinate property by using the underlying instance variable, but we wanted to use the property to let other classes set our annotation's coordinates. It's okay to redefine properties to be more permissive than the same property as declared in a protocol to which you've conformed, or as declared in your superclass. You can always redefine a readonly or writeonly property to be readwrite, but you have to explicitly use the `readwrite` keyword. Most of the time, that keyword isn't used because it's the default value and unnecessary.

Save *MapLocation.h* and switch over to the implementation file, *MapLocation.m*. Replace it with the following code:

NOTE: You can type the • character by pressing ⌥⇧8. Or you can just choose a different character to separate the address lines, if you prefer. Don't put a newline in the string, however, because it will be stripped out when displayed in the annotation's callout view. The default callout gives one line and one line only to the subtitle.

```objc
#import "MapLocation.h"
#import <MapKit/MapKit.h>

@implementation MapLocation
@synthesize streetAddress;
@synthesize city;
@synthesize state;
@synthesize zip;
@synthesize coordinate;

#pragma mark -
- (NSString *)title {
    return NSLocalizedString(@"You are Here!", @"You are Here!");
}

- (NSString *)subtitle {
    NSMutableString *ret = [NSMutableString string];
    if (streetAddress)
        [ret appendString:streetAddress];
    if (streetAddress && (city || state || zip))
        [ret appendString:@" • "];
    if (city)
        [ret appendString:city];
    if (city && state)
        [ret appendString:@", "];
    if (state)
        [ret appendString:state];
    if (zip)
        [ret appendFormat:@", %@", zip];

    return ret;
}

#pragma mark -
- (void)dealloc {
    [streetAddress release];
    [city release];
    [state release];
    [zip release];
    [super dealloc];
}

#pragma mark -
```

```
#pragma mark NSCoding Methods
- (void)encodeWithCoder: (NSCoder *)encoder {
    [encoder encodeObject: [self streetAddress] forKey: @"streetAddress"];
    [encoder encodeObject: [self city] forKey:@"city"];
    [encoder encodeObject: [self state] forKey: @"state"];
    [encoder encodeObject: [self zip] forKey: @"zip"];
}

- (id) initWithCoder: (NSCoder *)decoder  {
    if (self = [super init]) {
        [self setStreetAddress: [decoder decodeObjectForKey: @"streetAddress"]];
        [self setCity: [decoder decodeObjectForKey: @"city"]];
        [self setState: [decoder decodeObjectForKey: @"state"]];
        [self setZip: [decoder decodeObjectForKey: @"zip"]];
    }
    return self;
}

@end
```

There really shouldn't be anything there that throws you for a loop. For the `MKAnnotation` protocol method, `title`, we just return *You are Here!*:

```
- (NSString *)title {
    return NSLocalizedString(@"You are Here!", @"You are Here!");
}
```

The subtitle method, however, is a little more complex. Because we don't know which data elements the reverse geocoder will give us, we have to build the subtitle string based on what we have. We do that by declaring a mutable string, and then appending the values from our non-nil, non-empty properties.

```
- (NSString *)subtitle {
    NSMutableString *ret = [NSMutableString string];
    if (streetAddress)
        [ret appendString:streetAddress];
    if (streetAddress && (city || state || zip))
        [ret appendString:@" • "];
    if (city)
        [ret appendString:city];
    if (city && state)
        [ret appendString:@", "];
    if (state)
        [ret appendString:state];
    if (zip)
        [ret appendFormat:@", %@", zip];

    return ret;
}
```

Everything else here is standard stuff you've seen dozens of times, so let's move on to implementing the `MapMeViewController` class. Save *MapLocation.m* before proceeding.

Implementing MapMeViewController

Single-click *MapMeViewController.m*. Replace the existing template code with the following:

```objc
#import "MapMeViewController.h"
#import "MapLocation.h"

@implementation MapMeViewController
@synthesize mapView;
@synthesize progressBar;
@synthesize progressLabel;
@synthesize button;
#pragma mark -

- (IBAction)findMe {
    CLLocationManager *lm = [[CLLocationManager alloc] init];
    lm.delegate = self;
    lm.desiredAccuracy = kCLLocationAccuracyBest;
    [lm startUpdatingLocation];

    progressBar.hidden = NO;
    progressBar.progress = 0.0;
    progressLabel.text = NSLocalizedString(@"Determining Current Location",
        @"Determining Current Location");

    button.hidden = YES;
}

- (void)openCallout:(id<MKAnnotation>)annotation {
    progressBar.progress = 1.0;
    progressLabel.text = NSLocalizedString(@"Showing Annotation",
        @"Showing Annotation");
    [mapView selectAnnotation:annotation animated:YES];
}

#pragma mark -
- (void)viewDidLoad {
    // uncomment different rows to change type
    mapView.mapType = MKMapTypeStandard;
    //mapView.mapType = MKMapTypeSatellite;
    //mapView.mapType = MKMapTypeHybrid;
}

- (void)viewDidUnload {
    self.mapView = nil;
    self.progressBar = nil;
    self.progressLabel = nil;
    self.button = nil;
}

- (void)dealloc {
    [mapView release];
    [progressBar release];
    [progressLabel release];
    [button release];
    [super dealloc];
```

```
}

#pragma mark -
#pragma mark CLLocationManagerDelegate Methods
- (void)locationManager:(CLLocationManager *)manager
    didUpdateToLocation:(CLLocation *)newLocation
           fromLocation:(CLLocation *)oldLocation {
    if ([newLocation.timestamp timeIntervalSince1970] <
        [NSDate timeIntervalSinceReferenceDate] - 60)
        return;

    MKCoordinateRegion viewRegion =
        MKCoordinateRegionMakeWithDistance(newLocation.coordinate, 2000, 2000);
    MKCoordinateRegion adjustedRegion = [mapView regionThatFits:viewRegion];
    [mapView setRegion:adjustedRegion animated:YES];

    manager.delegate = nil;
    [manager stopUpdatingLocation];
    [manager autorelease];

    progressBar.progress = .25;
    progressLabel.text = NSLocalizedString(@"Reverse Geocoding Location",
        @"Reverse Geocoding Location");

    MKReverseGeocoder *geocoder = [[MKReverseGeocoder alloc]
        initWithCoordinate:newLocation.coordinate];
    geocoder.delegate = self;
    [geocoder start];
}

- (void)locationManager:(CLLocationManager *)manager
        didFailWithError:(NSError *)error {

    NSString *errorType = (error.code == kCLErrorDenied) ?
    NSLocalizedString(@"Access Denied", @"Access Denied") :
    NSLocalizedString(@"Unknown Error", @"Unknown Error");

    UIAlertView *alert = [[UIAlertView alloc]
                            initWithTitle:NSLocalizedString(@"Error getting Location",
                                @"Error getting Location")
                            message:errorType
                            delegate:self
                            cancelButtonTitle:NSLocalizedString(@"Okay", @"Okay")
                            otherButtonTitles:nil];
    [alert show];
    [alert release];
    [manager release];
}

#pragma mark -
#pragma mark Alert View Delegate Methods
- (void)alertView:(UIAlertView *)alertView
didDismissWithButtonIndex:(NSInteger)buttonIndex {
    progressBar.hidden = YES;
    progressLabel.text = @"";
}
```

```
#pragma mark -
#pragma mark Reverse Geocoder Delegate Methods
- (void)reverseGeocoder:(MKReverseGeocoder *)geocoder
        didFailWithError:(NSError *)error {
    UIAlertView *alert = [[UIAlertView alloc]
                             initWithTitle:NSLocalizedString(
                                 @"Error translating coordinates into location",
                                 @"Error translating coordinates into location")
                             message:NSLocalizedString(
                                 @"Geocoder did not recognize coordinates",
                                 @"Geocoder did not recognize coordinates")
                             delegate:self
                             cancelButtonTitle:NSLocalizedString(@"Okay", @"Okay")
                             otherButtonTitles:nil];
    [alert show];
    [alert release];

    geocoder.delegate = nil;
    [geocoder autorelease];
}

- (void)reverseGeocoder:(MKReverseGeocoder *)geocoder
        didFindPlacemark:(MKPlacemark *)placemark {
    progressBar.progress = 0.5;
    progressLabel.text = NSLocalizedString(@"Location Determined",
        @"Location Determined");

    MapLocation *annotation = [[MapLocation alloc] init];
    annotation.streetAddress = placemark.thoroughfare;
    annotation.city = placemark.locality;
    annotation.state = placemark.administrativeArea;
    annotation.zip = placemark.postalCode;
    annotation.coordinate = geocoder.coordinate;

    [mapView addAnnotation:annotation];

    [annotation release];

    geocoder.delegate = nil;
    [geocoder autorelease];
}

#pragma mark -
#pragma mark Map View Delegate Methods
- (MKAnnotationView *)mapView:(MKMapView *)theMapView
            viewForAnnotation:(id <MKAnnotation>)annotation {
    static NSString *placemarkIdentifier = @"Map Location Identifier";
    if ([annotation isKindOfClass:[MapLocation class]]) {
        MKPinAnnotationView *annotationView = (MKPinAnnotationView *)[theMapView
            dequeueReusableAnnotationViewWithIdentifier:placemarkIdentifier];
        if (annotationView == nil)  {
            annotationView = [[MKPinAnnotationView alloc]
                initWithAnnotation:annotation reuseIdentifier:placemarkIdentifier];
        }
        else
            annotationView.annotation = annotation;
```

```
        annotationView.enabled = YES;
        annotationView.animatesDrop = YES;
        annotationView.pinColor = MKPinAnnotationColorPurple;
        annotationView.canShowCallout = YES;
        [self performSelector:@selector(openCallout:) withObject:annotation
            afterDelay:0.5];

        progressBar.progress = 0.75;
        progressLabel.text = NSLocalizedString(@"Creating Annotation",
            @"Creating Annotation");

        return annotationView;
    }
    return nil;
}

- (void)mapViewDidFailLoadingMap:(MKMapView *)theMapView
                    withError:(NSError *)error {
    UIAlertView *alert = [[UIAlertView alloc]
                        initWithTitle:NSLocalizedString(@"Error loading map",
                            @"Error loading map")
                        message:[error localizedDescription]
                        delegate:nil
                        cancelButtonTitle:NSLocalizedString(@"Okay", @"Okay")
                        otherButtonTitles:nil];
    [alert show];
    [alert release];
}

@end
```

Let's take it from the top, shall we? The first method in our class is the action method that gets called when the user presses a button. This is the logical starting point for our application's logic, so let's look at it first.

As we've discussed before, we could have used the map view's ability to track the user's location, but we wanted to handle things manually to show more functionality. Therefore, we allocate and initialize an instance of CLLocationManager so we can determine the user's location. We set self as the delegate, and tell the Location Manager we want the best accuracy available, before telling it to start updating the location.

```
- (IBAction)findMe {
    CLLocationManager *lm = [[CLLocationManager alloc] init];
    lm.delegate = self;
    lm.desiredAccuracy = kCLLocationAccuracyBest;
    [lm startUpdatingLocation];
```

Then, we unhide the progress bar and set the progress label to tell the user that we are trying to determine the current location.

```
    progressBar.hidden = NO;
    progressBar.progress = 0.0;
    progressLabel.text = NSLocalizedString(@"Determining Current Location",
        @"Determining Current Location");
```

Lastly, we hide the button so the user can't press it again.

```
        button.hidden = YES;
}
```

Next, we have a private method called openCallout: that we'll use a little later to select our annotation. We can't select the annotation when we add it to the map view. We have to wait until it's been added before we can select it. This method will allow us to select an annotation, which will open the annotation's callout, by using performSelector:withObject:afterDelay:. All we do in this method is update the progress bar and progress label to show that we're at the last step, and then use the MKMapView's selectAnnotation:animated: method to select the annotation, which will cause its callout view to be shown.

> **NOTE:** We didn't declare this method in our header file, nor did we declare it in a category or extension. Yet the compiler is happy. That's because this method is located earlier in the file than the code that calls it, so the compiler knows about. If we were to move the openCallout: method to the end of the file, then we would get a compile time warning, and would have to declare the method in an extension or in our class's header file.

```
- (void)openCallout:(id<MKAnnotation>)annotation {
    progressBar.progress = 1.0;
    progressLabel.text = NSLocalizedString(@"Showing Annotation",
        @"Showing Annotation");
    [mapView selectAnnotation:annotation animated:YES];
}
```

In the viewDidLoad method, we gave you code to try out all three map types, with two of them commented out. This is just to make it easier for you to change the one you're using and experiment a little.

```
- (void)viewDidLoad {
    // uncomment different rows to change type
    mapView.mapType = MKMapTypeStandard;
    //mapView.mapType = MKMapTypeSatellite;
    //mapView.mapType = MKMapTypeHybrid;
}
```

Both viewDidUnload and dealloc are standard, so we won't talk about them. After those, we get to our various delegate methods. First up is the location manager delegate method where we're notified of the user's location. We did something here that we didn't do in *Beginning iPhone 3 Development*, which is to check the timestamp of newLocation and make sure it's not more than a minute old.

In the application we built in the first book, we wanted to keep getting updates while the application was running. In this application, we only want to know the current location once, but we don't want a cached location. Location Manager caches locations so that it has quick access to the last known location. Since we're only going to use one update, we want to discard any stale location data that was pulled from the location manager's cache.

```
- (void)locationManager:(CLLocationManager *)manager
    didUpdateToLocation:(CLLocation *)newLocation
```

```
        fromLocation:(CLLocation *)oldLocation {
    if ([newLocation.timestamp timeIntervalSince1970] <
        [NSDate timeIntervalSinceReferenceDate] - 60)
        return;
```

Once we've made sure we have a fresh location, taken within the last minute, we then use the MKCoordinateRegionMakeWithDistance() function to create a region that shows one kilometer on each side of the user's current location.

```
MKCoordinateRegion viewRegion =
    MKCoordinateRegionMakeWithDistance(newLocation.coordinate, 2000, 2000);
```

We then adjust that region to the aspect ratio of our map view and then tell the map view to show that new adjusted region.

```
MKCoordinateRegion adjustedRegion = [mapView regionThatFits:viewRegion];
[mapView setRegion:adjustedRegion animated:YES];
```

Now that we've gotten a non-cache location, we're going to stop having the location manager give us updates. Location updates are a drain on the battery, so when you don't want any more updates, you'll want to shut location manager down, like so:

```
manager.delegate = nil;
[manager stopUpdatingLocation];
[manager autorelease];
```

Then we update the progress bar and label to let them know where we are in the whole process. This is the first of four steps after the *Go* button is pressed, so we set progress to .25, which will show a bar that is one-quarter blue.

```
progressBar.progress = .25;
progressLabel.text = NSLocalizedString(@"Reverse Geocoding Location",
    @"Reverse Geocoding Location");
```

Next, we allocate an instance of MKReverseGeocoder using the current location pulled from newLocation. We set self as the delegate and kick it off.

```
MKReverseGeocoder *geocoder = [[MKReverseGeocoder alloc]
    initWithCoordinate:newLocation.coordinate];
geocoder.delegate = self;
[geocoder start];
}
```

NOTE: We didn't release geocoder here, nor did we release the location manager in the findMe method. In both cases, we autorelease the objects in the last delegate method we use.

If the location manager encounters an error, we just show an alert. Not the most robust error handling, but it'll do for this.

```
- (void)locationManager:(CLLocationManager *)manager
        didFailWithError:(NSError *)error {

    NSString *errorType = (error.code == kCLErrorDenied) ?
    NSLocalizedString(@"Access Denied", @"Access Denied") :
    NSLocalizedString(@"Unknown Error", @"Unknown Error");
```

```
UIAlertView *alert = [[UIAlertView alloc]
                     initWithTitle:NSLocalizedString(@"Error getting Location",
                         @"Error getting Location")
                     message:errorType
                     delegate:self
                     cancelButtonTitle:NSLocalizedString(@"Okay", @"Okay")
                     otherButtonTitles:nil];
    [alert show];
    [alert release];
    [manager release];
}
```

Our alert view delegate method just hides the progress bar and sets the progress label to an empty string. For simplicity's sake, we're just dead-ending the application if a problem occurs. In your apps, you'll probably want to do something a little more user-friendly.

```
- (void)alertView:(UIAlertView *)alertView
didDismissWithButtonIndex:(NSInteger)buttonIndex {
    progressBar.hidden = YES;
    progressLabel.text = @"";
}
```

If the reverse geocoding fails, we do basically the same thing we'd do if the location manager failed: put up an alert and dead-end the process.

```
- (void)reverseGeocoder:(MKReverseGeocoder *)geocoder
        didFailWithError:(NSError *)error {
    UIAlertView *alert = [[UIAlertView alloc]
                     initWithTitle:NSLocalizedString(
                         @"Error translating coordinates into location",
                         @"Error translating coordinates into location")
                     message:NSLocalizedString(
                         @"Geocoder did not recognize coordinates",
                         @"Geocoder did not recognize coordinates")
                     delegate:self
                     cancelButtonTitle:NSLocalizedString(@"Okay", @"Okay")
                     otherButtonTitles:nil];
    [alert show];
    [alert release];

    geocoder.delegate = nil;
    [geocoder autorelease];
}
```

If the reverse geocoder succeeded, however, we update the progress bar and progress label to inform the user that we're one step further along in the process.

```
- (void)reverseGeocoder:(MKReverseGeocoder *)geocoder
        didFindPlacemark:(MKPlacemark *)placemark {
    progressBar.progress = 0.5;
    progressLabel.text = NSLocalizedString(@"Location Determined",
        @"Location Determined");
```

Then, we allocate and initialize an instance of `MapLocation` to act as the annotation that represents the user's current location. We assign its properties from the returned placemark.

```
MapLocation *annotation = [[MapLocation alloc] init];
annotation.streetAddress = placemark.thoroughfare;
annotation.city = placemark.locality;
annotation.state = placemark.administrativeArea;
annotation.zip = placemark.postalCode;
annotation.coordinate = geocoder.coordinate;
```

Once we have our annotation, we add it to the map view and release it.

```
[mapView addAnnotation:annotation];

[annotation release];
```

And, then, to be good memory citizens, we set the geocoder's delegate to `nil` and autorelease it.

```
geocoder.delegate = nil;
[geocoder autorelease];
}
```

When the map view for which we are the delegate needs an annotation view, it will call this next method. The first thing we do is declare an identifier so we can dequeue the right kind of annotation view, then we make sure the map view is asking us about a type of annotation that we know about.

```
- (MKAnnotationView *) mapView:(MKMapView *)theMapView
           viewForAnnotation:(id <MKAnnotation>) annotation {
    static NSString *placemarkIdentifier = @"Map Location Identifier";
    if ([annotation isKindOfClass:[MapLocation class]]) {
```

If it is, we dequeue an instance of `MKPinAnnotationView` with our identifier. If there are no dequeued views, we create one. We could also have used `MKAnnotationView` here instead of `MKPinAnnotationView`. In fact, there's an alternate version of this project in the project archive that shows how to use `MKAnnotationView` to display a custom annotation view instead of a pin.

```
MKPinAnnotationView *annotationView = (MKPinAnnotationView *)[theMapView
    dequeueReusableAnnotationViewWithIdentifier:placemarkIdentifier];
if (annotationView == nil)  {
    annotationView = [[MKPinAnnotationView alloc]
        initWithAnnotation:annotation reuseIdentifier:placemarkIdentifier];
}
```

If we didn't create a new view, it means we got a dequeued one from the map view. In that case, we have to make sure the dequeued view is linked to the right annotation.

```
else
    annotationView.annotation = annotation;
```

Then we do some configuration. We make sure the annotation view is enabled so it can be selected, we set `animatesDrop` to `YES` because this is a pin view, and we want it to drop onto the map the way pins are wont to do. We set the pin color to purple, and make sure that it can show a callout.

```
annotationView.enabled = YES;
annotationView.animatesDrop = YES;
annotationView.pinColor = MKPinAnnotationColorPurple;
annotationView.canShowCallout = YES;
```

After that, we use performSelector:withObject:afterDelay: to call that private method we created earlier. We can't select an annotation until its view is actually being displayed on the map, so we wait half a second to make sure that's happened before selecting. This will also make sure that the pin has finished dropping before the callout is displayed.

```
[self performSelector:@selector(openCallout:) withObject:annotation
    afterDelay:0.5];
```

We need to update the progress bar and text label to let the user know that we're almost done.

```
progressBar.progress = 0.75;
progressLabel.text = NSLocalizedString(@"Creating Annotation",
    @"Creating Annotation");
```

Then we return the annotation view.

```
return annotationView;
}
```

If the annotation wasn't one we recognize, we return nil and our map view will use the default annotation view for that kind of annotation.

```
    return nil;
}
```

And, lastly, we implement mapViewDidFailLoadingMap:withError: and inform the user if there was a problem loading the map. Again, our error checking in this application is very rudimentary; we just inform the user and stop everything.

```
- (void)mapViewDidFailLoadingMap:(MKMapView *)theMapView
                    withError:(NSError *)error {
    UIAlertView *alert = [[UIAlertView alloc]
                    initWithTitle:NSLocalizedString(@"Error loading map",
                        @"Error loading map")
                    message:[error localizedDescription]
                    delegate:nil
                    cancelButtonTitle:NSLocalizedString(@"Okay", @"Okay")
                    otherButtonTitles:nil];
    [alert show];
    [alert release];
}
```

Linking the Map Kit and Core Location Frameworks

Before you can build and run your app, you need to right-click on the *Frameworks* folder in the *Groups & Files* pane and select **Existing Frameworks...** from the **Add** submenu. Select *CoreLocation.framework* and *MapKit.framework* and click the *Add...* button.

You should now be able to build and run your application, so do that, and try it out. Try experimenting with the code. Change the map type, add more annotations, or try experimenting with custom annotation views.

Go East, Young Programmer

That brings us to the end of our discussion of MapKit. You've seen the basics of how to use MapKit, annotations, and the reverse geocoder. You've seen how to create coordinate regions and coordinate spans to specify what area the map view should show to the user, and you've learned how to use MapKit's reverse geocoder to turn a set of coordinates into a physical address.

Now, armed with your iPhone, MapKit, and sheer determination, navigate your way one page to the East, err… right, so that we can talk about in-application e-mail.

Chapter 12

Sending Mail

Ever since the first public release of the iPhone SDK, applications have always had the ability to send e-mail. Unfortunately, prior to iPhone SDK 3.0, doing so meant crafting a special URL and then launching the iPhone's Mail application, which has the side effect of quitting your own application. This is obviously less than ideal, forcing a user to choose between sending an e-mail and continuing to use your application. Fortunately, the new MessageUI framework allows your user access to e-mail without leaving your application. Let's take a look at how this works.

This Chapter's Application

In this chapter, we're going to build an application that lets the user take a picture using their iPhone's camera or, if they don't have a camera because they're using an iPod touch or the Simulator, then we'll allow them to select an image from their photo library. We'll then take the resulting image and use the MessageUI framework to let our user e-mail the picture to a friend without leaving our application.

Our application's interface will be quite simple (Figure 12–1). It will feature a single button to start the whole thing going, and a label to give feedback to the user, once the e-mail attempt is made. Tapping the button will bring up the camera picker controller, in a manner similar to the sample program in Chapter 16 of *Beginning iPhone 3 Development* (Apress, 2009). Once our user has taken or selected an image, they'll be able to crop and/or scale the image (Figure 12–2). Assuming they don't cancel, the image picker will return an image, and we'll display the **mail compose view** (Figure 12–3), which allows the user to compose their e-mail message. We'll pre-populate that view with text and the selected image. Our user will be able to select recipients and change the subject or message body before sending the message. When they're all done, we'll use the label in our interface to give feedback about whether the e-mail was sent.

Figure 12–1. *Our chapter's application has a very simple user interface consisting of a button and a single label (not shown here)*

Figure 12–2. *The user can take a picture with the camera or select an image from their photo library, and then crop and scale the image*

Figure 12–3. *After selecting and editing the image, we present the mail compose view modally and let our user send the e-mail*

CAUTION: The application in this chapter will run in the simulator, but instead of using the camera, it will allow you to select an image from your Simulator's photo library. If you've ever used the **Reset Contents and Settings** menu item in the simulator, then you have probably lost the photo album's default contents and will have no images available. You can rectify this by launching Mobile Safari in the simulator and navigating to an image on the Web. Make sure the image you are looking at is *not* a link, but a static image. This technique will not work with a linked image. Click and hold the mouse button with your cursor over an image, and an action sheet will pop up. One of the options will be *Save Image*. This will add the selected image to your iPhone's photo library.

In addition, note that you will not be able to send e-mail from within the simulator. You'll be able to create the e-mail, and the simulator will say it sent it, but it's all lies. The e-mail just ends up in the circular file.

The MessageUI Framework

In-application e-mail services are provided by the MessageUI Framework, which is one of the smallest frameworks in the iPhone SDK. It's composed of exactly one class, a view controller that lets the user send e-mail, and a protocol that defines the delegate methods for that view controller.

Creating the Mail Compose View Controller

The view controller class is called MFMailComposeViewController, and it's used similarly to the way the camera picker is used. You create an instance of it, set its delegate, set any properties that you wish to pre-populate, and then you present it modally. When the user is done with their e-mail and taps either the *Send* or *Cancel* button, the mail compose view controller notifies its delegate, which is responsible for dismissing the modal view. Here's how you create a mail compose view controller and set its delegate:

```
MFMailComposeViewController *mc = [[MFMailComposeViewController alloc] init];
mc.mailComposeDelegate = self;
```

Prepopulating the Subject Line

Before you present the mail compose view, you can pre-configure the various fields of the mail compose view controller, such as the subject and recipients (to:, cc:, and bcc:), as well as the body. You can prepopulate the subject by calling the method setSubject: on the instance of MFMailComposeViewController, like this:

```
[mc setSubject:@"Hello, World!"];
```

Prepopulating Recipients

E-mails can go to three types of recipients. The main recipients of the e-mail are called the *to:* recipients and go on the line labeled *to:*. Recipients who are being cc:ed on the e-mail go on the *cc:* line. If you want to include somebody on the e-mail, but not let the other recipients know that person is also receiving the e-mail, you can use the *bcc:* line, which stands for "blind carbon copy." You can prepopulate all three of these fields when using MFMailComposeViewController.

To set the main recipients, use the method setToRecipients: and pass in an NSArray instance containing the e-mail addresses of all the recipients. Here's an example:

```
[mc setToRecipients:[NSArray arrayWithObjects:@"jeff@iphonedevbook.com",
    "@dave@iphonedevbook.com", nil];
```

Set the other two types of recipients in the same manner, though you'll use the methods setCcRecipients: for cc: recipients and setBccRecipients: for bcc: recipients.

```
[mc setCcRecipients:[NSArray arrayWithObject:@"dave@iphonedevbook.com"]];
[mc setBccRecipients:[NSArray arrayWithObject:@"secret@iphonedevbook.com"]];
```

Setting the Message Body

You can also prepopulate the message body with any text you'd like. You can either use a regular string to create a plain text e-mail, or you can use HTML to create a formatted e-mail. To supply the mail compose view controller with a message body, use the method setMessageBody:isHTML:. If the string you pass in is plain text, you should pass NO as the second parameter, but if you're providing HTML markup in the first argument rather than a plain string, then you should pass YES in the second argument so your markup will be parsed before it is shown to the user.

```
[mc setMessageBody:@"Watson!!!\n\nCome here, I need you!" isHTML:NO];
[mc setMessageBody:@"<HTML><B>Hello, Joe!</B><BR/>What do you know?</HTML>"
    isHTML:YES];
```

Adding Attachments

You can also add attachments to outgoing e-mails. In order to do that, you have to provide an instance of NSData containing the data to be attached, along with the **mime type** of the attachment and the file name to be used for the attachment. Mime types, which we discussed briefly back in Chapter 10 when we talked about interacting with web servers, are strings that define the type of data being transferred over the Internet. They're used when retrieving or sending files to a web server, and they're also used when sending e-mail attachments. To add an attachment to an outgoing e-mail, use the method addAttachmentData:mimeType:fileName:. Here's an example of adding an image stored in your application's bundle as an attachment:

```
NSString *path = [[NSBundle mainBundle] pathForResource:@"blood_orange"
    ofType:@"png"];
NSData *data = [NSData dataWithContentsOfFile:path];
[mc addAttachmentData:data mimeType:@"image/png" fileName:@"blood_orange"];
```

Presenting the Mail Compose View

Once you've configured the controller with all the data you want prepopulated, you'll present the controller's view modally, as we've done before:

```
[self presentModalViewController:mc animated:YES];
[mc release];
```

It's common to release the controller once it's presented, as there's no further need to keep it around, and your delegate method will be passed a reference to the controller later, so you can dismiss it.

The Mail Compose View Controller Delegate Method

The mail compose view controller delegate's method is contained in the formal protocol MFMailComposeViewControllerDelegate. Regardless of whether the user sends or cancels, and regardless of whether the system was able to send the message or not, the method mailComposeController:didFinishWithResult:error: gets called. As with most delegate methods, the first parameter is a pointer to the object that called the delegate method. The second parameter is a **result code** that tells us the fate of the outgoing e-mail, and the third is an NSError instance that will give us more detailed information if a problem was encountered. Regardless of what result code you received, it is your responsibility in this method to dismiss the mail compose view controller by calling dismissModalViewControllerAnimated:.

If the user tapped the *Cancel* button, your delegate will be sent the result code MFMailComposeResultCancelled. In that situation, the user changed their mind and decided not to send the e-mail. If the user tapped the *Send* button, the result code is going to depend on whether the MessageUI framework was able to successfully send the e-mail. If it was able to send the message, the result code will be MFMailComposeResultSent. If it tried, and failed, the result code will be MFMailComposeResultFailed, in which case, you probably want to check the provided NSError instance to see what went wrong. If the message couldn't be sent because there's currently no Internet connection, but the message was saved into the outbox to be sent later, you will get a result code of MFMailComposeResultSaved.

Here is a very simple implementation of the delegate method that just logs what happened:

```
- (void)mailComposeController:(MFMailComposeViewController*)controller
        didFinishWithResult:(MFMailComposeResult)result
        error:(NSError*)error {
    switch (result)
    {
        case MFMailComposeResultCancelled:
            NSLog(@"Mail send canceled...");
            break;
        case MFMailComposeResultSaved:
            NSLog(@"Mail saved...");
            break;
        case MFMailComposeResultSent:
            NSLog(@"Mail sent...");
            break;
        case MFMailComposeResultFailed:
            NSLog(@"Mail send errored: %@...", [error localizedDescription]);
            break;
        default:
            break;
    }
    [self dismissModalViewControllerAnimated:YES];
}
```

Building the MailPic Application

Now that we have a handle on the details, the next step is to put that knowledge to work building a mail-sending application of our own. Create a new project in Xcode using the *View-based Application* template. Call the project *MailPic*.

Declaring Outlets and Actions

Once the project opens up, expand the *Classes* folder and single-click *MailPicViewController.h*. Before we design our interface, we need to declare our outlets and actions. Replace the contents of *MailPicViewController.h* with this version:

```
#import <UIKit/UIKit.h>
#import <MessageUI/MessageUI.h>

@interface MailPicViewController : UIViewController
    <MFMailComposeViewControllerDelegate, UIImagePickerControllerDelegate,
        UINavigationControllerDelegate> {
    UILabel *message;
}

@property (nonatomic, retain) IBOutlet UILabel *message;
- (IBAction)selectAndMailPic;
- (void)mailImage:(UIImage *)image;

@end
```

This is pretty straightforward. We import the header `<MessageUI/MessageUI.h>` so the compiler has access to the class and protocol definitions that we need to use the Message UI framework. Then we conform our class to three protocols. We conform to `MFMailComposeViewControllerDelegate` because this class will be acting as the mail compose view controller's delegate. We also conform to the `UIImagePickerControllerDelegate` because we're going to use the image picker controller to get an image, and need to be the picker's delegate to do that. We conform to `UINavigationControllerDelegate` because `UIImagePickerController` is a subclass of `UINavigationController`, and we need to conform to this protocol to avoid compiler warnings, even though we won't actually implement any of that protocol's methods.

We have a single instance variable and property for the label that we'll use to provide feedback to the user, as well as two methods. The first method is an action method that will get triggered when the user taps the button on our interface. The second method will be used to actually present the mail compose view controller so the user can send the e-mail. We need a method separate from the image picker delegate methods to do that because we can't present a new modal view until the previous one has been dismissed. We dismiss the image picker in the image picker delegate methods, and will use `performSelector:withObject:afterDelay:` to call the `mailImage:` method after the camera picker view has been fully dismissed.

Building the User Interface

Save *MailPicViewController.h* and then expand the *Resources* folder in the *Groups & Files* pane. Double-click *MailPicViewController.xib* to launch Interface Builder.

From the library, drag over a *Round Rect Button* and place it anywhere on the window titled *View*. Double-click the button and give it a title of *Go*. Control-drag from the button to *File's Owner* and select the *selectAndMailPic* action.

Next, grab a *Label* from the library and drag it to the *View* window as well. Place the label above the button and resize it so it stretches from the left margin to the right margin. After you place the label, control-drag from *File's Owner* to the new label and select the *message* outlet. Double-click the new label and press delete to erase the word *Label*.

Save the nib file, close Interface Builder, and go back to Xcode.

Implementing the View Controller

Single-click on *MailPicViewController.m*. Replace the existing contents with this new version. We'll step through it when you're done:

```
#import "MailPicViewController.h"

@implementation MailPicViewController
@synthesize message;

- (IBAction)selectAndMailPic {
    UIImagePickerControllerSourceType sourceType =
        UIImagePickerControllerSourceTypeCamera;
    if (![UIImagePickerController isSourceTypeAvailable:
        UIImagePickerControllerSourceTypeCamera]) {
        sourceType = UIImagePickerControllerSourceTypePhotoLibrary;
    }

    UIImagePickerController *picker =
    [[UIImagePickerController alloc] init];
    picker.delegate = self;
    picker.allowsEditing = YES;
    picker.sourceType = sourceType;
    [self presentModalViewController:picker animated:YES];
    [picker release];
}

- (void)mailImage:(UIImage *)image {
    if ([MFMailComposeViewController canSendMail]) {
        MFMailComposeViewController *mailComposer =
            [[MFMailComposeViewController alloc] init];
        mailComposer.mailComposeDelegate = self;
        [mailComposer setSubject:NSLocalizedString(@"Here's a picture...",
            @"Here's a picture...")];
        [mailComposer addAttachmentData:UIImagePNGRepresentation(image)
            mimeType:@"image/png" fileName:@"image"];
        [mailComposer setMessageBody:NSLocalizedString(
            @"Here's a picture that I took with my iPhone.",
            @"Here's a picture that I took with my iPhone.") isHTML:NO];
        [self presentModalViewController:mailComposer animated:YES];
        [mailComposer release];
    }
    else
        message.text = NSLocalizedString(@"Can't send e-mail...",
            @"Can't send e-mail...");
}
```

```
- (void)viewDidUnload {
    self.message = nil;
}

- (void)dealloc {
    [message release];
    [super dealloc];
}

#pragma mark -
#pragma mark Camera Picker Delegate Methods
- (void)imagePickerController:(UIImagePickerController *)picker
didFinishPickingMediaWithInfo:(NSDictionary *)info {
    [picker dismissModalViewControllerAnimated:YES];
    UIImage *image = [info objectForKey:
        UIImagePickerControllerEditedImage];
    [self performSelector:@selector(mailImage:)
                withObject:image
                afterDelay:0.5];
    message.text = @"";
}

- (void)imagePickerControllerDidCancel:(UIImagePickerController *)picker {
    [picker dismissModalViewControllerAnimated:YES];
    message.text = NSLocalizedString(@"Cancelled...", @"Cancelled...");
}

#pragma mark -
#pragma mark Mail Compose Delegate Methods
- (void)mailComposeController:(MFMailComposeViewController*)controller
          didFinishWithResult:(MFMailComposeResult)result
                        error:(NSError*)error {
    switch (result)
    {
        case MFMailComposeResultCancelled:
            message.text = NSLocalizedString(@"Canceled...", @"Canceled...");
            break;
        case MFMailComposeResultSaved:
            message.text = NSLocalizedString(@"Saved to send later...",
                @"Saved to send later...");
            break;
        case MFMailComposeResultSent:
            message.text = NSLocalizedString(@"Mail sent...", @"Mail sent...");
            break;
        case MFMailComposeResultFailed: {
            UIAlertView *alert = [[UIAlertView alloc] initWithTitle:
                NSLocalizedString(@"Error sending mail...",
                    @"Error sending mail...")
                message:[error localizedDescription]
                delegate:nil
                cancelButtonTitle:NSLocalizedString(@"Bummer", @"Bummer")
                otherButtonTitles:nil];
            [alert show];
            [alert release];
            message.text = NSLocalizedString(@"Send failed...", @"Send failed...");
            break;
        }
```

```
        default:
            break;
    }
    [self dismissModalViewControllerAnimated:YES];
}

@end
```

The first method in our implementation file is the action method that's triggered when the user taps the *Go* button. We first need to determine which image picker source type to use (camera or photo library) by finding out if the device we're running on has a camera. If it does, we set `sourceType` to `UIImagePickerControllerSourceTypeCamera`. Otherwise, we use `UIImagePickerControllerSourceTypePhotoLibrary`, which will let the user pick an existing photo from their photo library.

```
- (IBAction)selectAndMailPic {
    UIImagePickerControllerSourceType sourceType =
        UIImagePickerControllerSourceTypeCamera;
    if (![UIImagePickerController isSourceTypeAvailable:
        UIImagePickerControllerSourceTypeCamera]) {
        sourceType = UIImagePickerControllerSourceTypePhotoLibrary;
    }
```

Then we create the image picker, configure it, and present it to the user.

```
    UIImagePickerController *picker =
    [[UIImagePickerController alloc] init];
    picker.delegate = self;
    picker.allowsEditing = YES;
    picker.sourceType = sourceType;
    [self presentModalViewController:picker animated:YES];
    [picker release];
}
```

The next method gets called after the user has selected an image and the image picker view has been dismissed. In it, we first check to make sure that the device we're on can actually send mail. Currently, all iPhone OS devices are capable of sending mail, but that may not always be the case, so we make sure this device supports e-mail before launching the mail compose view.

```
- (void)mailImage:(UIImage *)image {
    if ([MFMailComposeViewController canSendMail]) {
```

Then we create an instance of `MFMailComposeViewController` and set its delegate to self.

```
        MFMailComposeViewController *mailComposer =
            [[MFMailComposeViewController alloc] init];
        mailComposer.mailComposeDelegate = self;
```

We prepopulate the subject field with *Here's a picture*. Our user will be able to change this value, but they won't have to.

```
        [mailComposer setSubject:NSLocalizedString(@"Here's a picture...",
            @"Here's a picture...")];
```

Next, we use a function called `UIImagePNGRepresentation()` that returns an `NSData` with a PNG representation of a `UIImage` instance and pass in the image that the user took or selected. We also set the mime type to the appropriate type for a PNG image, and give the image file a generic name of *image*, since we don't have access to the name the camera assigned.

```
[mailComposer addAttachmentData:UIImagePNGRepresentation(image)
    mimeType:@"image/png" fileName:@"image"];
```

We also set the body of the mail to a short message.

```
[mailComposer setMessageBody:NSLocalizedString(
    @"Here's a picture that I took with my iPhone.",
    @"Here's a picture that I took with my iPhone.") isHTML:NO];
```

And finally, we present the mail compose view modally and clean up our memory.

```
    [self presentModalViewController:mailComposer animated:YES];
    [mailComposer release];
}
```

If the device we're running on can't send e-mail, we just notify the user by setting the text field's label.

```
    else
        message.text = NSLocalizedString(@"Can't send e-mail...",
            @"Can't send e-mail...");
}
```

There's no point in discussing `viewDidUnload` or `dealloc`, as they are both standard implementations, so the next method to look at is the camera picker delegate methods. The next method gets called when the user selects a picture. In it, we dismiss the image picker, grab the selected image out of the info dictionary, retaining it so it won't get autoreleased before we're done with it. Then we use `performSelector:withObject:afterDelay:` to call the `mailImage:` method half-a-second in the future, which will cause it to run right after the image picker is finished dismissing. Why the delay? We cannot put up a modal view until after our previous modal view has finished being dismissed. Because the first modal view animates out, we tell the run loop to wait half-a-second (that's the default animation timing) to make sure our second view doesn't step on the first.

```
- (void)imagePickerController:(UIImagePickerController *)picker
        didFinishPickingMediaWithInfo:(NSDictionary *)info {
    [picker dismissModalViewControllerAnimated:YES];
    UIImage *image = [info objectForKey:
        UIImagePickerControllerEditedImage];
    [self performSelector:@selector(mailImage:)
            withObject:image
            afterDelay:0.5];
    message.text = @"";
}
```

NOTE: In *Beginning iPhone 3 Development*, we implemented a different delegate method called `imagePickerController:didFinishPickingImage:editingInfo:`. That method has been deprecated in favor of the newer method `imagePickerController:didFinish PickingMediaWithInfo:` that we've used here. They both serve the same exact function, but the newer method is capable of returning video in addition to still images, at least on phones that support video. For the foreseeable future, `imagePickerController:didFinish PickingImage:editingInfo:` will continue to work, but you should use `imagePicker Controller:didFinishPickingMediaWithInfo:` for all new development.

If the user chose not to take a picture or select an image, we just dismiss the image picker view and set the label to identify the fact that they cancelled.

```
- (void)imagePickerControllerDidCancel:(UIImagePickerController *)picker {
    [picker dismissModalViewControllerAnimated:YES];
    message.text = NSLocalizedString(@"Cancelled...", @"Cancelled...");
}
```

Finally, the pièce de résistance, the mail compose view controller delegate method. In it, we check the result code and update the label to inform the user whether their mail was sent or saved or if the user cancelled. If an error was encountered, we show an alert view with the description of the error that was encountered.

```
- (void)mailComposeController:(MFMailComposeViewController*)controller
        didFinishWithResult:(MFMailComposeResult)result
                       error:(NSError*)error {
    switch (result)
    {
        case MFMailComposeResultCancelled:
            message.text = NSLocalizedString(@"Canceled...",@"Canceled...");
            break;
        case MFMailComposeResultSaved:
            message.text = NSLocalizedString(@"Saved to send later...",
                @"Saved to send later...");
            break;
        case MFMailComposeResultSent:
            message.text = NSLocalizedString(@"Mail sent...", @"Mail sent...");
            break;
        case MFMailComposeResultFailed: {
            UIAlertView *alert = [[UIAlertView alloc] initWithTitle:
                NSLocalizedString(@"Error sending mail...",@"Error sending mail...")
                message:[error localizedDescription]
                delegate:nil
                cancelButtonTitle:NSLocalizedString(@"Bummer", @"Bummer")
                otherButtonTitles:nil];
            [alert show];
            [alert release];
            message.text = NSLocalizedString(@"Send failed...", @"Send failed...");
            break;
        }
        default:
            break;
    }
```

```
        [self dismissModalViewControllerAnimated:YES];
}
@end
```

And that's all there is to that. There's just one more step before we can build and run it.

Linking the MessageUI Framework

Right-click the *Frameworks* folder in the *Groups & Files* pane and select **Existing Frameworks...** from the **Add** submenu. When the frameworks sheet drops down, select the *MessageUI.framework* and click the *Add* button. Now you are ready to build and run the application.

THE OLD FASHIONED WAY

You may, at times, have a reason to need the old way of sending e-mail, perhaps because you need to support older versions of the iPhone OS that don't have the MessageUI framework available. Here is how you would craft a mailto: URL to launch *Mail.app* with a new e-mail message, with the fields pre-populated:

```
    NSString *to = @"mailto:jeff@iphonedevbook.com";
    NSString *cc = @"?cc=dave@iphonedevbook.com,secret@iphonedevbook.com";
    NSString *subject = @"&subject=Hello World!";
    NSString *body = @"&body=Wow, does this really work?";
    NSString *email = [NSString stringWithFormat:@"%@%@%@%@", to, cc, subject,
        body];
    email = [email stringByAddingPercentEscapesUsingEncoding:NSUTF8StringEncoding];
    [[UIApplication sharedApplication] openURL:[NSURL URLWithString:email]];
```

One way to check if your device has the MessageUI framework installed is to try to load the MFMailComposeViewController class into memory:

```
        Class mailClass = (NSClassFromString(@"MFMailComposeViewController"));
        if (mailClass != nil) {
          // Use new way
}
else {
        // Use the old-fashioned way
}
```

If you are able to load the class, you're good to go with the technique shown in this chapter. If the class object returns nil, then you need to use the old-fashioned method shown in this sidebar.

Mailing It In...

In the course of this chapter, you've seen how to use the MessageUI framework's in-application e-mail services. You've seen how to prepopulate the message compose view with recipients, a subject, a body, and even attachments. You should now be equipped to add e-mail to any of your applications. When you're ready to move on, turn the page and we'll learn the art of iPod Fu.

iPod Library Access

The iPhone, in addition to being a phone, is a first-class music player as well. Out of the box, people can (and do) use it to listen to music, podcasts, and audio books. Of course, it goes without saying that the iPod touch is also a music player.

iPhone SDK programs have always been able to play sounds and music, but with the 3.0 SDK, we now have access to our user's entire audio library. This means, for example, that games can provide a soundtrack or allow users to create one from their own music library. In this chapter, we're going to explore the various aspects of finding and playing the user's own music.

This Chapter's Application

In this chapter, we're going to build an application that lets users create a queue of songs from the music stored on their iPod touch or iPhone.

> **NOTE:** We'll use the term **queue** to describe our application's list of songs, rather than the term **playlist**. When working with the iPod library, the term playlist refers to actual playlists synchronized from iTunes. Those playlists can be read, but they can't be created using the SDK. To avoid confusion, we'll stick with the term queue.

We'll allow users to select songs in two ways:

- Enter a search term for titles they want to add to their queue (Figure 13-1).

- Choose specific songs using the iPod's **media picker**, which is essentially the iPod application presented modally from within our application (Figure 13-2). Using the media picker, our user can select audio tracks by album, song, or playlist, or using any other approach that the iPod application supports (with the exception of Cover Flow).

Figure 13-1. *Our application's main page. The user can add songs to the list of songs to be played by entering a partial title into the* Title Search *text field and pressing the* Append Matching Songs *button.*

Figure 13-2. *Users can also use the iPod media picker to select songs to add to our application's queue.*

When our application launches, it will check to see if music is currently playing. If so, it will allow that music to keep playing and will append any requested music to the end of the list of songs to be played.

> **TIP:** If your application needs to play a certain sound or music, you may feel that it's appropriate to turn off the user's currently playing music, but you should do that with caution. If you're just providing a soundtrack, you really should consider letting the music that's playing continue playing, or at least giving the users the choice about whether to turn off their chosen music in favor of your application's music. It is, of course, your call, but tread lightly when it comes to stomping on your user's music.

As you can see in Figure 13-1, the currently selected song will have a small icon to the left of it in the table: either a small play triangle, if it's actually being played, or a small pause symbol, if it's paused. The user can play and pause, skip to the next or previous track, seek forward and backward within the current songs, and delete items from the queue.

The application we'll build isn't very practical, because everything we're offering to our users (and more) is already available in the iPod application on the iPhone or the Music application on the iPod touch. But writing it will allow us to explore almost all of the tasks your own application might ever need to perform with regard to the iPod library.

> **CAUTION:** This chapter's application must be run on an actual iPhone or iPod touch. The iPhone simulator does not have access to the iPod library on your computer, and any of the calls related to the iPod library access APIs will result in an error on the simulator.

Working with the iPod Library

The methods and objects used to access the iPod library are part of the **MediaPlayer framework**, which allows applications to play both audio and video. Currently, only audio tracks from our user's media library can be accessed using the MediaPlayer framework, but the framework also provides tools for playing back video files pulled from the Web or from an application's bundle.

The collection of audio files on your user's device is referred to as the **iPod library**. This is a generic term that applies to all the audio tracks on either an iPod touch or an iPhone. You will interact with several classes when using the iPod library. The entire iPod library itself is represented by the class MPMediaLibrary. You won't use this object very often, however. It's primarily used only when you need to be notified of changes made to the library while your application is running. It's pretty rare for changes to be made to the library while your application is running, since such changes will usually happen as the result of synchronizing your device with your computer.

A specific audio item from your iPod library is called a **media item**, which is represented by the class MPMediaItem. If you wish to play songs from one of your user's **playlists**, you will use the class MPMediaPlaylist, which represents the playlists that were created in iTunes and synchronized to your user's device. To search for either media items or playlists in the iPod library, you use a **media query**, which is represented by the class MPMediaQuery. Media queries will return all media items or playlists that match whatever criteria you specify. To specify criteria for a media query, you use a special media-centric form of predicate called a **media property predicate**, represented by the class MPMediaPropertyPredicate.

Another way to let your user select media items is to use the **media picker controller**, which is an instance of MPMediaPickerController. The media picker controller allows your users to use the same basic interface they are accustomed to using from the iPod or Music application.

You can play media items using a **music player controller**, which is done by creating an instance of MPMusicPlayerController. Music player controllers are not view controllers. They are responsible for playing audio and managing a list of media items to be played. Generally speaking, you are expected to provide any necessary user interface elements, such as buttons to play or pause, or to skip forward or backward.

> **NOTE:** Don't confuse MPMusicPlayerController with MPMoviePlayerController. Unlike MPMoviePlayerController, MPMusicPlayerController is not a view controller. A movie player controller is a view controller that takes over the screen completely. A music player controller, on the other hand, just controls the music, doing things like managing the queue, stopping, starting, and skipping forward through songs. Since it is not a view controller, it has no direct impact on your application's user interface or visual appearance. It is responsible only for playing and manipulating the playback of audio.

If you want to specify a list of media items to be played by a music player controller, you use a **media item collection**, represented by instances of the class MPMediaItemCollection. Media item collections are immutable collections of media items. A media item may appear in more than one spot in the collection, meaning you could conceivably create a collection that played "Happy Birthday to You" a thousand times, followed by a single playing of "Rock the Casbah." You could do that ... if you really wanted to.

Media Items

The class that represents media items, MPMediaItem, works a little differently than most Objective-C classes. You would probably expect MPMediaItem to include properties for things like title, artist, album name, and the like. But that's not the case. Other than those inherited from NSObject and the two NSCoding methods used to allow archiving, MPMediaItem includes only a single instance method, called valueForProperty:.

valueForProperty: works much like an instance of NSDictionary, only with a limited set of defined keys. So, for example, if you wanted to retrieve a media item's title, you would call valueForProperty: and specify the key MPMediaItemPropertyTitle, and the method would return an NSString instance with the audio track's title. Media items are immutable on the iPhone, so all MPMediaItem properties are read-only.

Some media item properties are said to be **filterable**. Filterable media item properties are those that can be searched on, a process we'll look at a little later in the chapter.

Media Item Persistent ID

Every media item has a persistent identifier (or persistent ID), which is a number associated with the item that won't ever change. If you need to store a reference to a particular media item, you should store the persistent ID, because it is generated by iTunes, and you can count on it staying the same over time.

You can retrieve the persistent ID of a media track using the property key MPMediaItemPropertyPersistentID, like so:

```
NSNumber *persistentId = [mediaItem
    valueForProperty:MPMediaItemPropertyPersistentID];
```

Persistent ID is a filterable property, which means that you can use a media query to find an item based on its persistent ID. Storing the media item's persistent ID is the surest way to guarantee you'll get the same object each time you search. We'll talk about media queries a bit later in the chapter.

Media Type

All media items have a type associated with them. Currently, media items are classified using three categories: music, podcast, and audio book. You can determine a particular media item's type by asking for the MPMediaItemPropertyMediaType property, like so:

```
NSNumber *type = [mediaItem valueForProperty:MPMediaItemPropertyMediaType];
```

Media items may consist of more than a single type. A podcast, for example, could be a reading of an audio book. As a result, media type is implemented as a **bit field** (sometimes called **bit flags**).

> **NOTE:** Bit fields are commonly used in C, and Apple employs them in many places throughout its frameworks. If you're not completely sure how bit fields are used, you can check out Chapter 11 of *Learn C on the Mac* by Dave Mark (Apress, 2008). You can find a good summary of the concept on Wikipedia as well: http://en.wikipedia.org/wiki/Bitwise_operation.

With bit fields, a single integer datatype is used to represent multiple, nonexclusive Boolean values, rather than a single number. To convert type (an object) into an

NSInteger, which is the documented integer type used to hold media types, use the integerValue method, like so:

```
NSInteger mediaType = [type integerValue];
```

At this point, each bit of mediaType represents a single type. To determine if a media item is a particular type, you need to use the bitwise AND operator (&) to compare mediaType with system-defined constants that represent the available media types. Here is a list of the current constants:

- MPMediaTypeMusic: Used to check if the media is music.

- MPMediaTypePodcast: Used to check if the media is a podcast.

- MPMediaTypeAudioBook: Used to check if the media is an audio book.

To check if a given item contains music, for example, you would take the mediaType you retrieved and do this:

```
if (mediaType & MPMediaTypeMusic) {
// It is music…
}
```

MPMediaTypeMusic's bits are all set to 0, except for the one bit that's used to represent that a track contains music, which is set to 1. When you do a bitwise AND (&) between that constant and the retrieved mediaType value, the resulting value will have 0 in all bits except the one that's being checked. That bit will have a 1 if mediaType has the music bit set, or 0 if it doesn't. In Objective-C, an if statement that evaluates a bitwise AND or OR operation will fire on any nonzero result; the code that follows will run if mediaType's music bit is set; otherwise, it will be skipped.

Media type is a filterable property, so you can specify in your media queries (which we'll talk about shortly) that they should return media of only specific types.

BITWISE MACROS

Not every programmer is comfortable reading code with bitwise operators. If that describes you, don't despair. It's easy to create macros to turn these bitwise checks into C function macros, like so:

```
#define isMusic(x)      (x & MPMediaTypeMusic)
#define isPodcast(x)    (x & MPMediaTypePodcast)
#define isAudioBook(x)  (x & MPMediaTypeAudioBook)
```

Once these are defined, you can check the returned type using more accessible code, like this:

```
if (isMusic([type integerValue])) {
    // Do something
}
```

> **NOTE:** additional constants are defined for media types: MPMediaTypeAnyAudio and MPMediaTypeAny. These could theoretically be used to check the returned type; however, there's currently little reason to use these constants in that way. Because the only media types currently supported are all audio, every valid media item will always check positive when compared to either of these constants.

Filterable String Properties

There are several string properties that you might want to retrieve from a media item, including the track's title, its genre, the artist, and the album name. Here are the filterable string property constants you can use:

- MPMediaItemPropertyTitle: Returns the track's title, which usually means the name of the song or podcast episode.

- MPMediaItemPropertyAlbumTitle: Returns the name of the track's album.

- MPMediaItemPropertyArtist: Returns the name of the artist who recorded the track.

- MPMediaItemPropertyAlbumArtist: Returns the name of the principal artist behind the track's album.

- MPMediaItemPropertyGenre: Returns the track's genre (e.g., Classical, Rock, or Alternative).

- MPMediaItemPropertyComposer: Returns the name of the track's composer.

- MPMediaItemPropertyPodcastTitle: If the track is a podcast, returns the podcast's name.

Although the title and artist will almost always be known, none of these properties are guaranteed to return a value, so it's important to code defensively any time your program logic includes one of these values. Although unlikely, a media track can exist without a specified name or artist.

Here's an example that retrieves a string property from a media item:

```
NSString *title = [mediaItem valueForProperty:MPMediaItemPropertyTitle];
```

Nonfilterable Numeric Attributes

Nearly anything that you can determine about a song or other audio track in iTunes can be retrieved from a media item. The numeric values in the following list are not filterable—in other words, you can't use them in your media property predicates. You can't, for example, retrieve all the tracks that are longer than four minutes in length. But once you have a media item, there's a wealth of information available about that item.

- MPMediaItemPropertyPlaybackDuration: Returns the length of the track in seconds.

- MPMediaItemPropertyAlbumTrackNumber: Returns the number of this track on its album.

- MPMediaItemPropertyAlbumTrackCount: Returns the number of tracks on this track's album.

- MPMediaItemPropertyDiscNumber: If the track is from a multiple-album collection, returns the track's disc number.

- MPMediaItemPropertyDiscCount: If the track is from a multiple-album collection, returns the total number of discs in that collection.

- MPMediaItemPropertyPlayCount: Returns the total number of times that this track has been played.

- MPMediaItemPropertySkipCount: Returns the total number of times this track has been skipped.

- MPMediaItemPropertyRating: Returns the track's rating, or 0 if the track has not been rated.

Numeric attributes are always returned as instances of NSNumber. The track duration is an NSTimeInterval, which can be retrieved from NSNumber by using the doubleValue method. The rest are unsigned integers that can be retrieved using the unsignedIntegerValue method.

Here are a few examples of retrieving numeric properties from a media item:

```
NSNumber *durationNum = [mediaItem valueForProperty:
    MPMediaItemPropertyPlaybackDuration];
NSTimeInterval duration = [durationNum doubleValue];

NSNumber *trackNum = [mediaItem valueForProperty:
    MPMediaItemPropertyAlbumTrackNumber];
NSUInteger trackNumber = [trackNum unsignedIntegerValue];
```

Retrieving Lyrics

If a media track has lyrics associated with it, you can retrieve those using the property key MPMediaItemPropertyLyrics. The lyrics will be returned in an instance of NSString, like so:

```
NSString *lyrics = [mediaItem valueForProperty:MPMediaItemPropertyLyrics];
```

Retrieving Album Artwork

Some media tracks have a piece of artwork associated with them. In most instances, this will be the track's album's cover picture, though it could be something else. You retrieve the album artwork using the property key MPMediaItemPropertyArtwork, which returns an instance of the class MPMediaItemArtwork. The MPMediaItemArtwork class has a method that returns an instance of UIImage to match a specified size. Here's some code to get the album artwork for a media item that would fit into a 100-by-100 pixel view:

```
MPMediaItemArtwork *art = [mediaItem
    valueForProperty:MPMediaItemPropertyArtwork];
CGSize imageSize = {100.0, 100.0};
UIImage *image = [art imageWithSize:imageSize];
```

Retrieving the Date Last Played

One last piece of data that you can retrieve from a media item is the date and time when it was last played. You can retrieve that in the form of an NSDate instance by using the property key MPMediaItemPropertyLastPlayedDate, like so:

```
NSDate *lastPlayed = [mediaItem
    valueForProperty:MPMediaItemPropertyLastPlayedDate];
```

Media Item Collections

Media items can be grouped into collections, creatively called media item collections. In fact, this is how you specify a list of media items to be played by the music player controller. Media item collections, which are represented by the class MPMediaItemCollection, are immutable collections of media items. You can create new media item collections, but you can't change the contents of the collection once it has been created.

Creating a New Collection

The easiest way to create a media item collection is to put all the media items you want to be in the collection into an instance of NSArray, in the order you want them. You can then pass the instance of NSArray to the factory method collectionWithItems:, like so:

```
NSArray *items = [NSArray arrayWithObjects:mediaItem1, mediaItem2, nil];
MPMediaItemCollection *collection = [MPMediaItemCollection
    collectionWithItems:items];
```

Retrieving Media Items

To retrieve a specific media item from a media item collection, you use the instance method items, which returns an NSArray instance containing all of the media items in the order they exist in the collection. If you want to retrieve the specific media item at a particular index, for example, you would do this:

```
MPMediaItem *item = [[mediaCollection items] objectAtIndex:5];
```

Creating Derived Collections

Because media item collections are immutable, you can't add items to a collection, nor can you append the contents of another media item collection onto another one. Since you can get to an array of media items contained in a collection using the instance method items, however, you can make a mutable copy of the items array, manipulate the mutable array's contents, and then create a new collection based on the modified array.

Here's some code that appends a single media item onto the end of an existing collection:

```
NSMutableArray *items = [[originalCollection items] mutableCopy];
[items addObject:mediaItem];
MPMediaItemCollection *newCollection = [MPMediaItemCollection
    collectionWithItems:items];
[items release];
```

Similarly, to combine two different collections, you would combine their items and create a new collection from the combined array:

```
NSMutableArray *items = [[firstCollection items] mutableCopy];
[items addObjectsFromArray:[secondCollection items]];
MPMediaItemCollection *newCollection = [MPMediaItemCollection
    collectionWithItems:items];
[items release];
```

To delete an item or items from an existing collection, you can use the same basic technique. You can retrieve a mutable copy of the items contained in the collection, delete the ones you want to remove, then create a new collection based on the modified copy of the items, like so:

```
NSMutableArray *items = [[originalCollection items] mutableCopy];
[items removeObject:mediaItemToDelete];
MPMediaItemCollection *newCollection = [MPMediaItemCollection
    collectionWithItems:items];
[items release];
```

Media Queries and Media Property Predicates

To search for media items in the iPod library, you use media queries, which are instances of the class MPMediaQuery. A number of factory methods can be used to retrieve media items from the library sorted by a particular property. For example, if you wanted a list of all media items sorted by artist, you would use the artistsQuery class method to create an instance of MPMediaQuery configured, like this:

```
MPMediaQuery *artistsQuery = [MPMediaQuery artistsQuery];
```

Table 13-1 lists the factory methods on MPMediaQuery.

Table 13-1. *MPMediaQuery Factory Methods*

Factory Method	Included Media Types	Grouped/Sorted By
albumsQuery	Music	Album
artistsQuery	Music	Artist
audiobooksQuery	Audio Books	Title
compilationsQuery	Any	Album*
composersQuery	Any	Composer
genresQuery	Any	Genre
playlistsQuery	Any	Playlist
podcastsQuery	Podcasts	Podcast Title
songsQuery	Music	Title

Includes only albums with MPMediaItemPropertyIsCompilation set to YES.

These factory methods are useful for displaying the entire contents of the user's library that meet preset conditions. That said, you will often want to restrict the query to an even smaller subset of items. You can do that using a media property predicate. Media property predicates can be created on any of the filterable properties of a media item, including the persistent ID, media type, or any of the string properties (like title, artist, or genre).

To create a media property predicate on a filterable property, use the class MPMediaPropertyPredicate. Create new instances using the factory method predicateWithValue:forProperty:comparisonType:. Here, for example, is how you would create a media property predicate that searched for all songs with the title "Happy Birthday":

```
MPMediaPropertyPredicate *titlePredicate =
[MPMediaPropertyPredicate predicateWithValue:@"Happy Birthday"
    forProperty:MPMediaItemPropertyTitle
    comparisonType:MPMediaPredicateComparisonContains];
```

The first value you pass—in this case, @"Happy Birthday"—is the comparison value. The second value is the filterable property you want that comparison value compared to. By specifying MPMediaItemPropertyTitle, we're saying we want the song titles compared to the string "Happy Birthday". The last item specifies the type of comparison to do. You can pass MPMediaPredicateComparisonEqualTo to look for an exact match to the specified string, or MPMediaPredicateComparisonContains to look for any item that contains the passed value as a substring.

NOTE: Media queries are always case-insensitive, regardless of the comparison type used. Therefore, the preceding example would also return songs called "HAPPY BIRTHDAY" and "Happy BirthDAY."

Because we've passed `MPMediaPredicateComparisonContains`, this predicate would match "Happy Birthday, the Opera" and "Slash Sings Happy Birthday," in addition to plain old "Happy Birthday." Had we passed `MPMediaPredicateComparisonEqualTo`, then only the last one—the exact match—would be found.

You can create and pass multiple media property predicates to a single query. If you do, the query will use the AND logical operator and return only the media items that meet all of your predicates.

To create a media query based on media property predicates, you use the init method `initWithFilterPredicates:`, and pass in an instance of `NSSet` containing all the predicates you want it to use, like so:

```
MPMediaQuery *query = [[MPMediaQuery alloc] initWithFilterPredicates:[NSSet
    setWithObject:titlePredicate]];
```

Once you have a query—whether it was created manually or retrieved using one of the factory methods—there are two ways you can execute the query and retrieve the items to be displayed:

- You can use the `items` property of the query, which returns an instance of `NSArray` containing all the media items that meet the criteria specified in your media property predicates, like so:

  ```
  NSArray *items = query.items;
  ```

- You can use the property `collections` to retrieve the objects grouped by one of the filterable properties. You can tell the query which property to group the items by setting the `groupingType` property to the property key for the filterable attribute you want it grouped by. If you don't set `groupingType`, it will default to grouping by title.

When you access the `collections` property, the query will instead return an array of `MPMediaItemCollections`, with one collection for each distinct value in your grouping type. So, if you specified a `groupingType` of `MPMediaGroupingArtist`, for example, the query would return an array with one `MPMediaItemCollection` for each artist who has at least one song that matches your criteria. Each collection would contain all the songs by that artist that meet the specified criteria. Here's what that might look like in code:

```
query.groupingType = MPMediaGroupingArtist;
NSArray *collections = query.collections;
for (MPMediaItemCollection *oneCollection in collections) {
    // oneCollection has all songs by one artist that meet criteria
}
```

You need to be very careful with media queries. They are synchronous and, if performed in an action or delegate method, will block the main thread while the search is performed, so if you specify a query that returns 100,000 media items, your user interface is going to hiccup while those items are found, retrieved, and stored in collections or an array. If you are using a media query that might return more than a dozen or so media items, you might want to consider moving that action off the main thread. We'll look at how to move operations off of the main thread in Chapter 14.

The Media Picker Controller

If you want to let your users select specific media items from their library, you'll want to use the media picker controller. The media picker controller lets your users choose songs from their iPod library using an interface that's nearly identical to the one in the iPod or Music application they're already used to using. Your users will not be able to use Cover Flow, but they will be able to select from lists sorted by song title, artist, playlist, album, and genre, just as they can when selecting music in the iPod or Music application (Figure 13-2).

The media picker controller is extremely easy to use. It works just like many of the other provided controller classes that we've covered in the previous chapters, such as the image picker controller and the mail compose view controller that we used in Chapter 12. Create an instance of MPMediaPickerController, assign it a delegate, and then present it modally, like so:

```
MPMediaPickerController *picker = [[MPMediaPickerController alloc]
    initWithMediaTypes:MPMediaTypeMusic];
picker.delegate = self;
[picker setAllowsPickingMultipleItems:YES];
picker.prompt = NSLocalizedString(@"Select items to play",
    @"Select items to play");
[self presentModalViewController:picker animated:YES];
[picker release];
```

When you create the media picker controller instance, you need to specify a media type. This can be one of the three values we talked about earlier—MPMediaTypeMusic, MPMediaTypePodcast, or MPMediaTypeAudioBook—or you can use MPMediaTypeAny to let your users select any media item in their library. You can also pass MPMediaTypeAnyAudio, which will currently return any media item, but if future versions of the SDK expand the media types that can be accessed using a media query, then the query will exclude those other types that might be added, such as video.

You can also use the bitwise OR (|) operator to let your user select any combination of media types. For example, if you wanted to let your user select from podcasts and audio books, but not music, you would create your picker like this:

```
MPMediaPickerController *picker = [[MPMediaPickerController alloc]
    initWithMediaTypes:MPMediaTypePodcast | MPMediaTypeAudioBook ];
```

By using the bitwise OR operator with these constants, you end up passing an integer that has the bits representing both of these media types set to 1 and all the other bits set to 0.

Also notice that we need to tell the media picker controller to allow the user to select multiple items. The default behavior of the media picker is to let the user choose one, and only one, item. If that's the behavior you want, then you don't need to do anything, but if you want to let the user select multiple items, you must explicitly tell it so.

The media picker also has a property called `prompt`, which is a string that will be displayed above the navigation bar in the picker (see the top of Figure 13-2). This is optional, but generally a good idea.

The media picker controller's delegate needs to conform to the protocol `MPMediaPickerControllerDelegate`. This defines two methods: one that is called if the user taps the *Cancel* button and another that is called if the user chooses one or more songs.

Handling Media Picker Cancels

If, after you present the media picker controller, the user hits the *Cancel* button, the delegate method `mediaPickerDidCancel:` will be called. You must implement this method on the media picker controller's delegate, even if you don't have any processing that needs to be done when the user cancels, since you must dismiss the modal view controller. Here is a minimal, but fairly standard, implementation of that method:

```
- (void) mediaPickerDidCancel: (MPMediaPickerController *) mediaPicker {
    [self dismissModalViewControllerAnimated: YES];
}
```

Handling Media Picker Selections

If the user selected one or more media items using the media picker controller, then the delegate method `mediaPicker:didPickMediaItems:` will be called. This method must be implemented, not only because it's the delegate's responsibility to dismiss the media picker controller, but also because this method is the only way to know which tracks your user selected. The selected items are grouped in a media item collection.

Here's a very simple example implementation of `mediaPicker:didPickMediaItems:` that assigns the returned collection to one of the delegate's properties:

```
- (void)mediaPicker: (MPMediaPickerController *) mediaPicker
  didPickMediaItems: (MPMediaItemCollection *) theCollection {
    [self dismissModalViewControllerAnimated: YES];
    self.collection = theCollection;
}
```

The Music Player Controller

The last component used to access the iPod library is the music player controller, which allows you to play a queue of media items by specifying either a media item collection or a media query. As we stated earlier, the music player controller has no visual elements. It's an object that plays the audio. It allows you to manipulate the playback of that audio by skipping forward or backward, telling it which specific media item to play, adjusting the volume, or skipping to a specific playback time in the current item.

The iPod library offers two completely different kinds of music player controllers: the iPod music player and the application music player. The way you use them is identical, but there's a key difference in how they work. The iPod music player is the one that's used by the iPod and Music apps. As is the case with those apps, when you quit your app while music is playing, the music continues playing. In addition, when the user is listening to music and starts up an app that uses the iPod music player, the iPod music player will keep playing that music. In contrast, the application music player will kill the music when your app terminates.

There's a bit of a gotcha here in that both the iPod and the application music player controllers can be used at the same time. If you use the application music player controller to play audio, and the user is currently listening to music, both will play simultaneously. This may or may not be what you want to happen, so you will usually want to check the iPod music player to see if there is music currently playing, even if you actually plan to use the application music player controller for playback.

Creating the Music Player Controller

To get either of the music player controllers, use one of the factory methods on MPMusicPlayerController. To retrieve the iPod music player, use the method iPodMusicPlayer, like so:

```
MPMusicPlayerController *thePlayer = [MPMusicPlayerController iPodMusicPlayer];
```

Retrieving the application music player controller is done similarly, using the applicationMusicPlayer method instead, like this:

```
MPMusicPlayerController *thePlayer = [MPMusicPlayerController
    applicationMusicPlayer];
```

Determining If the Music Player Controller Is Playing

Once you create an application music player, you'll need to give it something to play. But if you grab the iPod music player controller, it could very well already be playing something. You can determine if it is by looking at the playbackState property of the player. If it's currently playing, it will be set to MPMusicPlaybackStatePlaying.

```
if (player.playbackState == MPMusicPlaybackStatePlaying) {
    // playing
}
```

Specifying the Music Player Controller's Queue

There are two ways to specify the music player controller's queue of audio tracks: provide a media query or provide a media item collection. If you provide a media query, the music player controller's queue will be set to the media items returned by the items property. If you provide a media item collection, it will use the collection you pass as its queue. In either case, you will replace the existing queue with the items in the query or collection you pass in. Setting the queue will also reset the current track to the first item in the queue.

To set the music player's queue using a query, use the method setQueueWithQuery:. For example, here's how you would set the queue to all songs, sorted by artist:

```
MPMusicPlayerController *player = [MPMusicPlayerController iPodMusicPlayer];
MPMediaQuery *artistsQuery = [MPMediaQuery artistsQuery];
[player setQueueWithQuery:artistsQuery];
```

Setting the queue with a media item collection is accomplished with the method setQueueWithItemCollection:, like so:

```
MPMusicPlayerController *player = [MPMusicPlayerController iPodMusicPlayer];
NSArray *items = [NSArray arrayWithObjects:mediaItem1, mediaItem2, nil];
MPMediaItemCollection *collection = [MPMediaItemCollection
    collectionWithItems:items];
[items setQueueWithItemCollection:collection];
```

Unfortunately, there's currently no way to retrieve the music player controller's queue using public APIs. That means you will generally need to keep track of the queue independently of the music player controller if you want to be able to manipulate the queue.

Getting or Setting the Currently Playing Media Item

You can get or set the current song using the nowPlayingItem property. This lets you determine which track is already playing if you're using the iPod music player controller, and lets you specify a new song to play. Note that the media item you specify must already be in the music player controller's queue. Here's how you retrieve the currently playing item:

```
MPMediaItem *currentTrack = player.nowPlayingItem;
```

To switch to a different track, do this:

```
player.nowPlayingItem = newTrackToPlay; // must be in queue already
```

Skipping Tracks

The music player controller allows you to skip forward one song using the method skipToNextItem, or to skip back to the previous song using skipToPreviousItem. If there is no next or previous song to skip to, the music player controller stops playing. The music player controller also allows you to move back to the beginning of the current song using skipToBeginning.

Here is an example of all three methods:

```
[player skipToNextItem];
[player skipToPreviousItem];
[player skipToBeginning];
```

Seeking

When you're using your iPhone, iPod touch, or iTunes to listen to music, if you press and hold the forward or back button, the music will start seeking forward or backward, playing the music at an ever-accelerating pace. This lets you, for example, stay in the same track, but skip over a part you don't want to listen to, or skip back to something you missed. This same functionality is available through the music player controller using the methods beginSeekingForward and beginSeekingBackward. With both methods, you stop the process with a call to endSeeking.

Here is a set of calls that demonstrate seeking forward and stopping, and then seeking backwards and stopping:

```
[player beginSeekingForward];
[player endSeeking];

[player beginSeekingBackward];
[player endSeeking];
```

Playback Time

Not to be confused with payback time (something we've dreamt of for years, ever since they replaced the excellent Dick York with the far blander Dick Sargent), playback time specifies how far into the current song we currently are. For example, if the current song has been playing for five seconds, then the playback time will be 5.0.

You can retrieve and set the current playback time using the property currentPlaybackTime. You might use this, for example, when using an application music player controller, to resume a song at exactly the point where it was stopped when the application was last quit. Here's an example of using this property to skip forward ten seconds in the current song:

```
NSTimeInterval currentTime = player.currentPlaybackTime;
MPMediaItem *currentSong = player.nowPlayingItem;
NSNumber *duration = [currentSong valueForProperty:
    MPMediaItemPropertyPlaybackDuration];
currentTime += 10.0;
if (currentTime > [duration doubleValue])
    currentTime = [duration doubleValue];
player.currentPlaybackTime = currentTime;
```

Notice that we check the duration of the currently playing song to make sure we don't pass in an invalid playback time.

Repeat and Shuffle Modes

Music player controllers have ordered queues of songs and, most of the time, they play those songs in the order they exist in the queue, playing from the beginning of the queue to the end and then stopping. Your user can change this behavior by setting the repeat and shuffle properties in the iPod or Music application. You can also change the behavior by setting the music player controller's repeat and shuffle modes, represented by the properties repeatMode and shuffleMode. There are four repeat modes:

- MPMusicRepeatModeDefault: Uses the repeat mode last used in the iPod or Music application.

- MPMusicRepeatModeNone: Don't repeat at all. When the queue is done, stop playing.

- MPMusicRepeatModeOne: Keep repeating the currently playing track until your user goes insane. Ideal for playing "It's a Small World."

- MPMusicRepeatModeAll: When the queue is done, start over with the first track.

There are also four shuffle modes:

- MPMusicShuffleModeDefault: Use the shuffle mode last used in the iPod or Music application.

- MPMusicShuffleModeOff: Don't shuffle at all—just play the songs in the queue order.

- MPMusicShuffleModeSongs: Play all the songs in the queue in random order.

- MPMusicShuffleModeAlbums: Play all the songs from the currently playing song's album in random order.

Here is an example of turning off both repeat and shuffle:

```
player.repeatMode = MPMusicRepeatNone;
player.shuffleMode = MPMusicShuffleModeOff;
```

Adjusting the Music Player Controller's Volume

The music player controller lets you manipulate the volume at which it plays the items in its queue. The volume can be adjusted using the property volume, which is a clamped floating-point value. Clamped values store numbers between 0.0 and 1.0. In the case of volume, setting the property to 1.0 means play the tracks at the maximum volume, and a value of 0.0 means turn off the volume. Any value between those two extremes represents a different percentage of the maximum volume, so setting volume to 0.5 is like turning a volume knob halfway up.

> **CAUTION:** Setting volume to 1.1 will not make the volume any louder than setting it to 1.0. Despite what Nigel might have told you, you can't set the volume to 11.

Here's how you would set a player to maximum volume:

```
player.volume = 1.0;
```

And here's how you would set the volume to its midpoint:

```
player.volume = 0.5;
```

Music Player Controller Notifications

Music player controllers are capable of sending out notifications when any of three things happen:

- When the playback state (playing, stopped, paused, seeking, etc.) changes, the music player controller can send out the `MPMusicPlayerControllerPlaybackStateDidChangeNotification` notification.

- When the volume changes, it can send out the `MPMusicPlayerControllerVolumeDidChangeNotification` notification.

- When a new track starts playing, it can send out the `MPMusicPlayerControllerNowPlayingItemDidChangeNotification` notification.

Note that music player controllers don't send any notifications by default. You must tell an instance of `MPMusicPlayerController` to start generating notifications by calling the method `beginGeneratingPlaybackNotifications`. To have the controller stop generating notifications, call the method `endGeneratingPlaybackNotifications`.

If you need to receive any of these notifications, you first implement a handler method that takes one argument, an `NSNotification *`, and then register with the notification center for the notification of interest. For example, if we wanted a method to fire whenever the currently playing item changed, we might implement a method called `nowPlayingItemChanged:`, like so:

```
- (void)nowPlayingItemChanged:(NSNotification *)notification {
    NSLog(@"A new track started");
}
```

To start listening for those notifications, we would register with the notification for the type of notification we're interested in, and then have that music player controller start generating the notifications:

```
NSNotificationCenter *notificationCenter = [NSNotificationCenter defaultCenter];
[notificationCenter addObserver:self
    selector:@selector(nowPlayingItemChanged:)
    name:MPMusicPlayerControllerNowPlayingItemDidChangeNotification
    object:player];
[player beginGeneratingPlaybackNotifications];
```

Once we do this, any time the track changes, our `nowPlayingItemChanged:` method will be called by the notification center.

When we're finished and no longer need the notifications, we unregister and tell the music player controller to stop generating notifications:

```
NSNotificationCenter *center = [NSNotificationCenter defaultCenter];
[center removeObserver:self
    name:MPMusicPlayerControllerNowPlayingItemDidChangeNotification
```

```
    object:player];
[player endGeneratingPlaybackNotifications];
```

Now that we have all that theory out of the way, let's build something!

Building the Simple Player Application

Now, we'll create an application that leverages most of the iPod library functionality that was added with iPhone SDK 3.0. Our application will retrieve the iPod music player controller, and allow our users to add songs to the playlist by specifying partial song titles to search for or by using the media picker. We'll provide rudimentary playback controls that will let users pause and play music, as well as skip forward and backward. By tapping and holding the forward or backward button, they will be able to seek forward and backward in the currently playing song. We'll also provide a table that shows the current queue of songs to be played and allows users to remove songs from the queue.

> **NOTE:** As a reminder, the simulator does not yet support the iPod library functionality. To get the most out of the Simple Player application, you'll want to run it on your iPhone or iPod touch, which means signing up for one of Apple's paid iPhone Developer Programs. If you have not already done that, you might want to take a short break and head over to `http://developer.apple.com/iphone/program/` and check it out.

In Xcode, press ⇧⌘N to create a new project. Select the *View-based Application* project template and name the new project *Simple Player*. Look in the project archives that came with the book, in the folder *13 – Simple Player*, and find the image files called *empty.png*, *nexttrack.png*, *pause_small.png*, *pause.png*, *play_small.png*, *play.png*, *prevtrack.png*, and *remove.png*. Drag these to the *Resources* folder in the *Groups & Files* pane to add them to your project.

Expand the *Classes* and *Resources* folder, and then single-click the *Classes* folder to select it.

Adding Media Item Collection Functionality

MPMediaItemCollections are immutable, but we need the ability to manipulate collections in our application. So, we'll add a category on MPMediaItemCollection that will make it easier to create new collections based on existing collections. Press ⌘N to bring up the new file assistant, select *Objective-C class* under the *Cocoa Touch Class* heading, and make sure the *Subclass of* pop-up menu is set to *NSObject*. Name this new file *MPMediaItemCollection-Utils.m*, and make sure you also have it create *MPMediaItemCollection-Utils.h*.

Once the new files have been created, single-click *MPMediaItemCollection-Utils.h* in the *Groups & Files* pane and replace the current file with the following:

```objc
#import <Foundation/Foundation.h>
#import <MediaPlayer/MediaPlayer.h>

@interface MPMediaItemCollection(Utils)
/** Returns the first media item in the collection.
 */
- (MPMediaItem *)firstMediaItem;

/** Returns the last media item in the collection.
 */
- (MPMediaItem *)lastMediaItem;

/** This method will return the item in this media collection at a specific index.
 */
- (MPMediaItem *)mediaItemAtIndex:(NSUInteger)index;

/** Given a particular media item, this method will return the next media item in
    the collection. If there are multiple copies of the same media item in the list,
    it will return the one after the first occurrence.
 */
- (MPMediaItem *)mediaItemAfterItem:(MPMediaItem *)compare;

/** Returns the title of the media item at a given index.
 */
- (NSString *)titleForMediaItemAtIndex:(NSUInteger)index;

/** Returns YES if the given media item occurs at least once in this collection.
 */
- (BOOL)containsItem:(MPMediaItem *)compare;

/** Creates a new collection by appending otherCollection to the end of this
    collection.
 */
- (MPMediaItemCollection *)collectionByAppendingCollection:
    (MPMediaItemCollection *)otherCollection;

/** Creates a new collection by appending an array of media items to the end of this
    collection.
 */
- (MPMediaItemCollection *)collectionByAppendingMediaItems:(NSArray *)items;

/** Creates a new collection by appending a single media item to the end of this
collection.
 */
- (MPMediaItemCollection *)collectionByAppendingMediaItem:(MPMediaItem *)item;

/** Creates a new collection based on this collection, but excluding the specified
items.
 */
- (MPMediaItemCollection *)collectionByDeletingMediaItems:(NSArray *)itemsToRemove;

/** Creates a new collection based on this collection, but which doesn't include the
specified media item.
 */
- (MPMediaItemCollection *)collectionByDeletingMediaItem:
    (MPMediaItem *)itemToRemove;
```

```
/** Creates a new collection based on this collection, but excluding the media item
    at the specified index.
 */
- (MPMediaItemCollection *)collectionByDeletingMediaItemAtIndex:(NSUInteger)index;

/** Creates a new collection based on this collection, but excluding the media
    items starting with the objects at index from and ending with
    to.
 */
- (MPMediaItemCollection *)collectionByDeletingMediaItemsFromIndex:(NSUInteger)from
    toIndex:(NSUInteger)to;
@end
```

> **NOTE:** You don't need to type in the JavaDoc-style comments. We often include them with categories and other reusable code, but if you want to save yourself some typing time, we won't be offended if you choose to leave them out.

The method names in this header file are fairly self-explanatory. The first four items are shortcut methods to allow easier access to specific media items in the collection. The fifth method, `titleForMediaItemAtIndex:`, give us a one-line way to retrieve the title of a track, which we'll use later to display the titles from the queue in our table view. The rest of the methods create new collections in various ways. They will allow us to create new collections by combining collections or by adding or deleting items from an existing collection. Make sure you save *MPMediaItemCollection-Utils.h*.

Now, switch over to *MPMediaItemCollection-Utils.m* and replace its contents with the following code:

```
#import "MPMediaItemCollection-Utils.h"

@implementation MPMediaItemCollection(Utils)
- (MPMediaItem *)firstMediaItem {
    return [[self items] objectAtIndex:0];
}

- (MPMediaItem *)lastMediaItem {
    return [[self items] lastObject];
}

- (MPMediaItem *)mediaItemAtIndex:(NSUInteger)index {
    return [[self items] objectAtIndex:index];
}

- (MPMediaItem *)mediaItemAfterItem:(MPMediaItem *)compare {
    NSArray *items = [self items];

    for (MPMediaItem *oneItem in items) {
        if ([oneItem isEqual:compare]) {
            // If last item, there is no index + 1
            if (![[items lastObject] isEqual: oneItem])
                return [items objectAtIndex:[items indexOfObject:oneItem] + 1];
        }
    }
```

```
        return nil;
    }

- (NSString *)titleForMediaItemAtIndex:(NSUInteger)index {
    MPMediaItem *item = [[self items] objectAtIndex:index];
    return [item valueForProperty:MPMediaItemPropertyTitle];
}

- (BOOL)containsItem:(MPMediaItem *)compare {
    NSArray *items = [self items];

    for (MPMediaItem *oneItem in items) {
        if ([oneItem isEqual:compare])
            return YES;
    }
    return NO;
}

- (MPMediaItemCollection *)collectionByAppendingCollection:
    (MPMediaItemCollection *)otherCollection {
    return [self collectionByAppendingMediaItems:[otherCollection items]];
}

- (MPMediaItemCollection *)collectionByAppendingMediaItems:(NSArray *)items {
    if ([items count] == 0)
        return self;
    NSMutableArray *appendCollection = [[[self items] mutableCopy] autorelease];
    [appendCollection addObjectsFromArray:items];
    return [MPMediaItemCollection collectionWithItems:appendCollection];
}

- (MPMediaItemCollection *)collectionByAppendingMediaItem:(MPMediaItem *)item {
    if (item == nil)
        return nil;

    return [self collectionByAppendingMediaItems:[NSArray arrayWithObject:item]];
}

- (MPMediaItemCollection *)collectionByDeletingMediaItems:(NSArray *)itemsToRemove {
    if (itemsToRemove == nil || [itemsToRemove count] == 0)
        return [[self copy] autorelease];
    NSMutableArray *items = [[[self items] mutableCopy] autorelease];
    [items removeObjectsInArray:itemsToRemove];
    return [MPMediaItemCollection collectionWithItems:items];
}

- (MPMediaItemCollection *)collectionByDeletingMediaItem:
    (MPMediaItem *)itemToRemove {
    if (itemToRemove == nil)
        return [[self copy] autorelease];

    NSMutableArray *items = [[[self items] mutableCopy] autorelease];
    [items removeObject:itemToRemove];
    return [MPMediaItemCollection collectionWithItems:items];
}

- (MPMediaItemCollection *)collectionByDeletingMediaItemAtIndex:(NSUInteger)index {
```

```
    NSMutableArray *items = [[[self items] mutableCopy] autorelease];
    [items removeObjectAtIndex:index];
    return [items count] > 0 ? [MPMediaItemCollection collectionWithItems:items] :
        nil;
}

- (MPMediaItemCollection *)collectionByDeletingMediaItemsFromIndex:(NSUInteger)from
    toIndex:(NSUInteger)to {
    // Ensure from is before to
    if (to < from) {
        NSUInteger temp = from;
        to = from;
        from = temp;
    }

    NSMutableArray *items = [[[self items] mutableCopy] autorelease];
    [items removeObjectsInRange:NSMakeRange(from, to - from)];
    return [MPMediaItemCollection collectionWithItems:items];
}

@end
```

There's nothing here we haven't talked about before, but you should browse through the methods and make sure you understand what they're doing. They all use the same basic approach, accessing or copying the items property of self to retrieve a specific item or to create a new collection.

Save *MPMediaItemCollection-Utils.m* before continuing.

Declaring Outlets and Actions

Single-click *Simple_PlayerViewController.h* and replace its contents with the following code:

```
#import <UIKit/UIKit.h>
#import <MediaPlayer/MediaPlayer.h>

@interface Simple_PlayerViewController : UIViewController
  <MPMediaPickerControllerDelegate, UITableViewDelegate, UITableViewDataSource> {
    UITextField *titleSearch;
    UIButton    *playPauseButton;
    UITableView *tableView;

    MPMusicPlayerController *player;
    MPMediaItemCollection   *collection;
    MPMediaItem             *nowPlaying;
    BOOL                    collectionModified;
    NSTimeInterval          pressStarted;
}

@property (nonatomic, retain) IBOutlet UITextField *titleSearch;
@property (nonatomic, retain) IBOutlet UIButton *playPauseButton;
@property (nonatomic, retain) IBOutlet UITableView *tableView;

@property (nonatomic, retain) MPMusicPlayerController *player;
@property (nonatomic, retain) MPMediaItemCollection *collection;
```

```
@property (nonatomic, retain) MPMediaItem *nowPlaying;

- (IBAction)doTitleSearch;
- (IBAction)showMediaPicker;
- (IBAction)backgroundClick;

- (IBAction)seekBackward;
- (IBAction)previousTrack;
- (IBAction)seekForward;
- (IBAction)nextTrack;
- (IBAction)playOrPause;
- (IBAction)removeTrack:(id)sender;

- (void)nowPlayingItemChanged:(NSNotification *)notification;

@end
```

We start by conforming our class to three protocols: `MPMediaPickerControllerDelegate`, because we're going to be using `MPMediaPickerController` to let our user picks songs, and `UITableViewDelegate` and `UITableViewDataSource`, because our controller will be acting as the delegate and datasource for the table that shows the current queue of songs.

Following that, we have three instance variables that will be used as outlets to user interface items. One outlet will point to the text field where the user can enter title search values. We'll need a reference to that field so we can retrieve the typed value, and so that we can have it resign first responder status when we want the keyboard to retract. We also need a reference to the play/pause button so we can change the image it shows, toggling between a play icon and a pause icon. When a song is playing, we want to show the pause icon, and when it's stopped or paused, we want to show a play icon. The last outlet will be to the table view, which we'll need whenever our song queue changes so we can tell it to reload its data to let our users see the changes.

Next up is an instance of `MPMusicPlayerController`. This will be a pointer to the iPod music player controller, which we'll retrieve in `viewDidLoad:`.

The next three items work together. The first, `collection`, contains the current queue of songs. The second item, `nowPlaying`, is a reference to the song that's currently playing. `collection` will usually be `player`'s queue. There's an exception to that, however. When music is playing, the only way to add items to or remove items from the music player controller's queue is to create a new collection containing both the existing queue of songs and the new ones to be added or deleted, and then setting that collection as the player's queue, replacing the existing queue. Doing that while a song is playing will cause a small skip in playback, even if you save the currently playing item and the current playback time, and restore them after installing the new queue. As a result, we're going to wait until the song changes to update the player's queue. That's where the third instance variable, `collectionModified`, comes in. We'll set that to `YES` anytime a change is made to our collection. That way, when the currently playing song changes, we can install the new collection during the pause between songs, which won't be noticeable to the user.

The final instance variable, `pressStarted`, is used by the forward or back button methods. When the user taps and holds, we want to seek forward or back; if the user just single-taps, we want to skip. Each of those buttons will call two different methods: one when the user touches the screen, and another when the user lifts a finger off the screen after the touch. When the user taps down, we'll store the current time, and when the user lifts up their finger, we'll use the amount of time elapsed to determine whether we should skip to the next track.

After that, we define properties for our outlets, as well as for `player`, `collection`, and `nowPlaying`, and then declare our class's methods. The first two methods are triggered by two buttons on our application's user interface. `doTitleSearch` will be called when the *Append Matching Songs* button is pressed, and `showMediaPicker` will be called when the *Use Media Picker* button is pressed.

The method `backgroundClick` should look familiar. This is a technique we used in Chapter 4 of *Beginning iPhone 3 Development* (Apress, 2009) to allow our user to put away the keyboard by tapping outside the text area.

The next four methods are used by the forward and backward buttons. When they are tapped, either `seekBackward` or `seekForward` will be called. When the tap ends, `previousTrack` or `nextTrack` will be called. In those methods, we'll include the logic to determine if we should skip or just seek. The `playOrPause` method will be triggered by the button that's used for playing or pausing music.

The last method, `removeTrack:`, will be used by buttons on cells in our table view. This button will allow the user to delete a track from the queue. We'll use `sender` in this method so that we can identify which row triggered the delete, and remove the appropriate item from the playlist.

Make sure you save *Simple_PlayerViewController.h*.

Building the User Interface

Double-click *Simple_PlayerViewController.xib* to launch Interface Builder. The first order of business is to close the window labeled *View*. We're going to change the view's class, and we'll open the window again in a bit.

Once the *View* window is closed, click the icon labeled *View* in the nib's main window. Then press ⌘4 to open the identity inspector. Change the underlying class of the main view from *UIView* to *UIControl*. This will allow the view to trigger actions.

The icon labeled *View* should have just been renamed to *Control*. Now double-click the *Control* icon in the main window to open that *Control* window. Don't worry—even though the window is labeled *Control*, it's still a subclass of `UIView` and will still act as our application's main view.

The next step is to connect the content area of the view that is not covered by other active controls to the `backgroundClick` method. Select the *Control* icon, and press ⌘2 to open the connections inspector. Click in the circle next to *Touch Down*, drag over to *File's Owner*, and then select *backgroundClick*. Once we implement that method, clicking anywhere in our view that doesn't contain an active control will cause the keyboard to retract if it's showing.

Select a *Label* from the library, and drag it over to the window that's now labeled *Control*. Use the blue guidelines to place it in the upper-left side of the window, against the margins. Double-click it, and change its text to *Title Search*.

Now, grab a text field from the library, and add it to the *Control* window. Use the blue guidelines to place it below the label you just added, and then use the resize handles to make it stretch from the left margin to the right margin. Control-drag from *File's Owner* to this text field, and then select the *titleSearch* outlet.

Drag a *Round Rect Button* from the library and place it below the text field. Use the blue guidelines to place it against the right margin and the appropriate distance below the text field. Double-click the button, and change its title to read *Append Matching Songs*. You may need to adjust the button's position after changing the title so it's once again against the right margin. Control-drag from this button to *File's Owner*, and select the *doTitleSearch* action method.

Drag another *Round Rect Button* from the library; alternatively, you can option-drag the existing button to create a copy of it. Double-click the button, and change its label to *Use Media Picker*. Then place the button against the lower-right margins using the blue guidelines. Control-drag from this button to *File's Owner*, and select the *showMediaPicker* action.

From the library, grab one more *Round Rect Button*, or option-drag one of the existing buttons to make another copy. Then use the blue guidelines to place the new button above the *Use Media Picker* button, centered horizontally in the window. Press ⌘1 to bring up the attribute inspector, and change the button's *Type* from *Rounded Rect* to *Custom*. We're not going to assign an image to this button here. This will be the play/pause button, and the image it shows will depend on whether music is playing, so we need to set the image in code. Next, scroll down to the bottom of the attribute inspector to the *View* heading, and change the *Mode* to *Center*, which tells the button to center, but not resize, any image we assign to it.

You might want to select **Show Bounds Rectangles** from the **Layout** menu so that you can see where this button is. That option will draw a thin line around all interface elements, even empty custom buttons (Figure 13-3).

Figure 13-3. *The Show Bounds Rectangles option in the Layout menu will draw a thin line around all of the interface elements, including those that are empty or blank.*

With the custom button still selected, switch to the size inspector by pressing ⌘3. Set *w* to *30, h* to *27, x* to *145*, and *y* to *368*.

Next, we'll make two copies of this custom button: one on either side of our play/pause button. The left button will hold the previous track image, and the right button will hold the next track image. Hold down the option key and drag the custom button to the left, using the blue guidelines to place the new button.

With this new button selected, press ⌘1 to bring up the attribute inspector. Look for the *Background* combo box, and type in *prevtrack.png*. Now, press ⌘= to adjust this button's size to match the image.

Repeat this process to create the next track button. Single-click the empty button in the middle, and option-drag to the right this time to create another button. For this one, assign a *Background* of *nexttrack.png*. Then press ⌘= to adjust the button's size. You now have the three buttons used to control playback.

Select the next track button, and press ⌘2 to bring up the connections inspector. From the circle to the right of *Touch Down*, drag to *File's Owner* and select the *seekForward* action. Drag from the circle to the right of *Touch Up Inside*, and drag again to *File's Owner*. This time, select the action method *nextTrack*. Repeat this process one more time with *Touch Up Outside*, and connect it to the *nextTrack* method. Regardless of whether the user's finger was still inside the button, we need to stop seeking, so we connect both *Touch Up* events to the same method. We will have logic in that method to determine if we should actually skip to the next track.

At this point, the connections inspector should look like Figure 13-4. If you find anything out of place, you can always delete connections and redo them.

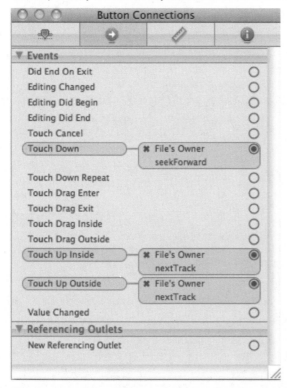

Figure 13-4. *All the connections needed to let the next track button handle both seeking and skipping*

Now, single-click the blank middle button. In the inspector, drag from the circle to the right of *Touch Up Inside* to *File's Owner*, and select the *playOrPause* action. Then control-drag from *File's Owner* to the button, and select the *playPauseButton* outlet.

Next, click the left-hand button. In the inspector, look for the *Touch Down* circle, and drag to *File's Owner*, selecting the *seekBackward* action. Drag again from the circle next to *Touch Up Inside* to *File's Owner*, and select the *previousTrack* action. Drag one last time from the circle next to *Touch Up Outside*, and again select the *previousTrack* action method.

From the library, grab a *Table View* and place it just below the *Append Matching Songs* button. Drag on the table view's lower-right corner to resize it to the right margin and just above the three buttons you just added. Control-drag from the new table view to *File's Owner* twice, connecting to the *delegate* outlet the first time, and the *dataSource* outlet the second time. Then control-drag back from *File's Owner* to the table view, and select the *tableView* outlet.

Save your nib, quit Interface Builder, and go back to Xcode so we can finish up.

Implementing the Simple Player View Controller

Back in Xcode, single-click *Simple_PlayerViewController.m*. Replace the existing contents with the following code:

```objc
#import "Simple_PlayerViewController.h"
#import "MPMediaItemCollection-Utils.h"

#define kTableRowHeight 34

@implementation Simple_PlayerViewController
@synthesize titleSearch;
@synthesize playPauseButton;
@synthesize tableView;
@synthesize player;
@synthesize collection;
@synthesize nowPlaying;

#pragma mark -
- (IBAction)doTitleSearch {
    if ([titleSearch.text length] == 0)
        return;
    MPMediaPropertyPredicate *titlePredicate =
        [MPMediaPropertyPredicate predicateWithValue:titleSearch.text
        forProperty:MPMediaItemPropertyTitle
        comparisonType:MPMediaPredicateComparisonContains];
    MPMediaQuery *query = [[MPMediaQuery alloc] initWithFilterPredicates:
        [NSSet setWithObject:titlePredicate]];

    if ([[query items] count] > 0) {
        if (collection)
            self.collection = [collection collectionByAppendingMediaItems:
                [query items]];
        else {
            self.collection = [MPMediaItemCollection collectionWithItems:
                [query items]];
            [player setQueueWithItemCollection:self.collection];
            [player play];
        }

        collectionModified = YES;
        [self.tableView reloadData];
    }
    [query release];
    titleSearch.text = @"";
    [titleSearch resignFirstResponder];
}

- (IBAction)showMediaPicker {
    MPMediaPickerController *picker = [[MPMediaPickerController alloc]
        initWithMediaTypes:MPMediaTypeMusic];
    picker.delegate = self;
    [picker setAllowsPickingMultipleItems:YES];
    picker.prompt = NSLocalizedString(@"Select items to play...",
        @"Select items to play...");
    [self presentModalViewController:picker animated:YES];
    [picker release];
```

```objc
}

- (IBAction)backgroundClick {
    [titleSearch resignFirstResponder];
}

- (IBAction)seekBackward {
    [player beginSeekingBackward];
    pressStarted = [NSDate timeIntervalSinceReferenceDate];
}

- (IBAction)previousTrack {
    [player endSeeking];

    if (pressStarted >= [NSDate timeIntervalSinceReferenceDate] - 0.1)
        [player skipToPreviousItem];
}

- (IBAction)seekForward {
    [player beginSeekingForward];
    pressStarted = [NSDate timeIntervalSinceReferenceDate];
}

- (IBAction)nextTrack {
    [player endSeeking];
    if (pressStarted >= [NSDate timeIntervalSinceReferenceDate] - 0.1)
        [player skipToNextItem];
}

- (IBAction)playOrPause {
    if (player.playbackState == MPMusicPlaybackStatePlaying) {
        [player pause];
        [playPauseButton setBackgroundImage:[UIImage imageNamed:@"play.png"]
            forState:UIControlStateNormal];
    }
    else {
        [player play];
        [playPauseButton setBackgroundImage:[UIImage imageNamed:@"pause.png"]
            forState:UIControlStateNormal];
    }
    [self.tableView reloadData];
}

- (IBAction)removeTrack:(id)sender {
    NSUInteger index = [sender tag];
    MPMediaItem *itemToDelete = [collection mediaItemAtIndex:index];
    if ([itemToDelete isEqual:nowPlaying])  {
        if (!collectionModified) {
            [player skipToNextItem];
        }
        else {
            [player setQueueWithItemCollection:collection];
            player.nowPlayingItem = [collection mediaItemAfterItem:nowPlaying];
        }

    }
    MPMediaItemCollection *newCollection = [collection
```

```objc
        collectionByDeletingMediaItemAtIndex:index];
    self.collection = newCollection;

    collectionModified = YES;

    NSUInteger indices[] = {0, index};
    NSIndexPath *deletePath = [NSIndexPath indexPathWithIndexes:indices length:2];
    [self.tableView deleteRowsAtIndexPaths:[NSArray arrayWithObject:deletePath]
        withRowAnimation:UITableViewRowAnimationFade];

    if (newCollection == nil &&
        player.playbackState == MPMusicPlaybackStatePlaying) {
        MPMediaItem *next = player.nowPlayingItem;
        self.collection = [MPMediaItemCollection collectionWithItems:
            [NSArray arrayWithObject:next]];
        [tableView reloadData];
    }
}

#pragma mark -
- (void)viewDidLoad {
    MPMusicPlayerController *thePlayer = [MPMusicPlayerController iPodMusicPlayer];
    self.player = thePlayer;
    [thePlayer release];

    if (player.playbackState == MPMusicPlaybackStatePlaying) {
        [playPauseButton setBackgroundImage:[UIImage imageNamed:@"pause.png"]
            forState:UIControlStateNormal];
        MPMediaItemCollection *newCollection = [MPMediaItemCollection
            collectionWithItems:[NSArray arrayWithObject:[player nowPlayingItem]]];
        self.collection = newCollection;
        self.nowPlaying = [player nowPlayingItem];
    }
    else {
        [playPauseButton setBackgroundImage:[UIImage imageNamed:@"play.png"]
            forState:UIControlStateNormal];
    }

    NSNotificationCenter *notificationCenter = [NSNotificationCenter defaultCenter];
    [notificationCenter addObserver:self
        selector:@selector (nowPlayingItemChanged:)
        name:MPMusicPlayerControllerNowPlayingItemDidChangeNotification
        object: player];

    [player beginGeneratingPlaybackNotifications];
}

- (void)viewDidUnload {
    self.titleSearch = nil;
    self.playPauseButton = nil;
    self.tableView = nil;
    [super viewDidUnload];
}

- (void)dealloc {
    NSNotificationCenter *center = [NSNotificationCenter defaultCenter];
    [center removeObserver:self
```

```
                name:MPMusicPlayerControllerNowPlayingItemDidChangeNotification
                object:player];
        [player endGeneratingPlaybackNotifications];

        [titleSearch release];
        [playPauseButton release];
        [tableView release];
        [player release];
        [collection release];
        [super dealloc];
}

#pragma mark -
#pragma mark Media Picker Delegate Methods
- (void)mediaPicker: (MPMediaPickerController *) mediaPicker
    didPickMediaItems: (MPMediaItemCollection *) theCollection {
        [self dismissModalViewControllerAnimated: YES];

        if (collection == nil){
            self.collection = theCollection;
            [player setQueueWithItemCollection:collection];
            [player setNowPlayingItem:[collection firstMediaItem]];
            self.nowPlaying = [collection firstMediaItem];
            [player play];
            [playPauseButton setBackgroundImage:[UIImage imageNamed:@"pause.png"]
                forState:UIControlStateNormal];
        }
        else {
            self.collection = [collection
                collectionByAppendingCollection:theCollection];
        }

        collectionModified = YES;
        [self.tableView reloadData];
}

- (void) mediaPickerDidCancel: (MPMediaPickerController *) mediaPicker {
        [self dismissModalViewControllerAnimated: YES];
}

#pragma mark -
#pragma mark Player Notification Methods
- (void)nowPlayingItemChanged:(NSNotification *)notification {
        if (collection == nil) {
            MPMediaItem *nowPlayingItem = [player nowPlayingItem];
            self.collection = [collection
                collectionByAppendingMediaItem:nowPlayingItem];
        }
        else {

            if (collectionModified) {
                [player setQueueWithItemCollection:collection];
                [player setNowPlayingItem:[collection mediaItemAfterItem:nowPlaying]];
                [player play];
            }

            if (![collection containsItem:player.nowPlayingItem] &&
```

```
                player.nowPlayingItem != nil) {
            self.collection = [collection
                collectionByAppendingMediaItem:player.nowPlayingItem];
        }
    }

    [tableView reloadData];
    self.nowPlaying = [player nowPlayingItem];

    if (nowPlaying == nil)
        [playPauseButton setBackgroundImage:[UIImage imageNamed:@"play.png"]
            forState:UIControlStateNormal];
    else
        [playPauseButton setBackgroundImage:[UIImage imageNamed:@"pause.png"]
            forState:UIControlStateNormal];

    collectionModified = NO;
}

#pragma mark -
#pragma mark Table View Methods
- (NSInteger)tableView:(UITableView *)theTableView
numberOfRowsInSection:(NSInteger)section {
    return [collection count];
}

- (UITableViewCell *)tableView:(UITableView *)theTableView
        cellForRowAtIndexPath:(NSIndexPath *)indexPath {
    static NSString *identifier = @"Music Queue Cell";
    UITableViewCell *cell = [theTableView
        dequeueReusableCellWithIdentifier:identifier];
    if (cell == nil) {
        cell = [[[UITableViewCell alloc] initWithStyle:UITableViewCellStyleDefault
            reuseIdentifier:identifier] autorelease];

        UIButton *removeButton = [UIButton buttonWithType:UIButtonTypeCustom];
        UIImage *removeImage = [UIImage imageNamed:@"remove.png"];
        [removeButton setBackgroundImage:removeImage forState:UIControlStateNormal];
        [removeButton setFrame:CGRectMake(0.0, 0.0, removeImage.size.width,
            removeImage.size.height)];
        [removeButton addTarget:self action:@selector(removeTrack:)
            forControlEvents:UIControlEventTouchUpInside];
        cell.accessoryView  = removeButton;
    }
    cell.textLabel.text = [collection titleForMediaItemAtIndex:[indexPath row]];
    if ([nowPlaying isEqual:[collection mediaItemAtIndex:[indexPath row]]]) {
        cell.textLabel.font = [UIFont boldSystemFontOfSize:21.0];
        if (player.playbackState ==  MPMusicPlaybackStatePlaying)
            cell.imageView.image = [UIImage imageNamed:@"play_small.png"];
        else
            cell.imageView.image = [UIImage imageNamed:@"pause_small.png"];

    }
    else {
        cell.textLabel.font = [UIFont systemFontOfSize:21.0];
        cell.imageView.image = [UIImage imageNamed:@"empty.png"];
    }
```

```
        cell.accessoryView.tag = [indexPath row];

        return cell;
}

- (void)tableView:(UITableView *)theTableView
        didSelectRowAtIndexPath:(NSIndexPath *)indexPath {
        MPMediaItem *selected = [collection mediaItemAtIndex:[indexPath row]];

        if (collectionModified) {
            [player setQueueWithItemCollection:collection];
            collectionModified = NO;
        }

        [player setNowPlayingItem:selected];
        [player play];

        [playPauseButton setBackgroundImage:[UIImage imageNamed:@"pause.png"]
            forState:UIControlStateNormal];
        [self.tableView reloadData];
}

- (CGFloat)tableView:(UITableView *)theTableView heightForRowAtIndexPath:(NSIndexPath
*)indexPath {
        return kTableRowHeight;
}

@end
```

Okay, flex your fingers a bit to rest them from all that typing, go get a beverage and tasty snack, and we'll take a look through the code to see what's what. Although the file is long, and a lot of subtle stuff is going on, we've already covered most of what we do in this controller class.

Our first method is the one that is called when the *Append Matching Songs* button is pressed. If the user hasn't typed a search term, we're just going to return without doing anything. In a real application, you might want to handle this situation differently, perhaps giving some feedback about why nothing happened when the button was pressed. The reason we ignore the press here is because a media query with an empty comparison value will return every media item in the person's library. On a 32-gigabyte iPhone—or, worse, a 64-gigabyte iPod touch—that could potentially be an awful lot of music. Since this method is firing on the main thread, that means the user interface will likely freeze while we retrieve every single item in their library, and we don't want that to happen.

```
- (IBAction)doTitleSearch {
        if ([titleSearch.text length] == 0)
            return;
```

Next, we build a media property predicate using the search term typed into the text field, and then create a media query using that predicate.

```
        MPMediaPropertyPredicate *titlePredicate =
            [MPMediaPropertyPredicate predicateWithValue: titleSearch.text
            forProperty: MPMediaItemPropertyTitle
```

```
    comparisonType:MPMediaPredicateComparisonContains];
MPMediaQuery *query = [[MPMediaQuery alloc] initWithFilterPredicates:
    [NSSet setWithObject:titlePredicate]];
```

If the query actually returns items, then we either append the returned items to collection or, if collection is nil, we create a new media item collection based on the results of the query and assign it to collection. We also set collectionModified to YES so that when the currently playing song ends or a new song is played, it will update the music player with the modified queue.

```
    if ([[query items] count] > 0) {
    if (collection)
        self.collection = [collection collectionByAppendingMediaItems:
            [query items]];
    else {
        self.collection = [MPMediaItemCollection collectionWithItems:
            [query items]];
        [player setQueueWithItemCollection:self.collection];
        [player play];
    }

    collectionModified = YES;
    [self.tableView reloadData];
}
```

After that, we just release our query, reset the text field, and retract the keyboard.

```
    [query release];
    titleSearch.text = @"";
    [titleSearch resignFirstResponder];
}
```

If the user presses the *Use Media Picker* button, then this method is called. We start by creating an instance of MPMediaPickerController, assign self as the delegate, and specify that the user can select multiple items. We assign a string to display at the top of the media picker, and then present the picker modally.

```
- (IBAction)showMediaPicker {
    MPMediaPickerController *picker = [[MPMediaPickerController alloc]
        initWithMediaTypes:MPMediaTypeMusic];
    picker.delegate = self;
    [picker setAllowsPickingMultipleItems:YES];
    picker.prompt = NSLocalizedString(@"Select items to play...",
        @"Select items to play...");
    [self presentModalViewController:picker animated:YES];
    [picker release];
}
```

If the user clicks anywhere in the view that doesn't contain an active control, we'll tell the text field to resign first responder status. If the text field is not the first responder, then nothing happens. But if it is, it will resign that status, and the keyboard will retract.

```
- (IBAction)backgroundClick {
    [titleSearch resignFirstResponder];
}
```

When the user first taps the left-arrow button, we begin seeking backward in the song, and make note of the time that this occurred.

> **TIP:** Generally speaking, an NSTimeInterval, which is just a typedef'd double, is much faster than using NSDate for tracking specific moments in time, such as we do here.

```
- (IBAction)seekBackward {
    [player beginSeekingBackward];
    pressStarted = [NSDate timeIntervalSinceReferenceDate];
}
```

When the user's finger lets up after tapping the left arrow, we stop seeking. If the total length of time that the user's finger was on the button was less than a tenth of a second, we skip back to the previous track. This approximates the behavior of the buttons in the iPod or Music application. In the case of a normal tap, the seeking happens for such a short period of time before the new track starts that the user isn't likely to notice it. To exactly replicate the logic of the iPod application would be considerably more complex, but this is close enough for our purposes.

```
- (IBAction)previousTrack {
    [player endSeeking];

    if (pressStarted >= [NSDate timeIntervalSinceReferenceDate] - 0.1)
        [player skipToPreviousItem];
}
```

In the two methods used by the right-arrow buttons, we have basically the same logic, but seek forward and skip to the next song, rather than to the previous one.

```
- (IBAction)seekForward {
    [player beginSeekingForward];
    pressStarted = [NSDate timeIntervalSinceReferenceDate];
}

- (IBAction)nextTrack {
    [player endSeeking];
    if (pressStarted >= [NSDate timeIntervalSinceReferenceDate] - 0.1)
        [player skipToNextItem];
}
```

In the method called by the play/pause button, we check to see if the music player is playing. If it is playing, then we pause it; if it's not playing, then we start it. In both cases, we update the middle button's image so it's showing the appropriate icon. When we're finished, we reload the table, because the currently playing item in the table has a play or pause icon next to it, and we want to make sure that this icon is updated accordingly.

```
- (IBAction)playOrPause {
    if (player.playbackState == MPMusicPlaybackStatePlaying) {
        [player pause];
        [playPauseButton setBackgroundImage:[UIImage imageNamed:@"play.png"]
            forState:UIControlStateNormal];
    }
    else {
        [player play];
```

```
    [playPauseButton setBackgroundImage:[UIImage imageNamed:@"pause.png"]
        forState:UIControlStateNormal];
    }
    [self.tableView reloadData];
}
```

Our final action method is called when the user taps the red button in the accessory pane of a table row, which indicates that the user wants to remove a given track from the queue. Each button's tag will be set to the current row number its cell currently represents. We retrieve the tag from sender, and then use that index to delete the appropriate item. If the item being deleted is the currently playing track, we skip to the next item.

```
- (IBAction)removeTrack:(id)sender {
    NSUInteger index = [sender tag];
    MPMediaItem *itemToDelete = [collection mediaItemAtIndex:index];
    if ([itemToDelete isEqual:nowPlaying]) {
        if (!collectionModified) {
            [player skipToNextItem];
        }
        else {
            [player setQueueWithItemCollection:collection];
            player.nowPlayingItem = [collection mediaItemAfterItem:nowPlaying];
        }

    }
    MPMediaItemCollection *newCollection = [collection
        collectionByDeletingMediaItemAtIndex:index];
    self.collection = newCollection;
```

As always, we don't actually update the music player controller's queue now, because we don't want a skip in the music. If the song that was deleted was the currently playing one, calling skipToNextItem will result in our notification method getting called, so we don't need to install the queue here. Instead, we just set collectionModified to YES so that the notification method knows to install the modified queue.

```
    collectionModified = YES;
```

Of course, we want the deleted row to animate out, rather than just disappear, so we create an NSIndexPath that points to the row that was deleted and tell the table view to delete that row.

```
    NSUInteger indices[] = {0, index};
    NSIndexPath *deletePath = [NSIndexPath indexPathWithIndexes:indices length:2];
    [self.tableView deleteRowsAtIndexPaths:[NSArray arrayWithObject:deletePath]
        withRowAnimation:UITableViewRowAnimationFade];
```

This last bit of code in the method may seem a little strange. If the row that was deleted was the last row in the table, we need to check to see if there's any music playing. Generally, there won't be, but if the music that's playing was already playing when our application started, there's a queue already in place that we can't access. Remember that we do not have access to a music player controller's queue. Suppose the row that was deleted represented a track that was playing, and it was also the last track in the queue. When we skipped forward, we may have caused the iPod music player to pull another song from that queue that we can't access. In that situation, we find out the new song that's playing and append it to the end of our queue, so the user can see it.

```
        if (newCollection == nil &&
        player.playbackState == MPMusicPlaybackStatePlaying) {
        MPMediaItem *next = player.nowPlayingItem;
        self.collection = [MPMediaItemCollection collectionWithItems:
            [NSArray arrayWithObject:next]];
        [tableView reloadData];
    }
}
```

> **NOTE:** The fact that we can't get to the iPod music player controller's queue isn't ideal in terms of trying to write a music player. However, we're writing a music player only to demonstrate how to access music in the iPod Library. The iPhone already comes with a very good music player that has access to things that we don't, including its own queues. Think of our example as purely a teaching exercise, and not the start of your next big App Store megahit.

In viewDidLoad, we get a reference to the iPod music player controller and assign it to player. We also check the state of that player to see if it's already playing music. We set the play/pause button's icon based on whether it's playing something, and we also grab the track that's being played and add it to our queue so our user can see the track's title.

```
- (void)viewDidLoad {
    MPMusicPlayerController *thePlayer = [MPMusicPlayerController iPodMusicPlayer];
    self.player = thePlayer;
    [thePlayer release];

    if (player.playbackState == MPMusicPlaybackStatePlaying) {
        [playPauseButton setBackgroundImage:[UIImage imageNamed:@"pause.png"]
            forState:UIControlStateNormal];
        MPMediaItemCollection *newCollection = [MPMediaItemCollection
            collectionWithItems:[NSArray arrayWithObject:[player nowPlayingItem]]];
        self.collection = newCollection;
        self.nowPlaying = [player nowPlayingItem];
    }
    else {
        [playPauseButton setBackgroundImage:[UIImage imageNamed:@"play.png"]
            forState:UIControlStateNormal];
    }
```

Next, we register with the notification center to receive notifications when the media item being played by player changes. We register the method nowPlayingItemChanged: with the notification center. In that method, we'll handle installing modified queues into player. We also need to tell player to begin generating those notifications, or our method will never get called.

```
    NSNotificationCenter *notificationCenter = [NSNotificationCenter defaultCenter];
    [notificationCenter addObserver:self
        selector:@selector (nowPlayingItemChanged:)
        name:MPMusicPlayerControllerNowPlayingItemDidChangeNotification
```

```
        object: player];

    [player beginGeneratingPlaybackNotifications];
}
```

The viewDidUnload method is standard and doesn't warrant discussing, but the dealloc method has a few things we don't normally see. In addition to releasing all of our objects, we also unregister from the notification center and have player stop generating notifications. This is good form. In our particular case, it probably wouldn't matter if we didn't do this, since notificationCenter will be deallocated when our application exits. That said, you really should unregister any object that has been registered with the notification center when the object that's registered is deallocated. The notification center does not retain the objects it notifies, so it will continue to send notifications to an object after that object has been released if you don't do this.

```
        NSNotificationCenter *center = [NSNotificationCenter defaultCenter];
    [center removeObserver:self
        name:MPMusicPlayerControllerNowPlayingItemDidChangeNotification
        object:player];
    [player endGeneratingPlaybackNotifications];
```

The rest of the dealloc method is pretty much what you're used to seeing. After dealloc, we begin the various delegate and notification methods. First up is the method that's called when our user selects one or more items using the media picker. This method begins by dismissing the media picker controller.

```
- (void) mediaPicker: (MPMediaPickerController *) mediaPicker
    didPickMediaItems: (MPMediaItemCollection *) theCollection {
    [self dismissModalViewControllerAnimated: YES];
```

Next, we check to see if we already have a collection. If we don't, then all we need to do is pass theCollection on to player and tell it to start playing. We also set the play/pause button to show the pause icon.

```
    if (collection == nil){
        self.collection = theCollection;
        [player setQueueWithItemCollection:collection];
        [player setNowPlayingItem:[collection firstMediaItem]];
        self.nowPlaying = [collection firstMediaItem];
        [player play];
        [playPauseButton setBackgroundImage:[UIImage imageNamed:@"pause.png"]
            forState:UIControlStateNormal];
    }
```

If we already have a collection, we use one of those category methods we created earlier to append theCollection to the end of the existing collection.

```
    else {
        self.collection = [collection
            collectionByAppendingCollection:theCollection];
    }
```

Next, we set collectionModified to YES so that the updated collection is installed next time there's a break between songs, and we reload the table so the user can see the change.

```
    collectionModified = YES;
    [self.tableView reloadData];
}
```

If the user canceled the media picker, the only thing we need to do is dismiss it.

```
- (void) mediaPickerDidCancel: (MPMediaPickerController *) mediaPicker {
    [self dismissModalViewControllerAnimated: YES];
}
```

When a new track starts playing—whether it's because we told the player to start playing, because we told it to skip to the next or previous song, or simply because it reached the end of the current song—the item-changed notification well be sent out, which will cause this next method to fire.

The logic here may not be obvious, because we have several possible scenarios to take into account. First, we check to see if collection is nil. If it is, then most likely, something outside our application started the music playing or triggered the change. Perhaps the user squeezed the button on the iPhone's headphones to restart a previously playing song. In that case, we create a new media item collection containing just the playing song.

```
- (void)nowPlayingItemChanged:(NSNotification *)notification {
    if (collection == nil) {
        MPMediaItem *nowPlayingItem = [player nowPlayingItem];
        self.collection = [collection
            collectionByAppendingMediaItem:nowPlayingItem];
    }
```

Otherwise, we need to check to see if collection has been modified. If it has, then the music player controller's queue and our queue are different, and we use this opportunity to install our collection as the music player's queue.

```
    else {
        if (collectionModified) {
            [player setQueueWithItemCollection:collection];
            [player setNowPlayingItem:[collection mediaItemAfterItem:nowPlaying]];
            [player play];
        }
```

Regardless of whether the collection was modified, we must see if the item that is being played is in our collection. If it's not, that means it pulled another item from a queue that we didn't create and can't access. If that's the case, we just grab the item that's playing now and append it to our collection. We may not be able to show the users the preexisting queue, but we can show them each new song that's played from it.

```
        if (![collection containsItem:player.nowPlayingItem] &&
            player.nowPlayingItem != nil) {
            self.collection = [collection
                collectionByAppendingMediaItem:player.nowPlayingItem];
        }
    }
```

No matter what we did above, we reload the table to make sure that any changes become visible to our user, and we store the currently playing item into an instance variable so we have ready access to it.

```
[tableView reloadData];
self.nowPlaying = [player nowPlayingItem];
```

We also need to make sure that the play or pause button shows the correct image. This method is called after the last track in the queue is played, so it's possible that we've gone from no music playing to music playing or vice versa. As a result, we need to update this button to show the play icon or the pause icon, as appropriate.

```
if (nowPlaying == nil)
    [playPauseButton setBackgroundImage:[UIImage imageNamed:@"play.png"]
        forState:UIControlStateNormal];
else
    [playPauseButton setBackgroundImage:[UIImage imageNamed:@"pause.png"]
        forState:UIControlStateNormal];
```

Of course, once we're finished here, we need to reset `collectionModified` back to NO so that we can tell if the collection is changed again.

```
collectionModified = NO;
}
```

Our last group of methods contains our table view datasource and delegate methods. The first one we implement is `tableView:numberOfRowInSection:`. In that method, we just return the number of media items in `collection`.

```
- (NSInteger)tableView:(UITableView *)theTableView
numberOfRowsInSection:(NSInteger)section {
    return [collection count];
}
```

In `tableView:cellForRowAtIndexPath:`, we dequeue or create a cell, pretty much as always.

```
- (UITableViewCell *)tableView:(UITableView *)theTableView
        cellForRowAtIndexPath:(NSIndexPath *)indexPath {
    static NSString *identifier = @"Music Queue Cell";
    UITableViewCell *cell = [theTableView
        dequeueReusableCellWithIdentifier:identifier];
    if (cell == nil) {
        cell = [[[UITableViewCell alloc] initWithStyle:UITableViewCellStyleDefault
            reuseIdentifier:identifier] autorelease];
```

When we add a new cell, we need to create a button and assign it to the accessory view. The button's target is set to the `removeTrack:` method, which means that any tap on any row's button will trigger that method.

```
UIButton *removeButton = [UIButton buttonWithType:UIButtonTypeCustom];
UIImage *removeImage = [UIImage imageNamed:@"remove.png"];
[removeButton setBackgroundImage:removeImage forState:UIControlStateNormal];
[removeButton setFrame:CGRectMake(0.0, 0.0, removeImage.size.width,
    removeImage.size.height)];
[removeButton addTarget:self action:@selector(removeTrack:)
    forControlEvents:UIControlEventTouchUpInside];
cell.accessoryView  = removeButton;
}
```

We assign the cell's text based on the title of the media item the row represents:

```
cell.textLabel.text = [collection titleForMediaItemAtIndex:[indexPath row]];
```

Then we check to see if this row is the current one that's playing. If it is, we set the cell's image to a small play or pause icon, and make the row's text bold. Otherwise, we set the row's image to an empty image the same size as the play and pause icon, and set the text so it's not bold. The empty image is just to keep the rows' text nicely aligned.

```
if ([nowPlaying isEqual:[collection mediaItemAtIndex:[indexPath row]]]) {
    cell.textLabel.font = [UIFont boldSystemFontOfSize:21.0];
    if (player.playbackState ==  MPMusicPlaybackStatePlaying)
        cell.imageView.image = [UIImage imageNamed:@"play_small.png"];
    else
        cell.imageView.image = [UIImage imageNamed:@"pause_small.png"];

}
else {
    cell.textLabel.font = [UIFont systemFontOfSize:21.0];
    cell.imageView.image = [UIImage imageNamed:@"empty.png"];
}
```

NOTE: Our application currently does not keep track of the index of the currently playing item. We could implement that for queues we create, but not for ones that are already playing. As a result, if you have multiple copies of the same item in the queue, when that song plays, every row that contains that same item will be bold and have a play or pause icon. Since we don't have access to queues created outside our application, there's no good solution to this problem here, and since it's not a real-world application, we can live with it.

We make sure to set the cell's delete button's tag to the row number this cell will be used to represent. That way, our removeTrack: method will know which track to delete. After that, we're ready to return cell.

```
cell.accessoryView.tag = [indexPath row];

return cell;
}
```

If the user selected a row, we want to play the song that was tapped. The only gotcha here is that we must make sure that the updated queue is installed in the player before we start the new song playing. If we didn't do this, we might end up telling the player to play a song it didn't know about, because it was added to the queue since the last track change.

```
- (void)tableView:(UITableView *)theTableView
    didSelectRowAtIndexPath:(NSIndexPath *)indexPath {
    MPMediaItem *selected = [collection mediaItemAtIndex:[indexPath row]];

    if (collectionModified) {
        [player setQueueWithItemCollection:collection];
        collectionModified = NO;
    }

    [player setNowPlayingItem:selected];
```

```
    [player play];

    [playPauseButton setBackgroundImage:[UIImage imageNamed:@"pause.png"]
        forState:UIControlStateNormal];
    [self.tableView reloadData];
}
```

Last, but certainly not... well, actually, this might be least. We're using a slightly smaller font size and cell height than the default values, and here's where we specify the row height to use. kTableRowHeight was defined at the beginning of the file as 34 pixels. By placing it at the top of the file, it's easier to find should we want to change it.

```
- (CGFloat)tableView:(UITableView *)theTableView
        heightForRowAtIndexPath:(NSIndexPath *)indexPath {
    return kTableRowHeight;
}
```

@end

Taking Simple Player for a Spin

Well, wow! That was a lot of functionality used in such a small application. Let's try it out. But, before you can do that, you need to link to the MediaPlayer framework. At this point, you should know how to do that, but in case your brain is fried, we'll remind you. Right-click the *Frameworks* folder in the *Groups & Files* pane. From the menu that pops up, select the **Add** submenu, then select **Existing Frameworks....** Check the box next to *MediaPlayer.framework* and click the *Add* button.

Go ahead and take the app for a spin. Remember that although Simple Player may launch in the simulator, the simulator does not currently support a media library, so you'll want to run Simple Player on your device. As usual, we won't get into the details here. Apple has excellent documentation on their portal site, which you'll have access to once you join one of the paid iPhone Developer Programs.

After your app is running on your device, play with all the different options. Make sure you try adding songs both by typing in a title search term and by using the media picker. Also try deleting songs from the queue, including the currently playing song.

If this were a shipping app, we would have done a number of things differently. For example, we would move the title search field to its own separate view with its own table view so you could see the results of your search as you typed. We would tweak the seek threshold until we got it just right. We would also use Core Data to add persistence to keep our queue around from one run of the app to the next. There are other elements we might change, but we wanted to keep the code as small as possible to focus on the iPod library.

Avast! Rough Waters Ahead!

In this chapter, we took a long but pleasant walk through the hills and valleys of using the iPod music library. You saw how to find media items using media queries, and how to let your users select songs using the media picker controller. We demonstrated how to use and manipulate collections of media items. We showed you how to use music player controllers to play media items, and to manipulate the currently playing item by seeking or skipping. You also learned how to find out about the currently playing track, regardless of whether it's one your code played or one that the user chose using the iPod or Music application.

But now, shore leave is over, matey. It's time to leave the sheltered cove and venture out into the open water of concurrency (writing code that executes simultaneously) and debugging. Both of these topics are challenging but supremely important. So, all hands on deck! Man the braces and prepare to make sail.

Chapter 14

Keeping Your Interface Responsive

As we've mentioned a few times in this book, if you try to do too much at one time in an action or delegate method, or in a method called from one of those methods, your application's interface can skip or even freeze while the long-running method does its job. As a general rule, you do not want your application's user interface to ever become unresponsive. Your user will expect to be able to interact with your application at all times, or at the very least will expect to be kept updated by your user interface when they aren't allowed to interact with it.

In computer programming, the ability to have multiple sets of operations happening at the same time is referred to, generally, as **concurrency**. You've already seen one form of concurrency in the networking chapters when we retrieved data from the Internet asynchronously and also when we listened for incoming connections on a specific network port. That particular form of concurrency is called **run loop scheduling**, and it's relatively easy to implement because most of the work to make those actions run concurrently has already been done for you.

In this chapter, we're going to look at some more general-purpose solutions for adding concurrency to your application. These will allow your user interface to stay responsive even when your application is performing long-running tasks. Although there are many ways to add concurrency to an application, we're going to look at just two, but these two, combined with what you already know about run loop scheduling for networking, should allow you to accommodate just about any long-running task.

The first mechanism we're going to look at is the **timer**. Timers are objects that can be scheduled with the run loop, much like the networking classes we've worked with. Timers can call methods on specific objects at set intervals. You can set a timer to call a method on one of your controller classes, for example, ten times per second. Once you kick it off, approximately every tenth of a second, your method will fire until you tell the timer to stop.

Neither run loop scheduling nor timers are what some people would consider "true" forms of concurrency. In both cases, the application's main run loop will check for certain conditions, and if those conditions are met, it will call out to a specific method on a specific object. If the method that gets called runs for too long, however, your interface will still becomes unresponsive. But, working with run loops and timers is considerably less complex than implementing what we might call "true" concurrency, which is to have multiple tasks (and multiple run loops) functioning at the same time.

The other mechanism we're going to look at is relatively new in the Objective-C world. It's called an **operation queue**, and it works together with special objects you create called **operations**. The operation queue can manage multiple operations at the same time, and it makes sure that those operations get processing time based on some simple rules that you set down. Each operation has a specific set of commands that take the form of a method you write, and the operation queue will make sure that each operation's method gets run in such a ways as to make good use of the available system resources.

Operation queues are really nice because they are a high-level abstraction and hide the nitty-gritty implementation details involved with implementing true concurrency. On the iPhone, queues leverage an operating system feature called **threads** to give processing time to the various operations they manage. Apple is currently recommending the use of operation queues rather than threads, not only because operation queues are easier to use, but also because they give your application other advantages.

> **NOTE:** Even though it's not available when using the iPhone SDK, another form of concurrency is multiprocessing, using the Unix system calls fork() and exec() or Cocoa's NSTask class. Using multiple processes is more heavy-weight than using threads.

If you're at all familiar with Mac OS X Snow Leopard, you've probably heard of **Grand Central Dispatch** (GCD), which is a technology that allows applications to take greater advantage of the fact that modern computers have multiple processing cores and sometimes multiple processors. If you used an operation queue in a Mac program back before GCD was released, when you re-compiled your application for Snow Leopard, your code automatically received the benefit of GCD for free. If you had used another form of concurrency, such as threads, instead of operation queues, your application would not have automatically benefitted from GCD.

We don't know what the future holds for the iPhone SDK, but we are likely to continue to see faster processors and possibly even multiple core processors. Who knows? Perhaps at some point in the not-too-distant future, we'll even see an iPhone or iPod touch with multiple processors. By using operation queues for your concurrency needs, you will essentially future-proof your applications. If Grand Central Dispatch comes to the iPhone in a future release of the iPhone SDK, for example, you will be able to leverage that functionality with little or no work. If Apple creates some other nifty new technology specifically for handling concurrency in a mobile application, your application will be able to take advantage of that.

You can probably see why we're limiting our discussion of "true" concurrency to operation queues. They are clearly the way of the future for both Cocoa and Cocoa Touch. They make our lives as programmers considerably easier and they help us take advantage of technologies that haven't even been written yet. What could be better?

Let's start with a little detour to look at the problem that concurrency solves.

Exploring the Concurrency Problem

Before we explore ways of solving the concurrency problem, let's make sure we all understand exactly what that problem is. We're going to build a small application that will demonstrate the problem that arises when you try to do too much at one time on the application's **main thread**. Every application has at least one thread of operation, and that's the one where the application's main run loop is running. All action methods fire on the main thread and all event processing and user interface updating is also done from the main thread. If any method that fires on the main thread takes too long to finish, the user interface will freeze up and become unresponsive.

Our small application is going to calculate square roots. Lots and lots of square roots. The user will be able to enter a number, and we'll calculate the square root for every number from 1 up to the number they specify (Figure 14–1). Our only goal in this exercise is to burn processor cycles.

Figure 14–1. *The Stalled application will demonstrate the problem of trying to do too much work on the application's main thread*

With a sufficiently large number entered, when the *Go* button is tapped, the user interface will become completely unresponsive for several seconds or even longer. The progress bar and progress label, whose properties will be set each time through the loop, won't actually show any changes to the user until all the values in the loop have been calculated. Only the last calculation will be reflected in the user interface.

Creating the Stalled Application

In Xcode, create a new project using the *View-based Application* template and call this project *Stalled*. Once the new project is open, expand the *Classes* and *Resources* folders in the *Groups & Files* pane. We'll start by declaring our outlets and actions and then go to Interface Builder and design our interface, then we'll come back to write the implementation of our controller and try it out.

Declaring Actions and Outlets

Single-click *StalledViewController.h* and replace the existing contents with the following:

```
#import <UIKit/UIKit.h>

@interface StalledViewController : UIViewController {
    UITextField     *numOperationsInput;
    UIProgressView  *progressBar;
    UILabel         *progressLabel;
}

@property (nonatomic, retain) IBOutlet UITextField *numOperationsInput;
@property (nonatomic, retain) IBOutlet UIProgressView *progressBar;
@property (nonatomic, retain) IBOutlet UILabel *progressLabel;

- (IBAction)go;
@end
```

We haven't seen a controller class header this simple in quite a while, have we? Nothing here should be unfamiliar to you. We have three outlets that are used to refer to the three user interface elements whose values we need to update or retrieve, and we have a single action method that gets fired by the one button on our interface. Make sure you save *StalledViewController.h*.

Designing the Interface

Double-click *StalledViewController.xib* to launch Interface Builder. Drag a *Round Rect Button* from the library to the window titled *View*, placing the button against the upper-right margins using the blue guidelines. Double-click the button and change its title to *Go*. Control-click from the new button to *File's Owner* and select the *go* action.

Now drag a *Text Field* from the library and place it to the left of the button. Use the blue guides to line up the text field and place it the correct distance from the button. Resize the text field to about two-third of its original size, or use the size inspector and change its width to 70 pixels. Double-click the text field and set its default value to *10000*. Press ⌘1 to bring up the attribute inspector, and change the *Keyboard* to *Number Pad* to restrict entry to only numbers. Control-drag from *File's Owner* to the text field and select the *numOperationsInput* outlet.

Drag a *Label* from the library and place it to the left of the text field. Double-click it to change its text to read *# of Operations* and then adjust its size and placement to fit in the available space. You can use Figure 14–1 as a guide.

From the library, bring over a *Progress View* and place it below the three items already on the interface. We placed it a little more than the minimum distance below them as indicated by the blue guides, but exact placement really doesn't matter much with this application. Once you place the progress bar, use the resize handles to change its width so it takes up all the space from the left margin to the right margin. Next, use the attributes inspector to change the *Progress* field to 0.0. Finally, control-drag from *File's Owner* to the progress view and select the *progressBar* outlet.

Drag one more *Label* from the library and place it below the progress view. Resize the label so it is stretches from the left to the right margins. Control-drag from *File's Owner* to the new label and select the *progressLabel* outlet. Then, double-click the label and press the delete key to delete the existing label text.

Save your nib, close Interface Builder, and head back to Xcode.

Implementing the Stalled View Controller

Select *StalledViewController.m* and replace the existing contents with the following code:

```
#import "StalledViewController.h"

@implementation StalledViewController
@synthesize numOperationsInput;
@synthesize progressBar;
@synthesize progressLabel;

- (IBAction)go {
    NSInteger opCount = [numOperationsInput.text intValue];
    for (NSInteger i = 1; i <= opCount; i++) {
        NSLog(@"Calculating square root of %d", i);
        double squareRootOfI = sqrt((double)i);
        progressBar.progress = ((float)i / (float)opCount);
        progressLabel.text = [NSString stringWithFormat:
            @"Square Root of %d is %.3f", i, squareRootOfI];
    }
}

- (void)viewDidUnload {
    [super viewDidUnload];
    self.numOperationsInput = nil;
    self.progressBar = nil;
    self.progressLabel = nil;
}
```

```
- (void)dealloc {
    [numOperationsInput release];
    [progressBar release];
    [progressLabel release];
    [super dealloc];
}
```

@end

Let's focus on the go method, because that's where the problem is. Everything else is stuff you've seen before. The method starts by retrieving the number from the text field.

```
NSInteger opCount = [numOperationsInput.text intValue];
```

Then, we go into a loop so we can calculate all of the square roots.

```
for (NSInteger i = 1; i <= opCount; i++) {
```

We log which calculation we're working on. In shipping applications, you generally wouldn't log like this, but logging serves two purposes in this chapter. First, it lets us see, using Xcode's debugger console, that the application is working even when our application's user interface isn't responding. Second, logging takes a non-trivial amount of time. In real-world applications, that would generally be bad, but since our goal is just to do processing to show how concurrency works, this slow-down actually works to our advantage. If you choose to remove the NSLog() statements, you will need to increase the number of calculations by an order of magnitude because the iPhone is actually capable of doing tens of thousands of square root operations per second and it will hardly break a sweat doing ten thousand without the NSLog() statement in the loop to throttle the speed.

> **CAUTION:** Logging using NSLog() takes considerably longer when running on the device launched from Xcode because the results of every NSLog() statement have to be transferred through the USB connection to Xcode. Although this chapter's applications will work just fine on the device, you may wish to consider restricting yourself to the Simulator for testing and debugging in this chapter, or else commenting out the NSLog() statements when running on the device.

```
NSLog(@"Calculating square root of %d", i);
```

Then we calculate the square root of i.

```
double squareRootOfI = sqrt((double)i);
```

And update the progress bar and label to reflect the last calculation made, and that's the end of our loop.

```
progressBar.progress = ((float)i / (float)opCount);
progressLabel.text = [NSString stringWithFormat:
    @"Square Root of %d is %.3f", i, squareRootOfI];
}
```

The problem with this method isn't so much what we're doing as where we're doing it. As we stated earlier, action methods fire on the main thread, which is also where user interface updates happen, and where system events, such as those that are generated by taps and touches, are processed. If any method firing on the main thread takes too much time, it will affect your application's user experience. In less severe cases, your application will seem to hiccup or stall at times. In severe cases, like here, your application's entire user interface will freeze up.

Save *StalledViewController.m* and build and run the application. Press the *Go* button and watch what happens. Not much, huh? If you keep an eye on the debug console in Xcode, you'll see that it is working away on those calculations (Figure 14–2) thanks to the NSLog() statement in our code, but the user interface doesn't update until all of the calculations are done, does it?

Note that if you do click in the text field, the numeric keypad will not disappear when you tap the Go button. Since there's nothing being hidden by the keypad, this isn't a problem. In the final version of the application, we'll add a table that will be hidden by the keypad. We'll add some code to deal with that situation as needed.

```
2009-11-19 18:02:36.119 Stalled[15896:207] Calculating square root of 9942
2009-11-19 18:02:36.120 Stalled[15896:207] Calculating square root of 9943
2009-11-19 18:02:36.120 Stalled[15896:207] Calculating square root of 9944
2009-11-19 18:02:36.120 Stalled[15896:207] Calculating square root of 9945
2009-11-19 18:02:36.121 Stalled[15896:207] Calculating square root of 9946
2009-11-19 18:02:36.121 Stalled[15896:207] Calculating square root of 9947
2009-11-19 18:02:36.121 Stalled[15896:207] Calculating square root of 9948
2009-11-19 18:02:36.122 Stalled[15896:207] Calculating square root of 9949
2009-11-19 18:02:36.122 Stalled[15896:207] Calculating square root of 9950
2009-11-19 18:02:36.123 Stalled[15896:207] Calculating square root of 9951
2009-11-19 18:02:36.123 Stalled[15896:207] Calculating square root of 9952
2009-11-19 18:02:36.123 Stalled[15896:207] Calculating square root of 9953
2009-11-19 18:02:36.124 Stalled[15896:207] Calculating square root of 9954
2009-11-19 18:02:36.124 Stalled[15896:207] Calculating square root of 9955
2009-11-19 18:02:36.124 Stalled[15896:207] Calculating square root of 9956
2009-11-19 18:02:36.125 Stalled[15896:207] Calculating square root of 9957
2009-11-19 18:02:36.125 Stalled[15896:207] Calculating square root of 9958
2009-11-19 18:02:36.126 Stalled[15896:207] Calculating square root of 9959
2009-11-19 18:02:36.133 Stalled[15896:207] Calculating square root of 9960
```

Figure 14–2. *The debug console in Xcode shows that the application is working, but the user interface is locked up*

If we have code that takes a long time to run, we've basically got two choices if we want to keep our interface responsive: We can break our code into smaller chunks that can be processed in pieces, or we can move the code to a separate thread of execution, which will allow our application's run loop to return to updating the user interface and responding to taps and other system events. We'll look at both options in this chapter.

First, we'll fix the application by using a **timer** to perform the requested calculations in batches, making sure not to take more than a fraction of a second each time so that the main thread can continue to process events and update the interface. After that, we'll look at using an operation queue to move the calculations off of the application's main thread, leaving the main thread free to process events.

Timers

In the Foundation framework shared by Cocoa and Cocoa Touch, there's a class called NSTimer that you can use to call methods on a specific object at periodic intervals. Timers are created, and then scheduled with a run loop, much like some of the networking classes we've worked with. Once a timer is scheduled, it will fire after a specified interval. If the timer is set to repeat, it will continue to call its target method repeatedly each time the specified interval elapses.

> **NOTE:** Non-repeating timers are no longer very commonly used because you can achieve exactly the same affect much more easily by calling the method performSelector:withObject:afterDelay: as we've done a few times in this book.

Timers are not guaranteed to fire exactly at the specified interval. Because of the way the run loop functions, there's no way to guarantee the exact moment when a timer will fire. The timer will fire on the first pass through the run loop that happens after the specified amount of time has elapsed. That means a timer will never fire before the specified interval, but it may fire after. Usually, the actual interval is only milliseconds longer than the one specified, but you can't rely on that being the case. If a long-running method runs on the main loop, like the one in *Stalled*, then the run loop won't get to fire the scheduled timers until that long-running method has finished, potentially a long time after the requested interval.

Timers fire on the thread whose run loop they are scheduled into. In most situations, unless you specifically intend to do otherwise, your timers will get created on the main thread and the methods that they fire will also execute on the main thread. This means that you have to follow the same rules as with action methods. If you try to do too much in a method that is called by a timer, you will stall your user interface.

As a result, if you want to use timers as a mechanism for keeping your user interface responsive, you need to break your work down into smaller chunks, only doing a small amount of work each time it fires. We'll show you a technique for doing that in a minute.

Creating a Timer

Creating an instance of NSTimer is quite straightforward. If you want to create it, but not schedule it with the run loop right away, use the factory method timerWithTimeInterval:target:selector:userInfo:repeats:, like so:

```
NSTimer *timer = [NSTimer timerWithTimeInterval:1.0/10.0
    target:self
    selector:@selector(myTimerMethod:)
    userInfo:nil
    repeats:YES]
```

The first argument to this method specifies how frequently you would like the timer to fire and call its method. In this example, we're passing in a tenth of a second, so this timer will fire approximately ten times a second. The next two arguments work exactly like the target and action properties of a control. The second argument, `target`, is the object on which the timer should call a method, and `selector` points to the actual method the timer should call when it fires. The method specified by the selector must take a single argument, which will be the instance of `NSTimer` that called the method. The fourth argument, `userInfo`, is designed for application use. If you pass in an object here, that object will go along with the timer and be available in the method the timer calls when it fires. The last argument specifies whether the timer repeats or fires just once.

Once you've got a timer and are ready for it to start firing, you get a reference to the run loop you want to schedule it into, and then add the timer. Here's an example of scheduling the timer into the main run loop:

```
NSRunLoop *loop = [NSRunLoop mainRunLoop];
[loop addTimer:timer forMode:NSDefaultRunLoopMode];
```

When you schedule the timer, the run loop retains the timer. You can keep a pointer to the timer if you need to, but you don't need to retain the timer to keep it from getting deallocated. The run loop will retain the timer until you stop the timer.

If you want to create a timer that's already scheduled with the run loop, letting you skip the previous two lines of code, you can use the factory method `scheduledTimerWithTimeInterval:target:selector:userInfo:repeats:`, which takes exactly the same arguments as `timerWithTimeInterval:target:selector:userInfo:repeats:`.

```
NSTimer *timer = [NSTimer scheduledTimerWithTimeInterval:1.0/10.0
    target:self
    selector:@selector(myTimerMethod:)
    userInfo:nil
    repeats:YES]
```

Stopping a Timer

When you no longer need a timer, you can unschedule it from the run loop by calling the `invalidate` method on the instance. Invalidating a timer will stop it from firing any further and remove it from the run loop, which will release the timer and cause it to be deallocated unless it's been retained elsewhere. Here's how you invalidate a timer:

```
[timer invalidate];
```

Limitations of Timers

Timers are very handy for any number of purposes. As a tool for keeping your interface responsive, they do have some limitations, however. The first and foremost of these limitations is that you have to make some assumptions about how much time is available for the process that you're implementing. If you have more than a couple of timers running, things can easily get complex and the logic to make sure that each timer's method gets an appropriate share of the available time without taking too much time away from the main thread can get very complex and abstruse.

Timers are great for when you have one, or at most, a small number, of long-running tasks that can be easily broken down into discrete chunks for processing. When you have more than that, or when the processes don't lend themselves to being performed in chunks, timers become far too much trouble and just aren't the right tool for the job.

Let's use a timer to get the *Stalled* application working the way our users will expect it to work, then we'll move on and look at how we handle scenarios where we have more than a couple of processes.

Fixing Stalled with a Timer

We're going to keep working with the *Stalled* application, but before we proceed, make a copy of the *Stalled* project folder. We're going to fix the project using two different techniques, so you will need two copies of the project in order to play along at home. If you run into problems, you can always copy the *14 – Stalled* project in the project archive that accompanies this book as your starting point for both this exercise and the next one.

Creating the Batch Object

Before we start modifying our controller class, let's create a class to represent our batch of calculations. This object will keep track of how many calculations need to be performed as well as how many already have. We'll also move the actual calculations into the batch object as well. Having this object will make it much easier to do processing in chunks, since the batch will be self-contained in a single object.

Single-click the *Classes* folder in the *Groups & Files* pane, then type ⌘N to create a new file. Select *Objective-C class* from the *Cocoa Touch Class* heading, and make sure the *Subclass of* pop-up menu reads *NSObject*. Name this new file *SquareRootBatch.m* and make sure to have it create *SquareRootBatch.h* for you as well. After the file is created, single-click *SquareRootBatch.h* and replace its contents with the following:

```
#import <Foundation/Foundation.h>

#define kExceededMaxException   @"Exceeded Max"

@interface SquareRootBatch : NSObject {
    NSInteger    max;
    NSInteger    current;
}

@property NSInteger max;
@property NSInteger current;

- (id)initWithMaxNumber:(NSInteger)inMax;
- (BOOL)hasNext;
- (double)next;
```

```
- (float)percentCompleted;
- (NSString *)percentCompletedText;
@end
```

We start off by defining a string that will be used for throwing an exception. If we exceed the number of calculations we've specified, we will throw an exception with this name.

```
#define kExceededMaxException    @"Exceeded Max"
```

Then we define two instance variables and corresponding properties for the maximum number whose square root will be calculated and the current number whose square root is being calculated. This will allow us to keep track of where we are between timer method calls.

```
@interface SquareRootBatch : NSObject {
    NSInteger    max;
    NSInteger    current;
}
@property NSInteger max;
@property NSInteger current;
```

Next, we declare a standard init method that takes one argument, the maximum number for which we are to calculate the square root.

```
- (id)initWithMaxNumber:(NSInteger)inMax;
```

The next two methods will enable our batch to work similarly to an enumerator. We can find out if we still have numbers to calculate by calling hasNext, and actually perform the next calculation by calling next, which returns the calculated value.

```
- (BOOL)hasNext;
- (double)next;
```

After that, we have two more methods used to retrieve values for updating the progress bar and progress label:

```
- (float)percentCompleted;
- (NSString *)percentCompletedText;
```

And that's all she wrote for this header file. Save *SquareRootBatch.h* and then flip over to *SquareRootBatch.m*. Replace the contents with this new version:

```
#import "SquareRootBatch.h"

@implementation SquareRootBatch
@synthesize max;
@synthesize current;

- (id)initWithMaxNumber:(NSInteger)inMax {
    if (self = [super init]) {
        current = 0;
        max = inMax;
    }
    return self;
}

- (BOOL)hasNext {
    return current <= max;
```

```
}

- (double)next {
    if (current > max)
        [NSException raise:kExceededMaxException format:
            @"Requested a calculation from completed batch."];

    return sqrt((double)++current);
}

- (float)percentCompleted {
    return (float)current / (float)max;
}

- (NSString *)percentCompletedText {
    return [NSString stringWithFormat:@"Square Root of %d is %.3f", current,
        sqrt((double)current)];
}

@end
```

Basically, we've taken the logic from our go method and distributed it throughout this little class. By doing that, we make the batch completely self-contained, which will allow us to pass the batch along to the method fired by the timer by making use of the userInfo argument.

> **NOTE:** In this implementation, you might notice that we're actually calculating the square root twice, once in next, and again in `percentCompletedText`. For our purposes, this is actually good because it burns more processor cycles. In a real application, you would probably want to store off the result of the calculation in an instance variable so that you have access to the last calculation performed without having to perform the calculation again.

Updating the Controller Header

Let's rewrite our controller class to use this new timer. Since our user interface will be useable while the batch is running, we want to make the *Go* button become a *Stop* button while the batch is running. It's generally a good idea to give users a way to stop long-running processes if feasible.

Single-click *StalledViewController.h* and insert the following bold lines of code:

```
#import <UIKit/UIKit.h>

#define     kTimerInterval  (1.0/60.0)
#define     kBatchSize      10

@interface StalledViewController : UIViewController {
    UITextField     *numOperationsInput;
    UIProgressView  *progressBar;
    UILabel         *progressLabel;
    UIButton        *goStopButton;
```

```
    BOOL            processRunning;
}

@property (nonatomic, retain) IBOutlet UITextField *numOperationsInput;
@property (nonatomic, retain) IBOutlet UIProgressView *progressBar;
@property (nonatomic, retain) IBOutlet UILabel *progressLabel;
@property (nonatomic, retain) IBOutlet UIButton *goStopButton;

- (IBAction)go;
- (void)processChunk:(NSTimer *)timer;

@end
```

The first constant we defined—kTimerInterval—will be used to determine how often the timer fires. We're going to start by firing approximately 60 times a second. If we need to tweak the value to keep our user interface responsive, we can do that as we test. The second constant, kBatchSize, will be used in the method that the timer calls. In the method, we're going to check how much time has elapsed as we do calculations because we don't want to spend more than one timer interval in that method. In fact, we need to spend a little less than the timer interval because we need to make resources available for the run loop to do other things. However, it would be wasteful to check the elapsed time after every calculation, so we'll do a certain number of calculations before checking the elapsed time, and that's what kBatchSize is for. We can tweak the batch size for better performance as well.

We're also adding an instance variable and property to act as an outlet for the *Go* button. That will enable us to change the button's title to *Stop* when a batch is processing. We also have a Boolean that indicates whether a batch is currently running. We'll use this to determine what to do when the button is tapped and will also use it to tell the batch to stop processing when the user taps the *Stop* button. We also added one method, processChunk:, which is the method that our timer will call and that will process a subset of the batch.

Save *StalledViewController.h* and double-click *StalledViewController.xib*.

Updating the Nib

Once Interface Builder opens up, control-drag from *File's Owner* to the *Go* button. Select the *goStopButton* action. That's the only change we need, so save the nib and close Interface Builder.

Updating the View Controller Implementation

Back in Xcode, single-click on *StalledViewController.m*. At the top of the file, add the following bold lines of code. The first will import the header from the batch object we created, and the second synthesizes the new outlet property we added for the button.

```
#import "StalledViewController.h"
#import "SquareRootBatch.h"

@implementation StalledViewController
@synthesize numOperationsInput;
@synthesize progressBar;
@synthesize progressLabel;
@synthesize goStopButton;
...
```

Next, replace the existing go method with this new version:

```
- (IBAction)go {
    if (!processRunning) {
        NSInteger opCount = [numOperationsInput.text intValue];
        SquareRootBatch *batch = [[SquareRootBatch alloc]
            initWithMaxNumber:opCount];

        [NSTimer scheduledTimerWithTimeInterval:kTimerInterval
            target:self
            selector:@selector(processChunk:)
            userInfo:batch
            repeats:YES];
        [batch release];
        [goStopButton setTitle:@"Stop" forState:UIControlStateNormal];
        processRunning = YES;
    } else {
        processRunning = NO;
        [goStopButton setTitle:@"Go" forState:UIControlStateNormal];
    }
}
```

We start the method out by checking to see if a batch is already running. If it isn't, then we grab the number from the text field, just as the old version did:

```
if (!processRunning) {
    NSInteger opCount = [numOperationsInput.text intValue];
```

Then, we create a new SquareRootBatch instance, initialized with the number pulled from the text field:

```
SquareRootBatch *batch = [[SquareRootBatch alloc]
    initWithMaxNumber:opCount];
```

After creating the batch object, we create a scheduled timer, telling it to call our processChunk: method every sixtieth of a second. We pass the batch object in the userInfo argument so it will be available to the timer method. Because the run loop retains the timer, we don't even declare a pointer to the timer we create.

Next, we set the button's title to *Stop* and set processRunning to reflect that the process has started.

```
[goStopButton setTitle:@"Stop" forState:UIControlStateNormal];
    processRunning = YES;
```

If the batch had already been started, then we just change the button's title back to *Go* and set processRunning to NO, which will tell the processChunk: method to stop processing.

```
    } else {
        processRunning = NO;
        [goStopButton setTitle:@"Go" forState:UIControlStateNormal];
    }
```

Now that we've updated our go method, add the following new method (place it right below go) that will process a chunk of the overall batch:

```
- (void)processChunk:(NSTimer *)timer {
    if (!processRunning) {  // Cancelled
        [timer invalidate];
        progressLabel.text = @"Calculations Cancelled";
        return;
    }

    SquareRootBatch *batch = (SquareRootBatch *)[timer userInfo];
    NSTimeInterval endTime = [NSDate timeIntervalSinceReferenceDate] +
        (kTimerInterval / 2.0);

    BOOL isDone = NO;
    while (([NSDate timeIntervalSinceReferenceDate] < endTime) && (!isDone)) {
        for (int i = 0; i < kBatchSize; i++) {
            if (![batch hasNext]) {
                isDone = YES;
                i = kBatchSize;
            }
            else {
                NSInteger current = batch.current;
                double nextSquareRoot = [batch next];
                NSLog(@"Calculated square root of %d as %0.3f", current,
                    nextSquareRoot);
            }
        }
    }
    progressLabel.text = [batch percentCompletedText];
    progressBar.progress = [batch percentCompleted];

    if (isDone) {
        [timer invalidate];
        processRunning = NO;
        progressLabel.text = @"Calculations Finished";
        [goStopButton setTitle:@"Go" forState:UIControlStateNormal];
    }
}
```

The first thing this method does is see if the user has tapped the *Stop* button since the last time the method was called. If it was, we invalidate the timer, which will prevent this method from being called any more by this timer, ending the processing of this batch. We also update the progress label to tell the user that we canceled.

```
    if (!processRunning) {  // Cancelled
        [timer invalidate];
        progressLabel.text = @"Calculations Cancelled";
        return;
    }
```

Next, we retrieve the batch from the timer.

```
SquareRootBatch *batch = (SquareRootBatch *)[timer userInfo];
```

After that, we calculate when to stop processing this batch. For starters, we're going to spend half of the time available to us working on the batch. That should leave plenty of time for the run loop to receive system events and update the UI, but we can always tweak the value if we need to.

```
NSTimeInterval endTime = [NSDate timeIntervalSinceReferenceDate] +
    (kTimerInterval / 2.0);
```

We set a Boolean that we'll use to identify if we have reached the end of the batch. We'll set this to YES if hasNext returns NO.

```
BOOL isDone = NO;
```

Then, we go into a loop until we either reach the end time we calculated earlier, or there's no calculations left to do.

```
while ((([NSDate timeIntervalSinceReferenceDate] < endTime) && (!isDone)) {
```

We're going to calculate the square root for several numbers at a time rather than checking the date after every one, so we go into another loop based on the batch size we defined earlier.

```
    for (int i = 0; i < kBatchSize; i++) {
```

In that loop, we make sure there's more work to be done. If there isn't, we set isDone to YES and set i to the batch size to end this loop.

```
        if (![batch hasNext]) {
            isDone = YES;
            i = kBatchSize;
        }
```

If there is another number to calculate, we grab the current value and its square root and log the fact to the debug console.

```
        else {
            NSInteger current = batch.current;
            double nextSquareRoot = [batch next];
            NSLog(@"Calculated square root of %d as %0.3f", current,
                nextSquareRoot);
        }
    }
}
```

After we're done with processing a chunk, we update the progress bar and label.

```
progressLabel.text = [batch percentCompletedText];
progressBar.progress = [batch percentCompleted];
```

And, if we're all out of rows to process, we invalidate the timer and update the progress label and button.

```
if (isDone) {
    [timer invalidate];
    processRunning = NO;
```

```
        progressLabel.text = @"Calculations Finished";
        [goStopButton setTitle:@"Go" forState:UIControlStateNormal];
    }
```

All that's left to do now is to take care of our new outlet in the `viewDidUnload` and dealloc methods, so add the lines in bold to your existing code:

```
- (void)viewDidUnload {
    self.numOperationsInput = nil;
    self.progressBar = nil;
    self.progressLabel = nil;
    self.goStopButton = nil;
}

- (void)dealloc {
    [numOperationsInput release];
    [progressBar release];
    [progressLabel release];
    [goStopButton release];
    [super dealloc];
}
```

Go ahead and take this new version for a spin. Build and run your project and try entering different numbers. As the calculations happen, your user interface should get updated (Figure 14–3) and the progress bar should make its way across the screen. While a batch is processing, you should be able to tap the *Stop* button to cancel the processing.

Figure 14–3. *Now that we're using a timer, the application is no longer stalled*

That's great, and our users are now able to start and stop the process and can continue to use the application while the calculations are being performed. But, if we had more tasks going on in the background, this option wouldn't be ideal. Trying to calculate how much time to let each batch use would be non-trivial. Fortunately, Apple has given us the operation queue and has put all sorts of non-trivial logic in it so that we don't have to reinvent the wheel. Let's take a look at operation queues now.

Operation Queues & Concurrency

There are times when your application will need to run more than just a few concurrent tasks. When you get to more than a handful of tasks, the amount of complexity quickly escalates, making it very difficult to try and use any form of run loop scheduling to share time amongst all the tasks. When your application needs to manage many independent sets of instructions, you have to look at other mechanisms besides run loop scheduling to add concurrency.

As we've mentioned before, one of the traditional tools for adding concurrency at the application level is called threads. Threads are a mechanism provided by the operating system that allows multiple sets of instructions to operate at the same time within a single application. In the case of both the iPhone and the Mac, the threading functionality is provided by the **POSIX Threads API** (often referred to as **pthreads**), which is part of the OS X operating system. You should rarely, if ever, need to actually use that API in Cocoa Touch applications, however.

The Foundation framework has, for many years, contained a class called NSThread, which is far easier to work with than pthreads, which are implemented as a procedural C API. NSThread was the recommended way, until fairly recently, to add and manage threads in a Cocoa application.

With Mac OS X 10.5 (Leopard), Apple introduced some new classes for implementing concurrency and is strongly recommending the use of these new classes instead of using NSThread directly. NSOperationQueue is a class that manages a queue of instances of a subclass of NSOperation. Each NSOperation (or subclass) contains a set of instructions to perform a specific task. The operation queue will spawn and manage threads as needed to run the queued operations.

The use of operation queues makes implementing concurrency quite a bit easier than the traditional NSThread-based approach, and worlds easier than using pthreads directly. The benefits of using operation queues are so clear and compelling that we're not even going to show you how to use the lower-level mechanisms directly. We are going to discuss threads a bit, but only enough to inform your use of NSOperationQueue. Although NSOperationQueue does make many aspects of concurrency easier, there are still a few gotchas associated with concurrency and threads that you need to be aware of when using operation queues.

Threads

As we've mentioned before, every application has at least one thread, which is a sequence of instructions. The thread that begins executing when the program is launched is called the main thread. In the case of a Cocoa Touch application, the main thread contains the application's main run loop, which is responsible for handling inputs and updating the user interface. Although there are some instances where Cocoa Touch uses additional threads implicitly, pretty much all application code that you will write will fire on the main thread unless you specifically spawn a thread or use an operation in an operation queue.

To implement concurrency, additional threads are spawned, each tasked to perform a specific set of instructions. Each thread has equal access to all of your application's memory. This means that any object except local variables, can potentially be modified, used, and changed in any thread. Generally speaking, there's no way to predict how long a thread will run, and if there are multiple threads, there's no way to predict, with any certainty, which thread will finish first.

These two thread traits—the fact that they all share access to the same memory, and that there's no way to predict what share of the processing time each will get—are the root cause of a number of problems that come along for the ride when doing concurrent programming. Operation queues provide some relief from the timing problem, since you can set priorities and dependencies, which we'll look at a little later, but the memory sharing issue is still very much a concern.

Race Conditions

The fact that every thread can access the same memory can cause any number of problems if you're not conscious of that fact while programming. When a program doesn't give the expected result because shared data is accessed concurrently by multiple threads, a **race condition** is said to exist. Race conditions can happen when any thread operates on the assumption that it is the sole user of a resource that is actually shared with other threads.

Take a look at the following code:

```
static int i;
for (i = 0; i < 25; i++) {
    NSLog(@"i = %d", i);
}
```

There's not really any reason why somebody would declare i to be static in this example, but it illustrates one classic form of race condition. When you declare a variable static, it becomes a single shared variable used whenever this method fires on any object. If this code runs in a program with only a single thread, it will work completely fine. The fact that there is only one variable i shared by multiple objects simply isn't a problem because as long as we're in the loop, no other code can fire and change the value of i.

The second we add concurrency into the mix, that's no longer true. If, for example, we had this code running in multiple threads, they would all be sharing the same copy of i. When one thread increments i, it increments it for all the other threads as well. Instead of each thread looping 25 times, which is likely the intent, all the threads combined would loop a total of 25 times. The output in such a case might look like this:

Thread 1:	Thread 2:	Thread 3:
i = 0	i = 2	i = 5
i = 1	i = 3	i = 10
i = 4	i = 6	i = 13
i = 7	i = 8	i = 18
i = 9	i = 11	i = 19
i = 12	i = 14	i = 24
i = 15	i = 17	
i = 16	i = 21	
i = 20	i = 22	
i = 23		

This behavior is almost certainly not what was intended. In this case, the solution is simple: remove the static operator from i. It won't always be quite as obvious as this, but you should understand the potential for problems now with shared memory.

Another example of a race condition can happen with accessors and mutators. Let's say, for example, that we have an object that represents a person with two instance variables, one to hold their first name and another to hold their last name:

```
@implementation Person : NSObject {
    NSString *firstName;
    NSString *lastName;
}

@property (nonatomic, retain) NSString *firstName;
@property (nonatomic, retain) NSString *lastName;

@end
```

If an instance of Person is being accessed from multiple threads, we could have problems. Let's say, for example, that the instance is being updated in one thread, and read in another thread. Now, let's say that the first thread, the one that is updating the object, is changing both firstName and lastName. For the sake of argument, let's say that we have an instance of Person called person, and it starts out with a firstName value of *George* and a lastName value of *Washington*. The code executing in the first thread is changing both firstName and lastName to new values, like so:

```
person.firstName = @"Samantha";
person.lastName = @"Stephens";
```

Now, concurrently with that, another thread is reading the values from person:

```
NSLog(@"Now processing %@ %@.", person.firstName, person.lastName);
```

If the NSLog() statement from the second thread fires between the two assignments we showed from the first thread, the result would be this:

```
Now processing Samantha Washington.
```

There is no such person as Samatha Washington. There's George Washington and there's Samantha Stephens. But, as far as that second thread's NSLog() statement is concerned, person represented Samantha Washingon.

Operation queues do not eliminate the problem of race conditions, so it's important to be aware of them. Sometimes, you can give each thread its own copy of a shared resource, perhaps an object or block of data, instead of accessing that shared resource from multiple threads. This will ensure that one thread doesn't change the resource out from under a competing thread. That said, there's some overhead with making multiple copies of data. Often, duplicating resources is just not a viable option, however, because you need to know the current value, not the value as it was when your thread started. In those cases, you need to take additional steps to ensure data integrity and avoid race conditions. The main tool we use to avoid race conditions is the **mutex lock**.

Mutex Locks and @synchronized

A mutex lock is a mechanism used to ensure that while a piece of code is firing, other threads can't fire that same piece of code or related code. The term "mutex" is a portmanteau of the words "mutal" and "exclusion" and, as you might suspect based on that, locks are essentially a way to specify that only one thread can execute particular sections of code at a given time.

Originally, locks were always implemented using the class NSLock. Although NSLock is still available, there's now a language-level feature for locking down segments of code: @synchronized blocks.

If you wrap a section of code in a @synchronized block, that code can only fire on one thread at a time. Here's an example of a @synchronized block:

```
@synchronized(self) {
    person.firstName = @"Samantha";
    person.lastName = @"Stephens";
}
```

Notice that after the @synchronize keyword, there's a value in parentheses: self. This argument is called a **mutual exclusion semaphore** or a **mutex**. To understand semaphores in the context of concurrency, the best real-world metaphor is the bathroom key you might find in some small gas stations. There's a single key to the bathroom, usually attached to a large keychain. Only the person who has the key can use the bathroom. If there's only one key, it's a mutual exclusion semaphore or mutex, because only one person can use the bathroom at a time.

@synchronize works pretty much the same way. When a thread gets to a synchronized block of code, it will check to see if anyone else is using the mutex, which is to say, if any other synchronized chunks of code that take the same semaphore are currently executing. If they are, then the thread will **block** until no other code is using that semaphore. A thread that is blocked is not executing any code. When the mutex becomes available, the thread will unblock and execute the synchronized code.

This is the main mechanism we'll use in Cocoa Touch to avoid race conditions and to make our objects **thread safe**.

Atomicity and Thread Safety

Throughout *Beginning iPhone 3 Development* (Apress, 2009), and up until now in this book, we've always had you use the `nonatomic` keyword when declaring properties. We've never fully explained what `nonatomic` does, we just said that atomic properties added overhead that we didn't need. A good chunk of the overhead we were referring to is mutex locking. When you don't specify `nonatomic`, the accessors and mutators get created as if the `@synchronized` keyword was used with `self` as the mutex. Now, the exact form of the mutator and accessor methods varies depending on the other keywords and the property's datatype, but here's a simple example of what a nonatomic accessor might look like:

```
- (NSMutableString *)foo {
    return foo;
}
```

As a contrast, here's what the atomic version might look like:

```
- (NSMutableString *)foo {
    NSString *ret;
    @synchronized(self) {
        ret = [[self retain] autorelease];
    }
    return ret;
}
```

The atomic version does two things that the nonatomic doesn't do. First, it uses `self` as a mutex around all the code except the return statement and variable declaration. This means that no other code that uses `self` as a mutex can run while the next line of code is executing. All atomic accessors and mutators block when any other atomic accessor or mutator on the same object is executing on another thread. This helps to ensure data integrity.

The second thing that this version does is put the object to be returned into the autorelease pool. The reason it does that is probably non-obvious. Suppose, immediately after `foo` was returned, a new value was assigned to `foo`. In that case, the old `foo` that was returned by the earlier call would still be a valid object because it's in the autorelease pool. If it wasn't in the pool, then between the time that the new `foo` was assigned and the time that the calling method attempted to use the old `foo`, the old `foo` was probably deallocated. Not a very likely scenario in an application using only one thread, but a very possible one in an application using concurrency.

When we declare a property to be `nonatomic`, we're removing these protections because, for some reason, we don't think we need them. So far, this has always been fine, because we've only been accessing and setting object properties from the main thread. For outlets, it's still the case that you can pretty much always declare them `nonatomic`, because you shouldn't use outlets on threads other than the main thread.

Most of the UIKit is not thread-safe, which means it's generally not safe to set or retrieve values from threads other than the main thread.

But, if you're creating objects that are used in threads or in operation queues, then you almost certainly want to leave off the nonatomic keyword, because the protection from atomic properties is valuable enough to offset the small amount of overhead.

It's important to note, however, that there's a difference between the concepts of **atomicity** and thread safety, and the fact that you've used atomic properties does not make your class thread-safe. In some simple cases, having atomic properties may be all that an object needs to be thread-safe, but thread-safety is an object-level trait. In our earlier example with the Person object, removing the nonatomic keyword from the two properties would not make the object thread-safe because the problem we illustrated earlier could still happen. You could still have one thread reading the object after firstName had been changed, but before lastName had been changed. To make the object truly "thread-safe," you'd need to not just synchronize the individual accessors and mutators, but also any transaction involving dependent data. In this case, you would need to synchronize code that sets the first and last name so that other code accessing either firstName or lastName would block until the transaction was finished.

The example that demonstrated @synchronized a few pages back shows an excellent way to ensure that the transaction is atomic. You need to lock down the transaction to make sure that no other code can read either value until both have been changed. In the Person class, you might consider adding a method called something like setFirstName:lastName: to synchronize the entire transaction, like this:

```
- (void)setFirstName:(NSString *)inFirst lastName:(NSString *)inLast {
    @synchronized (self) {
        self.firstName = inFirst;
        self.lastName = inLast;
    }
}
```

Notice that we've used mutator methods to set first and last name, even though those mutators are atomic, which means the code in that mutator will also by synchronized. This is okay, because @synchronized is what's called a recursive mutex, which means that a synchronized block can call another synchronized block safely as long as the two blocks share the same mutex.

However, you never want to call a synchronized block from within another synchronized block if they don't use the same mutex. Doing so puts you at risk of a situation known as a **deadlock**.

> **TIP:** Apple's API documentation will tell you if a class is thread-safe. If the API documentation doesn't say anything on the topic, then you should assume that the class is **not** thread-safe.

Deadlocks

Sometimes solutions have their own problems, and mutex locks, which are the primary solution to race conditions in concurrency, indeed have a very big problem of their own, which is known as a deadlock. A deadlock occurs when a thread blocks and then waits for a condition that can never be met. This can happen, for example, if two threads each have synchronized code that calls synchronized code on the other thread. If both threads are using one mutex and waiting for the one the other thread has, neither thread will ever be able to continue. They will block forever.

There's no simple solution to deadlock scenarios, but one really good rule of thumb that will help you avoid deadlocks is: Never have a synchronized block of code call another synchronized block of code that uses a different mutex.

If you find yourself needing to call a method or function with synchronized code in it, you may need to actually replicate the code from that method inside the synchronized block instead of calling the other method. This seems to violate the idea we've been pounding throughout this book that code shouldn't be unnecessarily duplicated. However, if you don't duplicate the code when necessary and attempt to call synchronized code from synchronized code, you could end up deadlocked.

Sleepy Time

If too many threads are executing, the system can get bogged down. This is especially true on the iPhone which, as of this writing, has only a single CPU with a single core. Even if you're using threads, your user interface can start to skip or respond slowly if you're trying to do too much in too many threads. One solution to this, of course, is to spawn fewer threads. This is something that NSOperationQueue can actually handle for you, as we'll see in a few moments.

There's another thing that threads (and by extension operations) can do to help keep your application responsive, which is to **sleep**. A thread can choose to sleep either for a set interval, or until a set point in time. If a thread sleeps, it blocks until it's done sleeping, which yields processor cycles to the other threads. Putting sleep calls in a thread or operation essentially throttles it, slowing it down to make sure that there's plenty of processor time available for the main thread.

To cause the thread where your code is executing to sleep, you can use one of two class methods on the class NSThread. To sleep for a specified number of seconds, you would use the method sleepForTimeInterval:. So, for example, to sleep for two and a half seconds you would do this:

```
[NSThread sleepForTimeInterval:2.5];
```

To sleep until a specific date and time represented by an instance of NSDate, you could alternatively use sleepUntilDate:. As a result, the previous example could be rewritten like this:

```
[NSThread sleepUntilDate:[NSDate dateWithTimeIntervalSinceNow:2.5]];
```

Note that you should never, ever, and we really mean never, use either of these sleep methods (or their pthreads API counterparts) on the main thread. Why? The main thread is the only thread that handles events and can update the user interface. If you put the main thread to sleep, your interface will just plain stop.

Operations

We're going to look at operation queues in a moment, but before we do that, we need to talk about operations, which are the objects that contain the sets of instructions that the operation queue manages. Operations usually take the form of custom subclasses of NSOperation. You write the subclass and, in it, you put the code that needs to be run concurrently.

> **NOTE:** There's a provided subclass of NSOperation called NSInvocationOperation that will allow you to run code concurrently without creating your own subclasses of NSOperation. NSInvocationOperation allows you to specify an object and selector to use as the basis for the operation. In all but the simplest cases, however, you will want to subclass NSOperation because doing so gives you a lot more control over the process.

When implementing an operation for use in an operation queue, there are a few steps you need to take. First, you create a subclass of NSOperation and define any properties that you'll need as inputs or outputs from the operation. In our square root example, we will create a subclass of NSOperation and define properties for current and max on it.

The only other thing you have to do is to override the method called main, which is where you put the code that makes up the operation. There are a couple of things you need to do in your main method. The first thing you need to do is wrap all of your logic in a @try block so you can catch any exceptions. It's very important that an operation's main method not throw any exceptions. They must be caught and handled without being re-thrown. An uncaught exception in an operation will result in a fatal application crash.

The second thing you have to do in main is to create a new autorelease pool. Different threads cannot share the same autorelease pool. The operation will be running in a separate thread, so it can't use the main thread's autorelease pool, so it's important to allocate a new one.

Here's what a skeleton main method for an NSOperation subclass looks like:

```
- (void)main {
    @try {
        NSAutoreleasePool *pool = [[NSAutoreleasePool alloc] init];

        // Do work here...

        [pool drain];
    }
    @catch (NSException * e) {
```

```
                    // Important that we don't re-throw exception here
                    NSLog(@"Exception: %@", e);
            }
    }
}
```

Operation Dependencies

Any operation can optionally have one or more dependencies. A dependency is another instance of NSOperation that has to complete before this operation can be executed. An operation queue will know not to run an operation that has dependencies that have not yet finished. You can add dependencies to an operation using the addDependency: method, like so:

```
    MyOperation *firstOperation = [[MyOperation alloc] init];
    MyOperation *secondOperation = [[MyOperation alloc] init];
    [secondOperation addDependency:firstOperation];
    ...
```

In this example, if both firstOperation and secondOperation are added to a queue at the same time, they will not be run concurrently even if the queue has free threads available for both operations. Because firstOperation is a dependency of secondOperation, secondOperation will not start executing until firstOperation has finished.

You can get an array of an operation's dependencies by using the dependencies method:

```
    NSArray *dependencies = [secondOperation dependencies];
```

You can remove dependencies using the removeDependency: method. To remove the firstOperation as a dependency from secondOperation, you would do this:

```
    [secondOperation removeDependency:firstOperation];
```

Operation Priority

Every operation has a priority that the queue uses to decide which operation gets run when and that dictates how much of the available processing this operation will get to use. You can set a queue's priority using the setQueuePriority: method, passing in one of the following values:

- NSOperationQueuePriorityVeryLow
- NSOperationQueuePriorityLow
- NSOperationQueuePriorityNormal
- NSOperationQueuePriorityHigh
- NSOperationQueuePriorityVeryHigh

Instances of NSOperation default to NSOperationQueuePriorityNormal. Here's how you would change it to a higher priority:

```
[firstOperation setQueuePriority:NSOperationQueuePriorityVeryHigh];
```

Although higher priority operations will execute before lower priority ones, no operation executes if it's not ready. So, for example, an operation with a very high priority that has unmet dependencies will not be run, so a lower priority operation could go in front of it. But, among operations that are ready to execute (which can be determined using the isReady property), the operation with the highest priority will be selected.

You can determine the current priority of an operation by calling the queuePriority method on it:

```
NSOperationQueuePriority *priority = [firstOperation queuePriority];
```

Other Operation State

By subclassing NSOperation, your class will inherit several properties that can be used to determine aspects of its current state. To determine if an operation has been cancelled, you can check the isCancelled property. The code in an operation's main method should periodically check the isCancelled property to see if the operation has been cancelled. If it has been cancelled, your main method should immediately stop processing and return, which will end the operation.

If an operation's main method is currently being executed, the isExecuting property will return YES. If it returns NO, then it means that the operation hasn't been kicked off yet for some reason. This could be because the operation was just created, because it has a dependency that hasn't finished running yet, or because the queue's maximum number of threads have already been created and none are available yet for this operation to use.

When an operation's main method returns, that will trigger the method's isFinished property to be set to YES, which will cause it to be removed from its queue.

> **NOTE:** NSOperation has another property called isConcurrent, and it's a little counterintuitive. If you're going to use an operation concurrently in a queue, you want to return NO for isConcurrent (which is actually the default value). If you return YES, then the operation queue will not create a thread for your operation. It will expect the operation to create its own thread. So, if you return YES for isConcurrent, and don't write code to spawn a thread by overriding the start method, then your operation will execute on the main thread and be decidedly non-concurrent. This property tells not whether an operation can be run concurrently, but rather whether the operation itself creates a new thread. We're not creating these types of operations in this chapter, but you can read more about them in Apple's Concurrency Programming Guide at http://developer.apple.com/mac/library/documentation/General/Conceptual/ConcurrencyProgrammingGuide

Cancelling an Operation

You can cancel operations by calling the `cancel` method, like so:

```
[firstOperation cancel];
```

This will cause the operation's `isCancelled` property to be set to `YES`. It is, however, the operation's responsibility to check for this in its `main` method. Calling `cancel` will not cause the operation to be force cancelled. It just sets the property and it's the `main` method's responsibility to finish processing and return when it detects that the operation has been cancelled.

The fact that cancellations are tracked at the operation level and not by the operation queue does cause some behavior that may seem wrong at first. If an operation in a queue that is not yet executing gets cancelled, the operation will stay in the queue. Calling `cancel` on a pending operation doesn't remove the operation from the queue, and the operation queue doesn't provide a mechanism for removing operations. Cancelled operations don't get removed until they are done executing. The operation will have to wait until it starts executing to realize it's been cancelled and return, triggering its removal from the queue.

Operation Queues

Now you know how to create operations, so let's look at the object that manages operations, `NSOperationQueue`. Operation queues are created like any other object. You allocate and initialize the queue, like so:

```
NSOperationQueue *queue = [[NSOperationQueue alloc] init];
```

Adding Operations to the Queue

At this point, the queue is ready to use. You can start adding operations to it immediately without doing anything else. Adding operations is accomplished by using the `addOperation:` method, like so:

```
[queue addOperation:newOp];
```

Once the operation is added to the queue, it will execute as soon as there is a thread available for it and it is ready to execute. It can even start executing operations while you're still adding other operations. Operation queues, by default, set the number of threads based on the hardware available. A queue running on a multi-processor or multi-core device will tend to create more threads than one running on a single-processor, single-core device.

Setting the Maximum Concurrent Operation Count

It is generally advisable to let the operation queue decide the number of threads to use. This will, in most cases, ensure that your application makes the best use of available resources now and in the future. However, there may be situations where you want to take control over the number of threads. For example, if you have operations that yield a lot of time by blocking for some reason, you might want to have more threads running than the operation queue thinks it should have. You can do that using the method setMaxConcurrentOperationCount:. To create a serial queue, which is one that only has a single thread, you would to this:

```
[queue setMaxConcurrentOperationCount:1];
```

To tell the queue to reset the maximum number of operations based on the hardware available, you can use the constant NSOperationQueueDefaultMaxConcurrentOperationCount, like so:

```
[queue setMaxConcurrentOperationCount:
    NSOperationQueueDefaultMaxConcurrentOperationCount];
```

Suspending the Queue

An operation queue can be paused (or **suspended**). This causes it to stop executing new operations. Operations that have already started executing will continue, unless cancelled, but new ones will not be started as long as the queue is suspended. Suspending the queue is accomplished using the method setSuspended:, passing YES to pause the queue, and NO to resume the queue.

Fixing Stalled with an Operation Queue

Now that we've all got a good grasp on operation queues and concurrency, let's use that knowledge to fix the *Stalled* application one last time. Open up that copy of the *Stalled* application we had you make earlier. If you didn't do that, you can just copy the *14 – Stalled* application from the project archives and use that as your starting point for this section.

This time, we're going to fix the *Stalled* application by using an operation queue. Tapping the *Go* button will add another process to the queue, and we'll add a table that shows the number of operations in the queue along with some information about their status. As you can see from Figure 14–4, the individual rows have a red button. In the last chapter, we used the red button to remove songs from the music player's queue. In this chapter, we're using it to cancel operations in the operation queue. To create that button, you'll need to grab the image *remove.png* from the project archive or grab it from the *Simple Player* application and add it to the *Resources* folder of this project. Do that now before proceeding.

Figure 14–4. *Our final version of the Stalled application will use an operation queue to manage a variable number of square root operations*

Creating SquareRootApplication

We're going to start by creating our NSOperation subclass. Single-click the *Classes* folder and press ⌘N to create a new file. Select the *Objective-C class* template from the *Cocoa Touch Class* heading and choose *NSObject* from the *Subclass of* pop-up menu. Name this new file *SquareRootOperation.m*. Make sure you have Xcode create *SquareRootOperation.h* for you as well.

Single-click *SquareRootOperation.h* and replace its contents with the following:

```
#import <Foundation/Foundation.h>

#define kBatchSize          100
#define kUIUpdateFrequency  0.5

@class SquareRootOperation;
@protocol SquareRootOperationDelegate
- (void)operationProgressChanged:(SquareRootOperation *)op;
@end

@interface SquareRootOperation : NSOperation {
    NSInteger    max;
    NSInteger    current;
    id           delegate;
}
```

```
@property NSInteger max;
@property NSInteger current;
@property (assign) id<SquareRootOperationDelegate> delegate;

- (id)initWithMax:(NSInteger)inMax
        delegate:(id<SquareRootOperationDelegate>)inDelegate;
- (float)percentComplete;
- (NSString *)progressString;

@end
```

We start off by defining two constants. The first, kBatchSize, will be used to set how many calculations we perform before checking to see if our operation has been cancelled. The second, kUIUpdateFrequency, specifies how often, in seconds, we update the user interface. We are going to be doing, literally, thousands of calculations a second. If we update the interface from every thread every time we do an update, that's an awful lot of updates. Remember, updates to the user interface have to be done on the main thread. We'll show how to safely do that from an operation in a moment, but doing it incurs overhead. Different threads can't talk to each other directly.

You don't need to understand the process that threads use to communicate, but you do need to understand that there is overhead associated with sending messages between threads. Fortunately, as you'll see in a moment, the complexity of inter-thread communication is hidden from us. But there's still a cost involved with that communication that will slow things down if we do it too frequently. By reducing the updates to every half a second, we eliminate a lot of unnecessary inter-thread communications. As you test your application, you might want to tweak this value. You might find that more or less frequent updates give a better user experience, but these settings seem to be a good starting point and give decent results both on the device and on the simulator.

```
#define kBatchSize          100
#define kUIUpdateFrequency  0.5
```

After that, we create a protocol for our thread's delegate. Our operation's delegate will be the controller class for our application's main view: StalledViewController. We'll call this protocol's only method to tell that controller that changes have been made that need to be reflected in the row that represents our operation in the table view.

```
@class SquareRootOperation;
@protocol SquareRootOperationDelegate
- (void)operationProgressChanged:(SquareRootOperation *)op;
@end
```

After that, things are pretty similar to our SquareRootBatch class from the timer example, except instead of subclassing NSObject, we subclass NSOperation. In addition to the instance variables and properties for current and max calculation, we also have an instance variable and property for our delegate:

```
@interface SquareRootOperation : NSOperation {
    NSInteger   max;
    NSInteger   current;
    id          delegate;
}
```

```
@property NSInteger max;
@property NSInteger current;
@property (assign) id<SquareRootOperationDelegate> delegate;
```

We have an init method that takes the max number of calculations and a delegate:

```
- (id)initWithMax:(NSInteger)inMax
        delegate:(id<SquareRootOperationDelegate>)inDelegate;
```

And we have two methods that can be called by our delegate to get the current values for the progress bar and label:

```
- (float)percentComplete;
- (NSString *)progressString;
@end
```

Make sure you save *SquareRootOperation.h* and then switch over to *SquareRootOperation.m*. Replace the current contents with the following:

```
#import "SquareRootOperation.h"

@implementation SquareRootOperation
@synthesize max;
@synthesize current;
@synthesize delegate;

- (id)initWithMax:(NSInteger)inMax
        delegate:(id<SquareRootOperationDelegate>)inDelegate {
    if (self = [super init]) {
        max = inMax;
        current = 0;
        delegate = inDelegate;
    }
    return self;
}

- (float)percentComplete {
    return (float)current / (float)max;
}

- (NSString *)progressString {
    if ([self isCancelled])
        return @"Cancelled...";
    if (![self isExecuting])
        return @"Waiting...";
    return [NSString stringWithFormat:@"Completed %d of %d", self.current,
        self.max];
}

- (void)main {
    @try {
        NSAutoreleasePool *pool = [[NSAutoreleasePool alloc] init];
        NSTimeInterval  lastUIUpdate = [NSDate timeIntervalSinceReferenceDate];
        while (current < max) {
            if (self.isCancelled)
                self.current = max + 1;
            else {
```

```
            self.current++;
            double squareRoot = sqrt((double)current);
            NSLog(@"Operation %@ reports the square root of %d is %f",self,
                current, squareRoot);
            if (self.current % kBatchSize == 0) {
                if ([NSDate timeIntervalSinceReferenceDate] > lastUIUpdate +
                    kUIUpdateFrequency) {
                    if (self.delegate && [delegate respondsToSelector:
                        @selector(operationProgressChanged:)])
                        [(NSObject *)self.delegate performSelectorOnMainThread:
                            @selector(operationProgressChanged:) withObject:self
                            waitUntilDone:NO];
                    [NSThread sleepForTimeInterval:0.05];
                    lastUIUpdate = [NSDate timeIntervalSinceReferenceDate];
                }
            }
        }
    }
    [pool drain];
}
@catch (NSException * e) {
    // Important that we don't re-throw exception, so we just log
    NSLog(@"Exception: %@", e);
}
}
}
```

@end

The init method is pretty standard, and the percentComplete method is just like the one we had earlier in the chapter for the timer-based version of the application. The first code we need to look at is progressString. All this does is return a string that represents the current amount of progress in the operation and will be used in the cell that represents this row (see Figure 14–4). The one extra step we take here to set the label to *Cancelled...* if the operation has been cancelled. Remember, earlier, we said that cancelled operations that haven't started executing sit in the queue with their isCancelled property set to YES until they get kicked off, at which point they don't do any processing and fall out of the queue. Since we don't have any way to remove these operations from the queue, we do the next best thing and update the label that is displayed in the table to show that the user requested that this operation be cancelled. Otherwise, we return *Waiting...* if the operation hasn't started yet, or a string identifying how many square roots we've calculated so far if we are executing.

```
- (NSString *)progressString {
    if ([self isCancelled])
        return @"Cancelled...";
    if (![self isExecuting])
        return @"Waiting...";
    return [NSString stringWithFormat:@"Completed %d of %d", self.current,
        self.max];
}
```

The next method is the soul of our operation, and it warrants some special attention. The main method is the one that gets called when this operation gets kicked off by the queue. Our operation is going to be running in a thread, so we start of by wrapping everything in a @try block and allocating an autorelease pool.

```
- (void)main {
    @try {
        NSAutoreleasePool *pool = [[NSAutoreleasePool alloc] init];
```

Then we declare and initialize a variable that will be used to keep track of how much time has elapsed since the last time we updated the user interface.

```
        NSTimeInterval  lastUIUpdate = [NSDate timeIntervalSinceReferenceDate];
```

Next, we start our loop until current is equal to max.

```
        while (current < max) {
```

Every time through the loop, we check to see if our operation has been cancelled. If it has, then we set current to one more than max, which will cause our loop to end, and will end our method.

```
            if (self.isCancelled)
                self.current = max+1;
```

If our operation hasn't been cancelled, then we increment current, calculate its square root, and log the result.

```
            else {
                self.current++;
                double squareRoot = sqrt((double)current);
                NSLog(@"Operation %@ reports the square root of %d is %f",self,
                    current, squareRoot);
```

We then use modulus math to determine if we should check the time. Remember, we specified a batch size constant that tells how often we should check if it's time to do a user interface update, so every time current modulo kBatchSize equals zero, then we've reached a multiple of kBatchSize and should check to see if it's time to update the user interface.

```
                if (self.current % kBatchSize == 0) {
```

If we've processed an entire batch, we check the current time and compare it to the time of the last update added to the update frequency. If the current time is greater than those values added together, it's time to push another update out to our controller so it can get reflected in the user interface.

```
                    if ([NSDate timeIntervalSinceReferenceDate] > lastUIUpdate +
                        kUIUpdateFrequency) {
```

We make sure we have a delegate and that it responds to the correct selector before using performSelector:onMainThread:withObject:waitUntilDone: to let the controller know that the row that represents this operation should be updated. This is a great method that allows us to communicate back to the main thread without having to deal with the nitty-gritty aspects of inter-thread communications. It's an absolutely lovely method, just ask anybody who's had to do it the old-fashioned way using Mach ports.

```
                        if (self.delegate && [delegate respondsToSelector:
                            @selector(operationProgressChanged:)])
```

```
[(NSObject *)self.delegate performSelectorOnMainThread:
    @selector(operationProgressChanged:) withObject:self
    waitUntilDone:NO];
```

After we update the interface, we're going to sleep for a fraction of a second. This is optional, and the exact value to use here would probably get adjusted as we tested our application, but it's often a good idea to block periodically to yield some time. As of the time this book was written, iPhones and iPod touches come with a single processor with a single core, so yielding some time to the main thread is going to keep our app a little more responsive than it might otherwise be.

```
[NSThread sleepForTimeInterval:0.05];
```

Finally, we update `lastUIUpdate` with the current time so the next time through the loop, we know how long has passed since we updated the user interface.

```
                lastUIUpdate = [NSDate timeIntervalSinceReferenceDate];
            }
        }
    }
}
```

Once we're done, we have to drain the autorelease pool, otherwise we'll end up leaking everything that's in the pool.

```
    [pool drain];
}
```

Finally, we catch any exceptions. In this application, we just log them. If you need to do something else here, like show an alert, make sure that you call methods on the main thread to do it. Do not do any UI work directly in an operation because UIKit is not thread safe. Yes, we did say that already, but it's important.

Oh, and by the way? UIKit is not thread safe.

Also, whatever you do, do not throw an exception here. Because this operation is executing on a non-main thread, there is no higher-level exception hander available to catch that exception. This means that any exceptions thrown here will be uncaught exceptions, which is a fatal condition at runtime (aka, a fatal crash).

```
    @catch (NSException * e) {
        // Important that we don't re-throw exception, so we just log
        NSLog(@"Exception: %@", e);
    }
}
```

Make sure you save *SquareRootOperation.m*.

Changes to StalledViewController.h

We no longer need our progress view and progress label on our user interface, but we do need a table to show the operation queue's operations. Before we go to Interface Builder to make the interface changes, we need to make some changes to *StalledViewController.h*:

```
#import <UIKit/UIKit.h>
#import "SquareRootOperation.h"

@interface StalledViewController : UIViewController
<SquareRootOperationDelegate, UITableViewDelegate, UITableViewDataSource>
{
    UITextField     *numOperationsInput;
    UIProgressView  *progressBar;
    UILabel         *progressLabel;
    UITableView     *tableView;
    NSOperationQueue    *queue;
}
@property (nonatomic, retain) IBOutlet UITextField *numOperationsInput;
@property (nonatomic, retain) IBOutlet UIProgressView *progressBar;
@property (nonatomic, retain) IBOutlet UILabel *progressLabel;
@property (nonatomic, retain) IBOutlet UITableView *tableView;
@property (nonatomic, retain) NSOperationQueue *queue;


- (IBAction)go;
- (IBAction)cancelOperation:(id)sender;
- (IBAction)backgroundClick;


@end
```

We imported SquareRootOperation.h, which is the header for the operation class we just created, and then conformed our class to the SquareRootOperationDelegate protocol in addition to the two table view delegates it was already conformed to. We also added an instance variable and property to serve as an outlet to a table view and another instance variable and property for our operation queue.

We added two methods, one that will be used to cancel operations and that will be called when the user taps the accessory pane of a row in the table. The backgroundClick method shouldn't need any explanation at this point. Because our table will be partially obscured by the keyboard, we need to provide a way to make the keyboard go away, which this method will do.

Save *StalledViewController.h* and double-click *StalledViewController.xib* to launch Interface Builder.

Adjusting the User Interface

Once Interface Builder opens up, if the window labeled *View* is open, close it. Now, click on the *View* icon in the main window, press ⌘4 to bring up the identity inspector, and change the underlying class from *UIView* to *UIControl*. This will allow background clicks to trigger action methods. Press ⌘2 to bring up the connections inspector, then look for the circle to the right of *Touch Down*, and drag from that circle to *File's Owner* and select the *backgroundClick* action.

Now double-click the *Control* icon, which used to be the *View* icon, to open our application's user interface back up. Single-click the progress view and hit the delete key. Then single-click the progress label (the empty label below the progress bar) and press delete again.

Look in the library for a table view and drag it over to the *Control* window. Place it in the window, then use the resize handles so that it takes up all of the window from the left side to the right (not the margins, the full window), and from the very bottom of the window until just below the existing text field, button, and label, using the blue guidelines for proper distance.

Control-drag from *File's Owner* to the table view and select the *tableView* outlet. Then, control-drag back from the table view to *File's Owner* twice. The first time, select the *delegate* outlet, the second time select the *dataSource* outlet.

Once you've done that, save the nib, quit Interface Builder, and go back to Xcode.

Updating StalledViewController.m

Single-click *StalledViewController.m* so we can make our final changes. At the top of the file, there are a few additions and a few deletions that need to be made:

```
#import "StalledViewController.h"

#define kTableRowHeight           40.0
#define kProgressBarLeftMargin    20.0
#define kProgressBarTopMargin     5.0
#define kProgressBarWidth         253.0
#define kProgressBarHeight        9.0
#define kProgressLabelLeftMargin  20.0
#define kProgressLabelTopMargin   19.0
#define kProgressViewTag          1011
#define kProgressLabelTag         1012


@implementation StalledViewController
@synthesize numOperationsInput;
@synthesize progressBar;
@synthesize progressLabel;
@synthesize tableView;
@synthesize queue;
...
```

The constants are going to be used to construct our table view cells. We're going to programmatically create a progress bar and a label and add them to our cells. These values define the location and size of these views, except the last two, which are values that we'll assign to the progress view's and label's `tag` property and that we'll use to retrieve the two views from dequeued cells.

We then get rid of the `@synthesize` statements for the two delete outlets, then add `@synthesize` statements for the new table view outlet and for the operation queue.

Next, look for the method called go and replace the current implementation with this new one:

```
- (IBAction)go {
```

```
        NSInteger opCount = [numOperationsInput.text intValue];
        SquareRootOperation *newOp = [[SquareRootOperation alloc] initWithMax:opCount
            delegate:self];
        [queue addOperation:newOp];
        [newOp release];
}
```

First, we retrieve the number of operations, just as we did in the last two versions. Next, we create an instance of SquareRootOperation with that number, passing self as the delegate so that we get notified of changes that impact the user interface. Finally, we add the operation to the queue and release it.

After the go method, insert the following two methods:

```
- (IBAction)cancelOperation:(id)sender {
    NSInteger index = [sender tag];
    NSOperation *op = [[queue operations] objectAtIndex:index];

    [op cancel];
    if (![op isExecuting])
        [self.tableView reloadData];
}

- (IBAction)backgroundClick {
    [numOperationsInput resignFirstResponder];
}
```

The first method you just added gets called when the user taps on one of the red buttons in the table view. We're using the same technique we used in the *Simple Player* application from the last chapter. The accessory button on each row has its row index assigned as its tag, so we retrieve the tag, and then use that index to retrieve the operation from the queue that corresponds to that index.

Once we have the operation, we cancel it. We check to see if the operation was executing, and if it wasn't, we trigger a reload of the table data so that the row's text gets changes from *Waiting...* to *Cancelled....*

The other method you just added just tells the text field to resign the first responder so that the keyboard will retract and we can see the whole table.

Look for the existing viewDidUnload and dealloc methods, and make the following changes to accommodate the changes we made in the header:

```
- (void)viewDidUnload {
    self.numOperationsInput = nil;
    self.progressLabel = nil;
    self.progressBar = nil;
    self.tableView = nil;
}

- (void)dealloc {
    [numOperationsInput release];
    [progressLabel release];
    [progressBar release]
    [tableView release];
    [queue release];
```

```
    [super dealloc];
}
```

After the `dealloc` method, add the following new method, which is an implementation of `viewDidLoad`, which gets called when our view loads for the first time.

```
- (void)viewDidLoad {
    NSOperationQueue *newQueue = [[NSOperationQueue alloc] init];
    self.queue = newQueue;
    [newQueue release];
    [queue addObserver:self
            forKeyPath:@"operations"
               options:0
               context:NULL];
}
```

The first thing we do in `viewDidLoad` is create a new instance of `NSOperationQueue` and assign it to queue. Then we do something kind of neat. We use something called KVO. That's not a typo. We're not talking about KVC, but it's a related concept. KVO stands for Key-Value Observation, and it's a mechanism that lets you get notified when a particular property on another object gets changed. We're registering `self` as an observer of queue for the keypath called `operations`. That key path is the name of the property that returns an array with all of the operations in the queue. Whenever an operation is added or gets removed from the queue, our controller class will get notified of that fact thanks to KVO. The `options` parameter allows us to request additional information about the change, such as the previous value of the changed property. We don't need anything over and above what basic KVO provides, so we pass 0. We also pass `NULL` into the final argument because we don't have any objects that we want to get passed along to the notification method.

Now that we've registered for the KVO notification, we have to implement a method called `observeValueForKeyPath:ofObject:change:context:`. Let's add that method to our class and then talk about what it's doing. Insert the following new method after `viewDidLoad`.

```
- (void)observeValueForKeyPath:(NSString *)keyPath
                      ofObject:(id)object
                        change:(NSDictionary *)change
                       context:(void *)context {
    NSIndexSet *indices = [change objectForKey:NSKeyValueChangeIndexesKey];
    if (indices == nil)
        return; // Nothing to do

    // Build index paths from index sets
    NSUInteger indexCount = [indices count];
    NSUInteger buffer[indexCount];
    [indices getIndexes:buffer maxCount:indexCount inIndexRange:nil];

    NSMutableArray *indexPathArray = [NSMutableArray array];
    for (int i = 0; i < indexCount; i++) {
        NSUInteger indexPathIndices[2];
        indexPathIndices[0] = 0;
        indexPathIndices[1] = buffer[i];
        NSIndexPath *newPath = [NSIndexPath indexPathWithIndexes:indexPathIndices
            length:2];
```

```
            [indexPathArray addObject:newPath];
    }

    NSNumber *kind = [change objectForKey:NSKeyValueChangeKindKey];
    if ([kind integerValue] == NSKeyValueChangeInsertion)  // Operations were added
        [self.tableView insertRowsAtIndexPaths:indexPathArray
            withRowAnimation:UITableViewRowAnimationFade];
    else if ([kind integerValue] == NSKeyValueChangeRemoval)  // Operations removed
        [self.tableView deleteRowsAtIndexPaths:indexPathArray
            withRowAnimation:UITableViewRowAnimationFade];
}
```

Any change to properties you observe using KVO will trigger a call to this method. The first argument to the method is the keypath that you're watching, and the second is the object that you are observing. In our case, since we're only watching one keypath on one object, we don't need to do anything with these values. If we were observing multiple values, we would probably need to check these arguments to know what to do. The third argument, change, is a dictionary that contains a whole bunch of information about the change that happened. We didn't pass in a value for context earlier when we observed queue, so we won't receive anything in context when this method gets called.

> **NOTE:** KVO is a neat feature of Cocoa Touch, but one that we're not covering in-depth. If you're interested in leveraging KVO in your own applications, a great place to start is Apple's *Key Value Observing Programming Guide* available at http://developer.apple.com/mac/library/documentation/cocoa/Conceptual/KeyValueObserving/KeyValueObserving.html

The first thing we do in this method is retrieve the value stored under NSKeyValueChangeIndexesKey. When the property you're getting notified about is a mutable array, which is the case here, any insertions or deletions will be accompanied by a set of indices that tell where the insertions or deletions happen. We're going to need those values to update our table view.

> **NOTE:** Even though operations is declared as an NSArray, the operation queue actually uses an instance of NSMutableArray to keep track of the operations in the queue. Since NSMutableArray is a subclass of NSArray, this is perfectly appropriate. The fact that operations is an NSArray is a hint to other objects not to change its contents, but it's perfectly fine to observe changes made by the operation queue.

```
    NSIndexSet *indices = [change objectForKey:NSKeyValueChangeIndexesKey];
```

If this returned value is nil, we've got nothing to do, so we return.

```
    if (indices == nil)
        return; // Nothing to do
```

If it's not nil, then we need to take the indices, which come in the form of an NSIndexSet object, which is an object designed to keep a collection of indices, and convert them into an array of NSIndexPath objects, which hold an index path that points to the section and row of our table. Since our table has only one section, we know that all rows are in section 0 and we can use that knowledge to craft index paths pointing to our rows:

```
NSUInteger indexCount = [indices count];
NSUInteger buffer[indexCount];
[indices getIndexes:buffer maxCount:indexCount inIndexRange:nil];


NSMutableArray *indexPathArray = [NSMutableArray array];
for (int i = 0; i < indexCount; i++) {
    NSUInteger indexPathIndices[2];
    indexPathIndices[0] = 0;
    indexPathIndices[1] = buffer[i];
    NSIndexPath *newPath = [NSIndexPath indexPathWithIndexes:indexPathIndices
        length:2];
    [indexPathArray addObject:newPath];
}
```

Once we get here, we have an array of NSIndexPath objects, each of which represents one row that was just either deleted or inserted into the queue's operations array. We can find out whether it was an insertion or deletion by grabbing another piece of information out of the change dictionary using the key NSKeyValueChangeKindKey. That will return an NSNumber that, when converted to an integer, will tell us what kind of change happened. If it was an insertion, then the integer representation of the returned value will equal the constant NSKeyValueChangeInsertion. If it was a deletion, it will equal NSKeyValueChangeRemoval. So, we use that information to tell the table to insert new rows, or to delete existing rows, as appropriate:

```
NSNumber *kind = [change objectForKey:NSKeyValueChangeKindKey];
if ([kind integerValue] == NSKeyValueChangeInsertion)  // Operations were added
    [self.tableView insertRowsAtIndexPaths:indexPathArray
        withRowAnimation:UITableViewRowAnimationFade];
else if ([kind integerValue] == NSKeyValueChangeRemoval)  // Operations removed
    [self.tableView deleteRowsAtIndexPaths:indexPathArray
        withRowAnimation:UITableViewRowAnimationFade];
```

Almost there, friends. Almost there. At the bottom of the class we have a few more methods to add. First, we need to add our SquareRootOperationDelegate method, where we update the user interface. Insert the following method just above the @end declaration:

```
- (void)operationProgressChanged:(SquareRootOperation *)op {
    NSUInteger opIndex = [[queue operations] indexOfObject:op];
    NSUInteger reloadIndices[] = {0, opIndex};
    NSIndexPath *reloadIndexPath = [NSIndexPath indexPathWithIndexes:reloadIndices
        length:2];
    UITableViewCell *cell = [tableView cellForRowAtIndexPath:reloadIndexPath];
    if (cell) {
        UIProgressView *progressView = (UIProgressView *)[cell.contentView
            viewWithTag:kProgressViewTag];
        progressView.progress = [op percentComplete];
        UILabel *progressLabel = (UILabel *)[cell.contentView
            viewWithTag:kProgressLabelTag];
        progressLabel.text = [op progressString];
```

```
    [self.tableView reloadRowsAtIndexPaths:[NSArray
        arrayWithObject:reloadIndexPath]
        withRowAnimation:UITableViewRowAnimationNone];
    }
}
```

We take the SquareRootOperation instance that called the method and find its index in
the operations array. We use that information to build an index path that points to the
row that corresponds to the operation that triggered the method call. We use that index
path to get a reference to the cell that displays the updated operation. If there is no
corresponding cell, then the row isn't currently visible and we don't need to do anything.
If the row is visible, we grab the percentComplete and progressString values from the
operation and use them to set the label and progress view for the operation's cell.

All that's left are the table view methods, and you all are old hands at these by now, so
just insert the following methods above the @end declaration:

```
#pragma mark -
#pragma mark Table View Methods
- (NSInteger)tableView:(UITableView *)theTableView
 numberOfRowsInSection:(NSInteger)section {
    return [[queue operations] count];
}

- (UITableViewCell *)tableView:(UITableView *)theTableView
cellForRowAtIndexPath:(NSIndexPath *)indexPath {
    static NSString *identifier = @"Operation Queue Cell";
    UITableViewCell *cell = [theTableView
        dequeueReusableCellWithIdentifier:identifier];
    if (cell == nil) {
        cell = [[[UITableViewCell alloc] initWithStyle:UITableViewCellStyleDefault
            reuseIdentifier:identifier] autorelease];

        UIProgressView *progressView = [[UIProgressView alloc] initWithFrame:
            CGRectMake(kProgressBarLeftMargin, kProgressBarTopMargin,
            kProgressBarWidth, kProgressBarHeight)];
        progressView.tag = kProgressViewTag;
        [cell.contentView addSubview:progressView];
        [progressView release];

        UILabel *progressLabel = [[UILabel alloc] initWithFrame:
            CGRectMake(kProgressLabelLeftMargin, kProgressLabelTopMargin,
            kProgressBarWidth, 15.0)];
        progressLabel.adjustsFontSizeToFitWidth = YES;
        progressLabel.tag = kProgressLabelTag;
        progressLabel.textAlignment = UITextAlignmentCenter;
        progressLabel.font = [UIFont systemFontOfSize:12.0];
        [cell.contentView addSubview:progressLabel];
        [progressLabel release];

        UIButton *removeButton = [UIButton buttonWithType:UIButtonTypeCustom];
        UIImage *removeImage = [UIImage imageNamed:@"remove.png"];
        [removeButton setBackgroundImage:removeImage forState:UIControlStateNormal];
        [removeButton setFrame:CGRectMake(0.0, 0.0, removeImage.size.width,
            removeImage.size.height)];
```

```
        [removeButton addTarget:self action:@selector(cancelOperation:)
            forControlEvents:UIControlEventTouchUpInside];
        cell.accessoryView  = removeButton;
    }
    SquareRootOperation *rowOp = (SquareRootOperation *)[[queue operations]
        objectAtIndex:[indexPath row]];
    UIProgressView *progressView = (UIProgressView *)[cell.contentView
        viewWithTag:kProgressViewTag];
    progressView.progress = [rowOp percentComplete];

    UILabel *progressLabel = (UILabel *)[cell.contentView
        viewWithTag:kProgressLabelTag];
    progressLabel.text = [rowOp progressString];

    cell.accessoryView.tag = [indexPath row];

    return cell;
}

- (NSIndexPath *)tableView:(UITableView *)tableView
  willSelectRowAtIndexPath:(NSIndexPath *)indexPath {
    return nil;
}

- (CGFloat)tableView:(UITableView *)theTableView
heightForRowAtIndexPath:(NSIndexPath *)indexPath {
    return kTableRowHeight;
}
```

Nothing in these table view methods should need much explanation. If you're unclear about the way we built the custom cell in `tableView:cellForRowAtIndexPath:` by adding subviews to the cell's content view, you might want to revisit Chapter 8 of *Beginning iPhone 3 Development*.

Queue 'em Up

Build and run the application and take it for a spin. You probably want to run this one in the simulator. Try spawning a whole bunch of operations and then watch them run, keeping an eye both on Xcode's debugger console and the application itself. Try deleting both executing and pending operations to see how they behave. If you want to run the application on your phone, you might want to consider commenting out the `NSLog()` statement in the main method of *SquareRootOperation.m*, but if you do, make sure you add a few zeros on to the number of calculations to perform or else increase the amount of time that each operation sleeps, otherwise the operations will finish so fast you won't even see the table update.

Make note of how many running operations there are when you run it on the device versus the simulator. We found that the queue defaulted to one concurrent thread on iPhones and iPod touches, but every Mac we tried it on had at least two threads. That makes sense, since every Mac right now ships with at least two processor cores, but every iPhone and iPod touch currently ship with only one. Try experimenting by setting the maximum number of concurrent operations in the queue and see how performance is impacted.

This chapter was just an introduction to concurrency, but you should have enough of a grip on both operation queues and timers to be able to effectively use both techniques in your iPhone applications. Once you've digested it all, turn the page and we'll get into the final frontier: debugging.

Chapter 15

Debugging

One of the fundamental truths of computer programming (and life) is that not everything works perfectly. No matter how much you plan, and no matter how long you've been programming, it's rare for an application you write to work perfectly the first time and forever under all circumstances and possible uses. Knowing how to properly architect your application and write well-formed code is important. Knowing how to find out why things aren't working the way they're supposed to, and fixing them, is equally important. This last part of the coding cycle, as you're probably well aware, is a process called **debugging**.

When it comes to mastering the process of debugging, experience is far and away the best teacher. Each time you fix a specific problem with your code, you're just a little less likely to make that same mistake in the future. In addition, with experience, the next time you encounter that mistake, you're probably going to find and fix the problem a little bit faster than you did the last time you encountered it. Obviously, we can't give you experience, but we can take you through the basic tools used to debug iPhone applications and show you a few of the most common types of bugs you will encounter.

In this chapter, we're not going to build and debug a complex application. Instead, we're going to create a project from a template, then show you different debugging techniques, one at a time, by adding code to demonstrate specific problems.

We're going to start by taking a brief tour covering the general process of debugging, then take a quick look at breakpoints, which allow you to pause the execution of a running program at a pre-specified point. We'll see how to look at the value of variables in a currently running program, and how to step through the program line by line using the debugger.

Next, we'll talk about static analysis, a new feature of Xcode available only in Snow Leopard, which analyzes your code for common problems and mistakes. Finally, we'll spend some time looking at several of the most common types of bugs you will encounter and talk about techniques for finding and fixing them.

Before we get started, let's create an Xcode project that we'll use to demonstrate debugging techniques. Use the *Navigation-based Application* project template and select the check box called *Use Core Data for storage*. Name the project *DebugMe*.

Once the project is opened up, expand the *Classes* and *Resources* folders in the *Groups & Files* pane.

The Debugger

As you probably have noticed, when you create a project in Xcode, the project defaults into what's called the **debug configuration**. If you've ever compiled an application for the App Store or for ad hoc distribution, then you're aware of the fact that applications usually start with two configurations, one called debug and another called release. If you look in the upper-left corner of your project window, you should see a pop-up menu that says something like *Device – 3.1.2 | Debug* (Figure 15–1). This tells us that our project is set to run on the device in debug mode.

So, how is the debug configuration different than the release or distribution configuration? There are actually a number of differences between them. The release configuration, for example, is set up so that the generated application will be optimized to be as small and fast as possible. But the key difference between them is that the *Debug* configuration builds **debug symbols** into your application. These debug symbols are like little bookmarks in your compiled application that make it possible to match up any command that fires in your application with a specific piece of source code in your project. Xcode includes a piece of software known as a **debugger**, which uses the debug symbols to go from bytes of machine code to the specific functions and methods in source code that generated that machine code.

> **CAUTION:** If you try to use the debugger with the release or distribution configuration, you will get very odd results since those configurations don't include debug symbols. The debugger will try its best, but ultimately will become morose and limp quietly away.

Like the compiler that Xcode uses (GCC), the debugger used in iPhone development is actually a separate piece of software called **GDB**, which is a quasi-acronym that stands for **G**nu **deb**ugger. Xcode launches GDB for you when it's needed. You don't have to ever interact with GDB directly if you don't want to, though there are some neat things you can do with it that can't be done otherwise, as you'll see a little later. Whenever you launch an application using **Build and Debug** from the **Build** menu or **Debug** from the **Run** menu, either in the simulator or on the device, you are both building debug symbols into your application and launching GDB along with your application. When you launch your application in this way, GDB is said to be **attached** to your application. Being attached to your project is what allows it do the cool things it does.

Xcode features a window called the **debugger console** (Figure 15–1), which you can bring forward by pressing ⌘⇧R. The debugger console is more than just a static log that shows the results of your application's NSLog() statements and runtime errors (though that's certainly one important role that it serves). It's also an interface to GDB's command-line functionality. You can do pretty much any of the debugging tasks that you can do through Xcode by typing commands into this console. Usually we'll use

Xcode rather than typing GDB commands directly, but for a few of the more important tasks, we'll show you how to do them using the debugger console as well.

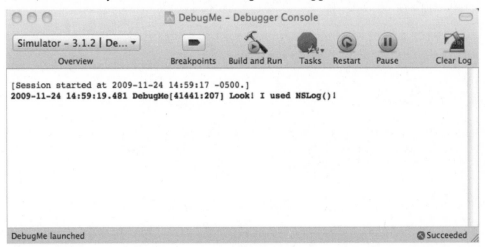

Figure 15–1. *The debugger window is actually an interface to the command-line program GDB, which is the debugger used by Xcode*

Breakpoints

Probably the most important debugging tool in your arsenal is the **breakpoint**. A breakpoint is an instruction to the debugger to pause execution of your application at a specific place in your code and wait for you. By pausing, but not stopping, the execution of your program, you can do things like look at the value of variables and step through lines of code one at a time. A breakpoint can also be set up so that instead of pausing the program's execution, a command or script gets executed and then the program resumes execution. We'll look at both types of breakpoints in this chapter, but you'll probably use the former a lot more than the latter.

The most common breakpoint type that you'll set in Xcode is the **line number breakpoint**. This type of breakpoint allows you to specify that the debugger should stop at a specific line of code in a specific file. To set a line number breakpoint in Xcode, you just click in the space to the left of the source code file in the editing pane. Let's do that now so you can see how it works.

Single-click *RootViewController.m*. Look for the method called viewDidLoad. It should be one of the first, if not the first method in the file. On the left side of the editing pane, you should see a column with numbers, as in Figure 15–2. This is called the **gutter**, and it's one way to set line number breakpoints.

```
 8
 9   #import "RootViewController.h"
10
11
12   @implementation RootViewController
13
14   @synthesize fetchedResultsController, managedObjectContext;
15
16
17   #pragma mark -
18   #pragma mark View lifecycle
19
20
21   - (void)viewDidLoad {
22       [super viewDidLoad];
23
24       // Set up the edit and add buttons.
25       self.navigationItem.leftBarButtonItem = self.editButtonItem;
26
27       UIBarButtonItem *addButton = [[UIBarButtonItem alloc] initWithBarButto
             (insertNewObject)]];
28       self.navigationItem.rightBarButtonItem = addButton;
29       [addButton release];
30
31       NSError *error = nil;
32       if (![[self fetchedResultsController] performFetch:&error]) {
33           /*
34            Replace this implementation with code to handle the error appropr
35
36            abort() causes the application to generate a crash log and termin
                  may be useful during development. If it is not possible to re
                  the application by pressing the Home button.
37           */
38           NSLog(@"Unresolved error %@, %@", error, [error userInfo]);
39           abort();
40       }
41   }
```

Figure 15–2. *To the left of the editing pane is a column that usually shows line numbers. This is where you set breakpoints*

TIP: If you don't see line numbers or the gutter, open Xcode's preferences and go to the Text Editing section. The first two check boxes in that section are *Show gutter* and *Show line numbers*. It's much easier to set breakpoints if you can see the gutter and the line numbers. Regardless of whether you have *Show Gutter* checked, the gutter will appear while debugging.

Look for the first line of code in viewDidLoad, which should be a call to super. In Figure 15–2, this line of code is at line 22, though it may be a different line number for you. Single-click in the gutter to the left of that line, and a little arrow should appear in the gutter pointing at the line of code (Figure 15–3). You now have a breakpoint set in the *RootViewController.m* file, at a specific line number.

```
 8
 9   #import "RootViewController.h"
10
11
12   @implementation RootViewController
13
14   @synthesize fetchedResultsController, managedObjectContext;
15
16
17   #pragma mark -
18   #pragma mark View lifecycle
19
20
21   - (void)viewDidLoad {
22       [super viewDidLoad];
23
24       // Set up the edit and add buttons.
25       self.navigationItem.leftBarButtonItem = self.editButtonItem;
26
27       UIBarButtonItem *addButton = [[UIBarButtonItem alloc] initWithBarButto
              (insertNewObject)];
28       self.navigationItem.rightBarButtonItem = addButton;
29       [addButton release];
30
31       NSError *error = nil;
32       if (![[self fetchedResultsController] performFetch:&error]) {
33           /*
34            Replace this implementation with code to handle the error appropr
35
36            abort() causes the application to generate a crash log and termin
                 may be useful during development. If it is not possible to re
                 the application by pressing the Home button.
37           */
38           NSLog(@"Unresolved error %@, %@", error, [error userInfo]);
39           abort();
40       }
41   }
42
```

Figure 15–3. *When a line number breakpoint is set, it will appear in the gutter next to the line of code where it will pause the program's execution*

You can also remove breakpoints by dragging them off of the gutter, and move them by dragging them to a new location on the gutter. You can temporarily disable existing breakpoints by single-clicking them, which will cause them to change from a darker color to a lighter color. To re-enable a disabled breakpoint, you just click it again to change it back to the darker color.

Before we talk about all the things you can do with breakpoints, let's try out the basic functionality. Select **Build and Debug – Breakpoints On** from the **Build** menu or press ⌘Y to build and run the application with GDB attached. The program will start to launch normally, then before the view gets fully shown, you're going to be brought back to Xcode, and the project window will come forward, showing the line of code about to be executed and its associated breakpoint.

NOTE: In the toolbar at the top of the debug and project windows is an icon labeled *Breakpoints*. As its name implies, clicking that icon toggles between breakpoints on or breakpoints off. This allows you to enable or disable all your breakpoints without losing them. Note that **Build and Debug – Breakpoints On** forces this setting to on and then launches the debugger. The **Build and Debug** menu item launches the debugger with or without breakpoints, depending on this setting.

Let's bring the debugger into the mix. Select **Debugger** from the **Run** menu, or type ⌘⇧Y to bring up the **debugger window** (Figure 15–4).

At the bottom of the debugger and most other Xcode windows, you'll see a message along the lines of:

```
GDB: Stopped at breakpoint 1 (hit count : 1)- '-viewDidLoad - Line 22'
```

That's Xcode passing along a message from the debugger, telling us that execution has paused at line 22 of *RootViewController.m*. That bottom portion of the window (you'll find it in the project and console windows as well) is called the c, and it's a good idea to keep an eye on it while debugging, as it will tell you the last status message from the debugger.

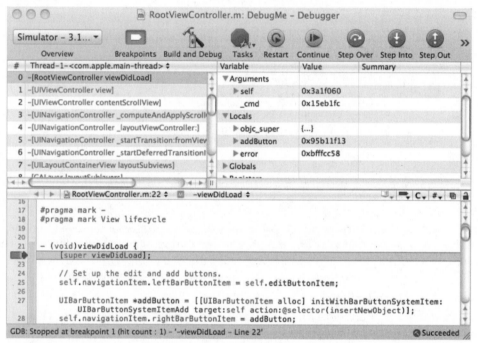

Figure 15–4. *Xcode's debugger window comes forward when the application stops at a breakpoint*

The Debugger Editing Pane

The bottom pane of the debugger window is an editing pane, just like the one in your project. You can edit your project's source code here. But notice that there's also a red arrow and a highlighted line in the source. That's our visual indication that we are currently stopped and using the debugger. The program is still running, but it's paused so we can see what's going on. This red arrow and highlighted line will start at a breakpoint, but as you'll see in a few minutes, you can continue the execution of the program one command at a time.

The Stack Trace

The upper-left pane of the debugger window is called the **stack trace**, and it shows the method and function calls that got us here. The call immediately previous to the call to viewDidLoad was a call to the view accessor method on an instance of UIViewController. You might be confused to see an instance of UIViewController in the stack trace. Don't be. Since we didn't override view, the UIViewController version of view was called and, therefore, that version of view was placed in the stack trace. When a class doesn't override a method implemented by its superclass, the superclass's version of the method shows up in the stack trace. In this case, that call to view was actually made on RootViewController, even though the stack trace is reporting it's being called on UIViewController. That's because the stack trace is showing you not what the object instance is, but where the code that was called exists, and the accessor method view exists on UIViewController.

The method before that was the method contentScrollView, also on an instance of UIViewController. The methods before that in the stack trace all have underlines at the beginning of their names, which tells us that those are Apple's super-secret internal methods that we don't have access to and should never, ever call.

Methods in the stack trace that are listed in black are ones for which we have access to the source code. Generally, these will be methods we've written, or at least that are contained in our project. Methods in the stack trace that are in gray are ones that are contained in frameworks or libraries that we've linked against and for which we don't have access to the source code. At our current breakpoint, only the method we're in is our own, the rest are gray, meaning we didn't write those methods.

If you click on a black row in the stack trace, the editing pane will show you the source code for that method. If you click on a gray row, then it will just show you the disassembly (the assembly language representation of machine code) for the listed method. You can step through disassembly, but unless you understand assembly language for the processor being used, it probably won't make much sense.

> **NOTE:** The disassembly you see will look very different when running on the device and when running in the simulator. In the simulator, you're looking at Intel X86 assembly, but when working on a device, you're looking at ARM assembly. A discussion of assembly language is way beyond the scope of this chapter, but you can find out more about ARM assembly by reading http://www.arm.com/miscPDFs/9658.pdf and you can learn more about Intel assembly by going to http://www.intel.com/products/processor/manuals/index.htm.

Although simpler bugs are often self-contained with a single-method, more complex bugs rarely are, and being able to track the flow of method and function calls that led up to a problem can be incredibly useful.

The Variable List

The upper-right pane of the debugger window is the **variable list**, and it displays all of the variables that are currently **in scope**. A variable is in scope if it is an argument or local variable from the current method, or is an instance variable from the object that contains the method. In fact, if you look at the variable list, you'll see that they're divided by type.

> **NOTE:** The variable list will also let you change a variable's value. If you double-click any value, it will become editable, and when you press return to commit your change, the underlying variable will also change in the application.

Global variables are also in scope for any function or method, but they are treated a little differently. By default, no global variables are included in the variable list. The reason for this is that there are potentially an awful lot of global variables spread throughout the various frameworks that you might link into your program. Even if your program doesn't explicitly declare any global variables, there could still be dozens, maybe even hundreds, of global variables, most of which you'll never care about. As a result, global variables are opt-in. You have to specifically tell Xcode you want to see a specific global variable in the list. If you click the disclosure triangle next to the *Globals* row in the variable list, instead of revealing a list of variables, it will pop up a new window (Figure 15–5).

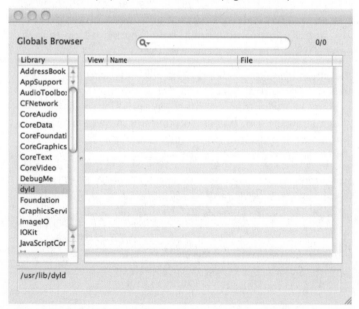

Figure 15–5. *Globals are opt-in. You select them from this window, either by browsing a specific framework or library, or by using the search field.*

This window is showing you a list of all the frameworks and libraries that are available to your application. If a framework hasn't been loaded or doesn't contain any global variables, that framework will have an empty list of global variables. Among the list of libraries and frameworks is one with the same name as our application. In our case, that would be a listing for a framework called *DebugMe*. That is where you would find any global variables declared in our application. When a global variable exists, it will be listed and will contain a checkbox to the left of it. If you check the box, the selected global variable will become visible in the variable list.

After the global variables are a number of other sections for processor registers. Registers are small amounts of storage on the processor that you can access very quickly. Unless you're hand-coding assembly, you won't generally be using registers directly. If you understand the architecture of the processors on your devices, these can yield some useful information, but generally you won't need these until you get to the point where you're doing some pretty advanced work, far beyond the scope of this chapter.

The Debugging Controls

In the toolbar of the debugger window, you'll see several buttons that you can use to control the execution of your program when stopped at a breakpoint (Figure 15–5).

Figure 15–6. *The debugging controls give you control over the execution of the program*

The leftmost button, when pressed, will restart your program. This is functionally equivalent to quitting your program and then re-launching using the debugger. This button doesn't cause your application to be rebuilt, so changes you've made to your code since the last time you built won't be included.

The *Continue* button resumes execution of your program. It will pick up right where it left off and continue executing as normal unless another breakpoint or an error condition is encountered.

The *Step Over* and *Step Into* buttons will allow you to execute a single line of code at a time. The difference between the two is that *Step Over* will fire any method or function call as a single line of code, skipping to the next line of code in the current method or function, while *Step Into* will go to the first line of code in the method or function that's called and stop there. When you use *Step Into*, the method you were in gets pushed down one in the stack trace, and the called method becomes the top method in the stack trace. When your program is stopped at a line of code that isn't a function or method call, these two buttons function identically.

The *Step Out* button finishes execution of the current method and returns to the method that called it. This effectively pops the current method off the stack trace's stack (you didn't think that name was accidental did you?) and the method that called this method becomes the top of the stack trace.

That might be a little clearer if we try it out. Stop your program. Note that even though your program might be paused at a breakpoint, it is still executing. To stop it, click on the stop sign in the toolbar at the top of the debugger window or select **Stop** from the **Run** menu. We're going to add some code that might make the use of *Step Over*, *Step Into*, and *Step Out* a little clearer.

NESTED MESSAGE CALLS

Nested method calls like this combine two commands in the same line of code:

```
[[NSArray alloc] initWithObject:@"Hello"];
```

If you nest several methods together, you will skip over several actual commands with a single click of the *Step Over* button, making it impossible to set a breakpoint between the different nested statements. This is the primary reason that we avoid excessive nesting of message calls. Other than the standard nesting of `alloc` and `init` methods, we generally prefer not to nest messages.

Dot notation has changed that somewhat. Remember, dot notation is just shorthand for calling a method, so this line of code is also two commands:

```
[self.tableView reloadData];
```

Before the call to `reloadData`, there is a call to the accessor method `tableView`. If it makes sense to use an accessor, we will often use dot notation right in the message call rather than using two separate lines of code, but be careful. It's easy to forget that dot notation results in a method call, so you can inadvertently create code that is hard to debug by nesting several method calls on one line of code.

Trying Out the Debug Controls

In Xcode, the file *RootViewController.m* should still be showing in the editor pane. Note that you can go back to the project window to edit your source code, but you can also do that in the debugger window. Makes no never mind to us.

If you don't see *RootViewController.m*, go back to the project window and single-click on *RootViewController.m* in the *Groups & Files* pane. Now, add the following two methods immediately before `viewDidLoad`.

```
- (float)processBar:(float)inBar {
    float newBar = inBar * 2.0;
    return newBar;
}

- (NSInteger)processFoo:(NSInteger)inFoo {
    NSInteger newFoo = inFoo * 2;
    return newFoo;
}
```

And insert the following lines of code into the existing `viewDidLoad` method:

```
- (void)viewDidLoad {
    [super viewDidLoad];

    NSInteger foo = 25;
    float bar = 374.3494;
    NSLog(@"foo: %d, bar: %f", foo, bar);
```

```
foo = [self processFoo:foo];
bar = [self processBar:bar];

NSLog(@"foo: %d, bar: %f", foo, bar);

// Set up the edit and add buttons.
self.navigationItem.leftBarButtonItem = self.editButtonItem;
...
```

Your breakpoint should still be set at the first line of the method. Xcode does a pretty good job of moving breakpoints around when you insert or delete text from above or below it. Even though we just added two methods above our breakpoint and the method now starts at a new line number, the breakpoint is still set to the correct line of code, which is nice. If the breakpoint somehow got moved, no worries; we're going to move it anyway.

Click and drag the breakpoint down until it's lined up with the line of code that reads:

```
NSInteger foo = 25;
```

Now, choose **Build and Debug** from the **Build** menu to compile the changes and launch the program again. If the debugger window is not showing, bring it to the front. You should see the breakpoint at the first new line of code we added to viewDidLoad.

The first two lines of code are just declaring variables and assigning values to them. These lines don't call any methods or functions, so the *Step Over* and *Step Into* buttons will function identically here. To test that out, click the *Step Over* button to cause the next line of code to execute, then click *Step Into* to cause the second new line of code to execute.

Before using any more of the debugger controls, check out the variable list (Figure 15–7). The two variables we just declared are in the variable list under the *Local* heading with their current values. Also, notice that the value for bar is red. That means it was just assigned or changed by the last command that executed.

> **NOTE:** As you are probably aware, numbers are represented in memory as sums of powers of 2 or powers of ½ for fractional parts. This means that some numbers will end up stored in memory with values slightly different than the value specified in the source code. Though we set bar to a value 374.3494, the closest representation was 374.349396. Close enough, right?

Variable	Value	Summary
▼Arguments		
▶self	0x3c13030	
_cmd	0x15eb1fc	
▼Locals		
▶objc_super	{...}	
foo	25	
bar	374.349396	
▶addButton	0x90	
▶error	0x4	
▶Globals		
▶Registers		
▶Vector Registers		
▶x87 Registers		

Figure 15–7. *When a variable was changed by the last command that fired, it will turn red in the variable list*

There's another way you can see the value of a variable. If you move your cursor so it's above the word *foo* anywhere it exists in the editor pane, a little box will pop up similar to a tooltip that will tell you the variable's current value and type (Figure 15–8).

```
28        [super viewDidLoad];
29
30        NSInteger foo = 25;
31        float bar = 374.3494;
          NSLog(@"foo: %d, bar: %f", foo, bar);
33
34        foo = [self processFoo:foo];
35        bar    NSInteger    foo  bar]         25
36
37        NSLog(@"foo: %d, bar: %f", foo, bar);
38        |
```

Figure 15–8. *Hovering your mouse over a variable in the editing pane will tell you both the variable's datatype and its current value*

The next line of code is just a log statement, so click the *Step Over* button again to let it fire.

The next two lines of code each call a method. We're going to step into one and step over the other. Click the *Step Into* button now.

The red arrow and highlighted line of code should just have moved to the first line of the processFoo method. If you look at the stack trace now, you'll see that viewDidLoad is no longer the first row in the stack. It has been superseded by processFoo. Instead of one black row in the stack trace, there are now two, because we wrote both processFoo and viewDidLoad. You can step through the lines of this method if you like. When you're ready to move back to viewDidLoad, click the *Step Out* button. That will return you to viewDidLoad. processFoo will get popped off of the stack trace's stack, and the red indicator and highlight will be at the line of code after the call to processFoo.

Next, for processBar, we're going to use *Step Over*. We'll never see processBar on the stack trace when we do that. The debugger is going to run the entire method and then stop execution after it returns. The red arrow and highlight will move forward one line (excluding empty lines and comments). We'll be able to see the results of processBar by looking at the value of bar, which should now be double what it was, but the method itself happened as if it was just a single line of code.

DEBUG HERE, DEBUG THERE, DEBUG ANYWHERE

The debugger window is not actually the only place where you can step through code using the debugger. If, while debugging, you go to the editing pane in your project's window, you'll see the same red arrow and highlighted line of code that you saw in the editing pane of the debugger window, and at the top of the editing pane, there will be a small set of icons that match the toolbar icons.

You can use these small icons exactly the same way you use the debugging controls in the toolbar of the debugger window, and can step through the code here if you prefer working in the project window.

But wait! There's more. Act now, and you we'll throw in a free mini debugger. If you select **Mini Debugger** from the **Run** menu, a small floating window will appear.

This window also shows the debugger controls and the source code with the red arrow and highlighted line of code. The difference with this window is that it stays on top of all other windows, even when Xcode is in the background, so you can step through code while the simulator is the frontmost application, which can be really handy. There's no One Right Way™ to step through your code. Use whichever option works best for you.

The Breakpoint Window and Symbolic Breakpoints

You've now seen the basics of working with breakpoints, but there's far more to breakpoints. Select **Breakpoints** from the **Run** menu's **Show** submenu, or type ⌘⌥B to bring up the **breakpoint window** (Figure 15–9). This window shows you all the breakpoints that are currently set in your project. You can delete breakpoints here by selecting them and pressing the delete key. You can also add another kind of breakpoint here, which is called a **symbolic breakpoint**. Instead of breaking on a specific line in a specific source code file, we can tell GDB to break whenever it reaches a certain one of those debug symbols built into the application when using the debug configuration. As a reminder, debug symbols are human-readable names derived from method and function names.

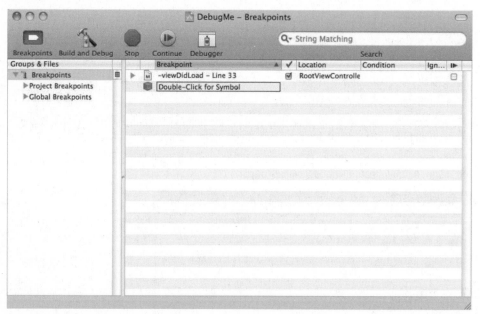

Figure 15–9. *The breakpoint window allows you to see all the breakpoints in your project, and also lets you create symbolic breakpoints*

Single-click the existing breakpoint (select the first line in the right-hand pane) and press the delete key on your keyboard to delete it. Now, double-click the row that says *Double-Click for Symbol*. Type *viewDidLoad* and then press return. We're telling GDB that we want to break on the symbol called *viewDidLoad*, which equates to stopping at the method viewDidLoad.

When you press return, a sheet will drop down (Figure 15–10). This happens because there's more than one symbol with that name. Symbols do not have to be unique. The same method name, for example, can be used in multiple classes. In a large project, you might have dozens of *viewDidLoad* symbols compiled into your application.

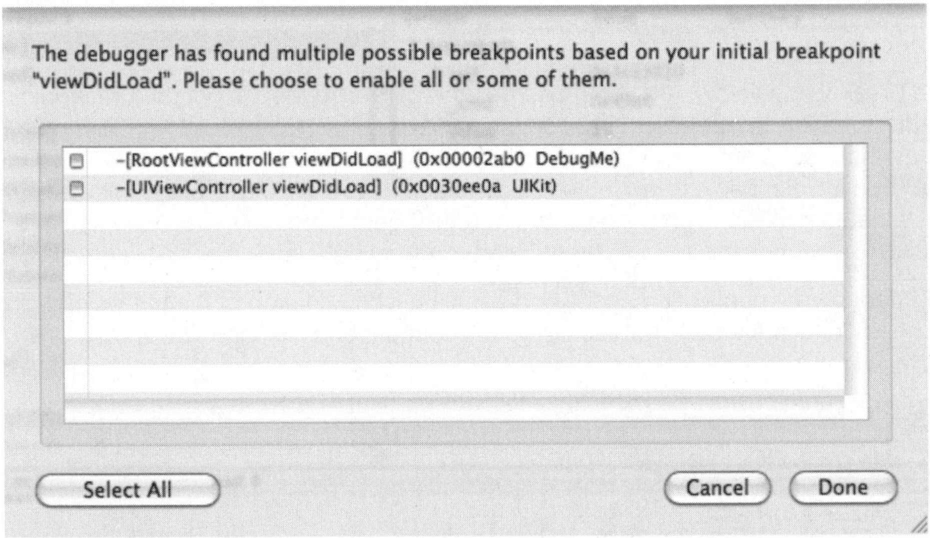

The debugger has found multiple possible breakpoints based on your initial breakpoint "viewDidLoad". Please choose to enable all or some of them.

☐   –[RootViewController viewDidLoad] (0x00002ab0 DebugMe)
☐   –[UIViewController viewDidLoad] (0x0030ee0a UIKit)

Select All   Cancel   Done

Figure 15–10. *When the same symbol exists multiple times, you will be asked to clarify which of those symbols you want to stop on.*

In this application, we have two versions of `viewDidLoad`. We have the version that we wrote, and the one from our superclass that we overrode. When we use debug configuration, not only do we compile debug symbols into our application, but we also link against frameworks that have the debug symbols compiled in as well, so we could even create breakpoints in code that's not ours.

In this case, let's just select the `viewDidLoad` in `RootViewController` by checking its check box, then click the *Done* button. If the application is still running, stop it by clicking the stop sign icon on the toolbar, and then select **Build and Debug – Breakpoints On** to re-launch it. This time, your application should stop again, at the first line of code in `viewDidLoad`.

Conditional Breakpoints

Both the symbolic and line number breakpoints we've set so far have been **unconditional breakpoints**, which means they always stop when the debugger gets to them. If the program reaches the breakpoint, it stops. But you can also create **conditional breakpoints**, which are breakpoints that pause execution only in certain situations.

If your program is still running, stop it, and in the breakpoint window, delete the symbolic breakpoint we just created. In *RootViewController.m*, add the following code, right after the call to super:

```
for (int i=0; i < 25; i++) {
    NSLog(@"i = %d", i);
}
```

Save the file. Now, set a line number breakpoint by clicking to the left of the line that reads:

```
NSLog(@"i = %d", i);
```

Go to the breakpoint window and look for a column called *Condition*. For the breakpoint that you just created, double-click that column and type in *i > 15*. This will tell GDB only to break at this breakpoint if the value of i is greater than 15. You might get a warning from GDB that it wasn't able to evaluate the condition. If you do, that's okay, because i is a local variable, so GDB won't know about it until it gets there. The variable i doesn't exist outside of the method and we're not in that method right now.

Build and debug your application again, and this time it should stop at the breakpoint just like it has done in the past, but look in your debugger console, and you should see this:

```
2009-11-25 11:25:00.772 DebugMe[46520:207] i = 0
2009-11-25 11:25:00.774 DebugMe[46520:207] i = 1
2009-11-25 11:25:00.776 DebugMe[46520:207] i = 2
2009-11-25 11:25:00.779 DebugMe[46520:207] i = 3
2009-11-25 11:25:00.780 DebugMe[46520:207] i = 4
2009-11-25 11:25:00.782 DebugMe[46520:207] i = 5
2009-11-25 11:25:00.783 DebugMe[46520:207] i = 6
2009-11-25 11:25:00.784 DebugMe[46520:207] i = 7
2009-11-25 11:25:00.785 DebugMe[46520:207] i = 8
2009-11-25 11:25:00.786 DebugMe[46520:207] i = 9
2009-11-25 11:25:00.787 DebugMe[46520:207] i = 10
2009-11-25 11:25:00.788 DebugMe[46520:207] i = 11
2009-11-25 11:25:00.789 DebugMe[46520:207] i = 12
2009-11-25 11:25:00.790 DebugMe[46520:207] i = 13
2009-11-25 11:25:00.791 DebugMe[46520:207] i = 14
2009-11-25 11:25:00.792 DebugMe[46520:207] i = 15
```

If you hover your cursor over i in the editing pane, it should show a value of 16. So, the first 16 times through the loop, it didn't pause execution, it just kept going, because the condition we set wasn't met.

This can be an incredibly useful tool when you've got an error that occurs in a very long loop. Without conditional breakpoints, you'd be stuck stepping through the loop until the error happened, which is tedious. It's also useful in methods that are called a lot, but are only exhibiting problems in certain situations. By setting a condition, you can tell the debugger to ignore situations that you know work properly.

> **TIP:** The *Ignore* column, just to the right of the *Condition* column, is pretty cool too—it's a value decremented every time the breakpoint is hit. So you might place the value 16 into the column to have your code stop on the 16th time through the breakpoint. You can even combine these approaches, using *Ignore* with a condition. Cool beans, eh?

Breakpoint Actions

If you look in the debugger window again, you'll see a column at the far right that doesn't have a name, just a symbol, a vertical line with a sideways triangle. You've seen that symbol before; it's the symbol used on the *Continue* button in the debugger controls. If you check the box in that column for a breakpoint, program execution won't pause when it reaches that breakpoint, it will just keep going.

What good is a breakpoint that doesn't cause a break? It's not much good by itself, but combined with **breakpoint actions**, it can very useful.

Stop your application.

Delete the condition we just added to this breakpoint. To do that, double-click on the condition, then hit delete followed by return. Next, check the continue box for the row so that the breakpoint doesn't cause the program's execution to stop.

Now we'll add the breakpoint action. At the very left of the row that represents our breakpoint, you'll see a disclosure triangle. Expand it now to reveal the breakpoint actions interface (Figure 15–11).

> **NOTE:** Don't let that *objc_exception_throw* reference in Figure 15–11 confuse you. That's a special global breakpoint that we'll discuss later in the chapter.

	Breakpoint	▲	✓	Location	Condition	Ignore Count	I▶
▶	● objc_exception_throw		☑	libobjc.A.dylib			☐
▼	[M] –viewDidLoad – Line 31		☑	RootViewController.m –			☑
	Click add button to incorporate breakpoint action.					⊖ ⊕	
	● Double-Click for Symbol						

Figure 15–11. *Clicking the disclosure triangle next to a breakpoint reveals the breakpoint actions interface*

Any breakpoint can have one or more actions associated with it. Click the plus button at the right side of the blue rounded rectangle to add an action to this breakpoint. Once you do that, you'll get a new breakpoint action. There are a number of different options to choose from (Figure 15–12). You can run a GDB command or add a statement to the console log. You can also play a sound, or fire off a shell script or AppleScript. As you can see, there's a lot you can do while debugging your application without having to litter up your code with debug-specific functionality.

Figure 15–12. *Breakpoint actions allow you to fire debugger commands, add statements to the log, play a sound, or fire a shell script or AppleScript*

From the **Debugger Command** pop-up menu, select **Log**, which will allow us to add information to the debugger console without writing another NSLog() statement. When we compile this application for distribution, this breakpoint won't exist, so there's no chance of accidentally shipping this log command in our application. In the white text area below the pop-up menu, add the following log command:

```
Reached %B again. Hit this breakpoint %H times. Current value of i is @(int)i@
```

The %B is a special substitution variable that will be replaced at runtime with the name of the breakpoint. The %H is a substitution variable that will be replaced with the number of times this breakpoint has been reached. The text between the two @ characters is a GDB expression that tells it to print the value of i, which is an integer.

> **TIP** You can read more about the various debug actions and the correct syntax to use for each one in the *Xcode Debugging Guide* available at http://developer.apple.com/mac/library/documentation/DeveloperTools/Conceptual/XcodeDebugging.

Build and debug your application again. This time, you should see additional information printed in the debug console log, between the values printed by our NSLog() statement (Figure 15–13). While statements logged using NSLog() are printed in bold, those done by breakpoint actions are printed in non-bold characters.

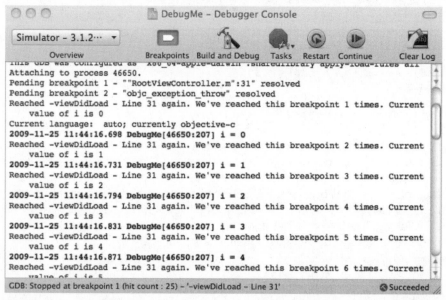

Figure 15–13. *Breakpoint log actions get printed to the debugger console but, unlike the results of* NSLog() *commands, are not printed in bold*

That's not all there is to breakpoints, but it's the fundamentals, and should give you a good foundation for finding and fixing problems in your applications.

The GDB Console

There's a huge amount of debugging functionality available through Xcode's user interface, and for many people, that functionality will suffice. However, GDB is an extremely robust piece of software capable of doing even more than what can be done using Xcode's debugger and breakpoint windows. We'll look at just a few GDB commands that you can use in the debugger console window, which lets you interact directly with GDB. Note that the debugger console only lets you interact with GDB while you are actively debugging a program and are stopped at a breakpoint.

Before you try any of the commands that follow, make sure that the debugger is running and that it is paused, either by selecting **Pause** from the **Run** menu or by stopping at a breakpoint. If you are using breakpoints, be sure you've got at least one without the *continue through breakpoint* check box checked.

The Info Command

GDB's `info` command gives you information about the currently running program. To use the `info` command, you have to specify what you want information about. You can get a list of the available info commands by just typing `info`, followed by a return, into the GDB console while debugging a program.

For example, if you type the following into the GDB console:

```
info breakpoints
```

GDB will list all of the breakpoints in your application. If you type:

```
info stack
```

GDB will give you the stack trace. Both of these commands just give you the same information that's already available in Xcode through the breakpoint and debugger window, though it can be useful to be able to get to that information without leaving the console window. Many of the other *info* commands will tell you things you can't get from elsewhere in Xcode. For example, if you type in:

```
info function
```

GDB will list all of the functions currently available to be called, including Objective-C methods and C++ member functions. It doesn't just include functions and methods from your application, either. This will list every function available, including those from linked frameworks, and even those that are private.

Working with Breakpoints

You can also work with breakpoints directly from the GDB console. You can do everything that the breakpoint window allows you to do, and more.

Creating Breakpoints

To create a new breakpoint, use the command break or b (they are the same, b is just a shorthand for break). Without any parameters, b will set a breakpoint where execution is currently stopped. If you want to set a breakpoint at a specific line number in the current file, append the line number, like so:

```
b 22
```

That would set a breakpoint in line 22 of the current file. To set a breakpoint in a specific file at a certain line number, you type the filename, then a colon, then the line number, like so:

```
b RootViewController.m:22
```

That would set a breakpoint at line 22 of the file *RootViewController.m.* You can also set a symbolic breakpoint using the b command by passing the name of the symbol as an argument:

```
b viewDidLoad
```

If there is more than one symbol with that name, you will be prompted to specify which one by selecting it from a list, not all that different from the way Xcode handles that situation. If you want to set a breakpoint for a symbol that hasn't been loaded yet, you can use the fb command, which stands for future break. Here's an example of setting a future break on a function in the Objective-C runtime.

```
fb objc_exception_throw
```

> **NOTE**: If you use the fb command and the symbol has already been loaded, then it will function exactly like the b command, so you don't have to worry about whether the symbol is loaded or not when you use fb.

Removing Breakpoints

If you are currently stopped at a breakpoint, typing

```
clear
```

will remove the current breakpoint. If you want to clear a specific breakpoint at a certain line number in the current file, you would append the line number to the command, like this:

```
clear 22
```

And if you want to remove a breakpoint at a specific symbol, you can append the symbol name to the clear command, like so:

```
clear viewDidLoad
```

If you want to delete all breakpoints, use the del command with no arguments:

```
del
```

Printing Data and Object Values

While in the debugger, you can print the values of any object or variable that's in scope. To print the value of a native datatype, you use the (surprise!) print command. To print the value of an Objective-C object, you use the po command, which stands for print object.

To print the value of the local variable foo, which is an int, for example, you would type this:

```
print (int)foo
```

> **TIP:** You can print in hex with print/x and in binary with print/t.

When you use the po command, GDB actually sends the object a description message and returns the result. Here's how you would print the description of an object bar to the console:

```
po bar
```

Calling Functions and Methods

You can do more than that, though. When you use the po command, you can actually send messages to objects in the debugger and have the po command called on the returned object. If we wanted to know the class of bar, we could type this:

```
po [bar class]
```

This would cause the debugger to send bar the class message and then print the results of sending description to the returned value. You can do the same thing with C functions using GDB's call command with a symbol.

```
call myFunctionThatTakesAnInt(5)
```

For Objective-C methods that don't return an object because they return void, or a native datatype like float or int, you can also use the call command, but you have to specifically cast the return value so GDB knows how to format it, like this:

```
call (float) [self methodThatReturnsAFloat]
```

or

```
call (void) [self methodThatReturnsNothing]
```

If you use call on an Objective-C method that returns an object, the call will work but the memory address of the returned object will be printed and not its description.

> **CAUTION:** GDB commands are not terminated with a semicolon, so don't add one after the po or call commands. Doing so will result in an error.

There's much, much more you can do with the command-line GDB console. We've barely scratched the surface of GDB's functionality in this section. If you're interested in becoming an advanced debugger, check out the GDB user manual at `http://sourceware.org/gdb/current/onlinedocs/gdb/`. For a quick reference to GDB's commands, you can open up a terminal session and type in man gdb. That will bring up the man page for GDB, which lists the available commands and gives a brief summary of what each does.

GDB INIT

If you create a text file in your home directory called *.gdbinit*, any GDB commands you place in this file will be automatically executed when GDB is launched and attached.

Static Analysis

Starting with Xcode 3.2 on Snow Leopard, Apple added a menu item to the **Build** menu called **Build and Analyze**. This option compiles your code and runs a **static analysis** on your code that is capable of detecting any number of common problems. Normally, when you build a project, you will see yellow icons in the build results window that represent build warnings and red icons that represent build errors. When you build and analyze, you may also see rows with blue icons that represent potential problems found by the static analyzer. Although static analysis is imperfect and can sometimes identify problems that aren't actually problems (referred to as **false positives**), it's very good at finding certain types of bugs, most notably code that leaks memory. Let's introduce a leak into our code and then analyze it.

If your application is running, stop it.

In *RootViewController.m*, in the viewDidLoad method, add the following code just after the call to super:

```
NSArray *myArray = [[NSArray alloc] initWithObjects:@"Hello", @"Goodbye",
    "So Long", nil];
```

Before you analyze, it's a good idea to select **Clean** from the **Build** menu. Only files that get compiled will be analyzed. Code that hasn't been changed since the last time it was compiled won't get compiled again, and won't get analyzed. In this case, that wouldn't be an issue, since we just changed the file where we introduced the bug, but it's good practice to analyze your entire project. Once the project is done cleaning, select **Build and Analyze** from the **Build** menu.

You'll now get a warning about an unused variable, which is true. We declared and initialized myArray, but never used it. You'll also get two rows in the build results from the static analyzer, one that tells you that myArray is never read after initialization. This is essentially telling us the same thing as the unused variable warning from the compiler. The next one, however, is one the compiler doesn't catch. It says: *Potential leak of an object allocated at line 30 stored into 'myArray'*. The line number might be a little different on your system, but you should still see this row in your build results. That's the static analyzer telling you that you might have leaked memory, and telling you the line of code where the object you might have leaked was allocated. To find out more about the potential leak, click the disclosure triangle to the left of the *Potential leak* message. Pretty informative, eh?

Before you begin testing any application, you should run **Build and Analyze** and look at every item it points out. It can save you a lot of aggravation and trouble.

Specific Bugs

You now know the basic tools of debugging. We haven't discussed all the features of either Xcode or GDB, but we've covered the essentials. It would take far more than a single chapter to cover this topic exhaustively, but you've now seen the tools that you'll use in 95% or more of your debugging efforts. Unfortunately, the best way to get better at debugging is to do a lot of it, and that can be frustrating early on. The first time you see a particular type of problem, you often aren't sure how to tackle it. So, to give you a bit of a kick-start, we're going to show you a couple of the most common problems that occur in Cocoa Touch programs and show you how to find and fix those problems when they happen to you.

Overreleasing Memory

Almost certainly the most frustrating and difficult type of bug in the Cocoa Touch world is the dreaded `EXC_BAD_ACCESS` exception, which happens when you try to use an object that has been deallocated. This usually occurs because you released an object that wasn't retrieved from `alloc`, `new`, or `copy`, and wasn't specifically retained. It can also happen if you don't specify `retain` in your property declaration, since using the mutator method for a property that's not specifically declared with the `retain` keyword won't retain the object for you.

Before we demonstrate this problem, delete the leaky declaration of `myArray` we just had you add to `viewDidLoad`.

Save, then switch over to *RootViewController.h* and add the following lines of code:

```
@interface RootViewController : UITableViewController
    <NSFetchedResultsControllerDelegate> {
    NSFetchedResultsController *fetchedResultsController;
    NSManagedObjectContext *managedObjectContext;

    NSArray      *stuff;
}

@property (nonatomic, retain) NSFetchedResultsController *fetchedResultsController;
@property (nonatomic, retain) NSManagedObjectContext *managedObjectContext;
@property (nonatomic, retain) NSArray *stuff;
- (void)doSomethingWithStuffArray;
@end
```

We're declaring the stuff array so we can overrelease it in a bit. We also declare a new method called doSomethingWithStuffArray which is where we'll try to access the array after it's been overreleased.

Switch over to *RootViewController.m*. First, synthesize the new array property we just created, right after the existing @synthesize declaration:

```
@synthesize stuff;
```

Then, add this new method right above the existing viewDidLoad method:

```
- (void)doSomethingWithStuffArray {
    NSString *oneString = [stuff objectAtIndex:0];
    NSLog(@"%@", oneString);
}
```

No magic there, we're just retrieving a string from the array and logging its contents. Now, in the viewDidLoad method, right after the call to super, add the following code:

```
NSArray *array = [NSArray arrayWithObjects:@"Hello", @"Goodbye", @"So Long",
    nil];
self.stuff = array;
[array release];
[self performSelector:@selector(doSomethingWithStuffArray) withObject:nil
    afterDelay:5.0];
```

At first glance this code might look okay, but we created array using a convenience factory method, which means it's not ours to release. Yet, after assigning it to the stuff property, we release it. Any object returned from a factory method is in the autorelease pool, so when we release it, it doesn't get deallocated immediately. That's what can make this problem so hard to track down. The actual problem won't occur until later, not at the time that we made the mistake.

Open the breakpoint window and look in the left pane. There you'll see listings for project and global breakpoints. Global breakpoints exist in every Xcode project, not just the one in which you created it. This fact can be very handy. We're now going to give you a global symbolic breakpoint that you should set and never, ever delete. As you'll see, this breakpoint can be extraordinarily helpful to have around. Let's set it now.

In the left pane of the breakpoints window, single-click *Global Breakpoints*. Next, double-click the single row that reads *Double-Click for Symbol*, type in *objc_exception_throw*, then hit return. This symbol points to the function that throws exceptions. If you're debugging an application and get an uncaught exception (which is about to happen), this breakpoint will pause the execution of the program when the exception is thrown, before the program terminates from the uncaught exception. This will give you a chance to look at the stack trace and examine variable values, to get a sense of what the heck happened.

OTHER GREAT SYMBOLIC BREAKPOINTS

The handy objc_exception_throw symbol is not the only symbol you might want to put into your global breakpoints. Here is a short list of other symbolic breakpoints that will pause execution before your application terminates in common error situations:

- **CGPostError**   Pauses execution when a Core Graphic error occurs

- **malloc_error_break**   Pauses execution when an overrelease error occurs when using malloc or calloc instead of Objective-C objects

- **_NSAutoreleaseNoPool**   Pauses execution when there's no autorelease pool in place. Typically happens when you forget to declare a pool in a thread or operation

- **_objc_error**   Pauses execution when Objective-C's default error handler is called

- **opengl_error_break**   Pauses execution when an OpenGL ES error occurs

Build and debug your application. Feel free to delete any breakpoints from earlier in the chapter, though you'll want to keep the *objc_exception_throw* breakpoint around forever. After the program has been running for about five seconds, you will kick into the debugger. If we hadn't set that breakpoint, your program would instead have terminated and given you a very ambiguous error message:

```
Program received signal:  "EXC_BAD_ACCESS".
```

Since we did set that breakpoint, that same information is available in the status bar at the bottom of the debugger, which should read:

```
GDB: Program received signal: "EXC_BAD_ACCESS".
```

This signal means you tried to access a piece of memory you don't have the right to access. In iPhone SDK programs, it's almost always the result of trying to use an overreleased object, though that's not the only way it can happen. If you were to call free() twice on the same chunk of memory, for example, or if a pointer got overwritten with an invalid value, you might get the same error.

Obviously, we know exactly where the problem is in this situation, but how would we go about finding it in a real application if we had no idea where it was coming from? Well, that breakpoint you just set is a great starting point. Look in the stack trace in the debugger window. It should look like Figure 15–14. If yours does not look like that, no worries, read the tech block that follows.

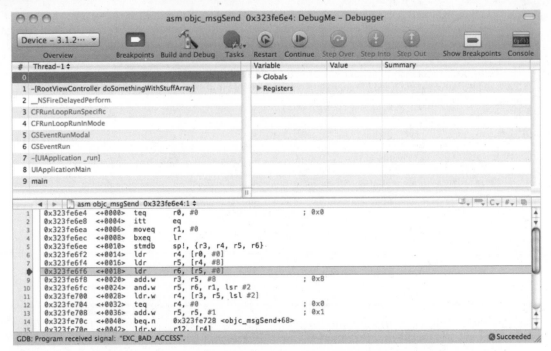

Figure 5-14. *The debugger is stopped at obj_msgSend, which is part of the Objective-C runtime*

> **NOTE:** If your stack trace doesn't look like 5-14, and doesn't include the call to doSomethingWithStuffArray, and instead you see a gray item at the same spot with three question marks instead of a proper name, it probably means you're running on the simulator. For some reason on the simulator, after receiving the EXC_BAD_ACCESS, sometimes the debugger is unable to match up code with the debug symbols and this is the result. Hopefully this will be fixed in a future release of the iPhone SDK, but we didn't want you to think you were doing something wrong. If you encounter this with your own applications, debugging on the device instead of the simulator should still work okay.

Trace the call stack back to the first method that's listed in black and click on it. It should be the second row (index 1) that represents the doSomethingWithStuffArray method, just like in Figure 5-14. When you click on it, lo and behold, the editing pane shows you exact line of code that triggered the error. Once you know that, you know the problem is with the stuff array, and you can go look at where you created it to make sure you're not overreleasing it (which, of course, we are in this case). If you aren't, you can then go check the property declaration, and make sure it's specified with the retain keyword.

Breaking on the exception won't always tell you where the problem is, though. Even worse, sometimes instead of getting an EXC_BAD_ACCESS immediately, your code seems to work for a while, and then suddenly crashes. Sometimes you get completely unexpected behavior. Instead of receiving an EXC_BAD_ACCESS, you get an error telling you that the object doesn't respond to the selector objectAtIndex:.

This can mean that the memory that was previously used for stuff might might have been reused for another object for our application. In that case, accessing that memory is perfectly fine, it's just that the object that's there isn't the one we're expecting to be there because it now represents a different object altogether. In these cases, the answer is to call in the zombies. What? Zombies? Yes, zombies.

> **NOTE:** The kind of unpredictable errors that you get when memory is reused for different type of object is commonly referred to as a **heisenbug**, which is a play on the term Heisenberg Uncertainty Principle. They can be some of the most difficult bugs to track down.

NSZombie

At this point, you're probably expecting us to explain the really lame joke about zombies at the end of the last paragraph. Only, it's not a joke. We really are going to call out the zombies. We're going to set an environment variable that will change the way object deallocation works in Cocoa. Instead of freeing up a deallocated object's memory so it can be reused, the system will start turning deallocated objects into **zombies**, which are valid objects. Because they're valid objects, their memory can't get re-used by another object. But, they don't respond to messages the way regular objects do; instead, they eat their brains.

Okay, that last bit actually was a lame zombie joke, sorry. That's not really what zombies do. What they actually do is report the fact that you've sent a message to them. Remember, without zombies enabled, sending a message to a deallocated object would have resulted in a crash or some other heisenbug. With the zombie still around, we won't crash and we know exactly what object was inappropriately sent the message, so we know where to look to fix it.

Zombies are awesome. Let's enable zombies and re-run our application so you can see how this works.

If your application is running, stop it. In the *Groups & Files* pane, look for *Executables*. Click the disclosure triangle next to it to reveal a single item called *DebugMe*. Double-click that item to open up a new window, then click the *Arguments* tab (Figure 15–15).

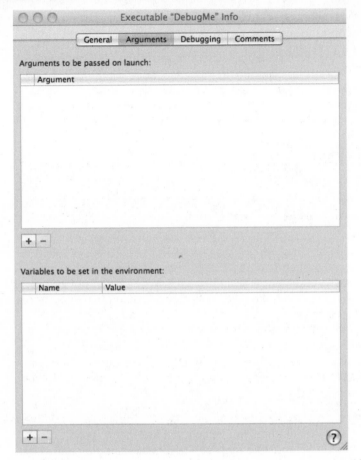

Figure 15–15. *The executable window allows you to specify, among other things, environment variables and arguments to be passed to the executable*

This window allows you to set certain parameters about the way your application is launched, but only when it's launched from within Xcode. These values don't affect the program when it's compiled and run elsewhere, either from the app store or using ad hoc distribution. On this tab, you can specify parameters that get passed to your application (Figure 15–15, top pane) and also can set environment variables for the application's run (Figure 15–15, bottom pane).

The bottom pane is the one we want. We need to set an environment variable, so click the plus button in the very lower-left of the window. This will add a row to the bottom table. Double-click the row on the *Name* column and change the variable's name to *NSZombieEnabled*. Then, double-click on the same row in the *Value* column and set the value to *YES*. Now you can close the window.

Build and debug your application again. This time, it won't crash. But if you look in the debugger console, you'll see a message like this:

```
*** -[CFArray objectAtIndex:]: message sent to deallocated instance 0x3a2d110
```

This message offers up some excellent clues to help us figure out which object was overreleased. We know it's an array, because `CFArray` is the core foundation counterpart to `NSArray`. We also know the message that was sent, which is `objectAtIndex:`, so we can search in our project for occurrences of `objectAtIndex:` or we could set a symbolic breakpoint for `objectAtIndex:` and see which ones fire before the invalid object is set.

Infinite Recursion

Another hard-to-debug problem is when you have a method or set of methods that infinitely recurse. A method that calls itself, or two methods that call each other, will keep running until the system runs out of space on the call stack for any more method calls. As you saw earlier with the stack trace, method and function calls in a program are kept track of in a stack. If that stack runs out of room, no more calls can be made and your application quits.

The reason these are hard to debug is that they generally don't give very much in the way of feedback. They keep running until the app runs out of room on the call stack, and then the application crashes. Typically, you don't get any indication in the debugger console at all about why it crashed.

In iPhone development, this problem frequently occurs when people forget that dot notation is just a shorthand for a method call. For example, you might create an accessor method like this:

```
- (NSString *)foo {
    return self.foo;
}
```

If you're thinking of dot notation the way it's used in Java or C++, this method looks okay. You're just returning the instance variable, `foo`, right? Alas, no. Calling `self.foo` is exactly the same thing as calling `[self foo]`, which means that this method is calling itself. And it will keep doing so forever, until the program dies.

When this happens, you'll get a sheet in the debugger window that tells you that Xcode is loading stack frames (Figure 15–16). There are going to be a lot of stack frames when this happens. A stack frame represents an individual row of the stack trace pane. Sometimes Xcode gets overwhelmed by the size of the stack trace and just crashes... just disappears without a trace.

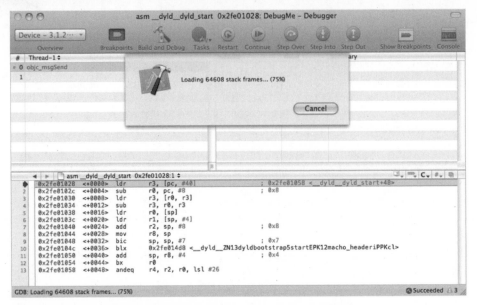

Figure 15–16. *The main indication that you've got infinite recursion going on*

But, if Xcode manages to hang on, the stack trace will make it pretty obvious what's going on (Figure 15–17). If you see the same method or set of methods repeated over and over in the stack trace after it finishes loading the stack frames, that's your clue that you've got a method or methods infinitely recursing.

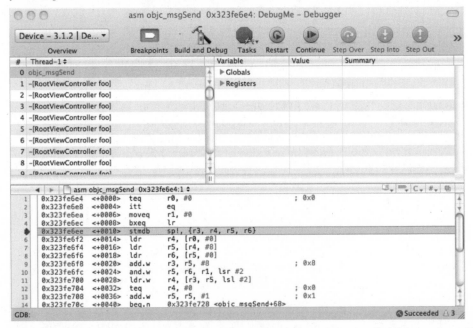

Figure 15–17. *A stack trace with the same methods repeated over and over is a tip off that you've got infinite recursion going on*

Missed Outlet and Action Connections

Sometimes, no matter how hard you look, no matter how many instructions you step through in the debugger, the results seem to be wrong. A method that should be getting called isn't getting called, or the wrong action is firing. If you encounter this sort of mystery, don't forget that not all bugs are contained in code. You can also make mistakes creating your nibs. You can forget to connect an outlet or action, or accidentally delete a connection after it has been made. You can connect the wrong control event, or unintentionally connect a control to multiple targets.

Failing to make an outlet connection in Interface Builder can often be a difficult problem to track down because messages in Objective-C can be sent to nil objects, and messages to nil objects do no harm. That means a nil connection is generally not fatal. It doesn't do what you want, but it doesn't trigger an error, either. Unfortunately, there's not really a good tool for determining if there's a problem with your nib, so you need to learn to recognize behavior that can result from missing or incorrectly connected actions and outlets.

If you set breakpoints in action methods, and they either don't fire at all, or don't fire when you think they should, you probably want to check your nib file and make sure that the connections are all what they should be. Make sure that all outlets are connected and that the controls that trigger actions are triggering the correct actions on the correct event.

If you control-drag from a control, the default action that you're connecting to with most controls is the *Value Changed* event. Interface Builder knows enough to use *Touch Up Inside* if you control-drag from a button, but with most controls, control-dragging connects you to the *Value Changed* event, which may very well not be what you want. As a result, you should get in the habit of making your connections to action methods using the connections inspector, and leave the control-dragging for connecting outlets.

GDB: Stopped at Concluding Paragraph

Debugging can be one of the most difficult and frustrating tasks on this green earth. It's also extremely important, and tracking down a problem that's been plaguing your code can be extremely gratifying. The reason the debugging process is so hard is that modern applications are complex, the libraries we use to build them are complex, and modern operating systems themselves are very complex. At any given time, there's an awful lot of code loaded in, running, and interacting.

It would be impossible to predict every bug that you might encounter, and any attempt to write an exhaustive chapter on the subject would be futile. But, we've packed your backpack with a few of the most useful debugging tools and some information on some of the most difficult and problematic bugs, which should give you a good starting point for your future application development treks.

As we stated at the beginning of the chapter, there's no teacher like experience when it comes to debugging, so you just need to get out there and start making your own mistakes and then fixing them. Don't hesitate to use search engines or to ask more experienced developers for help if you truly do get stuck, but don't let those resources become a crutch, either. Put in an effort to find and fix each bug you encounter before you start looking for help. Yes, it will be frustrating at times, but it's good for you. It builds character.

And with that, we're close to the end of our journey together. We do have one more chapter, though, a farewell bit of guidance as you move forward in your iPhone development travels. So, when you're ready for it, turn the page.

Chapter 16

The Road Goes Ever On...

You've survived another journey with us, huh? Great! At this point, you know a lot more than you knew when you first opened this book. We would love to tell you that you now know it all, but when it comes to technology, you never know it all. This is particularly true of iPhone development technologies. The programming language and frameworks we've been working with in this book are the end result of well over 20 years of evolution. And Apple engineers are always feverishly working on that Next Cool New Thing™. Despite being much more mature than it was just a year ago, the iPhone platform has still just begun to blossom. There is so much more to come.

By making it through another book, you've built yourself an even sturdier foundation. You've acquired a solid knowledge of Objective-C, Cocoa Touch, and the tools that bring these technologies together to create incredible new iPhone applications. You understand the iPhone software architecture and the design patterns that make Cocoa Touch sing. In short, you are even more ready to chart your own course.

Getting Unstuck

At its core, programming is about problem solving—figuring things out. It's fun and rewarding. But there will be times when you run up against a puzzle that seems insurmountable, a problem that does not appear to have a solution.

Sometimes, the answer just appears—a result of a bit of time away from the problem. A good night's sleep or a few hours of doing something different can often be all that you need to get through it. Believe us, sometimes you can stare at the same problem for hours, overanalyzing and getting yourself so worked up that you miss an obvious solution.

And then there are times when even a change of scenery doesn't help. In those situations, it's good to have friends in high places. Here are some resources you can turn to when you're in a bind.

Apple's Documentation

Become one with Xcode's documentation browser. The documentation browser is a front end to a wealth of incredibly valuable sample source code, concept guides, API references, video tutorials, and a whole lot more.

There are few areas of the iPhone that you won't be able to learn more about by making your way through Apple's documentation. And the more comfortable you get with Apple's documentation, the easier it will be for you to make your way through uncharted territories and new technologies as Apple rolls them out.

Mailing Lists

The following are some useful mailing lists that are maintained by Apple:

- `http://lists.apple.com/mailman/listinfo/cocoa-dev`: A moderately high-volume list, primarily focused on Cocoa for Mac OS X. Because of the common heritage shared by Cocoa and Cocoa Touch, many of the people on this list may be able to help you. Make sure to search the list archives before asking your question, though.

- `http://lists.apple.com/mailman/listinfo/xcode-users`: A mailing list specific to questions and problems related to Xcode.

- `http://lists.apple.com/mailman/listinfo/quartz-dev`: A mailing list for discussion of Quartz 2D and Core Graphics technologies.

Discussion Forums

These are some discussion forums you may like to join:

- `http://iphonedevbook.com/forum`: Forums that we set up and host for iPhone development-related questions. We also make sure that the most current version of the project archives that accompany this book are here, updated with all errata and running on the most current release of the iPhone SDK.

- `http://devforums.apple.com/`: Apple's new developer community forums for Mac and iPhone software developers. These require logging in, but that means you can discuss new functionality that's still under NDA. Apple's engineers are known to check in periodically and answer questions.

- `http://www.iphonedevsdk.com/`: A web forum where iPhone programmers, both new and experienced, help each other out with problems and advice.

- `http://forums.macrumors.com/forumdisplay.php?f=135`: A forum for iPhone programmers hosted by the nice folks at MacRumors.

Web Sites

Here are some web sites that you may want to visit:

- `http://www.cocoadevcentral.com/`: A portal that contains links to a great many Cocoa-related web sites and tutorials.

- `http://cocoaheads.org/`: The CocoaHeads site. CocoaHeads is a group dedicated to peer support and promotion of Cocoa. It focuses on local groups with regular meetings, where Cocoa developers can get together, and even socialize a bit. There's nothing better than knowing a real person who can help you out, so if there's a CocoaHeads group in your area, check it out. If there's not, why not start one up?

- `http://nscodernight.com/`: The NSCoder Night site. NSCoder Nights are weekly organized meetings where Cocoa programmers get together to code and socialize. Like CocoaHeads, NSCoder Nights are independently organized local events.

- `http://cocoablogs.com/`: A portal that contains links to a great many blogs related to Cocoa programming.

- `http://www.iphonedevcentral.org/`: A web site devoted to iPhone programming tutorials.

- `http://stackoverflow.com/`: Although not specifically oriented toward the iPhone or Objective-C, a great source for finding answers to questions. Many experienced and knowledgeable iPhone programmers, including some who work at Apple, contribute to this site by answering questions and posting sample code.

Blogs

Check out these blogs:

- `http://iphonedevelopment.blogspot.com/`: Jeff's iPhone development blog. Jeff posts sample code, tutorials, and other information of interest to iPhone developers.

- `http://davemark.com/`: Dave's little spot in the sun. Not at all technical, just full of whimsical ephemera that catches Dave's interest and he hopes you'll enjoy, too.

- `http://theocacao.com/`: A blog maintained by Scott Stevenson, an experienced Cocoa programmer.

- `http://www.wilshipley.com/blog/`: Wil Shipley's blog. Wil is one of the most experienced Objective-C programmers on the planet. His "Pimp My Code" series of blog postings should be required reading for any Objective-C programmer.

- `http://rentzsch.tumblr.com/`: Wolf Rentzsch's blog. Wolf is an experienced independent Cocoa programmer and the founder of the C4 Independent Developers conference.

- `http://chanson.livejournal.com/`: Chris Hanson's blog. Chris works at Apple on the Xcode team, and his blog is filled with great insight and information about Xcode and related topics.

- `http://www.cimgf.com/`: The Cocoa Is My Girlfriend site, which covers software development on both the Mac and iPhone using Objective-C.

- `http://cocoawithlove.com/`: A technical blog for Cocoa and Cocoa Touch developers, run by Matt Gallagher. It has many tutorials.

- `http://mattgemmell.com/`: Matt Legend Gemmell's blog. Matt is an experienced Cocoa developer. He is the author of several open source Cocoa frameworks, including the MGTwitterEngine framework, which makes Twitter integration with your iPhone apps a snap.

And If All Else Fails...

Drop Dave and Jeff an e-mail:

`daveandjeff@iphonedevbook.com`

Farewell

We sure are glad you came along on this journey with us. We wish you the best of luck, and hope that you enjoy programming the iPhone as much as we do.

Index

■ A

abstract entities, 53
accessors, 147
   virtual accessors, 151
action declaration
   MailPic application, 397
   MapMe application, 375
   missed connections, debugging, 525
   music playing application, 428–430
   setting up application skeleton, 331–333
   StalledViewController, 454
action methods
   action declarations, application skeleton, 333
   MapMeViewController, 384
   RequestTypes application, 353
Activity Indicator View, 334
addAnnotation method, 371
addAnnotations method, 371
addAttachmentData method, 395
addDependency method, 476
addOperation method, 478
aggregates, 188–189
album artwork, retrieving
   media items, iPod library, 413
alert views, 152, 245, 265, 266, 268
alertView:clickedButtonAtIndex method, 154
alertView:didDismissButtonWithIndex method, 76, 78
amAcceptingConnections variable, 234
AND operator *see* bitwise AND (&) operator
annotation object, MapKit, 370
   writing MapMe class, 378–380

annotation view, MapKit, 362, 370
   MapMeViewController, 388, 389
   providing map view with, 372
annotations, MapKit, 361, 369–373
   adding and removing, 371
   annotation object, 370
   annotation view, 370
   MapMeViewController, 388
   providing map view with annotation views, 372
   selecting annotations, 372
API documentation, 91
Apple documentation, 528
Apple mailing lists, 528
application architecture, 43
application delegate
   adding to, 45–46
   modifying interface, 44–45
application music player controller, 419
application skeleton, setting up, 331–336
   action and outlet declarations, 331–333
   designing interface, 333–335
   implementing stubs, 335
applicationMusicPlayer method
   MPMusicPlayerController, 419
applications, localizing, 100
applicationWillResignActive method, 240
applicationWillTerminate, 23–24
archiving objects, 235–236
ARM assembly, 501
arrays
   contentsForTransfer method, 293

controlling table structure with, 87–90

creating, 99–100

creating from set, 199–200

nested, 88, 89, 90

ordered, 199–200

outer, 88

paired, 87–88

paired nested, 89

populating, 99–101

removing, 193

subarrays, 88

artwork, retrieving

media items, iPod library, 413

aspect ratio

accommodating, 367

coordinate regions, map view, 365

assembly language, 501

assign keyword, 297

asynchronous data retrieval, 344–350

adding to WebWorks, 346–350

NSURLConnection delegate methods, 345–346

atomicity and thread safety, 472–473

attachments, adding to e-mail, 395

attribute controllers

fetched property, 216–218

attribute editors, 152

color, 158–161

date, 115–117

string, 112–115

using, 118–120

attribute types

Transient, 137

attributes, 19–20

adding to data model, 140–143

adding to entities, 54, 59–60

adding validation to, 142–143

calculated, 151

default values, 137, 146–147

displaying new, 161–163

editing, 55

formatting, 92–94

name, 54

read-only, 146, 166

setting type, 58–59

transformable, 138, 142, 146, 147, 155, 156, 161, 167

types, 56–59

view-only, 165–166

audio

see also music playing application

MPMediaTypeAnyAudio, 411

MPMediaTypeAudioBook, 410

tracks, specifying queue of, 419

autorelease pools, 472, 475, 485

creating SquareRootOperation, 484

AVAudioPlayer

retrieving data using Foundation objects, 337

awakeFromInsert method, 146–147

■B

b (break) command

creating breakpoints, GDB console, 514

backgroundClick action

building music playing application, 430, 435, 440

updating StalledViewController, 488

backing store see persistent store

bar button items, 110–111

batch object

fixing Stalled application with timer, 460–462

beginGeneratingPlaybackNotifications method, 423

Beginning iPhone 3 Development (Apress), 2

beginSeekingBackward method, 421

beginSeekingForward method, 421

Berkeley sockets API

online network play, 271

big-endian byte ordering, 279

Binary datatype, 57–58

bit fields (bit flags), 409

bitwise AND (&) operator

comparing mediaType, 410

returning media items meeting predicates, 416

bitwise macros, 410

bitwise OR (|) operator
 selecting media types, 417
blogs for further information, 529
Bluetooth, 225
Bonjour, 226, 281–288
 browser delegate methods, 286–287
 creating service for publication, 282–285
 delegate methods for publication, 284–285
 error codes/domains, 285
 publishing service, 283
 resolving discovered service, 287–288
 searching for published services, 285
 stopping service, 284
 valid types, 283
Boolean datatype, 57
breakpoint actions, debugging, 511–512
breakpoint window, debugging, 508–509
 Condition column, 510
 Ignore column, 510
 overreleasing memory, 518
breakpoints, 269, 497–512
 breakpoint actions, 511–512
 breakpoint window, 508–509
 CGPostError, 519
 conditional breakpoints, 509–510
 Debugger Editing Pane, 500
 debugging controls, 503–507
 GDB console, 513–514
  creating breakpoints, 514
  removing breakpoints, 514
 line number breakpoints, 497
 malloc_error_break, 519
 NSAutoreleaseNoPool, 519
 objc_error, 519
 objc_exception_throw, 511, 519
 opengl_error_break, 519
 stack trace, 501
 symbolic breakpoints, 508
 unconditional breakpoints, 509
 variable list, 502–503

Xcode moving breakpoints around, 505
browser delegate methods, 286–287
browsers
 creating peer browser for online network play, 311–318
bugs as examples for debugging, 517–525
 heisenbug, 521
 infinite recursion, 523–524
 missed outlet and action connections, 525
 overreleasing memory, 517–521
 zombies, 521–523
byte ordering, 279
 big-endian, 279
 CFNetwork, 280
 little-endian, 279

C

C language, resources for, 2
call command, GDB console, 515
callback functions
 declaring socket context, 275
 implementing socket callback function, 280, 281
 setting up listener, 274
callout, annotations
 MapKit framework, 362
  selecting annotations, 372
Cancel button, 193–196, 208
cancel method, 111, 195
 operations, 478
cancelOperation action
 updating StalledViewController, 488
Cascade rule, 177
categories, importing, 99
cellForRowAtIndexPath method, 90, 102, 114, 201–205, 210, 316
 building music playing application, 446
 updating StalledViewController, 493
CF prefix, 273
CFAllocators, creating sockets, 276
CFNetwork

byte ordering, 280
callback functions, 274
configuring sockets, 275–277
creating sockets, 276
delegates, 274
header file, 309
online network play, 271, 273
run loop integration, 274
setting up listener, 273–279
socket object, 306
specifying port for listening, 278
CFReadStreamRef, 309
CFRelease, 310
CFSocket, 275, 309
CFSocketContext, 275–276, 277
CFSocketCreate function, 276–277
CFSocketRef, 306
CFSocketSetAddress function, 278, 279
CFStream pointers, 288
CFWriteStreamRef, 309
CGPostError breakpoint, 519
checkForGameEnd method, 260–261, 321
Class category, Cocoa Touch, 293
class declaration, 245, 296
class methods, 208
class names, 156
class_copyPropertyList function, 220
classes
    adding fetched properties to, 189–190
    adding relationships to, 189–190
    renaming, 191–192
Classes folder, TicTacToe
    adding packet categories, 293
    implementing OnlineSession object, 295
clear command
    removing breakpoints, GDB console, 514
clickedButtonAtIndex method, 154
client-server model, 229–230, 231–232
clients, 229
CLLocation, 364
CLLocationManager, 384
CLLocationManagerDelegate, 376

Cocoa
    operation queues, 453
    related blogs, 529, 530
    related web sites, 529
    transmission type, 283
Cocoa Touch
    Class category, 293
    KVO (Key-Value Observation), 490
    listening for network connections, 274
    operation queues, 453
    related blogs, 530
    threads, 469
    using assign not retain for delegates, 297
collectionByAppendingXyz methods
    building music playing application, 425, 427
collectionByDeletingXyz methods
    building music playing application, 425, 427
collectionModified instance variable
    building music playing application, 429, 440, 442, 444, 446
collections
    media item collections, 413–414
    MPMediaItemCollections, 416
collections property, MPMediaQuery, 416
collectionWithItems method, 413
color attribute editor, 138, 139, 158–161
color models, 147, 156
colors
    default, 138
    displaying, 163–165
    editing, 138
comments
    beginning with //TODO, 74, 75
    javadoc notation, 91
    special, 74, 75
commitEditingStyle method, 38–39, 209
committed values, 195
committedValuesForKeys method, 195
communication models, network, 229–232
composition, 173

concurrency, 451, 453–454
 adding to application, 451
 creating Stalled application, 453–457
 multiprocessing, 452
 operation queues, 452, 478–479
 operations, 452, 475–478
 run loop scheduling, 451
 threads, 468, 469–475
 timers, 451, 458–460
Condition column, breakpoint window, 510
conditional breakpoints, 509–510
connection:didFailWithError method, 346, 349
connection:didReceiveData method, 346
connection:didReceiveResponse method, 345
connectionDidFinishLoading method, 346, 349
connectToPeer method, 234
constant operands, 183
constants see k prefixed constants
containsItem method
 building music playing application, 425, 427
contentsForTransfer method, 293
context, 22–23
 updating StalledViewController, 490
Continue button, debugging window, 503
 breakpoint actions, 511
controller classes, generic, 169–172, 190–216
controller:didChangeObjectColforChangeType method, 30–34
controller:didChangeSection method, 35
controllerDidChangeContent method, 30
controllerWillChangeContent method, 29–30
coordinate property, CLLocation
 annotation object, MapKit, 370
 user location, map view, 364

coordinate regions, map view, MapKit, 364–367
 accommodating aspect ratio, 367
 converting degrees to distance, 366
 setting region to display, 367
coordinates
 determining visibility of, 369
Core Data
 architectures, 12
 concepts and terminology, 12–13
 custom managed objects, 137–167
 data model, 13–16, 18
 data model editor, 13–14, 18–21
 expressions, 185, 188–189
 fetched properties, 178–188, 189–191
 fetched results controller, 25–39
 history of, 10
 managed objects, 21–24
 migrations, 133–136
 overview, 9–10
 persistent store, 13–14, 16–18, 24–25
 persistent store coordinator, 16–18
 relationships, 172–177, 179–185
 template application, creating, 10–12
 validation, 147
 versioning, 127–133
 Xcode template, 10–12
Core Foundation, 273, 275
 CFAllocators, 276
 implementing callback functions, 275
 Objective-C objects, 275
 toll-free bridging, 279
CoreData.sqlite, 17
CoreData.xcdatamodel, 13
CoreLocation framework
 building MapMe application, 376
 linking MapKit framework, 389
Cover Flow
 selecting audio tracks, 405, 417
currentPlaybackTime property, music player, 421
custom subclasses, creating, 143–144

■D

data
    packaging for sending, 235–236
    receiving from peers, 236
    retrieving asynchronously, 344–350
    retrieving synchronously, 339–344
    saves on terminate, 23–24
    sending to peer, 234–235
data model
    designing, 50–60
    multiple, 16
    NSManagedObjectModel, 14–16
    persistent store and, 13–14
    reviewing, 18
data model editor, 13–14, 18–21
    adding entities, 179
    creating fetched properties in, 179–
        188
    creating relationships in, 179–185
    entity pane, 18–19
    property pane, 19–20
data models
    about, 128–133
    adding attributes, 140–143
    changes to, 127–128
    compilation, 128
    migrations, 133–136
    updating, 140–143
    version identifiers, 131–132
    versions, 129–133
data modes, 235
data receive handler, 236
datagram sockets, creating, 276
datasource methods, 101–102
dataSource outlet
    building music playing application,
        433
datatypes
    attribute, 56–59
    Binary, 57–58
    Boolean, 57
    Date, 57
    Decimal, 57
    Double, 57
    Float, 57
    integer, 56–58

receiving data from streams, 291
    String, 57
    Transformable, 58
dataWithContentsOfURL method, 337
date attribute editor, 115–117
date attributes, 19
Date datatype, 57
date last played, retrieving
    media items, iPod library, 413
date picker view, 117
deadlocks, threads, 474
dealloc method, 101, 237, 264
    fixing Stalled application with timer,
        467
    MapMeViewController, 385
    music playing application, 436, 444
    OnlineSession object, TicTacToe,
        302
    peer browser view controller, 316
    StalledViewController, 456, 488
deallocated objects
    EXC_BAD_ACCESS exception, 517,
        519, 520
    zombies, 521–523
debug actions, 512
debug configuration, Xcode projects,
        496
debug symbols, 496
debugger console, Xcode see debugger
        window
Debugger Editing Pane, 500
debugger window, 496
    breakpoint actions, 511–512
    breakpoint window, 508–509
    breakpoints, 497–512
    bringing up debugger window, 500
    conditional breakpoints, 509–510
    debugging controls, 503–507
    interface to GDB, 496
    stack trace, 501
    StalledViewController, 456, 457
    status bar, 500
    symbolic breakpoint, 508
    variable list, 502–503
debugger, Xcode, 496
debugging, 269, 495

breakpoints, 497–512
bugs as examples for, 517–525
    infinite recursion, 523–524
    missed outlet and action
        connections, 525
    overreleasing memory, 517–521
creating Xcode project to
    demonstrate, 495
editing pane, 507
EXC_BAD_ACCESS exception, 517,
    519, 520
GDB (Gnu debugger) console, 513–
    516
gdbinit file, 516
Mini Debugger, 507
release or distribution configuration,
    496
static analysis, 495, 516
zombies, 521–523
debugging controls, 503–507
debugging window buttons, 503
Decimal datatype, 57
decimal numbers, 57
default values, 114
    for attributes, 137, 146–147
degrees
    calculating distance of one degree
        longitude, 366
del command
    removing breakpoints, GDB console,
        514
delegate methods
    alert view, 78
    browser delegate methods, 286–287
    delegate methods for publication,
        284–285
    fetched results controller, 29–35
    mailComposeController, 395
    map loading delegate methods, 368
    mediaPickerDidCancel, 418
    MFMailComposeViewControllerDele
        gate, 395
    NSNetService, 326
    NSNetServiceBrowser, 317
    NSURLConnection, 345–346
    OnlineListener, 325

OnlineSession, 325
peer picker, 323
region change delegate methods,
    368
resolving discovered services, 287,
    326
setting up application skeleton, 332,
    333
streams, 289
tab bar, 78
delegate outlet
    building music playing application,
        433
delegate property, setting to nil, 79
delegates
    building MapMe application, 376
    CFNetwork, 274
    creating OnlineListener object, 309
    map view delegate, 367–369
    publishing Bonjour service, 284
    using assign not retain for, 297
delete button, 209–211
DELETE request, HTTP, 350, 351, 357
delete rules, 177, 218
deleted objects, cleaning up, 218–221
deletes, 209–211
Deny rule, 177
dependencies, operation, 476
dependencies method, operations, 476
description method, 92–93
deselectAnnotation method, 372
destination entities, 173
detail view
    as grouped table, 84
    controlling table structure with
        arrays, 87–90
    declaring instance variables and
        properties, 96–97
    editable, 83
    editing challenges, 85–87
    editing subcontrollers, adding, 107
    formatting attributes, 92–94
    functionality, 106
    specifying sections and rows, 86
    tabled-based vs. nib-based, 84–85
detail view controller

creating, 94–96
  implementation, 97–103
  using, 103–106
detailController
  adding to MainWindow.xib, 104–105
  declaring, 103–104
  pushing onto stack, 105–106
device name
  advertising services, 283
didChangeObjectColforChangeType
    method, 30–34
didChangeSection:atIndex method, 35
didChangeState method, 233
didConnectToPeer method, 238
didDismissButtonWithIndex method,
    76, 78
didFailWithError method, 324, 346, 349,
    374
didFindPlacemark method, 374, 375
didFindService method, 286, 287
didFinish method, 402
didNotPublish method, 285
didNotResolve method, 287
didNotSearch method, 286
didPickMediaItems method, 418
didReceiveConnectionRequestFromPee
    r method, 234
didReceiveData method, 346
didReceiveResponse method, 345
didSelect method, 323
didSelectItem method, 78
didSelectRowAtIndexPath method, 316
disclosure indicator, 165–166
disconnectPeerFromAllPeers method,
    237
discovered services, 282
  browser delegate methods, 287
  resolving, 287–288
    delegate methods, 326
  searching for published Bonjour
    services, 285
discoveredServices array, 287, 312, 316
discussion forums, 528
display name, 233
DNS domain name, 282
documentation browser, Xcode, 528

doGetRequest action
  RequestTypes application, 353, 356
dollar sign, 184
domains
  advertising services, 282
  error domains, 149
  NSNetService, 285
doPostRequest action
  RequestTypes application, 353, 356
doTitleSearch action
  music playing application, 430, 431,
    434, 439
Double datatype, 57
Doxygen, 91
drawRect method, 370
dynamic keyword, 147

■E

edit mode, 197
editButtonItem, 25
editing pane, debugging in, 507
e-mail application, 391
  adding attachments, 395
  mail compose view, 391
  MailPic application, 396–403
  MessageUI framework, 394–396
  MFMailComposeViewControllerDele
    gate, 395
  prepopulating message body, 395
  prepopulating recipients, 394
  prepopulating subject line, 394
  presenting mail compose view, 395
  sending e-mail to old way, 403
encounteredError method, 310
endGeneratingPlaybackNotifications
    method, 423
endianness see byte ordering
Enterprise Objects Framework (EOF), 10
Enterprise Program, 4
entities, 13–14, 18–19
  abstract, 53
  adding, 51–52, 179
  adding attributes to, 54, 59–60
  adding fetched properties to, 181–
    187

destination, 173

editing, 52–54

inserting new, 37

naming conventions, 55

properties of, 19–21

relationships between, 20, 172–177,
180–181

entity pane, 18–19

error codes, 149

   NSNetService, 285

error domains, 149

errors

   didFailWithError method, 349

event codes

   NSStreamEventEndEncountered,
290

   NSStreamEventErrorOccurred, 290

   NSStreamEventHasBytesAvailable,
290

   NSStreamEventHasSpaceAvailable,
290

   NSStreamEventOpenCompleted,
289

Event entity, 13, 19

events

   handleEvent method, 289

exceptions, 111

   creating SquareRootOperation, 485

   EXC_BAD_ACCESS, 517, 519, 520

   main method, operations, 475

expressions, 185, 188–189

extensions, 198

■F

factory methods, adding, 211–215

false positives, static analysis, 516

faults, 188

fb (future break) command, 514

fetch requests, 21

   creating, 26

FETCH_SOURCE variable, 184, 185,
187

fetched properties, 21, 169

   about, 178

   adding to classes, 189–190

creating, 179–188

displaying, 190–191, 205, 216–218

fetched property attribute controller,
216–218

fetched results controller

   creating, 26–29

   declaring, 49–55

   delegate methods, 29–35

     controller:didChangeObjectColfor
ChangeType, 30–34

     controller:didChangeSection, 35

     controllerDidChangeContent, 30

     controllerWillChangeContent, 29–
30

   managed objects

     creating and inserting, 36–37

     deleting, 38–39

     retrieving, 36

   object updates, 32–34

   overview, 26

   references to, 62

   section name keypaths, 77

FETCHED_PROPERTY variable, 185

fetchedResultsController, 25–39, 76–79

filterable properties

   media items, iPod library, 409, 411

   media types, iPod library, 410

findMe action, MapMe, 376, 377

first-generation iPhones

   online network play, 271

firstMediaItem method

   music playing application, 425, 426

Float datatype, 57

form parameters, 351–352

forums, discussion, 528

Foundation objects, 273, 279

   retrieving data using, 336–339

FUNCTION macro

   implementing stubs, application
skeleton, 336

further information

   Apple documentation, 528

   blogs, 529

   discussion forums, 528

   mailing lists, 528

   web sites, 529

Xcode documentation, 528

G

GameKit, 225
  components, 225
  header files, 242–246
  importing, 240
  in-game voice functionality, 226
  Nearby play, 321
  packaging data for sending, 235–236
  peer picker, 225, 227, 237–239, 264
  project creation, 239
    interface design, 241–269
    view controller header, 242–246
  receiving data from peers, 236
  sending data to peers, 234–235
  sessions, 225, 232–234
    closing connections, 237
    creating, 232–233, 238–239
    finding and connecting to other, 233–234
  TicTacToe (sample application), 226–229
    game board design, 246–250
    interface design, 241–269
    playing, 268–269
    TicTacToe view controller, 252–268
    TicTacToePacket, 248–251
    view controller header, 242–246
GCD (Grand Central Dispatch), 452
GDB (Gnu debugger), 496
GDB (Gnu debugger) console, 513–516
  calling functions and methods, 515
  command termination, 515
  debugger console as interface to, 496
  info command, 513
  printing data and object values, 515
  working with breakpoints, 513–514
    creating breakpoints, 514
    removing breakpoints, 514
gdbinit file, debugging, 516
generic code, 169, 190

generic controller class, 169–172, 190
  creating, 190–211
  using, 211–216
GET parameters, 352
GET request, HTTP, 350
  RequestTypes application, 353, 356
getImageAsynchronously action, WebWorks, 346
getImageSynchronously action, 340
getImageUsingNSData action
  Foundation objects, 338
getTextAsynchronously action, WebWorks, 347
getTextUsingNSString action
  Foundation objects, 338
GKPeerPickerController, 237–238, 259
GKSendDataReliable method, 235
GKSendDataUnreliable method, 235
GKSession, 232–234
GKSessionModeClient, 233
GKSessionModePeer, 233, 234, 264
GKSessionModeServer, 233, 234
global variables, breakpoints, 502
go method
  fixing Stalled application with timer, 464
  StalledViewController, 455, 456, 487
Google
  MapKit framework, 360
goStopButton action
  updating nib, Stalled application, 463
Grand Central Dispatch (GCD), 452
grouped tables for detail views, 84
groupingType property, MPMediaQuery, 416
gutter, line number breakpoints, 497, 498, 499

H

handleEvent method, 289
handleReceivedData method, 325, 327
hash, 131
header files, 145–146
  OnlineListener, TicTacToe, 309

response header fields, 340
setting up, 242–246
updating, 152–153
writing peer browser header, 312
headerdoc notation, 91
heisenbug, 521
HeroEditController
adding view-only support, 165–166
creating, 94–96
declaring instance variables and properties, 96–97
displaying new attributes in, 161–163
implementation, 97–103
refactoring, 190–193
renaming, 191–192
using, 103–106
HeroListViewController, 44, 49
creating, 60–64
implementation, 66–79
interface design, 64–66
updating, 215–216
heroValueDisplay method, 93–94, 103, 163
htonl function, byte ordering, 279
HTTP
form parameters, 351–352
response codes, 340
specifying request types, 350–351
HTTP headers, mutable URL requests, 351
hybrid map type, map view, MapKit, 362, 363

IBAction keyword, 333
IBOutlet keyword, 333, 376
idle timer, turning off, 239
Ignore column, breakpoint window, 510
imagePickerController:didFinish method, 402
images, sending see MailPic application
imageView outlet, 334
index path, 86
indexOfObject method, 78

indexPath, 203
indices, 55–56
infinite recursion, debugging, 523–524
info command, GDB, 513
in-game voice functionality, GameKit, 226
initDieRollPacket method, 266
initWithFilterPredicates method, 416
initWithInputStream method, 301
initWithObjects method, 100
in-memory store, 18
insert button, 209–211
inserts, 209–211
instance variables, 61–62, 173
declaring, 96–97
naming conventions, 62
refactoring, 193
synthesized, 62–63
INT_MAX, 249
Integer 16/Integer 32, 56
Integer 64, 56–58
integer datatypes, 56–58
integerValue method, 410
Intel assembly, 501
Interface Builder, 47–49, 84
building MapMe interface, 376
building user interface, music player, 430–433
designing interface, application skeleton, 333
designing StalledViewController interface, 454–455
fixing Stalled with operation queues, 486
updating nib, Stalled application, 463
interface, user see UI (user interface)
Internet play, 328
Internet, retrieving data from
building RequestTypes application, 353–357
form parameters, 351–352
HTTP request types, 350–351
retrieving data asynchronously, 344–350

retrieving data synchronously, 339–344

setting up application skeleton, 331–336

using Foundation objects, 336–339

invalidate method, 459

inverse relationships, 176–177, 181

iPhone

creating queue of songs, 405

iPhone Dev Center, 3–4

iPhone Developer Program, 4

iPhone development

blogs, 529

discussion forums, 528

prerequisistes, 2–3

web sites, 529

iPhone simulator, 4

iPod library, 407–424

see also music playing application

media item collections, 408, 413–414

media items, 408–414

media picker controller, 408, 417–418

media property predicates, 408, 415

media queries, 408, 414

music player controller, 408, 418–424

different kinds of controller, 419

iPod music player controller, 419

iPod touch

see also music playing application

media picker, 405, 406

online network play, 271

iPodMusicPlayer method, 419

IPPROTO_TCP argument

creating sockets, 277

IPv4/IPv6, 278

isCancelled property, operations, 477, 478, 483

isConcurrent property, operations, 477

isExecuting property, operations, 477

isFinished property, operations, 477

isKindOfClass method, 125

isNew method, 195–196

isReady property, operations, 477

isReadyForUse method, 302

isToManyRelationshipSection method, 198–199

items property, MPMediaQuery, 416

specifying queue of audio tracks, 419

IUDatePicker, 117

■J

javadoc notation, 91

■K

k prefixed constants

kBatchSize, 463, 481, 484

kCFSocketAcceptCallBack, 277

kGameStateDone, 267

kSelectorKey, 207

kTableRowHeight, 448

kTimerInterval, 463

kToManyRelationship, 207

kUIUpdateFrequency, 481

updating StalledViewController, 487

key operands, 183

keypath property, 109

keypaths, 22

KVC (key-value coding), 21–22, 137, 173, 174

KVO (Key-Value Observation), 489, 490

■L

lastMediaItem method

music playing application, 425, 426

latitudeDelta

coordinate regions, map view, 364, 365, 367

lazy loading, 15, 17, 28, 62

Learn C on the Mac (Mark), 2

Learn Objective-C on the Mac (Apress), 2

lightweight migrations, 128, 134, 136

line number breakpoints, debugging, 497

gutter, 497, 498, 499

listeners
    OnlineListener, 292, 306–310
    overview of online network play, 273
    setting up, 273–281
        callback functions, 274
        configuring sockets, 275–277
        implementing socket callback
            function, 280–281
        registering socket with run loop,
            280
        run loop integration, 274
        specifying port for listening, 277–
            279
    specifying port for listening, 277–279
    stopping, 281
little-endian byte ordering, 279
localized strings, 100, 110–111
location
    building MapMe application, 376
    setting region to display, 367
    tagging specific locations, 369
    user location, map view, MapKit, 364
location manager
    MapMeViewController, 385, 386
locks
    deadlocks, 474
    mutex locks, 471
logging
    StalledViewController, 456
longitude
    calculating distance of one degree
        longitude, 366
longitudeDelta
    coordinate regions, map view, 364,
        365, 367
loops
    run loop integration, 274
lyrics
    see also music playing application
    MPMediaItemPropertyLyrics, 412
    retrieving, media items, iPod library,
        412

Grand Central Dispatch (GCD), 452
mail compose view
    e-mail application, 391, 395
    MFMailComposeViewController, 394
    MFMailComposeViewControllerDele
        gate, 395
mailComposeController delegate
    method, 395
mailing lists, Apple, 528
MailPic application, 396–403
    building user interface, 397
    declaring outlets and actions, 397
    implementing view controller, 398–
        403
    linking MessageUI framework, 403
MailPicViewController
    building MailPic user interface, 397
    implementing view controller, 398–
        403
main method, operations, 475, 483
MainWindow.xib
    adding instances to, 104–105
    setting up, 47–50
malloc_error_break breakpoint, 519
managed object cells, 203
Managed Object Class template, 143–
        144
managed object models, 128
managed object relationship cells, 203
managed objects, 16
    committed values, 195
    context, 22–23
    creating and inserting, 36–37
    custom, 137–167
    defined, 21
    deleting, 38–39
    key-value coding, 21–22, 85–86
    retrieving from fetched results
        controller, 36
    saves on terminate, 23–24
ManagedObjectAttributeEditor
    adding validation feedback using,
        152–154
    header file, updating, 152–153
    implementation file, updating, 153–
        154

■**M**

Mac OS X Snow Leopard

subclasses, updating, 154
ManagedObjectColorEditor, 158–161
managedObjectContext, 23
ManagedObjectDateEditor, 115–117
    updating, 155
ManagedObjectEditor, 191
    creating, 190–211
    using, 211–215
managedObjectModel, 15, 16
ManagedObjectSingleSelectionListEdito
        r, 120–125
    updating, 155
ManagedObjectStringEditor, 112–115
    updating, 154–155
map loading delegate methods, 368
map types, map view, MapKit, 362–364
map view delegate, 367–369
map view, MapKit, 361, 362–369
    building MapMe interface, 376
    coordinate regions, 364–367
    hybrid map type, 362, 363
    map loading delegate methods, 368
    map types, 362–364
    map view delegate, 367–369
    mapType property, 364
    providing with annotation views, 372
    region change delegate methods,
        368
    satellite map type, 362, 363
    standard map type, 362
    user location, 364
MapKit framework, 360
    annotation view, 362
    annotations, 361, 369–373
    building MapMe application, 375–
        390
    callout, annotations, 362
        selecting annotations, 372
    linking CoreLocation framework, 389
    map view, 361, 362–369
    release 3.0, iPhone SDK, 359
    reverse geocoding, 359, 373–375
MapLocation
    MapMe annotation object, 378, 379
    MapMeViewController, 388
MapMe application

building, 375–390
    building interface, 376–378
    declaring outlets and actions, 375–
        376
    linking MapKit and CoreLocation
        frameworks, 389
    MapMeViewController, 381–389
    opening screen, 360
    reverse geocoding, 361
    writing annotation object, 378–380
MapMeViewController
    declaring outlets and actions, 375
    implementing, 381–389
    MapMe application, 376
    MapMe interface, 377
mapping models, 134
mapType property
    map view, MapKit, 364
mapViewDidFailLoadingMap method,
        368, 389
mapViewDidFinishLoadingMap method,
        368
mapViewWillStartLoadingMap method,
        368
marketing version identifiers, 129
media item collections, iPod library,
        408, 413–414
    building music playing application,
        424–428
    creating derived collections, 414
    creating new collection, 413
    MPMediaItemCollection, 408, 413
    retrieving media items, 413
    setQueueWithItemCollection
        method, 420
media items, iPod library, 408–414
    filterable properties, 409, 411
    getting/setting currently playing
        media item, 420
    MPMediaItem, 408
    nonfilterable numeric attributes, 411
    persistent ID, 409
    playing queue of, 418
    property predicates, 415
    queries, 414
    retrieving, 414, 416

retrieving album artwork, 413
retrieving date last played, 413
retrieving lyrics, 412
searching for, 414
selecting specific media items, 417
type, 409
media picker controller, iPod library,
    408, 417–418
media picker, iPod touch, 405, 406
media property predicates, iPod library,
    408, 415
    MPMediaPropertyPredicate, 408,
    415
    nonfilterable numeric attributes, 411
media queries, iPod library, 408, 414
    synchronization, 417
media types, iPod library
    filterable properties, 410
mediaItemAfterItem method, 425, 426
mediaItemAtIndex method, 425, 426
mediaPicker:didPickMediaItems
    method, 418
mediaPickerDidCancel method, 418,
    437
MediaPlayer framework
    working with iPod library, 407
memory, overreleasing, 517–521
    zombies, 521–523
mergedModelFromBundles method,
    132, 133
message body, e-mail application
    prepopulating, 395
MessageUI framework, 394–396
    adding attachments, 395
    linking, MailPic application, 403
    MFMailComposeViewController, 394
    MFMailComposeViewControllerDele
        gate, 395
    prepopulating message body, 395
    prepopulating recipients, 394
    prepopulating subject line, 394
    presenting mail compose view, 395
    sending e-mail to old way, 403
methods
    see also delegate methods
    nested method calls, 504

MFMailComposeViewController
    addAttachmentData method, 395
    creating, 394
    implementing MailPicViewController,
        400
    setBccRecipients method, 394
    setCcRecipients method, 394
    setMessageBody method, 395
    setSubject method, 394
    setToRecipients method, 394
MFMailComposeViewControllerDelegat
    e, 395
    building MailPic application, 397
migrations, 133–136
    lightweight, 128, 134, 136
    standard, 128, 134
mime types, 395
Mini Debugger, 507
MKAnnotation protocol, 370, 378, 380
MKAnnotationView, 370, 388
MKCoordinateRegion, 364, 365
MKCoordinateRegionMakeWithDistanc
    e method, 366, 386
MKCoordinateSpan, 364, 366
MKMapView, 367
MKMapViewDelegate protocol, 368
MKPinAnnotationView, 370, 388
MKPlacemark terminology, 374
MKReverseGeocoder, 373, 386
MKReverseGeocoderDelegate, 376
MKUserLocation, 364
mom files, 128, 129, 132, 133
momd files, 132, 133
movie player controller, iPod library,
    408
MPMediaItem, 408
MPMediaItemArtwork, 413
MPMediaItemCollection, 408, 413
    music playing application, 424–428
MPMediaItemCollections, 416
MPMediaItemPropertyAlbumArtist, 411
MPMediaItemPropertyAlbumTitle, 411
MPMediaItemPropertyAlbumTrackCoun
    t, 412
MPMediaItemPropertyAlbumTrackNum
    ber, 412

MPMediaItemPropertyArtist, 411
MPMediaItemPropertyArtwork, 413
MPMediaItemPropertyComposer, 411
MPMediaItemPropertyDiscCount, 412
MPMediaItemPropertyDiscNumber, 412
MPMediaItemPropertyGenre, 411
MPMediaItemPropertyLastPlayedDate,
    413
MPMediaItemPropertyLyrics, 412
MPMediaItemPropertyMediaType, 409
MPMediaItemPropertyPersistentID, 409
MPMediaItemPropertyPlaybackDuration
    , 412
MPMediaItemPropertyPlayCount, 412
MPMediaItemPropertyPodcastTitle, 411
MPMediaItemPropertyRating, 412
MPMediaItemPropertySkipCount, 412
MPMediaItemPropertyTitle, 409, 411,
    415
MPMediaPickerController, 408, 417
    music playing application, 429, 440
MPMediaPickerControllerDelegate, 418,
    429
MPMediaPlaylist, 408
MPMediaPredicateComparisonContains
    , 415, 416
MPMediaPredicateComparisonEqualTo,
    415, 416
MPMediaPropertyPredicate, 408, 415
MPMediaQuery, 408, 414, 416
MPMediaTypeAny, 411, 417
MPMediaTypeAnyAudio, 411, 417
MPMediaTypeAudioBook, 410, 417
MPMediaTypeMusic, 410, 417
MPMediaTypePodcast, 410, 417
MPMoviePlayerController, 408
MPMusicPlaybackStatePlaying, 419
MPMusicPlayerController, 408, 419,
    429
    notifications, 423
MPMusicRepeatModeXyz modes, 422
MPMusicShuffleModeXyz modes, 422
multi-field validations, 147–148
multiple-attribute validations, 150
multiprocessing, 452
music

MPMediaItem type, 410
music player controller, 408, 418–424
    adjusting volume, 422
    application music player controller,
        419
    beginGeneratingPlaybackNotificatio
        ns method, 423
    beginSeekingBackward method, 421
    beginSeekingForward method, 421
    creating, 419
    currentPlaybackTime property, 421
    determining if playing, 419
    endGeneratingPlaybackNotifications
        method, 423
    getting/setting currently playing
        media item, 420
    iPod music player controller, 419
    MPMusicPlayerController, 408, 419
    MPMusicRepeatModeXyz modes,
        422
    MPMusicShuffleModeXyz modes,
        422
    notifications, 423
    nowPlayingItem property, 420
    nowPlayingItemChanged method,
        423
    playback time, 421
    playbackState property, 419
    repeat and shuffle modes, 421
    repeatMode property, 422
    seeking, 421
    setQueueWithItemCollection
        method, 420
    setQueueWithQuery method, 420
    shuffleMode property, 422
    skipping tracks, 420
    skipToBeginning method, 420
    skipToNextItem method, 420
    skipToPreviousItem method, 420
    specifying queue, 419
    volume property, 422
music playing application, 405
    see also iPod library
    caution turning off user's music, 407
    iPod's media picker, 405, 406
    main page, 406

use of terms 'queue' and 'playlist', 405

using simulator, 407

working with iPod library, 407–424

music playing application, building, 424–448

   adding media item collection functionality, 424–428

   building user interface, 430–433

   declaring outlets and actions, 428–430

   implementing view controller, 434–448

   trying it out, 448

mutable URL requests, 351

mutableSetValueForKey method, 175, 176, 210

mutators, 147

mutex locks

   deadlocks, 474

   threads, 471, 472

   using self as mutex, 472

N

name attribute, 54, 58–59

name_icon.png, 63–64

naming conventions

   instance variables, 62

   properties, 55, 62

navigation controllers, 44, 48–50

Navigation-based Application template, 43

Nearby play

   GameKit, 321

   online network play, 271, 272

   peer picker, 321, 324

nested arrays, 88, 89, 90

nested method calls, 504

netService:didNotPublish method, 285

netService:didNotResolve method, 287

netServiceBrowser:didFindService method, 286, 287

netServiceBrowser:didNotSearch method, 286

netServiceDidResolveAddress method, 288

netServiceDidStop delegate method, 285

network communication models

   client-server model, 229–230

   hybrid models, 231–232

   peer-to-peer model, 230–231

network play see online network play

network streams

   online network play, 271

networked games

   cheating in, 267

   interface design, 241–269

   TicTacToe (sample application), 226–229, 241–269

networking

   Bonjour, 281–288

   creating service for publication, 282–285

newGameButtonPressed method, 321

NeXTSTEP, 10

nextTrack action

   music playing application, 430, 435, 441

nib

   deleting instance from, 215

   updating, Stalled application, 463

nib-based detail view, 84–85

nil values, 90, 150

No Action rule, 177

nodes, 232

nonatomic keyword, properties

   thread safety, 472, 473

nonfilterable numeric attributes

   media items, iPod library, 411

notifications

   building music playing application, 444

   music player controller, iPod library, 423

   updating StalledViewController, 489

nowPlayingItem property, music player, 420, 429, 430

nowPlayingItemChanged method, 423, 437, 443, 445

NSArray, 83, 90, 293
NSAttributeDescription, 114
NSAutoreleaseNoPool breakpoint, 519
NSBinaryStoreType, 17
NSClassFromString function, 119
NSCoder Night web site, 529
NSCoding protocol, 249, 378
NSData, 57–58, 236
    adding packet categories,
        TicTacToe, 293, 295
    retrieving data using Foundation
        objects, 337
NSDate, 19, 93
NSDictionary, 21, 90
NSEntityDescription, 114
NSError, 148, 149, 337
NSFetchedResultsChangeUpdate, 32–
    34
NSFetchedResultsController, 25, 39
NSFormatter, 92
NSHTTPURLResponse object, 340
NSIndexPath, 207, 491
NSIndexSet, 490
NSInvocationOperation, 475
NSKeyedArchiver, 142, 155, 235
NSKeyedUnarchiver, 142, 155
NSKeyValueChangeIndexesKey, 490
NSKeyValueChangeInsertion, 491
NSKeyValueChangeKindKey, 491
NSKeyValueChangeRemoval, 491
NSLocalizedDescriptionKey, 149
NSLocalizedString, 110–111
NSLog function, 269
    debugger window, 496
    implementing StalledViewController,
        456
    race conditions, threads, 470
NSManagedObject, 21, 85–86
    custom subclasses, 137–167
    instance variable, 96
    isNew method, 195–196
    subclasses, 175
NSManagedObjectContext, 37
NSManagedObjectModel, 14–16, 132,
    133
NSMutableArray, 174

selecting annotations, 372
updating StalledViewController, 490
NSMutableData
    adding asynchronous retrieval to
        WebWorks, 348
    adding packet categories, 295
    building RequestTypes application,
        357
    implementing OnlineSession object,
        303, 305
    retrieving data asynchronously, 345,
        346
    setting up application skeleton, 333
NSMUtableSet, 174
NSMutableURLRequest
    building RequestTypes application,
        357
    HTTP request types, 351
    POST parameters, 352
NSNetService
    advertising services, 282
    delegate methods, 326
    device name, 283
    didNotPublish method, 285
    didNotResolve method, 287
    DNS domain name, 282
    error codes/domains, 285
    port numbers, 283
    publishing Bonjour service, 283
    resolving discovered service, 287
    service type, 283
    updating TicTacToeViewController
        for online play, 325
NSNetServiceBrowser
    creating peer browser for online
        play, 311
    delegate methods, 317
    didFindService method, 286, 287
    didNotSearch method, 286
    implementing peer browser view
        controller, 315
    searching for published Bonjour
        services, 285
NSNetServiceDelegate, 284
NSNull, 89, 100, 163, 166
NSNumber, 19, 57

NSOperation, 468, 475, 476
NSOperationQueue, 23, 468
    sleeping threads, 474
    updating StalledViewController, 489
NSOperationQueuePriorityXyz values,
        476
NSOutputStream, 309
NSPersistentStoreCoordinator, 16–18
NSSelectorFromString method, 208
NSSet, 174, 199–200, 219
NSSQLiteStoreType, 17
NSStream, 288
NSStreamEventEndEncountered, 290
NSStreamEventErrorOccurred, 290
NSStreamEventHasBytesAvailable, 290,
        292
NSStreamEventHasSpaceAvailable, 290
NSStreamEventOpenCompleted, 289
NSString, 19, 337
    constants, 137
NSThread, 468
NSTimer, 458
    see also timers
    invalidate method, 459
    scheduledTimerWithTimeInterval
        method, 459
    timerWithTimeInterval method, 458
NSURL
    retrieving data asynchronously, 344
    retrieving data synchronously, 342
NSURLConnection
    adding asynchronous retrieval to
        WebWorks, 347
    delegate methods, 345–346
    retrieving data asynchronously, 344
    retrieving data synchronously, 339,
        342
NSURLRequest
    HTTP request types, 351
    retrieving data asynchronously, 344
    retrieving data synchronously, 339,
        342
NSValueTransformer, 156
NSZombie, 521–523
ntohs function, byte ordering, 279
NULL, 150

Nullify rule, 177
numberOfRowInSection method, 199,
        446
numbers
    decimal, 57
    integers, 56, 58
numeric attributes, 19
numeric attributes, nonfilterable
    media items, iPod library, 411
numOperationsInput outlet
    StalledViewController interface, 455

■O

objc_error breakpoint, 519
objc_exception_throw breakpoint, 511,
        519
object updates, 32–34
Objective-C
    blogs, 530
    exceptions, 111
    extensions, 198
    resources for, 2
    runtime, 220
Objective-C 2.0 Programming
        Language, 2
object-relational mapping (ORM), 9
objects
    archiving and unarchiving, 235–236
    managed see managed objects
    retrieving, from nested arrays, 90
observeValueForKeyPath method
    updating StalledViewController, 489
online network play
    adding, 271
    Bonjour, 281–288
        creating service for publication,
            282–285
        publishing service, 283
        stopping service, 284
    finding players on local network, 271
    Internet play, 328
    Nearby play, 271, 272
    Online play, 271, 272
    overview of process, 273
    peer picker, 321, 324

reassembling objects, 292
setting up listener, 273–281
    callback functions, 274
    CFNetwork, 273–279
    configuring sockets, 275–277
    implementing socket callback
       function, 280–281
    registering socket with run loop,
       280
    run loop integration, 274
    specifying port for listening, 277–
       279
stopping listener, 281
streams, 288–291
updating TicTacToe for, 292–327
    adding packet categories, 293–
       295
    creating OnlineListener object,
       306–310
    creating peer browser, 311–318
    implementing OnlineSession
       object, 295–305
    updating TicTacToeViewController,
       318–327
OnlineListener, 292
    delegate methods, 325
    generic nature of, 328
    updating TicTacToe for online play,
       306–310
    updating TicTacToeViewController
       for online play, 320, 324, 327
onlineListener:encounteredError
    method, 310
OnlinePeerBrowser, TicTacToe
    building peer browser interface, 312
    updating view controller for online
       play, 320, 321, 324
    writing peer browser header, 312
OnlineSession, TicTacToe, 292
    delegate methods, 325
    generic nature of, 328
    updating for online play, 295–305
       view controller, 320, 323, 326,
       327
OnlineSessionDelegate, TicTacToe
    error methods, 327

implementing OnlineSession object,
    297
onlineSessionReadyForUse method,
    327
onMainThread method, 484
openCallout method, 385
opengl_error_break breakpoint, 519
operation queues, 452, 478–479
    adding operations to, 478
    fixing Stalled application with, 479–
       487
    NSOperationQueue, 468
    setMaxConcurrentOperationCount
       method, 479
    setQueuePriority method, 476
    suspending, 479
    threads and, 452, 478
operationProgressChanged method
    StalledViewController, 481
operations
    adding to queue, 478
    autorelease pools, 472, 475
    cancelling, 478
    concurrency, 452, 475–478
    dependencies, 476
    exceptions, 475
    main method, 475
    NSInvocationOperation, 475
    NSOperation, 468, 475
    priority for queues, 476
    state, 477
    try block, 475
operations array, queue, 491, 492
OR operator *see* bitwise OR (|) operator
ordered arrays, 199–200
ORM (object-relational mapping), 9
outer arrays, 88
outlet declaration, 103–105
    MailPic application, 397
    MapMe application, 375
    missed connections, debugging, 525
    music playing application, 428–430
    setting up application skeleton, 331–
       333
    StalledViewController, 454
overreleasing memory, 517–521

EXC_BAD_ACCESS exception, 517, 519, 520
zombies, 521–523

■P

packet categories, adding
    updating TicTacToe for online play, 293–295
packetQueue array
    implementing OnlineSession object, 297
packets
    packaging for sending, 235–236
paired arrays, 87–88
paired nested arrays, 89
parameters, form, 351–352
peer browser
    building interface, 312
    creating for online play, 311–318
    creating files, 311
    implementing view controller, 313–318
    writing header, 312
peer identifiers, 238
peer picker
    delegate methods, 323
    GameKit, 225, 227, 237, 238, 239, 264
    Nearby play, 321, 324
    online network play, 272
        creating peer browser for, 311–318
    Online play, 321, 324
    online view controller class, 292
peerPickerController:didConnectToPeer method, 238
peerPickerController:didSelect method, 323
peers, 230–231
    disconnecting from, 237
    handling connections with, 238
    receiving data from, 236
    sending data to, 234–235
peer-to-peer model, 230, 231, 232
percentComplete method, 483

percentCompletedText method, 462
performFetch method, 26, 79
performSelector method, 338, 342, 385, 389, 397, 401, 458, 484
persistent ID, media items, 409
persistent store
    access to, 16
    data model and, 13–14
    loading data from, 24–25
    multiple, 16
persistent store coordinator, 16–18
persistentStoreCoordinator accessor, 17
PF_INET argument
    creating sockets, 276
piece variable, 259
placemarkIdentifier, map view, 373
playback state
    music player notifications, 423
playback time, music player, 421
playbackState property, music player, 419
player see music player controller
PlayerViewController see music playing application, building
playlist
    use of term 'queue' compared, 405
playlists, iPod library, 408
playOrPause action, music player, 430, 435, 441
playPauseButton outlet, music player, 433
po (print object) command, GDB, 515
podcasts
    MPMediaItem, 409
    MPMediaTypePodcast, 410
pointers, 149
port numbers, 277
    advertising services, 283
ports
    application ports, 278
    manually assigning, 278
    registered, 278
    specifying for listening, 277–279
    toll-free bridging, 279
    well-known ports, 278

POSIX Threads API (pthreads), 468
POST parameters, 352
POST request, HTTP, 350
    RequestTypes application, 353
pragma line, 323
predicate builder, 182–184, 185, 187
predicates, 28, 178, 182–184
predicateWithValue method, 415
presentModalViewController, 395
pressStarted instance variable, 430
previousTrack action, music player,
        430, 433, 435, 441
print command, GDB console, 515
priority, operations, 476
private keyword, 61, 62, 97
processChunk method
    fixing Stalled application with timer,
        463, 464
Progress View
    MapMe interface, 377
progressBar outlet
    designing StalledViewController
        interface, 455
    MapMe interface, 377
    MapMeViewController, 384, 386,
        389
progressLabel outlet
    building MapMe interface, 377
    designing StalledViewController
        interface, 455
progressString method, 483
prompt property, media picker, 418
properties, 19–21
    see also fetched properties
    attributes, 19–20
    declaring, 96–97
    fetch requests, 21
    fetched, 21
    instance variables, 61–62
    naming conventions, 55, 62
    relationships, 20
property pane, 19–21, 54
protected keyword, 97
protocol family
    creating sockets, 276
protocols

service type identifying, 283
pthreads (POSIX Threads API), 468
publishing services
    creating service for publication, 282–
        285
    delegate methods for publication,
        284–285
    overview of online network play, 273
    publishing Bonjour service, 283
    resolving discovered service, 287–
        288
    searching for published Bonjour
        services, 285
    stopping Bonjour service, 284
PUT request, HTTP, 357
    HTTP request types, 350, 351

■Q

queries
    media queries, iPod library, 414
queuePriority method, 477
queues
    music player controller, 419, 420
    operation queues, 452, 478–479
    use of term 'playlist' compared, 405

■R

race conditions, threads, 469–471
read-only attributes, 166
readonly keyword, 62
receiveData method, 236
recipients, e-mail application
    prepopulating, 394
recursion, infinite, 523–524
refactor window, 192
refactoring, 190–193
region change delegate methods, 368,
        369
regionDidChangeAnimated method, 368
regions
    coordinate regions, 364–367
    setting region to display, 367
regionThatFits method
    accommodating aspect ratio, 367

regionWillChangeAnimated method, 368

Registered iPhone Developer, 2–4

registered ports, 278

regular expressions, 58–59

relationships, 20, 169
  about, 172
  adding to classes, 189–190
  creating, 179–185
  delete rules, 177
  inverse, 176–177, 181
  to-many, 174–176, 181, 197–211
  to-one, 173–174, 181

removeAnnotation method, 371

removeAnnotations method, 371

removeDependency method, 476

removeTrack action, music player, 430, 435, 442, 446, 447

repeatMode property, music player, 422

request object
  retrieving data synchronously, 339

request types
  building RequestTypes application, 353–357
  mutable URL requests, 351
  specifying HTTP request types, 350–351
  URL request, 339–344

RequestTypesViewController, 353, 354

Reset Contents and Settings, Simulator, 393

resolveWithTimeout method, 287

resources
  see also further information
  C language, 2
  Objective-C, 2

response codes
  200 series of, 342
  300 series of, 345
  retrieving data synchronously, 340

response header fields, 340

response object, 340

responsive interface see concurrency

Restart button, debugging window, 503

RESTful web services

specifying HTTP request types, 350, 357

result code, mailComposeController, 396

result sets, 186

retain keyword, deallocated objects, 517

reverse geocoding
  MapKit, 359, 373–375
  MapMe annotation object, 378, 380
  MapMe application, 361, 376
  MapMeViewController, 387
  MKPlacemark terminology, 374
  MKReverseGeocoder, 373

RGBA colors, 147, 156

root view controllers, 44
  setting, 48–49

RootViewController, 24

rowKeys array, 101

rowLabels array, 100

rows
  editing style for, 201
  selecting, 166
  selection updating, 205–208
  setting indentation, 197–199
  setting number of, 199

run loop
  integration, setting up listener, 274
  registering socket with, 280
  scheduling, concurrency, 451
  stopping listener, 281
  timers, 451

■S

satellite map type, map view, 362, 363

Save button, 193–196, 208

save method, 111, 114–115, 152, 154, 194–195

scheduledTimerWithTimeInterval method, 459

scope, variable list, debugging, 502

secret_icon.png, 63–64

section name keypaths, 77

sectionNameKeyPath, 35

sectionNames array, 101–102

seeking, music player, 421
    seekBackward action, 430, 435, 441
    seekForward action, 430, 435, 441
selectAnnotation method, 372
    MapMeViewController, 385
selectedAnnotations array, 372
selection list controller, 120–125
selection lists, implementing, 116–125
self, 187
    declaring socket context, 275
    StalledViewController, 488, 489
    using as mutex, 472
sendData method, 234, 268, 302
sender variable, 259
sendPacket method, 323
sendQueuedData method, 302, 304,
    305
sentinels, 100
servers, 229
service type
    advertising services, 283
services
    see also publishing services
    advertising services, 282
    domain, 282
    resolving services, 282
    searching for services, 282
session classes
    OnlineSession, 292
session identifiers, 232
session mode, 233
session:didFailWithError method, 324
session:didReceiveConnectionRequest
    FromPeer method, 234
session:peer:didChangeState method,
    233
sessions (GameKit), 225, 232
    closing connections, 237
    creating, 232, 233, 238–239
    delegate methods, 265
    finding and connecting to other,
        233–234
    listening for, 234
    modes, 233
setBccRecipients method, 394
setCcRecipients method, 394

setEditing method, 76
setMaxConcurrentOperationCount
    method, 479
setMessageBody method, 395
setQueuePriority method, 476
setQueueWithItemCollection method,
    420
setQueueWithQuery method, 420
setRegion method, 367
setSubject method, 394
setSuspended method, 479
setToRecipients method, 394
setValue:forKey, 21
SHARED heading, Mac, 281
Show Bounds Rectangles option, music
    player, 431, 432
showMediaPicker action, music player,
    430, 431, 434, 440
showSaveCancelButtons property, 194,
    196
showsUserLocation property, mapView,
    364
shuffleMode property, music player,
    422
Simple_PlayerViewController *see* music
    playing application, building
simulator
    music playing application, 407
    Reset Contents and Settings menu,
        393
single-attribute validations, 147, 148–
    149
skipToXyz methods, music player, 420
sleep, threads, 474
Snow Leopard, 2
SOCK_STREAM argument
    creating sockets, 276
sockaddr_storage, IPv6
    specifying port for listening, 278
socket programming
    setting up listener
sockets
    creating, 276–277
    datagram sockets, 276
    declaring context, 275–276

implementing callback function, 280–281

registering with run loop, 280

setting up listener, 274, 275–277

stream sockets, 276

songs

see also music playing application

choosing from iPod library, 417

sort descriptors, 26, 28, 77

sounds *see* music playing application

spinner outlet

designing interface, application skeleton, 334

SquareRootBatch

fixing Stalled application with timer, 460–462, 464

SquareRootOperation

creating, 480–485

StalledViewController, 488, 492

SquareRootOperationDelegate, 486, 491

stack trace, breakpoints, 501

Stalled application

creating to illustrate concurrency, 453–457

fixing with operation queues, 479–487

fixing with timer, 460–468

creating batch object, 460–462

updating controller header, 462–463

updating nib, 463

updating StalledViewController, 463–468

when timer firing occurs, 458

StalledViewController

application illustrating concurrency, 454

creating SquareRootOperation, 481

designing interface, 454

fixing Stalled with operation queues, 485

fixing Stalled with timer, 462–468

implementing, 455–457

updating, 487–493

standard map type, map view, 362

standard migrations, 128, 134

Standard Program, 4

startListening method, 310

startNewGame method, 260, 265

state, operations, 477

static analysis, 495, 516

status bar, debugger window, 500

Step Into button, debugging, 503, 505, 506

Step Out button, debugging, 503, 506

Step Over button, debugging, 503, 505, 506, 507

nested method calls, 504

stopListening method, 310

stream sockets, 276

streams, 288–291

CFStream pointers, 288

delegate methods, 289

implementing socket callback function, 280

NSStream, 288

NSStreamEventXyz event codes, 289, 290

opening streams, 289

receiving data from streams, 290

sending data through streams, 291

stream:handleEvent method, 289

string attribute editor, 112–115, 120

string attributes, 19

String datatype, 57

string properties, filterable media items, iPod library, 411

strings, localized, 100

stringWithContentsOfURL method, 337

stub methods

setting up application skeleton, 331–336

action and outlet declarations, 331–333

designing interface, 333–335

implementing stubs, 335

subarrays, 88

subcontrollers, 107

subject line, e-mail application prepopulating, 394

subviews, 49

superclass, creating, 108–111
SuperDB application, 42
  application architecture, 43
  application delegate, 44, 45, 46
  connecting outlets, 50
  data model design, 50–60
  detail view, 83, 125
  display problem, 163–165
  HeroListViewController
    creating, 60–64
    implementation, 66–79
    interface design, 64–66
  launching, 79–80
  MainWindow.xib, 47–50
  project setup, 42–43
  table view controller, 46–47
  updating, 90–92
switch statements, 86–87, 266
symbolic breakpoints, debugging, 508
synchronization
  media queries, 417
  retrieving data asynchronously, 344–350
    adding asynchronous retrieval to WebWorks, 346–350
    NSURLConnection delegate methods, 345–346
  retrieving data synchronously, 339–344
    URL request, 339–344
  retrieving data using Foundation objects, 337
synchronized block, threads, 471, 472, 473
synthesize statements, 61, 62
  overreleasing memory, 518
  updating StalledViewController, 487
synthesized instanced variables, 62–63

T

tab bar delegate method, 78
tabBar:didSelectItem method, 78
table structure
  controlling with arrays, 87–90
table view

architecture, 85–86
  delegate methods, 29–35
  edit mode, 197
  row editing style, 201
  specifying sections and rows, 86
  updating, 30–34
table view controller
  creating, 46–47
  subclasses, creating, 94–96
table-based detail view, 84–85
  controlling structure, with arrays, 87–90
  declaring instance variables and properties, 96–97
  detail view controller, creating, 94–96
  editing challenges, 85–87
  editing subcontrollers, adding, 107
  formatting attributes, 92–94
  functionality, 106
tables
  structure, 83
tableView:cellForRowAtIndexPath method, 90, 102, 114, 201–205, 210, 316, 446, 493
tableView:commitEditingStyle method, 38–39, 209
tableView:didSelectRowAtIndexPath method, 316
tableView:numberOfRowInSection method, 199, 446
tableView:titleForHeaderInSection method, 102
TCP (Transmission Control Protocol)
  creating sockets, 276
textView outlet
  designing interface, application skeleton, 334
thread safety
  atomicity, 472–473
  UIKit, 485
threads, 468, 469–475
  atomicity and thread safety, 472–473
  autorelease pools, 472, 475
  Cocoa Touch, 469
  communication between, 481